Stories of My Life

Ramona R. Mitchell

To Dianne, enjoy the
stories.
        Ramona

Bethesda Communications Group

Published by the Bethesda Communications Group
4816 Montgomery Lane
Bethesda, MD 20814
www.bcgpub.com

ISBN-13: 978-1-7357729-1-2
ISBN-10: 1735772917

The photos included are from the collection of Ramona R. Mitchell.

The front cover painting by Ramona R. Mitchell
Book design by Deborah Lange

To my grandson Benjamin Timm, whose expressed interest in the stories brought this book into existence

Contents

Acknowledgments

Many people have encouraged me in this journey and helped in the creation of this book. My grandson Benjamin Timm had the inner vision and was crucial in encouraging me before I felt any urge to write. My yoga teacher Swami Sivananda Radha was my guiding light, without which none of this could have been manifested, and my daughter Kirstin helped me with her quick mind and with her practical encouragement. Roger Steinmetz shoved me into saying "yes," and without Moira Collins and Debbie Lange I would not have found the courage or help with the design and editing of the manuscript. Michael Radford helped me with his technical ease when I barely knew how to use a computer and needed constant help. My gratitude goes out to the many people whose efforts helped in enriching my understanding of life's magical journey.

Introduction

I strive to live authentically, using my strength to gather the power to reach higher ideals. Searching for quality in all my actions was my first effort and my response to life, as I encountered the dark experiences of a war-torn childhood. In telling my stories to my grandson, I found that the truth was like an elixir that empowered the experiences of my life, giving them more value.

—Ramona R. Mitchell

"Every act is like a mirror, in which we see ourselves reflected, and which can allow us to understand who we really are."
— A yoga sutra of Patanjali from
What Are We Seeking by TKV Desikachar

1 Europe

Gathering Stories

"Grandma, tell me another story!" Ben requested. My little grandson was strapped in his car seat, and we were getting ready for the drive to my house in Eldorado from his house in Santa Fe. "But not one of these fairy tales! I want a true story, like those you told me last time. I want to know all that happened and from the beginning, so don't leave something out." I had previously related some of the events from my time in Egypt, where I had grown up, and I was scratching my mind for something appropriate.

My daughter had already warned me that, like any little boy, Ben was interested in guns and shooting. I told him not to shoot me, however tempting, because I had gone through a real war and was terribly afraid of guns. "Do you know what a bomb sounds like as it falls through the air from the sky? It whistles, and only after that it makes an unbearably loud bang!" Then I told him what it sounded like when bombs exploded. When he came back home, he started to build a lot of structures with his wooden building blocks. To his mother's surprise, he then began to smash them with appropriate sound effects. "What are you doing, Ben?" she asked. "Oh, I am bombing the city," he informed her. "Grandma told me how it's done."

Over the years, whenever I was with Ben, I was asked for stories and thus began my task of gathering my experiences, first in my mind, then telling the best ones to Ben. It was just a short step from there to writing them down. Like any good storyteller, I began my tales for him with "once upon a time..."

I was born in Berlin, Germany, right before the beginning of World War II. My parents, Karl and Leni Hilpert, named me Rosmarie. Dramatic events tend to imprint themselves deeply into memory, leaving a profound impression, which is perhaps the reason why my sister Gabriele's birth is one of my first memories. She was born in a hospital staffed by nuns, and this was the first time I saw women wearing black and white habits. I found this somewhat alarming, especially as one picked me up to show me a beautiful shrub with red berries outside the front door. My new baby sister lay in a little cot with a picture on the headboard. I was more interested in this image than the baby, while adults tried to direct my attention to the child. I recall watching my mother breastfeeding Gabriele, so I copied her behavior by trying to breastfeed my doll. The reason I remember this was that I was scolded as if indulging in some forbidden act.

Light

Before I could draw well myself, I went to my father with the request to draw a picture for me of a little girl with a light on her head. My father lifted me up on his lap, spread out a sheet of paper and began to draw. All went well until he got to the head. "How do you want me to draw the light?" he asked to my surprise. Did he not know how a little girl with a light on her head looked? He tried to put the star-like light behind the head; he placed it over the head. I was getting extremely upset because whatever he drew was not how the starlight on top of a little girl's head looked. I did not understand why he did not know this obvious fact. My explanations did not help, and eventually, he gave up. It puzzled me to no end that he obviously had not had a vision nor understanding of something that was completely natural to me. Many years would go by before I could acknowledge to myself that I saw lights or auras over the heads of people. In fact, I almost stopped seeing them in an effort to conform to the limited vision available to others. I also had many inner visions that manifested, allowing me to know events ahead of time and which helped me guide events in my life.

Father Karl Otto in the 1930s

Mother Leni in the 1930s

Karl Otto skiing in Austria, 1941

Rosie skiing in Austria, 1941

There were several incidents where knowing the future came to me. One of these occurred on our Berlin roof terrace. With a towel tied to my waist, I was dancing in circles before the sunset. I held one of my dolls. We were spinning faster and faster, and excitement gripped me. I could feel this tension in my belly, spreading right through me, as I went faster and faster, losing myself in the whirling motion, forgetting where I was, nothing but the motion to focus on. Suddenly, in my mind, I knew my parents were talking about going to the Palatine, to live there. I could actually sense a forest with trees and mountains and wildflowers. A conviction grew that I would be very happy there. Then I began to sing, "We are going, we are going to the Palatine." Indeed, we went to the Palatine, as women and children were soon evacuated to the countryside when the bombardments became worse.

Another early memory was at the age of three, when I went skiing with my parents in Austria, in Steinach am Brenner. A huge Baroque cross with a white bleeding man nailed to it hung in the dining room of the inn. Very realistic depictions of blood ran down his face and along his body. There was even blood dripping off his elbows. I refused to eat my food and my mother became alarmed. Needless to say, I could not explain how upsetting the "bleeding man" was to my young mind. After much effort and coaxing, she convinced me to eat some horrid red pudding which the "bleeding man" seemed to permit.

On our return to Berlin, I found that my little sister, who had been left behind under the care of Margarete, our nurse, had carefully and methodically pushed in all the eyes of my dolls and cut off their hair. She had not spared a single doll. I was horrified. My mother collected the damaged dolls to take them to the toy hospital, asking me to understand that my little sister was just a baby and did not understand. "Then why had she not blinded her own dolls or pulled out the legs of her teddy?" I asked. Throughout my childhood, my mother continued to ask me to forgive my sister for the damage she inflicted upon my things.

Gabriele and Rosie, 1941

Departure to the Palatine

When we returned to Berlin, all women and children were evacuated because of the sudden increase in bombardments on the city. It was decided we should live in the Palatine. My father was to remain in Berlin, and we were separated from him for the next two years. My mother, sister, and I traveled by train south to the Palatine, near the French border, a wine-growing region, from where my father's family came. A large part of the Hilpert family still lived in the region.

We took refuge with my father's stepmother, who owned an attractive little house. However, there was almost instant tension in the air, and she was hostile to us. I remember my mother's distress as we sat on a grassy area beside the road, waiting for a car to take us away. Our new home was a beautiful little country inn, surrounded by forest and slopes covered by vineyards, as I had seen in my vision. I ran wild and began roaming alone in the woods and meadows. An old man I encountered in the woods taught me where to find edible mushrooms and warned me of poisonous berries. In retrospect, this was a magical time for me, as I learned from nature and found a freedom I could never have discovered in a big city. My mother took frequent trips to Berlin to see my father, and one of the village girls looked after us while she was gone.

My maternal grandmother, Katharina, came to look after us. I don't recall that she disciplined us, or, for that matter, interfered with my wild excursions into the woods. I discovered spiders, worms, bees and all kinds of creatures for myself and carefully watched the snails. It was at this stage that I first noticed that the horizon line curved, that trees sang when the wind passed through them, and I began a silent communication with plants. I often stroked them and found they liked to be touched; they rewarded me in surprising ways by showing me their mysteries. I became very good at finding mushrooms. There was already very little food available, and children were sent out to collect edible chestnuts and pick blueberries.

It was on one of my father's infrequent visits that he discovered I could not speak with any degree of ease. He tested me carefully, telling me a story and asking me to repeat it. Unfortunately, I was unable to recount the story he had just told me, and I could feel his deep disappointment, and I also sensed a decision he made right then. I discovered it soon enough. My parents decided to send me to the little village Kindergarten in Kleisweiler. The village children were very nice and most curious. They asked me how old I was. I had no idea. They asked me what my religion was. Are you Roman Catholic or Protestant? Again, I had only an embarrassed silence in answer.

Every day I walked down the hill from the little inn and joined the vital crowd of children. It was very lively. First thing in the morning at school, we had to stand to attention and recite: "Folding little hands, bowing the head, think one minute of Adolf; Hail Hitler!" "Handchen falten, Kopfchen senken, eine

Sisters Gabriele and Rosie, Mother Leni,
Grandmother Katharina, and a family friend, 1942

Minute an Adolf denken, Heil Hitler." With the words: "Heil Hitler" we had to raise our right arm in salute.

During recess one day, we stood and looked at the sky filled with little silver crosses and which made a buzzing sound. These were the first planes I had ever seen, and we were told they were enemy planes going to bomb a city. The information was disturbing and confusing because I did not grasp the concept of what "bombing" meant. After that, I often saw the silvery planes high in the sky and watched them with puzzled amazement. They looked like crosses and I wondered if they had anything to do with Religion.

The village children had taken me to attend mass at the Roman Catholic Church. I sat at the very front and was told God would appear and that I should pay very close attention. That I did, for even now I can see the priest in his highly embroidered gown and the little altar boys waving incense back and forth, and I can hear the little bell being rung because the moment of transformation was supposed to come. But nothing visible happened, and I was disappointed and puzzled.

One day a whole group of children gathered to play. A game evolved. I don't recall exactly what happened. The boys were on top of a highly loaded hay cart, and I was furious at one of the boys. Backing away, I picked up a good-sized stone and took aim. To my surprise, the stone flew like an arrow and hit his head. In slow motion, I saw him twist and then fall from the cart down to the ground. The terrible thought took hold of me that I had probably killed him. I turned and ran as fast as I could up the hill and back to the safety of the inn. No one ever accused me, and I never asked if the boy had died. However, after this incident, I never doubted that I had the ability to kill a human being, a most uncomfortable thought.

The conversations of "killing and death" were in the air. In the inn dining room, a big radio announced the news and everyone listened in total silence to the latest events. Sometimes our noble Fuhrer spoke, and this attracted all sorts of additional people to the dining room. Everyone listened in rapt attention, and we children were hushed up. I did not like his voice; I found its high pitch and hysterical tones very unsettling.

When I was three and still living in Berlin, I turned the knob of our living room radio. In essence, I only wanted to know if anything would happen if I turned the knob, as I had seen my father do. Nothing happened. I did not realize that radios took quite a while to heat up in those days, and so no sound manifested until almost a minute had passed. Impatiently I began to turn the knob up, further and further up. Nothing happened until suddenly an ear-shattering volume burst forth. It was Herr Hitler giving one of his speeches. In terror, I fled not only the room but the house itself, as I tried to escape the monstrous volume of sound I had released.

My mother spoke several languages very well, including English and Italian. Interested in hearing outside news, she would sneak into the kitchen of the inn and would tune the radio to the BBC and listen to the British broadcasting service. Listening to outside information was prohibited in Germany and heavily punished. One day my mother was listening to the kitchen radio again, unaware that the radio was tuned to transmit its message into the dining room. When she was caught in the kitchen, she pretended total ignorance and insisted she did not know any English. Insisting she had only played with the dial and did not understand English saved her from being taken in front of the authorities. There was a Nazi staying at the inn who did not believe her and was very much set on reporting her.

On one of his infrequent visits, my father looked thin and gaunt. My parents spent all their time together, and I did not see much of them. However, we did go on a walk to a cemetery where my paternal grandfather lay buried. On the way, a rather long walk, my father asked me to pick flowers for the grave. Never having seen a grave, I was puzzled but obeyed the instruction. At one stage my father repeated: "put the flowers on the grave." Now in German, grab (a grave) and graben (a ditch) are very close in sound. Thinking, he wished me to place my little bouquet of field flowers into the ditch we were just then walking along, I made my way down into the rather deep ditch and let go of the offering. He exploded. I was unused to the volume of an angry male voice and horrified that a misunderstanding had occurred. The rest of the afternoon was rather unhappy for me. Although I saw my grandfather's grave, I had no idea that his dead body was buried there.

Having my father back was very intense and exciting. During the summer, there were rather heavy thunderstorms in the Palatine; they even washed away whole slopes and garden walls. The occasion of one big storm is a favorite memory. The rain was lashing down and the pine trees were bending under the intense wind. My father grabbed his two little girls and exclaimed, "We are off to join nature's wonderful wild dance," and we ran out of the little inn into the turbulence. "Karl! Karl!" my mother screamed, "The children will get wet." However, he was already in his game. Lifting his fist to the sky, he shouted: "We are not afraid, St. Peter, let it thunder and rain, we will not retreat!" Grabbing our hands, he rushed into the rain. I had fairly long hair at the time, and it was soon sopping wet and sticking to my neck. Our thin summer dresses stuck like wet paper to our legs. In short, we were soaked.

He ran with us, holding tightly to our hands and insulting the great God Wotan, insisting we were not afraid and nor were we. His rebellious enthusiasm rubbed off on us, so we too danced and jumped and stood under young pines, which he shook as we stood underneath them so that we were even wetter than before. The whole adventure was magnificent, and so freeing, savage, and liberating. On our return, my mother scolded him, saying we might catch a cold. He called her a brooding hen, afraid to let her chicks out of her sight. By her expression, I could read her displeasure, and that too was good to know, for I was learning the power of disobedience and liked it. He was a playful man and disrespectful of authority. His sense of humor was celebrated. Apparently, he could be put together with a group of serious, dull people and in no time, he would have them laughing and sharing stories. It seems he brought out an insubordinate quality in people and made them daring.

Another incident that touched me deeply during my childhood was a visit to a medieval castle. We walked quite a long way into a bright green spring forest. It was a beautiful day, and my father told me about the wars fought here centuries ago and how people had built fortresses with high protective walls around a castle, adding a moat filled with water as a further protective measure. Then we arrived at the ruins. The bridge across the moat was still there, and the moat was filled with slimy green water. Boiling pitch had been poured over the edge of the high wall onto the enemies below, and the black tar was still clinging to the stones. There was a horrible bottle-shaped dungeon where criminals were dumped into the darkness never to emerge alive. We walked through large splendid halls, up spiral staircases, into large festival gathering spaces, into the huge kitchen, and then into a special room where suits of armor were displayed. Swords and helmets hung on the walls, as well as other weapons that came into view. My father lifted a huge sword off its perch and asked me to lift it. I recall its dramatic weight and that its tip instantly touched the ground.

"You are now five years old." he said to me. "That is the age when a boy had to start learning how to fight." He then told me that he had learned how to fight with a saber and showed me the scar across his chin. Finally, we came up to the roof of the castle and were able to look out across the land and treetops. Here, women had little gardens with flowers. I actually found a columbine flower growing between the stones, and my father assured me this was a type of flower much loved then, probably a remnant of an ancient flower bed.

Potatoes

I loved my father dearly and longed for his presence and approval. Alas, approval was not so easy to gain. I hated eating potatoes. During the war, when food was already scarce, potatoes were valued and often the only available food. My father, when he came to the Palatine, used to give me a spanking under a pear tree for refusing to eat potatoes. This upset me greatly, as it brought a discordant note into the relationship.

The noble spud was not to my taste, and I only found out many, many years later why. In 1989, I took an important step in my spiritual development; I went to a Canadian Ashram in British Columbia. The Guru Swami Sivananda Radha, who had inspired me with her book, *Kundalini Yoga for the West*, had founded Yasodhara Ashram, and this is where I went.

The four-day workshop focused on the teaching of Kundalini yoga. A gentle, white-haired Swami taught the course. We were introduced to the five senses and their manifestations. The first chakra (center or lotus) was the sense of smell, and the second chakra was the sense of taste. In order to allow us to experience this sense, we were blindfolded and given a number of different items to taste. Among them was a tiny slice of raw potato. My mouth felt insulted. The object made my taste buds constrict. I tasted something bitter and vile and wished I could spit it out. Nauseated and disgusted, I discovered to my surprise I had tasted a potato slice, raw. When I was asked why my response was so extreme, so emotional, I had no answer. My response was irrational.

I was told to write and reflect and to examine my response to the potato. I recall writing down words like potato sack, potato cellar, dungeon, dark, dank, smelly open sacks, backs, brown shirts(the name for soldiers' uniforms), stabbing sacks... backs...and then suddenly an image began to flash in front of my eyes. There were trucks rumbling along the street under my window in Berlin. It was dusk. One truck followed the next. They were open truck beds loaded with what looked like sacks of potatoes. I had climbed up on a low stool in order to be able to look out of my bedroom window. It seemed like an endless chain of trucks rumbling on and on. Some of the sacks were open with arms or legs hanging out. Slowly it became apparent to me these were human limbs, gray and bloodied, stuffed into sacks. At one point the young woman, Margarete, who looked after us children, came and lifted me off the stool, telling me in a firm and frightened voice not to look out of the window.

When this memory flashed into my consciousness I reacted in horror, unwilling to believe this could possibly have happened. I began to feel sick to my stomach, and a cold sweat began to break out. Then I felt shaky and confused, as I must have felt as a three-year-old. It was very difficult to share this information with the group. My conscious mind was most reluctant to accept that I had tapped into a suppressed memory. Yet why had I always hated eating potatoes? Why did I have this violent reaction to a slice of raw potato, which most in the group found wholesome and earthy tasting?

Past Life Regression

This excursion left a profound impression on my young mind. Many years later I studied hypnotherapy. One of the experiences we were given was a past life regression. The class of students that I was part of was hypnotized and we regressed together. Asked to go back in time, I was astonished to discover that I was a male in the 13th century in France. My family was of noble origin, and we lived in a castle. From a very young age on, I was trained in sword fighting and became a warrior. There were constant skirmishes and unrest. I hated the violence and corruption and found myself embroiled in politics. After a number of further questions, we were taken forward in time and asked to witness how we died. While I lay asleep on a bed, an assassin entered my room. He stabbed me in the throat. I felt the warm blood gushing from the wound on the left side of my throat and tried to stop the hemorrhage by pressing my hands against my neck. Floating above my bleeding body and looking down as I reflected on my fading life, I swore to myself never to engage in politics again and never to be a man again. This, however, was not the end of the regression. Our instructor asked us to reflect on the experience and to look at our present lives with the intent of finding corroborating evidence for this past life. He asked us to think about what traits from back then were still active in our present life, what tendencies could we pin-point, and what beliefs and signs could we find.

At first, I drew a blank. The regression had certainly felt totally authentic. The big hairy man I was then felt right and real.

However, when I awoke the next morning, I remembered that I had an extensive dagger collection as a teenager. I had taken fencing instruction and been fascinated with judo. As a matter of fact, I became very good at judo and I was delighted that I was able to throw big and powerful men on the mat. Clearly, I enjoyed the martial arts! My mother was a little worried at times by my unfeminine interests. Another curious fact was my fear of betrayal and dislike and suspicion of politics. I did not trust politics.

In that past life, I died by having my throat cut. As I lay dying I held my neck, trying to stem the bleeding. Back then I felt my life-force fade and realized I was dead and floating above my body. Looking down, I saw my corpse with both hands holding the left side of my neck. This detail brought back the memory of my mother telling me on several occasions that I was born with quite a dent on the left side of my jaw. She was worried that this was a permanent deformity and asked the doctor. He assured her the indentation would disappear and was caused by my having both fists pressed against the left side of my neck during the birth.

In this past life as a French knight, I had died holding the wound in my throat. This was certainly a strange coincidence! I was told that I was born with shoulder-length black hair, which was very unusual. Something seldom mentioned was that my face too was hairy, at least for the first few days. My parents called me "little monkey," and later I had a favorite toy that was a little monkey. During that past life as a knight, I sported shoulder-length black hair. In fact, serfs had their hair cut short or shaved. Only free men were allowed to wear long hair. Of course, all of this could be called coincidence, but I feel that this past life was very real. Reflecting on my experiences opened me to question the conscious and subconscious aspects of my mind.

In September You May Get Another Egg

There came a rather worrisome period in the Palatine when I became confused because I did not know what was going on. My mother disappeared to Berlin. My grandmother came to stay and look after us. Only later did I learn my mother had to undergo an appendix removal. There were very few available doctors in Berlin, as all physicians were transferred to the front to treat wounded soldiers. After much searching, my parents found a Jewish surgeon still working in a Berlin hospital. He was willing to undertake the surgery, providing my mother was slim and he did not have to cut through layers of fat. My mother confirmed repeatedly that she was very slim, and so the surgery was performed. However, that very same evening an air raid over Berlin forced all the patients to get up and run for the bomb shelter. My mother told me how she had to get out of bed, still dizzy from the procedure, holding the draining tubes going into her wound in her hand while she had to walk to the elevator.

My parents, when I saw them again, looked very thin, and I was told there was very little food in Berlin. In the Palatine, food had also become scarce. A song circulated: "In life all events pass, all go by, and in September you may get another egg." My mother and I were walking past some large buildings tucked back among huge old trees. There was a rather splendid garden and extensive grounds where a number of women were walking. "Why do these women all have big bellies?" I asked. "Because they are all carrying babies in their bellies," my mother responded. "Why do they have babies?" I wanted to know. This upset my mother. "They are making children for our Fuhrer. He likes to have blonde, blue-eyed children, and the hired women have agreed to give birth to such."

At this point, my mother encountered a friend, and the conversation turned to what we had just witnessed. I listened intensely and learned that these breeding mothers were chosen because of their Aryan looks. Their children were to be raised in a specific discipline and would become part of the German Special Forces. The birth mothers would give them up after birth and relinquish all responsibility. Many years later, I heard the sad stories of these unwanted creatures. I heard that many of them were forced to live in stables with animals. Farmers did not want them on their property, and normal people shunned them.

Return to Berlin

I was six years old and it was early spring when we were forced to return to a disintegrating Berlin. An atmosphere of doom and despair prevailed, and there was limited food and little heat. A few days before our departure, there was a heavy rain in the Palatine. The flat, tarred rooftop of the little inn was covered with huge puddles of rainwater. I walked out after the storm and, bending over one of the large puddles, saw my head reflected against the large empty blue sky above me. Treetops silhouetted were exquisitely lacy with delicate foliage and were so sharply etched I felt I could touch them. My own face loomed against the backdrop of the vast empty expanse, and I felt dizzy, feeling as if I could drop into this void and disappear forever. It was an intense moment of consciousness, when I understood that life was about to change completely.

Back in the city of Berlin, I soon found myself in trouble. I had black hair and dark eyes and was now often called "Jew" or "gypsy" and had rocks thrown at me by other children. My father was upset when I told him that the boys had caught me and tied me to a tree. They told me they were going to kill me and danced around me like a bunch of savages. It was probably fortunate that I was too young to understand. However, one incident really stood out. Due to bomb attacks, one of the streets in our neighborhood had a section of damage and was being re-tarred. I was with a group of children watching the big machines work, the big roller flattening the surface, and we smelled the ugly smells. Some older boys took hold of me after the workmen took off for lunch. Calling me "Pechmarie," the name of a girl in a fairy tale who had pitch-black hair, they proceeded to smear tar into my long hair. I became hysterical and screamed all the way home where my poor mother spent hours removing the tar from my hair. Extremely upset, especially since the boys had told me I was going to die, I was inconsolable. Fortunately, my mother found out that they had put a curse on me. She gave me an antidote, a piece of chocolate. I ate it and lived.

I began to prefer my own company to that of others and spent delightful times investigating nearby bombed-out buildings and collecting treasures of colored glass from shattered stained-glass windows. I had been forbidden to play in the destroyed buildings, as they were not secure, but at least no nasty boys bothered me there. The bombardments became more intense and then came day and night. Before I went to bed at night my mother had us arrange our clothes so we could dress fast and efficiently. The first items were my underpants and socks, then came the rest. I had to be able to put the clothes on within seconds, as there was no time to waste. The horrible whining sirens announced the arrival of enemy planes and everyone rushed for cover in bomb shelters or, in our case, a cellar.

My father had a wonderful sense of humor, which became more pronounced as circumstances worsened. My parents were well-to-do, and we lived in an affluent area of Berlin called Grunewald. My father was the director of advertising with the Blaupunkt company, which made radios and other electronics. Blaupunkt was rated very high in the world industry. Even years later, the company thought so highly of my father that they kept his position open for five years after he was declared "missing" in Poland, hoping for his return.

My parents entertained frequently, had a maid and a cook, and were involved in the cultural life in Berlin. They subscribed to concerts and recitals given in private homes for Jews, who were no longer allowed to perform in public. Wilhelm Furtwangler, the famous music conductor, arranged this, so musicians could continue to earn a living. Many an evening, I sat on the stairs leading down to the living room, listening to concert music or lively talk.

We children did not spend much time in company of my mother. She came to kiss us at night, beautifully dressed with long, open hair smelling of perfume and cigarette smoke. A young woman named Margarete was hired to take care of us. On weekends, my father was at home, and mornings started with the sound of a coffee grinder, for he loved freshly made coffee. We were allowed into the dining room for breakfast, but not for other meals. My parents firmly believed that children should be seen but not heard. Thus, my father's workroom, where he executed his designs and wrote, was firmly out of bounds, as was my parents' bedroom.

Sometimes my father took me to a local pub on Sunday mornings. At the pub, men gathered to read papers, drink coffee or wine, and discuss the political situation. It was here my father introduced me to champagne. I recall the glass filled with bubbly fluid, which made me sneeze. The daughter of the owner of the wine tavern and I became good friends and played games together.

Quite often now, destitute people rang our doorbell. I remember my mother pulling them into the hallway and giving them food. She told me they were Jewish. An atmosphere of fear and suspicion hovered over everyone and people could no longer trust one another. I watched impoverished Jewish people pushing wheelbarrows along the street, crying a repeated refrain: "Lumpen, Knochen, Altpapier (rags, bones and old paper)." That was the only job the government permitted the Jews to have.

Both my parents repeatedly got into trouble with the Gestapo. The first time I remember was while shopping. My mother carried my younger sister on her arm while I walked beside her holding her hand. She also had a shopping bag suspended over one shoulder, and as I recall, held a handbag in her other hand. When a group of military personnel marched through the streets, it was expected that the citizens stop, raise their right arms in salute, and stand like that until the soldiers had marched past. Because of her burdens and the need to hold a child in her arms, my mother just stood, unable to raise her right arm in the expected salute. When the soldiers had passed, an angry man appeared and shouted at my mother. She argued with him but was unable to convince him. I remember that I began to scream in the loudest tone of voice possible and somehow that stopped things. My mother, however, was extremely upset, and I probably would have forgotten this incident were it not for the repeated retelling that happened later. Due to this, I also began to understand that she had felt very threatened and could have landed in jail.

It was 1944, and the air attacks were constant. They usually came just after we had been put to bed for the night. The food was scarce, and I remember feeling anxious and often very frightened. We were instructed to black out all of the windows. This meant black paper was glued to the interior of window panes, even on cars and buses. This was so no light could give away a house, tram, car, or another vehicle. Because of this, during the daytime the inside of our home was dark and gloomy. At night, searchlight beams illuminated the sky. Like long fingers, they passed back and forth across the darkness and sometimes caught a little silver cross in their beam. Then the quick chatter of anti-aircraft fire sounded, as the German military tried to shoot down the enemy airplanes.

My parents sacrificed their government-issued bread allowance for my sister and me, as we were rapidly losing weight. I noticed they smoked much more to combat hunger, and my father chewed coffee beans to stay alert. I remember becoming dizzy in the hallway and seeing black dots dancing in front of my eyes when I climbed the stairs. Eventually, there was a time when I had to pause whenever I tried to walk upstairs, as I ran out of energy. With these symptoms came a type of indifference, lassitude, and tiredness. I actually thought of death; it came up in conversation almost daily. I knew that children died and recognized the very real possibility that I could die. Somehow, I made the decision not to worry and directed my mind elsewhere.

My mother found a bunker where we children were placed during the nights. There were only children there, and some nurses were in charge. However, it was a toxic environment as childhood diseases rapidly spread from sick children to healthy ones. Both my sister and I tested positive for some horrible illness and had to return home, where the only adequate shelter from a bomb attack was a storage basement. Earth had been shoveled over the small basement windows and along the base of the house. We were ill for quite a while, and I do not recall very much from this period. When at last I was able to go outside again, I saw parents pulling children aside, and once I was even shouted at and told not under any circumstances to get near a little girl who had been my friend. I don't think I understood the whole notion of infectious diseases. I only felt like an outcast.

Winter came, and it was very cold. Our food supply became more and more scarce. My mother told me that they sold something called a fish salad which contained fish guts and sawdust. My father was gifted at somehow finding real food. Being from the Palatine and having contact with a large family of vintners, he could get not only wine but also the occasional pheasant or slab of bacon. The alcohol was very valuable, and one could get almost anything for a bottle of wine or Schnapps. People began to barter for firewood, coal, cigarettes, soap, and shoes. There was a terrible lack of everything. When Easter came, my mother somehow managed to make us a little basket filled with tiny little sweet egg-like shapes. I recall that they tasted nasty.

Strafing

One of the most terrifying experiences occurred one evening when my mother and I hurried down the street where we were walking, seeking a bunker for protection, as an alarm had just gone off alerting us to seek shelter. We ran as fast as we could from tree to tree in the hope of not being seen. The aircraft were flying very low and if they spotted us, they would start to shoot. There were no people in the streets, no cars nor buses. I was out of breath, and my heart was beating in my throat with terror. We stopped under some trees and I tried to get as close as possible to a tree trunk, hugging it for protection. We paused like this frequently, as we tried to regain some strength to continue our mad dashes from tree to tree. We had just found another group of trees, when a plane dipped low and then started to strafe us. The machine gun fire was ear-splittingly loud and so violent that it tore up and shredded the road surface. My mother grasped my hand and nearly pulled my arm out of its socket as she dragged me forward, shouting "Run! Run! Run!" I remember becoming confused as we rushed forward, wondering where we were going. The roar of the plane overhead came and then changed direction, as it strafed a different street. Torn up foliage lay on the pavement at my feet, broken off branches as well. My mother hugged me tightly to her chest and kissed my cheek. "Well done, we are nearly there. Come on." We then continued our journey home.

Déjà Vu

One evening, my father showed me a book from his library, a big book of beautiful photographs. The men with colorful feather headdresses were Indians and lived on a huge continent called America. I was fascinated. My father also told me he would like to leave Europe and go to Chile in South America "after this ugly war is over." After this, I asked to see the Indian chiefs repeatedly. Something in me woke up, something like a memory. The huge feather headdress was remarkable and symbolic for a huge aura of energy, or so I imagined.

Another event was a visit by a little girl, who quickly became my friend. We rolled over the floor, playing, talking, and showing each other what we could do. Suddenly, she placed her head on the floor and lifting her legs off the ground came into a full headstand. Something in me went wild. "Yes! I can do that too!" I thought, but however much I tried, I could not. I could remember clearly that I was very good at standing on my head. Confused, I swayed between a concrete reality and something I had a memory of, which struck me as absolutely authentic and clear. There was no doubt in my mind that I could stand on my head and had stood on my head many times before. Many years later during my first yoga class, the very same feeling returned. I felt certain I knew how to do yoga and was certain I had practiced, but where and when?

Another occasion presented itself with a similar déjà vu impact. It was an adult dinner party, and my parents and friends were discussing the ancient language of Sanskrit. They commented that it was the most lucid and clear language in the world, and it would be good to revive it, teach it and use it. As on a prior time, I was smitten with the message of Sanskrit, feeling that in some strange fashion it was very familiar and close to me. When first hearing Vedic chanting the familiar pull came, the feeling that this was it, this is what I needed to do. Decades later, I signed up for and began practicing Vedic chanting. I mention these events because in some inexplicable way, I touched on some other, totally unknown and remote reality and felt I was coming home, pulled by a thread of memory from a time and place I could not define.

During that springtime, I also had the most profound experience of love. During a dream, I found myself standing at the tram stop on our street, in front of our house. A tall man with long hair, wearing a long pale garment, was standing at the tram stop. I was just a little kid, yet I threw myself at this stranger, wrapped my arms around his neck and kissed him all over his face. "Take me with you!" I begged, forgetting my parents, my home, my dolls and everything that made up my life. He questioned me, but I insisted I was going with him. We boarded a tram with blacked-out windows and traveled for a long time. Then we came to a very different place, with a mountain and many rocks. The tram was gone, and I was desperately trying to keep up with his long strides as we began our ascent. He was never anything but kind and compassionate, but I was crying with exhaustion as we climbed higher and higher...the dream ended here.

On awakening I was filled with love—love for the leaves on the tree and love for my little sister. I absolutely loved everything with a profound and deep feeling. Going outside into the garden, I looked at buds on the trees, at clouds, at the sunshine, and heard the city noises...all and everything was compressed into a web of intense and joy-filled love. This experience did not just suddenly go away but stayed for days and days before becoming weaker and eventually dissolving. However, whenever I wanted, I could bring this feeling back. Of course, at the time, I had no expression for love. After all, I was only five years old, but I had the most powerful and intense experience of a sensation which I recognized as something extraordinary and unique.

Grenades and Parting from My Father

The bombardments worsened in the spring. For a short period, an attempt was made to let me go to school. However, the air attacks now came in the mornings as well. One day, released from school, the sirens began to howl as I ran home nonstop and out of breath. When I saw planes appearing in the sky, I threw myself under the rim of a sandbox in a small playground for children. The drone was unending, a terrifying sound increasing in intensity as the aircraft multiplied. Terrified, I stuffed my fingers into my ears, only to discover the drone was inside me as well. The sound became a drawn-out and soothing "OM." Fortunately, we lived in an outlying area of Berlin, and the attacks were not as intense as in the inner city. Even so, almost daily, houses in our neighborhood were turned to rubble. Streets were pitted by deep craters, and the traffic could no longer proceed along their accustomed routes.

One day, my little sister found something beautiful on the ground. It was a glittering little object, and she brought it home. Fortunately, my mother saw it, took it from her and called the bomb squad. Two serious-looking men came and defused the glittering object. They said it was a grenade made to look attractive to children and dropped by American planes. My mother was horrified and very grateful the deadly device had not exploded in Gabriele's hand. She was very tense for the rest of the day and repeatedly instructed us not to pick up anything, however pretty it might look. The officers had told her that some of the explosives looked like dolls. It shocked the adults that civilian children were targeted.

One event still sticks in my mind. The sirens had gone off, and I had just been put to bed. Now I was quickly torn from beneath warm covers and rushed downstairs to our basement shelter. Then we heard the planes come, the whistle of falling bombs, the explosions, and the unpleasant air pressure that followed a close hit. I had been told to put my head down and cover my ears. There were other people living in the apartment building as well, maybe even people from close buildings who also sought refuge in our shelter. I recall a large number in the cellar that night, and since the attacks were close, they all lay stretched out on the floor, covering their heads with their arms. For the first time, I heard people praying, pleading for their lives, for their survival. My father stood upright, cracking one joke after another. He made fun of the attackers, fun of our condition and fun of the government. After a while, I noticed the effect he was having on the group. People were not quite as terrified, and some even laughed. The majority were still praying loudly. It was totally surreal as a scene.

My father had a wonderful sense of humor, but eventually, he overstepped his luck. At the time anyone not called up to fight was required to do some other service for the war effort. My father was very myopic and wore heavy glasses, which exempted him from military service. I gather during one of the occasions when he was asked to "serve the war effort," he joked that it was beneath his dignity to polish bombs and wished for a more appropriate way to serve. He was called in front of a Nazi tribunal and condemned to go to the front as a soldier. In an effort to save his life, his company, Blaupunkt, sent him on a business trip to Romania. He was told to get lost. Suddenly, surprisingly, he was back, bringing my sister and me little red oriental slippers with pointed, curved-up toes.

At night, heated discussions rose from the living room. Later, my mother told me that she had tried to convince him to drive us all to the Swiss border one night, drop the car over the edge of the road in order to make it look like an accident, and walk across the border into Switzerland. My father argued that he was a man of honor, not a coward. My mother told him he was a fool. Most Germans no longer had any illusions and knew at this stage that the war was lost. The Russians were advancing steadily, and it was a bitterly cold winter. In 1944, shortly before Christmas, as punishment for his outspoken ways, my father was ordered into military training and was sent to the Polish front.

We were now short of food, and barter became common, as people exchanged cigarettes for bread, alcohol for eggs, and money seemed to lose its value more and more. We had stairs in our two-story luxury apartment and slowly getting up those stairs became difficult. It became more common for me to see black dots dancing before my eyes, and I felt faint, dizzy, and out of breath.

Then the horrible day of parting came. It was evening, and I can still see my parents, their arms around each other, walking ahead of my sister and me. They walked slowly, talking, while Gabriele and I jumped up onto a low wall lining the way and, balancing on it, followed them. Eventually, we were inside the railway station. My parents embraced for a long time, and then my father hugged me. "This bad war will end. I want you to be good. Promise me to look after your Mummy." I thought the request strange. Wasn't she supposed to look after me? Then we returned home without him.

Last Letters from the Polish Front

After my mother's death in 1990, when my sister and I looked through my mother's papers and files, we found a big bundle of my father's last letters, sent from the Polish front. We sat down and read them, trying to understand some of the carefully worded messages, which were obviously disguised and meant to be only understood by my mother. He was with a group of old men and very young boys, some no older than fourteen. They had been brought to an old farmstead and huge shed, where they slept on straw without heat and received very little food. He complained about the extreme cold and rough conditions. They had only icy cold water to wash and shave their faces. He begged her to send him any undergarments she could find, even her own silk underwear for heat. The men were in training to fight the advancing Russians. They were being trained with dummy rifles, carved out of wood, as real rifles and ammunition were in such short supply.

They were also trained to ride horses, as no vehicles were available anymore. It seems he enjoyed the horses and mentioned that he would like all of us to learn to ride after the war. My sister's birthday was after Christmas, and he sent a letter to her with the drawing of a horse holding a bouquet of flowers between its front legs. Then a letter came with the news that he had fallen off a horse and had broken his glasses. He was extremely myopic and could not see without them. He begged my mother to send him new glasses. Another request was that we stay in Berlin to wait for his return. He was witnessing the huge refugee streams heading west, with their plight of cold, hunger, illness, and death. He repeated warnings, asking my mother not to risk flight from the city. The food situation was becoming worse, and he asked her to send him food, if possible.

Eventually there came a day the letters stopped. The Russians were advancing. No one knew what had happened. My grandmother came from Mannheim so that my mother could make her way towards the front. But she could not find any information. She was very close to the shifting frontlines and could hear the firing and saw the streams of people fleeing the fighting of the advancing Russian army. Within two months after his departure to the front, my father's outfit of men was declared lost. For five years, my mother waited and hoped against hope for a miracle. My father never returned.

By January 1945, everything in Berlin had gone from bad to worse. My mother had a beautiful white Angora cat with fur as soft as down. We liked to play with her and put her into our doll's pram. One day the cat could not be found, and my mother was very upset about the disappearance of her pet. She placed a request in the paper asking for the return of the cat. A week later she received the answer. "Thank you for your white cat. She was a most delicious morsel."

Weakened by malnutrition, my sister and I became seriously ill. The air raids were practically nonstop. Every night, more houses around ours were hit and went up in flames. My mother carried me piggy-back down unlit stairs while holding my little sister in her arms. I recall my teeth chattering uncontrollably with terror and cold. Once in the cellar, my sister was placed in her old baby carriage, and I was put into a crib that was somewhat too short for me. The neighbors lay on the ground, praying for hours, while the earth trembled and shook and bombs whistled through the air. One night after a particularly heavy bombardment, we returned upstairs to our apartment and found the outer walls of our bedroom gone, with the cold night wind blowing through the room. We took refuge in my mother's large bed and snuggled under the warm quilt.

Departure

Friends advised my mother to leave the city in order to save our lives. There was no electricity at all now and no gas to cook with. People built little brick ovens and heated food over little fires made of sticks. It took a long time to get food hot in this way. The signs of starvation have now made themselves noticeable. Often, when lying down, visual hallucinations came. I would see bars, black and white, which moved apart, then together again, shifting constantly. My dreams of flying were probably the most marvelous experience, and very believable. Often a big, brown-skinned man with a shaved head wearing a white loincloth would appear and show me how to fly even higher. He came when I became anxious or frightened by the circumstances around me, assisting me in my mental escapes. When I was 21 years of age, I was shown photos of the Indian Yogi Gurudev Sivananda of Rishikesh, India, and could hardly believe my eyes. Here was the man I had seen in my dreams in Berlin in 1944. He was so familiar looking!

One morning I walked out of our house and sat outside on the entry step in the pale sunlight. A boy came and sat down beside me. "Do you want to see my wound?" he asked. Naturally, I was curious, and he showed me his knee, which looked as if he had smeared red jam on it. He proceeded to tell me a horrendous story of how a monster-man had come during the night and stabbed him in the leg and that he had barely escaped with his life. The man was going to come again, he had promised as much. "Are you scared?" I asked, believing in every word of his tall tale. "I have to go now," he said and left. The next morning, he was back. "I had to come and tell you," he said showing me his jam-covered red knee. "Look, it's much worse, he stabbed me more." I listened with horror to the monster tale, again believing every word even though I knew the blood was red jam. This went on for several days; then he stopped coming. Probably his house was bombarded during the night and the monster-man got him, I thought. I believed he was dead. We too would soon be dead. I waited to feel the sensation of horror, but there was nothing but indifference. All I knew, all that I loved and relied on was being taken; there was neither hope nor security. Then I became very ill, and life was dark.

Eventually, we departed on one of the last trains to leave Berlin. Trading a bottle of schnapps for the ride, my mother organized a taxi to take us and our luggage to the train station. There we found a sea of refugees crowding the platforms, sleeping on straw, hoping for transport out of the city. The train doors were no longer opened for fear of a human stampede, so passengers and luggage were lifted through the windows into overfilled compartments. Wrapped securely into a blanket, I was placed into a luggage net for the long, dark and cold journey into Denmark. I recall little of the trip as I was ill and hot with a fever. We arrived in Abenrade and were driven to a large Victorian house, decorated with gold-colored brick trim. Here we were given an attic room with a skylight, which was the only window. The house had no damp course, and the condensation ran down the inside walls like water in a shower stall. At some stage, a woman with gray hair walked in and smiling revealed huge buck teeth. My little sister stood up in her cot and yelled, "A witch! A witch!" This was a fine greeting for our generous hostess.

Denmark

My sister and I were both severely malnourished and ill. For four months, we were carefully fed small meals repeatedly in the course of the day. In addition, I was given drinks of beaten egg yolk mixed with cream and cognac. I could not eat very much in one sitting, and I recall the desire to finish what was on my plate. One day, my mother brought me a plate of hot porridge on a large tray and instructed it to be completely eaten, or else. I tried and after a couple of spoons I could eat no more. I began to dribble the porridge onto the tray and made a decorative border around the plate until the last bit of porridge was gone.

The first day on which I was permitted to go outside coincided with the day the war ended. The streets of the little town of Abenrade were filled with festivity and parades, and British soldiers were carried on the shoulders of Danes in honor. I was stunned to discover the winter had turned into summer, and all was lush and green. I realized I must have been ill for a very long time, many months in fact.

Denmark was a kind place. I learned the language rapidly, and my new best friend was the granddaughter of our Danish hostess, who had been kind enough to offer us refugees shelter in her attic. My mother, sister, and I shared this damp room for a while, but since the house was so large, we eventually moved into a more spacious room. My aunt and uncle arrived to stay with us as well. My uncle Christian had been working in the German Embassy in Norway until that became impossible. He was thus unemployed and at loose ends. My mother's older half-sister Alma was a very beautiful and capable woman. She showed me photos in books, mostly American Natives, and told me about these fascinating people. Christian was the silent type and did not like talking to children. He was mostly not in the house and perhaps worked somewhere.

In order to earn some income, my mother first worked in a toy factory, hand-painting dolls eyes, until her sight became affected, and then Alma and she designed stuffed animals for children. My mother had considerable artistic talent, which her father had refused to nurture since he believed that decent girls did not go to art school. Instead, she held a degree in social science, which never served her. Now she and Alma became so very successful as toy designers that they had to rent a workspace and hire other women to help them in their enterprise. Regrettably, they never gave my sister or me any of the loveable and beautiful animals they designed, for which my heart ached. We had lost everything in Germany, our father, home, our toys and friends, our language and security. We were in such desperate straits; it never occurred to my mother that her children yearned for a toy.

One late evening, my mother called me, and sliding the heavy curtain back, pointed into the dark night sky. "Look, do you see it?" I saw a cigar-shaped object with a bright yellow tail end. "What is it?" I asked her. She informed me it was a flying object, very rare to see. And thus, I saw my first "unidentified flying object." My first reaction to it was fear, and I asked where it came from and would it attack us. "No," she replied," it comes from outer space or so people say." The craft floated about for a while and I became bored watching it and left.

Nighttime was hard for my mother. She would cry after she thought we were asleep, but her sobbing woke me and I would crawl into her arms trying to console her. This made her control her emotions, as she did not want to cry in front of me. However, later in the night, she would sob again, and this time I just had to lie there and listen to the grief of a young woman whose husband had been devoured by the war. I began to understand the despair and lack of security confronting my mother, and how precarious our refugee situation was.

Frau Vogtmann, the kind Danish woman who had offered us her hospitality, was not always pleased with the two little girls who ran through her hallways and garden. There were times when we were warned insistently not to make noise and not to disturb, not to speak in German, and if possible, to become invisible. The situation was trying for all of us. At first, we were extremely poor, so poor that clothes of adults were altered and used to make garments for my sister and me. My mother learned how to make soap, as we didn't have any. Then she spun wool and knitted cardigans for us. I even recall a pair of underpants knitted of wool, which were most scratchy and irritating to my skin.

Our trips to the peat bogs remain a favorite memory. We needed to heat our rooms and were informed how to get to the ancient peat bogs, where we could cut peat with a pitchfork. In a truck, we drove to the moors, which stretched out in an endless plain under the gray skies. My mother and my Aunty Alma began to use their pitchforks and cut neat squares out of the peat, which was a soft, mossy substance. Once dried, this substance burnt well in an oven.

There were some unfortunate events as well. On a cold icy winter day, I went outside to join some children in play. A boy accused me of being German, although at the time I was fluent in Danish. I recall saying nothing in my defense, just looking at him. He and his friends began making snowballs and turning them in their hot hands until they hardened to a dense, icy consistency. Then they grabbed me, stuffed snow down my back and threw the hard icy balls at me, as I desperately tried to get away. One hit my eye, and I had a black eye for some days.

A birthday party for my little friend, the granddaughter of Frau Vogtmann, was a huge and impressive affair. Unused to extravagance, I was startled to see the beautiful table in the garden, decorated with flowers, loaded with cakes, ice creams, juices, and other delicacies. About 20 children came and the feast began. I can still see the long table standing on the tall green grass under an apple tree. My mother expressed great surprise at the luxuries available in Denmark. There was no shortage of milk, eggs, or other foods. Their beautiful old farmhouses were in fact painted with a mixture of milk and paint, which gave the walls a warm rich hue.

The Danes were a kind and generous people, and we did not suffer any deprivation. We were invited to gatherings, beach parties, mussel eating, and beautiful old farms, where the food was abundant. We learned to skate on frozen lakes, experienced Christmas decorations in store windows that riveted me, and saw the midnight sun. My favorite memory was a trip to the island of Barsoe, invited by my little friend. Her parents owned a wooden house on an empty, wide span of sandy beach. No one wore any clothes. From morning to nightfall, we played in the waves, found shells and transparent jellyfish, and decorated our naked bodies with slung strands of seaweed. I had never known such luxurious freedom. The adults left us completely alone. There was even an eclipse of the sun one day at about noon. Suddenly the beach darkened as before a storm, and the seabirds fell silent. A dark disk passed before the sun. We squinted our eyes looking up at the sky, and I felt a sense of unease. Having to go back to my ordinary life in Abenrade was not to my liking, and I was rather rude and ungrateful to my family on my return. Barsoe will always be in my memory as a wonderfully enchanted island where I first tasted freedom and unencumbered joy.

One day my little sister and I visited the house owner's bedroom. There were many tempting boxes on her dressing table, and we began to open them and look inside. This is how we discovered her jewelry box. In it was a little brooch made of filigree gold in the shape of a crescent moon with a star above it. A pearl pendant dangled beneath the moon. My sister loved it, and taking it into her hand, she studied it. She didn't put it back in the box, but hung onto it. When my mother discovered the theft, I was severely scolded and we had to go and apologize to Mrs. Vogtmann and return the broach. The kind lady, seeing how much Gabriele loved the little crescent moon, gave it to her as a gift. We found it again after my mother's death, 47 years later, and this time Gabriele claimed it as hers.

Denmark was a kind place. The people had big hearts and gave generously to the poor German refugees. However, all too soon we were asked to leave this haven, and we entered the no man's land of the border between Denmark and Germany. There began a horrible and most unpleasant experience which I did not anticipate.

The Refugee Camp

We ended up behind barbed wire in a refugee camp. People were treated like cattle, deloused regularly, and we slept in unheated Quonset huts on piles of straw. There were no windows in these metal huts, only openings for entry or exit. People were asked to leave an open walking space and arrange themselves on opposite sides of the aisle. The toilets, "open cubicles without doors or roofs," were outside, so people sat on the icy porcelain rim in rain or snow. At night, the starry sky looked down from above, serene and distant.

For the first time in my life, I experienced acute despair, as we were virtual prisoners. The food was a tasteless slop; the guards cold and unfeeling. During the night, locked in the airless sleeping quarters, there were frightening noises, crying, sobbing, snoring and moaning, sounds indicating the women were being beaten and violently abused. I peed my pants repeatedly in fear of being the next victim.

The days dragged on in gray monotony, and there was absolutely nothing to do. I felt furious about being imprisoned when I knew I was an innocent child and did not deserve incarceration. Soon, I met some other children, and the boys devised a plan to escape. They had figured out that there was an opening at the other end of the camp that was the only exit. Of course, it was guarded, and we had to slip past the guards somehow. A decision was made to try the escape, and we crept along behind low growing trees and bushes, staying out of sight. Then the gate came into view. The guards sat on a bench outside the doorway, drinking coffee and chatting. Our group had by now split up. I decided to seek a way past some smallish trees when a dog started to howl, and the guards looked up.

We did not know about the dog. I decided to make a run for it and rushed into the thickest growth of trees in an elevated area. I could not see well as I plunged along when suddenly a violent sting of pain slapped my face and abruptly threw me to the ground. A strand of barbed wire had slashed my forehead in three places. I felt dizzy sitting on the cold ground with blood running over my face and dripping into the pristine snow. For a while, I just sat still. The barking stopped. In front of my eyes, the barbed fence stretched itself in an uninterrupted extension, and I just needed to walk beside it to get back to the Quonset huts. To stop the bleeding and to soothe the pain on my forehead, I took handfuls of snow, which I used to clean up the blood as best I could. For a long while, I felt dizzy and frightened and I cried. Oddly, when I returned, not a single person asked about my wounds. The worst cut was between my eyes in the middle of my forehead. The scar remains to this day.

My mother wore a rather thick fur coat, which we called the "teddy bear" coat. She had cleverly lined the entire coat with loose cigarettes, more precious than gold in those days. She managed to bribe her way out of the refugee camp with her cigarette fortune, which meant many visits to the camp commander. One day her coat lining developed a hole, and she left a trail of cigarettes in the snow as she walked through the camp. Fortunately, she discovered the damage, and I was sent to pick up the lost cigarettes.

Return to Germany

Remote relatives who were farmers living in the Rhineland region near Cologne were forced to take in refugees from the East Zone of Germany that was now under Russia's occupation. When they were informed that we were searching for accommodation, they volunteered to take us in so they would not have to take in strangers. Thus, started our stay in a tiny Roman Catholic village, all prearranged through the trade in single cigarettes.

We traveled from Denmark's border in an old damaged German train. I was excited beyond belief in my sudden liberation. The train had to stop wherever the rail was damaged and missing, and people walked, lugging their suitcases until we came to a whole part, where another train would pick us up.

The journey was very drawn out and tiring. Our trip stopped in Hamburg, a big city by the sea, where an old and very close friend of my mother lived. Her name was Hertha, and she was very wealthy. Her home was large. It seemed like a palace after all we had been through. The house was big, undamaged, and with a garden. I can still see it in my mind's eye. Hertha had two daughters, Muckel and a younger daughter, Rosika, who was my favorite.

The first thing that struck me was that Hertha had a cook who prepared all the meals. She seemed to live in a large, sunlit kitchen on the first floor, and chickens lived there as well. There was scant food since it was after the war. Hertha had purchased some hens and a cockerel, so she could have eggs, something not available in stores. The kitchen became a very attractive place for me. The chickens lived in a corner of the kitchen, and the rooster would wake up the whole house each morning with his crowing. A rabbit would also rush around on occasion, but could not be caught.

The rooms were all very spacious and silent because they had double doors; there was a first door leading into a small foyer and a second door leading into the room. Since double glazed windows did not exist at this time, the windows were doubled up. One window was followed by a second window with a space between them. Inside the space between the windows stood flower pots with beautiful cyclamen. There was a certain routine to the day, which centered on mealtimes, but eventually I became bored.

How my maternal grandmother came to be in Hamburg, I cannot recall. She suddenly appeared and perhaps looked after my sister and me. I recall in the evenings we would go to my grandmother's room, and she read books to us. Then came the evening she fell downstairs and broke her arm. For some reason, I was to blame, perhaps I had not been in my room and she had come to look for me. Since there was no electricity, the house was dark at night, and one had to carry a candle in order to see where one was going. There was a lot of excitement that night before my grandmother was taken to the hospital, where her arm was set. I recall she was in pain. I suppose pain medication was also not available then. After she departed from Hamburg, I never saw her again. She died five or six years later.

Eventually, we departed by train to Cologne in the Rhineland. It was January and bitterly cold. We were dropped off beside the grey, vast, Rhine River sluggishly flowing with large ice floats drifting in the current. The bridge over the Rhine River had been destroyed during the war. A huge raft had been fashioned from heavy planks, and we stepped onto this heaving platform. The wide grey river was frozen, and big chunks of ice bobbed in the water, banging against the sides of the raft as we were slowly pulled across to the other shore. Everything was gray—the sky, the Rhine, and the faces of people. When we arrived, the city of Cologne was nothing but ruins.

The train station was right beside the Cologne Cathedral, one of the masterpieces of Gothic art. I recall looking up in surprise at this gigantic structure rising black against the darkening sky, while all around it the structures that had once been houses had been turned to rubble. I had never ever seen anything like this marvel of medieval architecture, and my eyes kept following the levels, the spires reaching up and up. It seemed to me that the cathedral looked like hands folded in prayer reaching up into the cold empty sky. There were just two dim street lights to illuminate the empty space in front of the cathedral.

We were to wait there for the relatives to pick us up. Dusk was falling; all was empty, dark and threatening. A man told my mother not to leave the bags unguarded, as they would be stolen. We were told to sit on the luggage pieces, my little sister and me. My mother was visibly worried. As time went by, she approached a solitary man walking along and asked if there were places that would give us shelter if our relatives failed to appear. He shook his head and said he knew of no shelters. It was full night by now.

Then, out of the darkness came the clip-clop sound of horse's hooves and shortly thereafter a carriage drawn by a brown horse materialized. This was Uncle Hein, coming to rescue us. He was a very tall, skinny man with short-cropped hair. It seemed that the journey had taken more time than he expected. Very few people had cars at this time in Germany. We were wrapped in a big, warm blanket inside the old coach and the luggage went on the back. He mounted the driver's platform in front, and off we went. There were hardly any lights to illuminate the city streets and the black, charred ruins stood against the somewhat lighter sky like a picture out of hell.

Frauweiler

Later we arrived in the small, empty village of Frauweiler, which had formed itself around a nun's convent and had only one main street. The village is now gone but the little Romanesque Church in the center, however, is still a landmark. My poor mother, being a city woman, was out of place in such a rural setting and was a constant target of criticism and harassment. Children ran after her whenever she left the house calling her names and claiming she walked on coals, as she wore heels on her shoes.

The room we received on the farm was an upstairs bedroom, quite spacious, with a view of the village square where all events took place. The Muesch family consisted of a warm and charming grandmother, her two grown daughters, Adelheid and Gertrud, and a tall, silent son, Hein, who was in charge of the farm. They were the siblings of my Uncle Christian. Adelheid, the youngest of the women, was unwell and spent much of her time in prayer or in the church. When we arrived, it was January and icy cold. In a short time, the grandmother became ill. I recall her brushing her long fading hair and then knotting it into an intricate bun at the back of her head. She was truly kind to us, as we were frightened and wary children. It was very shocking when, later on, I was told that she had died. Gertrud, the older daughter, took me to see the corpse. This was the first corpse I had seen. She lay on her bed, hands neatly folded on her chest, looking chalk-white in the face. There was a curious odor in the room. Gertrud kissed her mother on the forehead and wiped the tears from her eyes. Then she sprinkled holy water on the body and made the sign of the cross on her mother's forehead. Many people came at various intervals to pay their respects to the dead woman.

My mother helped financially with the funeral arrangements. She bought the candles and flowers for the church service. The only flowers available at this early time of the year were tulips. They were still tight buds glowing in many vases around the altar of the little Romanesque church. The tulips did not open for the longest time, and everyone became aware of how long they lasted. It was taken as a special omen. It was a grey and stormy day when the funeral took place. It hailed, and there was driving rain as we walked behind the hearse pulled by black horses with plumes attached to their heads. Everyone, I noticed, wore black and the women cried audibly. Fortunately, the walk to the church was not too long, but the cold in that stone structure was excruciating. I had not been in such a church before; it was interesting to look at the figures of saints and martyrs, the crucifixion and angels. The sermon was given from an elevated balcony, a structure supported by devils and serpents carved out of stone, and painted in primary colors.

After the death of the fine old lady, our lives began to take on a very different quality. This was God's country. Every meal began and ended with a prayer. Sundays were idle days, and not even a finger was lifted. Meals were prepared ahead of time and going to church was obligatory. The village priest was respected as an educated man. He faced his congregation each Sunday from the pulpit and bellowed, "There is a draft! Shut the church door!" The men had a way of entering the church only halfway, half inside and half outside. They arranged their bodies so that a foot or a cane held the church door of beautifully carved wood open by several inches. The men thus could hear the service without actually being inside the church. The women and children filled most of the front of the church and at the very front sat all the little tots, including my sister and me. The service only became exciting when the priest became truly frustrated with the congregation. He looked swollen to me

Rosie and Gabriele in the village Frauweiler, 1948

as he thundered at the men in his powerful voice while his face became beetroot red with anger. What he said was beyond my comprehension.

The people here spoke a dialect, which my sister and I picked up rapidly. It was called "Kolsch." I learned yet another type of language. Soon my mother complained that she could no longer understand her children. So far, I had been homeschooled, and this situation continued in part because my mother did not wish her children to become unable to speak High German. The village had a one-room schoolhouse, and we went to school every day from 8 am to noon. At first, the priest instructed us. Then a young teacher was hired, a soft-spoken sensitive woman. Since the state could not afford to pay her an adequate salary and the village needed a teacher, the families solved the payment problem by feeding her. Every day she ate breakfast, lunch, and dinner with a different family. Of course, I got to know her more at the dining room table. She seemed relieved to break the bread with more civilized people and let us know her appreciation, as she considered us above the rest.

Since so many children were undernourished and frail, the occupying force of Americans supplied a school lunch. We were instructed to come to school with a metal container with a lid to receive the soup, which quickly became known as "vomit soup." I do not know what it contained, but it tasted disgusting. We dutifully had our little containers filled, thanked them, and then went home. Once inside the farm courtyard, I poured my soup into the nearest pig trough. The pigs raced over snorting and really enjoyed the treat.

Village Life

There certainly was not enough food, and we had been spoiled in Denmark. Breakfast consisted of a thin slice of heavy black bread with slippery sugar beet syrup spread over it. Lunch often was a bean, pea or lentil soup, followed once a week by a custard pudding. Dinner was more varied; there were usually sliced fried potatoes or mashed potatoes, sometimes carrots or cabbage and rarely some meat. The men, aside from my two uncles, Hein and Christian, were hired laborers and ate with us. Gertrud explained that they needed more food because of their heavy fieldwork. They each had a soft-boiled egg for breakfast most days, and if there was a chicken, duck or goose served, they got the main servings. My sister and I received the necks, wings and in general, were given the carcass to clean out. For years, I preferred the hunt for a tasty morsel of forgotten flesh inside the carcass of a bird. I can still taste the wonderful, organic meats I was given on the farm.

We did not have milk or butter to eat until 1948. While the farm had cows and abundant milk, almost all of it had to be given away by law. The farmers had to deliver a quota, which rarely left them with enough for themselves. The huge and heavy milk containers were placed at the big gate for pick-up. There was also a ladle suspended from one container "for testing." I was forbidden to lift the lid up: in case something might fall into the milk. The temptation of fresh cool, creamy milk was too much for me. On many days I did the forbidden deed of taking the ladle and testing the milk myself...ah, delicious! During the time spent in the village, in spite of a shortage of food, I was almost never ill.

The farm's main buildings, living quarters, stables, sheds, and coach house were laid out in a big square within which lay a very large courtyard containing a huge round, walled enclosure. All the soiled hay, animal refuse, and rubbish went into this open pit. The pigs and sheep were also periodically inside the enclosure. Every few months, the smelly pit would be completely emptied of all hay, and a huge suction machine would slurp up the urine and feces. This mélange of manure would then be loaded onto open wooden carts. Sturdy Belgian horses with huge hoofs pulled the carts out to the fields, where the contents were spread over the soil before plowing began. The liquid remains were equally applied over the earth. It was heaven to all the village kids to get onto the carts and out to the fields for the sordid task of spreading the manure. What none of us recognized was that the smell transferred itself to our clothes, hair, and skin. Also, there was inevitable splattering.

The first adventure of this kind was greeted with horror and dismay by my mother. The farmers just laughed, but it actually was no laughing matter. Everyone only had a bath every four to six weeks. Water was difficult to heat, and so bathing was strictly limited. That is not to say that washing oneself with cold water was difficult—a cold sponge bath was routine. However, keeping small children clean was more of a problem.

I had long hair, which hung in two long braids down my back. Since my hair was seldom washed, I was quite used to an itchy head, but this became intense, and one evening Gertrud looked closer and announced, "She has head lice." My mother was horrified, but farmers of that time had remedies for everything. The next day, I sat with some horribly smelly stuff on my hair, all wrapped in a thick towel. After several hours the towel was removed, and my hair was washed repeatedly. A "louse comb" with teeth very close together was then used to comb out all the louse eggs, which were firmly attached to individual hairs. The process was repeated the following week to assure no lice escaped. Then the school was informed that we had lice among the children. I felt very fortunate my mother had taken such great care of me. Other children were not so lucky. Several girls and boys came to school with shaved heads—an easier way to deal with the problem.

Every Monday was "wash day." A special room was reserved for the huge amounts of laundry to be washed. It had a concrete floor with drains in the floor and hollow areas meant for holding fire. Cauldrons hung over the fires, suspended from big metal ceiling hooks. Fires were lit under the cauldrons, and water heated inside them. Then linens and towels, and other laundry items were thrown into the caldrons. Step ladders were placed in front of each cauldron, and women stood stirring the contents with a wooden paddle. The room eventually was filled with steam, in spite of open windows. It looked a bit like the devil's kitchen filled with white steam, with the biting heavy odor of soap stinging one's nostrils and flickering hazy flames. The figures of women were like dark shadows coming and going in the steamy mist.

I usually helped with the hanging of the laundry. A part of the back garden was reserved for this. Ropes were strung over high poles and stretched long distances. There was a special wooden fork that was used to support the sagging clotheslines once they were loaded with the laundry. Items that were spotted or stained were laid out on clean, green grass to be bleached by the sun. I can still smell the wonderful fresh odor of air-dried bed sheets.

During the years after the war, there was a shortage of shoes and clothing in general. All my clothes were made from garments that had once belonged to my mother and aunts, and from even pants belonging to my uncles. These were cut down to be made into small skirts, pants, or jackets. That still left the problem of underpants and stockings. These items did not exist for children. So, what did we wear? Nothing, as far as I recall.

The shoe problem was simpler. People returned to former methods of shoe-making. They carved wooden clogs like those in Old Dutch paintings of the 17th century. I loved my wooden clogs. They made a wonderful sound as I walked, and all the children did their very best "to make lots of noise" when entering or exiting the church on Sundays. We made a clatter that was deafening. My wooden clogs were often a little too big, which was deemed better than being too snug. The simple solution was to stuff a small amount of straw into the toe area at the front of the clog. I noticed when I ran a lot my ankles began to bleed, as the wood hit them constantly. I always seemed to have bloody ankles.

A Taste of Religion

Looking back to the years spent in Frauweiler, I believe I was happier and more entertained than in any other part of my childhood. This was a period of intense learning. We were living in this tiny village, yet we had a wonderful organ player whose music we enjoyed during the many church services we were obliged to attend. I heard wonderful music by Bach and the Italian master Vivaldi and other famous choir music. All of us were taught to sing, and naturally those early songs never faded entirely from my memory. Mass was held in Latin, and by the age of nine, I was taking Latin lessons from the parish priest. There were traditional festivals and old ceremonies, dances, and hunts.

The village had grown around a women's convent, hence the name "Frauweiler," which means "women's retreat." Religion was constant, and everyone was involved in the practice. Since I was eight years old, it was time for my first holy communion, and I joined the group of children being readied for this big spiritual experience. We sat on the hard wooden benches in the front rows of the little church while the priest told us that our parents had not known each other before marriage. He told us that they had been strangers to each other and were not related. This came as a big surprise to me. Then we were introduced to the 10 Commandments. All of this was fascinating and strange; however, nothing bothered me as much as the notion of "sin." Lying was sin, which seemed fair, but looking at another man's wife with "lustful intentions," whatever that meant, did not seem real to me.

It was only when the priest mentioned that any time, we touched our private parts we were sinning that I snapped inside. He said it was a mortal sin that would condemn us to everlasting and eternal hellfire. I was horrified, incredulous, and more upset than I had ever been. That day, I lost my innocence, and everything gained an undercurrent of evil and horror. I ran home in tears and told my mother I wanted nothing further to do with religion. Certainly, I did not want to go to the little confessional booth and tell the priest all my sins—that I had touched myself wiping my bottom or washing myself! All of which were such horrific sins that I would suffer all eternity in hell. My mother tried in vain to explain to me that I had misunderstood, that wiping one's bottom was not sinful, nor was washing one's private parts. I refused to believe that she would know better than the priest. I also suspected she was trying to console me by not telling me the absolute truth. I cried for a long time and felt as if caught in a spider's web.

During consequent religion lessons, we were introduced to more and more sins until I felt just being alive must be a sin. My little friends, the village children, just shrugged when I told them how horrible this whole way of thinking seemed to me. Then, just as if to underline some important part, the following happened. My sister and I had one of our rare baths and after splashing around in the tub as long as possible, we were told to dry ourselves and go to bed. After we had toweled ourselves dry, we ran naked towards our room, when we encountered Gertrud. She looked at us in a misgiving way as we streaked past and said: "It stinks here, it stinks!" This comment puzzled me and I kept mulling her remark over and over until I realized we had been naked, so being naked was a mortal sin, and she had not wanted to see us like this. To her, our innocent children's bodies were "dirty and they stank."

Holy Communion

The time for my first holy communion drew close, and a white dress was made for the occasion. I wore a little wreath of white flowers in my hair and had white socks and white shoes. My aunts explained that this was going to be the greatest moment in my young life. My mother seemed to go along with this whole ritual, but I couldn't help but notice that she was curiously indifferent. I never saw her with rosary fingering beads, nor did she attend the church service on Sunday. We children had to go twice and the more often we went, the holier we would be. I practiced saying the prayers while passing the beads of the rosary between my fingers. I expected something wonderful to happen, but however hard I prayed, nothing ever did.

Then the horrible day came for my very first confession. We had been instructed to count how many times we had told lies, how often we had disobeyed our parents, how often we showed disrespect to our elders, and how frequently we had indulged in dirty thoughts. We were also to count how often we touched our private parts and were expected to recognize if this touching had been a "pleasant sensation" or not. I tried to calculate as well as I could how often I had lied since birth and how often I had wiped my bottom (or maybe scratched an itch in that part). I realized that since it had never felt unpleasant, I must have enjoyed it.

The confessional was a big dark box of wood. The center was like a little room, which the priest entered to sit down. A mesh window of carved wood allowed him to look out, but anyone kneeling in front of the confessional window could not see the priest. He was a mere shadow. On his side, there was a velvet curtain, which he pulled open before the confession began. At the conclusion, he pulled the curtain shut, which indicated the end of the confession. I felt somewhat shaky as I knelt on the hard wooden board. Then the curtain was drawn, and the priest whispered a quick prayer, before asking: "My daughter, how can I help you?"

"My father, I have sinned," I recited as instructed and began to ramble off the litany of my heavy mortal sins which would roast me for all eternity in hell. He told me not to repeat such sins, and I wondered how I would fare if I did not wash or wipe my bottom. Then I was told to say so and so many "Our Fathers" and other prayers. Then, with the sound of sliding metal rings, the curtain closed. With great relief, I left the confessional and kneeling in front of the altar, I recited my penance prayers as fast as I could, so I could get out of there.

The next day I received Holy Communion, my first since I was now purified and clean. The symbolic white dress indicated as much. All children of a certain age group walked into church for this momentous occasion. Later, I was told my little sister had wanted to be part of all this as well and had come to church followed by a goose. She and the goose had managed to walk almost to the altar before someone stopped them.

Holy Communion meant kneeling in front of the altar along a long railing, closing my eyes and sticking out my tongue. When the priest came, he placed a paper-thin round, white wafer on my tongue. We were to allow it to melt in the mouth since it was the holy body of our Lord Jesus Christ. Under no circumstances were we to bite into it. It took a rather long time to melt, and the whole notion of it being the body of our Lord was well beyond me. I remember it was a beautiful day and during the afternoon I walked to some fields where hedges of fragrant white flowers were in bloom. I felt happy with the heady perfume of blossoms and felt the day held blessings.

The experience of first Holy Communion shattered many innocent illusions I had held. Clearly, adults did not follow the teachings very strictly and lived a double standard. The priest was often very frustrated with his congregation, and he expressed his frustration in a choleric temperament he made no effort to hide. I became more watchful, more aware and careful, as I did not want to go to confession ever again. It felt like a terrible invasion of my privacy. My mother told me that she only went to church when she felt like it and that God understood her needs. She said she felt more at ease connecting with him in nature, in the mountains or in a forest. Since as a Catholic, she was required to attend mass weekly, I felt very concerned that she was committing a mortal sin and would be damned, or worse still, ex-communicated.

I dutifully attended all the required masses and began to have some strange experiences. One Sunday, as the priest preached from the pulpit, I noticed a light around his head, just like the one I had seen around the heads of saints in books. Startled, I realized this meant he was a holy person. I stared harder and the light became stronger. To test myself I turned my head and looked at a woman. As I held a steady gaze, she too began to develop a light aura around her head. Now I tested my vision on as many people as I could, and everyone had an aura. This delighted me enormously, for it meant all these people were good and holy, but why did the Catholic books give these signs of an elevated person only to saints? Perhaps most people were saints. Such musings brought me few answers and much confusion. Another vexing point was the prohibition to read the Bible as written. The priest explained we would get confused. The Vatican had given interpretations to specific Bible passages. My mother disagreed with the priest. She had read Bibles that had not been "doctored." I learned from her what was written in those holy books had to be examined with intelligent care "because it isn't necessarily so!"

The villagers seemed to have a special love for the Holy Virgin Mary. Her statue stood in a little dark side chapel surrounded by candles. There were usually more people kneeling there than in front of the big altar. On my wanderings through fields and past stands of trees, at crossroads and other areas where old oaks stood, I would delight in finding little niches or tree hollows which contained a statue, sometimes primitive, often worn by time and weather, of the Goddess. It thrilled me somehow, for no reason I understood, to find this little figure inside a hollow in the tree. I noticed even men stopped to pray to her and ask her blessings for their fields. Usually, some withered daisies, cornflowers or poppies lay at the feet of the figure.

The Circus

There were many holy days in the Roman Catholic Church, and most were celebrated. There were also many fun fairs and other celebrations. The circus came at intervals. It took over the whole village green to erect a huge tent, which went up quickly. Then the fancy circus wagons and painted and decorated trucks arrived, along with the cages of wild beasts and performers who rode in on horses. It was a memorable entrance. Since our room overlooked the village green, I had a perfect spot to observe the whole drama. The village children gathered to see the unloading of cages and beasts. We stood transfixed to see a dwarf, the "fattest woman," clowns, trapeze artists, and the India rubber lady. There were colorful wagons in which the circus folk lived, and we were thrilled to see beautiful girls with waist-length hair in colorful gowns, who applied cream to their hands and arms while we stared in total fascination.

It was a time of great anticipation and excitement. When the tent was ready, a car drove through our one village street, and a man with a bullhorn cried out the time of the performances and announced the extraordinary and unique events we were invited to see. I went around the relatives begging for money so

I could see the shows and get onto the carousels. I recall being right at the front of a performance. The India rubber woman was announced. "She has no bones in her body; she can bend like rubber." It was the long-haired girl wearing a very tight bodysuit. She stood on the platform and slowly bent back until her face was almost on the ground. Then, with a quick flip, she had reversed herself and was back on her feet. Then she stood on her head and a man fed her long strands of spaghetti, all the while explaining how the food had to go anti-gravity to get to her stomach. I was so close to the girl I could see her efforts as she became a snake, then turned somersaults, and did the other acrobatic feats that the man demanded of her. She was extraordinarily double-jointed and flexible. Since I stood right in front of her, I could see her breathe and notice the beads of sweat on her brow. This all was deeply exciting and a revelation to me. Watching a group of singers perform, I had noted how the Adam's apples of the men vibrated. During the circus days, the entire population of the village gathered under the big top for feasting and dancing and entertainment. We children were sad when the big tent came down and the wagons were reloaded. The show went back on the road, and suddenly the village green was once again empty and only used for football by the young men.

Looking back, it seems to me the circus came quite often, as did Gypsy caravans. The Gypsies arrived riding on tiny horses and pitched tents on the village green. The Gypsies were not liked quite as much. The warnings would circulate that they stole if they could, and people would lock their sheds and stables. One dark and rainy night, the dogs began to bark steadily. We had just finished dinner. The men rose, looking grim and picked up their coats. I too wanted to go outside but was firmly prevented from doing so. Instead, I listened to the furious barking and howling of the dogs as they moved away towards the fields. The next morning, we heard the news. The dogs had been untethered and had led the men out to the fields, where thieves were busy stealing from a big shed where potatoes were stored. No Gypsies remained on the village green.

Visits to Cologne

My mother was clearly uncomfortable in the village. She left several times to take pottery and art courses. Then there were courses in making clay sculpture. She was inspired to make clay sculptures, so my sister and I were made to pose for her in our nightgowns. I still have her little sculpture of two girls, the older with a protective arm around her younger sister, who is leaning into the embrace. Symbolically, the piece indicates fragility and the need for protection, which is reflected in the position of the children. It also speaks of my mother's concern for her fatherless offspring.

My mother had wished to study art, but her father had not allowed that. Now she had an opportunity. The courses she took quickly brought results, as she was very talented. I recall her efforts to sculpt a horse. My job was to hold the horse and, if possible, to keep it still. It was a problematic undertaking, as the horse would jerk, paw the ground, swish its tail and wiggle impatiently. Nonetheless, she made a beautiful horse sculpture. Our relatives found all sorts of fault with the work, and I don't know what happened to it. She also had me pose for a life-size bust. Her sculptures won prizes, and a piece called "The Lost Son" was so highly regarded it ended up in the Cologne museum. Many photos were made of it, and I still have a very clear image of this particular sculpture in my memory.

In order to make a little income, my mother also made little cloth dolls. She referred to them as Biedermeier dolls. They wore long pants with hoop-skirts over them, carried a bouquet of flowers and, in my childish opinion, were adorable. I wanted one with all my heart. They sat on top of a dresser and when enough were ready, she would take me with her to Cologne where she delivered them to a little shop. Belgian soldiers bought them to send back home to their girlfriends in Brussels. It was my good fortune to be taken along when she visited Cologne. Sometimes we went to the zoo, and sometimes I was treated to ice cream, a very rare delicacy. It can't have been very good, because I vomited regularly after my treat. Basically, the ice cream was a sugar and water concoction.

Cologne was, if I recall correctly, mostly destroyed and a rather depressing sight. Charred ruins lined the roads everywhere, and huge amounts of rubble spilled into the streets. It was the women who cleared out the rubble. They were emaciated creatures, wearing scarves tied around their heads, turban style, who collected the rubble in buckets and baskets with bare hands and without any tools. As we stood at the road, trying to cross a street, an old, bent woman came along carrying a sack that she found very heavy. For a moment she lowered it to the ground. A man suddenly ran for it, grabbed it and raced away across the road. "Please, my coals!" she shouted, "Please I need them, I am old, and you took my only fuel for heat and cooking!" But he disappeared around a corner.

Another time while in Cologne, we witnessed a few heavy trucks rumbling down the road. They were filled with coals. Boys no older than 12 or 14 years of age waited at corners. When the trucks had to slow down in order to turn, they ran to the backs of the trucks and jumped up. Once on the truck bed, they began to throw down pieces of coal in rapid succession while older boys raced behind the trucks, picking up the pieces of coal. The whole process was well-coordinated and so fast it was amazing.

We traveled from the countryside to Cologne on old buses, and just the smell made me feel carsick. Usually, the journey ended with me vomiting. On one occasion, my mother started to talk to a man who claimed he was a palm reader. He lifted my hand and began to tell my fortune. Unfortunately, I do not recall much of what he said, but he claimed I was an unusual child with a very kind heart and much compassion. This startled me somewhat because at the farm I heard repeatedly how selfish, callous and unfeeling I was.

Farm Chores

At the farm, there were always jobs to be done, such as sweeping the chicken house, cleaning out the pigsty, and carrying heavy metal coffee containers out to the field where the men were laboring. I remember going barefoot since I had no sandals. It was late summer, the wheat had been cut and I had to walk barefoot across the sharp stubble, while hot coffee spilled onto the sides of my legs. Experiences like these made me try to avoid being seen around because I knew I would be asked to peel potatoes for dinner or darn socks of the laboring men (an almost nightly chore) or clean the mud-encrusted boots of the workers. I liked to hang out in the chicken house where it was quiet and I actually could read a book, or knit, a skill I was slowly learning.

I don't recall having personal friends. We seemed to hang out as a group, inventing group games and functioning as a little horde. As in every village, there was the "idiot" girl, a retarded child who was happy even when we beat her legs with nettles. There was the "Pollack," a Polish boy who was born in Poland but had German parents and was now a refugee in the village. He was tall and skinny and he spoke no German, which was the reason the priest beat him almost daily.

The priest, as mentioned, was choleric and always surprised us with his sudden outbursts of anger. To my horror, my sister once became his victim. Gabriele was small, very petite, with a head of curly white-blonde hair. Where I was dark, she was fair. I do not know what offended the priest, but he slapped her hard across the face, and then repeated it. She did not cry, smiling at him instead. He hit her again, for "dumb insolence." I went home and told my mother. I felt outraged. My relatives advised my mother not to complain; surely Gabriele had been naughty.

The remote relatives we lived with, the two sisters and two brothers, whom we called aunts and uncles, were exceedingly fond of my sister Gabriele. In many ways, she was a golden child. She had a very fast tongue and was able to defend herself expertly. They said she should become a lawyer. She was quick-witted and smart to an admirable degree and she understood how to wrap people around her little finger. Everybody loved her (except the priest) and she managed to organize the horde of village kids into following her ideas. In a sense, she was also fearless where I was hesitant.

On a farm, animals are raised to be killed for food. Farmers were not sentimental about sweet little bunnies, or birds, mice, or piglets. If a mouse was caught, it was thrown against a wall for a quick death. If a sweet little golden fluff ball of a chick had something wrong with it, the same fate was meted out to it. Pigs screamed blue murder before they were killed. Too intelligent not to realize death was looming, they made as much noise as they could in protest. Chickens were picked up by their feet, swung in a circle to distract them, and then their head and neck were deftly laid over a wooden block. Before they realized it, the hatchet descended, severing their heads. The bird was then let go and for several moments, the headless creature would run in a circle, spouting blood from its neck until it fell over and collapsed completely.

Gertrud would demonstrate the process to both of us girls and then ask me, as the older, to behead that lovely brown hen. I felt sick to my stomach already and could do no more than shake my head in horror and disbelief at her request. Gabriele was different. She was interested in the procedure and very capable. I watched as she beheaded her first chicken. Geese were dispatched by a different method, which involved a knife deftly plunged into a neck artery. After that, they were left to bleed until they fell over dead.

Autumn was the period when animal slaughter took place. Sheep and pigs, calves and bullocks, geese, turkeys, ducks, and hens were killed before the cold winter came. There were two reasons for the autumn slaughter. During the summer, the birds and animals had offspring and there was a certain abundance of young creatures on the farm. As older animals were no longer as fit and productive as before, they were killed in favor of younger livestock. During the long winter, when food was not plentiful, too many animals were a burden on available resources. The month of October was the chosen period for slaughter and celebration. The whole village was involved in the process and people helped each other. Early in the morning men and women came and were given a hearty breakfast and then the work started. One animal after the other went to its maker, and the vats filled with blood for making blood sausage. No part of the animal was thrown away. Pigs' trotters would end up in soups. Pig's heads became "head cheese," a type of jelly. Chicken feathers were used in down comforters, sheep's wool was spun and then used to knit sweaters. The skins were carefully prepared to make boots and leather jackets. Men stood around chatting with girls. The backs of the pigs were hung in a special chimney, where the meat was smoked, thus producing that particular taste of really good bacon. I recall sucking the rind that had been cut off the bacon, which was so delicious.

It was at that stage in my life I saw my first professional art in an art magazine my mother had bought. It contained images of the work of a German artist by the name of Max Ernst. An electric shock went through my being, as I carefully looked at these somewhat surreal images: the "Temptation of Saint Anthony," other images that looked like forest, rubbings of wood texture, and many strange visual designs. It was also at this time my mother introduced me to American jazz, and I heard music composed by black performers for the first time. My mother played the piano beautifully and taught me to sing "Lieder," a form of German art song and to accompany her on the piano. While I had no problem learning the songs, the messages in the songs dismayed me. There was the song "Das Veilchen" (the violet). The peasant girl comes along and the little violet thinks how wonderful it would be if the girl plucked it and pressed it to her bosom. Alas, the girl comes and steps on the little violet, which dies at her feet instead. "Das Heiden Roschen" was even more upsetting to me. The young man sees a little heather rose and wants her. But the rose warns him that she will sting him with her thorns if he should dare to touch her. Again, sadly, he is not impressed by her threat and tears her from the bush. She stings him, but in vain; she is the one who must suffer.

It was really only after I had left Frauweiler that the realization suddenly hit me that I had lost the most wonderful and free place I had ever known. To a large extent, the fact that I had not really been in a normal school until I was nearly 10 years old had given me a freedom to evolve, a privilege that very few children experience. My mother had educated me, probably better than any school was capable of doing. I had learned Latin from the village priest, had learned to respect the music of Bach while singing hymns in Church, and had a certain amount of misinformation put in my brain, but essentially my mind had been left in a healthy and intact state. I knew how to question the information I received and knew how to think for myself. The basic premise I clung to was that not much could be trusted. I continuously saw people behaving in stupid and irresponsible ways, and so much so, that I felt most people were in some fashion emotionally handicapped, usually by gross incompetence.

My Mother Returns to Berlin

That spring my mother became very ill, and I think now about how unhappy she must have been. Probably it was not surprising that she became ill. There was nothing for her to do in the village; she was an outsider, a city woman. She was sick enough to be sent to a sanatorium, a special healing center. There she wrote to old friends. Many of her teenage friends had been Jewish. One close friend had emigrated to Texas before the Holocaust occurred. The mother of her friend took pity on my mother, Leni, and sent her a generous amount of money. My mother had no income and would not have been able to make much by selling Biedermeier dolls, so this money was a huge injection of hope and raised her spirits. The first thing she did was to travel to Berlin, where we had lived until we had to flee.

The city was occupied by the Americans, the British, and the Russians. She had a great deal of trouble getting over the border. She told how she had paid a man who guided her through a salt mine on foot, a journey that lasted several hours and was very dangerous. "If the Russians had caught me, I would have been shot," she told me. In Berlin, she went to our house, now occupied by US military officers. She spoke fluent English and they were courteous but regretted to be of such little help. The paintings on the walls had all been cut out of their frames and most of the furniture had been looted, they informed her. After talking to the Americans, she looked up her neighbors. They were less welcoming, especially when she noticed paintings belonging to her on their walls and her arm chairs in their living room. Their excuse was "You were not here, you did not have to suffer through this time, and we are entitled to everything we took."

An old friend, a Jewish woman, related how the Russians had entered Berlin, raping every woman and child they could lay hands on. One of my mother's friends held out for days in a dank cellar until hunger drove her out. When Russian soldiers saw her, she pulled out her revolver and shot herself. The daughters of her Jewish friend fared better because they said they were Jewish, and the soldiers were respectful, having seen extermination camps. My mother had explained to me that there had been concentration camps, but that the German people had refused to believe such a horror existed. Because she was friendly with many Jewish people in Berlin, she had received more information. Some Jewish people were protected in northern Germany, especially in Berlin. It depended on having powerful friends in government. Thus, the Jewish doctor who took my mother's appendix out was spared because his profession was valuable. Jewish women married to Germans were often protected. Yet the wife of the famous painter Max Ernst was killed, and he missed being transported to a camp by taking the wrong train. Essentially, it was more luck than anything else if someone survived.

My father had been very outspoken and therefore been condemned. His telling the truth was a risky thing. I began to get a sense that in all things a double standard applied. While the priest asked us to tell the truth, saying that lying was a sin, adults all around me spoke mostly in ways that were of advantage to them. All through my childhood, there was a palpable sense of fear in the air, sometimes so thick it could have been cut with a knife. As I grew older, my perception was one of living in an extremely dangerous and untrustworthy environment. My mother told me how the city of Berlin was divided into two zones, one under American domination, one under the power of Russia. The poverty was extreme, and she had witnessed people fainting from hunger. Assistance would eventually arrive, and they gave the poor people hot water to drink. The heat was enough to revive them a bit, but the water had no nutritional value and so they fainted again after a short time. It seems my mother stayed with her Jewish friends, and they were receiving a huge amount of restitution funding for what they had suffered. Of her own property, my mother could save nothing, and it seemed to me that going back to her old house and seeing old friends had depressed her greatly.

She had also tried to find out what had happened to my father. As he had not been declared dead, the chance of a return was a possibility. At this stage, three years after the end of the Second World War, many men were returning from the east, my Uncle Willy among them. He had been a 17-year-old music student and had been lured into the Hitler youth movement with the promise of receiving a scholarship to study music. Once in it, there was no escape, and he had to go into military training. Almost immediately, he had been wounded and come home, only to be sent out again. He was captured by the Russians and tortured, and he became a broken man. He never talked about what happened to him, but his wife told some of the stories to the family.

It was usually at night, when adults talked, that I gathered information. My mother's brother Willy was in a prisoner-of-war camp in Russia when he contracted typhoid. Shivering with high fever, he was dragged out into the icy winter and covered with ice and snow. Perhaps this was actually a Russian method to help the sick and drive down their fever, but apparently this was executed with sadistic amusement. Willy was now emotionally and physically handicapped and was trained to be an upholsterer, and that is how he made his living. His health remained very poor and he was haunted by what had happened to him. I met him only once, many years later, when I was a student in Germany. He was fast-spoken, extremely well-read, and intelligent. He confessed that he would have liked to study psychology and that he liked philosophy. It struck me as tragic that he had not had much of a chance in his life. He was very likable and charming.

Gymnasium

In 1948, when I was 10 years old, my mother became busy. She traveled to Cologne repeatedly, had interviews with certain people, and spent time talking to Gertrud while I was not allowed to be present. My mother was never one to give much warning before some big change was instigated, but I never suspected she was planning to leave Germany.

In the interim, I had passed a required test that allowed me to attend high school. In Germany, children are separated by the age of ten according to their intellectual capacities, and those who are bright enough go to high school, or Gymnasium, which emphasizes academic learning. Those who are not inclined to academia enter the Oberrealschule, where they learn technical things, like carpentry, mechanics, or farming. I was thus obliged to travel by bike to Bedburg, a little town four kilometers away from our village, where a big, noisy high school spread out in the town center. Gertrud found a very stiff antique bicycle which was too high for me, and not even the saddle could be lowered. This vehicle was now my main means of transport. I stood in this bike, pedaling madly to get up the hills and pedaling backward to break my speed when I went downhill.

I was exhausted when I arrived at the big school building. There I had to find my classroom by myself, find the timetable for the courses on the bulletin board in the big entry hall, write down my courses, and then make my way to class. My classroom was huge, a room filled with noisy and unruly children. The teacher had a list of all the names, which were read out loud, and each student would answer "present" to acknowledge that he or she was there. I had my first English language classes at this school, despaired at not understanding math, and was very hungry by the time school ended at 2 pm.

Other children came with sandwiches to eat during the break; I don't recall having this luxury. I do remember having a bit of money in my pocket and actually stopping at a store to buy a scoop of sweet whipping cream, which was delicious. The ride home was often tedious as I cycled behind big trucks belching fumes that nauseated me. Nor had I received any instruction on how to behave in traffic and was rather terrified. I was also very concerned about my inability to understand or do my math homework. There was no one to help me, and I feared I would fail the class. When I finally arrived back at the village, I dismounted beside some fields where cabbage grew and would walk out to bite into the juicy green heads, never breaking one off, so as not to steal, just taking a bite to tide me over till dinner.

Spring moved into early summer and I cycled daily to Bedburg. I do not recall talking to any child in the school, nor to any teacher. I liked English and it seemed easy to learn, much easier than Latin. It was a huge relief when my mother told me one day that we were leaving soon. She failed to mention that we were leaving without my sister. The news of our departure was huge and most welcome, as I feared I had failed in math. I had been saved from an untenable situation, and I thanked in my heart to be freed.

At this time, some interesting things happened. I was taken on a pilgrimage by Gertrud and one of her friends. I had no idea what a pilgrimage was. We traveled to a faraway town, a rather lovely place which seemed to have suffered no destruction during the war. Here we stayed at an attractive little hotel, all of us in one room. I watched with interest as the women changed clothes. They did not have my mother's fine tight body and had saggy breasts. Since I had never seen this, it was a revelation to know middle-aged women looked like that. Later, we went to a cathedral, where an Easter service was taking place. The congregation stopped at every station on the road to Golgotha, the place near Jerusalem where Christ was crucified. As it were, we followed the route of his suffering, following pictures painted along the cathedral walls. He was shown carrying the coarse and heavy wooden cross, here was the point when a kind woman rushed from her house and pressed a cool cloth to his face, taking an image of his suffering away with her...and so it went on. I felt quite moved by the explanations and the images depicting Jesus' suffering.

Later, hymns were sung and we walked out into the countryside to a holy place where miracles had taken place since the Middle Ages. People brought their sick and crippled friends and relatives to this special spot to be healed. To my great disappointment, I saw no one being healed, but I must say the faith of those present and their deep devotion had its effect on me. I had a profound experience observing and participating in this ritual. Whatever it was, I never forgot the first time that I experienced people's faith and their belief in a higher realm. The lunch we enjoyed was on an open terrace in the fresh air which also was a new experience. I can still see the plate with mashed potatoes, green peas, and a pork cutlet. It tasted superb and amazed me. Normally, food did not taste this good.

The other experience at this time was a party, a costume party at a wealthy landowner's home on his farm. I had never before even known the young man, who was several years my senior, who gave the party. There was music and dancing, and every girl wore a pretty frock. This was the first time that I felt awkward and ugly, knowing I did not fit in. I watched in amazement as he danced with quite a few girls and all of them looked smitten. I longed to be one of them. He chased after them, and they squealed with delight at being caught. Later he noticed me and came after me too. However, I pulled away from him. A few days later he asked me to come to the farm, a rather prosperous one with lots of land and farm hands. He told me the village was to be destroyed and would become an open coal pit. His father's farm was to be sold to the government, and they would be given another one of equal value somewhere else. I was upset to hear this news, for even the cemetery was to be dug up and all the bones of the dead were to be reburied. It was clear to me that leaving this lovely village, though I loved it there, was the best thing. I had seen enough destruction without seeing Frauweiler destroyed as well.

The day of our departure arrived quickly, and the hasty farewells seemed too short. Even now, it was not really made clear to me, how long I would not see my sister. In her customary style, my mother merely indicated my sister would join us later. I felt rushed and everything was out of control. A car took us to Cologne, where we sat for a long time in an open park, well into the dark. Finally, we boarded a train. I remember being in and out of stations, a hard bench, tiredness, and an arrival in Munchen, where I saw hot dogs offered at the station. We traveled through the night, and a gray dawn arrived with the news that we were now in Italy. It had been very difficult for my mother to secure papers to enter Italy at a time when no one gave Germans entry visas. When she lost her husband, my mother was a well-to-do woman; now she had to live by her wits and ingenuity. She had saved some funds but they were not sufficient enough to take two children into a risky situation. She chose to take me, and she left my little sister behind on the farm for what she hoped would be a very brief period. Later, I discovered that the relatives held Gabriele in very high esteem. In fact, they wanted to adopt her and make her their heir, as none of them had offspring. They rightly saw her talent with animals and plants and her ability to organize and get along well with others. They esteemed her cheerfulness, cheekiness, and practical disposition.

Italy

In Italy, I again found myself in a country whose language I could not understand. As in Denmark, I was told not to speak in German, lest we offend someone. My mother spoke Italian fluently. We arrived in a huge train station in Rome, with bustling crowds of people, and found a small pension hotel in the heart of the city. Our room was tiny, with one bed, which we shared. This was all we could afford. My mother had sewn German money into her shoulder pads and in order to survive, had to stand on street corners and offer Deutschmark in exchange for Lire. Occasionally, some deal would be made in a hasty, furtive way that made me feel very uneasy. We lived frugally, subsisting on biscuits. Every day we walked the city. There were beautiful sidewalk cafes, where we occasionally sat down. My mother would have an espresso, and I would get a wonderful "Pellegrino Aranciata." The cafes usually featured two musicians plus an elegantly dressed female singer who performed popular songs. The music enchanted me, the violins sobbed and the singers lamented to the point of even shedding tears. I was informed that these were love songs. The other aspect of Rome that struck me was that though the city was old, it was undestroyed. There were no bombed out buildings present as far as I could see.

Eventually, I was even allowed to go out alone and wander around our block and look at all the beautiful dolls in the shop windows. It seems to me that we were in Rome quite a long time. We were becoming short on funds, and now we walked to the churches and nunneries, where my mother asked if they would give us refuge. I recall the hard faces of the nuns and the sound of the heavy metal gates clanging shut in our faces. One day, much to my delight, we sat in a sidewalk restaurant facing a beautiful square and a Baroque fountain with its soothing sounds of splashing water. My mother ordered spaghetti, and this was the first hot meal that I can recall having for a long time. She also bought me a banana from a passing donkey cart laden with fruit. It was the first banana I had ever tasted. After the meal, I wandered around the piazza and admired the beautiful fountain with its splashing water, so cooling on a hot summer's day. Eventually, I returned to my mother who sat smoking and seemed nervous and uncomfortable.

As we sat without leaving, I asked her why. "There is nowhere we can go," she said. "I have no money left." I felt a surge of total panic and fear. "But what are we going to do?"

Rome, Italy, with the Egyptian Football Team, 1948

I asked, unable to comprehend that we were at the end of our choices. She had no answer. We continued sitting as the afternoon faded into early evening, and the little street lamps switched on. We did not talk but observed the elegantly dressed people walking past. My mother was twitchy and nervous, and I felt deeply frightened.

Suddenly, my mother jumped up and rushed towards a group of dark-skinned strangers, who were just then walking past the cafe. She rushed to one, and there was hugging and a great deal of excitement. She was speaking yet another language, and I was totally in the dark as to what was going on. We walked with them to a beautiful Roman hotel with marble floors and were given a spacious, elegant hotel room with giant full-length mirrors on the wardrobe door.

Only then did I discover who these people were, as my mother finally found the time to tell me. Several years earlier, during the Olympic games in Berlin, my father had been stopped in the street by an Egyptian, who assumed that my dark-haired father was a fellow countryman. The Egyptian was in Berlin with his team of soccer players and wanted to know about the fabled Berlin nightlife. My father invited the whole

*At the Colosseum in Rome, Italy, with the girlfriend
of an Egyptian Football Team member, 1948*

group to his home and later showed them the sights of Berlin.
A friendship began between the Egyptian soccer team and
my parents, which was eventually cut off by the war. This was
the very same team that was now in Rome, playing against the
Italians when my mother saw and recognized them. For several
months, they very generously paid for all our expenses and
even arranged for an entry visa into Egypt. It was a miracle in a
time of desperation.

Life in Rome now took on new dimensions. We went
sightseeing with the Egyptian soccer team in grand style. My
mother's linguistic skills were much appreciated by them,
and we visited museums, the Vatican, the amazing Pantheon,
churches, the immense facade and soaring cupola of St Peter's,
and the Vatican libraries with endless galleries, which left
me overwhelmed and intoxicated. We visited gardens and
fountains, piazzas, and restaurants. I ate ice cream and drank
endless bottles of Pellegrino Aranciata. It became hot in Rome,
as it was summer, and my mother had to buy me a little dress,
in which I danced in front of the full-length mirror, delighted
with my looks. One of the sights that impressed me more than

the Coliseum was a church under which an immense network of passages spread root-like into all directions. Here in the Catacombs rested the remains of the men and women who died in ancient Rome for their new Christian faith. There were endless miles of skeletons, one on top of the other, and ribs covered the floor. The ceilings were artfully decorated with bones and skulls gazing out of empty sockets, and passage after passage was filled with the remains of martyred beings.

Then came the day the Egyptians left to return to their homes. My mother told me that quite soon we too would be departing and that I would be flying on an airplane. We would fly to Cairo. My mother had spent some time in Egypt as a very young woman, when for a period of time she assisted a very wealthy Florentine family with their children—two girls called Cupid and Kiara. She told me about the famous pyramids of Giza, about donkeys and camels that filled the streets, and that people wore very different types of garments. She also told me that I would be seeing my Aunty Alma again, whom I had last seen in Denmark. Once we were settled in Egypt, she would arrange for my sister to come and join us.

2 Egypt

Magical Egypt

At the age of 10, I was about to experience my first airplane flight, and it was to the foreign land of Egypt. We left late at night. The plane had huge propellers and made a hellish noise. We walked across the tarmac to the aircraft and were given our seats. Once in the air, the plane endured quite a bit of agitation, and it was not long before I was vomiting. In spite of my great excitement, the flight lost some of its glamor. Eventually, I fell asleep and woke up to a light-filled bright cabin. We were already in Egypt, flying over the town of Alexandria. I saw nothing but sand-colored space below, which was the desert. We landed, and it was very bright outside. A pleasant dry heat touched my body. While it was hotter than in Italy, the heat was less bothersome because it lacked humidity. Some people loomed at a distance, my aunt among them. I saw her waving. There were cordons and barriers, but I just ran past them and dodged under the cordons to reach her, and we had a heartfelt embrace. There was a particular smell in the air, which I later recognized as the smell of the desert, and which I grew to love.

Aunty Alma had come to Cairo after we were all sent out of Denmark. How she managed this, I never found out, and what she did reveal to me was quite shocking. Her grandmother came from a prosperous, aristocratic family, and had influenced the young Alma with intense advice, telling her to marry into money and to be wary of falling into love with someone of middle-class birth. Fortunately, Alma was a beauty and had much charm, so at the age of 18 years, she met a wealthy and corrupt count, who proposed to her. Among other real estate, he owned a castle in Heidelberg and lived in that charming university town. He was a gambler and spent the winter months in the south of France or in Italy, where he frequented the casinos. Alma soon discovered that he was unreliable and that she had married the wrong man. As a consequence, Alma asked her husband to establish her financial security by giving her a part of his wealth. She succeeded in investing her money well, and when I first knew her, she had amazing jewelry, especially diamonds. Already as a child, I was aware of her unhappiness and restlessness. As time went by, her husband began to lose money, and the couple separated. The bitter end came when one night, drunk and miserable, he lost all his wealth in a gambling casino in Monte Carlo. He sent a cable asking Alma, who was in Florence with friends, to help him out by covering his losses with her money. Alma refused, and in desperation, he shot and killed himself in front of the giraffe cage in the Berlin Zoo.

Alma was then a free and prosperous woman and spent the winter in Egypt, where she met a charming university professor of Egyptian-Armenian background. They married, but she soon discovered that in Egypt women stay at home and do not work. Furthermore, they lived with his family, and his family controlled the young married couple quite intensely. Alma also discovered she was unable to conceive a child, which became the reason the marriage was dissolved after 10 years.

Always ready to create a new way to live, Alma decided to start a business making orange jam, and she was very successful. She even exported the product. Eventually, she met Christian Muesch, the eldest son of a wealthy landowner and farmer, who worked in the German Consulate in either Morocco or Tunisia. The war broke out at this time, and the Consulate was changed or dissolved. At any rate, Christian left

North Africa and moved to Oslo, Norway. In the meantime, Alma met a charming Brit called Ray Jessup, a pharmacist, who was secretly working for British Intelligence.

Circumstances became very confusing and at some point, Alma and Christian married, and she moved to Oslo, joining her husband Christian. Why they came to Denmark in 1945 I do not know. Alma stayed in Abenrade until we were all forced to leave. Her connections in Cairo must have been very good, as she left without her husband for Cairo. Meanwhile, Christian returned to the family farm in Frauweiler and worked together with his brother and two sisters in managing the farm. It may have been Christian who arranged for my mother, my sister, and me to come to the farm as well. I do not know how these arrangements were made.

So now Alma stood on the hot asphalt and welcomed us to Egypt. She had started a small hotel that was a cool green oasis in the very heart of busy Cairo. Her little hotel was called "Horus House" and was located on the uppermost story of an elegant house. Her place had a huge rooftop veranda, where people could sit in the late afternoon and evening to enjoy a drink. The view was lovely. Looking out over the rooftops of most houses I saw chickens, rabbits and even turkeys living there. The houses were surrounded by gardens with trees, palms, and abundant flowers. It was on that spacious rooftop of Alma's hotel that I had my first view of Cairo. The hotel had about thirty rooms to rent, mostly to English and American guests. These were people who worked in embassies and consulates or who were teachers at the American University or professors of Egyptology at the large Cairo University. They were a merry crowd who congregated for high tea on the open veranda or got together for "Sundowners," mostly scotch and soda or gin and tonic.

My mother and I received a tiny, windowless room with two little beds. There was not much room for anything else. It was hot and airless, and my aunt had designed a curtain that was open at the top and did not reach the ground and so permitted some ventilation. My aunt explained that she could not keep us for very long and that my mother would have to find work to support us. If I remember correctly, she gave us a deadline of three weeks, after which we were expected to be out of her place. My mother was visibly upset, as she had not expected quite such a harsh reality to hit her as soon as she arrived. The next day, my mother made an appointment with General Fouad Hafez, whom someone in the football team had recommended to her. Fouad was the president of the football committee and head of the Egyptian Intelligence.

In the morning, we took a taxi through the hot, dusty, and crowded city and arrived at a huge impressive building, the Officers' Club. A veranda surrounded two stories and open archways gave a view down into an abundant flower garden with old trees. We walked up to the second floor and entered a huge office. A ceiling fan of amazing proportions hummed, and the room was pleasantly cool. General Fouad Hafez rose from behind his vast desk and welcomed us. He was a big man, slightly heavy, wearing a uniform with ribbons on his chest. His eyes were hazel, and his face was kind and smiling. He sat us down and called for a servant. I was offered freshly made mango juice, which I had never tasted before. My mother received a cup of Turkish coffee, and lovely pastries were brought in. He treated us as if we were important, which surprised me. Of course, I could understand nothing of the conversation, but it obviously went well as I could see my thin, elegant looking mother relaxing visibly. The mango juice was delicious, the fragrance of flowers drifted through the air, and beyond it, the sun-drenched city.

"He invited us to see the pyramids," said my mother as we left. "Are you excited?" I was very excited, as I had been told of these famous monuments and looked very much forward to seeing them. So far, my experiences had focused mainly on the view from Alma's terrace. I was able to look at life on the rooftops and gardens below. There were two sisters about my age who practiced piano every afternoon in a spacious garden room with French doors wide open to let in the scents of flowers and the cool air. To judge by their elegant clothes,

First Camel ride at age 10, 1948

they must have been French. I had nothing like those frocks. A gardener moved at a snail's pace from one flower bed to the next, watering the plants. I was informed that it rained perhaps just once a year in Egypt and without the Nile River and its water, the country was just desert.

I was fascinated by the way the Egyptians dressed. The gardener wore a long white gown, called a galabia, and a turban, as did all of my aunt's servants. Upper-class Egyptian gentlemen wore a red hat called a tarboosh. It looked just like an upside-down red flower pot with a black tassel hanging down from the top. The upper-class gentlemen did not wear galabias, but wore western-style suits instead. Women wore Malaya, black wraps that covered most of their bodies. They often also covered the lower parts of their faces with veils, so only the eyes were visible. They lined the inside of their eyelids with a black powder called kohl, with the result that their eyes looked startlingly beautiful. They also had a way of using their eyes to communicate, and I thought them very glamorous. Upper-class women dressed like Europeans and looked rather haughty. There were also lots of the Europeans, and since Egypt then was still under British dominion, the English language dominated. The ruler was a Turkish king called Farouk, who was more of a figurehead than an actual king. Along the Nile, where the Nile Hilton hotel now stands, used to be the British army barracks, a huge red brick building.

The trip to the pyramids of Giza took place on a sultry afternoon. We were driven in an American Ford Station wagon by a driver, and Fouad sat with us in the back, talking to my mother. Everywhere people saluted him, and the simple people bowed. I began to realize he was rather important, but he had no airs of importance about him. Once I saw a man coming to ask a favor of him. He plunged to his knees, and kissing Fouad's hand, he rapidly gave an account of his troubles, or at least he tried to. Fouad lifted the man up, patting him on his back as if he were the man's father, and made him sit down beside him. Then he listened to what the man told him. I was rather impressed by Fouad's humility. In Rome, I had seen people kissing the ring the bishop wore on his index finger. The bishop allowed people to kiss his ring. He even expected it and thrust his hand into people's faces, impatiently, or so it seemed to me.

We had left the city behind us by now and were driving through a vast quilt of checkerboard fields, all of which were the most amazing emerald-green color. There was a network of canals spreading amongst the fields, and every now and then we passed a brown mud-brick village. The villages consisted of square, box-like houses, with smaller and smaller boxes built on top of the flat roofs. There were water buffalo, camels and donkeys everywhere. The villagers, called Fellahin, wore galabias, and the women were all dressed in black Malaya.

When we arrived at Giza, I saw the huge sand-colored group of three pyramids. They hardly distinguished themselves from the desert in tone, and I felt a hint of disappointment. The chauffeur was instructed to drive into a very elegant hotel on the right, the Mena House hotel, which was a famous landmark. Here I was offered a cool glass of fresh lime juice and a better view of the great Cheops pyramid. Eventually, the adults rose, and we started up a steep hill towards the pyramids. It was only now that I began to get a hint of their true size.

The slope was tiring to walk, and the area opening up at the foot of the pyramid was vast, a platform of huge stone blocks. I ran ahead, excited at the prospect of getting closer to the monument. A number of Bedouins on donkeys, horses, and camels began to close in on us. They offered us rides and a faster mode of transport. I was offered a camel, and a photographer materialized to take my picture. The camel protested, but dutifully sank to its knees, and I mounted into the high saddle. Then, to my surprise, I was nearly thrown off backward, as the beast rose to its front feet. Then I was thrown into the opposite direction as it straightened up its back legs. I was high above the world with a magnificent view.

One of my mother's new friends was an elegant gentleman called Youssef, who actually lined his eyes with black kohl and wore a red tarboosh on his head. On his first visit, he brought a big box of chocolates called "black magic." They were entirely for me. I had never before eaten praline chocolates and was entranced with this sweet delicacy. I managed to eat the entire contents of the box, much to my mother's embarrassment and to Youssef's delight. Later on, in the night, I paid for my excess, but Youssef on his next visit brought me another box, which I again demolished within the shortest time. This time I felt so sick that thereafter chocolates no longer tempted me.

Rosie at age 11 with Aunt Alma, 1949

I soon discovered that my Aunt Alma had a lover. Ray
Jessup, her British spy friend from before her marriage to
Christian. He had the room next to my aunt's and was quite free
going and coming to her room. It became apparent to me that
the guests in the hotel were all more or less fun-loving, open,
and easy-going. When the sun began to set, everyone gathered
on the big roof terrace for cocktails, my mother among them.
Below us, gardens were being watered by gardeners patiently
standing with hoses in their hands, and the smell of damp earth
and fragrance of flowers rose. White clad servants moved
among the guests, delivering gin-tonics, beer, whiskey, and
wines. The party atmosphere spread as night descended, and
Arabic lamps were lit. A gong announced when dinner was
served.

My Aunty Alma was a very beautiful woman. It was said
that "she carried herself like a galleon in full sail." Tall and with
unusually blue eyes, she exuded a sense of self-confidence and
charm that served her well throughout life. Her two younger
sisters could not compete, and it caused much sibling rivalry,
especially between my mother and Alma.

Her room was always chaotic but filled with amusing things. She had a little dressing table covered with a silky fabric on which she displayed her creams, powders, crystal jars, make-up, dried flowers, silver hair brush and comb, and perfumes. Silk stockings hung over chairs, as well as silk nightgowns, and curlers, slippers, and high-heeled shoes abounded. I was allowed to put on her slippers, powder my face, make faces at the mirror, and amuse myself painting my eyes. Her room was a treasure trove of charms and temptations and in no way resembled my mother's tidy space. She enjoyed allowing me to style her abundant hair and, in my young mind, making her look more elegant.

The temptation rose to have a bit of fun. On her dressing table lay a number of clothes pegs. I had just completed brushing and styling her hair and noticed the hem of her silky skirt was caught in her belt. When she stood up her skirt hem just barely covered her underpants and her generous thighs were fully exposed. To help matters along, I now took the clothes pegs and hitched up more of her skirt, pinning it to her blouse at the back, where she could not see it. The gong was sounded for lunch and she now rose to her full height allowing me to see the transformation from behind. At the back, the skirt just covered her underpants and no more, while from the front her attire looked normal. The round, generous thighs were fully exposed, and I had to practice severe self-control not to burst into laughter. She marched off into the dining room, and several guests broke into loud laughter at the sight. One of the female guests caught my aunt's skirt and pulled it loose, thus ended the show. I don't think Alma ever took in what I had done.

Alma liked to show me off and often took me shopping or to meet with her friends. One of her great loves was the cinema. Cairo had numerous big opulent cinemas. During the hot time of the day, from 2:30 pm until close to 6:00, many people went to the movies. Movies were mostly in Italian, English, or French. Alma liked Italian. I went along, understanding nothing of the plot and having to guess at what was going on. Even now, I can still see some of the scenes in my head. Afterward, we went to the famous Groppi Cafe, where I was allowed an ice cream soda. Here characters gathered to be seen: rich women dripping gold bracelets and jewels, their eyes heavily ringed with kohl, and paunchy men of substantial girth carrying ivory canes and fly switches with horse hair tails to shoo away the ever-present flies. Tiny cups of strong Turkish coffee were drunk and pastries like Baklava tempted the customers.

I don't recall how long it took for my mother to find work, but she was now absent during the day and came home in the evening, totally exhausted. Probably Fouad Hafez, the general, had helped her. It was a government job, and she hated it. Because of her knowledge of languages, she found employment in the censorship office, opening letters from people who had been blacklisted for some reason. She was required to steam open the letter, read it, and then decide if there was some offensive or political message that warranted the destruction of the letter. She told me of one time where she opened a letter of a young Italian woman who was married to an Egyptian and homesick for Italy. She missed her family and was sending her mother the first baby tooth her son lost. My mother had to throw the tooth away and I was so horrified and saddened by that story.

Now I was usually on my own, as my aunt too was busy, and I was attracted by the kitchen. My aunt had a cook and a number of servants. People in Cairo were naturally multilingual. I spoke only German, so the kitchen staff set out to teach me Arabic. What are the first words one learns in any foreign language? Dirty words, of course! My Arabic vocabulary contained expressions like "You are the son of sixty-six dogs," "by the cunt of your mother," and "fuck you." It was not explained to me what I was saying, and the staff roared with laughter every time I uttered my new words. A young Coptic girl named Nadia was also employed, and she took me under her wing.

Most of the grocers in our neighborhood of Zamalek were of Greek origin, and Nadia and I would go out together to buy bread, olives, and feta cheese. The green grocer would

Leni, 1949

give me tastes of this or that, mainly cheeses, and was much amused that I knew so little about food. One time, Nadia took me to a little Roman Catholic Church in the area. We knelt in a pew right in the back. I watched my new friend. She prayed with her eyes shut. A fly landed on her hand. It crawled all over her brown hand, but she did not shoo it away. It began to crawl up her arm; still, she did not move. I was awed that her concentration on her prayer was so intense, that she did not find the fly irritating, something I would have been incapable of.

My impression of Cairo was heat and blinding brightness. It was very dry and dusty. Donkey carts, camels, and bicycles moved smoothly among cars and trucks. There was an incredible noise of honking horns, car radios blaring in competition with radios in street cafes, and the repeated call to prayers, chanted mostly by blind men, which happened every morning, at noon, once in the afternoon, and every evening. There was the most vibrant and colorful quality of life everywhere. I only needed to step into the street, and the adventure began.

Boarding School

I missed my sister very much, to the point of feeling deep grief. I also missed the village of Frauweiler, the freedom I enjoyed there, and the children. In Cairo, I had no friends. No other children lived near me, and I could not speak or understand the languages around me. I became bored and felt caged. Thus, I looked forward to the promise of school. We visited Saint Mary's English School in Shubra, an old district of Cairo, where I became a pupil. It was a convent school, run by British nuns.

Every morning the huge old school bus appeared at 6:45 am to pick me up at the corner of the block. For a full hour, the bus crisscrossed Cairo, then a city of 3 million inhabitants, to pick up little Egyptian girls. We were obliged to wear school uniforms, complete with a tie around our necks and a badge on our chest. The heavy brown shoes were uncomfortable in the heat, a reminder of good old England.

There was more than just one school bus picking up children. As I stood waiting, a very good-looking boy would come accompanied by his servant girl. She was taller and older than he and she carried his school bag for him. It puzzled me that he could not carry his own bags. Later children told me he was from a rich family, and they had slaves. The girl was his personal slave. The slaves were the children of the family's servants and were considered part of the family. They were never referred to as slaves, but in effect, they were owned and they served the family with no compensation given.

Since I did not speak English, I was put into a kindergarten class in my new school. It was ridiculous to think a ten-year-old would communicate with five-year-olds. I was moved to a class closer to my age. A lovely nun called "Mother of the Angels" was responsible for teaching. She was Irish and had a beautiful singing voice. I was instructed to call her "Mother" if I wanted to address her. "Mother of the Angels" taught poetry. And thus, I encountered William Blake, the great mystical English poet. The first poem I had to learn by heart was "Little lamb who made thee, dost thou know who made thee? He is called by thy name and he is himself a lamb..."

The school was strictly religious. Our days started with prayer and ended with prayer. I learned how to recite the "Our father who art in heaven" in English, and slowly forgot to recite it in my mother tongue. After the third day in school, a child walked up to me and asked; "Do you want to play?" I understood, and after that, I could speak English. At the time it seemed like a miracle to me how quickly I picked up this language, how fast I began to understand others, and that my mind worked to perfection. Of course, I had English classes in Germany, so something had already prepared me. It was in no time that I was moved up to the level appropriate to my age. This class was under the leadership of a great, big woman, who was most intimidating.

Then a problem came with the long bus journey to school. Often, overcome by petrol fumes, I became bus sick and vomited almost on a daily basis. My mother was informed, and it was decided I should become a boarder, which meant I only came home on weekends. My mother was irritated by the rules and requests the school made. I had to bring my own silver cutlery, inscribed with my name, plus sheets, towels, and napkins bearing my name. I also had to bring a certain number of clothes, far more than I possessed previously. It was a big financial sacrifice for my mother to provide all this. Once I was a boarder, circumstances went from bad to worse. The rules and laws imposed on children were medieval. There was to be no running anywhere, no singing, shouting, or talking when in bed. We were not allowed to stand in the shower for longer than a few minutes, sleeping without underpants was also not allowed, and permission was to be asked for nearly everything. I became very depressed and longed for my freedom.

The nights in the big dormitory were hot and airless, especially as we slept under mosquito nets.

The food was tasteless and coarse. It seemed to me that every meal came with thickly sliced, greasy French fries, which were cold. The nuns tried to force me to eat them. "But you are a German, you like potatoes," they admonished me. Oranges had to be cut with a knife and eaten with a spoon. Peeling oranges was not ladylike! We had an exercise class that met frequently under the direction of a priest. It was called "Come stride jumping with me." Twenty little girls in black bloomers and shirts exercised in the courtyard, hating every second of it.

On Saturday afternoons I walked through the foyer to the exit door and waited to be picked up. Often the Ford station wagon with the faithful driver was already waiting for me. I was to see my mother. This was the highlight of my existence. Very soon, my mother had her own apartment. It was a three-bedroom flat on the eighth floor of a tall apartment building overlooking the officers club. In no time she had two lodgers, both working as secretaries at the British embassy. They rented the rooms and received daily breakfast before going to work. My mother prepared the bacon and eggs with toast and tea and employed a handsome servant to bring breakfast trays to their rooms. He also cleaned the rooms, kitchen, hallway, and veranda.

The veranda was my favorite place. It skirted around the entire apartment, so there was an airy fresh quality to the space. When my mother had placed many plants with beautiful flowers there as well, it became a garden refuge. The view included most of Cairo, and I could watch all the activity that went on in the street below. Our house was the highest on the block; I could even see my aunt's Horus House Hotel in the distance.

On weekends, my mother took me to the big zoo in Cairo by cab. We walked in the beautiful garden setting and saw the wild animals. The zoo had been established by the British, and they liked big trees and water canals, islands within lakes, and the like. This zoo was a wonderful refuge from the heat. We walked around until we were tired; then my mother would take me to the "Tea island," which was situated inside a man-made lake, surrounded by flowers and trees and swarming with ducks, swans, herons, and all manner of birds. We would settle down, me for my favorite Italian spaghetti, and my mother for Wiener schnitzel. Usually, we stayed for quite a while since it was the heat of the day now. I would spend this time sketching waterfowl and watching Egyptian families and their children playing.

Once, while rounding a corner behind which a massive fence among thick shrubbery was visible, I wondered what animal was accommodated here. No sooner had the thought come than a huge beast came into view, seemingly irritated. It sprayed the fence. I stood transfixed and was not at all sure the fence was enough protection. Beyond the creature a large pond was visible, and it turned away from me and descended into the water. A sign on the fence said "hippopotamus." This was the famous Egyptian hippopotamus I had seen carved into temple walls and painted onto papyrus texts in the Egyptian museum. It snorted not far from me in its pool. I was fascinated with this creature and later bought myself a copy of a ceramic hippo sculpture in beautiful turquoise adorned with the plants of its habitat. Hippos were also sacred to Taweret, the divine midwife and goddess of pregnant women. Later in my adult life, I would own three sculptures of the Hippo Goddess, one carved of ivory, one from Kenya made of green malachite, and a massive black ebony carving also from Africa, and I eventually acquired several tiny carved ancient Egyptian pendants for necklaces. My chance encounter with a hippo developed into a curious identification with a culture to which I did not belong.

My study of Arabic was improving, for aside from learning English, I also had classes in classical Arabic. Spoken Arabic was referred to as colloquial, and it was the language spoken on the street. Classical Arabic was understood in any Arabic speaking country, mostly by the educated class. This was the written language and the language of the Koran. Our Arabic class was given by a young woman called Miss Helmy. We each had our Koran book, filled with words written in a script read from right to left. The book opened not from the front but from the back. Miss Helmy would chant out in her clear bell-like voice, "Allah Ho Akbar." Then we would repeat, "Allah Ho Akbar." Then the next line would be chanted. Eventually, we knew all this by heart. And that is how I learned Classical Arabic.

The school, although filled with little Muslim girls, did not allow any Arabic to be spoken on the playground. Children were meant to learn English with a good number of Christian values thrown into the bargain. This did not bother them, as many were Coptic Christians. Slowly, I discovered that upper-class Egyptian families valued a western education for their children, especially their girls. They spoke Arabic to their servants and English or French to each other. Their children were eventually fluent in Western languages and could go to a university in France or England.

My mother explained to me that even in Europe there had been a time when German was called the "language of the stable boy," and polite society chose to express itself in French. This reminded me that my own grandmother spoke in French to me when I was little, in part because she used French with her second husband, my grandfather, who came from Alsace, France.

We also spent many weekends with Alma and her group of friends. There were the Baglows, a military couple. He was very jolly and he loved a good laugh. There was a handsome American who was the Director for Coca-Cola in Egypt. I think my mother had a crush on him. Later she told me he had preferred an English woman who had a somewhat crooked mouth and a loud laugh. He married her. My mother said he did not like taking up with a woman who had children, as he did not like "raising another man's brood." I could see he had hurt her feelings on my sister's and my account and I was very glad to see him out of the picture. He also warned her not to give me Coca-Cola to drink, as it was "bad for the body, and if you don't believe me, put a rusty nail into the drink; it will dissolve," he said.

There were times when we were invited to parties and my mother dressed up to fit into British society. I watched with amusement as she put on a little "cocktail dress" and wore a hat and little white gloves. This was absolutely ridiculous in the heat of Cairo. The English always maintained their customs and wore a tie and jacket for dinner, and ladies wore gloves and hats. Since I was in an English boarding school, I began to understand the subtle undercurrent of a class system that looked down on Arabs and Egyptians and foreigners in general. If someone did not understand English, it was customary to raise the voice. The tone of voice got through eventually.

My health began to be affected by the poor food in the school. By Easter, I became very ill. When the summer holidays arrived, a doctor diagnosed some problems with my blood, perhaps anemia. He suggested a holiday by the sea. Alma offered to take me to Alexandria where she was going with Ray for a vacation. We drove in his car out past the great pyramids onto the highway leading down to the coast. It was a three-hour journey with a break at a mid-way rest-house.

The rest-house was a noisy cafe where tea and refreshments were served. Standing in the middle of a vast and empty yellow sand desert, it was the only place of refuge for many miles, and the most interesting people entered it. I saw men with brilliant eyes, eyes that were sharp and penetrating, as only someone who looked daily over miles of sun-scorched plains and honed his sight to distance could have. I saw women completely wrapped in black, with only their eyes still visible. There were special "harem rooms" where they secluded themselves. A monastery was nearby, founded after the death of Jesus Christ, right beside a salt sea, where men lived in complete seclusion, and they were Christian Copts. Apparently, the Egyptians were among the first to become Christians and remained so until the sixth century, when their country was conquered by the Arabs, who brought Islam with them. The invaders never left, so the country slowly became more Muslim than Christian.

The journey of three hours to Alexandria seemed very long to me, in part because there was so much of interest to see. As we neared the Mediterranean, the landscape shifted to places where huge papyrus thickets framed the highway. I saw kingfishers of brilliant blue, great white heron, gray heron, swallows, and egret. Eventually, at my insistence, we stopped the car and walked closer to the great green forest of reeds through which I saw bright blue channels of water. There was such a strong sensation of déjà vu that I was quite overcome with emotion. I longed to be on a barge going into the papyrus thicket, seeing all those wonderful birds and listening to their voices and the soft lapping of the water. My last vision was that of a kingfisher flying up, and I promised myself to return to this magical spot.

Alexandria

Alexandria, a Greek city in Egypt named after Alexander the Great, was a sand-colored town much like Cairo, except that the inky blue Mediterranean spread like a glittering girdle along its northern edge. A cornice, or broad avenue, bordered the coastline. Great blocks of black granite had been dropped down in certain areas to prevent the ocean from encroaching upon the town.

We stopped at a lovely beachfront hotel called Beau Rivage. A charming garden opened up within the inner part of the hotel. Huge monkey puzzle trees overlooked an area where guests were drinking tea, and white-clad servants rushed around. Our rooms overlooked the brilliantly blue Mediterranean. I stepped out onto the veranda, and the air was filled with the strong fragrance of salt and iodine.

All I wanted was to get to the water. It had a private beach reserved for hotel guests only. I spent most of my days by the ocean, jumping from tide pool to tide pool, finding shells and little crabs, entranced with the treasures of the sea. I did not know how to swim and so was permitted to go only thigh-deep into the water. My aunt was more interested in the night life, so I became part of these excursions, which I found torturous. These were mainly a place to eat and dance by the ocean and featured a band, singers and belly dancers. Those things were entertaining, but, being young, I was tired and could hardly keep myself awake after a certain time. However, Alma and Ray danced and joked and laughed and kissed, while I suffered and wanted nothing more than to get into bed. Sunburned and hot, the night air turned cold, and I shivered in my sundress feeling terribly miserable. It also occurred to me that my mother would never have kept me up so late. (Many years later, I discovered that my mother had suffered equally when Alma, who was ten years older, had kept her awake late into the night when she was the same age as I was then.)

The holiday had been good for my health, but I had also learned more than needed about my aunt's love life. Brought up as a Roman Catholic, I knew that being with Ray was not right and condemned according to the church, as she was married, Confused, and without anyone whom I could ask, I became more and more bewildered.

Back in Cairo, when I came home from school at weekends, my mother seemed tired and irritable. She complained of a backache and sore feet. It was not long before I was massaging her feet, something that seemed to help her a lot. In my heart I worried about her, she was the only parent I had, and I did not want her to get ill. She also had some strange requests. She would ask me to open her packages of cigarettes, then offer one to her, and light it. Flicking a lighter was too difficult for me, and often she had to light her own cigarette, which clearly spoiled the service she expected. Another service was making her a scotch. This was always after five o'clock and I was instructed to get a glass, pour a couple of fingers of scotch whiskey, add two ice cubes, and then fill the glass halfway with soda water. I did not mind doing these things at the time, but later I felt embarrassed when friends saw me light her cigarettes, pour her drinks, or rush a wrap to her.

I missed my sister very much. In school, I failed to make friends, and when the long summer holidays came, I was more of less imprisoned in the apartment all day long. My mother provided me with painting supplies, and I spent most of my days copying paintings by great masters. When she came home, I would massage her feet and her back for an hour. Sometimes a friend came; we would drive at dusk to the great pyramids and wander around the monuments. The temperatures in Cairo would drop as soon as the sun sank. The general population would then seek the outdoors, the gardens, the Nile cornice for walking, the parks, the clubs, and the desert. At the pyramids, it became so cool a cardigan was necessary after dark.

Suddenly the great news burst forth that my sister and Uncle Christian were coming. Alma's husband, Christian, had been part of the German diplomatic corps. As I mentioned earlier, his last posting during the war had been in Oslo, Norway. After the war, he was unemployed and he returned to his family's farm in Frauweiler in the Rhineland, where we, too, had found sanctuary. Now, it seemed, as Germany was slowly recuperating, he had been offered a position in East Africa, in Kenya. The circumstances behind Alma and Christian's separation and her ability to leave for Egypt at a time when no one of German nationality could get travel permits were never explained to me.

The Arrival of My Sister

In Egypt, great upheavals were taking place. King Farouk, a Turkish monarch, had been on the throne of Egypt when the British had occupied the country. A coup had taken place, and a general, Mohammed Naguib, seized power. The king was forced to leave Egypt on July 26, 1952, and he and his family and retinue were placed on a boat leaving for Italy. The day Farouk left from Alexandria was the same day my Uncle Christian and Gabriele were arriving by boat. Alma and my mother and some other people were in the Alexandria harbor, waiting for the ship

*Mother, General Fouad Hafiz, Aunt Alma, Uncle Christian,
Gabriele (age 13), Rosie (age 14)
at the arrival of Gabriele in Egypt, 1952*

from Europe to be allowed to enter. War ships cruised about, soldiers milled around, and confusion was everywhere. There was no shade and no food. We stood in the heat and I became very sunburned as the hours drifted from morning into the afternoon. The air was electric, canons were fired, shots rang out, and people shouted. In vain I looked for the king. It seems he was quietly whisked away in a motor launch out into the open sea to board the yacht that transported him to Italy.

There was shouting and jubilation when finally, the ship we had so patiently waited for came into sight. It was a big white ship, the sky was very blue, and the water sheer ink in color. An anchor was dropped and a stairway was placed against the side of the ship, and only then people descended. As the crowds milled around and we moved forward, I felt extremely happy and excited to have my sister back in my life. Soon we were embracing. She had two long brown braids and wore a white blouse. The trip we took back to Cairo has faded from memory, but I recall that Gabriele was very quiet, saying little. Reality was not as my imagination had painted it. We had grown apart;

she seemed distant and silent. Then a curious truth emerged. My mother and I had left Germany in 1948. We now picked up Gabriele in the middle of the summer of 1952. Throughout the years my mother always insisted that the separation from Gabriele lasted just a year. I had taken this statement as the truth, never really counting the months as they added themselves into years, never really examining the fact of a separation that amounted to four long years. My poor sister had been abandoned and left with no adequate explanation.

How could I reconnect to Gabriele? This burdened me, confused me, and alarmed me. She was silent. My mother asked her what she would like. She said she missed the farm animals. She would like some chickens, some rabbits, something alive. Now looking back, I think she must have felt traumatized, confused, and miserable. I felt as lonely as ever, maybe more so. My sister had not actually returned, she had been replaced by some unknown child, someone I did not know and failed to connect to.

Since my Uncle Christian was now in Cairo, he stayed at my Aunt Alma's Horus House Hotel, and we were invited quite frequently for lunch, dinner, or just for the sundowners on her big terrace. Ray seemed out of sight, and Christian was very much present at his wife's side, holding her hand or arm, indicating ownership if not infatuation as well. Alma was wearing amazingly low-cut dresses, revealing her ample bosom. I decided to scold her for indecency and pinned her dress together at the front. In retrospect, it amuses me that she allowed me to do this. Christian's stay was not long and after his departure, Ray was back at Alma's side. At the time I felt that there was a strong love between my aunt and Ray. In fact, I thought she was happier with him than with my uncle.

Soon we were back in Saint Mary's English Convent school as boarders. I had learned not to ask questions because the nuns disapproved of curiosity. I held my sister's hand tightly as we went in and was by her side during recess. I talked German to her. The nuns heard, and we were instantly separated. "Your sister is here to learn English," they admonished me," you are strictly forbidden to be together." Something in me exploded. There was little I could do, but I found means and ways to rebel. I spent my solitary lunch break in the classroom drawing a chalk skeleton on the blackboard. At first, nothing was said, but in time the teachers found it unsettling to find skeletons on blackboards, drawn in chalk on hallway floors and elsewhere. No one knew I could draw, so I was not suspected. Then I began to write on the blackboard, what exactly I cannot recall, but the nuns became irritated.

Shortly after this, my sister became ill with mumps. I insisted on using a phone and called my mother in her office. I told her she had to pick us up, it was unbearable and Gaby was very ill. The Ford station wagon was there that same afternoon, and we were out. It was just as well, as I had mumps too. A delicious free period followed. We were in the flat, high above Cairo and could play and escape the deadly routine in the convent school. It was at this point I realized that I found that routine unbearable. The years of being a refugee and moving like gypsies from place to place had left its mark on me. I preferred the unstable existence of our former lives to the deadly monotony of being a pupil in a convent.

At about this time, my mother had found a newly built apartment building in Zamalek, suitable for her dream of starting a small hotel. She had saved all her money to make a first down payment on a flat on the second floor. It was a huge apartment, spacious and cool. The entry had white marble floors, and a huge mirror in the center gave the appearance of space and opulence. Two elevators were available; this was luxury indeed. Of course, we did not instantly move in. In fact, this was a long drawn-out negotiation and a difficult decision for my mother to make. Perhaps there were financial considerations, a lack of funds. At any rate, the process took its time.

Eric

My mother met an Englishman named Eric. He worked for the Shell Oil Company in Suez and was a widower. I figured out instantly that something was going on. My mother was behaving in strange ways. One day when we were at Eric's house, I found her in the little bar area off the dining room, painting a heart pierced by an arrow with her red nail polish onto the wall. My first thought was: this is not her house, why is she painting a heart on the wall here? Then it dawned on me, and I became jealous and anxious. Eric was nice enough, a jolly Englishman with a ruddy complexion. He told me he had two daughters in England who looked much like me, a comparison I resented. He came to Cairo, and I was with them in a taxi witnessing how he massaged my mother's hands in a frantic and I thought, undignified way. He also sent her huge bouquets of flowers, which she arranged with unusual devotion. The whole thing both frightened and irritated me. I had seen enough of Alma and Ray together to feel this behavior was immodest and undignified.

Then Eric invited us to the Suez, and it was certainly lovely to be by the sea and to live in a rambling British-style bungalow surrounded by a lush almost tropical garden with palm trees and bougainvillea. There was a tame Fennec fox, a creature so exquisite and lovely I fell in love with it. I was warned that it was flea-infested, and I decided it needed to be washed in kerosene to free it of fleas. The young son of the gardener brought me the fuel and I forced the little creature to be washed in this smelly stuff. Some adults appeared and pointed out that this was a cruel and poisonous, perhaps a lethal flea treatment, and I let go of the fox, feeling terribly sorry and upset to have hurt the little creature. My other memory of our stay was that there were quite a few guests. After dark, when all the guests had left and I was supposed to be in bed asleep, I crawled along the wooden veranda that surrounded the house and listened to the sounds coming from behind wooden-shuttered doors. The squealing and laughter, moaning and heavy breathing was most mysterious and intriguing. I tried to figure out who was with whom and what was going on.

Upsetting news was not long in coming. I overheard Eric imploring my mother to marry him. He wished to return to England and start a chicken farm. The girls—Gabriele and I— would be sent to a good boarding school, and all would be lovely. A wave of nausea rolled over me. My mother belonged to me, not to this stranger. I did not want to go to England nor to a dreary boarding school. In desperation, I turned to prayer. Fervently, I prayed to the holy Mother to remove the man who was threatening my sister's and my own existence through wishing to marry our mother. I was terribly determined in my quest and prayed on every occasion—on weekends, Sunday mornings in church, afternoons, and evenings. It is worth mentioning that I was quite religious at this time, and although my mother did not go to church, she insisted we go on any and every occasion. There was a little Roman Catholic Church in Zamalek that was run by Italian nuns, and it was there that I performed my ritual.

All this took place during our summer holidays. Back in Cairo, our mother was at work while Gabriele and I amused ourselves as best we could. My mother had bought a typewriter for herself, and as we were alone in the flat, we hatched a plan and decided to type her a letter. I clearly remember the long hours as Gaby and I typed, painfully slowly, as every other word had to be retyped and mistakes had to be corrected. We spent most of the day on our masterpiece. We decided the letter should be a note to her from Eric. It was a very brief note, terse in fact.

Dear Leni,
I am sorry I won't be coming to Cairo this week. Here is a pound note to buy the children a chicken. I hope you enjoy it. With love.
Sincerely yours,
Eric.

Eric had been in the habit of buying us a chicken or giving my mother the money for one. Of course, we had no money to put a pound note into the envelope, and we also thought that she would notice very quickly that this was a fake letter. We steamed a couple of stamps off an old envelope, addressed the letter in a wobbly hand, sealed the envelope and then we took the elevator down to the first floor and stuck the letter in the mailbox with my mother's name on it. We went back to play and forgot all about our letter.

My mother returned after four in the afternoon. She was irritated and upset. "I could have sworn I saw it float down," she said. "What was floating down?" I asked. "Oh, this wretched pound bill," she exclaimed. Only slowly it occurred to me what she was talking about. I tried to tell her it was a hoax, that we had written the letter. There was no pound bill! She heard not a word. Instead, we took the elevator down and, finding the Boab, the concierge, a Nubian from Upper Egypt, she insisted he take her into the elevator shaft to search for the pound bill. The empty square socket of gray cement had big oil spots in its inner circle. There was no pound bill! They must have gone into the shaft and taken the loot, she muttered to me as we made our way back upstairs. Again, I told her that we had written her a letter on her typewriter and put it in the post box downstairs, but she turned away in silence.

I remember it was May, spring in Egypt with a lot of trees in bloom. We were home from boarding school, and Eric had come up from Port Said and was staying at Horus House, my aunt's place. That morning, I had been at church and prayed that Eric would go away and leave my mother alone. I had become sullen and jealous, often impolite to Eric and annoyed with my mother. It was not only that their relationship troubled me; I was becoming aware of physical changes in myself, swelling breasts and pubic hair and awkwardness.

That night we heard that Eric was very ill. The next morning, we visited him in the Anglo-Egyptian hospital. His face was very red and swollen like a balloon. He had become infected with a cold and used a Vicks nasal stick to clear his nostrils.

After frequent inhalations the sinus cavities became infected, and the infection spread into his head. Later, his heart became affected and in a couple of days he died. I recall my shock at the suddenness of his death, and worse still, I began to believe that my prayers had caused his demise. To my surprise, my mother was totally cool. I did not see any grief or tears. Some months later she stated he could not tempt her to return to Europe. People in Britain were still using ration cards, and after years on a farm, she had no desire to return to village life. I need not have worried so much as my mother was a smart woman.

Changes in School, Home, and Egypt

The situation in Saint Mary's English school, however, became more and more difficult. I was forgetting my German, and my mother learned that there was a German school in Cairo run by the nuns of the Saint Borromaer Order. To my enormous relief, we would no longer have to be boarders but would take a daily bus to this German school and back. Also, my mother was giving up her job at the censorship office and would be running her new little hotel, named "Pension Zamalek." The move came suddenly and was swift. My sister and I now shared a big room with flowering trees outside our balcony window. The area was quiet in comparison to living over a big main street crossing the island of Zamalek. Much had been seen by me from that high vantage point of the eighth floor in our former home.

In the early fifties, there was great political upheaval in Egypt. The country had been under British occupation since 1872 (or protection, as some referred to it). British manners and style of life dominated. Upper-class families sent their children to English schools, while still speaking French in the home. Arabic was considered low class. On January 26th, 1952, rebels against the continued presence of the British in Egypt set the European part of Cairo on fire. I was home that day and I recall the thongs of angry people swarming down the main arteries of Zamalek, overturning cars, which they set on fire, shouting

Entry to Hotel Zamalek in Cairo, Egypt

slogans and bringing themselves into a frenzy of passion and anger. I watched it all from the eighth-floor balcony much like someone in a box at the opera. King Farouk left Egypt on July 26, and his son Ahmed Fouad II was declared king. By 1953, Fouad was deposed, and Egypt was declared a Republic. Gamal Abdel Nasser became the head of state by 1954, the final victory of the coup of 1952. Nasser ruled until 1970, when his vice-president, Anwar el-Sadat, became the president. Sadat ruled for 11 years and was assassinated in front of a worldwide audience at a military parade. But I am ahead of myself.

After 1952, the English began to leave Egypt and the radio stations in Cairo became multinational. News was read in Arabic, Italian, French, and English. Music was equally divided to serve a multinational public. I learned Italian and French songs, heard American jazz and blues, and listened to Ella Fitzgerald. During special festivities we could hear the great Om Kalthoum, known as the Arabic Nightingale, singing at a huge concert in the officer's club below our eighth floor balcony.

Rosie, 1953

Egypt had an unbroken history of civilization stretching back at least 7, 000 years. Many invaders came and went over the centuries, and the Egyptians had to learn to be adaptable and tolerant. Their most charming trait is a delicious sense of humor and unequaled hospitality to foreigners. As a young refugee from Europe, I began to feel at home in Egypt and fell in love with the country and its people, a love and sense of belonging that I had never experienced before. I had dark hair, tanned easily, and learned Arabic rapidly. I fit in, and most people

Rosie, 1953

assumed that I was Egyptian. My sister was blonde and stood
out as unusual. Egyptian women and children would reach
out to touch her hair, and men and boys were attracted to her
foreignness.

At about this time, an elderly woman who was an
Egyptologist invited my sister and me for a visit to the pyramids
of Giza. She was very simple and plain, I thought at the time,
and not given to small talk. We took a bus and tram all the way
out to the ancient monuments and walked into the desert.
She then introduced us to the great ancient history, starting
with the tombs of the queens. As she talked, history began
to become alive for me, stunning me with its intensity. We sat
down after some time at the entry of an ancient tomb, and
she unpacked the sandwiches she had brought. As we ate, she
explained more, and we listened in silence. Then she fell silent,
and we simply sat there.

I cannot now tell if my imagination was running in overdrive
during that moment of silence. A strange sensation began
to come to me. It was a stillness and peace so intense it
was palpable. A literal atmosphere of heavy stillness and
timelessness invaded my consciousness to such a degree
that I felt as if I were in an alternant reality. The sun was

shining, a small wind stirred, sand was all about, there were ancient rocks and structures, a blue sky was above...nothing else, and yet all within me had changed. These experiences repeated themselves, and now I think that I had been led to a portal of some ancient place, and had stumbled, like Alice in Wonderland, down some ancient staircase into another dimension.

My mother's small hotel soon attracted visitors such as university lecturers, archaeologists, consulate personal, or people from the United Nations who stayed for long periods of time in Egypt. I began to see the strain in her, and as my survival depended on her, I was often anxious.

Crisis in the Hospital

My childhood of malnutrition had left its mark, and throughout my first years in Egypt, I was frequently ill. For months on end, I would walk daily to a little pharmacy run by the Catholic nuns of Zamalek and receive shots for this or that. By my early teenage years, I had already spent a lot of time in the Anglo-Egyptian hospital despairing of ever being well. During the long nights there, my thoughts turned inwards, reflecting on the meaning and purpose of life. I wondered what my destiny was to be.

One day a monk entered my hospital room, his face glowing, and, kneeling, he prayed for me at the foot of my bed. I felt embarrassed, hoping he would soon leave. He kept returning, always looking aglow and hot. This time he sat on the edge of my bed and told me God loved all the little children. He spread his hands over me in blessing, but they came lower and lower over my body. A thought of warning hit me as he tried to touch my covers. "Get out of here!" I screamed at the top of my voice, as I pulled my covers to my chin. "Get out, don't ever come back!" He fled with a bright red face. This was not the last time a pedophile priest tried to touch me; however, I never told my mother about these events, as I feared she would not believe me. The first time I told her about someone trying to touch me she had insisted that I was mistaken.

Academy des Beaux-Arts

My concerned mother kept me indoors during the long summer holidays. I spent many hours drawing and painting to keep myself entertained. My artistic gift had shown itself early, and since my mother had not been permitted to study art, she tried to provide me with the stimulation and support denied her. An artist was found who gave lessons. We visited her in her studio, and I looked closely at the work of her pupil, who was painting a woman holding a baby. The child's head was beautifully rendered, and I was amazed at the skill. However, my mother was unimpressed. Instead, I continued copying Italian Renaissance masters. When I turned thirteen, I received my first oil paints. Full of fire and enthusiasm, I painted my first terrible oil painting and got paint on the bedspread as well. Finally, at the age of fourteen, I enrolled at the Academy des Beaux-Arts in Cairo, which I attended twice a week until I was nineteen, in addition to going to regular school.

The Academy was a reputable school for artists. The Head of the Academy was a Czech national, trained in Paris. His wife, a French pianist, gave piano lessons to exceptional music students. On my first visit, I walked up the four flights of stairs of the big building, probably dating to the 18th century. The stairway was very large and spacious. Arriving at the top, I found a very long, wide hallway that led past various entries to apartments occupied by a variety of businesses. Then, suddenly, there was a shift as potted trees, shrubs and sculptures began to line the hallway. I was in a different zone.

At this point, the entry to the Academy des Beaux-Arts appeared with a doorway filled with potted flowers. This opened up into a huge atelier. Like a big sail, a canvas cover was stretched across the huge glass window descending diagonally towards the floor. The north light in this space was excellent for viewing art, which was spread around the walls. There were enormous canvases of the desert, of Egyptian feluccas sailing down the Nile, of veiled women, funeral processions, and ancient monuments illuminated by the setting sun, of surreal images and portraits—in short, an impressive variety of finely

Dining room of Hotel Zamalek with a painting by Rosie

executed images that delighted the eye. Perhaps the most astonishing coincidence was that except for one letter, my future teacher had the same name as I did. He was called Jaro Hilbert, and my last name was Hilpert.

Jaro Hilbert guided me to the studio. A group of about 12 pupils of varying ages sketched or painted in a spacious studio that opened up to a big open rooftop. It was airy and cool even in the heat of summer. It was in this studio I experienced my most permanent and profound lessons, which later served me well and guided me towards becoming an artist. I studied with Jaro Hilbert for four years, until I left for my studies abroad. He was a kind and generous teacher and he taught art in the classical style. We started drawing from plaster casts, progressed to still life, then to skulls and skeletons, and finally to portraits. More advanced pupils would then learn all about landscapes and painting the human nude. Jaro brought in colorful figures from the street, models that posed patiently or fell asleep within seconds. They usually were poor people who were happy to make some income by just sitting still. It was an invaluable and humbling lesson to see the naked human body in

Dining room of Hotel Zamalek with a painting by Rosie

all its forms and stages of aging, from vibrant youth to old age. I never could embrace the American notion of the importance of the body being kept young and artificial. I had had a lesson in what life truly looked like. Any romantic or idealized vision of the body also left me cold. In fact, I was quite drawn to social-realism, drawing beggars and the poor.

From the age of fourteen to nineteen, I went to the center of Cairo for three hours of art instruction two or three times weekly. When I left the Academy of Art, I returned to Zamalek by bus or tram. Coming out of the focused state of attentiveness in which I had spent the last three hours, the city, the people, and the lights all looked different. My vision was enhanced, expanded and transformed through the art training. A feeling of visual excitement rushed through me as I passed the Nile River with the city lights reflected on the water at night fall. The people looked more unusual, more vital and alive; everything assumed an energy that would eventually fade. However, more and more it stayed and became my normal experience.

My mother had transferred us to the Catholic school of the Borromaer nuns. This school, although in central Cairo, still meant long bus trips twice daily, and I easily succumbed to car sickness. In a sense, I enjoyed the bus journey, as I saw much of Cairo. The busy, colorful food markets spread into every little square. Here the vendors erected their sun shelters and offered tables loaded with fruits and vegetables of all sorts. Chickens were held in little cages piled on top of each other. When a customer wanted a chicken, the bird was pulled out of confinement, carefully examined and then the seller would behead it with the swift thrust of a knife. The headless chicken now ran in a circle for a while, its neck pulsing blood until it fell over. The buyer would depart with his chicken wrapped into a newspaper. Because of the heat, all meat had to be absolutely fresh. Pork was unknown, and for a long time so was cow's milk. We had rich water buffalo milk instead. Many women, perhaps most, spent their lives secluded in their homes. I often saw a basket being lowered from a window or balcony to a vender below, and merchandise would be haggled over and then deposited into the basket to be pulled up by a rope to the unseen female above. Basket shopping was very popular in Cairo and a fast and easy way to get groceries.

Departure of Alma

Around this time my Aunty Alma decided to join her husband Christian in Nairobi, Kenya, his new German Consulate posting. To some degree I was privy to her inner struggle when she left Ray. She sold Horus House, and the many lively and entertaining occasions on her big rooftop came to an end. The sad day of parting arrived. Alma and Ray took me with them to Alexandria, perhaps as a type of chaperone. We stayed in Alexandria in a nun's convent.

During the day, she allowed me to take a bus to Rushdi, a beach where her close friend, an Austrian woman, had a cabin. Rushdi was a big rounded cove where the rock had been terraced and lined with wooden cabins. It was big enough to store beach furniture and umbrellas, and people rented or bought these, and then the family could spend the whole day by the ocean. The general public could not enter this beach. I was fourteen years old and it was quite an adventure taking a bus to go to the beach.

The family of the Austrian woman was at the Rushdi cabin, and so I met some young people there, her two teenage sons to be exact. They spoke only French, no German and no English. My French was as yet unpolished in those days, so I understood little and misunderstood much. The young men were probably 16 to 17 years old, racially mixed, and they had bright blue eyes and shiny black hair. With their sun-bronzed skin and smoothly muscled bodies they looked like young gods. The girls were hanging around them like flies, chattering excitedly and flirting. After swimming I also hung around the cabin, where I was offered food and drinks. They asked a few questions, and realizing that my French was rudimentary, they began to discuss me, commenting on my figure, hair and suit, right in front of me. Most of this I understood and it shocked me how I was seen. They found my body mature and ripe for picking. They said I had a nice pair of breasts and shapely legs. I was "très jolie!" I felt very flattered and kept going over the French phrases in my mind to see if I had indeed understood correctly. As I did so, I suddenly realized they had not said "jolie" at all. They had used the word "jeune," which means young. They had found me too young! My balloon had burst.

When I got back to the convent, Alma was standing at the gate with Ray, sobbing. I went up to the room and looked at them from above. It was just like in the movies, they kissed and hugged and cried. It made me very sad for them. Years later, I learned from Alma that she had made a big mistake in not separating from Christian then. She arrived in Nairobi, Kenya, and instead of finding the lovely house Christian had described to her, she found herself in a primitive shack, surrounded by a maize field, in which she later discovered a Mau-Mau hiding spot. (In those days the Mau-Mau were a dangerous group of Kenyan Freedom fighters.) Furthermore, she discovered Christian had an English mistress whom he unabashedly visited nightly. Having sold her business, she could not return to Cairo. She was also too proud to tell Ray what had happened until much later.

Without the influence of Alma, my mother began to thrive. Alma had been insistent that my mother connect to "English people of importance," as well as to Germans who often seemed to look down on my mother. This now stopped. My mother, because of the guests who came to her hotel, made very different friends. Alma and Leni had a competitive relationship as sisters. Alma frequently complained that Leni had such good taste, was so much smarter than she was, and was so creative in so many ways, and that it was all because of her French father.

His family was aristocracy from the Alsace region, where there was a fortress, "Bitsche," after the family name. Their shield was the image of an Ouroboros. It is an ancient symbol depicting a serpent or dragon with its tail in its mouth. Originating in ancient Egyptian iconography, the Ouroboros entered western tradition via Greek magical tradition and was adopted as a symbol in Gnosticism and Hermeticism and most notably in alchemy. The first known appearance of the Ouroboros is in the *Enigmatic Book of the Netherworld*, an ancient Egyptian funerary text in KV62, found in the tomb of Tutankhamun in the 14th century BCE.

In the family, no one ever talked about my grandfather except my mother. He died before I was born so I never knew him. He was a widower when he married my grandmother Katharina, just as she was a widow. Alma, her oldest daughter, still a child, did not approve of her new stepfather. My grandfather had large properties in the border region between France and Germany. He was a French Huguenot and hence a Protestant. His family originally moved to Germany to avoid persecution in France.

Pets

Because my sister missed animals, one morning after breakfast my mother presented both of us with a flower pot filled with sand. "Put it on the balcony into the sunshine," she said. "Check it daily and you will be surprised." She actually had to keep reminding us to look at the pots, because we were not particularly interested. Thus, I was astonished one morning to find a tiny little tortoise in the flower pot. They had just hatched. I think altogether we had four or five tortoises. It was an amazing miracle to watch these tiny little creatures, which from now on lived on the big veranda. They were fed with vegetable scraps from the kitchen and they loved red watermelon. My mother was in the habit of painting her fingernails and toenails red, and one day, as she walked onto the balcony, the tortoises rushed her feet, trying to bite her toenails, which must have looked like watermelon. This was very funny to us young girls. What my mother had not realized was that these creatures were giant African spurred tortoises. They grew at a steady rate and were very fast on their feet. One lazy summer afternoon during our school holidays, Gabriele and I amused ourselves by placing a sunhat over a tortoise and then laughing as we watched the poor beast racing about in desperation.

At some point we lost interest and did not realize that the tortoise had made its way out of our room and was now moving down the long hotel hallway. An English lady resting on her bed during the heat of the day became aware of a gentle scratching sound, and then to her horror saw a hat gliding across the floor towards her. She screamed repeatedly, and we rushed into her room to rescue our pet. But this was no laughing matter. Her husband scolded us severely, telling us she was pregnant, and this fright could have caused a miscarriage. The tortoises eventually became so large they had to be given to the Cairo Zoo, where they might still be alive now because they can live to be one hundred years old.

The Hot Days of Summer

Fouad Hafez introduced us to an officer's club situated at the end of Zamalek Island. Here was a lovely swimming pool of aqua-blue water to refresh mind and body. I fell in love with the water and swam at every opportunity, constantly pestering my mother to take us. I can still taste the wonderful fresh water. The pool was scrubbed nightly by six men, their long gowns tied around their waists. They attacked their job with big brushes in one hand and a bar of soap in the other. In the early morning, the pool slowly filled with clean, cold Nile water, and it sparkled like a jewel in the sun.

A team of Egyptian swimmers came daily to train under the direction of their trainer, Alex, who was a Czech. I began to swim alongside the young swimmers, and one day Alex stopped me. "Girl, swim a length for me, I want to see how good you are," he said. I threw myself into the water and raced through the pool. He stood by, stopwatch in hand. "You are fast. Would you like to join the team?" I was very excited by this and so joined the team. I began to swim competitively and trained for hours. The swimming, perhaps because of the rhythmic breathing, healed me completely from the ill health that had clung to me. As it strengthened me physically, I was rarely ever ill again.

Swimming became a large part of my life in the hot desert climate of Egypt. I loved the cool, clear element of water, which made the heat easily bearable, refreshing my body and allowing me the freedom of leaving the seclusion of the house. My mother felt that a sport was a good thing for a young person and allowed me to go for training as a swimmer. Of course, initially I had to fight to get her permission to go alone to a club. This meant a 45-minute walk to the end of the Zamalek Island, where the club was, and after training, another 45 minutes to return. I went to the club daily, walking along the Nile River as fast as my feet could carry me under a canopy of red blooming flame trees. I was extremely restless physically, and the opportunity to walk and swim was very important to me.

My first official swimming competition took place in a club in Heliopolis, a city founded by the Greeks 2000 years ago. It was they who found the mineral springs that filled the huge Olympic sized swimming pool with pale turquoise water. It was explained to me that the mineral content of the water was so high that

احدى سباحات الاهلى تساعد زميلتهافى الخروج من
الماء بعـــد تمرين متواصــل من أجل البطـــولة ..

Newspaper announcement of award-winning swimmer Rosie, 1958

the liquid actually looked foggy. I fell in love with this pool and
looked forward to every opportunity for swimming there. I was
so nervous about my upcoming first competition, I could not
sleep for most of the prior night. The next day, all the swimmers

met at the club and were taken to Heliopolis by bus. We had 30 minutes to exercise a bit in the water before the start of the event. I was in a high state of anticipation. As I stood poised on the starting block, waiting for the signal, I fell into the pool before the shot was fired. As a consequence, I was disqualified.

My coach, Alex, gave me some advice after that, insisting I had to be calm, without my heart beating rapidly like a drum. The rhythm of my breath had to be undisturbed and even. "But how do I control my breath or my heart or my tension?" I asked, feeling miserable for having failed. "You need to learn to control your mind!" he answered. Fortunately, I quickly learned how important it was to stay calm. Alex then began testing me with a stopwatch. I was asked to swim a certain distance while he timed my swimming speed. I recall my surprise as my body cut through the water like an arrow flying through the air. It was completely effortless, I had plenty of breath, and I became one with the water like a fish. It was an amazing sensation, and this repeated itself during every competition I took part in. As a consequence, by age sixteen, I had won my first competition and eventually became champion of Egypt in breast-stroke, butterfly, and dolphin-stroke for the next four years. I had to commit to a daily training period through summer, autumn, winter and spring. I swam daily. My body became lean and powerful, and my health was perfect.

I so disliked wearing a bathing cap on my head, which was a requirement for anyone with long hair, so I went to a hairdresser, a young Italian, and asked him to give me a really short haircut. He did. When my mother saw me, she wept and pulled at the short spikes which stood straight up all over my head. The Arabs then referred to me as "ya walad," meaning "boy."

My mother was in the habit of going to an air-conditioned cinema in Cairo every afternoon to escape the extreme heat. I stubbornly refused the many invitations to join her, forgoing a movie in favor of the freedom swimming gave me. The time I spent in Egypt healed more than my body, it also stimulated the emotional and spiritual healing I desperately needed from my childhood experiences. Having lost my father, my home, my country, and all my possessions, I was psychologically disoriented. Even my mother tongue was often forbidden, and a sense of shame attached itself to being German. It was pointless to cry, complain, or rebel; my feelings became numb and frozen. All emotional pain was pushed down into the unconscious layers of my being. Swimming freed these feelings and allowed my soul to be as clear as the water.

Happiness of the Earth

Egypt is completely covered by desert except for the narrow area of land bordering the Nile. In those days, before the Aswan Dam was built, the Nile waters rose yearly in August, as they had done for a millennium, and flooded the banks, inundating the fertile land and leaving behind a rich alluvial mud. The flooding caused extreme humidity, and during August the humidity caused a heavy fog to blanket all of Cairo, which only lifted by eleven o'clock in the morning. It also caused much heat. As a consequence, people shuttered their windows early in the day and then closed the glass part as well to retain the cool night air for as long as possible. Once the sun started to sink, windows and shutters were once again thrown open. Among the Bedouin there is a saying: "The happiness of the earth lies on the back of a horse!"

It was in August, the hottest month, when my sister and I discovered the desert. We took a bus to the Cheops pyramid of Giza, which was far out of town at that time, and roamed around the ancient monuments. Becoming hot and tired, we decided to rent a couple of horses. A Bedouin supplied us with mounts and so we experienced a new pleasure. The Arabs are correct that "the happiness of the earth lies on the back of a horse."

After we learned to ride, we cantered into valleys of powdery, soft sand, found out-of-the way tombs and sandstone rocks of the most bizarre shapes, trotted through villages forgotten by time, and discovered an ancient world hidden in the desert. We returned home, caked with dust and so filled with enthusiasm that we convinced our mother to join us on our next adventure. She did, and eventually bought a beautiful, pale palomino horse to ensure that she was forced to return to the desert on a regular basis, mostly on weekends. This was very therapeutic for her because at this time she was deeply depressed about her life and circumstances.

Our expeditions usually started before dawn and lasted for most of the day. Eventually they led us to far pyramids, forgotten and unmapped, where we found mummies in reed coffins, funerary vessels, tiny plates and bowls for the dead, Greco-Roman coins, and mountains of ancient garbage which contained undiscovered treasures. To this day, I still have a number of ancient doll heads and shards we found there. We also became friendly with the Bedouin stable owner, Mohamed Ghounem, who aside from horses, camels and donkeys, kept a number of slaves. This was standard. He gave them room and board, and they worked for their master but had no rights to salary or independent lives. Over many years I frequently took the long tedious bus journey out to the desert and sat among the Bedouin, sketching and painting the mud villages at the foot of the pyramids. I often had to ask permission to sit on a rooftop, as children would come and throw sand at me, ruining my painting. Muslims believe it is wrong to make images, so I was seen as being or doing evil by some.

Arab Wedding

In the process of painting watercolor images, I became friendly with the village people. One of the young women was getting married and invited me to the wedding, which I felt was a big honor. I came at the appointed day. Her hands were completely covered with a beautiful henna design of vines and flowers, and her palms and the soles of her feet were bright orange. She wore a new bright silk dress and had heavy gold jewelry from her family on her head, ears, fingers, arms, toes, and ankles. In fact, she jingled when she moved. The older women were all around her, singing and beating little jug drums called tabla. Every now and then one of the women would make a shrill ululating sound with her tongue, then the rapid drumming would resume.

The arrival of the groom was announced with shots fired into the air. Night had fallen and the groom and retinue of his friends arrived on horseback. The horses were decorated with silver chains and colorful tassels hanging from their manes and tails. The groom, a handsome young man and was beautifully attired. Both he and the bride had their eyes heavily lined with kohl, an ancient eye make-up already used in Pharaonic times. It lends the eyes great depth and mystery to be so powerfully outlined.

Then the feasting began in the house. There were several tables heavily-ladened with food, and everyone was encouraging me to eat, eat more, and even more! This is the custom of Egyptian hospitality. Musicians dressed all in white arrived and settled down on the ground. A belly dancer appeared, and then the rafters reverberated with the shrill sound of flutes, drums and stringed instruments. Somehow, I missed the actual ceremony amid all the excitement. The groom and bride had vanished.

A few days later I decided to visit the bride. On the front wall beside the entry gate of the mud house a huge golden bedspread had been displayed. In the middle of it a small smudge of blood announced the great news, that the bride was a virgin. The young wife greeted me with a big smile, and I had to come in and see her bedroom. The whole ceiling of the room had been painted a midnight blue spangled with stars. The stars were the exact same design as those painted in the tombs of the pharaohs. Some customs don't change.

Education

Egypt at this point was a rich tapestry of people from all over the Middle East and southern Europe. Almost everyone spoke several languages fluently. Once I learned to speak Arabic, I fit in completely. People never questioned that I was not Egyptian, and for the first time in my life, I began to feel comfortable and at home. The Egyptians knew how to relax and enjoy themselves, and it calmed me to be in their accepting, all-embracing company. They lacked the critical, judgmental approach brought by the Greek civilization, and as I began to study Islam, my respect for the culture increased.

The call to prayer rang out from the tall legion of minaret towers of the mosques in Cairo from dawn to dusk. Our servants stopped to pray six times a day, stopping in the middle of work to collect and center themselves. They knew how to withdraw inside themselves. People prayed everywhere, on the street, in parks, in gardens, on rooftops, beside swimming pools, and in the desert beside their camels. Little mats were unrolled, and some worshippers just had a piece of cardboard reserved for this purpose. Having come from the little German village whose people were very religious, I could literally feel the spiritual intensity of the people in Egypt. It manifested in a type of faith, a trust that they were taken care of. They were incredibly patient, long-suffering and able to laugh at themselves. "Malesh," which means "never mind," was a standard expression.

The Westerners around me did not seem capable of understanding the Egyptians. "Oh dear, they are so fatalistic," was a common phrase I heard. Accusations of laziness abounded: they were always late, taking nothing seriously. Westerners could not abide their music, they thought their Ramadan fasting period was ridiculous, and they felt shamed by the generosity of the much poorer people who generously gave, offering their food to total strangers. In my young mind again and again, the comparison between my European roots and the values embraced by the Egyptians made me feel uneasy. I thought the more ancient values were superior, and so a slow gradual shift began within me. It first manifested against the religious upbringing my mother imposed on me. I began to question things, and my mother and particularly the nuns, who were educating me in school, became aware of my discontent.

I had become friendly with a young, blonde girl from Austria who had just arrived from Europe. She was much more used to contact with boys, and as her parents were busy setting up an apartment in town and not paying much attention to her, she began to find the attention young Egyptian men paid to her very exciting. Several times I invited her to my place; we visited sites with my mother and shopped in the bazaar. Everywhere she went, she attracted great attention because of her fair hair. "Ah, the moon has risen," the guys whispered to her. Compliments such as "Oh, antelope, let me catch you" and "my beautiful little lemon" rained down on her, and she responded, even though I warned her not to pay attention.

What happened to her, I never really knew. I guess she bragged to some innocent girl at the school. They expelled her for "unfitting behavior," and since I had been her friend, I was called to talk to the headmistress. Without asking a single question, she confronted me in hot anger. "You will lose your virtue with a dirty Arab, have a baby at sixteen, and be shunned by society. You will be nothing but a whore," the nun informed me. I stood silently and heard her in amazement and disbelief. It never even occurred to me to argue or defend myself. After all, what can a 14-year-old say? At home my mother talked to me. She believed her child, not the nun. The subject was not raised again. The school year ended and I was "dishonorably" expelled. In Zamalek, a small embassy school was to be started in the autumn, so once again, my sister and I were enrolled into another different school.

The teachers were high quality; most of them had Ph.Ds. A challenging curriculum was to be imposed, and classes were small. Thus, at the age of 15 I entered "Die Deutsche Evangelische Oberschule," from which I would graduate with the high school diploma of "Abitur." I loved my school and most of the teachers. For the first time, I was being challenged academically and with just six pupils in a classroom, there is nowhere to hide from a teacher. We had to be constantly alert and attentive. Our language teachers actually were French, English, or Egyptian, and I became fascinated with the French poetry I was being introduced to. I was able to learn it by heart easily and some of it stayed with me my whole life. Our English teacher was Miss Moneypenny, a true character who could be incredibly funny. She would scold me when I was not paying attention, and would say, "Rosemarie, I would like to put you in a sack and shake you up." We read and studied *The Vicar of Wakefield*, a book so English and so remote from the lives we lived, and yet I remember it well, perhaps because it contrasted so much with my reality at the time.

Insects in Egypt

Where in the world would insects be found who preferred one race over another and did not sting selected groups? Mosquitoes did not bite the Arabs. Windows in Cairo had no screens and the insect world flew in and out freely. There were the ever-present flies, huge cockroaches, biting gnats, mosquitoes, and locusts. You never knew what you would find. The nights became cool, even in summer, but evenings were too hot, so windows stayed open. Every night I was plagued with the whining sound of mosquitoes. It was too hot to cover myself with a sheet and so they feasted on me. One night, in desperation I decided that I did not care if I was bitten or not. I lay in submissive surrender to the onslaught, and much to my surprise, I hardly ever had mosquito bites after that.

Another lesson about insects came when we visited the graves of the Apis Bulls found in Sakkara. Though it was only May, the desert was hot. We stood outside the entrance waiting for the prior group of tourists to emerge. It was close to noon, and the sun stood over us. As the people began to emerge from the tomb below us, I saw what looked like a dark wave in front of their feet. Then as the group began to slap at their legs, it became clear that a heaving wave of black fleas was at their feet. The fleas jumped on their bare arms and legs. The Arabic guides laughed, amused at the tourists slapping away. Not a single flea ventured near the guides. I saw this type of immunity to insects many times and later in East Africa.

One June, we had a locust invasion. The sky turned pink, then dark. A whirring sound preceded the swarm which eventually covered the whole sky. Milanos, (birds of prey that were plentiful in Cairo), had a feast, and every now and then a half-consumed huge pink locust would drop from above. The insects had fat upper legs and looked well nourished. They flew over the city, and thankfully, did not devour the tree tops or other vegetation. However, it gave me a sense of the possible devastation these insects could engender, and how a whole country could lose their food supply. After they passed by, the ground was littered with the half-eaten corpses left by the birds.

At this time, a young German couple moved into my mother's hotel. Heddie was a lanky, tall blonde, very attractive and likeable. She was very excited to be in Egypt, and so my mother invited her along when we visited the bazaar or went horseback riding. In short order, a friendship developed. One morning, Heddie came with alarming news. "Frau Hilpert, I fear we have mice in the room. I hear them chewing away at night." The room was searched and scrubbed from corner to corner. No sign of mice was found. But Heddie insisted that she heard the chewing every night.

A few days later she burst in at breakfast time. "Look, unbelievable!" She held up a handful of elegant European underwear, silky panties, lace-trimmed and pastel-colored. Each pair had the crotch area completely chewed out. My mother asked her where she had kept her underwear. It turned out she had put her soiled underwear into an open brown grocery bag on the floor of her big wardrobe. "So, this is what you had been hearing," my mother said. "Not mice, but cockroaches." Heddie was horrified. My mother had informed her at the beginning of her stay never to leave any dirty clothes lying around overnight. Each room had a large clothes bag hanging in the closet for soiled garments. Our cockroaches had very selective taste.

I had a similar experience. I was wearing a nice dress and was carrying a birthday cake in a cardboard box, when the wind flipped the lid open and a smudge of sugar icing appeared on my chest. I wiped it off, and forgot about it. In the morning, my dress had a nice hole where the icing had touched the fabric. This was a pity because it was my best dress!

My sister and I shared a room, and it was our nightly ritual to hunt cockroaches. The moment we switched on the light, we would see the insects heading for the open windows, but some slid down the walls to hide in a dark corner. We would take off our sandals and jumping on chairs or the bed, would make our way towards them. With a sharp bang, we hit and dispatched them. We learned to be dexterous and did not squish them, because splattering them on the wall meant a major clean-up.

The Red Sea

A trip to the Red Sea was a big adventure for us, especially as we would go to a hot spring called Ain Sokhna that flowed in a narrow stream from a rocky bed down to the ocean. It was surrounded by tall reeds, low shrubs, and a few trees. Otherwise, the coastline was totally bare. High, rocky mountains beyond the beach formed a protective rim. The first time I went, I was surprised that the water was blue and crystal-clear and not red.

I soon found out why it was called the Red Sea. At sunset, the mountains turned red and threw their reflective light onto the water surface, turning it into a sea of scarlet! We camped at the hot springs and brought rough old tents along for that purpose, as well as all our drinking water and food. With a minimum of shelter and ocean water that was very salty, sunburn was almost impossible to avoid. On old photos taken at the beach our faces are bright red. On one occasion, we took our friend Heddie along, warning her of the dangers of severe sunburn. She loved the vast empty coastline where only a beach patrol of a single policeman on a fast camel came riding along twice a day.

The only other visitors to Ain Souchna were Bedouin groups with herds of goats. The women filled huge ceramic jugs with the warm water for drinking and for their animals. These people were stick-thin and very shy, and they tried not to look at us. The women wore long veils covered with gold and silver coins, a sign of their prosperity. Their dresses were decorated with bright embroidery, while the men wore galabias and turbans on

Age 18, at the Red Sea

their heads. We did not dare to take their photographs, as they seemed fiercely independent and proud. Often tribal people think a photograph will steal their souls, and we were aware of this belief.

The warm stream bubbled up in a rock and then ran along a fair distance and down to the ocean's edge, and since it was surrounded by reeds, shrubs, and other vegetation, it was shielded and protected from the sun. We all instantly removed our swimsuits and allowed ourselves to be carried from the source all the way to the ocean's edge in the soothing warm currents of the spring water. As an experience it was sensuous and fabulous drifting under a canopy of low hanging branches which permitted only dappled light to pass through the foliage. The ocean itself was a feast for the senses with fish so tame, they would swim between our fingers to nibble at bread we offered. Most of these tropical fish were of extraordinary color and fantastic shapes. Under the water, huge heads of blue coral and amazing sea fans delighted the eye.

On this occasion when Heddie came along, she stripped off and was as bare as God had created her, when from a distance, the beach patrol on his high fast camel came trotting along at a good pace. Alas, it was too late for Heddie to run out of the water to cover her nudity with a towel. The sea water was so clear and transparent it did not really cover a nude body. Heddie assured us "Don't worry, I shall just dive deep under the water; he will not be able to see me." When the camel came alongside, the policeman called "Marhab!" in greeting. Heddie believed herself to be deep under water. We laughed hysterically later on considering what a vision the police patrol must have had, for Heddie's huge voluptuous white bottom had risen above water, shining like a full moon.

Magic and Sufis

You only needed to leave your house or apartment in Egypt and the adventure would begin. I regularly witnessed people who knew of a reality that went beyond the material. Feasts were loved, and there were often magic shows called Gala-Gala. Magicians made eggs come out of their sleeves, and then the eggs would become chicks. There were tables that levitated, and there were cards that would move on the table and answer people's questions. At a big party at the officer's club in Cairo, I saw a powerful, bald Turk who was said to be over 100 years old. He bent iron bars with ease and could not be cut by knives. Nails hammered into his flesh did not penetrate his skin, and several strong young men could not lift him. Obviously, he was akin to an Indian Sadhu, a holy man, and able to perform amazing feats.

Once, when I was older, my mother took me to a Bedouin feast in the desert. Sweet tea was passed around in dirty glasses, tea so black and strong it caused drunkenness. The Bedouin call it the "whisky of the desert." Dancing began to the hypnotic beating of drums. The increasingly rapid rhythm forced us to dance faster and faster. I had joined in, not knowing that we were among Sufis who would dance and spin until their lips foamed and they fell down to the ground in an ecstatic swoon. As I spun around, I found myself dissolving into joy, when suddenly my mother's hand firmly grabbed me and I was dragged away. I sat bored and disappointed watching the dancers spin. "They are in a trance," my mother explained. "You can't join that; you will lose yourself." My curiosity and interest in this other world caused much conflict with my mother because she was afraid that I might go astray.

Semit Bread

Twice a month, Fouad Hafez would invite us to an open-air cinema in the center of Cairo. The theater usually showed great Hollywood films like *Quo Vadis* and *Singing in the Rain*, and by then, I loved going to see a movie. The large open floor space filled with chairs was surrounded by houses. Their balconies were packed with viewers, able to see the films at no cost. The city noises, cars, bicycle bells, calls to prayer, music, and voices of newspaper vendors penetrated into the space and the delicious smell of semit wafted through the air. Semit was sesame-seed bread shaped into a ring and eaten with salt. It was sold by vendors walking through rows of viewers before the feature film started. Once we were settled into our chairs and holding warm semit bread in our hands, the adventure started, and we were transported into a different reality.

I recall staggering into the city night after such an evening. The crowds pressed out into the brightly illuminated street. Overhead neon lamps spread a garish light, and the faces of

people were sharply defined. I remember an incident where
a young girl pressed forward. She could not have been much
older than twelve years of age. A smell of poverty clung to her,
and her headscarf was ragged. She held a baby in one arm and
reached out with her free hand begging for money. I looked at
the chalky face of the baby and saw the deep, dark sockets of
its eyes. Slowly the understanding formed in my reluctant mind
that I was staring at a dead baby. People were dropping coins
into the girl's palm and then moving away hurriedly, as if to deny
what they had seen. I stood rooted in horror, trying to stop the
questions that rose like a flock of disturbed pigeons. What was
she doing holding a dead baby? Was it hers or her mother's
child? How long ago had the child died...or was I mistaken? My
mother pulled at me hissing, "Come on, don't look." The image
haunts me still!

Gamal Fahmy

My mother did not allow me to have boyfriends. I had been
explicitly forbidden to become involved with an Arab, a Turk, a
Syrian, a Greek, an Armenian, or an Italian. That left Germans,
English, French, Dutch, Russians, Jews, and Spaniards.
Furthermore, until the age of nineteen, I always had to be home
by sunset, which was at six o'clock in the evening. I was given a
minimum of freedom, and my independence was limited to the
training period at the club or the three afternoons I spent in
the Art Academy. Because of my extra activities, I had to do my
homework at night and that usually kept me up until midnight.

All my free time was spent swimming, so it was not surprising
that I fell in love with a young Egyptian swimmer, Gamal Fahmy,
when I was 16 years old. Gamal was a champion swimmer and
spoke little English, but he had a fine and generous spirit. I did
not tell him I had a crush on him. He seemed to be interested in
an exotic Saudi girl who was a graceful roller skater. However,
late one afternoon, he walked me home from the club after
training and held my hand. Unable to phone each other or
make any kind of meeting arrangements, I was forced to rely
entirely on my intuition to know when he was coming to the

club. I started to experiment in making psychic contact with him. Amazingly, it worked. I knew when he thought of me, when he was worried or ill at ease, and what time he was coming to the club. One day he told me that his mother, a widow, was a psychic and made her living by reading people's fortunes from Turkish coffee grounds left at the bottom of a cup. This suggested to me that he too might be psychic. I was fascinated with my own newfound ability and wanted to develop it to my advantage.

One day as I walked to the club, I became overwhelmed by anxiety. Upon arrival, I was told that Gamal had been hit by a tram car while cycling to school. No one knew how seriously he had been hurt. I walked home rapidly, stole some money out of my mother's bag, and took a taxi to the area of Cairo where Gamal lived. I did not know his address. When the taxi reached the area, the driver asked me where I wanted to go and I confessed that I did not know. "What is the name?" he asked and then leaned out of the window and shouted to a coppersmith hammering his wares on the street nearby. "Do you know where Gamal Fahmy lives?" "Is he the son of Fatima?" came the reply. I remembered Gamal telling me that his mother's name was Fatima, so I nodded vigorously.

An address was given and the driver proceeded into the ever-narrowing streets of the old town until there was only a narrow passage left that the vehicle could not pass through. The fatherly taxi driver explained the last few steps I had to take on foot that lay ahead of me. With some hesitation, I proceeded into this very ancient part of Cairo. Houses were leaning into each other, so old they were falling apart, and I was grateful that his house was a newer one at the dead end of the street. As I rang the doorbell, a little dark-skinned Sudanese boy opened the door and ushered me into a large waiting room. Black-robed women sat along the walls, drinking tiny cups of Turkish coffee. I started to back out, but a delicate, small woman caught my dress and told me to sit. I, too, received a cup of coffee. Slowly, one woman after another was called into a room, and after a time came out and left. Eventually, it was my turn.

I came face-to-face with Fatima, a small woman that was obviously Gamal's mother. She smiled and said, "I know you have come to see my son." She then took me to his bedroom where he lay with his ribs bandaged. He was lucky as he just had some bruises. Gamal grinned at me in embarrassment, and I felt foolish and awkward. Meanwhile, Fatima took my coffee cup into her hand and turned it upside down so the suds ran down the sides forming a pattern. She had very large and intense black eyes and, looking at me, began to tell me my future by saying: "You love Gamal, but he is not for you. He will die in a war between Egypt and Israel when he is 31. In three years, you will receive a scholarship to study in the USA. Your younger sister will marry before you do. Your husband will be a tall man from the high north of Europe with two children. He will bring you to the USA and you will live beside a big water, but it is not the sea. It is a lake and very large. Your mother will leave Egypt and move to East Africa. Yes, I know you don't like this news."

I felt hot with anger, shame, and irritation. How dare she say I loved her son, when even he did not know this. Meanwhile he was grinning openly at me. I began questioning her about her abilities. After all, she had not even looked at the markings in the coffee cup, so how could she make such predictions? I asked her what a "psychic" gift was, and if she was always correct in her predications or sometimes only partially right. I wanted to know if I too could learn this.

This meeting with Fatima was the first of many. I was totally fascinated. We became friends, and she introduced me to the magical ancient practice of palm-reading. Through her, Egypt opened its inner doors. I experienced rare events like Sufi dances, whirling dervishes, ceremonies of driving out the devil, fertility rites, and many other forms of rituals that she would inspire me to experience. Incidentally, all of her predictions made about my life and future came true and are absolutely correct. My friendship with Gamal turned into an unconsummated love relationship lasting three years. We were severely handicapped by the strict rules in practice in Egypt at the time. I wore a large black Malaya which covered my head when I ventured into a meeting with him, and when in town, I walked several paces behind him just as a Native female would do. All this was to safeguard my reputation and prevent my mother from finding out about us.

Sakkara Tombs

The guests in my mother's little hotel were often fascinating people. They were writers, Egyptologists, linguists, doctors, and people from the United Nations. On weekends, one of the Egyptologists would invite all the guests out to Sakkara to show them new discoveries. Thus, I was privy to fascinating experiences. On one occasion, alabaster vases had been discovered inside an ancient storeroom. They were all placed on long tables inside a sealed shed, and light bulbs were suspended inside each alabaster vase. Most of them were fairly large and when illuminated from within, they looked magical. Some were golden with orange markings. In others the stone had green-gray veining; there were vessels of pink-rose hues and others more cool-white in color.

The professor explained that they did not understand the purpose of these alabaster vases. However, they reminded him of lamps, and thus they had illuminated the inside of each to see how they would look. Indeed, they looked magical, and the experts were fairly convinced that they must have been used as lamps. Why else would the ancient Egyptians have chosen such varied selections of colored alabaster? However, the great mystery was, how did the ancients illumine these vessels? What was their light source? How did the artisans paint and carve the inside walls of tombs located deep in rock chambers? No source of any kind of light had been found. Centuries later, great pitch-lamps had left sooty marks on tomb ceilings. However, these were not the means used by the ancients. There were similar puzzling questions about how stone was cut, or transported for that matter. The only tools were made of bronze, which were not strong enough to cut or polish granite.

I began to pay careful attention to the Hieroglyphic images I saw in tombs and became very capable of reading the messages they conveyed. In fact, I recall some people were very astonished at my grasp and understanding of the images. When I was bored in school, I practiced drawing Egyptian figures until I could feel them and render them accurately. This gave me a sense of how these ancient people felt, saw themselves, and interpreted the world around them. A deep fascination with the culture, history, and belief system of the ancient Egyptians began to spread through me.

Because my mother now had a horse that needed to be ridden and looked after, we spent more and more time in the desert. On horseback we investigated ancient sites and had access to forgotten temples and mud brick pyramids. One Sunday when we stopped to rest the horses at the foot of a mud brick pyramid, I made my first discovery of a burial. Sitting in the sand, resting against an ancient wall while idly scratching into the ground with a shard, I encountered something solid. After clearing the surface more, I realized it was a wooden coffin, definitely ancient, judging by the carvings on the surface. Within a short time, I had freed the top from the sand, and continuing to dig furiously, I uncovered enough to be able to open the coffin. Inside was a mummy, meticulously wrapped in what looked like tarry-black bandages. When I touched them, the material crumbled to dust between my fingertips. It was so old, just looking at it seemed to dematerialize it.

Eventually I held the head, still partially wrapped, in my hands. I recall the lock of hair on the forehead, the eyelashes, but it all crumbled to dust. The skin of the mummy looked leathery, but it too dissolved. Then my mother called. It was time to leave. I took off my headscarf, wrapped the skull into it and returned to my horse. At home I carefully laid the ancient skull on my shelf and surrounded it with shards, beads, and other treasures I had collected. Surprisingly, my mother said little, but the servants refused to enter and clean my room, so

I had to clean it myself from then on. This experience affected me deeply. The Bible says we are dust and shall return to dust. When I held the mummy, it did just that. The skin and hair transformed itself into dust, however carefully I handled it. This gave me much to think about—the brevity of life, how all would become dust, and that nothing could stop this process of disintegration.

During my classes at the Academy des Beaux Art, our teacher Jaro Hilbert suddenly presented us with a full human skeleton for drawing. In addition, we had to draw skulls from all directions and with different mediums, starting with charcoal, then with pencil, then with ink, then conte crayon, then oils. Not only did I now sleep with a skull in my bedroom, I also drew and painted skulls and I brought my drawings home and hung them all over the walls of my room. It was a deep contemplation on the most feared and inevitable experience to be faced, death. Such images were called "memento mori" during the Renaissance in Italy, when the dreaded event of the plague rose frequently to confront the population and people reflected on death. Much later in life, when I read that Yogis slept in cemeteries with the dead to contemplate the reality of their demise, I realized I had done just that through my fascination with mummies and by my continued collecting of skulls.

At this time a young friend of ours, an American girl named Genie, contracted polio. She ended up in an iron lung in the Anglo-Egyptian hospital. Her parents asked us to visit her when she was a little better. Gabriele and I went, unaware of what would confront us. When we opened the door of her room, we saw her parents, and then a bald Genie, as all her hair had fallen out. She was as thin as a skeleton, her limbs stiff and twisted and the moment she saw us she began to cry loudly, wailing that she wanted to be well, she wanted to walk again and be alive again. My eyes filled with tears that rushed down my cheeks in a torrent of grief and horror. We were unable to say anything, and the parents guided us out of the room, not having expected their daughter to be so upset. They thanked us for coming. Genie eventually returned to the United States and healed completely.

Tomb Robber

On another occasion, an Egyptologist and guest in our hotel took us to view an old tomb that had been robbed and where he had done much research. Inside the huge, carved granite sarcophagus lay only a skull, claimed to be of the great vizier Ptah Hotep, from the old Kingdom. I had read a beautiful teaching from this vizier, which had impressed me. The advice the vizier gave was not to rely on the treasures, which the Gods may gift you with, as all wealth is transient. By showing a good heart and having a noble, decent character, a person has something that remains and is remembered.

When the professor took the group to the next room, I reached into the sarcophagus and lifted out a skull. I stuffed it under my shirt. I rode my horse with the skull firmly held next to my heart. Many, many years later I told my six-year-old grandson the story of stealing the head of this great vizier. He went to school the next day and told his teacher that his grandmother was a "tomb robber." I had never considered what I had done in these terms, but of course now I see this was theft. So, I was a tomb robber!

Our small group of pupils in the German school bonded intensely. We had an adventurous head teacher who liked the desert and monuments and who saw to it that we had as many excursions as possible. She even found a "chalet," a type of guest house situated beyond the pyramids of Giza in the desert. We would all rent horses from our Bedouin friends at the foot of the pyramids and ride to the chalet. Food and bedding would be transported as well. We all shared the big living room, which was turned into sleeping quarters at night. We did not have sleeping bags, so we lay rolled into blankets. A hurricane lamp served as a source of light at night.

We would wake with the dawn and stepping into the cold morning, watch as the early light illuminated all the red and pink quartz rocks liberally scattered all over the sandy plain.

The rocks were round and smooth and soft to the touch. We had the freedom to roam and found our way to the tombs of the Persians, near an Arab cemetery. These tombs were nothing more than square shafts descending deep down into rock, maybe twenty feet deep. The boys found that there were clearly marked indentations in the walls, like foot and hand holds. Someone would start the descent, and soon, we all decided to investigate the tombs. But we were smart enough to understand we needed a long, sturdy rope, just in case someone fell. Then, armed with a rope, the six of us made the descent.

We descended to the bottom of the shaft, only to discover sand had filled the square-cut passages almost up to the ceiling, passages that fanned out into different directions. We dug the sand away with our hands until we were able to squeeze through the openings and drop down a slope of powdery sand onto a solid stone floor on the other side. The sides of the passages had shelves carved into the rock, which had held coffins. Our biggest concern was scorpions and large spiders, which we had to be able to see in the beams of our flashlights. Soon we were in total darkness because the flashlights had stopped working, and a couple of girls opted to return.

Those of us that continued found a huge sarcophagus that almost filled the passageway. It had been ransacked long ago, but we found several items, including an ancient doll, which we took with us. On our return we showed the items to the head teacher. "Outrageous! give me those stolen items at once. We must check their value and decide what to do with them." Needless to say, we never saw them again. They remained the honored property of the teacher.

On another occasion, a blustery cold winter day, one of the boys and I climbed the Cheops pyramid. In those days, there were no guards around. I found the climb hard, as the blocks of stone reached up to my chest and I had to lift myself up with the strength of my arms, an exercise that became very tiring. We made it to the top and stood in awe, looking across the land from this high point. A lush valley of green checkerboard fields stretched into the distance, and beyond that, the sand-colored city of Cairo spread out to the Mokkatam Hills. The wind moved beneath us and we saw the vast empty expanse of the sandy Sahara moving on and on. Far in the distance rose other pyramids, other tombs, and monuments. We even managed to carve our initials into a block of stone, as many visitors had done before us.

Our other climb up a pyramid was a little more dangerous. Several of us decided to try the second pyramid, which was never completely denuded of its alabaster mantle. Thus, a hat of white alabaster crowns this monument. Needless to say, when we reached this formidable rocky overhang, we decided to forgo the top. It is known that the citadel of Mohammed Ali on the Mokattam Hills was built out of the white alabaster mantle stolen from the great pyramids across the valley. It must have been a sight to see, these huge pyramids sparkling in icy white in the Egyptian sun before they were stripped by Arab invaders. These days and nights in the silence of the vast Egyptian desert are my most treasured memories.

Full Moons Rides

One of the great delights was our many horseback rides on full-moon nights. These were often arranged by my mother. We arrived before the moon came up and usually set out while it was pitch dark. At first, riding into the dark night was somewhat unnerving as one had to trust the horses completely, since they can see somewhat. After some time, the eyes became accustomed to the night and then suddenly the huge orange moon rose at the edge of the horizon, casting a spell of light over the desert landscape. All the little mounds and hills became sharply delineated, and everything looked magical and unfamiliar. The moon stirred the birds and foxes. Then there was barking and hooting of owls, and the horses became frisky and wanted to race through the powdery sand.

On one such occasion, when our horses thundered into an area between hills and smaller temples, we were warned by our Arab guide that we were entering haunted territory. No one paid much attention to this information. Surprised, I wondered what he meant, when my horse, as well as the other animals, began to show signs of agitation. The horses suddenly reared up, almost throwing some of the riders. The animals pawed the ground, whirled, and neighed, and they were clearly alarmed and frightened. Not one of us could advance. The horses tried to turn back, and we had trouble getting them to stand still. It was as if an invisible line drawn across the plain stopped us.

Our guide pointed into the distance. A figure stood out, pale against a dark hillside. "That's him, that's the phantom." Perhaps it was, perhaps it was just a man. The Egyptians said that a pharaoh never found peace and haunts the site. Eventually, we turned, and the horses raced into another direction. It was an eerie situation, and a strange feeling stayed with me. However, this experience repeated itself several times, and there was no doubt, something stopped the horses every time we tried to cross this particular plain.

The discovery of the desert made our life in Egypt very rich and exciting. Sitting on a horse lifted me above the crowd, and I was able to ride through villages and get to places one could not drive to. Mohammed, the Bedouin stable owner, was very kind to us, and one day, instead of my usual mare, he insisted I ride Salam, a white stallion with a very long tail. He has been in the movies many times, Mohammed told me. Unfortunately, I neglected to ask him what role Salam the horse had played in the movies. But I was soon to discover what it was.

Salam was frisky and impatient. We rode up the hill to the base of the great Cheops pyramid where a crowd of tourists had gathered and were waiting to be guided into the temples. Salam began to dance with tight little steps. Then suddenly, without warning, he reared up on his hind legs and pawed the air with his front hooves. I was lucky not to fall off his back. Salam neighed again, danced a few steps and then again rose on his hind legs. By now all the tourists were looking in our direction. When the horse, with an elegant shuffle, repeated his favorite routine, the tourists began to applaud. That was the sign he had waited for. He lifted his head and lightly cantered away. Clearly, the horse liked the attention and applause, and whenever we passed any group of people, he would become a movie star and rise up on his hind legs.

Hands Talk

One of my fellow students was called Renate. I had learned some palmistry from Fatima by now and often found myself the center of attention with everyone holding out a hand, wanting their fortunes told. That day Renate held out her hand. "What do you see in my hand," she asked. I looked carefully and to my surprise saw the major lines ending abruptly and a feeble heart line. "Renate, don't trust this or think it true. I have just begun to learn how to read palms, so I am not proficient in it. Your lines seem to indicate that you have a short life and a weak heart, but I feel certain this is wrong." She looked at me calmly. "I do have a weak heart. That is why you never see me at sports. Furthermore, I have been told by the doctors that I can't expect a long life. Does it say how long I have to live?" I felt hot and uncomfortable. This was unexpected. She stretched her hand out to me once more. I calculated carefully and came up with 24 years. But I did not say so to her. I gently held her hand in both of mine and said, "I am not God, and the length of life cannot be correctly estimated."

When I was a student in Germany, years later, I received a letter from my mother informing me that Renate had died at the university in Hamburg. "It is so very sad," she wrote, "The poor girl had a weak heart and died at the age of 24." This was my first confirmation of the accuracy of palmistry. By then I had begun to study palmistry very seriously and found it answered many questions for me and indicated future events for other interested individuals.

Visit to Lebanon and Syria

We had a lovely elderly American couple living with us in the hotel for two years. When they were transferred to Beirut, Lebanon, they invited my sister and me to visit them for a month. It was a huge adventure traveling by ourselves on a boat to the "Switzerland of the Middle East." But as soon as we left the harbor, the water became rough, and my sister assured me my face was green. I felt dreadfully seasick throughout the voyage.

Bob and his wife Ray picked us up at the harbor in an elegant American car sporting a little flag on the hood. Their apartment overlooked gardens and was part of the American University grounds. Huge old trees grew everywhere. The place looked affluent. I had never lived with a couple who were obviously in love and visibly dedicated to each other. They could not have children, and so they decided to invite us two teenagers for a spell. It quickly became apparent that there was a large group of Americans in Beirut, and that they all knew each other and regularly met in the club. This too was new to me, for other nationalities did not cling together like this. It seemed to me that Americans preferred to eat and go to parties together, make excursions together, and generally refrained from any effort to meet or talk to the Lebanese. I felt we were in some form of protective cocoon, isolated from the people of the country.

They had a scale in their bathroom and I quickly found myself gaining weight. Was it the hamburgers, hot dogs, and other delicacies new to me that were to blame? The biggest temptation was the ice cream, which we were generously given every time we visited the club. A new discovery for me was American magazines and all the references to body shape, artificial beauty, and sex. One magazine had long excerpts of the Kinsey report, and I learned a great many interesting things about sex and relationships.

Bob and Ray were also keen to take us on excursions. A whole group was formed for this purpose and together we visited Sidon and Tire, the great Roman temple, the last remnants of the vast Cedars of Lebanon on the mountain, Damascus, and other places of interest. What stayed with me much more than the sights was the genuine warmth of the Americans I met, as well as their generosity and outspoken love for each other, especially in Ray and Bob's case. We also visited the beautiful beaches and went swimming. As I was an excellent and fast swimmer by now, I chose as my goal a black rock to which I would race. A young man in our group decided to follow me and when I reached the rock, so did he. Without as much as a word he reached out and tried to pull me to him, touching my breast. I backed away from him and then sank deep down, out of his reach, pivoted, and raced back as fast as I could. I felt disturbed by the event but I was glad I had the strength and ability to get away.

The Lebanese people spoke French as well as Lebanese, and there were both Christians and Muslims in Beirut at the time. A young woman around my own age was employed by Ray to help her with her mother, who was very old and mostly in a wheelchair. The old lady was very sweet, and she seemed to like being on the large veranda, where she sang Christian hymns and prayed. The Lebanese girl and I talked together in French, and she told me how unhappy she was. She came from a good family who had fallen on hard times and so she had to go to work as a domestic servant.

I suddenly realized how very fortunate I was to be able to go to school and study with the potential of having a choice eventually in how I wished to live. My young Lebanese friend talked about the strained situation between Muslims and Christians and said that there was a great fear of conflict. She also spoke of the fear of invasion by Israel. I have often thought of her and how all her fears came true many years later. When I saw the destruction of Beirut in papers, I had trouble believing that elegant city had been wrecked, and for what purpose? Eventually, I became eager to return to Cairo. My visit to Lebanon had opened my eyes to my own good fortune: how much freedom I enjoyed, how lucky I was to be in a very good school, and how grateful I had to be for the lioness that was my mother, Leni.

My mother's little hotel was thriving, and there were many important people who spent several weeks staying with us. Others stayed for months and even years. There was an amazing Chinese doctor who talked to me like an equal and from whom I learned so much. There was a charming South Indian couple with their 11-year-old daughter, Shoba. The mother, hearing that I painted so well, asked me to paint her portrait. I took her to the Academy, and she posed there for the whole class. She was an exquisite woman with a deep brown complexion and silky black hair down to her waist. I threw myself into the task of painting her with great enthusiasm, but no one commented on the painting. Much later my mother told me the poor lady had been most upset by the mysterious, dark image I had painted of her. She saw herself as a light-skinned Indian and had expected something different.

Fortunately, I was usually indifferent to the criticism of others, unless it was from my teacher Jaro Hilbert. Whatever criticism he voiced stung like a viper. I now conclude that already at the young age of 15, my confidence in my capacity as a maker of images was developed, and I was indifferent to casual opinions. The Indian couple eventually took a flat not far from our house and on many occasions asked me to babysit for Shoba. The 11-year-old was amazing to me. She had such clarity of mind and read very advanced books. One evening, we talked about souls. She told me animals had souls. This surprised me, and I argued that animals were not on our level of evolution. We argued for a long time. She managed to persuade me that animals did have souls. She brought up reincarnation, Buddhism, and Hinduism. After I had put her to bed, I stood on the dark little balcony looking out into the night and went over the information I had been given, feeling I had received a great gift. Somehow, I had touched the ancient wisdom of India.

Object in the Sky

One day at the Officer's Club, I had just completed my two hours of swimming and was resting from the training. Stretched out in a beach chair, I dried my hair with a towel and enjoyed the beautiful early spring day. The sky was blue and cloudless and soon I would depart so I could arrive home by one o'clock for lunch. Most of the other swimmers had completed their training and were hoisting themselves out of the pool and would also be departing.

Suddenly, I saw a huge object in the sky. It had the shape of a saucer and looked just like silver. Many little round portholes were visible. I sat up in surprise just in time to see other people around the pool calling out and pointing to the sky. The object stood motionless above the pool, but it was impossible to gauge the distance. Then it spun like a spool of thread changing its location before it froze and stood still once more. This shifting and moving continued for a while. Sometimes it rose higher, sometimes it dropped, sometimes it stopped. All its movements kept me from feeling bored, and I never thought of looking at my watch. In fact, we all seemed frozen in time and no one talked or left. The object shot about with amazing speed, then suddenly darted up and sideways, and was lost to sight.

I had heard of UFOs before and felt oddly calm as I walked home. "Where have you been?" my mother asked as I walked into the dining room. "Do you know it is three o'clock and the kitchen has just closed!" To my surprise, I said absolutely nothing, giving no excuses or explanations. I was silent. What had happened to the three hours at the pool? I was actually missing hours of time and I had no recollection of what transpired after the sighting. Also, none of the other witnesses at the pool that day ever mentioned our mutual experience.

Not long after this, I discovered that the sightings of strange objects in the sky may actually predate the emergence of modern man. Flying saucers were seen in the Hunan province of China, and one of the first accounts is written down on an Egyptian papyrus that was part of the annals of Thutmose III, who reigned around 1504-1450 B.C. The papyrus is more than 3,400 years old and records the sighting of numerous brilliant round objects in the sky by Pharaoh Thutmose III, his army, and his scribes. The Pharaoh ordered the event be recorded so that it may be remembered. I did not speak of this experience for many years, and I don't know why.

Sweet Seventeen

When I turned seventeen, my mother permitted me to have a birthday party. This was the first birthday party I'd had since we had left Berlin. I invited my five schoolmates; my sister and her little group of fellow pupils came too. I also brazenly invited Gamal Fahmy. Gamal made no bones about his attraction to me, and we were both as innocent as ducks. The photos of the birthday party show a lot of young people dressed up for a costume party and having a wonderful time. We danced and laughed and hopped around. My mother wisely said nothing until much, much later.

My fellow classmates must have gossiped about Gamal and me, and after the party, it dawned on me that I was being excluded by Germans from some gatherings. Did they too see me as "l'Egyptienne" and no longer as a German? I certainly suspected as much. I had become a champion swimmer of Egypt some time before. My photo appeared in the papers; I was asked to pose for the cover of a magazine in my homemade two-piece bathing suit. It was extremely difficult to find bathing suits in Cairo, so I was forced to make my own on an old Singer sewing machine. Perhaps it was my imagination, but I felt certain teachers were less friendly all of a sudden. An exhibition of young artistic people was held in Cairo, and both my sister and I won acclaims. Again, our pictures were in the paper.

Because I had become a champion swimmer, we received a free membership in the Gezira Sporting Club, something my mother appreciated, since this was the best club in Cairo and it was close to our home. Considering all this, it was somewhat of a shock to me when I received a C grade in sports and a C grade in art. My mother went to the headmaster and complained, bringing medals and paintings of mine to prove her point. She warned me to be especially nice to all the teachers. Diplomacy and her wisdom won the day. The teachers changed my grades to As.

It was around this time my mother insistently asked some of her guests for advice on how she could send me to

Age 17, at a costume party

*Seventeenth birthday party, dancing
with Jamal (first boyfriend), 1957*

university after my Abitur, which was the German certificate for completing secondary school. Though she now made a good income, she was not allowed to send money out of the country for the education of a child. We were advised that we needed to apply for scholarships, a very difficult undertaking. At this time an American Professor from Idaho said he had some connections that might be helpful, providing I had excellent grades. My mother looked at my reports from school and invited the head teacher for consultation. While most grades were good, I was weak in math and French. To remedy this shortcoming, my mother decided on a plan. The following summer, my sister and I went on a two-month student trip to France. It was a total immersion venture; no other language aside from French was to be spoken. As far as I recall, my mother revealed nothing about the nature of the adventure we were to undertake. The trip started in Alexandria, where we were to board a boat leaving for France.

Summertime in Europe

We took a train to Alexandria, where a large group of our young people met, and were escorted by French teachers to the harbor. There we boarded a French ship bound for Marseille. On arrival in southern France, we took a bus to the Dordogne, where our tour began. We were offered hospitality in a large, rambling old house for students. Surrounded by forest, farms, and gentle hillsides, the location was truly beautiful. In the Dordogne, there are the Lascaux caves where 20,000-year-old images painted by ancient men astonish visitors. There is a gentle river valley with an equally mild climate that allowed ancient people to thrive and hunt game.

Among the students, groups were formed, and assignments were given to visit villages, walk to medieval centers, castles, markets, and cathedrals, and write short essays about the experience. My companion was a young man from Cairo whose parents were French. He had been to France almost every summer and told me this program was very stimulating. We walked to a Romanesque cathedral and began to make notes on the architecture and history of the place. I was enthralled and ever after found the history of medieval France fascinating. In the late afternoon, we returned through the magical forest and in a very large dining room enjoyed a truly fabulous feast that displayed the French culinary skills.

Quickly, connections were made with the other students, and after some games outside, we retired to our dorms. The teachers were excellent, enthusiastic representatives of France and its culture. Their endeavor was not only to teach us about the history of France but to give us an unforgettable experience. After two weeks, my French became fluent and my writing improved. Not long after that, I caught myself thinking in French.

Once during this trip, we visited Les Grandes Caves de Perigord. A highlight of my trip was descending deep into a huge cavern and then traveling in a little boat under the glittering ceiling of stalactites. Water dripped constantly from the high overhead vault, so we had to wear raincoats and rain hats. It was a magical adventure and very beautiful. Later on, we traveled by bus throughout France and visited famous sights, cathedrals, and castles with *son et lumiere* shows. We wrote essays daily, made drawings, saw plays in theaters, saw fashion shows in Paris, and visited the great fresh outdoor food market called Les Halles.

For two months, we traveled by bus through France, Switzerland, and Italy, mostly to the Naples region to see Vesuvius and the Isle of Capri and to experience the excavated ancient Roman site of Pompeo. In the Alps, we saw how cheese was made and visited chocolate factories. We drove south to the flower fields of Grasse and visited perfume factories. Then a small side trip was organized to visit the area where Picasso, the greatest artist of the twentieth century, lived! I was very excited and at the same time apprehensive. We entered a small chapel where Picasso had created several large murals. I was astonished at the liberties he took. Someone said he used boat paint for this work, and it was not going to hold up. Then we saw a little museum. Here were huge canvases of enormous women with pea-sized heads. I began to get a sense that he saw women as nothing more than sex objects. I remember writing my mother a long angry letter, declaring that this great artist was making fun of women and everyone took it seriously. In my opinion, he clearly had no respect for the female.

Return to Egypt

After two months, our journey was complete, and both my sister and I were totally fluent and at ease in the French language. We boarded our ship in Marseilles. A band played on board, a type of farewell for all the visitors to France. I stood at the railing, glad to be returning to Egypt, even though I had experienced a most civilized and fascinating time in France. I came back to my daily training in swimming, to my art courses at the Academy, to my friends at the club, to horseback riding in the desert, and to moonlight dances held in ancient temples beside the great pyramids. There were still some weeks of summer vacation left, and I was grateful for every moment, as I now appreciated Egypt more than ever. I understood one had to leave a place to appreciate it and see its qualities in a new light.

Gamal was very happy to see me again. He had finished his school education and had decided to join the army, as that was his only choice for continuing his education and preparing for his career. He was going to be a cadet with shorn hair and would stay for several months in some army barracks without home leave. I was horrified at his choice. Hadn't his mother foretold that he would die in a war!? His father had been an officer; he felt it was only right that he too should join the ranks.

At about this time, my mother was very busy. A number of new guests had arrived in the hotel and their passports had to be presented first thing in the morning to the authorities in a big government building. There the passports were stamped and the accompanying forms my mother had filled out were collected. She asked me to go to the Gomhouria government building at the Midan Tahrir and hand in the paperwork. I set out on a bus and reached my destination. The building was huge with white marble stairs, which although cleaned daily, always looked dirty. I pushed past the people milling about and ran up to find the office I had been told to go to. As I entered, the official rose and offered me a chair. This is certainly unusual behavior towards a young girl. I had never in my many visits to this government building been treated to anything but long waits while sullen officials self-importantly and loudly stamped the papers. This young official thanked me as I handed him my bundle. "Can I offer you a Turkish cup of coffee or lemonade," he inquired. "And how is Abu (daddy)?" "Oh, very well." I answered, trying not to give away my surprise. He handed back the passports. "Give your parents my Salaams," he said in parting.

As I bounced down the stairs, I began to think that the afternoon visits Fouad Hafez paid my mother, under the guise of assisting her with the huge task of bookkeeping that had to be done in Arabic, possibly had developed into more than just a working friendship. I recalled an exchange between my mother and Fouad I overheard late one night. I had awakened from my sleep and had heard their voices in the room next door. "Let me take you away from all this, marry me," he pleaded.

"Be ashamed of yourself, you are a married man," my mother answered. I believed them to be nothing more than friends. Did this mean that she had married him secretly? Was Fouad Hafez my stepfather by Egyptian law? Had he divorced his Turkish wife to get my mother? But then I thought the official must have been mistaken. There was nothing in the relationship between my mother and Fouad that suggested they had changed their arrangement. They quarreled frequently, and I felt sorry for him when my mother was as nasty as she could be. In fact, I had determined never to become like my mother. Her temper often got the better of her. She told me her nervous system was damaged when she became ill for a whole year, suffering lockjaw at the age of 12. Indeed, she was very delicate, even though she was very determined and a survivor.

A Day in Alexandria

I was seventeen, and it was a very good year! It was during the summer vacation when Gamal suggested we spend a day in Alexandria at the ocean. My mother had traveled to Europe, and I was in charge of the hotel. We decided to leave with the earliest train on a Sunday morning and take the train back at night. I told Gamal that since it was Sunday, I had to go to church. No big deal, we would find a Roman Catholic Church, and he actually sat beside me throughout the service. He said he found it interesting to experience the congregation of another faith.

We found our way to a beautiful Alexandrian beach, changed into bathing suits, rented a big wooden board for wave skimming, and ran into the deep blue Mediterranean. The water was crisp and fresh and the waves brisk and foamy as we threw our tanned swimmers' bodies into the brine. Only youth can know such a delight. We were tireless, filled with energy and joy as we swam out into the deep, and then waited for a big wave and threw ourselves onto the board, which was broad enough for two skinny kids. The wave lifted us up on its glassy back, and we slid effortlessly almost to the edge of the beach. We did this over and over again, timing the exact moment when to jump on the back of the wave, stumbling as we reached the beach, suddenly clumsy and physical.

When hunger announced itself, we found a vendor on the cornice who sold his food out of a little wooden cart. He had Arabic bread filled with beans, falafel, eggs, cucumbers and white cheese. He seasoned everything with a pinch of coarse sea salt, and we were in heaven. The afternoon suddenly turned to sunset; it was six o'clock sharp. I was very sunburned in spite of my tan and felt shivery in the cool moist evening air. Gamal gave me his jacket, and we went to the train station. It turned out we had made a mistake about the train schedule for the return to Cairo. There was no train until four o'clock in the morning.

We settled down to wait on a hard station bench, fighting tiredness and sunburn. The hours drifted past very slowly. Even if we had had the money to pay for it, there was no question of seeking out a hotel. We knew we were no more than teenagers. Gamal and I agreed with each other that we did not want to try the temptations of love. At four in the morning, we boarded the train for the three-hour trip to Cairo. I felt this day had been the happiest of my young life. We traveled second class. At some stop in a quiet little town, a mature man boarded with five sleepy young women, each carrying a child. They settled on the hard wooden benches. The women were so young, wrapped in the black Malaya of the married woman, and each already had a child. The man was probably their husband. He would get up just in time to stop a child from sliding off the lap of its mother, and often adjusted the sleeping women with a cane he carried. I felt sorry for him and felt very sorry for the young, tired women, none of whom had ever had as good a day as I had just experienced.

Boulak

Often after school or before my art classes I would make a quick diversion into the forbidden district of Boulak. No one had actually forbidden me, but if my mother knew, she would have been horrified. This was one of the oldest, poorest areas of Cairo, and as I slipped off the bus, I pulled out a big black scarf and covered my head and shoulders. This was for disguise as much as protection. If I forgot my scarf and went bare headed into this area, little children would run after me shouting "charmuta," which means "whore." It always felt like a huge adventure to venture into the ancient streets, just broad enough for a donkey to pass through, slipping past ancient, once beautiful old houses, now worn with age and leaning precariously towards each other. It was always a relief to see the one modern house at the end of the street, Gamal's house. Fatima or the little Nubian servant boy would open the door, and she and I would chat about this and that before she explained more palmistry to me.

While visiting Fatima, I discovered that Gamal's father had died by being poisoned. Muslims are allowed to marry up to four women. At that time in Cairo, many Egyptians had more than one wife. Usually, they had to be affluent and kept their wives in separate accommodations. This also avoided jealousy and strife between the women and their offspring. Fatima came from a Bedouin family. She had the sharp features of the desert tribes, a hooked nose and brilliant huge, black eyes. She was very slender and small. As a child, she contracted polio and was paralyzed until the age of 16. She could not even speak. Suddenly, as if through a miracle, she could move again. Her first spoken sentences were all predictions. She foretold the sex of a child about to be born to an aunt, she saw an accident ahead of time, and she warned people of bad events. In no time, she was accused of being a witch. A wise person told her she needed a medium through which she could pretend to learn of future events. The reading of coffee grounds was chosen since it is the generally accepted medium for a fortune-teller. Fatima began to make money for herself and became a healer of souls.

At about this time, an Egyptian officer came for a reading. He was very handsome and had been married by his parents to a woman he found very difficult to live with. He fell in love with the young fortune-teller, Fatima, and married her as his second wife. Fatima warned him about the danger of jealousy and that his first wife was very vengeful. He was careful for several years never to neglect his first wife. However, when Gamal was born, the situation changed and he wanted to be around his family more. The first wife had no children. Fatima was aware that he was in danger, but did not know the kind of danger that threatened her husband. When she was informed by the police that he had died, no one knew what the cause was. Fatima knew now it was poison, but she could not prove anything. She was very accepting of her fate and her gift, and said it was only by the "grace of Allah." During the course of our friendship, she married again. Gamal said that his stepfather was a kind man.

Threat of War

Although I was very much engaged in my schoolwork and enjoying studies like never before, a sudden cloud loomed on the horizon. Israel was about to attack Egypt. During the night, bridges had sandbags placed around them, ancient monuments were encased in protective wooden structures, sirens practiced alarms, and schools were closed. There were sirens going off in the middle of the day, fears of air attacks, and people hoarding food supplies. Fortunately, the war did not happen in the capital, but it was an unnerving situation nonetheless. I feared most of all for Gamal and his life, now that he was in the army. Anxiety hit me like a sledgehammer. I had trouble sleeping. Fears and images of the past world war invaded my mind. My consciousness became alert to a sharp degree. It was as if I saw everything for the first time.

During this period, I trained for my swimming right through the winter months, walking daily to the club that was quite close to my house. I had to cross the Nile River from Zamalek Island to reach the club. Often at this time the bridge was open to let the feluccas through with their high sails shaped like scimitars. A few rowboats took people across the river for a few piastres (the Egyptian coinage of the day), I among them. On the opposite shore stood a huge, ancient tree covered with white ibis and egret birds. The tree was so large its canopies

Age 17, swimming at the club

offered a space wide enough for merchants to spread out their wares, for beggars to sleep, for women to sit breastfeeding their babies, and for children to run about. It was a colorful corner. (Alas these ancient trees were all cut down later to make room for wider streets.) After completing my daily training regime, I left the club, my hair hanging wet and clammy down my neck, and I returned home by walking over the bridge. It was now dark and the little stalls of vendors were lit with colorful lights, and music played everywhere. I remember how relaxed and happy I felt as I made my way home and how much I feared the threat of destruction and the horrors of war.

Since our private Embassy school had to close, and I was in my last year leading to the Abitur degree, the teachers decided to ask our little group of six pupils to come to a gathering at their private homes. The idea was greeted with much enthusiasm by pupils and parents alike. We met at a teacher's home, settled in their living rooms, and enjoyed a whole morning's worth of history, English literature, or math. Then we went to another teacher's home for the afternoon.

Since the school was a German high school it was under the watchful eye of the German Ministry of Culture and had to conform to the high educational standards of Germany. It was considered an educational experiment by the German Education Department since it was the first school of its sort in Cairo, so we were to be tested in 16 subjects, on every subject that was being taught. This was a very intense time of study for all of us. We would meet with fellow students and study in a group. We also composed a little book about a two-week excursion we made to Upper Egypt, where we visited all the sights from Luxor to Aswan under the supervision of our head teachers, completing our accounts with images made from linoleum cuts, mostly cut by me and then printed. The whole educational experience was an intense immersion, and I worked so hard and was so stressed out that my hair was falling out by the handful.

Our finals came into sight, and I recall studying for three days nonstop. For our Abitur, we had written compositions in

Rosie at Luxor, 1955

German, English, and French, as well as a short written exam to show our mastery of the Arabic language. All science subjects were tested extensively, and we had to be able to speak fluently in English, French, and Arabic, and of course German. A group of German examiners were present, sent all the way from Europe to evaluate us. It was by far a more rigorous examination than the exams that Abitur contestants experience in Germany, and probably the most difficult examination I ever had.

We all did well, and I scored the marks I needed to be able to apply for a scholarship. Our friends from Wyoming wrote to their Rotary friends, and the wheels started to turn, which eventually led to my receiving a scholarship for the University of Georgia in Athens, Georgia. Meanwhile, our close-knit little group of fellow students got together for a celebration at the famous Mena House Hotel, just in front of the Giza pyramids, for a graduation dinner. They had already heard I was to receive a scholarship to the USA and go to a university there. A lovely bracelet had been purchased as a gift for me, and I felt quite stunned by so much love and affection. We sat beside a swimming pool illuminated under the water and listened to a band play while we enjoyed our dinner. Then we danced under the great dome of stars until one in the morning. I have always regretted losing touch with these precious friends.

Driving Out the Devil

During that summer, Gamal came to get me to witness a "driving out the devil" at his mother's house. I was very excited to be seeing a very ancient, and in some circles, forbidden, practice. When we arrived, the room was already filled with women, all dressed in their black Malayas. Sitting down cross-legged in a corner of the room on the floor, we waited. The shaman entered. He was a tall skinny man, dressed in a turban and wearing a broad wrapping around his hips to which innumerable seashells of varying sizes were attached. As he moved, so did the seashells. The seashells made a hissing sound as if snakes filled the room. Musicians arrived and soon I heard the drumming of tabla, with their clear high-pitched sound. Some women got up and swayed to the music.

Then with a sudden leap, the shaman entered the center and began to sway and shake his hips in a most erotic way. His gyrations became intense, and the women began to respond to the motions, swaying like reeds in the wind. The movements increased in intensity, becoming wild and rhythmic and keeping up with the rapid beat of the drumming. The women had their eyes shut, but the expressions on their faces became tortured, pained and unnatural. They began to howl and bark, hiss and sob. Foam began to appear on their lips, and the heat in the room became stifling. One fell to the floor, then another, and another. They began to writhe as if in agony, baring legs and completely losing all composure. I stared in horror, unable to believe that human beings could look like this. The shaman pulled at them, as if pulling invisible strings, and they responded by moving towards him and howling like animals. Their eyes were expressionless and glassy, and the expressions on their faces were horrible. One young woman lay on the ground having convulsions, white froth streaming from her mouth. The shaman stood over her. "Go away!" he ordered in a firm voice and repeated it. The voice which came from the young woman had now nothing human to it. Rather it sounded like a tortured wild beast. "Go!" said the shaman again.

All of a sudden there was silence. The body of the young woman on the ground looked motionless, devoid of life. I sat without breathing, shaken to the core. A woman wiped the young woman's face with a wet cloth as she slowly sat up. Then she guided her from the room. Gamal now said we needed to go, as the space was needed for those possessed. I felt shaken as I left and realized that there was an intense stench in the room. Gamal told me this ancient practice was most successful in driving out "the evil one." He said that mostly the spirits attach themselves to women because women are more easily influenced. "We call these spirits Shaitans; they are a form of powerful elementals."

Choices

Fatima's predictions all came true. It was now three years after she made them, I was 19 years old, and after finishing my Abitur, I had received a Rotary scholarship for a one-year study at the University of Georgia in Athens, Georgia, in the USA. I felt overwhelmed with excitement.

At the same time, my trainer, Alex, was still clocking my swimming, and to his delight found I swam with extraordinary speed. The Olympics in Rome were going to happen the following summer, and he wanted me to represent Egypt in breaststroke and butterfly stroke. I was elated by this good news. My mother, wisely, did not dash my hopes or argue. A good friend, very educated and sophisticated, was chosen by her to talk to me about my choices. I still recall very clearly visiting this gentleman in his apartment, which was filled with beautiful books and works of art, and being treated like a lady.

"My dear," he said, "you are a multi-talented young woman confronted with a huge decision, sports or art. Probably at this point in your life they are both equally attractive and tempting. But I ask you to consider that as a swimmer you have a limited time when physical strength can allow you to gain success and recognition. How long is the time when most people practicing a sport can shine? Maybe ten years, maybe less! You are equally talented in painting and you have been offered a scholarship, a merit scholarship no less. Painting can stay with you throughout life, can be your career, and can bring you many years of pleasure, even success into old age. Consider your options and make a wise choice. If you lose the scholarship you may kick yourself later on, because it will be much, much more difficult to find another one." Needless to say, I had not thought ahead, not even reflected on the choice I was confronted with. I thanked him for his wisdom and advice and chose to go to university.

The time before I left Egypt was deliciously free and unencumbered by concerns. My mother gave me full freedom for the first time in my young life. Gabriele and I were allowed to go out in the evenings with our many young friends and go to parties. Horseback rides were arranged in the desert during full moon nights, and often we ended up at the great temples at the foot of the pyramids for impromptu dancing. The nights were silken under the star-spangled canopy of the velvet sky as we danced to music on tapes that some young man had set up. We danced on cool smooth sand between the ancient stone walls of the temple, the evening air refreshing on our faces after the heat of the day. We were free and danced with the abandon of youth until exhaustion. After midnight we dragged ourselves wearily to the cars and drove back into the city.

Our excursions into the desert continued, mostly on horseback, and we went further and further in search of lost temples and ancient pyramids. Going into nature meant going into the desert and the pull of the Sahara became intense. Venturing into the environment of sand, dunes, ancient rock formations and blue sky was always an exhilarating adventure. We never knew what we would find. The desert meant freedom and was magically transformative. The deep silence, only broken by the wind, wrapped me into a different mind state. When I returned from my adventures I felt well, calm, and centered.

Meeting a Sage

On one of these excursions, I had an unusual experience. We had ridden to some ancient monuments, and I went off by myself towards a tomb. As I stepped from the blinding desert brightness into the dark entry, feeling the coolness on my skin, I noticed an old man sitting on a low rock in the corner. "Ed Fadel, ed Fadel, enter," he said, his face lighting up. He was paper-thin, with the most luminous eyes.

"Please share my food." he said, as he spread a white piece of cloth on the floor in front of him. Then he pulled out bread. "Oh, I do not mean to disturb," I said. "Thank you, I can't take the little you have to eat." He laughed and pointed to something. A tiny, pretty, white mouse was coming forward. He placed a crumb of bread on the cloth, and the mouse daintily hopped forward and holding the crumb in its front paws, began to eat. "Sharing is a blessing," the man said, his face sparkling with joy. "I share all I have, and you?" "I have come to see this tomb, are you guarding it?" I asked. "Yes, it holds valuables, see the gate is locked." He pointed to a metal gate behind him. "You sit here every day?" I asked. "I have a friend," he said, pointing to the mouse. "My friend comes and goes to the mummy of the pharaoh."

As he said this, the mouse ran behind him underneath the metal gate and looked back at us, as if to demonstrate the accuracy of the old man's words. "I don't mind serving the pharaoh. He is still here and shares his wisdom with me." He pulled off some more bread for the mouse, and this time the little creature hopped onto his hand, taking the bread from his fingers. "Sharing and serving bring happiness. Yes, much happiness, and peace of mind. Everything is connected. Everything serves something else." He laughed heartily and I could see his missing teeth.

Then I realized how blissful I felt, as if the old sage had projected a wonderful sensation. "Ah, you feel it." He laughed again. His laughter was ringing in the small entry, and I felt it came straight from his heart. I placed my left hand on my heart center and with the right hand I gave him the Muslim salute, touching my chest, my lips, and my forehead with my right hand as I bowed to him. Then I left the tomb. I had learned that some beings have the gift of touching the soul with their presence. The memory remains as clear to me as if the encounter took place yesterday.

Egyptian Nightlife

I had a good number of friends on the swimming team, at the club, and at the Art Academy. Many of them were wealthy, and since we seemed to form tight groups, those who had money paid entry fees for night clubs and restaurants for those who had no money. It was an unspoken agreement that those who could would take care of those who could not pay. Neither I nor my sister had any spare money. Yet we visited the best dancing spots in Cairo where live bands from Cuba, South Africa, Italy, and Greece played. We went out every evening, first to some good dining spot in Cairo, and then to dance on houseboats on the Nile or in the cooler areas near the pyramids.

Our favorite was Sahara City, a place in the desert, way beyond the pyramids of Giza. Here were belly dancers, performers from Africa, and whirling dervishes. Excellent food was served while we were seated on oriental cushions. Hookahs were passed around among the young men, and the girls watched to see on whose lap the belly dancer would sit. They always found a woman they liked and settled in her lap. It was explained to me, that most of them were lesbians and that they did not dance for the men but rather tried to appeal to other women.

At that time in Egypt, female sexual mutilation was still widely practiced, as it has been since Pharaonic times. As I understood it back then, most women were uninterested in sex and found it painful. While I was at St. Mary's English boarding school, many girls left the school suddenly, mostly in their thirteenth or fourteenth year. They came back for a final visit showing off a fat diamond ring on their finger and looking slightly shocked at what was to befall them. It was also murmured that they'd had the operation and that their clitoris had been removed. One of the signs was that they were having trouble urinating. Their marriages were arranged by their parents and usually to a man of middle age. One of my friends called Isis was married in this way. I met her again years later in the club. "I did not love him. He was so much older than me." she confided. "But what to do! I ended up loving him after all. I have two children by him!" Her eyes filled with tears. "I would like to be free as you are, to swim and to go dancing and to flirt and to lose my heart to a man of my choice. I feel caught in an ancient spider web, where all I am allowed to do is give birth to children, care for my family, get old, and die."

Timor

That was the summer I met Timor, a judo master from Mongolia, trained from childhood in Japan. He had come to train Egyptian soldiers in the art of self-defense. He set up a practice tent at the Gezira Sporting Club, and after witnessing a session, I was enthusiastic to start judo. Timor was a stocky young man with a body as hard as a rock. His knuckles on his hands were bruised and scarred from practicing his martial arts against a wooden pole. He demonstrated his ability to split blocks of ice with one direct hit with the side of his hand. He could also split bricks piled on each other and his hands actually were registered with the police as lethal weapons.

Timor was very kind in giving my sister and me two judo uniforms with the request that we pay when convenient. We never did pay him, which I now find inexcusable. Every afternoon we visited the judo tent and practiced this ancient martial art. I simply loved it and soon became good enough to throw big Egyptian men weighing far more than I did. Realizing what a wondrous gift it was to be able to defend myself lent wings to my practice. Timor saw something in me; perhaps it was my enthusiasm, or perhaps my lack of formal respect, which he might have found refreshing. I certainly was not the normal student. Cheeky and full of bubbly laughter, I teased him remorselessly. Soon my sister Gaby and I were the best female students he had, and he delighted in allowing us to demonstrate how easy it was for us to throw huge guys through the air to the ground. When we walked in our judo outfits through the pool area to the practice tent, there was always a stir of interest and yes, respect, or so it felt.

One of the handsome young men with whom I practiced a great deal was Burmese, and when he told me he was going on a retreat for a month, I was shocked. I asked him why and also inquired what a retreat was what it meant. He told me he was a Buddhist and was training how to meditate. He gave me a great deal of information and I was startled to realize how superficial my own spirituality was. My respect for my teacher grew when I realized how intensely he practiced and how dedicated he was. He often invited the whole class to a juice shop, where we all received freshly squeezed fruit or vegetable juices. At nine o'clock sharp, his wrist alarm clock sounded and he excused himself to go home to sleep. No amount of begging for another half hour of his company could persuade him otherwise. In retrospect, I recognize how he tried to be a model for us, demonstrating his firmness, resolve, and dedication.

We often brought Timor to our house. My mother found him fascinating. One evening, my Burmese friend called to tell me he would like to talk to my mother that evening on Timor's behalf. Of course, I should be present as well. I was totally casual. "Sure, come over, it will be fine." Totally unaware of the significance or intention of the visit, I listened in shock to the carefully worded request from my friend, asking for permission for Timor to marry me. He told us of the noble and old lineage of Timor and his family, going back to Genghis Khan, and his intentions of traveling and eventually settling in Asia. My mother was charming and most diplomatic as she declined for me. I sat there like a stunned goose, having had no idea that Timor had fallen in love with me.

We never ever mentioned the proposal or talked to each other about feelings, but I could sense Tiimor's deep disappointment. Every summer when I returned from my studies in Europe to spend the summer in Cairo, I returned to judo with my instructor Timor, who was someone I respected deeply. I recognized a noble soul in him, and it hurt my heart that I had disappointed him so deeply. I eventually achieved my brown belt rank in judo.

3   University

University and the New World

The United States was a unique adventure, especially as I
traveled on a Dutch cargo boat from Alexandria and saw what
the thousands of immigrants must have seen when they first
arrived—the Statue of Liberty holding up the torch! It was
evening, and the city lights had just switched on. Everything
looked aglow, soft pink, unreal to me. The boat glided past the
French sculpture, the tugboat hooted, and the harbor slowly
came closer and closer. The air was soft and balmy.

I found New York terrifying and exhilarating. A fellow
passenger offered to take me in his taxi into the city. We found
rooms on the 16th floor of a hotel. That evening, I made my
way to the famous Bird-Land Jazz Club and spent a few hours
drinking in live jazz. The next day, a Greyhound bus took me
via Washington D.C. to Athens, Georgia, to the University
of Georgia. On the bus, I sat beside an interesting man who
turned out to be a Native American. "If you want to know this
country you must go to New Mexico, to a town called Santa Fe."
he advised. He began to tell me about the Carlsberg Caverns,
huge magical caves, and about the Indians in New Mexico.
His stories brought to life the Native Nations, most of them
displaced by the government of the white man. If I visited the
Southwest, he told me, I would be able to see a magical land

and very different people. I was intoxicated with his stories as they awakened my childhood interests in these noble people.

When we reached Georgia, he was removed from my side and ordered to the back of the bus. I was asked if he bothered me since he was just a "drunk Indian." My protests to the contrary did not get him returned to his seat beside me. After meeting him, I wanted to go to New Mexico, and I saved up my money to go there at the end of my study time. A young woman called Marie had a car and was equally keen to go. However, she let me down at the very last moment, and it took me over thirty years before I finally did get to New Mexico.

At the University of Georgia, I studied art. The head of the Art Department, Lamar Dodd, was a charming and engaging man who brought his enthusiasm for art into the classroom. He showed us slides that were almost abstract, proving one did not need to cling to the convention of seeing in representational ways. I found myself thrown into a class where people painted abstractions; yet I had no idea how to go about painting something that was not representational. It did not take long before I experimented, and the ideas began to flow rapidly. Every night, there were fascinating lectures and I became completely addicted to all this information. Robert Frost, the poet, delivered a profound and memorable poetry reading, which has stayed with me to this day. I also learned about Chinese ink and brush paintings, the United Nations and politics, hypnosis, Greek philosophy, jazz, the plight of the black slaves in the South, haiku poetry, football games, square dancing, theater, pottery, design and more, which were all completely foreign to me.

Everyone was amazingly generous and kind. Every Sunday, I joined a group that watched selected films of great quality. I saw *Raisin in the Sun*, *To Kill a Mockingbird*, and *Mahalia Jackson in Concert*, just to name a few. Since I didn't have a car and the campus was large and my classes far from the dorm, I had to hitchhike to get around. There were large patches of beautiful forest on campus and a generous squirrel population. I loved to walk through those woods, which gave me some exercise. I was unused to so little physical movement and began to put on weight in an alarming way. The girls in the dorm soon informed me what not to eat. They starved themselves, and though they selected a lot of foods for their trays during lunch, they just pecked at their choices like birds and most of it was thrown away. I watched in amazement how much food was wasted.

One thing that was not explained to us was that my scholarship did not include room and board. My mother was unable to give me any money, as the Egyptian currency had no value outside Egypt. About a week into my stay, I suddenly realized something was very wrong, so I visited the campus secretary. This nice lady told me to return the following day. My student visa stated clearly that I was not allowed to work in the United States. On my return, the secretary told me how she had spoken with some administrators and a solution had been found. I could work as a waitress in the Continuing Education Center from 1 to 3 pm and make enough money to pay for my room and board. She smiled when I mentioned the law and promised that my job would be kept quiet. Thus, for the duration of my stay in Athens I worked as a waitress.

I was quickly instructed on how to set a table and how to approach guests and serve them. None of this was hard. I had already learned in my mother's hotel how to greet guests and make them feel welcome. I was given a section of the restaurant tables to serve and I started. One of the more difficult jobs was carrying a fully loaded tray on my shoulder. After finding nearly every server dropped the contents of the tray on occasion, I stopped worrying. I had also been told that if another server was not getting around to some people in her section, and if I had the time, I was to take those tables in addition to mine. It turned out that I was very fast and in no time was working the tables of my colleagues as well. That earned me a certain respect and also dislike. Because of my accent, I was referred to as the "Yankee."

There were a great number of foreign students on campus, and we were introduced to each other on several occasions

The art student in Georgia, 1957

and at festivities that were laid out in our honor. We were to
perform some dances from our countries, sing, or entertain
in other ways. The South Americans sang beautiful songs
and drummed, the Koreans danced gracefully, the Swedes
and Norwegians danced national group dances, and most
of us had a very good time. I met a hauntingly beautiful girl
from Finland called Senta, who was a real character. She

introduced me to music of the great composer Sibelius and told wonderful stories about her country. Some of the foreign students somehow managed to buy a cheap little car, since it was such a problem getting around the huge campus. It was a big bonus if I could catch a lift with some of my new friends. Senta found a Persian who was fascinated with her beauty and who chauffeured her everywhere. She traveled with her feet in pink pumps hanging out of the window. Her attire was always outrageous—she often wore slacks—and the proper Georgia girls were aghast. This was the time of tight sweaters and bobby socks. No slacks were allowed for females.

After meeting the Native American on the Greyhound bus, I had the firm intention of going to New Mexico. A fellow art student named Joe offered to teach me how to drive a car, and we settled into his old vehicle and I drove around and around in the cemetery until I managed to drive to his satisfaction. During my next visit to a Rotary club member, I mentioned my desire for a driver's license and he offered me his powerful Cadillac and graciously took me to the Motor Vehicle Division for my driving test. I had only driven the old little car of my friend, and so was completely surprised by power steering and a bench seat too difficult to adjust to my short stature. In fact, the whole vehicle felt like a huge truck I could not steer. In those days, part of the test was to drive around little flags. Much like a slalom skier I threw myself at the obstacles, gaining more and more speed as I spun around each little flag until I lost control. With lightning speed, the examiner slid towards me on the bench seat and firmly thrust his foot onto the brake, bringing the adventure to a full stop. He then took over the car and smoothly drove it to the exit. It took another 12 years before I acquired a US driving license.

So as I completed my USA stay, instead of going to New Mexico, I traveled up north to New York and Niagara Falls and into Canada before returning to Egypt on a Greek cargo ship. There were four passengers on the ship. It became instantly apparent that the captain and his crew were not on speaking terms. The first officer told me they had a mutiny on board and

ART STUDENT FROM CAIRO, EGYPT
Rosie Hilbert Displays Work

Newspaper photo of the art student in Georgia, 1957

had to sail to the island of Crete to drop their captain. A new captain would then take over. So instead of landing in Piraeus, we sailed down to Crete. It was a unique opportunity, as this allowed the passengers to visit the ruins of ancient Knossos and take a taxi around the island. I remember the sparkling ocean and the scent of trees and flowers as we neared Crete. The island, baking in the summer heat, was still, quiet, and inviting. I instantly fell in love with the light, the ocean, the ruins, and the images on the palace walls. The atmosphere was simply enchanting. In the museum, I saw the little figurines of bare-breasted snake-goddesses, images of slender young male bull-dancers, vases, and beehives. At sunset we found a little tavern and settled down for a wonderful Greek dinner accompanied by the chant of the island crickets.

Return from the USA

My arrival at Alexandria was enhanced by the exciting discovery that I needed an entry permit, which I should have arranged to get at the Egyptian Consulate in New York. It was too late now, and it was uncertain if I would be allowed to enter the country without the document. Briefly, I considered my options and then made the decision to divert the attention of the officer who was to check my papers. I had gained weight in the USA, and my clothes were somewhat tight. I chose a low-cut figure-hugging outfit. It looked like a sausage skin, it was so tight; and my breasts were squeezed and popped over the rim of the décolleté like overripe fruit. I chose very high heels I had bought in New York and finished my attire by wearing a little enameled Koran.

In this attire, I teetered out to the waiting group of custom and passport inspectors. The young man who asked for my papers, I greeted in fluent Arabic, telling him how ecstatic I was to be home once more. He asked me to sit and I leaned forward giving him an ample view of what I had to offer. He was instantly drawn to my Koran necklace, reaching forward to grasp it. "Oh, so you are Muslim," he exclaimed." "But of course," I lied. Then I began to ask him for news of Egypt and inquired what had happened in the year while I was at university. After ten minutes he had invited me to dinner, and I accepted, and he arranged to pick me up at a certain meeting place. My papers were all stamped as being in good order, and I walked down the ramp to meet my mother and sister, who were waiting for me at the dock.

Egypt had never looked better to me. The cool sea breeze of Alexandria was filled with the fragrance of jasmine and fragrant white flowers used to make necklaces, which were sold at night to ladies. As I sat in the taxi that whisked us to our hotel, night came quickly and the city was vibrant with lights and music and people walking along the seafront. This kind of liveliness I had missed in America. The city looked old, worn, and—compared to the cities of the USA—like a ruined remnant of ancient times. Yet I was ecstatic and filled with excitement. I called the passport official and his mother answered. I told her that I had to cancel the arranged meeting since my family was taking me back to Cairo with them.

Like Alexandria, Cairo looked dusty, sand colored, and ancient. In my wallet I had $100 left from my year in the USA. I intended to keep this sum as a reminder to return to America. I had no plan and no clear idea how I would manage this, but the intention was in my mind that I would return. Also, curiously, I had no doubt that it would come about.

Egypt had been my home for 10 years. I could pass for an Egyptian, I spoke the language, and I was happy there. In the USA, I had seen racism and a society trying to embrace immigrants as kindly as possible. In Egypt immigrants had been coming for thousands of years and been assimilated. There seemed to be no friction until Gamal Abdel Nasser. Suddenly my Jewish friends, one after the other were leaving and going to South Africa, Brazil, or to the USA. Greek families who had lived in Cairo for generations were returning the Greece. Italian and French boutiques closed. Department stores were nationalized and on closer inspection, it turned out they were not owned by Egyptians.

When I had visited Toronto, Canada; I had met some wonderful Egyptian families. "What are you doing in Canada?" I asked. Their information had shocked me. They had been offered immigration status in Canada because they were no longer welcome in their own country. Arabians had been pouring into Egypt since the sixth century, and the real Egyptians, who were Copts and had been the first Christians, were now in the minority in Egypt. They were being squeezed out.

My year in the USA had opened my eyes to an uncomfortable reality. Egypt was changing, and nothing ever stayed unaltered. As my friends were leaving to go to other countries, it became obvious to me that the haven I had found in Cairo was no longer solid. Gamal had joined the army to become an officer, and our paths were rapidly separating. My mother was looking in the direction of Kenya and had visited her sister Alma in Nairobi. Africa promised a lifestyle less challenging than Egypt.

She tried to talk General Fouad Hafez into coming with her to Nairobi. He refused. After all, his entire family was in Cairo. Fouad Hafez had been born a Turkish prince, I discovered. Educated at Sandhurst in England, he became an army man just as his father had been. Under King Farouk, who was Turkish, the young Fouad was transferred to Cairo to serve the monarch. Also, at that time, Egypt was part of Great Britain. Fouad told me about being sent to the Anglo-Egyptian Sudan and then further south to quell rebel tribes when he first came to Egypt. It was unbearably hot, and they were obliged to wear heavy fabric British uniforms meant for a temperate English climate. His men were suffering terribly from the heat and lack of water. They passed through dense savannas of very high grass, where attacks from wild animals came as sudden, unseen ambushes. Finally, they found a small pool of water. After careful inspection for crocodiles and testing that the water was potable, they also allowed their horses and camels access to the pool. He was lying in his open tent, resting, when a horrible scream sent him running to the water. The camp cook had gone somewhat deeper into the pool to get clear water that had not been stirred up by their animals. Looking down he found a mound of rotting corpses of murdered and mutilated Africans submerged in the water. The young Turkish Officer, sick to his stomach vomited. "It was hell in Africa," he said, "I do not want to return."

Was it the shame that was imposed on him that gave him a bad heart? When I returned from the States, Fouad Hafez had problems with his heart. He was by that stage a retired General. He had enjoyed a reputation for kindness and was honest to a fault. During his career, he had paid his taxes and remained incorruptible, unlike so many other men in his position. Under the new Arab regime, an effort was made to tidy things up. As a consequence, all retired government officials were scrutinized and pulled into court for investigation. Fouad had carefully kept all his papers and proofs, but in spite of that he was accused of siphoning off funds and enriching himself. An apartment building he had built with his own savings was confiscated, as well as an orchard and other property, such as a house he built for his daughter when she got married. When I expressed my horror, he just sighed and said those who examined his case were as corrupt as the ones in the prior government.

Circumstances were changing, and reality in Egypt was multilayered. A new fundamentalism was rising, and Fouad warned of the Muslim Brotherhood. The greatest warning he gave was for the West Bank and Gaza. "This is a huge tragedy in the making," he told me. "Unless there is an effort made to help and settle the Palestinian problem, an explosion of hate and war will rock the entire Middle East." How right the prediction he made in 1958 was!

My mother was also visibly uneasy. Having been through two world wars, she did not wish to witness more. Already Gamal's mother had predicted that my mother would leave and go south to East Africa. I had no reason to doubt her prediction. And she was proven correct, for in 1965, ten years later, my mother quietly began the big change. By that time General Fouad Hafez had died of a heart attack, a fact she mentioned to me in passing, as if it were of no importance. I never quite knew how to respond to such cool, unemotional behavior. Before his death, he had brought his son, Abdul-Aziz, an officer in the army, to our house. I was present when the son walked in, looking very much like his father. He was taken to my mother's room, where they conferred for some time. All that my mother told me was that Abdul-Aziz was told to take care of her should Fouad die. He wished to protect her, as a single woman in an Arab country needed the protection of a powerful male. Sadly, Abdul-Aziz was killed in 1967 in the Six Day war. My mother was left without protection when she most needed it.

However, my mother had many friends, some powerful, some simple. Every week for many years, Karima came to wash our laundry. She was our "living, walking, talking, washing machine," as someone from England said. Patiently, she sat all morning in front of a big washing bowl and took care of our dirty underwear, soiled dresses, and sweaty blouses. She washed sheets and towels, all by hand, squeezing the fabric against the sides of the basin, till the water ran clear. I recall her sigh as she rose occasionally to pick up a big pitcher heavy with water and poured the water into the basin, hour after hour going by. When she finished, her hands were red and probably sore from washing. When I took a ceramic course at the University of Georgia in Athens, I made a little sculpture of her and presented it to my mother as a gift. Now that sculpture of Karima is in my possession, sitting on a shelf, a little plump figure dressed in a black Malaya. I caught her exactly as I remembered her, after her labors were completed, as she sat on our balcony resting.

We also had a one-eyed servant from upper Egypt called Mahmoud, who was a character. He could neither read nor write, but he could count and do math in his head so rapidly he put most of us to shame. Mahmoud thought of us as his family; we belonged to him. After his Friday day off, he would return Saturday morning still under the influence of his beloved hashish. As a consequence of the prior evening's enjoyment, he felt very sensitive and vulnerable and was not quite with the world. He would often bring the breakfast tray to a guest without tea in the teapot, or he would forget the sugar bowl or the toast. My mother would raise her voice in reprimand, while Mahmoud covered his ears lamenting: "Not so loud please, please, I have a terrible hangover!"

One day he came to me asking me to teach him how to dial the phone number of our Greek grocer, Butchelati. "It is important that I let him know I am coming and which groceries to prepare for me," he said. I guided his hand across the round dial, showed him the numbers, and repeated the lesson until he had it right. Thereafter, Mahmoud called the grocery store daily, then more than daily, until the store owner became irritated and complained to my mother. "I am just practicing the numbers, so I remember them," Mahmoud assured my mother with a big smile.

It was during the hot summer after my return from the USA that I was taken to a top tailor in Cairo for a warm winter coat. My mother chose a beautiful, rich material of a cool, pale red color. She allowed me to choose the design, a short coat and a figure-hugging skirt. It was a most elegant outfit, which I wore for many years. During my time in America, she had worked on securing a scholarship for me in Germany at a prestigious art school in Kassel. The school had already started in the spring, but they were willing to allow my late entry because of my high grades. I would not be required to work as a student. The scholarship would cover everything, even my books and art supplies, as well as accommodation, clothing, and food. It was a German merit scholarship offered by the government to deserving individuals. I felt grateful to have such generous support, which would make my life as a student infinitely easier than it had been in the States.

Europe

I embarked for Europe early in September on a small Greek vessel sailing to Venice, Italy. The ship was to dock in Piraeus for a day. As I left my mother, I could feel her pain at seeing me leave yet again. During my year in the States, my sister had left to be with our Aunt Alma in Kenya. This meant my mother had let go of both her daughters, and I am sure that it was difficult for her. There was a teary, drawn-out farewell in the Alexandria harbor, and I stood for a long time at the railing of the ship as the coastline slowly disappeared. A young Saudi Arabian man stood not far from me. Dressed in rich white gown and head cloth, he stood out from the other passengers. He made his way towards me, and not wishing to talk to him, I left the railing.

The next day as I was enjoying some fresh air on deck, the young Saudi was back, determined to talk to me. As his Arabic was different from the Egyptian Arabic I spoke, we switched to a mix of Arabic and English. He boasted he was from the royal family of Arabia and taking a tour of Europe. "I would like a companion." he announced. It never seemed to occur to him to ask any questions of me, neither my name, nor my destination.

I listened to all his bragging in bored silence. Suddenly he whipped out his wallet, opened it in a dramatic gesture and showed me the bulging content. It was stuffed with high denominations of bills. "What do you cost?" he asked bluntly.

I stared at him in amazement. "I am not for sale." I turned away from him. But he was in front of me in a second. "Here, I give you 100 dollars." he offered. I laughed. He doubled, and then quadrupled the sum, clearly upset he had miscalculated my worth. "No, *you* made a mistake about me." I said forcefully. He looked shocked. "But you are a woman, I can buy you. How much? Money is no object." This time I became even more annoyed, for he was from such a backwater he seemed unable to comprehend there were free women in other countries. "I am a student, on my way to a university in Germany," I informed him. "You cannot buy me for all the money in the world." He became angry, clearly not believing me and thinking this was my way of bargaining for more.

At this point I spied one of the ship officers and quickly walked up to him. "Can you help me please, this Saudi is trying to buy me, and he does not understand there are free women in other countries." The officer smiled, took my arm and led me away. "We shall make him believe you belong to me, since that is probably all he can understand." He invited me for a Turkish coffee in the bar and told me some of the funny and amazing experiences he had as a ship's officer with passengers. The wealthy Saudi left and did not bother me again.

Familiar Venice

I had seen paintings by Canaletto, a famous Venetian painter, and had marveled at the incredible precision and craftsmanship of this artist. The emerald green waterways and canals astonished me. Could they really be so green? I entered Venice on a ship through the waterway leading past the glorious Piazza San Marco, the Doge's Palace, and other famous buildings. The water in the canals was as green as Canaletto had painted it. The city was a jewel and of such unbelievable beauty that

I became intoxicated and most anxious to have all the entry formalities behind me.

The ship finally docked, and we descended to an open warehouse where custom formalities were completed. I had come with a big, old, and very heavy suitcase which burst open, as the locks broke. The Italian officials were charming. One man carefully and skillfully tied the monster suitcase together with a length of cord, like a rolled meat roast. Then I set off by taxi for the youth hostel, which to my surprise was next to Piazza San Marco. Music was drifting from the square, and I rapidly changed into a dress and descended back down to the street.

It was late afternoon by now, warm and enchanting. The houses were old, beautifully made, and golden hued in the light of the slowly fading sun. I took off fast, drinking in the atmosphere like someone intoxicated with the excitement and curious about finding cathedrals and palaces I had read about. I did not for a moment stop to think where I was or how I would get to where I wanted to go. Some part of me seemed to know and led me with total assurance through narrow streets and across endless bridges.

Eventually at nightfall, I found myself back in the vast illuminated Piazza San Marco. One cafe and restaurant followed another, rimming the entire square. In each establishment, a little band of musicians were playing. They all seemed to play the same songs, so there was a garland of music stretching right around. Pigeons fluttered overhead and lovers strolled arm in arm. The musical My Fair Lady was in vogue, and when the song "I Could Have Danced All Night" was played, people rose and began to dance in the piazza Di San Marco. And, so did I. Alone, I danced until after midnight under the star-spangled sky, spinning in utter ecstasy. Then I walked to my little hostel and slept like a log.

The cooing of a pigeon on my window sill woke me the next morning. Hungry, I set out. Alas, I needed to buy a map, I got lost again and again; the effortless saunter through Venice was impossible today. How had I been able to find my way and to experience what I did yesterday? Very puzzled, I reflected for a long time how it could have been possible, without getting any answer. It occurred to me that I must have known this city intimately before, and what I experienced yesterday had been like a return to a well-loved and familiar place. Had I lived here during another life? Was there more than one life?

I strolled to a park where the Biennale, an international art exhibition, was located. A tall blonde handsome young German introduced himself, and from then on, we walked everywhere together and shared meals. He was a student from Munich who was interested in art, music, and architecture. A pleasant friendship was formed, and I promised to look him up when I passed through Munich.

After a week in Venice, I took a train to Florence, where the Abele Family, old friends of my mother, had promised to put me up. I took a taxi from the train station and stopped in front of a handsome, elegant building. At first, I thought it must be a mistake—the distinctive aristocracy of the place was unexpected. A dark entryway led to an illuminated spacious living room. Here I met Martha Abele and her daughter, who were perfect hosts and gave me an unforgettable education on the beauties of Florence.

I stayed for over a week and set out each day with a list of museums, palaces, and churches I was to visit. I saw the Uffizi when canvases were still fully illuminated, and no crowds inhibited my vision of the Ghiberti baptistry doors. The town squares were open, displaying marvels of architecture, and there were very few cars to interfere with the people. I could walk across the piazzas at leisure, admiring the architecture, the spaciousness, and the beautiful stores with expensive dresses. I remember having lunch in an elegant, intimate restaurant as the only customer and being served by two waiters, one more handsome than the other. They made me feel very special as I dined from beautiful plates and drank my favorite Aqua Pellegrino from a sparkling wine glass.

Kassel and Art School

Only too soon I was bound for Germany and the town of
Kassel, once the residence of the Kaiser, where I would spend
the next four years as a student of art. The train journey to
Germany seemed long, and the stations we passed were tidy
and everything looked so orderly. On arrival in the city of
Kassel, I hailed a taxi, and all my luggage was piled into it. I gave
the address of the art academy that was part of the University
of Kassel. To my surprise, the driver did not know where it was,
and I understood why when we reached the destination. It was
a pre-war military barrack-building, grey and cold looking. On
the second floor I found a secretary's office. Everything else
seemed to be closed. I introduced myself and asked where I
could stay. She looked uncomfortable as explained that there
were no dorms at the school and that it was customary for
students to find their own accommodations, usually in an attic
room in the house of a widow or in a little garden house on
someone's property.

I would have to go to a hotel for the night and would look
in the ads section in the newspaper for rentals in the morning.
Then she had an idea and called the number of a widow she
knew, who had a spare room available. The arrangements were
quickly made, and I traveled up to the Brasselsberg into an
attractive area with modern houses. There, I met my future
landlady, Gerda Jacob, whose house stood on a wooded lot
and had a garden at the back. Gerda herself was an attractive
36-year-old woman with a 6-year-old son called Wenzie. The
rental room was a maid's room in the basement area of the
house. It included a small bedroom with a tiny bathroom in the
entry. A wood burning stove heated the room. I did not need
more and gratefully accepted the new home.

Gerda knocked on my door sometime later and invited me
to have dinner with her. We were in the suburbs, far from any
stores and restaurants, and there would have been no food
for me that night. She was an opera singer by profession and
had a beautiful living room with a large full picture window
looking onto the back garden. Quality works of art, all modern,

decorated the walls, and a floor-to-ceiling bookcase held elegant books. She was lively and immediately likeable, and thus began a long friendship which lasted until her death many decades later. Months later she told me that when I entered her life, I looked like a tropical, exotic bird with colorful plumage and that she found me beguiling. With her help, I learned how to acquire a season's ticket for the tram car, how to get back to the art academy, and where to shop for food. In short, she taught me how to live as a student in Germany.

The art academy housed in the drab barracks was nothing to write home about. The students looked uniformly drab as well, dressed in muted colors. Under a gray sky, the light did nothing for their faces, which looked pale. Most seemed to have grey or blue eyes, and most had dark blonde hair. Their eyes held very little emotional expression, and I felt I was actually looking through them, like through a hole. No one showed any interest in me, and for a full three weeks I talked to no one and no one talked to me. Clearly, I was the outsider, the foreigner. Gerda was my guide and confidante and without her I might have felt that the place was unbearable.

After three weeks a very pretty, tall blonde talked to me as we were both leaving the classroom. Her name was Monika, and she became a very close friend. She introduced me to the German custom of afternoon coffee and cake. That broke the ice and after this, the mostly male students who hovered around my worktable chatted with me. Invitations to parties followed. These were referred to as "cellar feasts." As it turned out, a lot of the male students had their lairs in basements, some of which were very large. They usually had a large empty beer barrel as a table, surrounded by stools. The only light source at these parties were candles stuck inside wine bottles, which was nice because you couldn't see if there was dirt on the floor.

Student Life in Germany

The first time I went to a cellar feast I dressed in a cocktail frock and high heels and stood out like a neon light. All the other girls wore long black pants, black tops, enormous amounts of eye makeup, and messy hair. Needless to say, I felt very out-of-place and awkward. The students of the art academy thought they were already artists. They were also from very bourgeois backgrounds, so they tried to be as wild and Bohemian as possible. They aimed to shock and wanted to do everything in a new way. They were attracted to existentialism and the work of French philosopher Jean Paul Sartre. Simone de Beauvoir had just published *The Second Sex*, so there were wild discussions going on about these topics.

Students got drunk, couples paired up, and some stopped studying and spent all their time in bars.

It was during this period that my fellow students decided that my given name, Rosemarie, did not suit me. They carefully explained that there was a famous callgirl named Rosemarie Nitribitt who was involved with some members of government and therefore implicated in many scandals. Because of my dark hair, they suggested I looked more Egyptian, and they wanted to change my name to Amun-Ra, the Egyptian God of the Sun. I explained to them that the name was a male designation and would not work, so they came up with the idea switching the letters around and turning it into "Ra mon a," which became Ramona, and that stuck with me for the rest of my life. Even my mother approved!

I very quickly decided the cold, damp cellar feasts were not to my taste. Besides our studies, our creative art work load was huge and there were hardly enough hours in the day to do everything. We had to attend endless lectures and write papers on art history, design, and art education. To my distress, I found my German language skills were not as advanced as those of my classmates. Some lectures were hard for me to understand, and the first papers were very difficult to write. The educational system was very demanding in that it gave little outer structure. It was up to the student to figure out how to research the history of art in the library, and no one told me that the books the professor mentioned casually during a lecture were expected to be read by the students.

Egypt was a place full of decadence and corruption, but somehow no one paid much attention. However worldly I felt, European corruption was unknown to me, and I fell straight into the trap. My landlady Gerda was very lonely. Her husband had died a few months before my arrival, and she was trying to adjust to her very different life. Her husband had been a womanizer and had had many affairs that were previously unknown to her. One morning, a French woman had stood before her door, demanding to see Mr. Jacob. Gerda invited her in, showed her the house and then gently told her that the man she was so desperate to find had died of cirrhosis of the liver two months earlier. They cried together, and then the woman left in great sadness.

Gerda lost no time in trying to find herself some consolation and perhaps even hoped that renting a room to a young female would bring some young men into her circle. To my horror, when young men came to call on me, Gerda opened the door wide, inviting them in, treating them to coffee and cake or opening champagne bottles. None of this was with my approval and I was disturbed to be set up in this fashion. Furthermore, I was unused to the aggressive European male behavior. In Egypt, perhaps because of the Muslim code of respect for women, I had not been threatened sexually.

A student party had been organized one weekend, and so I went to the event, wearing my cocktail dress and high heels, which of course was all wrong in Germany. One of the older students asked to dance with me. He immediately squeezed me so close to his body I could barely breathe. "Please give me some space. I don't like dancing this close. I feel constricted in my movements," I said to him. He disagreed and squeezed me even closer. Well, I thought, I shall only unbalance him a little bit. No sooner had I thought of this when, moving closer, I laid my hand on his shoulder and, hanging on to his arm, unbalanced him in a smooth judo throw. I held onto his arm to break the fall somewhat, as I did not intend to hurt him physically. He fell sideways like a sack and his jacket sleeve tore at the shoulder seam, leaving me holding half his sleeve in my hand. "Oh, you

Rosie and Martin in Kassel

tripped! I am so sorry." I said as I helped him rise off the floor. He never knew what had happened to him, and I felt not an ounce of remorse.

One day a fellow student invited me to a party in his loft. He and his roommate lived over a bakery. When I arrived late in my little cocktail dress, I found an orgy taking place. My friend was locked into his bedroom with an under-age school girl. I fled in disgust. On my way out I noticed the key was in the front door lock. I turned the key, locking them all inside. My landlady thought this was the joke of the season. I later learned they had quite a difficult time getting out.

An older art student, Martin, became more than casually interested in me. He pursued me relentlessly, and since Gerda invited him to coffee and cake on Sundays, he would show up in his Sunday clothes, bathed and clean-shaven. Every time he left; my landlady would encourage me to take the big step to losing my virginity. Since I did not love him, I resisted, which fired his passion up more and more.

Our entire class had traveled to Hamburg to visit a large exhibition of the Russian-French artist Marc Chagall. I was smitten with the beauty and sensitivity of his paintings and felt the dreamy love depicted in his images. Lovers floated over the rooftops of Paris at dusk, and the romantic moments spoke deeply to me. Perhaps this influenced me in some fashion, as eventually, against my better instincts, I had my first sexual experience with Martin at the early age of 21. I gave in to Martin's pressures and thought that he would lose interest in me once he had what he wanted. We were staying in a sordid little harbor inn that was hardly romantic, and the adventure made me feel cheap. It confirmed what I had suspected, that sex did not intrigue me, and I wrote the experience off as a stupid mistake. However, Martin did not lose interest in me; rather he became even more insistent and persistent in his amorous advances.

When summer came, I was eager to return to Cairo, to my familiar life there, to my friends, horseback riding in the desert, excursions to the Red Sea, trips to temples, and dancing on roof-top restaurants to the music of excellent bands. Martin wanted to come with me, much to my irritation. I distinctly remember telling him that there was no way to have an affair with him once I was home, that I did a certain amount of work for my mother in the hotel, that I had friends I wanted to be with, and that I was not about to hang out with him. None of that registered. He and his roommate arranged to go stay on a little Greek island for a month, and then Martin was planning to show up in Cairo. My mother even agreed that he could have a room in the hotel free of charge.

Martin, his roommate, and I set off for Athens by train, traveling through Germany, then east through Yugoslavia and down into Greece. The journey was horrible. Hard wooden benches as seats for three days became intolerable and no sleep was possible, as there was no way to lie down. We were grateful when we arrived in Athens and found ourselves a clean, airy hotel in the old part of Athens. After a long afternoon nap, the three of us set out in search of food. A tiny inn in Plaka served wonderful food and Retsina wine. The two males were in heaven and got quite drunk, much to my annoyance.

The following day I took off alone, boarding a cargo ship bound for Alexandria. I felt excited and free of my companions, happy to be by myself, happy to be returning home. I slipped back into my old life with ease: horseback riding, sketching Bedouins at the foot of the pyramids, and hanging out in the Gezira sporting club. Athens had been horribly hot; Cairo seemed comfortable in contrast. Only now I became aware of how uncomfortable I had been during my year in Germany. There had been so many disturbing lessons. I had to shed my illusions about what it meant to be an artist, as well as beliefs as to what constitutes success in life. The lessons I had to learn showed me where I was lacking in skill and where I needed to be more attentive. My formative years in Egypt had filled my eyes with color and light and raised excitement and joy in my soul. I was open to curiosity and stimulation, eager to learn with high expectations.

Eventually, Martin arrived in Cairo, and to my irritation, my mother actually liked him. I agreed to be his guide to many of the sights, but I spent as little time with him as possible. After a month, Martin returned by himself to Germany and I returned about a month later via cargo ship, my favorite means of travel, especially since it was the most economical.

Yoga

Germany at that time seemed so very different. This was a period of nihilism and existentialism. My fellow students were cynical and critical. Everything was open to a very negative evaluation. In fact, I felt the joy in life was being killed by all this negativity. The paintings done then reflected the black anguish of their inner states, which was considered very desirable. I made images filled with color while the general trend was a palette of gray, black, and some pale tones of pink or green. Feeling that I had very little in common with my fellow students and that I could not embrace their values and ideals, I missed Egypt and its essence very deeply.

As I searched for relief, I discovered books on Zen and Buddhism. Later, I found a traveling yoga group who taught hatha yoga once a week in the local high school. I joined and instantly found myself responding to the practice. Just an hour and a half of hatha yoga practice offered amazing relief by separating my mind from the concerns with which I struggled. I found my spirit lifted above the concerns that burdened me, onto another more balanced and peaceful level. As I sat in the tramcar that took me back to my little room, I marveled at the change in my being. I felt free, light, and joyful. Yoga made a huge difference to my state of mind and sense of well-being.

The art school in Kassel was considered very avant garde and was staffed with the former pupils of the great teachers of the Bauhaus School of Design, which Hitler had closed. My teachers had been trained by Paul Klee, Wassily Kandinsky, Walter Gropius, Johannes Itten, Oskar Schlemmer, Lazlo Moholy-Nagy and Joseph Albers, just to name a few. The thrust was towards truth in visual perception. Meticulous exercises developed by Paul Klee schooled our minds into seeing the reality around us in expanded, unconventional terms. Form and color alone were used to express meaning, forcing the viewer to a new level of awareness. The use of symbol was considered to be the key to the unconscious layers of the mind.

Challenges of Art

It was an uneasy transition for me to drop all my acquired skill of painting representational images and to start with a totally empty mind. The Dadaists had tried automatic writing and drawing in order to release the hold of the rational mind. It was their belief that the subconscious layers of the mind only found expression if given open space. A type of "tabula rasa" was necessary.

The schooling was tough because the given guidance only extended to exercises. We were expected to do our own research and we were obliged to judge the quality of our

Studying art in Kassel

pictures. Only our own sense of taste was valid; we were our own critics and only we could know if our paintings contained that essential kernel of truth, thereby becoming valid. A French master artist once stated that "The most difficult thing to learn is to learn to see." Mostly our vision is clouded by what we expect to see, or want to see, or are accustomed to seeing. Anything we have seen before is familiar, something never seen before, could be "invisible" or just difficult to focus on. Just because it is so new, it reads as strange or alien. An art student needs to ask herself: do I paint a particular composition and color scheme to please others? Do I choose a subject that I know will appeal? Do I allow a style to influence me because I know that artist is successful with the public, or do I stay true to my own inner vision?

I found that my own inner vision was the difficulty. I did not dare to leave what I had just painted alone. It was so strange, so new, so shocking. I did not expect what came out of me and had trouble accepting what I expressed. I had to learn to turn a painting "face to the wall," so I no longer saw it and then wait for a few days. Usually by then I was curious to see how awful or how well that image looked. If I did not give myself this inner distance through waiting, I usually destroyed what I had done by painting over it. In other words, I could not accept my own message.

Self-acceptance

I was often desperate for some type of approval to know I was progressing. The desire to conform, to be part of the herd, is probably the strongest instinct within us. I craved the approval of my teachers and fellow students. Instead, I had to learn to be self-reliant and to be unimpressed by either success or failure.

Creating art is like love. Creative energy is elusive. It can be neither tamed nor fettered. It is a process of playing with color and form, much like a child plays in effortless joy. Any intention to direct or control the energy culminates in failure. The message from our teachers was "work, work, work!" "Art," they said, "is 99 percent application and 1 percent talent."

The other problem with my art education was that I had received a scholarship on the promise that I would become an art instructor at the conclusion of four years. My dream and all my inclinations were to be an artist, someone who could paint and sell her work with ease. I had never considered whether I was talented enough to make a living this way, nor if I had anything to say that would attract buyers, nor even if I had a message. I read voraciously about the impressionists and cubists, about Braque, and Picasso, and my understanding slowly grew, as I realized what great difficulties I was facing if indeed I were to choose to be an artist.

My fellow students all were much more realistic, aware that being a free-lance artist was the path to starvation. Only the most gifted succeeded, and as the history of art shows, even talent was often not rewarded. Van Gogh committed suicide; others lived a miserable life of poverty. Under these circumstances I decided it might be better if I were qualified to be an English teacher as well as an art instructor. I took the train to the nearby university town of Gottingen, where I applied to be admitted for a degree in English. I was totally fluent in that language and I expected to be able to cope with the workload. Much to my disappointment, the university turned me down because they considered it impossible for anyone to study at two institutions of learning at the same time; it had never been done before.

As a consequence of this refusal, I applied to art school in my birth town of Berlin. It seemed to me the art academy in Kassel was limited in that they did not instruct us in figure drawing, painting from life, and other academic disciplines to which I was drawn. Furthermore, they had refused to allow me to study photography. There was only limited room in that class, and so only males were considered. A similar rejection came to my request to be allowed to make sculptures. The teacher was very charming, but he said to me, "Young lady, you are a girl without the necessary strength to swing the hammer necessary for chiseling stone. It would only be a disaster to find you hurting yourself and failing in your enterprises. We have never had women consider sculpture; that is much too hard for the female!"

I wrote to the university in Berlin. Very carefully, I explained to the head of the Berlin Art School that I had a scholarship from the German government, I was not satisfied in Kassel, and I wished for the best possible art education. I received an acceptance letter and I packed my bags. I said goodbye to Gerda Jacob and thanked her for her kindness and took a train to Berlin. There I found myself a room in fast order and showed up at the Berlin Art School the next day. On the way in I admired excellent life drawings by the students and an exhibition by the faculty. I congratulated myself for having found the right place with the type of instruction I had expected.

Alas, when I went to talk to the administration, they informed me I could not change schools because my scholarship was valid only for Kassel. "You mean to say you allowed me to come all the way to Berlin, to break down all my bridges in Kassel, to rent and pay a month's fee for a room here, when you could have phoned to tell me this?" Incredulous, I left the school, picked up my suitcase, and headed back to the train station. The only positive thing was that the art school in Kassel had not yet started and that I had not yet canceled my attendance there.

Gerda Jacob allowed me to return to her house and gave me back my room for another half year. Martin was happy to see me, and the weather was grey and cold. My friend Monika was sensitive and compassionate, inviting me to go to a cafe for a cup of coffee together with a delicious piece of cake. It consoled me just a bit.

A friend from Cairo, an English woman who lived in London, invited me to visit her during the Christmas vacation. Since I had nowhere to go during the holidays, and no relatives in Germany had invited me, I jumped at the opportunity. I also wrote to the Baglows, whom I knew from Cairo, and asked if I might visit them. I secured three weeks of hospitality in England.

Betrayal

I flew to London and found the big city was very impressive. With the enthusiasm of youth, I embraced everything from the Tower of London to Madame Trousseau's wax museum to plays, musicals, castles, the Tate museum, and the British Museum. I even went to Trafalgar Square, fed pigeons, and stood in front of Buckingham palace. My friend introduced me to Chinese restaurants, a treat I had not so far enjoyed, and took me to a famous botanical garden. The British at home were very different from the British abroad, I found. There was an easy-going attitude about the people, so different from what I had experienced in Germany. Though a capital city, London did not seem intimidating; rather its quaint customs and humor made it very likeable. I saw an immense amount of really great art in the museums and galleries; much of it surprised me by its high quality. The theaters were equally impressive and I could have stayed far longer, as I found treasures wherever I went.

What sticks most in my mind was the way men and women related to each other. I was invited into private homes and surprised that fathers washed the dinner dishes, put the children to bed, and pushed the pram with the baby in it. In Germany at that time, no man would have washed the dishes or changed his child's diapers. The women seemed much more liberated than the Italians, French, or German women. My mind took note of this; there definitely was more freedom and equality in England, and I liked the English men I met. I am certain this influenced me in my choice of men in later years.

After three lovely weeks I returned to Germany. The flight was late and I missed my train to Kassel, having to make a later connection. Martin had promised to come to Gerda's house to meet me on my return. He brought a good bottle of wine with him to celebrate my being back. Gerda, the merry widow, invited him to join her in her spacious living room and opened a bottle of champagne. Thus, they waited. It was about midnight, when I finally made it back to the Brasselsberg. The house was dark, and I pulled out my house key and let myself in. Briefly I paused in front of the door to Gerda's living room. It was too late to disturb her. I tiptoed down the steps to my little room and went to sleep.

Several days later Gerda called me into her room. She asked me if I had noticed any change in Martin's behavior. She then confessed that on the night of my return they had waited for me, become amorous and eventually had succumbed to the temptation. They heard me arrive and pause outside the door.

I was not shocked nor particularly surprised. I knew Gerda was lonely. I could easily forgive her, but not Martin. I broke off the connection there and then. He had been a mistake and I should never have allowed myself to be talked into a relationship with him.

Dokumenta and Joe

That summer, the fourth Dokumenta, an international art exhibition, was to take place in Kassel. The Dokumenta happened every four years and was much admired in Europe. The whole town began to prepare for the occasion, and a park, a part of the old palace, and exhibition halls were transformed. My friend Joe, the fellow art student from the University of Georgia who had graciously tried to teach me how to drive, was now stationed as a soldier in Germany. He wrote, asking if it was possible for me to arrange a room for him in an inn so he could see the great Dokumenta.

Joe arrived in Kassel. Through Gerda, I had located a nice little room for him on the Brasselsberg. The weather was warm and sunny; the hillsides bloomed with flowers, and the Dokumenta was extraordinary. Many of the famous names in the art world were represented, from Picasso to Henry Moore to Jackson Pollock, and I drifted through the exhibit halls in a state of excitement and awe. I danced around the sculptures placed in the vast park surrounding the exhibition, and Joe and I drank the first of the bubbly harvest of beer called "Berliner Weisse," which tasted like champagne and left me pleasantly intoxicated. The days with Joe were magical and fulfilled, as we danced in the square and in the park, ate in the old palace, and visited the castle and its beautiful park. Stretched out in the sun on a hillside surrounded by Margaritas, we talked and laughed and kissed. Ah, youth.

The relationship with Joe developed from friendship into a full-blown love affair. With hindsight I would say we were both truly happy with each other, naturally filled with joy. It was easy to love him; he had a beautiful soul and was kind and generous. Being together with him made life much easier and better than it was without him. He, being in the United States army, was miserable, and so he naturally was attracted to me. We sought out every opportunity to be together. We traveled to Sicily, to Venice, and to Nuremberg and we ended up getting engaged. We bought our ring on the bridge across the Arno River in Florence, where there were famous jewelry shops.

Emotional Crisis

When we separated and I took my usual cargo ship back to Egypt, I sat on the front of the ship watching dolphins jumping deep below me, marveling that I was now engaged to such a wonderful man, and watched the sunlight sparkles on the gold band on my finger. When I arrived in Cairo, I waved my hand in front of my mother's eyes. "Look Mummy, I am engaged!" My mother looked at me briefly, and then said, "Take off that stupid ring and stop talking nonsense. Don't you dare tell anyone you are engaged!" I removed the ring from my finger, realizing that she had spoken the truth. I was in an enchanted mind-state, in love with some illusion. Life was not that easy? Or could it be?

In fact, what did I know about love? My mother had always had a way of making me doubt my own experiences. When I was little, she would accuse me of lying—so much so, that I became uncertain of myself. What was truth, and what was a lie? The result of my denying my feelings for Joe brought me into a deep emotional crisis. I became sad, contracting inside. My feelings had to be denied; they were invalid, not believable. I could not trust my own heart. Had I sat down then, in that hot

Cairo summer and examined my mind, feelings and hopes, had I reflected and contemplated what Joe really meant to me and sifted through the confusion within, I might have gained insight and clarity. But at that point in my life, I knew none of these methods. All I felt was a huge shuddering earthquake rocking me to the foundation of my being.

Helplessness and hopelessness rose. How could Joe and I marry? What made me think we could make it? My European degree was not valid in the USA. That meant no job! What did Joe have in terms of credentials and job possibilities? In my mind barriers rose to the height of skyscrapers and hope fled. Emptiness engulfed me, which only now I can define as a depression. I was not fully aware that I was beginning to embrace destructive tendencies as well as a loss of innocence, hope, and faith. No, I did not cry or mourn. I just stood like a stone; cold, empty, soulless, watching with detached observation what would unfold, watching my own responses. My soul was sick. This inner state made me reach out for distractions; nothing mattered any more or held value. I read "The Alexandria Quartet" by Lawrence Durrell. The novel Justine reflected my own inner state and I could identify with Justine's "deconstruction" and denials. After all, that is all one could do.

Facing the Unknown

At the end of the summer, I returned to Europe by boat, but this time instead of traveling via Greece, I was to travel to Naples and up the Italian coast to Genoa, from where I intended to take a train to Germany. Also, at my mother's suggestion, instead of traveling as a deck passenger, I rented a cabin to be shared with another woman. On board ship, I met a young medical student, Michelangelo, who was Swiss. When we reached Naples, the boat docked for several hours in the harbor and passengers could leave and visit the city. Michelangelo suggested we go to the aquarium, which he had seen before and claimed to be amazing. I shoved my locked suitcase underneath my bed, put a comb and my passport into my jeans back pocket and took a cardigan, just in case.

We prepared to set off on our adventure. As we left, I saw a swarthy man with a small suitcase filled with sample ties board the ship. It puzzled me that a salesman was allowed on board. The aquarium was indeed amazing and well worth the visit. When we returned to the ship and I entered my cabin, the suitcase under my bed was missing. It contained all I had, my train tickets to Germany, my money, jewelry, and clothes.

The first officer of the ship told me that the shipping line was not responsible for stolen suitcases. He shrugged his shoulders when I explained my plight. How was I to continue my journey? I had no money, no train tickets, and no change of clothes. However, I had a passport (thank God) and a comb. As I sat at the very front of the ship with my legs dangling over the edge, I reflected on my problem. I had a day's grace period before I would be dumped in the harbor of Genoa with nothing. It filled me with dread and horror and my imagination painted fearful fantasies of the worst kind. I had absolutely no idea what to do and how to get out of this bind. I determined I needed help. Again, I went to the ship's first officer. "You can't just dump a young woman on the street in Genoa; this shipping line is morally responsible! I saw a man board with a case of ties he was selling. People like that are probably responsible for the theft of my suitcase. I am happy to repay any sums later, but you must help me, please!"

One of the passengers aboard ship heard me talking to the officer. He was an Englishman and he joined into the conversation. It made no difference; the officer said their line was not responsible. The Englishman was outraged, and taking my arm, assured me he would help.

As it turned out he was an angel, and good to his word took the whole situation into hand. "When we arrived in Genoa," he said, "We will go to Thomas Cook and Sons, a worldwide insurance agency. I shall ask to be given the phone number of the German Consul, which is not in the phone book. We shall call and request help from him. Your Consulate is responsible for its citizens, and we must engage their assistance."

The following day, my newfound protector and I, with a signed letter from the Captain, stating my suitcase had been stolen from my cabin, ventured forth to visit the Firm of Thomas Cook and Sons, right in the harbor of Genoa. Michelangelo came along as well, as support. They first phoned the German Consulate, but their offices were closed for the weekend. He demanded to be given the number of the German Consul. There was hemming and hawing, but after a while the Englishman extracted the phone number and dialed the Consul. The following arrangement was agreed upon: a room in a certain hotel was reserved for me, and I did not have to pay for it. On Monday morning I was to present myself at the Consulate. There I would be given, not money, but a ticket to the Austrian Border. There I was to present myself to the station master, who would give me a further ticket to Mannheim, where my nearest relatives lived. No money was given to me for food for the coming day, or the day after that. I was very grateful to the angel of an Englishman, who had gone to the trouble of helping, and saved me.

Michelangelo turned out to be my other angel, for he decided to stick around Genoa for the next day, a Sunday, and share his food with me. He did not have much money left, but in the harbor street, vendors sold bits of fish, shrimp, and a whole variety of seafood, very cheaply. We would be able to share this. But first, he guided me to a scruffy hotel in the neighborhood, where the Consul had reserved a room for me. It was more of a broom closet than a room, having no window and situated under the stairs. However, it did provide a bed. I slept badly as feet were coming up and down the stairs all night long and at dawn the traffic noise in the street became very loud. The next morning, a Sunday, Michelangelo picked me up and we wandered the streets, mostly in the harbor. It rained off and on, so I was grateful I had a cardigan and his company.

Monday morning, I somehow found my way to the German Consulate and was ushered into an office. I introduced myself, laid the letter from the ship's first officer in front of the man behind the desk, and explained my case. I don't think it helped that I looked scruffy, or that I was a German living in Egypt. I was asked a lot of questions, and I could feel the suspicions filling the man's mind. He wanted to know where my nearest relatives in Germany lived. That would be my uncle and aunt in Mannheim. My uncle was the director of Braun Bavaria. I failed to mention this piece of information. Much later, when I talked to my uncle, he asked: "Why did you not say that I was the Director? He would have treated you very differently and with much more respect." That afternoon, I boarded my train for Lorrach, Austria, a little border town. I was very hungry by then and chilled, as my clothes were still damp. A lively group of young Italians boarded and when dinner time came, they unpacked sandwiches and other food. I was immediately included and invited to share their food when they saw that I had none. Later, I dozed as the train made its journey through the night.

At 4 am we reached Lorrach, and I stumbled out of the train. It was as yet dark, the station was empty, the benches cold. Not a soul was around. To stay warm, I walked around the station, then got bored and ventured into the street. It was a typical little Austrian town, neat houses with flower-filled window boxes. As I strolled along a single car pulled up beside me, a police car. I told the officer I had become cold sitting in the train station; this is why I was walking. "Get in," he ordered, "it is warm in the car." In the back seat another officer was snoozing. We chatted as he drove out of the little town and along country roads past fields. Larks were rising and their songs filled the dawn air. I pretended to be very innocent, as he kept asking me about boys and sex, probably testing the waters. From the back seat the other officer said," Leave her alone, she is just a young girl."

Eventually, to my relief they let me out in front of the station and I went in search of the station master. He had already been notified and had a ticket ready for me. I would be reaching the city of Mannheim early in the afternoon. He also allowed me

Rosie, the serious Kassel art student

to use his phone to call my uncle. With a great sense of relief, I boarded the train for Germany. My disturbing adventure was over. I was back on track. My uncle picked up his disheveled niece at the train station. My aunt and I did some shopping for clothes, underwear, shoes and a suitcase, for I had nothing. Then they graciously paid for my trip to Kassel. When we said goodbye, my uncle slipped me two hundred Deutsch Mark. I felt very touched by their kindness and concern, especially as I could feel my uncle had worried about me. I returned to my studies in Kassel for another academic year.

Writing a Dissertation

When it was time to write my dissertation, I came up with the idea of writing about a wonderful project that had an impact on the lives of poor children in a region near Cairo. So, on my next time home to Egypt, I started what was to be three years of research. Near the pyramids of Sakkara, there lies a little village where a group of children weave amazingly beautiful carpets. The year before, I had met a charming and very humble architect of Coptic origin called Visser Wassef. He told me of his country house, which he built based on methods used thousands of years ago. The house, in the village of Harrania, was cooled naturally and never became too hot in summer. Over time, he met and got to know the villagers, and he discovered they didn't have a school. Children were bored, having nothing to do, and they hung around his construction site as he built his house. He decided to give them some creative outlet and brought a weaver, looms, wool, and dye into a large open shed on his premises.

A number of young people decided they wanted to learn and came regularly. The weaver left as soon as the children understood the process and Professor Visser Wassef encouraged the children to show him what they could do. To his utter amazement, they wove the delightful images based on their country life, showing farm animals and birds, trees and plants and people during festivals dancing and enjoying themselves. After some years, he had gathered a number of outstanding examples, and these carpets soon travelled to New York and to museums in Europe. Some sold at high prices and the carpets were very much in demand. Visser Wassef was wise though, as he realized success could destroy the talented young artists, and exploitation was ever lurking in the shadows. He did not allow the children to look at magazines or TV, as he had already discovered that this kind of influence destroyed the simple vision of the children. Some of them also did not manage to be creative after puberty. Some of the girls were married by their parents after the age of twelve and soon lost interest. Others begged to be allowed to continue with their weaving, which most parents and even husbands allowed, as it brought the family a good income from their craft.

It seemed like a wonderful topic for me to write my dissertation on as it meant I could do it all in Egypt. I went out to Harrania, spent time talking to the children, found out about their lives and their creative vision and ideas. Though shy at first, they all opened up to me once they found out I was studying art. My mother owned a beautiful Palomino horse that she kept at the pyramids, and since there was no public transport to the village, I took a bus to the pyramids and then rode my mother's horse to Harrania. I photographed the carpets, the weaving process, and the children, and I helped them dye the wool and string up the looms.

It was a charmed experience, and I had a wonderful time writing about the children. Someone said I should approach a publisher, but I was young and foolish. Two years later a big book appeared in the bookstores, written by a Czechoslovakian, all about the weavings of Harrania. I had missed my chance.

Finding a Room to Rent

Upon my return to Europe, via cargo ship as usual, I had the unpleasant task of finding new lodgings. I'd given up staying at Gerda Jacob's house because she needed my basement room for her expanding family of children that she had taken in. I think part of the problem of renting student quarters for me was that I looked exotic, foreign, with tanned skin and long black hair. For a full month, I was even forced to camp on the floor of another of my art student friend Ingeborg's rooms. Eventually, my blonde friend Monika, my first friend at the art school, had a birthday on the 8th of December. She invited me for the celebration, so I made my way to her student quarters. She had a very pretty room in a nice contemporary building. We enjoyed her good cake and a number of good cups of coffee while we chatted the time away. I recall it was eight o'clock in the evening when I realized it was getting late, and I left to take the tram back to my rather shabby place.

Monika, upon hearing of my predicament in finding a place of my own, decided to take charge of my situation. We selected the best possibilities to be found in the newspaper and then made appointments to see the rooms. She came with me and initially she did all the talking and questioning, as if she were the one wishing to rent. After a while, she introduced me to the owner, explaining that I came from abroad and that it was I who needed the accommodations.

It was interesting how many Germans were unwilling to rent me a spare room. One of the landladies insisted that hers was a Christian house and that she could not rent a room to a non-believer. My defense that I was Christian did not persuade her in the least. Even the director of the art school had questioned my racial origins, telling Gerda Jacob, that I probably was the offspring of an Egyptian, due to "a side-step of my mother," as he put it. Such narrowmindedness was certainly insulting, to say the least. Thus, as I entered the lovely rental room my friend Monika was able to live in, it brought me a feeling of sadness. I was seemingly unacceptable in my native country.

The Usefulness of Judo

When I had left Monika's house late in the evening after her birthday party, I realized I had drunk a lot of coffee and was more alert than normal. My path led me down a narrow lane and along a fence, behind which ran the railway line. I walked quickly as darkness was beginning to fall. My judo training helped me to be more physically aware, and I had learned to sense when someone approached me from behind, as was the case just now. I moved to the other side of the lane, giving no indication that I was aware of being followed. A furtive glance had informed me that there was a man in a trench coat, rapidly catching up with me.

My only prayer was that he would not hit me over the head or attack me with a weapon. I could feel him get closer and closer and finally he made his move. A very strong arm grasped me around the neck, so I sank into a low squat position, bringing my left arm up behind me and over his head, and, using my right arm, lifted him up onto my back and slammed him forward overhead and down onto the ground as I screamed like a wild animal in terror. I saw his face and the open front of his pants, indicating he had meant to rape me. The fight and flight response had set in and I felt the adrenaline rush as I ran like a rabbit until I reached the tram stop. Then, trembling from head to foot, I got into the tram, grateful for my judo training, which had saved me from a horrible experience. I did report it to the police, but they could not find my attacker and I could not identify him in their fat book filled with mugshots that they insisted I look at.

Unexpected Shifts and Changes

During my last year in Kassel, the Institution called together all students to inform us that our qualification of "art Instructor" had suddenly become superfluous. The Ministry of Education found they had a glut of art teachers. We would be forced to go to a university and choose another minor subject such as Biology, English, or History to become employable at high schools. Most of us were horrified, as this meant another two years of university on top of the four years we already had studied. At the end of the year, I would earn a Master's Degree in Fine Arts from the University of Kassel, but what to do with it was an unanswered question.

This threw me back into the mindset of wanting to become a free-lance artist and to do nothing but paint. If only they would have allowed me to go to Gottingen University to study English as a second major, I would not be in this situation. It was also ironic that now, in the last year at the art school, we were allowed the freedom to paint our own compositions. Our teacher was a well-known German artist called Fritz Winter, and he lived and painted on his farm in Bavaria. Already in those days, painting as a subject was not given full value. Had I not spent years learning to paint from Jaro Hilbert in Cairo, I would have been most disappointed.

Fritz Winter showed up twice a semester for what seemed a very short week—maybe it was only a weekend—to give us assignments. Then we would paint and work alone, trying to master a subject no one had really instructed us in, eventually producing something valid or invalid. During his critiques, Fritz Winter spared no one. He demanded passion from us, a vision, and independence of spirit to hash it out. Often, I felt very disheartened, and my friend Ingeborg and I wandered the landscape searching for some suitable subject matter, which we slowly abstracted.

It was during this crisis that I discovered the teachings of Paul Klee, who had taught at the Bauhaus School of Design. Klee wrote a book on how to see and paint abstractions for his students, and this volume became my lifesaver. To move from realism to abstraction is not an easy task. The Cubists also had an effect on me, as I contemplated the checkerboard fields of Egypt and the mud hut villages, where one little square box grew out of the next. It was simple to see a pattern in these compositions, as I found the rooftops in the Giza village beside the Cheops pyramid suggested such patterns, which I viewed from a higher vantage point.

Art or Yoga

The question now arose as to what I was to do after my graduation which, in itself, was a complete letdown after all the years I'd worked. My classmates and I were called into a lecture room where we were presented with our graduation degree and without any further acknowledgements or celebrations. Now, I would have to decide to search for a private school somewhere in Germany or add two more years of university to my education, just so I would be employable in my native country. It is odd how in such moments of confusion opportunities arise. At this point, my yoga instructor offered me a teacher-training program in hatha yoga in Heidelberg. He and his little group of yogis traveled in a Volkswagen bus through German towns, teaching evening courses in high schools. I could join them. He felt I had potential as a yoga teacher. For three years I had been practicing hatha yoga and felt many surprising benefits from this practice.

When I sifted through my mind how much effort my mother had put into securing scholarships for me so that I could study art, it seemed like a horrible letdown for her if I chose yoga as a career. I was tempted indeed, but I was also still in the grip of a conventional mindset. The older I became, the more I realized that the world was a dangerous and deceptive place, and I only trusted my mother. As I pondered this predicament, my Aunt Alma came forward with a tempting suggestion. "Come to Kenya, stay with me, and paint for a year." What a great idea and what a generous offer! In one blow my life was being redirected. I wanted to paint and sell art. So here was the call! I chose to go to Nairobi in Kenya, East Africa.

Changing Events

Meanwhile, my sister Gabriele had lived with my aunt and uncle in Nairobi for a couple of years to repair her health. The dry desert heat of Egypt affected her negatively and she suffered from migraine headaches. Fortunately, she applied for and then received a scholarship to a school in Georgia, USA. She was a rebel and disliked the narrow-minded institution in which she found herself. She traveled to Tallahassee in Florida to see what the university there was like. There she met some young, free-thinking students who even offered her accommodations, and there, she fell in love with Klaus (Nicholas) Ritter, a student of engineering and architecture. They later married. Thus the second prophecy of Gamal Fahmy's mother came true, when years ago she foretold that my younger sister would marry before me.

Before I left Germany and after my graduation, my sister and brother-in-law arrived in Hamburg. I had been invited to come and meet his family—his father and aunts and uncles. It was a very touching encounter. The family had an estate in some woods north of the city of Hamburg. They were an old and well-to-do family. Nicholas's father had been an officer in the German army and had spent years as a prisoner of war in Russia. He had just completed a book, a bestseller. Klaus's mother was a teacher and a US citizen and had returned to Alabama with her children during the war. The parents had divorced. Just recently Klaus had rediscovered his father and been reunited with him and the German part of his family.

Reconnecting with Gabriele

On my arrival in Northern Germany, I met my little sister Gabriele, and we drove to the estate belonging to the Ritter family. It was surrounded by forests and farmlands. Over the old, arched, stone entry, flowers had been lovingly arranged, and I was pleasantly surprised by these warm and welcoming family members. Klaus was a nice-looking man with a shock of red hair and a red beard. He seemed relaxed and easy-going, which somehow gave a false impression because he was a thinker with a crisp and critical mind and was no one's fool. We enjoyed a lovely meal and conversation and then withdrew to a little garden pergola for dessert and coffee. There was limited space in the little garden house, and we squeezed together around a garden table. New drinks were offered, and liqueurs were poured into little delicate glasses, as everyone toasted the young couple. To my surprise and consternation, I found several male hands trying to caress my knees under the cover of the embroidered tablecloth. I never really found out whose hands they were. I removed them gently but firmly every time they started to grope.

As darkness fell, we were transported back into the nearby village, where a room had been reserved in the local inn. There had only been one room with a king-size bed available, so I joined my sister and Klaus in this big bed. During the conversation that followed, I discovered that Klaus believed in "open marriage" and my sister seemed to be in agreement with him. Somewhat disturbed by this, I told them my reasoning as to why this was an immature and stupid way to start a marriage.

The next day, I noticed that my sister was still wearing a little light cotton dress made for her years ago in Cairo. She also had no reasonable shoes for the northern European climate. We all set out to buy her shoes. Klaus insisted on the type of shoes old ladies wore. My sister seemed incapable of having her own opinion. All of this disturbed me.

When we all returned to Hamburg we were put up in Klaus' father's flat. His second wife was in the hospital recovering from an appendix surgery and was not present. He was completely incapable of providing us with dinner, so my sister and I fixed us something to eat. He was an amusing storyteller and very entertaining, that was until he began flirting with me, which embarrassed me very much as I had no interest in something like this. Eventually, he invited me to come with him on a "business trip," which I declined. The behavior of the men in the Ritter family was not to my taste and caused me concern about my sister. In time, this would become only too obvious. Herr Ritter was, however, a gentleman in most respects and he drove me back to Kassel, from where I was soon to leave for Egypt.

Elba

That last summer in Europe, Gerda Jacob invited me to join her on a car trip to Italy and spend time with her on the island of Elba, where she rented a little cottage in Proccio sur Forno. She went there every year for a month, taking her little son Wenzi with her. It was a lovely ride through the Alps and to the Garder Sea, which continued down the Italian coastline where we soon saw the island of Elba at a distance. We boarded a ferry boat, and in half an hour we landed on Elba. Napoleon Bonaparte had been held a prisoner on this island, and there was still a big fortress where he was incarcerated. The air sparkled, and the sea was a brilliant blue-green. The cove of Forno on Elba was breathtakingly lovely and unforgettable. The cottage we rented was small and right beside the ocean. Behind it, rocks rose, and vineyards spread on the higher levels. The pounding of the waves was a constant companion, day and night. We spent most of our time on an open-air veranda covered with vines. The most delicious meals were served in a restaurant higher up, overlooking the ocean. After all the studies and stresses of graduation, this place was sheer heaven, and I loved swimming around the little cove. The inhabitants were all fishermen and had colorful little boats and one motorboat anchored towards the deeper end of the cove.

One day, just before noon, Gerda and I stood on our little veranda when a small row boat came into view. A man was standing upright in it. With arms extended in a dramatic pose, he was singing his heart out. As the boat came closer, we heard him more clearly. He was an opera singer, singing the tenor part of a famous love duet. The rich tones rang across the water, and suddenly my friend Gerda, whom I had never heard sing before, stepped forward and sang the female response to the love duet. The voices mingled and rose and sobbed and trilled, and there was nothing more sublime than this chance duet. The boat landed right on our stretch of beach, the tenor jumped out, Gerda ran towards him, and both embraced as they finished. People in the restaurant above were whistling and clapping, everyone gathered and applauded. Those I saw had tears in their eyes. We were invited to join the tenor, which we did, and we drank a few bottles of beautiful wine together. I spent the next two weeks enjoying the atmosphere of the island life and unwinding from the effort of my academic studies before returning to Egypt.

Return to Egypt

My return to Egypt was by cargo ship from Venice and turned out to be short and uneventful. Meeting with friends and fellow students in Cairo, I found that all our lives were quickly changing. We were no longer students, jobs had to be searched for, and we made choices about where to live and with whom. I missed Joe, who was back in the States. I felt curiously empty and hollow. The highlight of that summer was the arrival of my sister Gabriele and her husband Klaus in Cairo. They came on his motorbike, traveling from Hamburg down to Gibraltar, then through Tunisia, Morocco, and Libya along the Mediterranean coastline. My mother was in a high state of concern. But they made the journey without mishap, arriving looking dusty and windblown.

Almost immediately Klaus began to upset my mother in small ways. I think she admired him, but at the same time his wild ways caused her to worry about my sister. As for me, I began to see things through his eyes and noticed what I had been indifferent to, what I had taken for granted. Every day a Hurley-Gurley man came to our building. A little girl, perhaps his daughter, danced when he played his music. The girl was maybe eight years old and charming. People stepped onto their balconies to listen and threw coins down to the child. They also had a baboon who could do certain tricks to entertain children. Klaus photographed the activities, recorded the music, and talked to the people. He was so awake, alive, and interested in every aspect of life in Cairo, while I had become indifferent.

One day in Khan al Kahlil, the bazaar, Klaus had a long drawn-out argument with an Arab who had overcharged him. "You don't seem to respect me as a fellow human being and only see me as the stereotype of the rich American," he complained. "I am not a rich American. I am a student and I came here to your country to meet the Egyptian people, to experience your ways, and to learn from such an ancient race. Now you, you really disappoint me." He did not let go of the man, insisting that he had to meet him "man to man." He invited him to a nearby restaurant for a cup of sweet Turkish coffee, and they continued to argue back and forth until the Egyptian had a sense of who this strange individual was. Probably forever after he would think twice about trying to cheat tourists.

Klaus was not an easy man as he always seemed to find some new concern he needed to address. Much of his thinking and ideas I approved of, while some came as a shock. One of the pleasant surprises was the transformation of the dark entry of my mother's little hotel. He turned it into an inviting, colorful, and comfortable spot: an old Egyptian mosque lamp with hand-blown glass now illuminated the space, a big circular brass table held the phone used by guests, and inviting Arab cushions acted as seats.

Hafla

My mother decided to offer the couple an unforgettable "hafla," a feast in the desert. This was her idea of a wedding gift. It was arranged to take place in a chalet, a simple little building in the desert beyond the pyramids, which one could rent for such occasions. She also ordered Bedouin tents with colorful hand-appliqued designs on the inside. Food was prepared by our cook and driven out to the desert. I arrived on horseback with everyone else, as there was no road to the chalet. Having had no idea what to expect, I was amazed.

When night fell, a fire was lit, and the tent was sparkling with light. We sat on carpets in front of round brass tables, enjoying our first drinks and finger food. There was lively music played by a group of musicians, and there were dancing horses, splendidly decorated with brightly colored tassels and saddles. The tent was wide open on one side, making the dancing horses and their riders visible. Rifle shots were fired into the air in celebration, and a pretty, young belly dancer began her gyrations in the flickering light of the fire. I had brought my sketchbook with me and I furiously sketched the musicians, the horses, and the belly dancer. I still own the drawings. It was a wonderful and unforgettable event. Later that night, the full moon rose and I wandered off across the desert, feeling the cool sand between my toes, while the stars hung above like a glittering chandelier.

Visit to Dime

One of the guests in the hotel was very eager to see something of old Egypt and asked if I could guide him, as he did not know how to find really good places. We decided on the desert Oasis of Fayum. Since he had a Mercedes Benz, I would be traveling in style. We set off driving on a road I barely remembered, but I was full of self-confidence. Eventually, we left the desert and entered the oasis. The large spread of the Fayum Lake lay before us.

This area was well known in antiquity. King Faruk came here to hunt gazelle in the desert. We walked down to the edge of a rather dirty lake where a group of Bedouin were washing their camels. The animals were not keen to oblige and were beaten into the water, then splashed until deemed clean. A kind-faced fisherman approached me and asked if we wanted a boat to go out onto the lake. As it was very hot, I instantly agreed and within minutes he had rowed us into a clean depth of lake, so clear I could see the fish. "There is a Roman city on the other side, just ruins of course. Would you like to see it?" he asked. He proceeded to inform us that the Romans had built a town called Dime as well as a harbor on the shore of Lake Fayum. The lake, however, started to shrink and soon the town was too far from the lakeshore. Eventually, the ancient town was abandoned.

He rowed us to a little cove and then pointed out the direction to which we needed to walk. "You will come to a Roman road built of black granite. Just follow it and soon you will be there." In total trust and without hesitation, we set out and soon came upon a raised black granite road stretching in a straight line into the desert. After a while, the walls of Dime appeared, shaped like fangs. The mud-brick walls had been gnawed by the wind and sandstorms until only a shell of walls was left. However, the sand had also protected the site, as it buried many lower structures. We found only the tops of archways were visible; the rest of the columns were buried in sand.

There was a domed Roman bath, so with some difficulty, we crawled into it. The dome was in perfect condition; tiled floors led to various rooms and all within was still intact. There were marble basins, broken ceramic jugs, and even Roman coins. I found ten coins that afternoon. Later, we found what must have been the town dump. The sand had been blown away and exposed a vast heap of broken shards. Among them, I found little heads of women. These I picked up and much later figured out that the delicately formed heads, with elaborate hairstyles and no sign of any breakage, were dolls' heads. The heads were made out of terracotta, but the bodies must have been made of cloth and made soft enough for a child. These and other discoveries made us forget all sense of time, and as we hurried back to the cove, we prayed that our fisherman would still be there.

He was, and he again rowed us into the middle of the clear blue lake. He saw that we were very hot and suggested we take a swim. It was delicious to drop overboard into the cool water and to swim along as the fisherman rowed his boat. I had removed none of my clothes, knowing a Muslim would be shocked. Fortunately, my blouse and jeans dried quite rapidly once I was back in the boat, and I felt very much refreshed by the swim. We thanked our new friend very much for the discovery of Dime and asked if there was a way to drive there by car. He shook his head; there were no roads, but he indicated that one could drive through the desert. We had both agreed we needed to return to the Roman town to take photos and investigate further.

It was decided that for our protection, we needed several cars for the trip into Dime across the desert. A little group of mostly Germans professed an interest, and we had three cars for the journey. This time we had cameras and water plus food since we were planning a long stay. As we entered the desert, we found old tire tracks and very soft sand, which is difficult to drive through and can easily stall a car. To my delight, we came across a pack of desert wolves. They were small and grey, but were clearly wolves. Eventually, the walls of Dime came into sight. The desert around the city was extraordinary, filled with strange eroded rock formations, many shaped like giant mushrooms. Somewhere south was Bahariya Oasis, known for its white desert and unique white limestone formations of amazing beauty. There were some of these formations here in Dime as well and I was determined to investigate the terrain. Soon most of the group sought out shady, cool spots, and I excused myself. The desert was very hot, and my clothes struck me as an unnecessary burden. I stripped off all my clothes and hid them at the base of a character rock of strange shape and ventured forth in my birthday suit. I twirled and danced, ran and rolled in soft sand, and jumped from rock to rock. It was magnificent freedom. The rock formations were straight out of "Alice in Wonderland."

In Egypt, the sun always sets at six o'clock in the evening. Suddenly, I realized darkness was approaching. Where was my rock, where was my clothing? I ran from place to place. Suddenly everything looked different, as the light cast long shadows and nothing looked familiar anymore. I began to imagine having to return to the group stark naked. What was I going to tell them? How embarrassing! The sunlight was slowly turning to crimson, and I still failed to see my rock. Then suddenly I stood in front of it and, feeling grateful, hurriedly slipped into my clothes and ran back to Dime. A group of sunburned faces spoke as if from one mouth: "Where have you been, we were becoming worried!"

4 Africa

Departing Cairo

I spent about six months in Cairo after my return from Germany. By Christmas, my stay was slowly coming to its end, and my mother was planning to accompany me to Nairobi in January. Her hotel business had prospered, and she was very generous to me. The transition from having been a student for five years to being without aim or goal was not exactly easy. The days slipped past, and I was aware of the big changes Egypt was undergoing.

One day my mother took papers up to the offices in the Gomhouria government building in Midan Tahrir, and unable to find a parking spot, left me in charge of the car. With the motor running, I sat by the sidewalk and watched people walking past. It was still early in the morning and a grey, wintry day. As I sat, focused on nothing, a feeling suddenly assailed me about the people streaming past. They did not seem alert or awake, rather, they reminded me of sleepwalkers. They seemed drugged, perhaps by exhaustion, helplessness, or despair. The more I looked at them, the more I saw it, a type of fatalism or indifference seemed to mark them. What were their chances in life? Had they had a choice at all? It depressed me profoundly and I felt very sad for them. From that day on, I looked at all sorts of Egyptians and asked them outright how they felt about their life and opportunities. Most shrugged as if the question was uncomfortable and had to be quickly discarded. "Insha Allah (Allah be willing)" was the way they began to answer. They had dreams and hopes, as it turned out, but they felt trapped, bound to an ancient system which gave no growing space and no opportunities. I realized that though I loved Egypt, though this had become my home and I even had once considered getting an Egyptian passport, there was as little future here for me as for them.

The last days in Cairo were so miserable that it made my departure easy. Although it was winter, there were extensive sandstorms. The atmosphere was sand-colored, skies were grey and everything looked drab, tired and dull. A fine powder penetrated beneath windows and doors and soon every surface was covered with grit. There was a crunch of sand between my teeth and I was glad to be packing to leave.

The arrival in Khartoum, Sudan, stands out as a shocking experience. We had an hour stop in the capital of the Sudan. We disembarked and walked to the main airport building. As soon as I stepped through the doorway of the plane I was engulfed in a wave of heat. It felt as if I had stuck my head into the middle of an oven. It was so hot, I felt as if I could not breathe. Fortunately, the waiting lounge was air-conditioned.

East Africa

Nairobi lies at a height of 6000 feet above sea level. Big-bellied clouds floated above, casting their shadows on the land below. There is a constant flow of shadow and light, and the colors are quite brilliant. Since this area lies on the equator, the sun stands right overhead and so the leaves on the trees sparkle with light and the faces of people are in shadow. There is a particular atmosphere in East Africa, somehow weightless and carefree. As we drove through Nairobi to our destination, my aunt and uncle's house in Westlands, I felt stunned by the brilliance of color everywhere. There were islands of tropical flowers in abundance in the median of the highway, arranged by a well-known landscape gardener. The red-blooming flame trees were in flower, and high hedges of bougainvillea trailed their scarlet branches towards the ground. The Africans themselves were dressed in bright garb, and everyone smiled in greeting. My response to this enchantment was excitement and disbelief. I had landed in paradise.

My aunt's house was a charming cottage, almost smothered in blossoms and very inviting. I met her servants, Virginia and Peter, both handsome people. I wondered about the names and discovered these were certainly not their real African names. My aunt cheerfully gave any African the name she felt like bestowing, totally disregarding the often difficult native name. Alma had become heavier in the intervening years and held on to all the mannerisms of those endowed with wealth and title.

I received a very small room in her house facing the driveway, with heavily barred windows. I soon discovered all houses have bars on their windows due to the frequent robberies in Nairobi. Much of it was known as "fishing." A long pole with a hook was inserted into the window between the bars and then articles of clothing and anything within reach and interest could be hooked and pulled out. I soon discovered that it was a game to steal from white people. If my aunt bought a carton of 12 eggs, two of them were missing as soon as the eggs were deposited in the fridge. Tea and coffee, as well as bacon, were favorite items that shrank the moment they entered the kitchen.

It was useless to scold or accuse an African. They were very sensitive, and heavy-handed behavior only caused endless arguments and protests of innocence. My aunt was very impressed with my method, learned long ago in Cairo. If I found something missing, I simply said: "Oh, Injirogee, you must have put the leftover chicken somewhere else, I can't find it. Please find it. I am just going to talk to my aunt for a bit and then I shall be back." The vanished item always reappeared. The idea of sharing food was a strongly ingrained custom and eventually my aunt fed her employees because it was easier than having to guard her groceries.

Virginia

My aunt's servant, Virginia, had been my aunt's treasure for six years. During this period, she had managed to have four children, all without the help of a husband. She was happy as the day was long and loved braiding her little girl's hair into stiff little braids, interspersed with beads. She dressed in wonderful fabrics of vivid colors, which looked fabulous on her, and knew how to wrap everyone around her little finger. First thing in the morning, my aunt stood among the flowers, a water hose in her hand. Virginia set the table on the open-air veranda and brought out the big stacks of toast my aunt called "kudja m'toto." Then Virginia's little children came running naked through the garden, shrieking with delight as my aunt sprayed them with the garden hose. They had to run through the water several times until deemed clean, and then they had to run until they were dry. It seems towels were a "disappearing item," so Alma no longer bothered with this luxury. Once they were dry, the little totos (children) presented themselves at the breakfast table to receive a thick slice of bread with butter and jam on it and a glass of milk. "Africans don't eat breakfast," Alma informed me, "so I feed them. The children get hungry and breakfast keeps them healthy." This ritual was a daily occurrence and was most entertaining.

We had arrived in Kenya in January, at the height of the African summer. I remained stunned by the beauty everywhere and fell in love with the land and people. It's impossible to imagine how wonderful Kenya was. At the time it was still a British colony, but there was a strong effort by the people to gain independence. Their leader was a man called Jomo Kenyatta, whom the British held in jail. They offered him all the gin he could possibly drink to ruin his health, but Jomo remained healthy and sober. A year and a half after my arrival, "Uhuru," Independence, was achieved by the population of Kenya, and Jomo Kenyatta became their first president. He had been educated in England, and I read *Facing Mount Kenya*, the dissertation he had written.

This book gave me much information and insight into the life of Africans. The missionaries had failed to understand the ancient ways that suited the population. For example, children were brought up in groups of the same age, both boys and girls. Once they reached puberty, a certain amount of freedom was permitted to both sexes, but pregnancy was not permitted. Once a couple found each other, the young man had to prove his sincerity by providing a suitable bride price, often in the form of cattle to be given to the father of the girl. Furthermore, he had to build two huts, one for his bride and one for both of them.

After the marriage, the wife usually became pregnant and was no longer able to attend to the fieldwork. She then chose a girl of her age group, one who had not found a husband, whom she asked to be the second wife. If the girl agreed, the husband built another hut, this one for his new wife who was there to help and assist the first wife. After the birth of their child, the first wife was taboo for her husband and slept alone in her hut nursing her baby for 2 years. Children were carried by their mothers and were never separated from her. As a consequence, children rarely cried, and in my time in Africa I never heard an adult shouting at a child or punishing it. The second wife, because she was not the choice of the husband, was free to have other men (of her choice) as lovers. The children of such unions were the responsibility of the husband, and he was known as their father. In this fashion, women, who usually outnumber men, were given both status, protection, and above all else were valued members of the family. Unfortunately, the missionaries destroyed this custom, calling it "evil," with the result that many women who had not found a husband lost their status, didn't have a family, became poor, and usually ended up as prostitutes.

Mombasa on the Indian Ocean

I celebrated my 25th birthday in Kenya. For the occasion, my uncle and aunt invited my mother and me to join them in Mombasa for a holiday. We set off with my uncle Christian driving. I sat in the back holding onto Waldie, the dachshund. This was my first excursion into the African countryside and I was looking forward to seeing my first wildlife and the Bush, as it was called. We left the Highlands of 6000 feet to move down to the sea level, which was tropical and very humid and hot. We had all taken the precautionary Malaria pills.

On the way, I saw repeated signs stating "Elephants have the right of way." This meant one had to stop if elephants happened to be on the road and wait for the huge beasts to move out of the path. My uncle entertained me with a story of some impatient travelers who had honked at the jungle giants to induce them to move. The elephants trumpeted loudly, advanced towards the travelers, and turned their car over. That is why, if seeing an elephant, one should always keep the motor running and plot an escape route. As we neared the Amboseli national wildlife refuge, the promised elephants materialized in our path. They were feeding on plants by the roadside and had no intention of moving anytime soon. The little dog in my arms was shaking with fear, and I hoped he would not bark or pee on me in distress.

Eventually, the giants of the jungle moved along, the road was open, and we drove on. As we neared the city of Mombasa, the landscape became tropical. Coconut palms and huge old mango trees lined the checkerboard fields. The people here belonged to the Griyama tribe. They were dressed in colorful garb, and the women wore white sisal skirts shaped much like a ballerina's tutu. They were bare-breasted with a broad strap tied across their upper chest above the breasts. If their breasts began to sag, the strap was lowered in order to keep the breasts looking perky and full. Some older women wore their strap quite low, and below it the breast stood to attention. The figures danced across the road in front of us, twirling like big, white blossoms in the breeze.

We were to stay in a huge, elegant hotel called the Nyali Beach Hotel, right on the Indian Ocean. But first, we had to drive onto the ferry, which was nothing more than a big wooden platform that was pulled across the water by strong human arms. The hotel, when it came into sight, looked like a palace. A rich warm sun turned the stone to a golden color. I realized it was built by Hindus, of which there were many in Kenya. Women in saris drifted on the garden paths and all had a magical quality of beauty and novelty. Our room was small and hot, and the beds had mosquito nets suspended over them. The humidity and heat began to affect me. I raced to the beach and found that the sand was the finest powder and snowy white, and the ocean was green and translucent and lined with huge coconut palms. I was in heaven, and I walked along the breezy oceanfront feeling amazed and overwhelmed with the sheer beauty that met my eyes everywhere.

My aunt wished to dine in the hotel's dining room—a spacious, huge, open-air veranda. A band was playing and some guests were dancing. By now I was feeling sick, as the heat, humidity and excitement was having its effect on me. I excused myself, realizing I was causing her great displeasure, and fled to my airless, humid room to sleep under a white mosquito net. I felt better by the next morning.

Malindi and Lamu Island

A few days later we moved up the coast and rented a villa. It was splendid, surrounded by old trees and bougainvillea hedges, with cool tiled hallways, an encircling veranda, and lovely big easy chairs. The Griama cook spoiled us with tasty meals of freshly caught fish and lobsters, mangoes, papayas, and other tropical fruit. Here, for the first time in my life, I ate like a queen, and the good food spoiled me forever. After this culinary experience I no longer liked mediocre nourishment.

I spent my days swimming in the translucent waters of the Indian Ocean, going on long beach walks, and reading books by Ouspensky, a mathematician and mystic who formulated a philosophy based upon the mathematical concept popularly known as the Fourth Dimension. By means of this he built a bridge between Western rationalism and Eastern mysticism. I was completely smitten by his work and his teachings. One of his books consists of verbatim records of his oral teachings from 1921 until 1946. In *The Fourth Way* and In *The Search for the Miraculous*, he shows the way for inner development to be possible while following the conditions of ordinary life. He put me in touch with the mystic Gurdjieff and his teachings that aimed for the development of consciousness in man. Suddenly my yogic interests began to expand into a new direction.

Birthday in Africa

Alma bought me a beautiful African silver bracelet for my 25th birthday and gave me a further trip, this time up the coast to the Island of Lamu, which she assured me, was the place the Egyptians under Queen Hatshepsut visited and named "The Land of Punt." We set off in the Volkswagen with me holding the dachshund on my lap. We encountered a river and needed to be ferried across. A big truck was already ahead of us, waiting to be ferried. I stood there with my little camera and caught the disaster when the truck slid off the wooden platform and no number of ropes could hold it. With a big splash, it slid into the river, turning sideways. The Indian who owned the vehicle was dancing with anger and fury, but there was nothing to be done. We were next in line, and our car made the journey across without mishap.

The island of Lamu lies off the north coast of Kenya, an island with a population of Arabs and native Africans. Arabic was still spoken there, and the way of life is governed by the Muslim religion. Women wear Malaya, as they do in Egypt, and veil their faces. We had to park the car on the mainland and board an Arab dhow, a big heavy sailing boat made without nails. A short journey across the water brought us to the Island of Lamu, fringed with thick mangrove swamps, which we skirted. The water had become rough, and the little dog was unhappy, so I cuddled him in my arms. When we arrived at the harbor, a lot of children ran up to see who had arrived. They took one look at the dog and backed away crying "Simba, Simba," which means "Lion." Clearly, they had never seen a lion before. They ran after us, keeping a respectful distance from the dog, marveling at our courage to keep a lion.

The island had no vehicles of any type nor electricity and only narrow lanes open to foot traffic. We ambled through a street, admiring the beautifully carved house doors. The houses were all white-washed and had heavy roofs made of palm fronds. The air sparkled with light and a cool sea breeze rustled through the foliage of the coconut palms. Soon we entered the hotel of Colonel Pink, a British gentleman who owned the only hotel available on the island. The hotel sported a bar and restaurant, which made it the big attraction and a place where everyone congregated. We were escorted to our second story rooms, which had a beautiful view of the ocean below.

Later, when we sat down for dinner in the only restaurant on the island, which of course was also Colonel Pink's, I was amazed at the clientele that frequented the premises. There were young black ladies all swathed in their black shawls and gowns, who sat sipping mango juices from straws pushed under their face veils. Pieces of food were pushed up under their veils, never to be seen again. Colonel Pink had also told us that Lamu Island was referred to as the "paradise of the gays." This was in 1963, and I barely understood the problems the gay people were having at the time.

At night, the full moon rose in all her luminous glory, and I actually managed to photograph her just hand-holding my little camera. The sea murmured a hypnotic repetition, while wild birds interrupted the near silence with screeches. We found a flashlight, ventured into lanes broad enough for only a donkey, and found ourselves in a crowd. As there was no electricity, there were no street lights. Circles of white lights from flashlights danced ahead of hurrying feet and the fragrance of perfume surprised me. The whole population of the tiny village seemed to be hurrying somewhere. We walked under banana palms and tall coconut palms onto the moon swept white beach, the sand under my feet feeling like slippery silk. I am no poet and cannot do justice to the magic that enfolded me that night.

The next day everything was lovely, without the mystery. The white-washed houses and palms surrounded a majestic

Portuguese fort built long ago. There used to be an active slave trade in East Africa between Portugal and the Arabian Peninsula. The slave market was still visible and is a tourist attraction. Metal rings were still in place and brought back the vision of human beings tethered to them. A little gutter had been thoughtfully carved into the rock so that the prisoners could urinate. Dhows took the slaves from Lamu Island across the Indian Ocean to the Arabian Peninsula, where they became the property of the wealthy. It seems the last slave sales were as recent as 1928.

Lamu

I felt overwhelmed with gratitude for the rare chance of being on Lamu, which my Aunt Alma had so kindly arranged for me. Intoxicated with the environment, I raced along the beaches taking photos. The mangrove swamps surrounding part of the island had been harvested. The mangrove wood was buried on the beaches under mounds of sand after having been put on fire. Some days later it turned into black charcoal, which was then sold as cooking fuel to East Africans.

Another curious discovery was the piles of hand-painted shards, said to be of Chinese origin. Chinese ships had been driven to the shores of Lamu during storms and had perished. Their broken goods survived. Every now and then a young African with slanted Oriental eyes would attract my attention. It seems the Chinese left more than their shards on Lamu! However, the language spoken on the island was Arabic. In fact, along the coastline of Kenya there had been beautiful Arab settlements, now abandoned, and many African women wore the black Malaya of the Muslims. The other remnant of a foreign people were the East Indians. They had been imported to help build the railway lines throughout East Africa, when it was a British colony. They remained in Kenya, and added to the magic through their colorful saris and other silken garb.

Each morning, I rose early and ran outside to discover more of this magical Island. I did not want to be forbidden to roam, which I suspected would happen if I mentioned my intentions.

The beach was wide that morning, rippled and snowy white. Far out, I saw the turquoise ocean and decided to go for a swim. The beach was so soft I sank in with every footstep, which became very tiring especially as I saw how far I still had to go. Plodding on, nevertheless, it seemed to me that I must have walked for at least 10 minutes before I saw the first veil of aqua water. Then, I was splashing through water, but it did not become deeper and stayed at a level of about a foot. How far I walked I can't remember, but when I turned to look back at the island, it looked far, far away, almost washed out in the blinding glare of the light. At my feet the water was no deeper than before, just covering the sand and gently rocking back and forth. In front of me the water gave no indication of growing deeper. Somehow, I felt suspended in a surreal world of light and ocean, and I abruptly turned to head back. When I finally reached the normal shore, it seemed that I must have walked over an hour.

Later that day, we visited the local market, a colorful place. I shall never forget the mountains of fruit and vegetables offered by beaming locals. We struck up a conversation in Arabic with one of the men. "Do you fish often?" I asked. "Only when I am hungry and there is nothing left to eat." was the reply. "So how often is that?" I asked. "Oh, maybe every five days, because in my family, someone cooks plantains, or beans, or meat. We all eat, so no need to work or worry or go out in the boat." He gave us his sunny smile. Obviously, life was good. Colonel Pink later told us that the men play games most of the day. The women build the houses, make the thatched roofs, weave, sew, raise kids, cook, and tend the chickens. It is a paradise for men.

Many months later I learned that Colonel Pink was dead. He had been murdered by a jealous lover. Lamu was no longer a good place to visit, as his was the only hotel on the island. He had been a most colorful and amusing host, and I felt his shortened life was a sad loss.

Malindi

Our next stop was a place called Malindi. It had a few shops along the highway and sported a couple of big luxury hotels. These were British hotels, and I encountered the extraordinary luxury of English breakfasts. Tables were loaded with tropical fruits, sliced meats, kippers, baked goods and breads, cheeses, fruit juices, and great coffees and teas. The beaches were snow white, and the Indian ocean rolled in lazy waves of aqua blue into shore. Again, I felt I had landed in paradise. The local Griyama women in their white sisal skirts, handsome silver earrings and necklaces, and black, shiny skin balanced large loads of tropical fruit on their heads as if they were fancy hats.

My aunt had found a villa for rent, so we moved into a lovely house surrounded by a garden filled with mango trees and dripping with bougainvillea hedges. Giant hibiscus blossoms caught my eye, and the ocean lay just beyond the boundary of the garden. My bedroom was on the second floor, cool and airy even during the hottest time of the day. Here I continued my studies of Ouspensky between intervals of refreshing swims in the Indian Ocean.

Life in Nairobi

Like all magical holidays, our stay came to an end, and we returned to Nairobi. My mother flew back to Cairo, and my life in Kenya began in earnest. My Aunty Alma was a woman with vision. She felt it was high time I met a suitable man and settled into married life, and she had the means to arrange it. Certainly, without her invitation to Kenya, my life would have been very different. I owe her a great deal, even if at times her vision and mine clashed and brought about misunderstandings.

Eventually, my crates filled with paintings and student work from Kassel arrived in Mombasa and then came by truck to Nairobi. When my aunt saw the amount of art I had produced during the last years, she determined I had to sell it somehow. But first I needed a studio. Amazed at her energy and determination, I fully agreed to everything. I had fifty pounds saved up, so we both drove to the industrial district of Nairobi and searched for a builder and for remnants of buildings. We found several big windows dismantled from an old structure, as well as parts of walls made of wood. A door was found as well as a young African, a carpenter, which is called "fundi," who turned out to be an impressive builder. His name was Kuku and we hired him to build the studio. I made the designs, indicated the size, length and width of the structure, where the windows were to be placed, where shelving was needed, etc. Kuku was smart, fast and capable. We poured the cement floor together, and dug a rain ditch around the floor base, something I had not considered.

The rainy season in Kenya is like a monsoon and requires careful drainage for buildings. We planned a tin roof, which was cheap and the only material that was new. The studio grew to impressive proportion, and Aunty Alma confessed herself delighted. The structure was erected at the end of her garden property, and I was allowed to dig up some small banana palms with which I surrounded the studio. In Kenya the soil was so fertile that one needed only to cut off a small branch from a shrub and stick it into the ground, and a few weeks later it became a bush. My banana palms grew into beautiful, abundant trees and surrounded the studio in a most charming manner. Once the studio was complete, I moved out of my stuffy, tiny room in the main house and, borrowing a camping bed from my aunt, I began sleeping in my own place. I had electricity, but no water or toilet, so I borrowed a big basin for emergencies.

After having lived for so many years in student digs, in shabby rooms and basements, I was delighted with the light-filled studio, with its open spaciousness and the fact that I could now paint to my heart's content. On full-moon nights, the moonlight traveled across the floor like a carpet of white blossoms. I made beautiful flower arrangements for my shelves, brought out my books, of which I had quite a few, and hung up my best paintings. This was my first real home.

Alma, of course, soon decided it was dangerous for a young woman to sleep alone in a glass box, which offered no protection and which had no bars across the windows to prevent thieves from entering. I stubbornly refused to move back to the main house. She provided me with a child's water pistol and a police whistle for protection. I think that the studio, because it was undefended, offered no temptation, and I was never robbed.

New Stanley Hotel Gallery

Our next move was to find a gallery for selling my work. Alma was quite clear that I needed to make some money. She was also determined to find a suitable marriage partner for me. However, that is another chapter. We drove to town together and I introduced myself to Mr. Brown, the director of the New Stanley Hotel Gallery. The New Stanley Hotel was at that time a landmark in Nairobi, hosting all sorts of important events, exhibitions, fashion shows, grand dinners and balls. I brought some slides of my paintings and a few actual examples of my work. Mr. Brown was a businessman and was not interested in young artists. He looked bored, as he glanced at my work and shook his head. I received a similar response from all other galleries, which left only one other option, the Sorsbie Gallery, which was the National Gallery of Kenya. Alma was determined and resourceful, and though she did not know the director of the Sorsbie Gallery and was not on their guest list for openings, she had friends who were invited regularly.

A plan was set in motion. While we were waiting for this opportunity, Alma was determined that I needed to meet some people who were important in her eyes. A lovely party was arranged in her house and garden. Mostly English and wealthy Germans were invited. She had quite a knack for bringing people together and creating a lively event. The garden was beautifully arranged for this with a bamboo bar in the center of the lawn. Outdoor garden lights hung in trees and bushes, shedding a colorful light. A small band of African musicians was also engaged to bring a festive atmosphere into the event. I didn't have a party dress, so I was sent off into town to find something. A lovely red dress, which lasted for many years, was my first buy, and I was set.

The guests certainly were the upper crust. Prince so and so, and Count so and so were introduced to me. There were loud and self-important voices, shrill feminine laughter, expensive gowns, and fragrant perfume. The African servants on bare feet moved silently and invisibly between the guests, dressed in the uniforms my aunt had made for such occasions. The little children of Virginia were hiding in the hedges, watching all this with huge dark eyes. It did not take long before I was bored. Conversations were not forthcoming. My uncle Christian was much in demand. I soon realized he had a reputation of being a crack shot and a superb hunter, and the men were eager to engage him in a hunting safari and were trying to set up dates. At this time, hunting was still the big sport in Africa and especially in Kenya, where one could see herds with thousands of animals stretching from one end of the horizon to the other.

Soon, we moved indoors for the meal, and here the conversations became loud and lively. I enjoyed a very good meal and talked a bit to some of the English men. Then an invitation followed for "after dinner drinks" for the men, and a suggestion for the women to go upstairs. I felt disinclined to go with the women, and when the men rose saying "Let's look at Africa," I, too, rose and went out into the grounds with them. Here to my surprise, they separated and disappeared into the darkest corners of the garden to seek some privacy. It only then dawned on me that they were all peeing.

My aunt's next ruse was to invite me to accompany them to the Donovan Maul Theater, run by a local English theater group. I enjoyed the plays very much, as I had had little chance to see plays during my student years. Of course, these occasions brought opportunities for Alma to show off her little niece, and so I met quite a few Nairobi oldtimers, as well as young staff from the German and British embassies. Among them was a young man whose company Alma and Christian enjoyed and who liked to drop in before dinner to play his guitar for them. Basically, he played for his supper. I had little time for him, but Alma asked me to encourage him. I looked at her in disbelief:

"Alma, don't you realize he is gay? Surely you don't think I should go out with him?"

My First Art Exhibition

Then, one day the magic opportunity arose to go to an opening at the Sorsbie Gallery in Nairobi. I slipped into a simple green frock, put on my Italian sandals, and was ready. The lady who was taking me chatted away as we drove into a posh area of Nairobi with huge villas and splendid gardens. We entered the gallery grounds, and to my amazement, I saw that the building was a copy of Le Grand Trianon de Versailles. The lady agreed and said, "It was built by a Frenchman who went bankrupt after its completion. Sir Mailin Sorsbie bought it from him and had the National Gallery installed within. A very impressive structure indeed," she added. A stair laid out in a semi-circle of marble steps led up to the entry that was shaded by columns. At the top of the steps, the Director, Alex Mitchell, stood welcoming the guests one by one. I moved up behind the line of visitors and sneaked a look at him. He was in evening dress and had a short, pointed beard and curly hair. Then my turn came. I introduced myself and quickly informed him that I was an artist, and would really welcome his opinion about my work and some advice. At this stage, a tall willowy woman stepped beside him, dressed in a beautiful strapless gown. "Where have you been?" he barked at her. Clearly, there was some domestic problem and so I moved on, regretting the timing, for he surely would not remember my conversation.

I wandered through the halls, beautifully hung with interesting contemporary art. I knew no one and thus was able to focus on the exhibition. After some minutes, to my great surprise, the director stood before me, apologizing for the interruption and saying he would very much like to see my paintings. Could I tell him a little more about me? Thus, ensued a conversation, and I told him I had just graduated from Kassel, was now a guest of my aunt and uncle in Nairobi, and wished to exhibit my work. An arrangement was made for a meeting, and I left in high spirits.

The next meeting came a week later, when my aunt and I drove to the Sorsbie Gallery to invite the Mitchells to dinner, during which occasion I was planning to show him my paintings. We walked up the imposing marble staircase and an African museum guard conducted us to the office, a bright spacious room with a big desk. My aunt was at her most charming, and I was at my most tongue-tied awkwardness. Alma was spewing superlatives about me—how talented I was, ever since early childhood, and how much it would mean to the whole family to receive some advice and support for me. Much later, Alex told me how amused he was to see me rolling my big brown eyes in embarrassment. A date was set, and then Ildiko, his wife, walked in. I did not recognize her as the elegant woman in the strapless evening attire. She was so plain that I thought she must be the secretary. Alma was charming and took all the tension out of the room.

Two weeks later, the Mitchells and another couple were invited to dinner. The house was too small and dark to show my pictures adequately, and so I found a way to hang them from the trees in the garden. It looked like a lovely little exhibition. Additionally, my portfolios with drawings, watercolors, and ink sketches were set on a large table so they could be opened and looked at.

I was not in the least bit nervous this time. Alex was very gracious and walked through the grounds beside me, carefully examining the paintings hanging from the tree trunks. Then we settled side by side on a narrow bench looking at the portfolios. There were far too many, but in my ignorance of how these things should be done, I showed him every sheet of paper. While we were thus engaged, I glanced at his hands, which were elegant long-fingered, strong hands. I was in the habit of checking out palms and whatever I could find out about a person. He saw me looking, and so I told him I could read palms. He instantly opened his right palm and asked me what I saw. "You nearly died at the age of six, something to do with your abdomen. Then you were very sick at fifteen or sixteen years of age." He looked surprised. "You are correct. I nearly died of appendicitis at the age of six, and had jaundice at the age of sixteen." He seemed to be examining me with added interest and then asked me how I had learned to read palms. At this stage, we were asked to go in for dinner. I had not told him I had also seen his marriage ending in a painful divorce for him.

At the dinner table, Ildiko was the center of attention. She had the manners and attitude of someone important, which was underlined by her elegant and expensive gown. She mainly talked of her two children, David and Fanny. After the meal, they left rather quickly because of the babysitter. The other couple then disclosed that the marriage was not going well for them. Ildiko was unhappy and was spreading rumors. My palm reading had been accurate.

Alex asked me to meet him in a little cafe in Nairobi, where we sat outside for a cappuccino coffee. He told me what he thought of my paintings and what he could propose. He was very positive about my work, but warned me not to have expectations. "The type of art sold here mostly to tourists is of wild animals, colorful Africans, and of course the wonderful landscapes of Kenya. No gallery here in town will pick up an abstract painter. If you wish to sell paintings, you have to paint subject matter that tourists can recognize. I propose that you join me in an exhibition, just a weekend, here in the New Stanley Gallery. The gallery director, Mr. Brown, will agree to change my show to a two-person exhibition, I am sure of that. You have four weeks' time. Can you paint 20 paintings, moderate size; say two by three feet, in one month? Also, they need to be properly framed; a frame helps a lot towards the sale of a picture."

I sat there, feeling shocked to the core that this man would share his exhibition with me and furthermore advise me on how to go about selling my work, framing it, and so on. He then took me in his car to the Sorsbie Gallery, where he showed me very interesting representational work by some African artists, including some big canvases done by him. This gave me an opportunity to see how he worked. His paintings were in bright, dramatic colors and mostly of Africans, landscapes, and beach scenes featuring huge driftwood pieces. "Can you come up with twenty paintings in a month?" he asked again. I had not painted anything representational in six years, but I agreed to the challenge. Alex helped me further by showing me how to choose Masonite boards and gesso them myself. This was a cheaper surface than canvas, which was not of high quality in Kenya and were imported from abroad.

I don't recall how I managed to paint 20 paintings in a month. I just painted from morning till night, totally focused on my work. I painted a herd of cattle driven by a young African just as the sun set, Elephant herds in Amboseli Park, the African gardener—basically things I had experienced in Kenya and which had made a visual impression on me. Degas, the famous French painter, had said: "Paint only what you remember; the rest is unimportant." I took his advice.

Art

When the paintings were ready, Alex came and inspected them. Then he loaded them into his car, and we went to an Indian picture framer in Nairobi. Alex chose the frames. I was not exactly sure I liked them, but said nothing. Two weeks later, I stood in front of the paintings, feeling stunned. They looked good and complete, which had not been the case before they were framed. We took them to the New Stanley Gallery. Mr. Brown was all smiles and charm. What a contrast to the cold reception I had received when I had asked him to look at my work.

We hung the pictures on a Friday. The opening was set for that evening. While I had hung shows before, Alex was a professional. He set the paintings, his and mine, down along the gallery walls. Then he chose the most powerful images and placed them in the center of each group, arranging the rest of the pictures around them. He often paused for long intervals of time, just looking at the arrangement. At noon, we broke and had lunch. I asked him questions about his process of choosing images and how he knew what would be surprising and what would be lost beside a powerful image. Mostly, I was impressed with his pace. He stood a lot and just looked and looked. Then he moved with a rapid speed, and the whole arrangement just fell into place. I had never seen anyone work at such a pace and yet do so little.

The evening came, and I felt nervous. A huge crowd of people had gathered at the New Stanley Gallery. Tourists and locals walked about, drinks clasped in their hands, looking and not looking at the exhibition. The director had illuminated the paintings with overhead lights, and they glowed like jewels on the walls. At some point, a woman came up to me and indicated all the red dots alongside my paintings. "You have sold a lot," she said. I had sold all but one, "Landscape with Zebra," over the weekend. Alex had so far sold nothing, but when I asked him, he was most cheerful. "Oh, don't be concerned. I shall sell everything after the show. You see my prices are high, so people who really want a painting will come to me privately and save themselves the commission they would have to pay to Mr. Brown."

Then he turned away and conversed with an American interested in buying a rather strange image. It was of a beautiful nude; the eye instantly went to her body and feasted on the voluptuousness of the form and silky skin. It was almost as an afterthought that the eye moved up to see the face. But there was none, only a set of teeth. The American wanted Alex to paint in a face, but he refused. Much later he told me that the nude was based on the figure of Ildiko, his wife. "The picture shows what I think of her!"

We became good friends. Alex helped me get two jobs teaching drawing, one at the Kenya Art Society and one at the University of Kenya. One day, the opportunity came to tell him what I had seen in his palm. I told him his marriage was going to fail. He was neither upset nor surprised. He disclosed that his Hungarian wife had fallen in love with the French Consul General and was leaving him and their two children. The flight had already been booked, and she was departing at the beginning of the summer. Alex was very amusing, intelligent, and delightful to talk to. He did not burden our conversations with the events of his past, which gave the present moment a chance to shine. He was circumspect about his personal disappointment over the failure of his marriage, something I much admired, for it showed his self-control. Neither of us was interested in an amorous relationship, and this allowed our friendship to ripen into true affection.

Hans

Sometime later, at a party of young foreigners, I spotted a man I thought to be an American. However, he turned out to be a German veterinarian named Hans, in Kenya on a research project. We talked, and Hans invited me to come to Muguga outside Nairobi, where he was stationed, and to go horseback riding with him. I was missing my riding excursions and happily accepted. The afternoon in Muguga turned out to be very much fun. He owned a horse and borrowed another one for me, and we set off into the Great Rift Valley, a huge earth chasm often compared to the Grand Canyon in the USA and filled with jungle and rivers and rich wild life. After several hours, we got back to his house, tired and stiff. He offered me a warm drink, and we sat around talking and getting to know each other.

One of the problems I had been encountering in Kenya was that most men had an expectation of a woman that I was not willing to meet. I did not feel that an invitation to a meal in a restaurant entitled the man to have sex with me. I tried to be as charming as possible when I turned them down, but the men often showed extreme anger. I was told I was a bitch, that I was sexually frigid and selfish. Also, because I painted, I would show them my studio. They seemed to expect me to drop everything to go out with them at a moment's notice. When I said I was painting that afternoon and was not free, their amazement was huge. "Do you mean to say, you would turn me down in favor of painting a picture?" was the astonished reply. This happened often with men of all sorts and of different nationalities. As a consequence, I became much more careful in my choice of companions. In fact, I usually elected to be with groups of friends rather than going out with a stranger.

My aunt and uncle were off to Europe during the African winter, which is summer in Europe. They had agreed to rent their house to a young diplomat. He was to give me access to the bath and kitchen, as I had no facilities in my studio. As soon as they left, the parties started. By seven in the evening, cars pulled into the courtyard and guests arrived. Things got louder and louder as the evening progressed, and if I was not careful, I could not get into the bathroom, of which there was only one. I would stand and wait in the hallway and wait and wait. Eventually it dawned on me that there was a couple inside making love. This was when I heard the phrase "Are you married or do you live in Kenya?" The sheer beauty and wildness of the place was intoxicating and with it came a desire for tasting life to the fullest.

The German veterinary scientist, Hans, asked me to join him on many outings into the bush. He also needed a photographer for recording his scientific experiments on animals. I had the wonderful opportunity to see game parks while camping in the bush, an activity that was not permitted to the ordinary citizen. There was usually a group of scientists travelling in a number of jeeps in convoys. It was a fairly tough journey across roadless terrain into wilderness areas where animals could be found and their habits and movements studied. We went with several French zoologists, a German photographer, a Belgian scientist, and a few veterinarians. Sometimes, especially if some animals had to be shot for scientific reasons, we also had African guides. The French scientists could not survive without proper food and took along a cook and servants so they could live in a more comfortable style in the wilderness.

I shared a large tent with Hans. He instructed me on how to behave in the bush when needing to follow the call of nature. This was easier said than done. The first time I was so frightened that I was constipated for days. If I found a protected area with a bush or tree, I also had to make sure no wild animal was taking shelter there. There were safari ants racing across the ground. If you stepped upon them, they attacked. There were ticks that would climb up a leg rapidly and be a huge problem to get rid of. There were lions resting in the shade, snakes sunning themselves, and curious baboons. However, it all amounted to a huge adventure, and I loved every second of it.

One of the most frightening occasions was a safari to the Mara Masai to look for elephants. In dense ancient forest growth, we found a herd. When we stopped, the car motor had to be kept running and the car had to be turned to face the open road so an instant departure was possible. One man had engine trouble and the motor on his car died. There we stood, in the vicinity of a huge herd of munching forest giants. There was no alternative; some of the men had to leave their vehicles and try to get the jeep motor running again.

I stood in the back of a jeep with my camera, ready to capture the elephants the moment they emerged out of the thicket, but I never even took a single photo. With a loud trumpeting, the first old tuskers led a group into sight, and I was so terrified by their sheer size that I just froze. There was nothing between them and us. The jeeps were pathetically small, the elephants enormous and lords of the jungle. It soon became apparent why they were so roused. A single warthog, its tail raised vertically into the air, stood confronting the old male elephant. The elephant stood swinging his head, flapping his big ears, and dancing uncomfortably in place, as if trapped by the little warthog. Clearly, he was very frightened. One of the men whispered to me that elephants have poor eyesight, and the old tuskers was not aware of the small size of the pig. More elephants moved into the clearing and we were completely surrounded by the herd. After about half an hour, I got a little used to them. They were mostly peacefully chewing and eating and ignoring our presence. A young Austrian climbed out of his vehicle, and with two more men began to fix the malfunctioning engine. One of the men even crawled under the vehicle. Eventually they managed, and with a roar the engine sprang back into life. The elephants moved back into the forest one by one, and so we gradually began to move too.

On another occasion, we drove to the northern frontier of Kenya. The landscape changed dramatically into mostly thorny shrub and very dry earth. Here we saw camels loaded with goods and driven by Somali traders. We stopped in a store run by an Indian Sikh to buy something cold. He had big ice boxes filled with a single huge block of ice around which bottles of Pepsi and Coca Cola were arranged. It was cool in his shop, and I recall feeling the ice-cold drink in my hands with gratitude. As we were standing there, a Somali entered with a teenage girl. She had the delicate features of the Nilotic desert people and a slim body. The Somali approached one of the men in our group with an offer and an agitated conversation followed. I did not understand the dialect.

After we moved outside, several men came to talk to me, as I was the only woman in the group. "The Somali is trying to sell us the girl for fifty pounds. We could buy her and then give her freedom in Nairobi. What do you think? Should we buy her, is it a possibility? We had no idea that they are still selling human beings here in Kenya." I remember feeling my heart contract and feeling nauseous. "Have you thought of the obligations you have, if you buy the girl?" I asked. "She needs shelter, feeding, papers, clothes, and we cannot even speak her language. We don't know if she is healthy or ill. We can't dump her on a street in Nairobi, what would she do? We all would like to help her, but if we buy her, we have a huge responsibility. Huge!"

We spent another half hour talking and debating what to do with the girl. 50 pounds was nothing. We could raise the money easily enough, but not one person in the group felt ready to take on the responsibility for another human being. In the end we sped away in our vehicles, appalled and ashamed by the knowledge that we could not set the girl free.

Elephants

Once, after camping at the northern frontier with a group of friends, someone shouted an alert. An elephant was approaching our camp. I stuck my head out of my tent and saw this huge, massive creature coming. Grabbing my camera, I slid forward and out of the low entry. As I straightened up, the elephant was already towering above me, just a few paces of distance between us. I saw in magnified detail the remarkable wrinkled skin, powder grey with dried mud, and the tiny eye with dusty eyelashes. The tusks of this old bull were huge, and the large feet advanced soundlessly as he moved forward. The elephant paid no attention to me, moving at such a fast pace I had to run to keep up with his speed.

I wanted to take a picture of him, but just as I was running faster to get a small advance on him, my sandal strap broke and I lost my shoe. I remember looking down to the ground, then back up at the elephant, only to see the swinging rhythm of his tail moving back and forth as he rapidly disappeared into the dusty savannah. As I paused, observing the quickly disappearing elephant, I felt myself to be in a breathless state of awe. I was unaware of fear, but I was trembling so violently I could not have taken a photo. The creature was a force of nature, monumental and totally present in its environment. I recall thinking it had a hard life. The wrinkled skin indicated dryness. It followed its path, moving undistracted and steadily into the direction it had chosen. There was no barrier between us as in a zoo, and yet I could trust the elephant totally. I had the strong feeling the bull was conscious and gentle, accepting my sudden presence and humbly sharing the moments of our encounter by giving me a taste of its energy and strength. It carried the quality of being a great miracle of creation. Its presence produced the feeling that I had received a great and valuable gift.

Evil in Paradise

Hans was an attractive man, much sought after by the ladies. Whenever he asked me to come out to Muguga, I would find traces of female visitors in his bathroom or kitchen. I teased him about it, but he never made excuses. He was professionally very ambitious and was in hot pursuit of a disease called Babesiosis, a blood disease that lay dormant in certain wild animals. For example, the capture and transport of zebras to zoos abroad mostly failed, as the animals died. They had this dormant blood disease which would erupt under stressful circumstances and claim its victim. Lions also carried the dormant illness.

Hans needed a photographer who would film the process of his investigative surgeries, all in the service of science, during which he removed an animal's spleen. These animals were sheep, cows, donkeys and horses, which he purchased for this purpose. After they had recovered from the surgery, the animal was infected with Babesiosis. I cannot recall the complex system through which Hans tried to get antibodies and develop a serum. The work was very interesting and he taught me how to film, how to inject animals, and how to collect blood samples and do other procedures. However, I soon began to ask myself if this type of investigation was really necessary or was just based on his curiosity, or on my curiosity to see what would happen. The more I looked around me, the more I saw interferences which seemed unnecessary or wrong.

Muguga was a British station that housed zoologists and wildlife scientists from different countries. Each house sat on a nice open parcel of land with a garden and meadow around it. The occupants had access to gardeners and servants, mostly living in an African village close by. Hans had invited me to go horseback riding with him, and he picked me up at the bus stop. It was a beautiful day for a ride. In Africa, the sun sets at 6 pm and so around this time we trailed back towards Muguga and passed the African village, which was surrounded by dense, thick shrubbery and trees. Little "mtoto" (African children) hid in the hedges to watch our approach, and one little boy courageously ventured beyond the shrubbery. We were riding our horses slowly side by side. Suddenly, Hans swung his horse around and with a loud whoop galloped towards the boy and the hedge. There were loud screams as the children fled from the hedges, and the horse's hooves thundered to a stop. Turning his horse, Hans rode towards me with a big grin. "That will give them a bit of excitement," he laughed.

My heart had skipped a beat and pounded in my chest.
People called Hans the Nazi. Did he really think terrifying
African children was amusing? I felt cold and shivery. Noticing
this, he offered me a little brandy to drink. His house felt cold
to me, and I asked him to drive me back. We both rose at the
same time, and he kissed me hard on the mouth. Again, I was
surprised by the suddenness and the clumsiness and I did not
respond. That is when I should have stopped associating with
him.

Gossip

Hans moved within groups of people, and since we were
never alone, it did not seem too risky after all. He afforded
me the opportunity to see something of Kenya. I also became
friendly with Jacqueline, a Belgian scientist, who was part of
the group. It was Jacqueline who opened my eyes to the vicious
rumors going around in Nairobi. I told her about the exhibition
Alex had shared with me, and how generous that was. "Oh,
be careful," she advised. "His wife is involved with the French
Consul General, Jean Francais. The Consul has four children
and his French wife is furious with her husband and Ildiko. In
France, you take affairs of the heart with a bit of style; you don't
sacrifice your career or family life for it." She shook her head
in disapproval. "And Ildiko, the Hungarian, she is pure drama.
She is passing a rumor around that Alex is an alcoholic and
impotent." There was so much more that my head was spinning,
and I did not want to know all this dirt! My aunt and uncle
had insisted that I was to cause no problems, as they were
embassy people and could not afford scandal. If I did anything
that caused a rumor, I had to leave. "You may not associate
amorously with an African, an Asian, a married man, or anyone
we do not approve of," Alma had instructed me. Well, I had no
intention of doing that.

Meanwhile, an invitation had arrived from the Sorsbie
Museum. I and a companion were invited to the opening of
a new exhibition. "Would you like to experience an evening
among artists?" I asked Hans. He accepted. It was a mistake

right from the beginning. I was looking forward to immersing myself in a group of intelligent people—writers, musicians, poets—the upper crust of Kenya society, mostly Brits, Italians, French, Asians, and some Africans as well. I had no idea how much "small-town mentality" ruled Hans.

As he did on the first occasion when I was invited to an opening, Alex met the guests on the broad staircase leading to the museum entry. Everyone was greeted warmly. In our case he made certain we knew we were invited to dinner following the exhibition. Hans was being difficult and moody. He did not like the show or the people. We went downstairs to join the other guests for dinner. The food was delicious; I still can see the wonderful spread of delicacies across a wide table. Hans did not like the food, the choice of wines, or the humor. I think that Alex noticed it instantly. He jokingly asked Hans if he needed some castor oil to make him feel better.

For a time, Hans disappeared into the garden. Everyone was a bit tipsy, and in the garden an amorous male was crying at the feet of his beloved, begging her not to leave him. That was the last straw for Hans. "I am leaving. If you don't come you will have to walk home," he said. My arguments fell on deaf ears. We slipped away from the party without saying goodbye. And that was the start of an enmity between Hans and Alex.

5 Alex

Invitation

The African winter begins during the European summer. One day, Alex invited me to go out with him for a meal. We talked and he mentioned that Ildiko would soon be departing for France, to Dijon, where she was taking an intensive language immersion program, as she needed to be utterly fluent in the French language. Jean was hoping to become an ambassador at his next posting, and as his wife-to-be, she had to speak perfect French. Reading my mind, Alex explained that he had offered Ildiko psychological counselling and had begged her for the sake of their two children to accept therapy. However, she refused, telling him her love affair with Jean was like Tristan and Isolde and was beyond understanding. For him she would give up everything, including her children.

Furthermore, she had become disturbed after the birth of Fanny, their second child. "This makes me wonder," he said, "if the childbirth had caused the change in her. Many women suffer some sort of inner shift and depression after the birth of a child." He continued to explain, "Ildiko claims to be of a noble, old Hungarian aristocracy. I actually tried to find out about this and checked the Almanach de Gotha, but found nothing. When we first arrived here, the high position, the interviews for the press, the mixing with wealthy people, and having servants for the first time in her life seemed to have gone to her head. Nothing was good enough anymore. She needed expensive clothes and she paid less and less attention to the children. Instead, she went to the club and got herself invited to go on safaris. Unfortunately, I was so busy establishing the Sorsbie Gallery, arranging shows, etc., that I could not find time to take her on safaris. The chairman of the board had also insisted I take no vacation for a year, until the museum was established."

"But that was three years ago," I interrupted. "Well, yes." he replied. "But now I really don't have the time to traipse through the jungle. The job comes first." Did I detect a streak of stubbornness and pride? I wondered a little at his lack of flexibility.

After the dinner, we went to an African nightclub. African politicians hung out with white girls and the alcohol flowed. There was a strip-tease show that was so awkward and clumsy that we were giggling nonstop. Late, we drove back to my place, but we sat for another hour in the car, talking until 3 am. Finally, I said goodnight and walked up to my studio home.

The next day he called, telling me that Ildiko was infuriated by his absence and late return. How dare he spend the evening without her? She insisted on knowing with whom he had gone out. He told her it was none of her business. She named several women, and my name was among them, much to his amusement. It was in June when Ildiko left for her new life in France. She had sewn herself a whole wardrobe of beautiful clothes, and she left Alex with a huge bill for fabrics and other materials she had used. He reported that the children were coming to terms with their mother's absence.

New Feeling

An invitation came my way from a young diplomatic couple of the German Embassy. It was a garden party in their lush and tropical grounds, which were intoxicatingly beautiful. To my delight, Alex was there as well. For the first time a very odd thing happened. We fell into a natural and easy conversation, such as very old friends do. As we conversed

a part of me stayed alert, a type of observer watched and
enjoyed the movement of words, and the facility with which we
communicated. For a moment, it seemed I stepped forward in
time, into a future situation and witnessed the same comfort
and ease as now. Then the situation switched, and I had the
strange feeling I had known him long ago, that this encounter
was predestined, like picking up pieces established long ago
and reviving a very familiar relationship. With it came a feeling
of trust and security, as if I knew him well, knew his character
and personality from before. I shocked myself out of this state,
feeling disturbed by the discovery. What was this after all?
Was my imagination playing tricks on me? I think this was when
I really looked at Alex for the very first time. He was slender
and tall, with thick curly hair. He sported a short beard and
moustache. His nose was long, and his eyes sparkled with a
quick wit and an expression of attentiveness. He looked very
aristocratic and also unpredictable. Most impressive was his
use of language and his quick mind.

Time seemed to move slowly in Kenya. It became cool, and
grey skies hovered over the land. My uncle and aunt left for
Germany on their annual vacation. I remained behind, living
in my studio, painting, and teaching. I had settled into my new
life. A letter came from Joe. He was in California, in Big Sur.
He loved it there. He had met Jessica and they were planning
to marry, he wanted me to know this. I sent him heartfelt
congratulations and told him a bit about my present life.
"Clearly, this was the right choice for us," I said. "I am glad for
you and wish you a wonderful life with Jessica." I did not cry,
only my heart did.

During a party, I heard the music of "Ella in Berlin" and was
amazed by Ella Fitzgerald's singing. I must have mentioned it,
because the next time I saw Alex, during lunch at his house,
he surprised me by playing "Ella in Berlin." This was the
second time at his place. I had previously seen his apartment
only during a party filled with guests. Now I could evaluate
it properly. The first thing I noticed was that it was a man's
environment. There was not a single feminine touch in the

rooms. Elegant Danish furniture combined with large paintings of driftwood and African beggars, which clearly were by his hand. Ildiko had by this time left for her new life in Europe. The children now looked much happier and more relaxed than I remembered from my prior meeting. For the first time, they actually talked and looked like spontaneous, carefree children. Alex's main servant was also the cook. He must have sensed that this new woman might be the new mistress, and so he did his best to impress me. The platter from which I served myself held the largest serving for me, while Alex received a smaller portion. We both noticed and were very amused. After lunch, Alex pulled out his new recording of "Ella in Berlin" and others. He had quite a collection and clearly relished my interest.

Probably what I liked best about the luncheon were the children. Fanny, the little girl, aged two, only spoke Kiswahili and was very cheeky and funny. David was a lovely five-year-old. In no time, I was playing with the children and we went out into the garden to inspect David's stick houses. Looking back, it must have impressed Alex that the young woman he had invited liked children and knew how to play with them. Perhaps, a new possibility was slowly forming in his mind, now that he didn't have a wife.

Hans and Alex

Hans had decided I needed a horse of my own. An English farmer had a horse for sale, a cheap deal, as the animal had a problem with its spine. Hans put this new horse in the same stable with his own horse, but it was for me to ride. This put me under obligation to go out to Muguga regularly, as the animal needed to be ridden. I did not exactly relish this deal.

A curious insensitivity began to show in Hans. He obviously did not feel it necessary to discuss some plan or decision of his with me or to gain my approval. He took it for granted that I would accept whatever he wanted. I would often have to wait for hours for him, as he ignored pre-arranged appointment times. Eventually, having waited for a reasonable amount of time, I learned to give up on him. I just would return to my home. There was never mention of these missed rendezvous or an apology.

One evening he drove me back home and before I could say "thank you and good night," he began to talk about "when we get engaged and return to Baden-Baden to marry." "But, Hans!" I interjected, "Where did all this come from? Have we even ever talked of a possible relationship? Have we even ever talked about love?" He looked hurt and instead of continuing the topic, withdrew into himself. It made me feel discordant and confused and also slightly guilty for not understanding his deeper feelings or intentions. I asked him about past relationships or loves. He refused to tell me anything, referring to probable girlfriends as "acquaintances." In one case he mentioned getting beaten up by a rival suitor, and I got the impression he liked to fight for his women.

The summer progressed, and I became very busy with painting, as I had managed to get into a little gallery run by a British couple. I submitted elephant paintings and landscapes with African huts, as well as watercolors of mountain scenes. In the late afternoon, it was my custom to roll out my blanket on the lawn and practice an hour of hatha yoga asanas. My existence condensed just to that present moment of late afternoon light shining through the hedge, the chatter of African women in the next compound, and the smell of early cooking fires being lit. Africa was all about smell and fragrance, and they were powerful and intoxicating.

I loved living in Nairobi, but, with a degree of sadness, I realized I would not be able to live there beyond a limited time. There was a big snake in the Garden of Eden, and sooner or later I would have to leave this paradise. I knew this with total certainty. Kenya was for the African people, not Europeans.

One evening Jacqueline and Hans unexpectedly dropped by and we sat for a bit in my studio, talking. They had come from a party and were a bit tipsy. They were on the point of leaving when a very drunk Alex roared through the gate in his Citroen station wagon. Hans called out an insult, Alex responded with another, and before I knew it they were locking horns.

"You little man, come up into my hand and let me look at you," shouted Alex. I was wearing my favorite little green silk dress as I ran to the door of Alex's vehicle and held it shut, as he was threatening to come out and make "mincemeat" out of Hans. Meanwhile, Hans was dancing around the car, shouting encouragement for a fight. Alex tried to open his car door, but I threw my weight against it, tearing the sleeve of my dress in the process. "Go home," I begged, "This is ridiculous. You can't make a scene and have a fight on my relatives' property as I will be sent away for having instigated a scandal." The verbal insults continued for a bit. Then, obviously my words had an effect, as he turned the car in the driveway, and shouting an insult roared out of the entry, scraping the side of the car on the gate as he exited.

It took me by surprise to find Hans taking a sudden interest in me, when before I had just been one in the group of friends. I also put two and two together, coming to the conclusion that he liked competition. I had suddenly aroused the interest of Alex and also of Hans. Flattering as it was, I didn't have real interest in either of them. In fact, it disturbed me, and my aunt's warning made me careful. I withdrew myself to some degree, not accepting invitations and even going to the extent of refusing to answer phone calls.

However, there was an invitation to a fancy-dress ball that I accepted, and since I had a sari, I carefully disguised myself as an East Indian, changing my hairstyle and wearing appropriate jewelry. What I would never have believed happened; nobody recognized me, certainly no one I knew. I was just another Indian girl invited to the party. I sipped my lemonade and felt the evaluating looks of Westerners gliding down my body, felt the disrespect and racial prejudice. I talked at length with an Asian art supply salesman, who just talked about his job and looked uneasy because I had the wrong accent. I made no effort to approach people I knew, as I was more curious about how they treated Asian Indians. One man I was acquainted with did the unpardonable by touching me and trying to raise my skirt. I began to feel vulnerable and I left. I felt exposed, in the wrong place, and with people who disrespected women and Indians. I recalled when I had passed customs entering Kenya and was obliged to fill out a sheet with questions. One was: "What race are you? Black? White? Asian? Arab?" I had written "human," just to make a point.

I really liked the Africans. They were beautiful and gentle and kind to their children. Babies stayed with their mothers, each one tied to the mother's back wherever she went. There was no infant crying, no sound of any scolding, no violence. My studio was right beside the compound of African domestics. I watched in amazement as these people washed themselves several times per day. Our servant told me one day that the white man stinks of acid. "It is the meat you eat and the harsh soap you wash with," he said. I had to agree with him.

Alex called me frequently and we talked. He was facing a number of problems, one of which was being a single parent. Sunday was his day off, but with two children, there was no day of rest for him. He had to take care of his kids. I considered helping him out one time, but then I changed my mind. Instead, old friends visited and helped him. One evening, he invited me for dinner together with his best friend, Michael Croydon, and Michael's current girlfriend. The evening was charming, funny, and very pleasant. Michael was a sculptor, a very talented man with the gift of telling the most amusing stories. We ended up going to a dance place in Nairobi, where a live band was playing the twist, a dance then in favor. Alex wore a waistcoat and a jacket over it on this pleasantly warm evening. In no time he was soaked in sweat, his Scottish attire quite inappropriate for the dancing. I watched in amazement and disbelief. Did he need to do this for my approval, or was he stuck in a gentleman's dress code dating back to the 19th century? I never could quite believe the unbreakable customs of the British, who still insisted on going to dinner in ties and jackets in tropical Africa.

Much to my horror, Hans called me a few days later threatening to ruin Alex's reputation if I continued seeing him. How did he know I had accepted some invitations, and why did he care? Saying almost nothing in reply, I immediately called

Alex and asked him if he had any idea what was going on. He was equally perplexed, but he did mention that this was a small town and that Ildiko had made sure he had enemies. I assured him that under such circumstances I wanted nothing to do with ruining his reputation, and I felt the threat was meant in all seriousness and thus I would not see him for some time.

Shortly thereafter my horse died. Hans gave no actual explanation and I felt relieved to be free from having to go to Muguga. Whenever he called, my excuse was that I was too busy. My aunt and uncle had returned from Europe. At about this time I acquired a new job. I was to teach a German language class at the Goethe Institute of Nairobi. I was given some instruction, and then, as I had a language teaching certificate, I was let loose to do what I could. It was lots of fun to teach without books or writing material, just with words and repetitions. My students were Sikhs and Africans, and much to my surprise, they were fast learners. Within six months, most of them became quite fluent in German, with a good enough proficiency to express themselves and say what they wanted in a difficult European language. My reputation soared at the Goethe Institute, and I was given additional jobs, such as arranging display windows and hanging art shows.

Romance at Diani Beach

It was now September, and Alex and Michael planned a seaside getaway to the coast in February, I gave some suggestions. Michael was bringing his girlfriend and Alex was bringing his children, the children's ayah (nanny), and a servant. At the last moment, Michael cancelled. I decided I would like to go for a week, so we took off for the eight-hour journey down to the tropical coast of Kenya. We arrived in a hotel recommended by my aunt and each of the grownups had a bandha—a little cottage with a palm frond roof overlooking the ocean. The air was soft and moist and the sand snow-white powdered corral. We all had dinner together, then the ayah put the children to bed. Alex invited me for a drink, but since I did not drink Scotch, I chose to take a beach walk instead, alone.

During the night the crying of Fanny and David awoke me. Both were screaming for their daddy. The ayah was trying to calm them, but was unsuccessful. I wondered if I should get up, but then chose not to interfere. Eventually, I fell asleep and then awoke in the morning to the soft murmur of the Indian Ocean and the sound of birds chattering in the huge trees. Later on, I asked Alex about the commotion during the night; he was embarrassed and explained he had slept heavily due to the Scotch and had heard nothing. I realized that he had made a mistake and he felt very ashamed.

After breakfast, we left the children with the ayah and drove to the south coast in search of a Mrs. Wales, who rented out cottages. We had to drive onto a big local ferry boat which transferred all vehicles to the other side of a large lagoon. A couple of Englishmen in a small car were parked next to Alex and his Citroen. They were in a rush to get off the ferry when we landed and instead of waiting for instructions, they tried to squeeze past Alex's vehicle, scraping the side of his car on the side he had scraped on my aunt's garden gate, which had just been repaired. Alex flew into a rage, shouting at the guys and ordering them to wait for him just beyond the landing platform. Needless to say, they preferred having nothing to do with an irate Scot and blasted away, so fast that Alex could not catch up with them.

The south coast, called Diani, was a tropical paradise. We found Mrs. Wales and then rapidly rented several bandas on a big patch of beach. The cottages stood among coconut palms, and monkeys swung through the treetops of huge ancient baobab trees. They had outhouses and the showers were also located within a bamboo fence in the open air. I thought it was heaven. We went back, picked everyone up, and drove down and looked for food stores. I remembered the native market, where we found the most colorful assortment of tropical fruits and vegetables. We loaded up several big baskets with the produce and went back to our cottages. There was a main house with a large veranda where we could cook and I took over the kitchen, knowing nothing about cooking. However,

I had already decided that Fanny was not eating properly and planned to change that. I fed the children big glasses of freshly squeezed juices, made fruit desserts, and was delighted that fishermen came daily offering us their catch-of-the-day. Somehow, we made the most fantastic and wholesome meals, and everyone was happy. I noticed that Alex stopped drinking Scotch. We went on long beach walks and raced the children. We collected seashells and made sand sculptures and castles for David.

One stormy and grey afternoon, heavy clouds brought rain and I walked the beach alone, my hair wet and disheveled. As I walked the deserted beach, the cry of seabirds in my ears, I asked myself what I was doing here alone with a wounded, lonely man and his little children. I noticed he was happy and that he looked at me in a different way. Long ago, he had confessed that the end of his marriage caused him to lose all faith and he was not interested in another relationship. This suited me perfectly. We had become friends and by now had known each other for six months. However, what was I doing joining a married man and his children on a vacation in tropical Kenya?

I walked back to the cottages and prepared a dinner for everyone. When the children had gone to bed and darkness had fallen, Alex and I were alone in the main house. We sat together on an old sofa and talked. Our only light source was a hurricane lamp, as there was no electricity on the premises. He asked me questions about my life and I talked readily enough and laid out the difficult years of my youth and our long stint as refugees.

Suddenly, I noticed a tear on his cheek. "You are not crying," I said in alarm, suddenly feeling self-conscious and foolish. "No, no, I am just touched and filled with compassion for the hardships you have had to endure. You tell a good story; it must have been very difficult for you." He smiled at me and reached for another cigarette. There was a period of silence, an awkward silence. For a brief flash, I contemplated saying good night and leaving the room. Instead, I remained. He looked at me and his face seemed to move very slowly, closer and closer and closer to mine. I seemed to see all this in slow motion. Then our lips touched and the sensation was the most unexpected, like falling slowly down a deep well or like being Alice in Wonderland falling down the rabbit hole. I lost myself so deeply and so completely, that I have no memory beyond this.

Alex pulled himself together at some point. "This won't do, I don't wish to take any advantage of you. This will have to wait until we can go to Mombasa and buy some protection." I agreed with him. After a last kiss, we walked to our separate bandhas to sleep. But instead of sleeping, I stood by the window and looked at the white beach glowing in the moonlight, wondering what had happened to my heart.

There was a knock on my door which woke me. Little David stood outside when I opened. "My daddy says he is pining for you," he informed me. I was unfamiliar with the term "pining," but I put on my dressing gown and walked over to his banda. He sat in his rumpled bed with Fanny beside him. The children cuddled close, giggling and laughing, and I sat down on the edge of the bed, as there was no chair in the room. Alex's face was alight, glowing with joy and life. He looked at me without taking his eyes off my face and we locked eyes. "I am pining for you; we need to go to Mombasa. "

An hour later, wearing a pretty white dress of my mother's which had been altered to fit me, we were off, back to the ferry, back to the coastal city filled with Sikhs, Indians and Arab traders to find a pharmacy. We drove along a main street which boasted two enormous elephant tusks opposite each other, bordering the street. We stopped in a little sidewalk café to order cold drinks. It was intensely humid and hot, and Alex was drenched in sweat. In contrast, I hardly perspired and he was amazed that I stayed physically so cool to the touch. The sensation that he loved me was so novel and strange to me and at the same time so endearing and wonderful, that I felt unable to do anything but to be alive in the delectable present moment. We found the little pharmacy and bought what we had come for.

Stormy Weather

The road back to Diani beach was exquisite. We drove through a plantation of coconut palms, their foliage a lime green mixed with a soft yellow, all swaying in the soft breeze while beyond the Indian Ocean gleamed in purest turquoise against the snow-white beaches. It was utterly lovely. We strolled along the beach with the children after lunch. The sky had become cloudy, and a wind had sprung up and the tide was rushing in. We were content to splash through the shallows and watch the seabirds. Far out, fishing vessels were moored, a string of brightly painted boats bobbing on the waves. An Englishman walked past us and with a brief greeting, threw himself into the waves.

"I would not get into this churning water, even though I am a good swimmer," I remember saying to Alex. "This is very rough and probably dangerous; I hope he knows what he is doing." We walked on and turned back when it began to rain. At the point where the Englishman had entered the water some people had gathered. "Can you swim?" they asked us, "someone by the boats is in distress." I looked out across the water now foaming and white and decided I could not help anyone out there. Just then a young, strong man ran to the water's edge, put on flippers and threw himself into the currents. He crawled out in the direction of the boats and I could see that he was struggling against the strength of the currents. I could see no one by the boats. We stood there, as the minutes passed, waiting and looking. I had a horrible feeling. Later the Englishman's body was found. Coming near the boats and trying to heave himself up into one of them, he must have received a heavy bash which knocked him out.

This experience was like a slap of wet seaweed in the face, sobering in its intensity. It took the magic out of the day by reminding me of the brevity of life. The moon was a sickle of brightness in the night sky. Seaweed had drifted onto the beach and lay there in dark clumps. A single luminous path sparkled on the dark waters of the ocean. We walked along in each other's arms.

Sometime during the night, I awoke and felt it was all too much, too hot, too intense. I walked out of Alex's banda onto the beach into the coolness of the night and listened to the steady rhythm of the ocean as I cried. Did I know something then, which was a warning, but was incomplete and therefore incomprehensible? We were in Diani beach only for 10 short days. These were strung together like a precious necklace of pearls. This time together was to set the tone for all that was to happen later. I vacillated between feeling a great tenderness and loving admiration for Alex, and then thinking it was all too good to be true and negating what I felt. Basically, I felt out of my depth; this man was older than I, sophisticated, experienced, and worldly.

Then came the evening he invited me to the Mombasa Club, in an old Portuguese fort on the edge of the ocean. At dusk, we drove down to Mombasa. The moon was already spreading its light over the Indian Ocean and casting deep shadows between the buildings. The air was moist and soft. We entered the ancient gate, guided by silent African waiters. A guest book had to be signed and I noticed Alex's hand formed beautiful calligraphy. Yes, he admitted, he was trained in Italic writing. The dining area was an open roof terrace, and below spread out the vast tropical ocean. So, we sat under a canopy of stars and each table held only a tiny little lamp as a source of light, so as not to take away from the magical night sky.

Alex looked happy and young, and once we sat down; he held my hand. To my great astonishment, he told me he loved me. This took me by surprise, for I could not fathom how anyone could fall in love so fast; surely, he needed to consider this more carefully. Then he proposed marriage to me. He laid out his thinking in a clear and logical fashion, walking me step by step through his thought processes. He could feel his time in East Africa was coming to a close. Uhuru (independence), was fast approaching and Kenya would soon gain independence. Mailin Sorsby, the chairman of the board of the Sorsby Gallery, would probably close the gallery or transfer the museum into African hands. This meant Alex would have to find a new direction. His divorce from Ildiko would come through in several months' time, after which he would like to marry me. He felt I had enough talent as an artist and did not wish to stand in my way. He would make sure I would be able to paint and to develop my talent. He proposed that he work in the marketplace, for which he had a talent, and leave me to be the artist that I already was. He would not drag me into the social arena or expect for me to be the hostess. He was persuasive, charming and with all my heart I wanted to believe him.

The night was perfect, the wine tasted like nectar, and I felt like a queen. This evening went beyond my wildest imagination. I tried to imagine my life as his wife. Suddenly, the moon hid behind a cloud. Now there was only the little table light between us and the night around us was dark. I don't recall giving him any answer and certainly, in my heart, I had none. In any relationship one partner might be more passionate, more advanced, more in love than the other. Now that I knew what he felt for me, I was more sensitive towards him and I studied him more closely. He had stopped drinking altogether and was losing weight. He looked happier and lighter, less burdened by worry. I can still see his face, suntanned, bending over me, his smile pure joy as he tells me how beautiful I am. He admired my swimmer's muscles and my cool skin. "How can you stay so cool in this tropical heat?" he asked repeatedly without expecting an answer. I took wonderful pictures of the children, who were by now well used to me. Fanny was cheeky and she stuck her tongue out at the camera.

We both painted in the afternoon, when the heat was too intense to go outside. I still have a lovely little watercolor of that beach. But now, it has a hole in it. Still, I am tempted to frame it for old time's sake. It was a perfect time, as perfect as time ever can be. We walked the beaches and, on our return, still found some of our footprints left in the white sand. He told me about his life in Scotland, about his student days and wild times. He found my stories of Egypt fascinating and encouraged me to talk about art, about my thoughts and dreams. I suspected that he wanted to find the key to who I was. He felt my reticence and tried to smooth out my fears, but I was very hesitant and I refused to be rushed. Then it was time to leave paradise.

On our drive back, when we were in Tsavo Park, the right front tire of the Citroen station wagon burst. We had to get out and change the tire. Fortunately, no lions appeared. We decided to keep our affair private, since Alex had enemies and did not want to jeopardize his divorce proceedings. On arriving at my place, Alex carried my suitcase up the steps to my studio. Both of us were conscious of the different circumstances and for some moments we clung to each other. Then a distance grew between us and isolated us once more.

Acceleration

Back in my old life, but too altered to fit into my former lifestyle, I was beset by restlessness and confusion. We talked on the phone in the evening. He was starting to suffer and began to express it to me, while I felt helpless to deal with his loneliness. The days seemed grey, and my rose-colored glasses began to slip off. As it was, I saw things differently now. A change has taken place within me and within him. Every evening, I withdrew to the garden and practiced yoga, which calmed and sustained me in so many ways. My mind cleared, and my emotions found peace at the end of a practice.

The Kenya Art Society, where I taught drawing, was not happy with me. Carefully, Alex explained to me that the ladies who took courses came for the fun of it, for the social get-together, not for learning how to draw. I am expecting too much of them and treated them like art students, which they were not. However, the harm was done, the ladies dropped the course, and I was out of that job. At the university, my art classes continued well and I met other faculty. However, I insisted on my free weekends. I joined my group of friends to seek out the wilds of Africa. Alex would have liked me to join him at the weekends, when he was trapped with his children. His personality was optimistic, generous and loyal, all of which I admired, but I also saw a strong urge towards self-indulgence, and he was quite reckless at times. Occasionally, he had driven at 80 miles per hour through Nairobi.

I turned down his invitations quite often, but unlike other men I had known, he was a total gentleman about it, never becoming annoyed or aggressive. I enjoyed his warm and optimistic nature and his lovely sense of humor. It has to be admitted too, that I was an unreliable, flighty person at that time, quite unpredictable and often depressed. He must have seen something in me I did not see in myself, or he would never have put up with me. My demons were quite destructive, and I had binges of hopelessness. Alex had a spirit of expansion and the ability to cope with the external world. He fit easily into any kind of society and was a good mixer. For some incomprehensible reason, he thought that I was "quite something." Now I know that he probably admired my honesty and fearlessness. Clearly, I was neither spoiled nor one of those self-indulgent party girls.

Lillian and Waldi

I can't recall why I asked him on one occasion to take care of my aunt's dachshund, Waldi, for the day. He reported the dog instantly loved him and sat on his feet under the desk. The surprise came when his secretary entered the room. With a hearty growl, the little dog charged towards the woman to attack her feet. She managed to withdraw behind the door just in time. This "possessiveness" of Waldi's became a bit of a problem, as Lillian, his secretary, just could not enter the room without being attacked. My intuition picked up the sign instantly. "So, you had an affair with Lillian?" I asked. "Yes," he admitted. "Some months ago, after a party with too much booze to drink, we became a little too intimate. She was unhappy in her marriage, and I with mine. That brought us together."

Waldi's other disgrace was that he trailed little Fanny when she was eating a piece of chocolate. She was only two years old and her hand above Waldi's head was conveniently reachable. He gently took her chocolate out of her hand and ate it. She cried and was given a second piece of chocolate. Again, he gently trailed her and in an unexpected moment took her chocolate away.

Lillian was not my friend. She was a handsome Scottish woman married to a well-to-do man, a member of the upper classes. It seems she was a superb secretary. Obviously, she had secret hopes that Alex might be interested in her. After Ildiko had been gone for some time, Lillian received a letter addressed to her, in which Ildiko begged her to give some news of her children and of Alex especially. She hoped and prayed that there was still a chance of returning to her husband and children. She described her anguish, missing the children dreadfully and being very unhappy. Her circumstances in France were miserable, and she confessed to having made a huge mistake in leaving her husband.

Lillian wrote back to her that there was no chance of a return or reunion with Alex. This correspondence was never mentioned to Alex. All this was discovered a year later when Alex met Ildiko face-to-face in France. Unfortunately, Ildiko never wrote to Alex directly to beg for a reunion, having trusted the false voice of Lillian instead. She believed there was no hope any longer, when there might well have been every possibility of saving the marriage.

My memory of the autumn in Nairobi is hazy. I worked, saw little of Alex, and phoned him a lot. I can't really remember the days. It felt as if I was suspended, not living in the present but in some future dimension. We talked and made plans. Alex had been right about the effect of independence, Uhuru. The Sorsbie gallery was moving into African hands. Alex's time in Kenya came to its end. He had an offer to become the director of the National Gallery of Johannesburg in South Africa. Invited to a fairly wild South African party, he met a lot of important Boers. One of them asked: "How are you with a rifle?" Alex replied he was a crack shot. "We want you, man! When they threaten independence in South Africa we are going to wade in blood. We need good men like you. Come to South Africa!" Needless to say, this was a complete turnoff for Alex. To wade in blood was not to his taste. A museum in Tennessee also was interested in him. He put it on hold, since they wanted to interview him in the USA.

New Plans

I had suggested something else. We had read some very amusing stories from an English writer who lived in Greece on an island. "How would it be to live in Greece for a year with the freedom to paint? The children could visit a Greek kindergarten. It would probably do them no harm. After a year we would see a new direction." Alex liked the idea. He had been working far too hard and that for too long, so having some free time, especially creative time, appealed to him. Greece at the time was very inexpensive.

There was one last dinner invitation for Alex at my aunt's place. Immediately on her return from Germany, she had found out that he was interested in me. My hesitation was inexplicable to her way of thinking. The day after the dinner, Alex wrote her a charming little thank you note. She asked me to come to her room. There she waved the note in front of my eyes and asked me to read it. "Are you not impressed?" she demanded. "That is a gentleman. That is the kind of man you should be looking for." "But, Tante Alma, he is a married man with two children!" She turned on her heel, ready to leave the room. "You are a stupid goose!" was her final remark before the door shut behind her.

We arranged to meet in Cairo after Christmas, at my mother's hotel. I did not have the intention to venture into a relationship with Alex unless my mother approved of him. I departed Nairobi before him and spent Christmas at home, giving my mother a full account of the situation. Alex had warned me that he would be removing his beard and that I should expect him to look differently. When I saw him again, he looked much younger and quite handsome. He and the children had received a nice, big room on the first floor of the hotel. My mother was wonderful with the children. On the first evening after dinner, we sat in her room discussing our situation with her. For a while she sat silent, obviously thinking over what I had said. Then she looked at me with a funny little grin and said "If you won't marry him, I will!"

For the brief ten days in Cairo, Alex was introduced to the ancient monuments, Sakkara and the Egyptian Museum, the bazaar, and the desert. The children were looked after by my mother's favorite woman, Linda. One morning a French guest came in great excitement to tell us, "Zee children are locked in the bathroom and can't get out." With great calm Alex gave David instructions on what to do and they were free in seconds, emerging with little white, frightened faces.

Perhaps it was my mother's experience with life and with people which made the situation so comfortable. Fanny, who had up to then never mentioned her mother or indicated missing her, began to open up to Leni. My mother often just lifted the child into her arms in a warm and understanding embrace. "Are you my mommy?" Fanny asked one day. "I want you to be my mommy." My mother was deeply touched and also very sad for the child. Fanny also had trouble liking food. Again, my mother's experience triumphed. She introduced the child to pate de foie gras, which became an instant favorite, as well a honey and Arabic bread. Alex had decided to return to Scotland, Edinburgh, and stay with his parents for a bit until his divorce became final. We agreed to meet in London in March, and then we would see how we could manage to get to Greece.

The ancient Egyptians had a very wise method for couples who wished to marry. They suggested a full year's trial period. Pregnancy was forbidden, but in every other way the couple lived like man and wife. If after a year's time, they were still determined to marry, then that was that. However, often the magic was gone, and then they were obliged to separate. This "trial period" is what I suggested to Alex. In Nairobi, we had sought out an old Hindu astrologer who had made a chart for us. It was very accurate over many years, although Fatima's predictions were still the most accurate, and every one came true.

While I returned to Nairobi, Alex flew into the Scottish winter. His first letters were terribly depressed. It seems his parents were horrified at how much he had aged and shocked that Fanny spoke only Kiswahili. His father was upset about Ildiko and had great trouble understanding how she could have abandoned her children.

The Trees Have No Leaves

On arriving in Edinburgh, David had said, "Daddy, it is strange here. The trees have no leaves."

Alex wrote to me that he sat in front of his parents' fireplace for the first three days and just drank Scotch. I felt unable to help in any way. His letters poured in, 10 pages of tightly typed script per day, typed on his father's old machine. I complained occasionally that it took me two hours to read his letter, but he was not deterred.

As spring began to arrive, I organized my departure, packing all my paintings and other possessions so they could be shipped in my absence. Some of my Indian students helped me, which made things much easier. I gave up my various jobs at the Goethe Institute and at the university and went to Egypt first. I planned to visit Upper Egypt one last time, as there might not be another opportunity. Somehow a room was rented in the house of Chech Ali Rassoul, who was known to be a grave robber and who sometimes had nice antiques for sale. His lovely Arab house sat just behind the Colossi of Memnon, two massive statues of King Amenhotep III of Thebes. They made strange singing and humming sounds, and people said it was caused by the changing temperatures at dusk and dawn. Later, the sculptures were repaired, and the singing stopped.

I loved the wonderful location, which had once held the mortuary temple of the king. Fields extended out to the statues, and in the evenings, the bats took over in a dramatic swirling by the thousands. Mourning doves cooed all day long, and it was a perfect location for making some paintings. Did I have a premonition that slides of the monuments would be required for future art history courses at Lake Forest College? I spent days wandering through the ancient sites, photographing everything. Returning to the quiet garden, my eyes drank in the beautiful view of Arab villages, and I sat in the stillness there painting watercolors. Timelessness prevailed unlike anywhere else.

A Visit to Scotland

After a short visit to Cairo to see my mother, I flew to London, where Alex was planning to pick me up for the start of our grand adventure together, living on a Greek Island. Unfortunately, Alex loved his Citroen car too much and made the mistake of shipping his station wagon to England. The vehicle had a hydraulic suspension system, which was mishandled, and when he drove the car from the coast up to Edinburgh, the cylinder block cracked. The repairs were so expensive that any notion of going to Greece and living there for a year were completely shattered.

After my arrival in London, we drove up the Great North Road to Edinburgh with me eating cheddar cheese and oatmeal biscuits, my newly discovered delicacy, while Alex filled me in on the sad tale of the Citroen car disaster. We drove to his parent's house, the home in which he had grown up. It was a small house, filled to capacity with huge wardrobes, bookcases, and Victorian furniture. It was explained to me that the furniture was from Brechin, the old family residence, and was far too large for the house. His father had great difficulty letting go of furniture that was now obsolete. He hung on to it, unable to shed what was inherited and of great value in his eyes. Alex's mother felt burdened by these huge furniture pieces.

His mother, Lizzie, was a charmer, red-haired, fun-loving, and warm-hearted. I immediately took to her. Alex's father, Alistair, was much more challenging. He was an extremely handsome man, well-built, and an amusing raconteur. However, he felt uneasy with his potential daughter-in-law. I looked far too young. One aunt of Alex's thought I was a school girl, and I guess the whole family was buzzing with the story of Alex bringing back this very young girlfriend who seemed to everyone wholly unsuitable to be a mother to his two children. Alex also made the error of introducing me to apple cider. I loved this drink and having no idea that it contained alcohol, drank much more than prudent. I realized how much I upset Alistair when I was giggling and tipsy one afternoon.

After arriving, Alex and I had set out to find an inn, as we could not stay with his parents. They had already taken in the two children and were busy coping with their small charges. Alex was tense and one place after another failed to be suitable. I recall him saying: "This is it; I don't know what to do!" We had just left a place where the bed was so short that Alex at six foot two inches did not have enough leg room. When we mentioned this to the proprietor, she shrugged, saying in a severe clipped Scottish accent, "In your country men tend to grow a lot taller."

I don't know where she thought Alex came from, since he had a Scottish accent. I encouraged him to drive just one more turn around the corner, and there we found the accommodation we wanted. Again, and again, I would find myself relying on my intuition and being guided in a most amazing way.

We were both tense about our potential suitability as marriage partners. As a consequence, I had asked Alex if he could find an astrologer who would cast our horoscopes. He did and presented me with the documents compiled by a well-known London astrologer. I recall my irritation at reading that "our marriage would not be made in heaven." What would anyone know of heaven!? However, on the whole, the prospects looked good. Therefore, I agreed to the union. We were together for three weeks while Alex introduced me to Scotland, his hometown of Edinburgh, theatre, art, food, the countryside, and all his favorite places. Standing on Princes Street, looking up at the castle built on top of the black rock overlooking the street, I shuddered so visibly with cold that Alex kept on mentioning it for many years. Gale force winds had blown grey, black clouds over the castle, and the impact was unforgettable.

Patsy

It was at this time that Alex told me of Patsy, his first great love. He explained he'd met her at the University of Edenborough during his student days, and he described her as a beautiful young woman with long flowing hair the color of golden-ripe wheat and with eyes like crystalline blue water. She was half Scots and half Aussie, sensuous and bewitching. He maintained that he'd never told her that he was three years younger than she was, but, for whatever reason, the relationship didn't last. Alex said he'd like to introduce me to her and her husband Bill, and this came about. I shall never understand why he did not marry her. When she saw me, she blushed to the roots of her hair. I saw her qualities instantly and valued her immensely.

One of our main problems was the divorce papers. Although it was now April, they had not yet been issued, and Alex's father was visibly worried that our being together would jeopardize the divorce. He had an amazing capacity for projecting his inner concerns, and it was making me quite uncomfortable. Again, and again, I mentioned to Alex that I could feel his discomfort with the situation, that his family did not approve of me, and I had made a poor impression on everyone. As the days went by, I became more and more affected by his father's disapproval, and it began to weigh on me.

Alex told me that before he came back to Edinburgh, his father had undergone a hernia surgery. All went well, but the medication upset his father and made him cough. He burst his stitching and had to be put under again in order for the wound to be re-stitched. This time, he suddenly experienced tightness across the chest and a heart problem was diagnosed. Alex confessed to his extreme concern for his father and the fear that his father would not live beyond the year.

It was true that his father was strange, eccentric, and somewhat unpredictable. I recall a mealtime when Lizzie had prepared dinner and called him to say the meal was ready. But instead of coming into the house, he told her he would be back in a little while. She put the dish back into the oven to keep it warm and he returned a long time later. Meanwhile, she fed the children and herself. At the time his behavior struck me as rude and inconsiderate, and I admired Lizzie's self-control.

As May came, I voiced my discomfort. "Alex, I feel the weight of his psychic disapproval and I feel so uncomfortable being with you, feeling so guilty for causing him discomfort and concern, that I really must leave and return to Kenya." He was the complete gentleman. The daffodils had just come out and the landscape of Scotland was moving into a lush and beautiful spring. It was the beginning of May.

He took me to the airport on May 5. I felt strangely empty and dead inside as we said goodbye. We made no promises or pledges to each other, wept no tears, and sighed no sighs. It was over. It did not work and this was the best thing to do, I told myself.

I had not counted on my subconscious. I was in a kind of agony that was hard to describe. After landing in Cairo, I took a taxi back to my mother and the little hotel. My mother disapproved of my leaving Alex; her face told me clearly how upset she felt. I don't know what I did for these three weeks in Cairo. It felt like a dead zone inside me. I walked along the edge of the Nile River in a restless mental state. May is the month of the Ham sin, sandstorms and heat. Fine sand covered the windowsills, tabletops and countertops after a sandstorm. Sand crunched between my teeth, and sand irritated my scalp and skin. A first letter from Alex contained the good news that the divorce papers had arrived on May 13, which was his birthday. "What a gift," he said. "If only you had stayed a few more days!"

I had written to my Aunty Alma in Nairobi, informing her of my return. Her response was an unexpected shock and very painful. She did not want me back. My mother was called to intercede on my behalf. Eventually, a compromise was reached, but it was just for a limited time. It was clear to me I had outgrown the nest; my own family wanted me to be independent or married. Neither my aunt nor mother approved of the situation I had managed to put myself into.

Unwanted

Three weeks later, I was happy to land in Nairobi once again. The air was clear, the landscape lush. No one was at the airport to receive me. A taxi took me back to the house in Westlands. I have no memory of the first days nor my reception by my aunt. My bed in the studio was an old safari camp bed loaned to me by Alma. One night the canvas ripped right in the middle. I fell onto the floor. My aunt was not interested in my comfort; no effort was made to replace the canvas cot. From then on, I slept on the floor. I was out of money and didn't have an income.

My effort to get a job in the Goethe Institute backfired. I was told I had been unreliable, leaving the job in the middle of the year, and they had hired a replacement. The University College of Nairobi had replaced me as well, and so I was stuck. Unimpressed with all this, I called up my African language students, my Indian Sikh students, and anyone whose phone number I still I had and offered them German classes at a discount in my home studio in Westlands. They came and so I had my classes back and some of my income. I offered a number of animal paintings to a gallery in town and made a few sales, which helped my financial situation a lot.

Hans heard that I was back in town and paid me a visit. His time in Nairobi was coming to a close, and he was returning to Germany at the end of the summer. That was the last time I saw him. The energy in Kenya had changed with Uhuru (independence). Africans finally once more became visible, and their fear of an exploitative white elite was very much in the minds of the old white settlers. My aunt and uncle had no desire to return to Europe. They wanted to live out their last years in beautiful Kenya, which they had come to love. There were quite a number of white settlers intent on staying. The Sorsbie Gallery, now that Alex was no longer the director, was handed over to a talented African painter, who ran it for a short period. Thereafter, the property was sold, and it became the Belgian Embassy. The waves of change were disconcerting for me. I keenly felt that I lived in a paradise and would soon have to leave this haven.

Waves of Change

The situation in Egypt was becoming worse, and my mother must have keenly felt the loss of Fouad Hafez, who died suddenly of a heart attack, and the loss of his protection. In her letters to me, she talked of thinking about retiring now that she had reached her sixties. She did not mention any grief or regret over the death of Fouad Hafez. She mentioned that Alma was looking out for properties in Westlands that might become available as English people left Kenya.

Alex wrote to me daily. Up to 10 pages of tightly-spaced script would arrive to tell me all the details of his humble life in Edinburgh. I think he felt trapped, with the burden of children, no wife, and no income. Any idea of an idyllic time in Greece, where we had planned to live a creative life free of responsibilities, had died with the cracked cylinder block of the Citroen station wagon.

One day an old friend of my aunt asked to speak to me. She actually drove to Westlands and came up to my studio. There she confided to me that Alma opened the letters Alex sent to me. As she could not understand some of the complex English he wrote, she phoned her friend repeatedly to ask what certain passages said. The lady thought it was a shameful thing to do and no longer wanted to be part of this. I thanked her, feeling rather shocked, and wrote to Alex asking him to seal his letters with Scotch tape so that she could not steam them open. A week later, Alma actually said to me, "How irritating that some people don't seem to trust me, having to seal their letters with tape." I never said anything to her, but since I had no safe place to keep all the letters, I burnt a certain amount rather than letting Alma read them.

Bush Baby and Other Wildlife

One day, one of my Asian students showed me a very sweet little creature he kept in his shirt breast pocket. It was a Galago bush baby, a tiny grey lemur with a lemon yellow belly and a fur as soft as a chinchilla. "Oh, I would love to have one of those," I said. He obliged, and two weeks later he brought

Bush baby

me two little bush babies. "Just feed them some milk with bread and bananas," he advised. I quickly figured out they were Insectivores and tried to find them beetles and moths in the late afternoons. I gave them the studio space as a home and being nocturnal, they slept all day and then leapt through the room at night, chasing each other and jumping enormous distances from a standing position. Both of them were wild, and I had as yet not tried to tame them.

Alex told me about the time when he first was in Nairobi, and was invited to the home of a wealthy man. An African servant admitted him to the house and asked him to step into the living room while he called the host. Alex was about to seat himself when a fully grown lion entered the room through the open French doors. Terrified, he backed away trying to escape, but the lion walked up to him, and rising to his hind legs, placed his huge paws on either side of his head. At this point the owner entered. "Dougal, what are you doing?" he said, and tapped the lion with a ruler. The huge beast dropped to the ground, and purring like a cat, rubbed his head against the Englishman's thigh. "Sorry, old chap," the Englishman said, "I forgot Dougal was inside. I bet he gave you a fright. Care for a drink?" "Yes," Alex responded. "Neat Scotch, no water, no ice."

So many people kept wild animals in Kenya, it was tempting to follow their example and yet it was not right. I met a woman who had two serval cats. They resemble cheetahs in some ways, with the same regal body structure. The added challenge is that they need to eat creatures with claws and fur, because they must have the extra nutrients from the consumption that a whole creature provides. The serval cat enchanted me, but there was no way I could keep a creature like that.

New Horizons

Alex had not yet found a job, and he asked me in one of his letters if I would join him if he left Britain. I suggested he try the USA, there might be more opportunities there than in Britain. He took my advice and had an offer to run a museum in Tennessee and another potential offer for a job as the Chairman of the Fine Arts Department at Lake Forest College. This college was near Chicago, and having spent two years in Toronto, Canada, he was not tempted by the climate, as the winters were very long. There was also the problem of the children; both were still very small. He could not expect his parents to continue to look after them.

At this point, he received a first letter from Ildiko. After their divorce in May, he had had no further connection with her. In her letter she deplored her situation, saying she was very unhappy and missing her children. She was now married to Jean, who had received the ambassador position in the Central African Republic, a small country in West Africa. She wanted desperately to see her children before they left for Africa. Was there any way Alex could bring them to her in Paris? Alex saw that this was a good opportunity. The children needed to see their mother, and he also hoped they maybe could work out some arrangement, as he was unable to take care of them, especially until he had another position and, hopefully, a wife. I had cheerfully agreed to take care of David and Fanny and even decided to forgo having children of my own. It did not seem very important to me to put more children into this world, especially as I wanted to be an artist. As Edgar Degas, the great French artist, said, "There is love and there is art; but I have only one heart."

I discussed much of this with my mother, who agreed and advised me not to join Alex until he had a new position and until I could see my future more clearly. Thus, Alex took the children to Paris, spent a couple of weeks in the French capital and allowed Jean to show him the city. Ildiko, he told me in a letter, was skin and bones, and had clearly suffered a lot, missing her children. They all got along very well for the time, and Jean had suggested Alex leave the children with Ildiko and himself in Paris until Christmas. They were not to leave for Africa and his new posting until January. Ildiko wished to see her parents in Canada. It would be an easy solution for everyone if she kept her children until then. If Alex accepted a job in the USA, he could easily come to Toronto and pick up the children. This proposal looked good and would help them all find an easier entry into their new lifestyles.

The one thing that made me uneasy, was that Ildiko had approached Alex asking, "Darling, do you still love me? I shall come back to you if you do." Alex told me that he responded in the negative, telling her she had hurt his feelings so deeply he could no longer go back to the way things had been between them before the divorce. He also reminded her that she now was married to Jean Francais and had forged new bonds. It seemed absurd to try to patch things at this stage.

I remember my unease and still wonder if this was all. I wrote to him saying that if he still loved her, he should make every effort to get her back. I assured him I would prefer that to marrying him, wrapped in an illusion that we would find happiness together. "You can't turn off feelings like you turn off the tap." It was quite clear to me that he had to be completely free from Ildiko emotionally if our relationship was to have any future. Ten years of marriage is a long time and could not be dissolved just like that. Now, many years later, I see I had every reason to be concerned, for I think he carried the thorn of rejection in his soul, and never really let it go, no matter what he told me. Every now and then, he would recite lines of a poem which ended with the line: "But oh, she left the thorn with me."

There was also another bit of something nasty. Ildiko had informed him, "This girl Ramona is not what she seems" and was, according to her spies in Kenya, involved with a whole lot of other men. "How could he be such a fool, not to see how vicious and evil that girl was!" This information at least showed me her true colors and that she was willing to destroy my reputation and the relationship between Alex and me. Was she not also willing to destroy her former husband, given half a chance? Knowing what I did at the time, I accepted her as someone selfish and destructive and untrustworthy. Alex and I had now been separated from May to November of that year, a long separation.

New Choices

I'd thought hard about my choices, trying not to be driven by some romantic idea of love and desire and happiness. I was 26 years old, and in the mirror, I saw the signs of aging. Alex's proposal was very sincere and passionate, and he was a sensitive and kind man. Why was I so reluctant? And he knew it, felt it, and tried to assure me in every letter he wrote. He, in the words of the "Godfather," tried to make me an offer I could not refuse. His long daily letters continued and slowly, gradually, I began to believe that we could find harmony and happiness together.

Alex had applied for the job of chairman of the Fine Arts department at Lake Forest College. An interview followed, and he was asked to come to London, where he met the college president, William Graham. They got on extremely well, joking and laughing, and at the conclusion of the interview, Alex said that he would like the job and would Mr. Graham let him know within the week, as he had other opportunities. On the train, traveling back to Edinburgh, he looked through some papers Bill Graham had given to him and discovered that President Graham was also an ordained minister of a church. He remembered their wild conversation and the many jokes and concluded he had been a bit too liberal and probably would not get the position. However, he had a good feeling about their meeting, and by the end of the week received a call confirming his appointment.

He now gave Ildiko permission to keep the children until after Christmas, when they had agreed to meet in Canada. There the children would be handed back to him, and he would bring them back to Lake Forest. After the divorce, he had received legal custody over both children from the Scottish court, as their mother had abandoned them.

The summertime in Europe is the African winter, and it was grey and a bit dreary during that period. I decided to throw my lot in with Alex, so my time in Nairobi was quickly coming to an end. My decision was final as I approached the US Consulate with the request for a visa. My reason for travel was for the express purpose of matrimony. There was the usual complex dance to get all the required documents. I decided to travel to Egypt first, to say goodbye to my mother, then to continue to Switzerland to visit a friend in Geneva, and finally to make a stop with friends in Reutlingen, Germany. I was to arrive in Chicago on the 24th of November.

6 America

Lake Forest

Meanwhile, Alex had left Europe and sent me first impressions of the town of Lake Forest. It was called a "village" and a big highway sign described it as an "oasis." Situated beside a huge lake called Lake Michigan, the area was very attractive and Alex felt I would approve. I remembered Fatima telling me I would marry a divorced man from the high north, who had two children. We would live beside a big water, but it was not the ocean! Clearly, her prediction was coming true.

Alex found his first accommodation in a dorm at the college. He needed a car to get around before he could rent an apartment. He had been instructed to come to the dining room at the college for his meals. When he came in on his first morning, still tired and jet-lagged, he was stunned to see the amazing size of the young students. They were huge hulks, extremely muscular and powerful. They loaded their trays with six fried eggs, a mountain of hash browns, toast, and other things. Then, having consumed all that, they went back for seconds. Only much later, he discovered these young men were not normal students but a football team practicing for their upcoming game. Everybody was very kind and helpful, and after a week, Alex found an apartment over what had been a stable. It was on the grounds of a very beautiful property beside the lake and it belonged to a millionaire. He must have felt very happy to find such a place for us.

He advised me not to bring my little bush baby (as I now only had one) to the New World, but I was already too attached to the little creature. I bought a special bag for the bush baby to travel in. However, the little animal was very smart and managed to get out during my flight to Egypt. I had not asked for any permission to take the little creature out of Kenya and so he was an illegal immigrant. The plane landed in Cairo and fortunately was almost empty. People left and I searched under seats, inside magazine racks, anywhere I could think of, but in vain. Eventually, the steward came and said, "Miss, what are you looking for. You must leave the plane now!" "Oh, I have this little animal and it got out," I explained. It was a stroke of good luck to see its tail sticking out beside a seat and I quickly grabbed it. The steward thought it was beautiful and wanted to stroke it. Bushy bit him instead and drew blood. I was grateful when I made it back to my mother's place without any further excitement. The bush baby was nocturnal which made it easy to travel during the daytime. However, once he woke up, he wanted out.

In Kenya, I had picked up an intestinal parasite. The doctor prescribed codeine, which was the only thing that would control it. I had lost so much weight, that I was a slim 96 lbs. While now visiting my friends in Germany, I ran out of these magic pills. A visit to the pharmacy brought the information that I could not get codeine without a medical prescription. What to do? My friends were from farming stock, from the Black Forest in southern Germany. Remembering a grandmother's prescription for parasites, they offered that, and I agreed to try it. A huge bag of autumn chestnuts was bought. My dinner consisted of roasted chestnuts and red wine, which was most delicious. Much to my amazement, I was completely healed by the next day and I remained well.

Probably due to the climate, the bush baby developed a cold and was sick. We took it to the vet, but she could not do much for him. I decided to give the little creature some time to recover fully. He hopped around my friend's art studio at night and had several restful days before I decided to fly off to Chicago. I sent a cable to Alex, who was patiently waiting for me to arrive, saying: "Bush baby sick, flight delayed to November 24. Love me, love my bush baby."

On the day of the flight, I bought a winter coat, as I had no need for such a garment in Africa. The flight left in the afternoon. By evening the bush baby was restlessly trying to fight its way out of its bag. The bag had little air vents, which I had cut into its sides. At intervals, little hairy arms or legs would stick out, to be withdrawn and then stuck out somewhere else. Fortunately, the people around me were asleep and did not see this strange event. Finally, the plane dropped down over the city of Chicago, invisible because of a dense cloud cover. And then I stepped out into a winter night at O'Hare airport in Chicago and my new life began. In those days the aircraft landed on the runway and the passengers walked to the terminal. An icy wind blew and snow drifted across the runway as I made my way down the metal steps of the aircraft and walked to the terminal. Neon lights illuminated tired faces. During customs check and passport check, no one even looked for a smuggled bush baby, much to my relief.

I rushed forward to the tall, slightly stooped figure of Alex, who had patiently waited for me for hours because the plane was late. His new car was no Citroen but a Chevy. He bundled my luggage into the car and then we drove through the evening along highways of several lanes and finally passed the sign that said "Lake Forest Oasis." A good sign! Although it was the middle of the night for me, we stopped in Lake Forest at the house of a charming woman named Ruth Winter, a new friend. She had a lovely, simple house and was a warm, loving person. Alex had stayed at her place when he first came to Lake Forest, and because she was very keen to meet me, he had agreed to bring me by after my arrival. Ruth was slender with a ready smile and she was soon was holding the bush baby in her hand. We eventually said goodbye and drove to the house by the lake and the small apartment that was to be our home for the next six months.

Living in Sin

Walking up a steep flight of stairs, we entered the kitchen and an attached living room. Two bedrooms completed the place. The bush baby was liberated from its confinement and it roamed throughout the night through the new spaces, investigating every nook and cranny. It preferred the last bedroom, which became its space. I remember a very neat kitchen space and dishes neatly placed in a dish rack from Alex's last meal. I do not recall much from my first days in the USA. I was tired from my journey, and being catapulted into winter was somewhat of a shock. There was a great silence all about, and it snowed almost daily. Alex was very attentive and actually brought me my breakfast in bed.

Each day he left to teach at Lake Forest College and returned at one pm for lunch. Thoughtfully, he had purchased an easel and paints for me so that I could amuse myself during his absence. I did not paint right away. Instead, I ventured outside and investigated my new environment, walking to the lake behind the house. The lake was a huge body of water of deepest blue lying at the base of a steep bluff. The mansions on top of the bluff obviously belonged to very wealthy people. The center of Lake Forest had a charming market square with little shops around it. It took me only a twenty-minute walk to get there.

Driving

In Nairobi, Alex had taught me how to drive his Citroen station wagon, and I had acquired a driving permit in Cairo. When Alex let me drive the Chevy, however, I felt totally insecure, as the bench seat did not suit my short stature. I could not look over the hood properly and driving this vehicle felt like trying to steer an ungainly mattress. As a consequence, I did not drive in the States for the first few years. This meant that Alex and I did all our shopping together, and my movements were somewhat limited.

As I began to get a picture of my new environment, I also became intimidated. All was vast: the lake, the highways, the city of Chicago, the skyscrapers. Much was a man-made environment and incredibly ugly. As the winter deepened, it became very cold and storms were frequent. To my amazement, even the lake froze and began to resemble the Arctic. The ice broke during storms and began to build itself up into icebergs or melted enough so that patches of ice resembled rounded lotus leaves. They would clank together like ice cubes in a whiskey glass, making a beautiful tinkling sound.

On the weekends, we would venture into the big city of Chicago. I really admired Alex's courage as he drove into the fast-paced traffic and many-laned highways and somehow found his way to where he wanted to go. We discovered the Art Institute of Chicago, the Field Museum, galleries, libraries, jazz clubs, stores, restaurants, and the Opera. Alex happened to be an opera buff, and one of his first purchases was a stereo system so he could listen to his records. Thus, we got to know each other and to share what we enjoyed. Slowly, I began to trust my new environment and to open myself to the people I met. They were the most charming Americans, mostly very wealthy, and all of an older vintage. They invited us for dinners, for Thanksgiving, for Christmas Day, to the opera, to the Art Institute of Chicago, and to big events of all kinds. I guess it was mostly because Alex was a charming and entertaining man. They referred to him as "a good mixer."

To me, those motherly women were kind and supportive. Perhaps more than I can imagine, they understood the huge step I had taken to leave all I knew behind me to join my future husband. Years later, I picked up a little enameled box standing on my dresser. Alex had given this to me as a present in Nairobi. It came from Russia and depicted a young man leaving a palace-like building with a spade in his hand. A young woman followed him as he ventured out into the unknown. The symbolic meaning declared itself to me only then, thirty years later.

The faculty of the college were initially less appealing. When Alex introduced me, one couple turned to him with a frown and asked why he was dating a student, as this was not appropriate for a faculty member. Alex smiled and said, "But this is Ramona, my fiancée. She has just arrived from Africa." Their faces registered huge surprise. I suppose I did not meet their expectations. To wear boots was a novelty. I guess the Europeans were ahead at that stage since women there were wearing high boots, tights, short smocks, loose open hair, and lots of eye makeup. These were still the days when women in America wore their hair in tight curls, female students were not allowed to wear anything but skirts in the freezing temperatures of the Chicago winter, and a professor had to wear a tie to lecture.

In order to get married, we needed to get an official medical clearance declaring that we did not have venereal disease. I used this opportunity to ask the doctor for a birth control method. In Europe, such a protection was readily available, but not alas, in the USA. I was informed I could apply for this only once I was officially married, and I had to bring my marriage certificate as proof.

Our other mistake was in assuming that it was all right for a couple to live together in an unmarried state. We were cheerfully sharing an apartment. At a party, the president of the college pulled me aside and asked when we were going to tie the knot. I said that such a serious step as marriage was not something I was going to hurry into and that I would only make that decision once I felt secure and ready. At this point, he told me it was not appropriate in the USA to "live in open sin." Meanwhile, he had his hand on my shoulder and was bending down to kiss me. I ducked out of this, but it was not the first nor the last time that married faculty member made an open pass at me.

Our favorite friend at the time was the first black professor Lake Forest College had hired. Nathan Williams was actually mixed race and had told Alex, "All my white blood is Jewish." Being a graduate from Harvard, he was refreshingly irreverent and outspoken. Thus, he and Alex got on together like old buddies. I think Nathan enjoyed educating Alex about the United States. Alex confessed he had not even noticed that Nathan was not white, as he did not look like an African or the people, he had become used to in Kenya.

Obstacles Galore

Alex asked me if now was the right moment to go through a civil marriage. December had come, and at the end of the month, he was flying to Toronto, to visit his former in-laws and to confer with Ildiko and Jean about the fate of his two children. We were hardly ready to rent a bigger space and to take two children into our lives. He had already looked at the schools and found them to be very inflexible about accepting two foreign children in mid-year. There were more questions than answers. We looked at our health certificates only to discover they had become invalid after three weeks. We would have to be tested for venereal diseases all over again. We decided to wait longer with the marriage until our lives were more stable and we knew what we were doing.

As a start, Alex began to ask around about houses. It turned out there were almost no houses to rent. People in the US owned their homes, and Lake Forest was a wealthy place. We would have to think about buying a place in a small town where most people were unthinkably rich. The college had some rentals in what was called the Faculty Circle on campus. All of these were taken by heads of departments. Then we discovered most faculty lived elsewhere, not in Lake Forest, which was too expensive. We would have to try the small neighboring towns like Lake Bluff, Highwood, or Highland Park. Lake Bluff was very small, a village really. Highwood was mostly Italian and difficult to get into. Highland Park was a mostly Jewish community, a twenty-minute drive away. We would need to buy a car I could drive, something small. Somewhat overwhelmed with all the rising obstacles, we threw up our hands and decided to do nothing as yet.

Alex in Lake Forest, 1965-66

The winter was fascinating, and I had never experienced anything like it. The snow would fall until the staircase disappeared in high snowdrifts and Alex would have to shovel it clean first thing in the morning. Snowplows came by daily, clearing roads and driveways. We had to drive into Chicago to buy winter clothes for me. The bush baby now slept wrapped in my cashmere shawl during the day. I started to paint, first self-portraits, then abstractions. Alex, fortunately, was not very busy at this point, so we were able to spend time together. We walked along Lake Michigan on many afternoons. Alex took pictures of the growing icebergs, the trees completely covered in ice crystals, and the mounds of snow on the beach that were sometimes so high it was impossible to cross through them. I remember sinking up to my hips into the snow and how difficult it was to crawl out.

On Sundays, we drove to the city. There were wonderful films shown in Chicago, as well as jazz in the Old Town area. Usually, we had lunch in a French restaurant and then caught a movie or a concert or saw the latest exhibition at the Art Institute. Alex was a font of information, and with hindsight, I now appreciate how much he taught me about food, wine, film, jazz, and photography. He showed me what I had not learned about painting in art school. He provided me with technical knowledge of how to paint and how to use painting mediums. As an art historian, he enlightened me about the Italian Renaissance, Dutch still life paintings, and the Impressionists. He was the first to teach American Art at a small liberal arts college, the first to teach about women in the arts. Chicago was famous for its architecture, and Alex was delighted to introduce me to the world of skyscrapers. He was very careful not to interfere in my artistic vision or in how I expressed myself. He never gave a critique to guide me. I had to learn by looking.

He was also a lover of music and poetry and a wonderful singer, full of joy and love for life and with an abundance of energy. He did not suffer fools gladly. He could get bored and irritated or make one joke after another. His lectures, of which I witnessed too few, were a hoot. People waited for the jokes and wit to emerge. A colleague commented after one of Alex's lectures that it had been "too funny to be scholarly." That comment had the feeling of jealousy embedded in it.

The students voted with their feet in attending classes and soon Alex had huge classes in art history. The Art Department began to grow. He was a good administrator and he began to build up the slide library and to choose faculty for the new courses. He always worked with the strengths of his teachers, placing them in situations in which they could shine. When the Christmas holidays came, he left for Toronto, Canada. I spent my lonely hours painting a self-portrait and a first really sweet abstraction. The time alone gave me a chance to reflect on our suitability and to examine my heart and soul. I remember this time as being very cold and dark and I remember that I missed him.

He returned without the children, as I had expected. There had been long discussions between the parents, the Hungarian grandparents, and Ildiko's husband Jean, now a newly established French Ambassador. In June he would start his new post in La Republique Centrafricaine, on the West coast of Africa. There would be a house with a swimming pool, servants, a chauffeur-driven limo, a cook and a governess to teach the children. The request from Ildiko was that the children remain with her for that first year. On the face of it, it made sense and seemed rational.

David Mitchell would turn seven the following August, and Alex wanted his son to be brought up in his own language and culture. They parted with a clear understanding, that Alex expected his firstborn to join him in the United States in six months' time. I had a sour taste in my mouth but said nothing. I felt this was all too slick and convenient to be real. It was now January and a few days later a call came from Scotland with the news that Alex's father had just died of a heart attack. Alex had repeatedly told me he feared his father had not long left to live. This news left him with a great dilemma. There was no way he could go back to Britain just now; no way he could support his mother over the difficult time ahead. His courses at the college had started and he was obliged to remain here. I looked at this whole turmoil with mixed feelings. It seemed so unfair to me how fate dished out one problem after another. Alex did not deserve so much misery.

Mystery

As the days wore on, Alex cried more and more. I held his shaking body as he sobbed and sobbed for the loss of a father he had loved deeply and for his poor mother. The worst for him, I think, was the feeling of not being able to help, of being so far away and unable to grieve with his family. I went down the snowy outer staircase and walked through the thick, deep snow towards the lake. It was almost evening, and I felt there had been enough pain and misery for one day. "Enough, enough," I said to myself. "God, this is not fair. Stop the pain." To my huge surprise, I heard the voice of Alastair Ferrier Mitchell. The voice of Alex's father! "Marry my son. If you care for him, marry him." "What, what is that, a voice, Alex's father?" I did not expect an answer. I was deluded, imagining things, and this was a crazy illusion. "Yes," the voice said, "Marry him."

I burst into tears. I howled and covered my mouth. Was this even possible? A dead man was telling me from the other side that I should marry his son. A great calm and stillness began to spread through me like a warm balm. The snow was real; the voice was real. Swaying, I stood in the darkening evening, the bare-branched trees surrounding me, with a feeling of great peace in my soul and with profound gratitude for what had just happened. There is more to the world than we know; there are more realities than we believe in. Slowly, I made my way back into the house. I found Alex and hugged him, just held him. I never told him what had happened.

Later, we learned that hundreds and hundreds of people came to the memorial service in Scotland. It seems his father had a long record of kindness, and the people of Edinburgh came out in droves to honor him. There was no room for them all in the church, and they formed long lines outside the door, all the way down the street.

The Wedding Dress

Our marriage was set for January 24. Repeatedly, we went into Chicago and visited one store after another in search of a wedding dress for me. I was a petite, weighing 96 pounds. There seemed to be no small dresses to be found. We went to more and more exclusive and expensive stores without results. In the end, I decided on an elegant black cocktail dress. Again, I did not realize what a stir this would cause. For as long as six years later, people at the college were still talking about my inappropriate wedding attire. At the time, I was happy with my elegant dress; plus, there was no other choice available. Perhaps out of gratitude that we had finally set a date, the president of Lake Forest College and his wife Doris offered their house for the wedding ceremony. I had only one request—to make it as simple as possible.

On the appointed day, a huge storm rolled into the state and covered every blade of grass, every branch on a tree, every car, house, in short, everything, with a thick layer of ice. We awoke to a world covered in a glittering mantle of rainbow sparkling ice. It was utterly magical, a glass world that tinkled and sparkled in red, blue, and yellow colors. Soon huge branches broke under the weight of the ice, power lines were downed and the electricity went out. In fact, we were without electricity for many days.

That afternoon, wearing heavy boots, a cocktail dress under a coat, and a shawl wrapped around my head, we descended the steps and found the car covered with so much ice it was impossible to open the doors. Alex got buckets filled with water, which we poured over the car until the ice sheet fell off. Carefully, we drove on the unaccustomed glassy surface of the roads and arrived at the home of the president. Upon entering, I noticed all the open archways had blankets tacked over the openings to keep out the cold. The living room was illuminated by a roaring fire and some candles. It was here, surrounded by people I had barely met, that we exchanged our vows. There was a little wedding cake and beautiful bottles of champagne, gifted by our landlord, who happened to be one of the richest men in America. The guests were all lovely people and very kind. Their wedding gifts were touching, especially considering that they did not know me. I used the gifts, so thoughtfully chosen, for many years in gratitude.

Married Life

After the ceremony, we left with Nathan Williams, our best man, and I made dinner in our little rustic kitchen. The men were drinking Scotch and having a lively conversation when there was suddenly an enormous crash in the pantry. Opening the door, I saw the floor-to-ceiling shelves, which held pots and pans, crocks and vases, had collapsed, and the broken glasses were sparkling on the floor. Alex suggested that we should just shut the door and cope with the mess tomorrow. Thus, started my married life!

On weekends, when he was not teaching at the college, Alex brought me breakfast in bed, often scrambled eggs, croissants, caviar, and champagne. His talents surprised me. He could cook a number of Scottish dishes, all of them very tasty. He could recite poetry by the yard, imitate "Hell and Brimstone" preachers, and sing like a bird. Because he had acted on the stage as an amateur actor, he could entertain me with impersonations of Russians, Cockneys, French writers, hysterical prima donnas, African cooks, and alas, his disturbed Hungarian ex-wife. I screamed with laughter, which encouraged the performances. He had wit and a most amusing assortment of sayings, limericks, and dirty jokes. His performances also encouraged me to tell him stories from my life, and thus we got to know each other. His great love was music and art. He was an opera buff and could sing whole arias and imitate various famous singers. In retrospect, I have to say of him, that he was far more than I had expected. There was never a dull moment, and he was extremely sensitive to my needs. He realized that he had left me alone and to my own devices much of the day and that he had to rely on my being able to be self-sufficient. He made a point of coming home for lunch in the middle of the day.

The outside world was frozen, inhospitable and since I knew no one, not worth venturing into. However, Alex had a beautiful camera and so I found myself walking to the shores of Lake Michigan, just steps from the apartment in distance, able to take photos of this extraordinary world of ice floes, snowdrifts and the lake in all its changing moods and hues. At first, I did not paint this world, but within a few months, the first impressions began to find their way into my abstractions. I painted in the kitchen, which was spacious. The linoleum floor had a pattern of colored dots and any paint drips just disappeared into the general design.

Of course, there were faculty parties galore. I discovered to my surprise that Americans of that generation were very fond of drinks. This being the sixties, people seemed to be very liberated, at least to me. In contrast to professors in Europe, people here were outspoken and willing to take risks. Once in Kassel, I had been invited to a dinner with professors from the university. To my horror, the entire evening was spent discussing the safe subjects of the varieties of toothpaste and toothbrushes. In Lake Forest, the faculty at that time was amusing, wild, and excited about research, teaching, and creativity. I was very shy at first and kept my distance.

Alex, in contrast, instantly joined into everything and anything. One of his first lectures I attended was a full house. Even before he began to speak, I could feel the anticipation of the audience and then he managed to say such amusing things that everyone was waiting for the next laugh. In time, however, he realized that this was not making him popular with the faculty. One evening, the head of some department phoned and accused him of "empire building." Jealousy arose quickly and his success at building up the Fine Arts Department was felt as a threat. The number of students attending lectures in Art History increased dramatically and the dean and the president of the college voiced their approval. However, right from the start, there was conflict within the department, as faculty began to sense the ability of their new head of the Fine Art Department and felt threatened. Alex had been hired from abroad because the administration had been unable to find anyone capable of building up their Fine Art Department in the US. He was hired as a professor of art history for one year, and then would become chairman after proving himself. He had a mission to accomplish and was ambitious to succeed.

The winter seemed endless. We planned to have a honeymoon in Mexico in the summer. I actually bought Spanish tapes and spent many an hour learning Spanish. Friends told us about Zihuantanejo, a small village by the ocean in Mexico. We planned to go there.

First House

The change from winter to summer was sudden in the Midwest. From one day to the next, the climate changed. We had a tiny little balcony overlooking a ravine with trees and the lake beyond. I remember the sudden warmth and sitting on the balcony listening to Scottish ballads. There was magic in the air and the unaccustomed warmth and the sudden onset of green foliage bursting out everywhere made that afternoon imprint itself in my memory. Perhaps because the winter was suddenly over, perhaps because I was waiting for Alex, I became aware of our deepening love and felt profoundly happy. He came home and told me he had found a house for us. "A house?" I said in disbelief. I was a gypsy at heart; a house was not in my imagination at that point.

We drove to the house, a grey two-story structure inside a long strip of property and like all houses in Lake Forest, surrounded by forest. Properties had no fences, and everything looked wide open. The house was rented to an artist and his wife. Expecting their second child, they were now considering a move to a bigger place. I did not like the house, especially when I stepped inside it. The floor in the small living room had been painted black, so had a floor to ceiling built-in bookshelf. The cooking space was a galley kitchen, basically, a hallway transformed into a kitchen. A stairway led upstairs to two bedrooms and a smaller room. The bathroom was tiny. The house was old and had been built before people had indoor plumbing. There was a big attic and a basement. Alex assured me that we could transform it into a very livable house, something he had done several times already.

We rented the house for $140 a month and within three weeks we had transformed it. The black fir-wood floors had been sanded and sealed. The walls were painted and, in the living, and dining room, the ceilings were painted a slate blue color. The effect was that it lifted the ceilings and made them high so that the rooms gave the impression of being very spacious. The windows had been very badly painted and were dirty. We worked every day from morning till nightfall to complete the task of cleaning them. As we didn't have furniture, we had to acquire some. The stores in Chicago were so expensive, that we gave up. In spite of asking several people, no one seemed to have an answer for us. Then we discovered the Unpainted Furniture Store. It was a bit of a puzzle to see the same type of furniture later in the houses of people we had asked for help. Why had they not enlightened us? With some second-hand furniture we bought from the prior renters, our little place became our home. The Sears bed we ordered failed to arrive in time and we had to buy a frame and mattress somewhere else. Then for a full month Sears failed to pick up the bed we had canceled!

For the first time since my childhood, I now lived in a private house. My mother's place in Cairo was a hotel, and so I had never felt actual privacy. The bush baby too loved its new space and raced through the rooms at top speed, jumping amazing distances much like a kangaroo. Our landlord was retired. His wife, Eileen M., worked at the college. The drive to the college was five minutes, an ideal distance. The house was a block from Lake Michigan, which meant it was cool in the summer because of the proximity of the large body of water. I remembered the prediction of Fatima "You will live beside a large body of water, but it is not the ocean." I could walk to the lake anytime, and often during the hot August months I swam in the refreshing coldness of the sky-blue water. Every other day I practiced yoga. Now that I had a garden, I brought my blanket into the shade of the huge old maples surrounding the lawn. From upstairs Alex could see our other neighbor peering through the hedge to see me standing on my head in a bikini. "I hope he had a thrill!" he told me later.

When July rolled around, we decided to drive to Mexico. Everyone told us we could do it in three days. We did not realize that Americans covered the huge distances of their country by driving relentless extended hours almost nonstop for days. The drive to Mexico City took us a week instead of three days. Since I could not drive, Alex did all the driving and we drove no more than five hours a day. Also, we encountered car trouble when we reached Arkansas. The mechanic who worked on the vehicle said: "I love working on transmissions, but the funny thing is, the car only goes backward, not forwards." Alex looked at the manual with the mechanic and worked out why the car only went backward. Thereafter we were back on the road, heading south. In San Antonio, Texas, we had to become members of a club in order to get a bottle of beer. It was a very dry state! The motel cost us $5. Ah, those were the days!

Mexico

On arrival in Mexico City, we gave up driving. Already the traffic was too much to handle. I got a bladder infection and was uncomfortable in the sudden cold of the high mountain regions we had travelled through. Alex suggested I lie in a hot bath and drink cranberry juice. The next morning, all symptoms were gone.

Alex continued to surprise me. He was psychic, but he failed to trust his inner knowing. He would insist he knew something and consequently did not listen to anyone else. I now know from carefully observed incidents that I am capable of having the right answers, but Alex for some obscure reason did not trust me and did not listen to me. This caused a barrier between us...was it because he had to be bigger, or better, or in charge? Was it because a man cannot listen to a woman?

Alex found the Mexican art in the museum in Mexico City too disturbing to look at. Something about the sculptures and images was deeply cruel and spoke of suffering. Therefore, I wandered through the exhibitions alone and emerged into the bright, sunlit exterior, where he was waiting beside a great disk, an Aztec calendar. He did not like the Aztec pyramids or other structures. So, we drove south. Everywhere the villagers we saw were sad, depressed people who looked miserable and exceedingly poor.

Darkness was already falling, when, following a bus, we encountered a river. The bus drove through the river and up the opposite bank. Alex stopped, and then decided to risk the trip through the river. The water was quite deep and he was tired and unsure. However, we emerged on the opposite shore all in one piece. This was Zihuantanejo, the small Mexican village that our friends had told us about. We stopped at the only hotel we saw and got a room. The donkeys brayed and the dogs barked all night through.

"I am leaving," Alex said, "This is awful." Our friends had talked of a hotel by the ocean, and this was not it. I left him sitting and drinking his coffee and walked over a hill to the ocean side. No sooner was I at the top of the hill than I saw the cottages on the slope and the main building of the hotel we had missed last night. I am sure I was disheveled looking and red in the face with exertion when I walked into the lobby. A European-looking man was behind the desk. His German accent was instantly recognizable. I introduced myself and told him my husband was an art historian. He enthusiastically told me that he too was an art historian. We could get a hillside cottage at a reduced rate, all meals included, and he would be delighted to have us here on our honeymoon. I had solved our problem.

I crossed back over the hill, down to the jungle and the village hotel, and brought Alex the good news. Then we made our way to the beach. The German owner was charming and was charmed by Alex. He had a beautiful German girlfriend who knew how to swim the high and dangerous waves of their little bay. We joined them for a drink before being guided to our cottage. Then to my huge surprise, Alex asked me what I thought of that "nice man!" Instantly, it clicked in my mind. He was too old, he was too slick, he was a Nazi. Had I not been told many times how many of these criminals managed to escape to South America and set up hotels there or other businesses? Still, I felt shocked, unwilling to believe, and yet I knew Alex had instantly recognized something I had been unwilling to see. Having been in the military, Alex recognized the unmistakable style of a career officer. He also trapped the so-called art historian into making a major mistake. His knowledge of art was strictly limited and it was apparent he was lying. He had obviously not studied art history.

Zihuatanejo

Our time in Zihuatanejo was charmed. The beach was a beautiful bay with huge waves rolling in. By afternoon the tide set in, and the ocean became so rough I avoided swimming. The beautiful blond German woman was far out flowing over the waves like a mermaid. It was magical to watch her as she moved with the ease of a fish. We tested out all sorts of alcoholic fruit drinks brought to us on the beach by a smiling waiter and joined the French, Portuguese and English guests on a shady veranda for meals.

Then alas, Montezuma's revenge caught up with us. We had brought some medication with us but it proved to be totally useless. After three days of misery, we drove to a pharmacy in the village. The gentle Mayan pharmacist handed us two packages and smiling, assured us we would be better by morning. And, so we were. The pills worked like magic.

Our stay of ten days was soon over. Alex looked much better for his vacation and much slimmer, thanks to Montezuma. We drove back past Mexico City and to a mountain town well known as a mining area for precious metals, mostly silver. We bought a bracelet and enjoyed the special architecture and the hotel filled with American tourists. My favorite place though was a magical Mexican village with ancient ruins nearby. The hotel there was so different from anything I had ever seen. Set beside a sky-blue lagoon, it had meandering water channels containing caves that were home to colorful fish. I could drift through this network of channels at my heart's content. Much later I read that such types of places were created by the Maya and were found in many places.

We were heading back when our car broke down on the highway. Fortunately, a guardian angel appeared. A man had seen the event, and speaking perfect English, came to our rescue. He made sure the mechanic understood and completed the repair quickly. Our return journey took just three days. We had learned to drive the American way; driving almost nonstop was the only method.

Lake Forest was hot and humid. A young student, Carol, had been in our house during our absence to look after the bush baby. Two days after our return a cop showed up in the driveway. "Are you the person who reported the attempted rape?" he asked me. "What happened?" I asked and explained who I was. The story emerged that Carol had been at a party and had flirted with a young man and then invited him to come to the house. Meanwhile, another girl was in the other bedroom, sleeping there at Carol's invitation. While Carol took her time getting back, the amorous young man arrived at the house and believing the sleeping girl to be Carol, silently undressed and slipped in beside her. Nothing happened beyond that, but the girl called the cops, and the young man ran away.

Loss

I had chosen the smallest upstairs bedroom as a studio and set up my easel. Meanwhile, Alex was ready to have his possessions in Edinburgh shipped to the US. Instead of the crates of books, drawings and paintings, a notice arrived telling him some hooligans had set the storage place on fire, and all his crates had been burned. Only one painting packed inside a wooden crate had survived. Could someone in the family confirm that this was Alex's property? His mother Lizzie went to the burnt-out building and confirmed the painting in question was a full-length portrait of Ildiko, his ex-wife. Thereafter Alex jokingly said Ildiko was indestructible. He offered her the painting and had it shipped to her in Paris. She had agreed to pay for the shipping costs, but she never did.

Losing his book collection and all his best drawings and paintings was a blow for Alex. It was as if his whole past was now wiped out. I reminded him what my Aunt Alma, who was good at laying Tarot cards, had told me in Nairobi. She laid a card she interpreted as "loss of valued property through theft or fire." This pertained to Alex. Neither of us had made much of it until this happened.

Betrayal

The new semester began at the college and since Alex had now been there for a full year, he assumed the position of Chairman of the Fine Arts Department. However, the raise the president had promised in London was not forthcoming. The president claimed he did not remember such a promise. Alex responded by saying he would bring the letter he had written to me, detailing the terms of the agreement he had made in London. A weekend went past. Alex was depressed and very angry at the betrayal and ungentlemanly behavior. He had not expected to be treated this way.

On Monday, he received a note from the president. He informed him that they had found some money and were willing to pay him the requested amount. Alex did not forget this betrayal; it soured his enthusiasm and he no longer trusted the integrity of the president of the college. It makes life more difficult if one is unable to trust people or their word. As for me, I began to feel uneasy with many of Alex's colleagues. As a result, Alex and I began to cling together much more than we might have otherwise. I recall a group of women asking me to go out for lunch with the "girls." It was a well-meant suggestion. I turned them down, saying I preferred to have lunch with my husband. Some women who became friends much later told me they had seen me as someone unapproachable.

I had completed a number of paintings and applied to juried shows in Chicago. This required my sending in a few slides with a fee. I did not expect to be selected, but I was, and the following weekend we ventured forth to the big city to deliver the selected painting. Alex had put a sales price on the work, and I was shocked at the high price. However, as Alex had claimed, if the price was too low, people did not trust the work, if it was just right, they respected the quality. Thus, to my enormous surprise, I sold my first painting in the US.

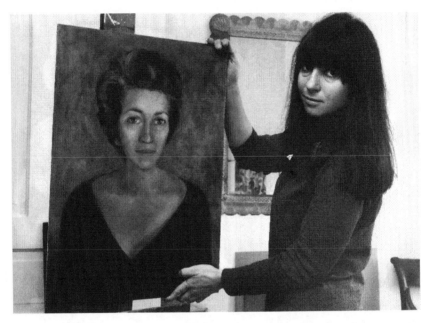

Portrait of the Lake Forest College president's wife, 1966

The autumn in the Midwest is the most beautiful time of the year there. The weather is mild and cool at night, but the most pleasant time is during the day, neither humid nor mosquito-infested, just mellow and beautiful. Slowly, the frosty nights begin to turn the leaves from green to golden, then to orange, and eventually to fiery red. The Indian summer, as it is called, mostly lasts three weeks. Then the honking geese flying south begin to be heard as they leave the area, and the lake becomes rough, as the weather becomes colder. The foliage of the many trees slowly begins its descent, falling and spinning through the air. The sky I remember as being a brilliant, deep blue and cloudless. This very special season of the year made me love the Midwest, and I spent hours photographing the birds, changing leaves, mushrooms, and brooks that reflected the splendor of autumn color. I was very aware of the sudden onset of the cold. There was a deeply felt regret that I could not fly south like the birds but instead was forced to stay.

We made more friends now, and often were invited to very lively parties. As time went on, I settled into this new life and marriage and felt more at ease. It was about this time Alex took me to a film called "The Pawnbroker." It was a powerful and heart-wrenching film, and when we left the cinema, I turned to Alex and burst into tears. There we stood in the middle of a busy street of Chicago, with me sobbing away. I felt my heart had finally opened and I was able to feel fully again. I think Alex was startled and also a bit embarrassed at what people would think, as we stood there. I tried to explain to him in the car how I had been unable for so long to feel anything but a numbness and total hopelessness, when I should have been feeling compassion, pain, sadness, etc. There was a sensation of huge relief that I had been able to open up. I saw it as a healing.

The winter in the Chicago area is very long and tedious. By February, it felt as if nothing would ever change and one was stuck in a never-ending ice age. The news from my mother in Egypt was not good. My mother feared another war and began to look for a safer place. As luck would have it, my Aunt Alma found a house for sale across the street from her own property in Westlands, Nairobi, and my mother was able to purchase it. The move to East Africa was difficult and treacherous. Only much, much later, did I find out how bad it had been. My mother would also, as Fatima had predicted, sell her little hotel in Cairo, and she stayed in Kenya until her death in 1990.

With the approach of summer, Ildiko wrote suggesting a visit and time for Alex to be with his children. Our arrangement that David join his father at this stage was not mentioned. She wanted to take Jean to Hungary to show him where she had grown up, followed by a visit to Canada to see her parents. They would send the children to us for the summer and pick them up in Illinois on their way back to France after the Canada visit. This was not the plan they had agreed to and Alex was puzzled, but held back his opinion for now. We made a bedroom ready for the small people. The children would fly from Paris to New York alone, and Alex would meet them at the airport there, and then fly with them to Illinois.

At the appointed day, Alex drove himself to O'Hare Airport and set off for New York to meet the children. I settled down to do some sewing. I still couldn't find clothes that fit me and so was forced to make my own. Alex had bought me a second-hand Swiss sewing machine, which was fabulous, and I was learning how to sew many different things. I did very well too, learning by trial and error. I recall sitting there and working and by midnight wondering if they would ever come. At around one in the morning Alex drove in with two exhausted, white-faced children. I packed them into bed as fast as I could and gave them a glass of warm milk with honey to calm tangled nerves. The children had disembarked from the plane, each one with a large white paper taped to the chest, stating the name and address in the USA. They also had been taught to say in heavily accented English "My father is called Professor Alex F. Michell. He lives in Lac Foret, Illinois."

Reunion with David and Fanny

The first thing I noticed about the children was that they were unkempt and dirty. David was black behind his ears and clearly his hair had not seen shampoo in a long time. Fanny had bands of dirt around her neck. Both chewed off their fingernails because the governess did not bother to cut them. Then there was the little matter of breakfast. It seemed they were not used to receiving anything to eat in the morning. I took them to the Lake Forest beach, played with them, and then took them to the woods and a parade in Lake Bluff. They seemed bored and indifferent to almost everything.

After discussing the situation, we decided to take them to the seashore in Florida. We packed our car and set off, Alex doing all the driving. Through a connection with one of his students, Alex had managed to rent a beach house in Clearwater, Florida. It was a very humble little shack and too small. A phone call and complaints got us better accommodations. Thus, we spent four weeks by the ocean. As long as one looked out to sea it was beautiful, but on the shore, there was an ugly assortment of beach shacks belonging to people of humble means, mostly of Greek origin. Florida offered much entertainment, from Busch Gardens to Water World with jumping dolphins to swamps and glass bottom boats showing the fish in the water below. We took many of these side trips to entertain the children.

Fanny was five years old and deeply disturbed. Her mother had told her she would be seeing her father, whom she did not remember. Then, to add insult to injury, that she was so lucky as to have two Mommies, I being her second mother. That did not sit well with the child. Basically, she was among strangers. She spoke very little English, as the language with which she was most familiar was French. Alex spent hours with her in an effort to reconnect.

David had no such problems. He remembered his father and quickly became very content to be in his company. At six in the morning, he would sneak into our bedroom and set up his little toy soldiers on the bed spread. He developed a fair fascination with my long black hair and would sit there combing his fingers through it. After a week, the children were used to us and everyone began to relax. A morning of painting transformed Fanny into a work of art. She painted her entire body in glorious colors and looked very funny. Both children understood the art of conning their father into buying them toy cars, Barbie dolls, and other toys as well as swimsuits and shoes. Fanny was particularly clever at getting her way. It seems she was used to eating in front of a TV, so lunch times became battles. Eventually, Alex gave in as there was no point in alienating Fanny when she was there for such a brief time.

Washington

Alex had painted a very successful portrait of Congressman McClory of Lake Bluff during the spring, and as a consequence we were now invited to Washington to see the painting in the congressman's office. I don't think we realized what a long drive we were in for. When we finally arrived in Washington D.C., we were offered a huge hotel suite with a swimming pool on the rooftop. Washington was extremely humid and so the pool was a great distraction for the children. We were also invited to see the White House and had lunch at the Pentagon. As usual, Fanny did not like her food. The Congressman would have none of it and fed the little blond princess with his own hands. She ate everything. I began to appreciate the power of persuasion as demonstrated and learned to use it.

Once we returned to Lake Forest, we booked a nice hotel room on Lake Michigan for Ildiko and Jean, who arrived within

Alex presenting a portrait to Congressman
Robert McClory in Washington, D.C., 1966

Alex, Congressman Robert McClory, Ramona,
David and Fanny Mitchell, 1966

days from Canada. Our little house in the woods must have
seemed charming to Ildiko, as she was clearly jealous. I did my
best to provide good meals and made a wiener schnitzel for
their arrival. Fanny and David both began to complain loudly,
"I don't like this, I want something different." they both cried.
"But darling, this is your favorite. This is what Mummy makes for
you on special days. You love this." Ildiko cooed. The power of

persuasion again won the day. Both children ate without further complaint.

It became clear to David that he would soon leave with his mother and Jean and he orchestrated a drama hard-to-beat. He hid himself; he hid his clothes when his mother tried to pack a suitcase, sulked, cried, and upset everyone. Ildiko started sobbing in the living room and Jean disappeared into the garden. I found David in the back garden and took him down the road to the beach. I told him that his father wanted him to be here with us and asked him to be patient, please! We would set everything in motion to unite him with his father. Slowly, I calmed him down. David seemed so mature and capable of understanding what I told him that I thought he had understood.

Ildiko was red-eyed and still sobbing when we returned to the house. Alex was conversing with Jean, and later we had an in-depth discussion about the children. Alex wanted his son to be brought up as a Scot and wanted him to come and live here and to go to school here. Ildiko rolled her eyes and threatened that she would kill herself. I suggested reading their palms. I still have the palm prints and looking back over the many years that passed, I read them very accurately. I saw that Ildiko would have more children and eventually would have her uterus removed and have breast cancer, as well as diabetes. Later that night, Alex told me that Ildiko had cried when she saw her old china plates and cups, her cooking pots and household things she left behind when she left Nairobi to join Jean in France.

The renewed threat of separation from his father upset David greatly, and all the adults saw how desperately the child wanted to be with his father. It was heartbreaking. Fanny showed no attachment, but then she was also much younger. In my opinion, she did not understand the mixed-up relationships of her parents. Alex composed a long letter after they departed. In it, he insisted on his right to have his son back, especially since the courts had granted him custody of his children. He was deeply upset, and I felt his profound grief. Letters flowed back and forth for months.

By spring a short note came from Jean saying Ildiko had tried to commit suicide. They were in West Africa at this stage, and the hospital was far from their embassy home. She had taken some lethal pills and the ambulance would have been too late to get her to the hospital in time. A doctor in the vicinity came and pumped out her stomach, thus saving her life. Jean begged Alex to refrain from upsetting her more at this stage. He promised a reunion with the children in the coming summer, when they would return to France for the holidays. David was now nine years old. There were occasional letters and photos exchanged, but the communication was not easy, in part because David was being educated in French.

In those days, long distance phone calls were prohibitively expensive, and computers did not exist as-of-yet. It was 1967, I had not seen my mother in a while, and Alex needed to visit his mother. So we planned to fly to Europe and to stay there for the whole summer. This would allow me to fly to Kenya to see my mother for three weeks. Alex would travel to Northumberland, at the border of Scotland, where his mother had joined her sister. They shared a lovely little house in the country. Once we had done our duties with visits to our mothers, we would see the children in France.

Complicated Family Problems

When I arrived in Nairobi, I discovered my sister and brother in-law Klaus had also come for a prolonged stay, in part to assist my mother in renovating the old British style bungalow she had purchased. Klaus, who was an architect and engineer, had already created a dramatic layout for the land, terracing it and removing a tennis court. Almost immediately, I noticed a certain discord and felt my sister was not happy. However, I did not involve myself, preferring to enjoy my brief stay.

A trip to the South coast of Kenya had been planned. We stayed in a lovely, old fashioned English Hotel on the fabulous Diani Beach. I had forgotten the sheer splendor of the Indian Ocean, the blinding white coral beaches, and the slender dark figures of the Africans. The skies were often grey during the summer, and the contrast to the aqua blue ocean was startling. It was here the friendship with Alex had blossomed into love; here my life had taken such a huge shift. I missed him on my long beach walks, missed his presence and conversation. I noticed how superficial some people were, how trite. The owner of the hotel began to make advances toward me, and I met a group of curious English characters. What was considered fun or amusing, did not amuse me. I had become more discriminating, as Alex and his ways had rubbed off on me. Life was shallow and dull without his presence, and I was glad when the time for my flight came. During the night I had a nightmare, dreaming my plane crashed, and I was dead. The vision of my death was so intense that I prayed to be spared this fate, and I promised myself I would not leave Alex again. My life without him was meaningless.

The Flight

The flights to and from Africa are mostly at night. My family drove me to the airport in the evening. Then they hung around for an hour to say farewell and then departed. As time passed, I watched the sunburned tourists shivering in the cool of the night—someone had malaria, someone had a shipment of tropical fish he was bringing to Germany, the hours dragged by, and our plane was still sitting on the tarmac. Then finally we were allowed to board the plane. Strapped into the seats we felt the plane shudder and rise and then suddenly reverse down and sag towards the ground and with a sharp jolt hit the tarmac. Wide, frightened eyes looked around, voices asking, "What was that?" Did we nearly crash? My dream still sat in my cells like a shrill scream..."NO"! We disembarked. Shivering, cold, shocked passengers asked for information. More hours dragged past. The sun rose like a ball of fire. Then an announcement: "A replacement for our original plane just landed. We will board shortly." It was an old battle-scarred machine. Was it safe? It lifted like a bird and the African landscape unfolded beneath us. Many hours later I landed somewhere in Germany. I was supposed to land in London! Over the intercom my name was called. Alex was trying to reach me. It was a relief to hear his voice, melodious, concerned. There were more hours of waiting until the plane for the short flight to London appeared.

"You look more beautiful than I remember," he said. I clung to him, feeling the support of being held. The nightmare was over. I had survived and I related my dream to him. I told him we did not crash, but we almost did. "I won't leave you ever again; life without you holds no meaning for me." Soon, we were on the road again heading for Scotland, where we stayed in a charming little country house. Alex's mother still had red hair, unlike her younger sister, whose hair was white. There was an uncle who was amused that I smiled so much. He called me "the smiler." It seems the Scots don't smile a lot. He took me to the fence where he fed buns to his favorite cows. "The farmer does not like it, but he can lump it. I like feeding the cows." Then I met Tommy, a cousin who was a veterinarian—a very handsome man he was, married to an English woman. It seems she cried when he proposed to her. He was so handsome, and she was not, so she could not believe he wanted to marry her. We walked the moors, which are barren hills where sheep graze. I ran after one of those fluffy, cuddly sheep, but it was impossible to catch. Tommy told me the grass is so coarse that their teeth are eventually ground down. They give them false teeth made of metal when that happens. At his home we were invited to lunch; a meal of four courses, starting with soup. Ailsa, his wife, did not wash the vegetables, I was warned. "Don't eat all the soup, because the bottom of the plate has earth in it." And indeed, at the bottom of the plate was a little heap of earth.

Battle for the Children

After a brief stay in Scotland, we travelled to the South of France to meet Ildiko and the children. They were at Saint Jean Cap Ferrat, living in a vast 18th century villa with a magnificent view of the ocean. It was the home of Jean Francais's parents, who were spending the summer in their Paris home. We were guided into a beautiful room where every chair was covered with silk, the huge drapes were silk, and the balcony looked out over an ancient bougainvillea hedge in full bloom. I had never been in such a luxurious house before. It was startling to hear the litany of complaints from Ildiko. The sink was stopped up, the washing machine was old, and the maid had broken the hand-painted plates which could not be replaced. The children had bounced on the silk covered couch, and the silk being old, had split in half.

Later, I met a beautiful young girl called Fleur, Jean's daughter from his prior marriage. She was there for the summer. We went for a walk together a few times, which was good for my conversational French, and she cried as she related the horrible shock of finding her parents' divorce papers on a desk in Paris. Her whole life had fallen apart, and Ildiko was treating her very badly here. I soon noticed just how badly, when Ildiko referred to her as a slut and a whore. After our arrival and the first welcomes from the children, we sat down to talk, a discussion that went on all night long and ended at five o'clock in the morning. Essentially Ildiko refused to hand over David and stated her children were her only reason to live. David, she insisted, now needed her more than ever and would be scarred psychologically. She suggested we observe his behavior and that we would come to agree with her. Indeed, David was tongue-tied and evasive. He even avoided eye contact and seemed solitary. He was building a big fort on top of a shed, completely engrossed with planks of wood, a hammer, and nails. However, he and I soon re-established a connection. Ildiko constantly hugged Fanny and said the child was her most treasured possession, the "joy of my life."

After a few days passed, Alex and I went to the village alone and had a coffee in a sidewalk café to talk things over. I told him my observations first. "Have you noticed that Fanny limps?" I asked. "She also does not like to walk and avoids it as much as possible. However, she enjoys it if I carry her." Yes, he had noticed and assumed her walk was based on her being very double-jointed. He was going to bring it up with Ildiko. We both concluded that David had been influenced by his mother and frightened in some way. He avoided his father. Alex's face was intense with pain. "I also do not want to be the cause of so much anguish that she tries to commit suicide again. I don't want to be responsible for her death, and the children would hate me forever if I were to cause their mother's death. There is no possible solution, except to allow her to have the children full time and to raise them as French citizens. I have lost them!"

Returning to the beautiful villa, Alex now relayed his decision to Ildiko. Later on that day, her Hungarian mother Eta arrived from Canada. She was a plump little woman with a kind face. To my astonishment, she treated me with disdain, avoiding all conversation with me. Eventually, I asked Alex if she spoke English. He explained later what transpired. He had approached Eta, to find out why she avoided me. He commenced by asking her how she liked Ramona. At this point, she spat out all her poison at him. "That whore, she has destroyed my daughter's life. She has destroyed the children's ability to be raised by both their parents. She is a harlot. I hate her." Alex patiently explained that this was not the truth and tried to inform Eta of the facts. He told her that she had been misinformed and that he did not expect her to believe him. However, he asked her to confront Ildiko if she wanted to learn the truth. Probably she did just that because Eta became more polite to me from then on.

Options

To entertain Ildiko's mother and ourselves, we visited a number of sites and locations of interest on the Cote D'Azur. One of these was a visit to Eze Sur Mer, a huge rock outcropping overlooking the Mediterranean. A narrow path wound itself up to Eze, which means "Isis" and was founded in ancient Egyptian times. Here we found a beautiful garden of giant cacti and an ancient village. Artists had moved into the old buildings and the whole street consisted of one craft store after another. A jeweler sold beautiful necklaces, and I was attracted to a blue one, which looked very Egyptian. As soon as Alex had bought me the one I liked as a gift, Ildiko wanted the same, but the others were slightly different. Alex bought her one too, just to stop her complaints. For some minutes, she was happy, then she again wanted the one I had. This is when I realized the yogic training had transformed me over the many years, as I had already practiced it. I had no attachment to the jewelry. Without the slightest misgivings, I passed her my necklace and took hers instead. Looking back over the events and the curious behavior of the players involved, I somehow managed to keep a distance from the drama and remained unperturbed and uninvolved. Clearly, Ildiko had a hard time letting go of her former husband and somehow, I did not feel like a threat to her. She even told me she didn't see a difference between her former and her present husband.

During the last few days there, a fun fair began to be installed in the village. David got some pennies from his mother and at a shooting stand, he won a prize of a little colorful butterfly in a tiny plastic box. While he did not open up to his father, pretending indifference, he did converse with me. That day he came with a little wrapped box, a gift for me. I was totally surprised to receive such a delicate and beautiful present from the child. I thanked him profusely. He returned to the fairground and an hour later brought me a second butterfly. Now I was truly startled, especially as we later were told he had gone and stolen the money for the shooting stand out of his mother's purse. Ildiko was quite angry with him and possibly jealous of the recipient of her son's affection. Having had to give up his children was hard for Alex, and his only hope was that his former wife would facilitate the promised yearly visits of their children.

When departure loomed and we decided to travel to Portugal, Lisbon. The weather was glorious and we saw marvelous cathedrals, museums, a botanic garden, palaces and in the evening, the Fado places. Unfortunately, Alex was sad and managed to get drunk every lunchtime. He did not wish to talk about his feelings, and I was hoping that in time healing and acceptance would follow. Hoping somewhere else would be better for him, we traveled to Porto where the coast was said to look spectacular. It did, but the water was glacial and the toe I sampled the water with nearly fell off from the cold. I think I stepped into the water no deeper than my feet. Then there was the question of accommodation. We found no real hotels and ended up in a front room of a little village house. The road passed right in front of the building, and all night long we heard the motorbikes and trucks turning the corner and accelerating past the house. A beautiful plastic, glowing Jesus looked down on our bed. We were out of this haven bright and early and had breakfast in a street cafe in Porto. We had reached the western edge of Europe and beyond lay nothing but the Atlantic Ocean. Where to go?

Mid-Atlantic and Sinking Fast

It was good when we reached this point of nowhere because it forced Alex to use his good mind and forget his troubles. He came up with a wonderful idea. Why not fly part way home? "By now we are mid-Atlantic and sinking fast. Let's go to Madeira and San Miguel Island." He sang me the song "Have Some Madeira My Dear" just to underline the desirability of visiting this island. We booked a flight, and then to while away the time we found a bullfight. In Portugal, the bulls are not killed. When the animals lose interest and are no longer able, the fight is over. I was glad not to be witnessing a Spanish bullfight; I clearly had no stomach for this kind of blood sport.

We landed in Madeira and found it instantly enchanting. It was a volcanic island with some of the most handsome people I had ever seen. A wonderful luxury hotel took us in. Lunch and dinner consisted of six courses, and the customers were mostly French. There wasn't a beach. A beautiful garden ended at a carefully carved-out pool which led into the open ocean. The water was delicious, and I spent hours swimming out into the inky blue Atlantic. One day we rented a taxi to take us into the high mountains, perpetually shrouded in mist. The road was lined with hydrangea shrubs of blue, pink and pale violet, and the hillsides were rich with trees and unfamiliar plants, all nurtured by the rich, volcanic soil. When we reached the top, the view took our breath away. Rocky, ancient peaks surrounded us. But it was so cold up here I shivered in my white summer dress and we soon had to leave.

Once we were back in America, Alex began to paint this peak. He had difficulties and worked for several months, feeling his way into the image as he remembered it. Eventually, it became an arresting picture of a peak resembling a head with an open mouth, bared teeth and a look of greed. In some fashion, it reminded me of a painting of Goya called: "Mars devouring his children."

After two more delightful weeks in Madera, we visited San Miguel, a sister island. Here was what people called the remnant of Atlantis, an area below sea level which had tropical vegetation and had been owned by one of Portugal's kings. It naturally contained a lovely palace and magnificent gardens as well as natural springs. One was a pool with red water, considered very desirable for spa visitors. We stayed in this tropical paradise for several days, and I explored all the mineral pools. At the time, I had a nice white bikini swimsuit. Unfortunately, the iron pool changed its color to pink forever.

The last visit was to the Santa Maria Island, much of it an American military base. Here I had a rather strange experience. We were visiting a sardine factory, and no one spoke anything but Portuguese. There were a lot of women who cleaned the fish and laid them in neat rows into the cans to be sealed and then cooked. For some bizarre reason, I began to understand what was being said to us, especially a young man who gave us much information about fishing methods and boats, times when the sardines were plentiful, and the success of the small sardine factory. I kept telling Alex what was told to me. At the conclusion of the visit, Alex said to me: "I am amazed, since when do you understand and speak Portuguese." "You are right," I said," I don't know how that happened." The visit to this sardine factory made sure we never ever ate sardines again. Also, I have never understood how I managed to understand and speak Portuguese.

In Madera, Spain, 1965

A New Life

After our return to America, Alex seemed to settle into his life more comfortably, and I felt he had accepted the loss of his children to some degree. As I had counted on David and Fanny joining us, the idea of having a child of my own never crossed my mind.

But I did eventually become pregnant. The doctor who delivered my baby had not seen me through the pregnancy, but he had diagnosed it. I had gone to the doctor because my menses were no more than a spotting. While I thought I might be "in pod," I did not dare to believe it fully. I recall it was a late afternoon in autumn. His office lamp was already lit and a rich golden glow came from this light. As he confirmed that I was indeed pregnant, I looked steadily into this light, amazed, marveling, moved, and in awe. A new light, a new life would come into this world. As the months went by, I tried to imagine who this child would be, male or female, blonde or dark-haired? I spun my web of imagination and dreams. Alex was delighted. Some of our new friends invited us to dinner to celebrate this big event. Women told me what birth had been like for them. I realized that my old life would be over forever, as I now was committed to being responsible for a new life. I was completely calm. As the weeks passed, my belly grew. I felt extremely well and continued to practice yoga. Looking back, I realize how inwardly focused I became. Most afternoons during the later months, I lay down after lunch for a brief rest. From the upstairs bedroom window, I saw the mighty magnolia tree and a bird that was building its nest in the top branches of the tree. The bird and I were both preparing to produce offspring and so I felt a kinship with the bird. I tried to visualize this new life in my belly. I told it stories and especially while listening to music could feel a communication with the embryo. Also, I continued to paint, and big sensitive compositions emerged. There was a rather lovely green-red composition resembling roots painted in this period which now graces my child's bedroom. Oddly, in later years I never again saw a bird building a nest in the magnolia tree.

And so, the months passed. The baby was expected to arrive in July. My mother set everything in motion to be there for the birth. Only after her death did I find documents showing how difficult it had been for her to find the money for this trip all the way from Africa to the USA. As the weeks of my pregnancy went by, I became more easily tired and by nine in the evening,

I had to go to sleep. Someone gave a big party and we were invited. I excused myself; however, Alex accepted. He promised to be home by midnight. I awoke with a start; the bed beside me was empty. Switching on the light I saw it was well past midnight on the clock. I called, and eventually a very giggly and slightly inebriated Alex came on the line. "You won't believe what happened. I shall be home in ten minutes."

He came in, smelling of cigarette smoke and whisky. It was a very strange evening he told me. Three women, all friends of mine, had offered to have sex with him, since, so they implied, he was probably very needy. I felt as if a strange evil wind blew through the house. What possessed these women to make passes at a married man, simply because his pregnant wife was not by his side? What sort of friends were they? I had counted them among my friends. Could I trust no one?

Sanibel Island

This incident made me feel very vulnerable and isolated. Fortunately, I had a dear friend in Ruth Winter, an older lady on whose support I could always count. She was wealthy, and like all wealthy people in Illinois she left for warmer, sunnier places when winter became too long. This was usually in the early spring, when there was a general exodus for Florida or Mexico. Ruth went to Sanibel Island in Florida every winter. She would return suntanned and vital. I think she could see that I was becoming depressed and lonely. Out of the blue, she invited both of us for a week into her classy old hotel on the beach of Sanibel Island. The flights were paid for, as well as our food and accommodation. It was a wonderful gift for me to arrive on a balmy beach covered with seashells. Even old people walked with a child's plastic bucket dangling from their hand, eyes fixed on the ground, collecting seashells. Sanibel was famous for its shell banks, and after a storm sometimes even rare and beautiful shells could be found. I was up early scouring the area for treasures and enjoying the sea air and glassy, clear ocean. Sea gulls hovered over the shore line, and the crows had a haunting call I shall forever associate with Florida.

A narrow neck of land connected Sanibel to the next island, called Captiva. It was said to have been a haven for pirates who dropped off their women on this island, from which they could not escape. Hence the name "Captiva!" A week is a short time, but it was such a huge relief for me to be by the ocean and out of the bitter Midwestern winter. In essence, this stay in Florida broke the back of winter. I felt healed and refreshed as I faced the last few months of pregnancy.

There is a kindness in Americans that is hard to beat. Because I could not drive, I was more or less stuck and did not go far except for my daily walks. A few times I voiced concern about a crib for the baby, clothes for the child, or a pram. Alex, who knew all about having children, assured me we could find an empty drawer and that I was not to worry about things. One day the doorbell rang and a delivery truck was outside. I had to sign for something and then the delivery man unloaded parcel after parcel, much to my huge surprise. Some of them were large indeed. After he left, I started to unwrap things. Another very wealthy, kind-hearted lady, Eleanor Douglas, had also taken me under her wing was the fairy godmother. There was a crib, a baby basket, a little bathtub, a stroller, mountains of diapers, baby clothes of assorted sizes, blankets, in short, everything one could possibly need for a newborn. I recall sitting down among the piles of wrapping paper and presents and looking at this avalanche of gifts in total disbelief with tears of gratitude in my eyes. I would never have known what to get and where to buy it, nor did I have the faintest idea there was so much available in terms of choices. This was all a completely new adventure for me.

The other huge surprise was a shower, a literal gift shower organized by one of the faculty wives. "Oh, I don't want to go all alone." I said to Alex, "I don't even know these people." On the appointed day he dropped me off. I felt shy and awkward meeting a big group of women, who had no idea that I did not know what this was all about. Again, the generosity and kindness was a huge surprise, and the discarded wrappings piled up at my feet as I opened present after present. There were baby clothes, a teddy bear, a children's book, socks and booties, and a beautiful nightgown and dressing gown made of a fabulous fabric that looked like spun gold. I felt somewhat overwhelmed to say the least, since these customs were all new to me. The night attire was the most beautiful I have ever owned, and I wore it with gratitude for many years. In the end my baby daughter took it away from me, as it became her "Beety" without which she could not sleep. It had to have just the right silky texture and perfumed smell or she became inconsolable. By the time she was three, it had become a dirty rag, but replacing it was impossible. She lost it somewhere in Madrid, Spain, and it was a huge drama to find a replacement that did not consist of a pair of my silkiest panties.

Birth of Kirstin

My mother arrived for the birth of the baby all the way from Nairobi. I was very grateful for her presence and help, as having a child was more time consuming than I expected. The birth was much more difficult than I had anticipated and I struggled for many hours. The general verdict was that my athletic disposition was to blame; in other words, I was too fit. I was not conscious during the birth. They knocked me out, something I have always regretted. The child came with difficulty, presenting its face first, which they called the military position! When I came back into consciousness, the doctors and nurses had gone; except for one. I was lying on a narrow table and beside me, on another table lay a serious, bright blue-eyed, little creature. Her eyes were huge, and she looked very serious, very aged and wise. They had just taken an impression of her foot-soles, so her feet looked dirty. "Oh, she has dirty feet, just like I do," I said. The nurse told me I had had a little girl. Then I was wheeled away and transferred to my bed.

Giving birth is now a much better situation than it used to be. I was not given the opportunity to hold my child. The next day they brought her into my room, but I again was not allowed to hold her. The other woman who shared my room was allowed to hold her child because she was not breastfeeding. They gave her a bottle so she could feed her baby. "Why," I asked her. "Oh, my husband does not want me to get ugly breasts, so I chose this." she answered. My milk was not yet flowing they explained, so the child would only be given water. I felt terribly upset by this stage, ready to scream and lament with pain and horror because I was not even allowed, after a full day to touch and hold my baby.

A deep depression settled on me. When Alex came in with a large gift of flowers, I asked him to bring me a bottle of red wine, some of which I drank with dinner. It helped a great deal. I walked repeatedly into the hallway to look at my little daughter through the thick glass partition. Her eyes were always open, alert and intelligent. She did not sleep or cry like the other infants. I missed her terribly and cried myself to sleep. Upon waking up, I became aware that I was developing a fever. I had ignored some pills I was supposed to take, so I swallowed them now.

Then finally, the next day I was actually allowed to hold her. She was so tiny and delicate, with long fingers. When she yawned, I had to laugh because she looked exactly like her father. I prized open one of her fists and looked at her palm. As yet she had no line of destiny. She was very gentle, and fragile like a blossom and infinitely sweet. Actually, that turned out to be her disposition and it was recognizable from the very start. When after a day she began to breastfeed, they agreed I could now go home. I struggled into a dress I had worn before pregnancy. My hips had spread, though I weighed exactly 106 lbs., which was my weight before pregnancy.

7 Motherhood

Motherhood

I was thirty years old and I had a baby. As I left the hospital, the staff cheerfully called out: "See you again in a couple of years." No, you won't, I thought and I kept my promise.

Alex was very nervous driving us home. It was beastly hot and humid and this heat lasted all summer. As yet, the child didn't have a name. All the names I had considered did not match the being that came into life. The baby was therefore referred to as "the Bun." In the hospital the newspaper woman came again and again inquiring about the child's name and each time was told I had not yet decided. Alex brought a huge book filled with names. He had only one request:" Don't give her a name that can be abbreviated to "Lulu" or "Wheezy" or "Gini." So, I searched in vain. There was a Scottish song from the Hebrides which I had played frequently and which I loved. A love song from the Isle of Skye called Kirsteen. How symbolic; the Isle of Skye, an island of heaven far to the north. The north is the spiritual direction and so the name of Kirstin was what I chose. We only changed the spelling so the name would be crisper. Though the name comes from the far north of Europe and was not sentimental and rarely heard, it was a surprise that it would become so popular.

My mother had planned to stay all summer. She was wonderful, as she took over most of the cooking and taught me a lot, both about the kitchen and about child care. She was very concerned about the length of the labor, 36 hours, and had wanted to come to the hospital to tell the doctors what to do! When an exhausted Alex finally returned to the house at 577 East Spruce, where she had been pacing the floor, they managed to drink a whole bottle of Scotch at the start of the fourth of July. Kirstin missed being born on that date by 30 minutes.

My mother cooked a superb meal for me on my return from the hospital. It was an Italian Veal dish with homemade noodles, which she had dried over the back rests of our Shaker chairs. This memorable dish was a one-time experience for it was never repeated. Leni was a terrific cook, but not used to cooking daily. Life was very different after the birth. Hours were spent quietly breastfeeding and holding the naked little baby, for it was beastly hot that summer. We both sweated profusely and the child developed a bad heat rash that no baby powder would heal.

My mother cooked all the meals and Alex provided the music, conversation and general entertainment. After 10 pm we went out into the garden. The grass was lush and fireflies flitted around. By this stage the mosquitoes had gone and a gentle coolness revived us.

At this time very few people had fans or air conditioners and for some unknown reason we did not think of buying even one fan. There was a new sense of responsibility now that the child was born. I never left her with anyone but the grandmothers or Alex. We didn't go to movies or parties and it never crossed my mind that I was missing anything. We never ever bought a television.

Michael's Arrival

That August, Michael Croydon arrived in Lake Forest and brought a baby hyena with him in a wooden cage. The hyena was named Liz. He had saved her as a baby and could

Michael Croydon, 1968

not be separated from her when he left Kenya. He also had shipped his red Alfa Romeo car to Lake Forest. He became an instant attraction as he roared through the streets with his exotic beast in his fancy car. He arrived in our back yard one afternoon, depositing the baby hyena in its cage next to the pram containing Kirstin. My mother hovered in fear and terror lest the beast somehow get out of its box and devour her grandchild.

We were extremely fortunate, for Kirstin never cried unless there was a good reason, and slept well. She was very gentle and never greedy or hungry as were other babies I had seen. In fact, I worried that she was getting enough milk as she fell asleep while feeding and I had to wake her again and again. Soon enough her cheeks began to fill out, and her second growth of white blonde hair came in. She had the biggest, bright blue eyes, which remained blue for a full year before becoming green-brown.

Thus, the summer went. The back of the garden had been just lawn, surrounded by old maple trees. Leni went to buy plants and Alex was coerced into digging them in at the back of the house. Suddenly we had flowers and color, which was a huge improvement. My mother was full of good ideas and eager to help. "I am very proud of my daughter," she confided in Alex. "Your little house is quite charming, but I do wish she would put cloth napkins on the table instead of paper ones." She also placed a vase with fresh flowers on the dining room table, something I continued to do after she left.

There were just two grocery stores in the little town at that time and my mother was forever in need of items then not available in the Midwest. "How can people here not know about bird's custard powder," she complained. "I really need some curry powder and yogurt, or I cannot make a proper Indian curry." Alex spent much time driving around trying to find ingredients for Leni, for her pizza, her cheesecake, or her stews. My mother would then delight us with foods I did not know how to cook, soufflés, cold avocado soup, peach ice cream and Italian ravioli.

Through Michael we met Kay and Ted B. Ted collected vintage sports cars and had a whole garage filled with them. He would come around in his Model T Ford to take us all on a ride through Lake Forest. Lake Forest was aptly named, for

Ramona and Kirstin at the Lake Forest Art Show, 1969

then it was a forest. Dandelions bloomed everywhere; houses were modest or huge, but set back from the roads and barely visible. There were no flower borders and no fences anywhere. It was impossible to tell where a property began or ended. The people we knew were kind and unhurried and they liked to chat. Alex was amused that the bank manager chatted with him for thirty minutes. That is how leisurely things were. People had parties in their backyards and went to Ravinia for concerts, highlights which took place every summer. Swimming in the lake was not recommended because the water was polluted, which was very sad during the hot summers.

Three weeks after Kirstin's birth I picked up my paint brushes again. I asked my mother if two children would be an obstacle for me if I wished to be an artist. Her answer was decisive and wise: "One child is plenty. Large families were a necessary insurance at one time because so many infants died; this is no longer the case. You can only focus fully on one child.

With more children you also burden the relationship with your husband. Be wise. Don't fall into the trap of greed." I viewed myself as a painter and so I needed to paint. Kirstin was placed into the studio in her basket or high chair and thus I was able to paint for several hours daily. Vincent Van Gogh had written, "If you hear a voice within you saying: you are not a painter, then by all means paint...and that voice will be silenced."

I recognized the need to continue my own development, for we can only give to others if we have something to offer. I made careful choices in how I used my time. Also, I made every effort to put quality into our life. Candles were lit on the dining room table at dinner time, and I made every effort to learn how to cook. Later I danced with Kirstin most evenings and played with her until her bed time.

Holiday in Makriamos

Kirstin was almost two years old when Ildiko finally determined that it was time for the children to see their father again. He had not seen them in three years. Ildiko made this decision for her own comfort, as she wished to spend the summer on a Greek Island called Makriamos. Jean, her husband, did not like the idea of her driving alone from France through Yugoslavia into Greece. We made the arrangements, flew over, and arrived at the Chateau de St Mauriz, their country residence. Certainly, she was in her temperamental phase and quite difficult. Her car was brand new and she would not allow Alex to touch it, let alone drive it. However, she insisted he sit beside her and do the map reading. More often than not, she called him "darling" and right in front of me. I was relegated to the back seat together with Fanny and David, with Kirstin on my lap. In retrospect, I think we were all most polite and probably naïve to be so agreeable.

By the time we reached Padua in Italy, the emotional atmosphere was very heated. Claiming she hated art, Ildiko said she would be sick if she had to look at another cathedral or work of art. This was in response to Alex's asking if we could visit the famous Giotto paintings in the Arena Chapel. She insisted she wanted to shop for shoes. We parted company and we went to the Arena Chapel while she dragged the kids through shoe shops. When we met again all hell broke out. I had never seen such a demonstration of viciousness and below-the-belt attacks as what she was capable of. It was actually awesome and amazing. The children were in shock and Fanny took her mother's hand. Alex suggested we go our separate ways, as clearly there was no possibility of civilized behavior on Ildiko's part. I felt like an outsider privy to the strange tensions between a man and woman no longer able to get on together. With hindsight I think I should have stood up and insisted on leaving. But in those days, I often made no judgement and simply went with the flow. Now I have to say that I probably made a very wise decision.

Getting through Yugoslavia

The drive through Yugoslavia that followed was bad. Ildiko drove almost without stopping. She wanted to get to Greece fast. She refused to stop when I needed to change Kirstin's diaper, which forced me to balance the child on my lap in a moving car and to throw the soiled diapers out of the car window in transit, as the older children held their noses in disgust. No food was available in stores as the country was too poor. We found some chocolate biscuits somewhere and drank some excellent red wine. Milk for the children could not be found either. We spent a night in a Communist hotel, which had only rooms with two single beds. These were covered with coarse grey blankets, and no baby cribs were available for Kirstin. The bathroom had a showerhead in the center of the ceiling and a simple drain beneath it. Anyone taking a shower sprayed the whole room with water, including the untiled walls.

At dawn there was a big commotion. David hammered on our door. "Daddy, come quickly Mummy needs you." David had a room to himself while Ildiko and Fanny shared the other one. Ildiko had not locked her room so that David could enter at any time. At dawn a young man drunk on Slivovitz and clad only in his underpants entered her room and tried to get into bed with her. At this point, David came to get Alex who chased the young man away. That was the end of our night's rest and we left at 5:00 in the morning.

By noon we reached the Greek border and there somehow lost our way. Another tourist in his car gave us directions on how to find the border crossing, and we proceeded. Suddenly an angry Yugoslav police man in his car crossed our path stopping us. He shouted abuse. Ildiko pulled out her diplomatic passport, rolled down her window and without turning to look at the man, flipped the diplomatic document in his face. To his shouts of anger in a language which no one in the car understood she repeated: "Passport Diplomatic!" There was nothing he could do. She never even made eye contact with him. After some moments he just waved us on. I guess we had crossed the border by some back exit.

Greece seemed civilized in contrast. We found a roadside restaurant and for the first time in two days there was fresh food and milk for the children. The only problem was the bathroom, which had an oriental toilet consisting of a hole in the ground with an elevated platform on either side of the hole for the feet to step onto. Ildiko was wearing long, floppy, flowing bell-bottom pants. As we waited for her a wailing rose and she emerged trailing shit covered bell bottoms. A change of costume was found in the trunk. Then we stood in a circle around her, holding towels between us, to shield her from view as she rid herself of her offensive and smelly garment. Then we continued on our journey.

Whenever Alex offered to help her with the drive, she was vehement that HER car would not be driven by anyone but herself. As she became more and more tired, she grew more and more irritable. We reached a large Greek city by evening and with Alex map reading and guiding us we found our hotel, where advanced bookings had been made.

We were shown into our separate bedrooms and while admiring the marble bathroom and glossy stone floors an S.O.S. knock came at the door. The toilet in Ildiko's bathroom was overflowing. Could we get help? This was easier said than done.

By the time a bellboy with a plunger arrived, Ildiko's bathroom was under water. Alex suggested that we all go for dinner and leave the hotel to deal with the mess. "Oye, youi, youi yew," moaned Ildiko, "this is what always happens to me. One disaster after the other." The dining room was elegant and spacious and the meal wonderful after our two days of nothing but wine and chocolate biscuits. Kirstin was fast asleep on my lap when we finally went up to our rooms.

The next morning, Alex helped Ildiko find a beauty parlor, where she had arranged to have electrolysis done on her legs. She had become very hairy and had to undergo this treatment to remove the offending hair, and so I was asked to take the children to a nearby beach for a swim. With everyone holding hands we crossed a very busy intersection and came to a beach covered with big boulders and rocks. Beyond it the ink blue ocean sparkled in the sunlight. We spread out a beach towel and ran into the water. After days in the car this was wonderfully refreshing. I had not noticed them, when we arrived; the beach had seemed empty, but now all of a sudden there were young boys and men galore. They splashed around in the water obviously trying to get our attention. By degrees they came closer and closer, and eventually diving below the water would manage to emerge right beside me. Pretending they were invisible worked only so long, and when one tried to grasp my hand, I spun around confronting him, and pointed to my wedding band. He laughed, shrugged his shoulders and disappeared under the water only to emerge again on the other side. Several came up to me and in sign language indicated how smitten they were. I must say I found it amusing. After years in the USA, I had forgotten these ancient customs and how men in Europe flirt and try to pursue and woo the female. Also, I had forgotten that I just might still be attractive and young-looking. Their game and attention was very flattering and uplifting.

In the afternoon our journey continued, this time by boat to the island of Makriamos. We boarded the ship and Ildiko insisted on staying in her car in the hold, while Alex, I, and the three children stood by the railing watching the deep blue

waters, screeching seabirds, and other fellow passengers. Later
we made the acquaintance of a well-known Greek opera singer
called Antigone Scourdas and her partner, a Dutch tenor. Alex,
who loved opera, was an entertaining conversationalist and
soon we were laughing and joking. They estimated that the
children were clearly the offspring of Alex, but were puzzled
about me. Later they told us they had thought I was a dancer.
Meanwhile Ildiko was roasting in the hot hold of the ship.

On arrival at the island, we were shown to a wonderful
hotel. Built into a gently sloping horseshoe-like cove above
a magnificent bay, it was on a slope was covered with well-
designed cottages for guests. The cottages spread out among
trees and local shrubs and were simple but attractive. The main
building was a structure of white marble with open halls and
terraces leading down to the water. It is ironic that the very late
lunch we had that first day at the hotel was the best meal they
ever served us. In fact, the food was so good we thought we
had really scored. The place was truly beautiful and amazing.

David and his sister shared their mother's cottage. That
evening David burst into our place asking us to come quickly.
Something was amiss with his mother. Ildiko lay in bed when
we arrived. "Darling," she said, "I am having a miscarriage. I
did not tell you I was pregnant?" She rolled her big black eyes
dramatically. "I need some menstrual pads. Here is my car key.
The pharmacy in the village is sure to have some." I began to
question her. Should we find a doctor, was she sure she had
lost the baby? How bad was the bleeding? She began to answer
some of my questions and out of that a conversation ensued.
It seems she lost the embryo. She did not wish to consult a
doctor, as nature would take its course. I agreed with her but
insisted that she stay in bed and rest. Also, I expressed regret
she had told us nothing about her condition and had insisted
on doing all the driving for three days, taxing her stamina and
resources, and Alex was allowed to drive her car for the first
time. After buying a huge pile of feminine napkins we returned
to the hotel. Thereafter she allowed Alex to drive her car any

time at all. After a few days she clearly was better and began coming down to the beach.

David woke early like most children and started to come to our cottage at 6 am to be with his Daddy. Kirstin fell in love with her big brother and they would horse around until we made our way down to the dining room for breakfast. The hotel restaurant was located under the open sky on a big platform, spreading out just above the ocean. We all had breakfast together underneath a big sunshade. Ildiko would arrive at 9 am or later, hostile and impolite. Neither she nor Fanny could say "good morning." Alex was admirable as he greeted her and Fanny with cordial good humor and tried to keep a conversation going. It was clear to me that Ildiko was consumed with envy and unable to control her emotions.

One morning an unhappy David come to our cottage and with a long face announced he had been forbidden to come to our cottage from now on, nor was he allowed to join us for breakfast. His mother did not wish it. What then was the point of us being here, if Alex was not allowed to see his children? Jean, the French ambassador, was expected in a few days. He had to stay in Africa at the embassy through Bastille Day, on the 14th of July. We were hoping his presence would cheer Ildiko up and make a difference in her attitude and behavior towards us.

Meanwhile I enjoyed the beautiful bay with its clear water. I swam back and forth across it many times. Kirstin was like a little seal, completely fearless and at home in the water. She had just celebrated her second birthday in Makriamos. Her great thrill was to cling to my long black hair as I swam back and forth, much to the amusement of the hotel guests. Kirstin was so comfortable she often swam with her face under water. Tiny children were allowed to be naked in Greece and so we enjoyed leaving Kirstin "au naturel."

Little Accident

One day Kirstin wandered off in the direction of the great reception hall of the hotel. It was a fabulous architectural design adorned with Grecian columns and snow-white marble floors. I found Kirstin sitting in the middle of this expansive, pristine, shining hall; a tiny brown, naked little figure clearly enjoying the cool floor. I swept her up in my arms and a downward glance showed me a neat little brown pile of poo. Fortunately, there was no one present behind the reception counters as I carried my little bundle of joy back to the beach. I asked Alex if I should brave the embarrassment and clean up the floor. Laughing, he said; "she left a fine comment! I would not bother; they will assume it was a dog."

We met some charming people, aside from the Opera singers. They were a British couple with two little girls, who soon became our new friends. Alex discovered the joys of Ouzo, a very strong Greek drink to which the Englishman introduced him. They had invited us to their cottage for "sundowners." When it was time to go down to the restaurant for dinner, Alex, instead of walking to the front door, marched into the closet, looking rather startled and confused. A strong drink indeed!

On the whole, we spent a wonderful month on the Greek island. Evenings were spent in the company of Antigone Scourdas and her partner, a huge Dutchman with a meltingly beautiful voice. Kirstin managed to get herself carried by him and he sang all kinds of songs for her as we walked to the village, where we ate in open air taverns. Delicate little fish were grilled on open fires, seasoned with herbs and Antigone managed to introduce us to all sorts of Greek delicacies. Since we stayed past a child's normal bedtime, Kirstin usually fell asleep on my lap. As a consequence, we had a long nap every afternoon. Sadly, Ildiko continued to be discontented with life. The food was not to her liking, someone stole her beach chair, David had gone off on his own, Fanny was bored. However, it was true that Ildiko seemed to attract bad luck. Now our new-found friends became a thorn in Ildiko's eye. She complained that we sat around with people who drank too much and who were loud and vulgar.

At this stage Jean arrived, and life definitely began to look up for Ildiko. Jean liked antiques and he found many different places to visit. The children were left with us. Fanny had decided to name herself Fa-Fa. It was not a name I liked or seemed to remember. She was mostly together with her mother and could be very rude, copying the behavior of the adults around her. She became increasingly annoyed with me for calling her by her birth name, Frances.

I had been under the impression that Alex was coolly coping well with this situation, only to realize I had been mistaken. What caused his emotional breakdown I do not recall, except that it took me by surprise. For over half an hour I held this shattered, sobbing man, as he confronted the pain of having lost his children. He saw little advantage in the way they were being raised, in spite of Jean's wealth. He felt guilty to have let them down, and helpless to do anything about it.

The day of our departure loomed, and David became terribly upset. He sulked and refused to eat. In order to help him over his grief, we all agreed to meet in Austria in a charming country inn recommended by Antigone. We planned that David would join us for a train trip to Auxerre, where Jean was remodeling a chateau he had bought. David's birthday was to be celebrated in the French countryside and he had extracted the promise from Alex he would get what turned out to be an outrageously expensive; a train set!

Despite this arrangement, when our departure from the Makriamos harbor occurred, David sat on the pier in a state of extreme upset, his long legs dangling down to the water. He refused to get into the car to drive back to the hotel with Jean, thus forcing the adults to stay and hang around until our ferry finally departed from the harbor. We had to take a train journey to Austria, which turned out to be lovely. The little inn in Austria was charming, just as Antigone had said.

Le Chateau in France

Two days later, at two in the morning, Jean and Ildiko finally arrived, having miscalculated how much time the drive would take. David was ecstatic to see his father again and now continued to travel with us, while Jean and Ildiko and Fanny drove to France by car. We took the train to France, a highlight in David's experience. The so-called "chateau" consisted of the remnants of a medieval fort; high walls surrounded by a moat still filled with water. A large arched entryway led into a courtyard where an old farmhouse built of pale yellow stone greeted the eye. Much had been recently renovated and been reconstructed in good taste. I liked being in France, and we were invited to visit Madame Boudoir, a neighbor with a big farm, who supplied milk, cream, butter, eggs, bread, and vegetables to the Francais kitchen. Alex and the children went to see her to bring back some milk. It turned out she was a character. She zoomed around on an expensive motorbike and had an eye for men. She invited us to sample her apple brandy, and in the course of the conversation discovered that Alex was Ildiko's ex-husband. She exclaimed that she was appalled. How could Ildiko prefer the little Frenchman to such a handsome Scottish gentleman? "Mon Dieux! What a mistake!" We laughed all the way back. David's birthday was celebrated with an overabundance of gifts, and the expensive train set was the highlight. Fanny made the extraordinary remark that "in her family, excessive gifts were a substitute for love." Then it was time for us to return home.

Though we lived in the States, in most ways we remained very European in our lifestyle. We chose not to have a television set and brought Kirstin up to be bilingual, to listen to music, and to read books. Alex often remarked that we and our friend Michael Croydon were like a little island unto ourselves. We hung out together, shared many meals, visited Chicago together, and discovered the countryside. My quest was to find something wild, untouched, and remote in nature. However, much as we searched, I found no large forests, no wilderness, nothing ancient or magical. The best thing was the shoreline of Lake Michigan. Later, when I was in a plane and looked down, all I saw was an extensive area of suburban sprawl. It made me sad, for in Europe, forests had been saved and parks were established in most towns and cities for the use of the population. Here the malls and vast shopping areas ate up all the empty space. Over the years I lived there, the farms disappeared, the open land turned into yet another development, and no dandelions remained in the green, green Roundup-treated lawns of Lake Forest.

Change came very quickly, and the ease of the hippy era gave way to a more driven time, where informal get togethers in backyards vanished, and people stopped greeting each other. Suddenly, Alex had far too many faculty meetings and stayed at work until 5:30 or 6:00. I was alone all day, alone with my wonderful little girl. Although I had sort of learned to drive in Cairo, I lacked sufficient practice. This forced Alex to come shopping with me and to drive me wherever I needed to go. In fact, I was totally dependent on him.

After Kirstin's birth, he had bought me a present of a Raleigh folding bike on which I cruised through Lake Forest, mostly to the beach and back. During the very long winters, I mostly walked. Since there weren't any forests or parks, only the beach offered some open space. This lack of open land was very hard on me, and I missed the freedom the Egyptian desert offered or the forests of Germany, where I could walk to my heart's content during my student years. Our little house in time began to feel like a very constricting box, limited in space. Friends suggested we buy a house, but we didn't have the money for a down payment, and Alex believed he would not stay in Lake Forest. His department had grown, and Art History was the fourth largest department at the college, which indicated he needed to move on.

When I look back, I feel amazed at how much we did, how inventive we were, how much joy we were capable of, and how happy we were even when things were difficult. Alex was full of good ideas, inventiveness, and confidence and was like a happy songbird. When we discovered Florida, we decided to drive there during the Christmas holidays to get a break from the long, cold winter. Our first visit to Captiva Island occurred when Kirstin was only five months old and my mother-in-law had just arrived from Scotland. We rented a humble cottage on the beach and had a wonderful time by the sea. We had to drive back over New Year's Day and couldn't find a vacancy in the motels along the way, forcing Alex to drive through the night nonstop until we were back in Lake Forest. We drove from tropical warmth and color into the freezing cold of the icy north.

Sabbatical Leave

After seven years, faculty at Lake Forest College received a sabbatical year of freedom. For Alex, this happened after eight years. He intended to go to Austria and write a book on Sir Peter Paul Rubens, a famous Flemish artist. We were familiar with Vienna, and of course I spoke the language, but we had no idea how difficult it would be to find an apartment or house there. It was really distressing to search the suburbs of Vienna for a whole month without finding anything even remotely suitable. There were some old apartments for rent, but the single bathroom located in the hallway was shared with the occupants of another flat. With a small child in tow, bathrooms and a washing machine seemed crucial, but neither of these could have been such a concern in the 18th century when these houses were built.

Eventually we moved to a charming village called Puschberg am Schneeberg, where a most delightful Austrian inn offered us extraordinary food and a cheery room. Very soon, I realized the drawbacks of charming old Europe. There were not enough showers, not enough heating during the winter months, expensive clothes, and expensive travel. We had started out in France, where we bought a Citroen car, sand-colored and a dream to drive. After only one week, eating only one meal in a restaurant, we found France too expensive for our means. We drove over the Alps into Italy, and at the recommendation of friends, ended up on the coast in a mosquito infested tourist area called Bungalowdorf Rosa Pineta or "Bungalow Village Pink Pine."

In Roman times this had been a swamp area, and it still is. During the first night there, Kirstin received 39 bites on her face, and Alex had been so savaged one of his eyes was swollen shut. As the linguist in the family, I marched into the office and demanded our money back. Lo and behold, the manager could speak no English, no French, or German, and failed to understand my poor Italian. When Alex however raised his voice, he understood English perfectly. We argued back and forth telling him that such mosquito-infested accommodation was not worth a cent, and why didn't they put up mosquito screens? If we swore not to tell other guests, he agreed to cover the windows with screens, and he hoped we would then be happy. When we returned in the evening the windows were screened, and seemingly other guests did not notice this change. We used Rosapineta as a place to sleep and went on daily excursions to Venice, Ravenna, and other places of interest. Everywhere the food was fabulous, the sights extraordinary and the works of art exquisite.

Alex was a great teacher and during this sabbatical year I learned a great deal about art history and painting. Alex pointed out the technique of using glazes that made the Venetian painters so famous. He taught me about architecture and Ravenna, which left a deep impression on me. I can still see the glittering golden mosaic of the cathedral.

Venice

While in Venice, I was always fearful that Alex might have a heart attack. He discovered woodworm in a famous painting on a wooden panel. Pointing it out to the guard brought nothing more than a bored shrug. Clearly, there was so much art in Italy that it was taken for granted. On a visit to the Palace of the Doge in Venice, we trailed behind a large group of tourists who blocked our vision. Kirstin, who always wanted to see everything, became bored. In the vast audience room of the Doge a red cord stretched across the room to prevent the visitors from stepping upon the raised platform of fine wood on which rested the opulent throne of the Doge. Quick as a wink, my three-year-old slipped under the cordon and ran up to the throne, then heaved herself up into the silken pillows. Here she sat gleefully taking in her surroundings and no amount of loudly whispered commands could bring her to vacate the throne. Fortunately, the guard was absent from the room, but I expected to hear a chilling "Madonna mia!" any moment and a torrent of Italian abuse. Eventually, in what seemed a long time, she turned herself around in the chair and slid out of it. Then, she quickly ran across the parquet floor and slipped under the red cordon. I heaved a sigh of relief until I caught sight of the wooden floor decorated with the little footprints of a child, clearly visible on the dusty surface, which had not seemed dusty before. The footsteps led to the throne and back to the cordon. We laughed, thinking of the surprise awaiting the guard when he saw the footprints on the dusty floor.

Kirstin loved Venice, particularly the pigeons. When we settled down for lunch in a charming outdoor restaurant beside a canal, she twirled like a little ballerina matching the twirling Paloma pigeons in their mating dance. In spite of constant warning not to get close to the edge of the canal, she was drawn to the pigeons and to the water. It became hard for me to enjoy meals, as she was always too excited to settle down inside a chair. Either she was under the table enjoying the long tablecloth that gave her the chance to pretend she was hidden in a tent, or she was fascinated with the carts displaying desserts of all shapes and sizes. She would stand in front of them hoping we would not notice her finger reaching out to one particularly tempting delicacy, so she could at least have a fingertip of taste.

Another favorite activity of hers was to inspect the toilets. This was usually our first obligation after we sat down in a restaurant. "Mummy, I need a pee, let's go!" and that even if she had just had one. The inspection was only complete after she had looked under every door and counted the feet of the ladies. There were periods when she just picked at her food, eating very little and periods when the ordered food came too late, and she would be lying across my lap fast asleep.

Ramona Mitchell

Unfortunately, this was the daily case in Spain, where people only ate dinner after 10:00 pm.

Alex solved this problem by finding tapas bars. Here an early alcoholic beverage did wonders for the spirit and the little delicacies offered for tapas were enjoyed by Kirstin. We discovered we could also order her a toasted cheese sandwich, and this became her favorite for dinner. After our month in Rosa Pineta, the true summer tourist crowds arrived in Italy. We were somewhat tired of sight-seeing and needed some downtime for Kirstin. However, the most urgent reason for trying to settle down somewhere was the bank strike in Italy. Italy always has some strike or another, but without money we could not function. This was the time before credit cards. We received our monthly payments from the Lake Forest bank.

I remembered my stay in Prochio sur Forno, a little cove on the island of Elba, where I spent some delicious days during my time as a student with my landlady Gerda Jacob from Kassel. I still had the phone number of the Florentine Professoressa who owned houses in Prochio. I called her and was delighted to find she had a place for us on the hillside overlooking the bay. She offered us a bedroom with private bath. Perfect! We set off and drove towards the coast, found the Elba ferry and boarded ship. The sea air was intoxicating, the water deepest ultramarine in color, and we felt ready for a holiday from sightseeing. Kirstin insisted on her bathroom inspection routine.

Elba

Leaving Alex standing by the railing outside, I took our daughter around the ship, showing her the bar and cafe as well. Suddenly, someone called my name and I turned around to see my old friend Gerda Jacob. She, too, was once again arriving on Elba to spend her summer vacation there. We hugged and chatted away, since I had not seen her in seven years. Gerda always had an eye for men, and now she told me about a really good-looking type she had seen at the railing. "Too bad he is too young for me" she said, sighing. Across the room Alex pushed the door open looking for me. He advanced towards us.

342

Gerda touched my arm, exclaiming "That's him, the man I saw outside." Alex came closer, and I said to her, "May I introduce you to Alex, my husband!" She looked as if she had been hit! What surprise! We arranged to meet in Procchio for a drink, once we got to our house. What an amazing coincidence it was to run into her on Isola Elba.

The bay looked unchanged, except that the forests that stretched along the rim of the bay had been replaced by vine orchards. Our accommodation offered me the opportunity to cook if I so desired. The bathroom was a surprise. It was laid out in the most expensive and beautiful varieties of marble with a huge bathtub and washbasin. I decided to wash Kirstin a bit and quickly discovered the water pressure to be very low. The owner's wife explained to me that there was a shortage of water just now, mostly the houses lower down were using up too much water. Over the month of our stay, this situation became quite challenging at times. On one occasion Alex soaped up his whole body, expecting to be able to shower it off. Alas, the water came out as a thin trickle. The only way to get rid of the soapy foam was to use the tiny stream of water like a knife, carving off the soap inch by inch. And so, we settled comfortably into our new life on Elba.

Alex, being an opera buff, knew quite a bit of mostly operatic Italian. A tiny grocery store run by the family's grandmother provided us with milk, cheese and eggs for breakfast. Alex would enter and say in his best accent, "Bon giorno Senora, lei commo va oggi?" Among other things that enchanted the old lady were comments like, "Your eyes are alight as stars, your tiny hand is frozen, let me warm it into life," or "in questa tomba oscura, lassa me riposar" which means "in this dark tomb let me rest." He managed to use these somewhat antiquated expressions with great success and the old lady was deeply moved by his compliments to her beauty and talent, mostly stolen from La Tosca. The other joke was that Alex was often mistaken for an Italian and this truly pleased him. When this happened, he found himself confronted by a torrent of fluent Italian, much beyond understanding or the chance to respond to. In response he would thoughtfully stroke his beard. How deep can you be?

The first big friend he made during our stay was an Italian writer and his Russian wife. The wife was truly amazing, funny and very dramatic. Their house was never cleaned. The sand walked in on many feet and slowly collected along the edges of walls and the corners of rooms. "Excellent Feng Shui," she said. Tragically she had just had surgery for her heavy Russian upper eyelids. The surgeon was very good, but had removed too much lid from the right eye, so that now she was obliged to sleep with a partially open right eye. "I never sleep; I am obliged to see everything," she said.

Then the hippies arrived in Procchio: young Dutch couples, Germans with long golden manes, English girls with remarkable breasts, and a young Italian from Milano. They were students, artists, musicians and poets. The guitars were strummed when the sun went down; people's terraces became dance floors. There were skinny dippers on full-moon nights, poetry readings on the beach, and wonderful singing under the stars. The wine flowed. Visitors took some of the couples into their rental cottages, where they slept on couches or rugs. Those not so fortunate slept behind a bush on the beach. Everyone was always invited to the restaurant for food. After all, they sang for their supper. The restaurant was on an open rooftop overlooking the bay. The chef, the son of a fisherman, had been trained in Switzerland and was a superb cook. The food was just so varied and wonderful I shall pine for it forever. We ate all of our lunches and dinners there. After dinner the music would start somewhere and everyone was invited to the dance. Kirstin ran wild with the hordes of children and never had so much fun.

Surprise

The next surprise was the arrival of Martin (my first boyfriend) in Elba. He arrived with his wife, an infant, and six-year-old son, Till. Till was cross-eyed. The young wife was vulnerable and overwhelmed, not surprisingly so, as her husband also brought along his long-time mistress from Paris,

who, as he told me, was a prostitute and had taken him into
her flat when he was without means and living the life of an
artist in Paris. Her name was Millu, and she was quiet and
shy. Gerda had told me he was coming to Elba with his family,
so I was not surprised by his visit. I was standing on an open
veranda overlooking the ocean when he arrived. It had been
10 years since we last saw each other and I was surprised at
my reaction to him. He looked so sensitive and vulnerable and
shy, not how I had remembered him. But it did not take more
than two days for him to try to corner me to talk. I shied away
from any contact that could be misconstrued or cause some
apprehension in Alex. Martin however persisted and there was
really nowhere to hide. I would catch him staring at me with
longing written all over his face. Perhaps it was my beautiful
Italian bikini. I never found out because any time he actually
walked straight towards me, I got up and ran into the ocean and
swam away.

He would follow me into the water. Still being an excellent
swimmer, I had no difficulty outpacing him and I swam far out
into the bay before I stopped and looked back. He had given
up and was making his way back to shore. Then, however, he
cornered Alex and invited him to his cottage for a drink. Alex
was gone for a long time and came back most amused. It seems
Martin was still trying to explain to himself what had happened
to the great love affair with me. He told Alex in great detail
how much in love he had been with me, and how I treated him
with great cruelty and indifference in return. When he invited
himself to Cairo during the summer holidays, he had intended
to ask my mother for my hand in marriage, something he never
told me. Alex was impressed with Martin and said that he would
hire him on the spot as a teacher of art.

Gerda's son Wenzi was the next arrival. Now a young man
in his twenties with a bountiful mane of dark curly locks,
he brought with him a young girl who was instantly named
Brunhilde because of her long, golden hair trailing down to the
back of her thighs. She was taller than him by several inches,
which amused me. Wenzi also brought along his sailing boat, a

sizable ship which would be used for day excursions along the Italian coastline.

And now the Dolce Vita began! What none of us had counted on was the reaction of the local population, the fishermen and merchants and owners of rental cottages. Newspapers began appearing on the beach, looking innocent enough, until one began to translate the Italian text. The locals felt there was an invasion of hippies—immoral, evil, and corrupt young people who were coming in like a horde of cockroaches. They took over the beaches of Italy, left excrement behind shrubs and plastic bags on the sand. They had no money and no manners. They were a plague and lived by panhandling. The worst thing, they smoked pot, corrupting the well-brought-up Italian youth. A story circulated that a corpse of a Dutch girl was found whose eyelashes and teeth and nails had been pulled out before she was killed.

Another article I read in an English publication described a group of American hippies on a somewhat remote island who had all been found shot to death. I never saw this story published in any of the big papers elsewhere, and I looked and searched in vain. Gerda's son Wenzi was the first to sound the alarm. The owner of Gerda's cottage came to tell her that she would never again be allowed to have his house for the summer if she and her son did not get rid of all the hippies. He blamed Wenzi for attracting these young people to the island and the bay of Procchio sur Forno. Wenzi spoke excellent English and asked Alex what he should do. In essence he had not had anything to do with all the young hippies who came. Long discussions followed on the beach and over cappuccinos on the large veranda overlooking the water. Most of the young people found Alex sympathetic and came to trust him with their individual stories. One afternoon a number of Italians were invited to the discussion. Alex lobbied for the young people. However, the minds of the Italians were made up, their verdict inflexible. Either the young people would have to leave or all those who came as annual visitors would be out of luck in the future, and that included Gerda. Alex was a master at gentle persuasion and talked the young people into departing, as no one wanted trouble with the angry locals. They all left that same afternoon and Wenzi drove them to the small harbor, where they boarded the ferry travelling to the mainland.

These events put a definite cloud over our stay. The cove was quiet and empty once more. Martin's son Till amused himself by standing on a rock at the edge of the ocean. Most of the children ran about naked, Till included. One day he began to massage his little penis until it stood to attention. His mother rushed to their cottage for the camera to capture this important event, obviously delighted.

This was the summer a book called *Papillion* came out. It was the story of a convict and it was a bestseller. I recall being completely absorbed in this story and disturbed by it. Then Alex developed a very itchy rash. We stopped eating shellfish, thinking it was the culprit. A German doctor arrived and taking one look at Alex, told him these were "no-see-um bites," not a rash caused by shellfish. Further conversations evolved during which Alex asked him about his high cholesterol, something a doctor in Illinois had diagnosed. The doctor smiled. "You know, olive oil does not cause high cholesterol, nor does the diet you describe. We Europeans see these matters in a different light and think the American consumption of excessive amounts of fatty meats and dairy products is the culprit." A year later American physicians would agree with him.

When our time in Italy came to a close, we decided to drive to Austria, but we couldn't find a convenient house to rent. Because of that, and as winter comes early in Eastern Europe, we decided to drive through France and south into Spain.

Spain

We rented a house in Marbella on the Costa del Sol, thinking to spend the winter there. The house was called Villa Christina and it belonged to what they called an Urbanization, which was a corporate housing development. It was a lovely white house, designed in a strictly Spanish style, and it was very comfortable. What we had not counted on were mosquitoes. They came at night, but turning on the indoor lights kept them away. Of course, as in Italy, mosquito screens were unknown. Alex was the most affected by the insects, and thus he spent his nights reading and slept during the day. I was left to my own devices with my little girl. We walked through the countryside, most of it sheep region, and picked wildflowers. The beaches were a disappointment. So much black oil had come ashore that the soles of one's feet were soon covered with tar, which had to be scraped off with a knife and then worked on with a solvent like turpentine. The beaches were narrow and bordered by skyscrapers, and the local fishing villages, which used to be there, were mostly gone. To my surprise I found a lot of foreigners lived here—Saudi Arabians, Swedes, English, and Danes. I was told by locals that their land had been invaded by northern Europeans and the coastline was no longer theirs, but now owned by Urbanizations. They also complained of the shoddy building materials being used and they predicted that many houses would look like slums in ten years. While we were there, quite a few roofs actually did cave in. Of course, the invading foreigners brought with them their own tastes in foods. The bakery was Swedish, the restaurant provided fish & chips and bangers & mash, and tour buses loaded with Brits stopped there for lunch. The more elegant restaurants were French-owned and very snooty (which meant they did not like children.)

We did the usual thing, which we had already resorted to in Italy. We drove to great sites of interest like Cordoba, Granada, Valencia, Tarragona, and Barcelona, and I fell in love with Spain. The land looked ancient, the cork tree forests called to me, Andalusia was magical, and when a side trip was longer, we stayed in the parador hotels, which were beautiful old mansions or palaces made available by the government to house tourists. For more than a month we toured Spain before deciding we were tired of travel and needed a place free of mosquitoes. We turned north and drove back through the center of Spain so we could see Madrid and its sights. By this time Kirstin was quite used to falling asleep on my lap in a restaurant, as dinners started after 10 at night. We used a Michelin guide to find top-notch restaurants, and I must say that we scored. My taste buds were never the same after the magnificent meals I enjoyed in Spain. When I returned to the USA, I cooked a different meal each day for a full year and only stopped doing so because of the request for repetitions of certain favorite dishes.

Madrid remains in my memory due to the shock of seeing the black paintings of Goya in the Prado. No reproductions had given me a clue of the impact I would feel finally seeing these works of art. I felt stunned and walked around in a high of sorts for days. Of course, we visited the Prado daily. Kirstin would stop in front of some paintings and show her appreciation and excitement by waving her arms up and down. Our slow pace did not suit her and though warned repeatedly not to rush ahead, she did just that. We decided she needed a lesson and one day we purposely hid ourselves until she noticed our absence. The child had a loud and clear voice, and suddenly we heard her shouting with such force the sound reverberated from the stone walls: "Daddy, where the fuck are you?" I rushed to calm her and Alex pretended he had nothing to do with her, as people were turning their heads to look at us.

Kirstin had, as any child would, her blanky, which she called "Beety." Originally it had been a beautiful negligee, a gift to me at her birth. Naturally three years on, this garment had become a rag and been replaced by an expensive silk slip. She had to have this piece of cloth and nothing that lacked the silky feel or smelly smell of the fabric could console her when she went to sleep. In fact, Beety was with her always, and because of our travels, Beety was somewhat grimy. Mosquito bites had been scratched bloody and Beety had soothed the itches, so naturally it was bloody as well. Going out to an expensive and luxurious Madrid restaurant one day, Beety was left under the table where Kirstin had played in her usual way. The loss was discovered as I was pushing her stroller along an elegant avenue. "My Beety," was her loud howl of distress, "I need my Beety." Alex refused to go back to the restaurant. "What will the waiter think if we retrieve a blood-stained woman's silk slip from under the table? What will he think we did? I hate to think!" So instead, we went to a fancy clothing store, and after sampling dozens of fabrics by rubbing them across her cheek, Kirstin eventually found one that was acceptable, even though it did not smell quite right yet.

We met one of our colleagues from Lake Forest College, a professor of Spanish language, for lunch. He was a very charming man and our restless little girl amused him a lot. I must say the Spanish are very accepting of children and their ways, for the waiter in this particular establishment took Kirstin with him behind the bar. A wooden platform there made a wonderful noise. He showed her some flamenco steps and thereafter she practiced rattling the boards nonstop and had the best time. To our surprise, none of the guests complained.

Driving to Scotland

Alex had called an old friend in Scotland and asked her if she could find him an affordable place to rent. This she did, in a village called Dalkeith, near Edinburgh. We were ready to settle down a bit. "But what are we going to do?" moaned Kirstin. "I want to see more castles and museums and cathedrals. And I want to eat toasted cheese sandwiches in pubs." "No," Alex told her, "in Scotland little children are not allowed in pubs." This resulted in screams of sorrow from Kirstin, who begged not to be taken to such a boring country. At top speed we made our way up to northern Europe, Germany this time. My mother was visiting Germany from Kenya and this was an opportunity to see her, and, far more important, for her to see Kirstin. The Citroen car could be driven at high speed up the Autobahn and it was amusing to see Germans deciding that they would not stay behind a French car but would instead overtake us. Meanwhile Kirstin was in the back with all her stuffed toys, serenely playing.

We reached Cologne, where naturally I needed to see the Cologne Cathedral, which I had not seen since that black night after the war when we waited for the horsedrawn carriage to take us to Frauweiler. Back then, it stood like a lonely sentinel among the charred ruins of the city, reminding me of praying hands. What a surprise to see it surrounded by banks and hotels, and so tightly squeezed in that it was literally losing all of its power to the glass and steel buildings of the 20th century. But I was assured that in the old medieval Cologne it had always been squeezed in. During that afternoon we also visited a famous German artist in his studio. He was most gracious and he impressed me with his humility. He showed us painting after painting and some wonderful drawings. I saw for the first time the type of life an artist must live in order to work, the environments that were needed for an artist to be productive, and the faith in oneself needed for creativity. In a sense, he was a model for me, showing me what was required.

We met up with my mother and she joined us for the drive to Berlin, which at the time, was still a city divided in half by a concrete and barbed-wire-topped wall. One sector was under American supervision the other dominated by the Soviet Union. All those many years after the Second World War, the city was still split and so was the population. Those in the East Sector could not visit the West Sector. The West Sector in fact was an island inside what was referred to as East Germany. We reached the border quite quickly, driving at 100 km an hour, and found it a pain to be reduced to the slow driving speed of 60 km an hour. Big warning signs along the way threatened us with arrest if the reduced speed was not kept. At one place we were stopped and the car was searched; then we were allowed to resume our journey. As we regained speed, I saw two men walking, one behind the other. The second man held out his arms in a curious way, holding something. Then I realized that he held a revolver in one hand and was supporting his right arm with his left hand. "Did you see that," I asked, suddenly aware we were in a dangerous and unpredictable place. Alex had seen it in a flash as we drove past.

At the border we had to go into a large room to have our passports examined. The border policeman was seated behind a high barrier of wood, peering down on visitors from this lofty height. I stood on tiptoes to hand in two passports, that of my American daughter and my own British passport. When I dropped down to the soles of my feet, I could not see the official and all he saw of me was the top of my head. I heard the shuffling of papers, the thud of a stamp applied. Then silence. Suddenly he shouted: "Where is the American, I want to see him instantly." "It is a baby girl," I answered in German from below. "Where? Where?" he shouted, this time in rapid-fire German. It sounded just like the shouting resorted to constantly during the third Reich. Kirstin was sitting peacefully on the floor in a bright yellow dress. He shouted again, "I want to see the American." At this point Alex lifted up his daughter, high enough for the official to see her. He looked a bit sheepish as he stamped her passport.

Now my mother handed over her German passport. "Oh, young man," she said in a sugary tone of voice, "I have not been back to Berlin, which used to be my home for many years, could you tell me how to get to..." and she named a famous street in the West Zone of the city. The official did not answer, not even when she repeated her question. He looked angry. When we returned to the car, I asked my mother: "Why did you ask him this question, he seemed most irritated with you." She giggled: "He has never been to the West Zone, too young, but his pride forbids him to reveal he does not know the streets in West Berlin. I wanted to embarrass him after his behavior, when he shouted to see the American. He could have looked at the passport photo to see it was a child."

Visit to Berlin

Finally, we made our entry into a grey city. It was already November and the weather behaved accordingly. After some time, we were on our way to the old pre-World War II house, where my sister Gabriele and Klaus lived on the third floor. The outside of the building was still pock-marked by flack impacts and the building had once been much higher with many floors. Now only three remained. The hallway was dark and one had to push a button on the wall to get a light to switch on, which lasted only long enough to walk up one flight of steps. By then,

darkness would fall once again. Eventually we stood before
the door of the rather spacious flat and greeted my sister and
brother-in-law. To my surprise, the place was almost empty of
all furniture. There was a translucent plastic blowup easy chair
and a battered square table. The naked light bulb over the
table dangled inside an aluminum tin can punctured with many
holes to let the light out. A three-legged stool and battered
chair were the only other seats I saw. On the wall hung a huge,
famous black-and-white poster photo of Yoko Ono with John
Lennon naked on their bed.

We were shown our room which contained only a mattress
on the floor with a large blanket thrown over it. My mother's
room was just a little more civilized and prompted her to repeat
over and over again, "Oh, how charming!" She never removed
her coat for the evening and continued to wear her gloves.
The hallway contained a wondrous selection of photos of
nude students cavorting at a party. As we dropped our luggage
on the floor, Alex remarked, "My, how the other half lives!"
I needed to bathe Kirstin and asked for the bathroom. The
bathtub was black with grime. In the toilet a big turd bobbed
up and down. I tried to flush it away, but it returned again
and again. Klaus was delighted. "Do you like my trick turd," he
asked. I asked for something to clean the bathtub and was given
some cleanser and an apology. It seems they did not live here
anymore. The flat was rented to a student. Also, they were now
separated. This was surprising news, and bit by bit we received
more details.

Klaus now lived with another woman, who had a little girl. My
sister did not tell me where she lived, but in the course of the
next days, when walking through the Free University of Berlin
and being introduced to friends, she kissed several men on the
mouth in a most intimate fashion.

Klaus seemed bored with our company and invited Alex to
visit some pubs with him. The two men departed and came
back later for a wonderful Japanese dinner concocted by my
sister. He was to say much later that the only civilized member
of the family was Alex. That night, with Kirstin between us, we

slept under a small blanket on the mattress on the wooden floor. We woke up early and were ready to visit the Pergamon museum in the east sector of the city. My sister carefully explained the bus system to us, but after we left, we rounded a corner and hailed a taxi to take us first to a delightful café on the Kurfuersten Dam and then into the East Sector, where the museum awaited us. It was a very special experience and the art was intoxicating.

During the next few days, we saw many more exciting museums and places of interest before saying goodbye to everyone and heading for the ferry that would take us to the British Isles. The sea was rough and the sky overcast as we stood on deck waiting to see the white cliffs of Dover. There was a tricky two hours' drive past London. Kirstin played with her toys in the back of the Citroen, as we blasted up the Great North Road in the direction of Scotland. When we entered Scotland, the highway narrowed to a two-lane road, and the houses in the villages looked much poorer than those in England. Eventually we reached Dalketh, outside Edinburgh, and took possession of our rental house. Someone explained the complex computerized heating system, and after this, we unloaded the car and put our child to bed. Dalketh was a new, modern development, with fairly large gardens surrounding pleasantly designed houses. The gardens backed onto old forest with huge old trees and had access to trails along a stream which afforded me hours of wonderful walks in nature. In many ways it was so much better than the Urbanization Villa Christina on the Costa del Sol. The artificial element in the development was not obvious here. These houses were built for local people and not as an investment for foreigners. The house we rented was reasonably-priced, spacious without being ostentatious, and simple while providing us with all the comforts we needed. It was also a relief to be back in an English-speaking part of the world, and here Alex could sleep at night without the whine of mosquitoes. He relaxed visibly and Kirstin soon made many friends among the local children. She now rode a tricycle we brought up with us from Germany, and up and down the empty road outside the house she would ride, attracting other children. She invited them home and generously told them just to help themselves to the huge bowl filled with fruit that I was in the habit of placing on the dining room table. Alex explained to me later that the Scots are not in the habit of eating fresh fruit on a daily basis, and those children would not hesitate to help themselves to several apples at a time. Hence the fruit bowl could empty within an hour or so.

Six Month Stay in Scotland

In no time Kirstin was picking up the local accent and talking in a broad Scottish brogue I could not understand. One morning a little boy no older than four tugged at my sleeve and in a broad accent which I failed to understand, asked for a "phish." I went to Alex saying I could not understand the child. He got up and talked to the little chap. "He just needs a pee, take him to the bathroom."

I protested, "But I don't know how to take a little boy to the bathroom. What do I have to do? Perhaps you should take him." Alex replied, "Oh, it's not hard, just hold his little whatnot and direct it into the bowl." Somewhat self-consciously, I did as I was told. Later, barely able to hold back his mirth, Alex asked me how it had gone with the little boy. I told him and he howled with laughter. Apparently, the child was perfectly able to pee by himself!

We stayed in Scotland from December until late spring. There were old friends of Alex's with whom contact was resumed; we visited his closest friend in Aberdeen, for a spell, as they say there. He was head of the Aberdeen Art Academy and a well-known artist in Britain. I was really taken with some of his paintings and it was easy to understand why Alistair was Alex's best friend. They shared a mutual ability to guide young artists and to teach them. However. the new difficulty was that now young people in Aberdeen no longer wanted to learn the methods and techniques of painting, drawing, or sculpture. They wanted to do something amazing and different.

They refused the instruction and assignments given by their teachers. The standards of art were rapidly changing and students believed that, as the song says, "anything goes." Alex was grateful that students in the USA were still enthusiastic about the art history and "applied art" taught there.

Aberdeen was called the "granite city," and the houses built of that hard rock had walls at least two feet thick. I recall that it was very cold there, the damp cold that penetrates the bones. I liked the Scottish people very much and most of those I met were real characters with a wonderful sense of humor. We would drive to Edinburgh to pick up our groceries for the week and shop in stores known for high quality. Among them was an Italian grocery that sold Italian cheeses, breads, and chestnuts, etc. We usually had Kirstin with us. On one occasion we put the groceries on the back seat of the car, beside her. Back at home when I unpacked the bags, I found the Italian loaf of bread surprisingly light and when I looked at the end of the loaf, I saw it had been totally hollowed out by little hands. Only the backed shell remained.

The time spent in Dalketh was relaxing and pleasant; however, Alex gave up on the idea of writing a book and dedicated himself instead to playing with his little daughter— playing for hours building structures with Lego blocks. I returned to my favorite pastime: painting pictures in the kitchen and visiting many museums, galleries, and art shows. We took one extended trip to the cold north to visit Scottish castles, lochs, and islands.

I was very keen to visit the Isle of Skye, the Findhorn gardens, and Loch Ness, famous for the great monster that was reputed to dwell in its dark waters. The month of May had come, and we set off only to find the rain continuing day after day, with little intervals of brilliant sunshine that illuminated the countryside like a floodlight just long enough for a photograph. When we reached Loch Ness, Kirstin and I set off on a walk along the shore, but no matter how long we stayed, the monster did not show itself. Alex was having a beer in a pub and there we saw an abundance of photos taken by many people who had

had the good fortune of seeing the monster. The endless rain was dreary, and in the highlands, it turned to snow. The people up here were renowned for possessing the power to see into the future and were often very taciturn.

This was also the first time I saw what were referred to as the "Black Scots." They were black-haired, dark-eyed, and of darker complexion than other Scots. No one could quite explain why they were different; perhaps an older tribe from the highlands mixed with blood of lowlanders. We also stayed in some of their splendid castles with beautiful surroundings— gardens and hunting grounds—reminiscent of an older time when this country had not been a colony of England. These people were extremely proud of their heritage. The thistle, I was told, is the national flower of Scotland, which fits as the Scots have such a prickly nature—they are sensitive and quick to take offense.

Cousin Robin the Psychic

It was during this time, while traveling in the car, I learned a bit more about the family I had married into. It seems Alex's grandmother was almost pure Scandinavian from the high north of Scotland and she was psychic. She would know when someone in the family was ill or about to die. Alex also had a cousin, Robin White, who was a spiritualist and no one talked about him—he was just not mentioned. When the cousins were all little boys, they would play together when the various family members met during holidays.

Robin would talk about a "white lady" who sat by his bedside when he went to sleep. He saw ghosts and other beings and was made fun of in school. Obviously, this embarrassed the family. However, he also was respected as being strange and not to be messed with. On our way back from the highlands we stopped in a little village where we wished to visit an uncle and aunt of Alex. These people were the parents of Robin. Aunt Lila brought out fabulous homemade liquor and as this loosened my tongue a bit, I asked about her son Robin. "Aye," she said, "he is a Spiritualist minister and very capable. As a child he would tell me all about the "white lady" who came every night and sat by his bedside. Many famous people, especially film stars, have consulted him, including many Americans." She then showed me a picture of her son. I looked at him and thought that I would like to meet him tomorrow. I was curious to see if he was genuine.

The following morning, just as we rose, the doorbell rang. A very tall man stood outside with his short little wife, who had bright red cheeks and a healthy complexion. "Ah," he said, as he shook my hand, "you wanted to meet me. Well, here I am. You don't have to speak it verbally for me to understand the message."

A very interesting day ensued. Robin had a heavy Scottish accent and much of what he said had to be translated to me by his cheery wife. For a start, he said he was reincarnated and had been a Roundhead during the reign of King Charles the First. He gave me one of his rings to try, to see if I could remember something of my past lives. I could. Then he read my aura and told me I had some glandular trouble brewing, which turned out to be correct. In my diary from that period, I found a notation that he was startled to see, as he put it, "a big man standing 'ahind yee' (behind you). You are well protected; he is an Egyptian, by the looks of him, and from Pharaonic times."

In Alex's case, he saw him jump off a high wall in Kenya with the result of a damaged shoulder caused by the fall. He certainly could not have known about this, as Alex had not revealed it to anyone. He had been excessively drunk that night in Nairobi and really managed to hurt his shoulder and arm and had trouble shaking hands with people for the next few days.

For me, it was fascinating that this man could verify so many of my own experiences and advise me to trust myself. It made me realize there was more to life than what was commonly accepted. I wanted to know more; moreover, I also wanted to support this ability I seemed to have, and which I had never totally accepted. Alex was very uneasy around his cousin and assured me there were some dark forces at work. I did not feel this way, in fact I felt well and free around Robin. His advice was that I should mentally ask for what I felt I needed or wanted. "You will be given what you ask for" he said.

It was interesting to notice that Robin was instantly given what he admired or liked. My mother-in-law gave him a little cake stand because he admired it. Alex had a huge old L.P. record collection, which must have been of quite some value. He gave it instantly to Robin, and then later complained for years about the loss of his collection. He had been a little boy when he began buying opera recordings of great singers. In fact, he spent all his pocket money on this. "But why did you give it to Robin?" I often asked without ever getting an explanation.

We had bought a Citroen in France, a car not often seen in Scotland at this stage. Robin admired our car a great deal and on our next visit he surprised us by driving up in an identical Citroen. The encouragement I received from Robin allowed me to open my mind. One of the first books I bought as a consequence was by Carlos Castaneda, *The Teachings of Don Juan: A Yaqui Way of Knowledge*. I also began to ask for spiritual guidance. As summer was approaching, our time in Scotland ended.

A Return to Kenya

We had made the decision to spend the next months in Kenya with my mother. Kirstin became four years old in Africa and her birthday was so successful we had to celebrate three days in a row. My aunt and uncle, now retired, lived across the road and they too had to celebrate Kirstin. Alex enjoyed the huge and extraordinary garden my mother had established and settled happily back into an armchair for his studies and reading. We also reconnected with some of his old Kenya friends, went on Safaris, and painted.

Our best time was spent in Diani beach on the coast. The snow-white coast shaded by coconut trees under a deep, dark grey sky was shockingly beautiful. Here Alex and I had made our first connection and it was deeply gratifying to return to this amazing paradise. We rented a Banda (cottage) with a huge palm frond roof sloping over the whitewashed walls. There were no glass windows, only metal bars to prevent thieves from entering. As we soon discovered, everything else had easy access. There were black and white Colobus monkeys that smelled my neatly stacked fruit and with lightning speed entered and then disappeared with bananas, mangoes, and papaya.

Other monkeys came more timidly, some just to check out the space and curious to land on a table. Insects had easy access, as did lizards, who hunted the insects. When night time came, hurricane lamps were brought in by the servant, and this was our only source of light. Lizards soon found their way into the rooms to hunt the night moths and other insects that were attracted by the light. When the full moon rose, everything became so bright that sleep became difficult. The ocean had a glowing path of luminosity spreading through it and huge fish would jump high into the air and then splash back into the deep. The wind softly rustled in the palm fronds and the snowy frangipani blossoms intoxicated us with their fragrance. Distant drumming announced African ceremonies and dances. It was wonderful to be back in Africa.

The Art Business

When we returned to Lake Forest after our year abroad, we found that the couple who had rented the house had failed to move out and we had nowhere to go. Friends put us up for a few days. When we finally saw our house, it was a shock to see the state it was in. The hood over the stove was black and charred from a fire. The bathroom downstairs had guinea pigs in the bathtub who had eaten the edge of the shower curtain in frustration. A lame dog with a white scarf tied around one leg limped through the house. Obviously, our request to the agent not to rent the house to people who had pets had been disregarded. In the basement, in my crates for shipping art, huge plants were growing. All our standing lamps were placed around them fully lit. As we toured the house with some colleagues, I asked: "What are those plants? What do you grow in a basement aside from mushrooms?" "This is marijuana!" he said, amused at my ignorance of the happy weed.

After the renters moved out of the house and I took full inventory of the place, we found they had opened our private crates stored in the attic, pulled out antique silver coffee pots and trays, including our expensive china, taken out our typewriter, Kirstin's toys, and tricycle, and lost my radio and bike. The house was so filthy that four of our friends actually helped us clean the kitchen for one day. Still, it took me two full months of daily labor before the place was habitable once more. After that experience, we never ever entrusted the house to strangers again.

After our return to the USA, there was a distinct shift in the air and in our lives. My paintings had been selling well for almost ten years and I seemed to be gaining a small reputation for my work. Then suddenly the art market changed. I asked our colleague Franz Schulze for advice. He suggested I rent a studio and invite dealers into my work space. "You are not an artist if you paint in a bedroom. Your success has to be visible. They want to engage a real artist; someone whose work sells." "But my pictures have sold and very well," I responded. But he shook his head. "Your art has to be visible in your studio, in your environment, in your appearance. This is not Europe. You have to look the part, act the part, be the part."

Over the course of thirty years, the art critic Franz Schulze, a friend and colleague, not once reviewed my paintings when they were shown in exhibitions. I guess he did not think I was an "artist." Alex advised me differently." You are as an artist what you are as a human being," he said. "What Franz is advising is a role to play. Be yourself and be true to yourself; that is what I would suggest." He was right, but I did double my efforts, spending days in Chicago making the rounds of the Galleries and talking to dealers. However, I was uncomfortable doing this. Most of them were clearly not interested in wasting time looking at the pictures of some unknown woman.

One dealer even scolded me for not making a prior appointment. Another dealer with whom I had an appointment was on the phone for half an hour telling a client not to buy the work of an elderly artist because his work was not going to increase in value. "You have to collect the work of someone young and impressive in order to advance your blue-chip portfolio," he advised. These visits to dealers became a humbling and soul eroding exercise, as I was not treated with either respect or sensitivity. It was all about making money, about exploitation, and had nothing to do with love for art. Alex was very kind and helpful. Often, he used his only free time to go with me to visit a specific gallery and dealer. He was charming and he promoted me with sensitivity, but this did not work either.

Chicago is known as the windy city, the city of "broad shoulders." The wind always blows there. It is not an easy place to live in or to succeed in. The most successful gallery in town was something invented by the Women's Board of the Art Institute of Chicago. They named it the Art Rental and Sales Gallery. The gallery space was located in a huge basement underneath the museum. Here paintings by the talented artists of the Chicago area were hung and could be rented for certain desired time. If the client liked the art work, the rental fee could be applied against the purchase of the work. This took the guesswork out of buying a picture, as people could take their chosen image home and hang it on the wall. If the painting or sculpture did not please, they returned it. If they fell in love with it, they could now pay it off over time, paying the rental fee month after month.

At three-month intervals, artists were asked to submit three new pieces, which were juried by a committee of art experts. Sometimes all three pictures made it into the gallery, sometimes none was accepted. For me it was a very lucky and lucrative method and I sold a great many very large images. I found that I preferred working on a large scale and obviously there were enough wealthy people looking for big paintings to buy them. One day I received a telephone call from one of the ladies of the board asking if I would be interested in an exhibition of my work at the Art Institute of Chicago. They would come out to Lake Forest to look at my paintings and choose the most appealing ones.

I could hardly believe my ears and felt stunned and in disbelief. The Art Institute is the largest museum of the city of Chicago, and this offer was huge, with wonderful implications for possible success. When Alex came home for lunch, I told him the great news. There was one huge problem, however. Our house was so small that we could not show more than three pictures at a time in our living room, which happened to be the only large room in the house. Alex thought this over for a few moments and then said, "it's May, it is warm, and we can go outside. In Nairobi you showed me your paintings by placing them under trees. We have a pleasant back garden lined with huge old trees. Why don't we put the pictures under the trees? People can walk around, have enough space to walk up to a painting or stand back from it, it would be just perfect." We did exactly as he had suggested.

The women of the board arranged to come out on a Saturday afternoon. The day was sunny and beautiful and the chosen paintings glowed under the trees. A gentle breeze stirred through the foliage of the ancient maples surrounding the property. I was surprised at how many came. I think they were 20 people in total. We dragged out garden chairs, a bench, and blankets to sit on. Alex brought out white wine and juices. I remember talking a great deal, answering questions and explaining my painting methods. The whole event felt like one big, lively party. Suddenly a wind sprang up. We lived one block from icy Lake Michigan and it was early in the year. The wind brought with it cold blasts of air and within minutes the temperature dropped by 20 degrees. Everyone was rushed into the shelter of the house and after many compliments and assurances they confirmed the exhibition and gave me a date.

The summer lay ahead and we would have to make many frames. Alex had bought a big radial saw and took over the making of frames, which were very expensive to buy from a framer. Hence, we decided to make them ourselves.

I threw myself into the upcoming exhibition, aware of the singular opportunity this event offered, hoping that it would make my work more recognizable in the city. Aside from frames to be made, we had to select monotypes and large oil paintings which worked together and made a cohesive statement! Alex, with his knowledge of how to hang an exhibition, was an invaluable asset. The days passed quickly and the day for delivering the pictures to the museum arrived. We had nothing to do with hanging, so I was very curious how they would look.

Opening at the Art Institute of Chicago

The opening was on a Friday evening at five o'clock. I put on a beautiful dress I had sewn myself, made out of cloth hand-printed in Africa, red in color with abstracted black lions. It was summer and I was sun-tanned and with my long black hair I looked exotic, or so I was told.

It was a huge surprise to see the beautifully hung paintings glowing against the walls. A waiter offered a glass of wine to me and surprisingly, after only one sip, I felt tipsy. Soon people poured into the gallery. I was surrounded by well-wishers with hundreds of questions about my work technique and subject matter. Most surprising to me was the large number of Lake Forest College faculty who came, including the dean.

Dean Donnelly was a superb photographer, and the photos he took of me are probably the best ever taken. The evening seemed to move with surprising ease. Then a man who was the big Chicago art critic introduced himself to me. I knew how important his opinion was and hoped he would mention my work in his upcoming article on Chicago exhibitions. He immediately focused on one large painting, telling me repeatedly that he liked this one best. "If I were to want to buy one, this one would be my choice." I thanked him, pointing out some other pieces and asking his opinion. But he seemed oddly stuck on his particular favorite and after a while the conversation came to an end.

Later, Alex found me and we left, driving to a Greek restaurant for dinner. All this had been arranged beforehand

My first big art exhibition at the Art Institute of Chicago, 1975

and I was delighted to be surrounded by so many friends. As the evening wore on, I became very tipsy, not so much from alcohol as from excitement, and did not cover myself with glory when I thanked everyone for their support and presence. "I did not expect such an outpouring of kindness; in fact, I thought a lot of you did not really like me." A good friend, Moira, who was sitting beside me, drew in her breath and said: "My God, you dare to be so incredibly candid."

This was my one great, impressive exhibition at the Art Institute of Chicago. The following day an artist friend of mine phoned eager to hear about the event. She asked if the art critic had come to view the exhibition. "Oh yes, and he kept on about one large oil painting, saying that this one he liked best and would choose as his favorite." "So, I hope you gave it to him," she said. "What! I was supposed to bribe him with one of my best images?" I said in utter disbelief. "Oh yes," she said. "You did not know this? He won't write a line about you if you don't give him the image he likes. He owns a huge art collection and he did not buy a single painting himself. They all were gifts from artists." I did not offer him my painting and his article, when it came out, did not mention my paintings.

Years later, when he retired, an enormous art exhibition of his collection was offered for sale in one of the big galleries. Everyone flocked to see what treasures he had amassed. Alex, wise as always, consoled me saying: "Well, I am not surprised. This is Chicago, after all! Art is a business."

When the show came down, I was very delighted to discover three paintings had been bought by someone called Dunn. "Bless him," I said to Alex, "how amazing!" Alex smiled, "Wilson Dunn is my millionaire cousin from Canada. He was here for a sale and decided to give you a little boost." Later in the week Wilson Dunn came for dinner and turned out to be a most amusing character...and he was a self-made millionaire! When he heard that I could read palms he insisted on having his fortune told. His palm revealed he was in business together with another man, a partner whom he did not trust. I told him this, and since he had not informed either Alex or me that he had a partner, he was very impressed that this could be read in his palm. He took what I told him seriously.

Wilson did not feel secure about his partner and must have had an intuition or some reason for the lack of trust in him. His palm showed that he ran a severe risk of suffering a financial loss, and I suggested he find the weak points in his business. Wilson took my suggestion to heart. On his next trip to Chicago, he again came for dinner and brought a lavish gift for me. He had dissolved the association with the partner and in the process discovered that this man had planned to cheat him. After that, on every occasion when he was in Chicago, I was asked to read his palm. Eventually I knew him well enough to tell him something about relationships with women, which I saw in his palm. He frankly confessed: "Everyone has a hobby. Some men collect stamps. I happen to collect women." One Christmas a few years later he invited us to drive up to Toronto in Canada to spend Christmas with his family. We did, and had a very interesting time. He had married when very young, and his wife was Greek. "If my husband ever cheated me, I would leave him instantly," she volunteered. "How blessed I am to have such a good man who is a good provider."

Daily Life in Lake Forest

Time went by and our visits to Europe became less frequent. We didn't own our house, as we didn't have the savings required to buy. We also didn't have a TV, and seldom went to the movies. Instead, we listened to classical music, painted pictures, and read mountains of books. Eventually, I had to beg Alex not to buy more books. Our small house was overwhelmed with both books and gramophone recordings. Weekly I cleaned our house, shopped for food, and cooked all our meals. After Kirstin was born, I also decided to teach her German, with great success. I baked all our bread, and even made yogurt. Looking back, I am amazed at the amount of energy I must have possessed. I credit my almost daily yoga practice which continued as the years fled by.

I read extensively about yoga and taught myself asanas and breathing techniques from books. In those days there were very few teachers of yoga. Occasionally I would venture out and sample some teacher of high reputation. How my weekly yoga group of friends came about I do not recall. I certainly did not set myself up as teacher, but somehow, I guided the group of friends and we all progressed and enjoyed our sessions for many years. Some women wore skin tight leotards and came with colorful yoga mats; others came in shorts and practiced on blankets.

A book written by Swami Vishnu Devananda and dedicated to his Guru Swami Sivananda of Rishikesh was my main source for asanas. I had purchased this book in Cairo when I was 22 years old and used it until I was almost 50. This book was my main source, even though I failed to understand it fully. There was lively talk of yoga during those years, especially about the need to find a guru. However, I was not drawn to trying to find a master. When I did eventually meet my guru, not only was it a woman, but she came from the lineage of Swami Sivananda of Rishikesh and she had studied with Swami Vishnu Devananda, who had taught her asanas. I had the right book and guidance for those many years. No coincidence—I was being guided!

When Kirstin was five years old, I was hired by Lake Forest College as a part-time lecturer in art. Initially it was to replace Michael Croydon, who was on a leave of absence from the Art Department. Later it spread into teaching four days a week. I painted every spare minute I could find, especially on weekends.

One day a sad little girl said to me: "Other parents take their children sledding and ice skating; my parents only work." This comment truly shocked me and I tried to make amends by taking her swimming at the Olympic-sized college swimming pool in the evenings and on weekends. When she was a little older, we bought her cross-country skis and we had some delightful times skiing. I also managed to hang a swing on a high branch of a huge old elm tree in the back garden so she could have a swing like other children. Unfortunately, we lived in an extravagantly wealthy town. For one of her birthdays, we had handwritten invitations she handed out to children in her class. A couple of children did not come to the birthday party. Several days later on a walk with Kirstin we saw the two little girls and Kirstin asked them why they had not come. "We don't go to poor people's houses," they responded.

If Kirstin suffered social deprivation, she never let us know. However, by the time she was seventeen, she bought a little TV set so that her boyfriend, when visiting her, was not deprived of the sports games he insisted on watching. She learned to speed-read like her father and consumed vast amounts of books weekly. Kirstin gained quite a reputation in the Lake Forest Library, because she walked out with seven or more books under her arm at least once a week, much to the delight of the librarians.

She made friends easily and forged friendships with some wealthy girls. However, she rarely talked about these individuals and we got only occasional glimpses into the lifestyle of the very wealthy. "Daddy, why don't you have a big glass bowl to stuff dollar bills into, like the G's have. It makes it easier to have pockets empty of single bills, and if you need some bills, you just reach into the bowl."

When Kirstin first went to school she spoke with an English accent. It seems she was made fun of by the other children. In about three days' time, she acquired a very acceptable American accent. She also picked up a style of behavior that allowed her to get instant attention from the shop girls when she entered a store. Kirstin was a delightful child and very intelligent. One could fault her with nothing and we felt blessed. She was healthy, almost never ill, and had her first cold when she was five years old. Because she never had to learn how to blow her nose, she stood in the kitchen stamping her foot in frustration, wailing: "I can't breathe, Mummy, do something."

Kirstin

Kirstin did not approve of being called a girl nor did she play with dolls, which were thrown into a corner of her room. She insisted that she was a tomboy and thus had much more freedom than those girly-girls. Instead of dolls, she collected stuffed animals to such an extent that there was no empty space on her bed. When we drove to Florida for our annual summer holidays, she packed the backseat of the car with her furry friends and we had a major battle about leaving some of them behind. She also insisted on lengthy bedtime stories, and I had to make many of them up as I went along. The difficulty arose when I was asked to repeat a favorite and I could not recall it. Alex bought a tape recorder and my tales were recorded. Her father had a more difficult task. She had certain preferred opera death scenes, like the death of Othello. Not only had this to be reenacted with conviction, it also had to be sung. Alex hammed the whole bit as he stabbed himself and collapsed onto the ground while singing in Italian. She sat on her bed with glowing eyes enjoying every sob.

Kirstin was full of surprises and often amazed us with her audacity. While shopping at the supermarket, I encountered one of my neighbors, who approached me and said, "You will be as amused as we were. Did you know that Kirstin comes to our house fairly frequently with a big bag of rocks she selected? She claims that they are special and she sells them for a few cents. She is quite persuasive and good at selling her special rocks. We find her a delightful little girl."

I was quite amazed to say the least and found out later on that she sold her rocks at several mansions. On other occasions Kirstin came back home with tomatoes and berries she had bought for me from an elderly, white-haired neighbor, Swedish by birth, who grew her own vegetables. This prompted me to start growing my own berries and vegetables.

Kirstin and her best friend, Jennifer Galloway, were in the habit of roaming through the wild forested ravines at the end of Spruce Street that led down to the beach. They felt free to do what they liked and spent hours sliding down the muddy bluffs to the beach on a large piece of cardboard and building dams to block the water flow in the ravines. I usually cleaned up Jennifer's face just a little bit before sending her home.

One weekend, I trimmed the bushes and painted the outside back porch white. A few days later, Jennifer came over to play, and the girls went to the beach and collected clay from the bluffs in buckets. They then proceeded to plaster my beautiful white porch with it. On my return from teaching, I was greeted by a messy brown mud porch. Small handprints spreading out in all directions gave away the culprits, who beamed at me, thrilled with their great work of art.

The Bush Baby

My beautiful little bush baby lived for nine years. During its lifetime, we never had a mouse or cockroach or ant in the house. During the nights it roamed freely through the house and became fairly tame due to Alex's loving attention. He would hold out his hand and tell it to hop up, and it did. After he trained the little Lemur to jump up into his hand, the bush baby would jump onto his head and commence to groom his curly hair. It would coo in a throaty voice as it separated his curly strands of hair, grooming his head thoroughly with great

Kirstin, age 4, looking up at a sculpture
displayed at Lake Forest College, 1972

attention. Alex waited with bated breath for the next phase, when Bushy lifted a leg to pee into its right front foot, and then rub both soles of his feet, before marking his territory, which was Alex's head. This was the loving reward Alex received on an almost daily basis from his little friend. No one else received these signs of affection.

371

When I became pregnant, the little animal disliked my smell and avoided me completely. After Kirstin was born, it was affectionate once more and played for long periods of time with my hands. We had to keep it separated from the baby because it wanted to play with her. It seemed to have no sense of its own size and we would laugh ourselves silly when it tried to drag the full-length window curtain into a big brass pot standing in a corner of the room. He would establish a number of nests in the house in which he chose to sleep. Some soft baby clothes began to disappear, as well as silky underwear, only to be found months later in the bush baby's brass pot or some other unlikely nesting spot.

These creatures are said to have a digestive system much like human beings, only they choose to consume insects in place of meat. Certainly, he liked booze, and Alex had to guard his sherry or whisky glass carefully. Several times he managed to drop his head into the whisky glass and became tipsy. We did not want him to fall. He was a master at catching insects in flight and he held loud conversations with squirrels. In the summer time I would go out and catch insects for him: moths, crickets, worms, and beetles. I would release these creatures in the house in the evenings and watch the little hunter catch them. In Africa lemurs are tied to a stake outside huts or tents as they hunt the scorpions, snakes or spiders and thus protect the people. Another delicacy he enjoyed was chocolate. A box of truffles still wrapped and sealed was found opened in the morning with a considerable amount missing. He had carefully stashed some and eaten the rest. Perhaps the most touching thing was that he played with Kirstin's toys.

One morning Kirstin got up early and ran downstairs before Alex. "Daddy! Daddy!" she called, "Come quickly! Daddy, Bushy is sleeping on the floor." I buried him in the garden and mourned for weeks. I never wanted to own another pet to be kept as a prisoner in my house. For many years I dreamt of my little bush baby.

Tina

We were introduced to Tina at a party. She was an extremely wealthy woman and she lived near Boston. A summer residence on Cape Cod, a huge palace of a house, was where she lived during the summer, as well as in Bermuda. When she discovered Alex painted portraits, she immediately fancied having herself portrayed. Since money was no object, I encouraged her to be courageous and to choose a more generous canvas size, large enough for a half-length or even full-length picture of herself.

She came to our house to look at the full-length painting of a very beautiful woman on which Alex was working at the time. I could see that she was impressed and delighted at the notion of emerging out of a virginal, white canvas like magic and discovering how extraordinary she actually looked. However, she chose a size of canvas only large enough for a full head and shoulders, what artists refer to as a bust because the figure is cut off just under the shoulders.

Alex arranged for a number of sittings. Tina had shoulder length brown, softly curling hair and large, dark eyes. She was certainly attractive and Alex "laid-in" what is called a "ghost," a start to the picture that looked very promising. Alex was a very talented portrait painter with a great deal of experience. He easily could bring forth the true personality of the sitters while he conversed with them and kept them entertained and lively. He always claimed that he allowed them to move, talk and laugh, as otherwise there would be no life in the portrait. He did not require his subjects to sit still; rather he enjoyed capturing the energy and life force through engaging them in an animated conversation. He asked Tina to tell him something about herself, what she liked and what interested her.

The studio was upstairs and when she came downstairs after her second sitting, she looked flushed and excited and told me it had been a most significant time and experience in her life. "He is extraordinary," she told me. "He pays total attention and listens to me, and I feel as if he is able to see straight through me and he sees my soul." That remark should have been a warning to me, but though I heard it, I did not attach particular importance to it.

There was a pause of about a week between sittings. Tina flew back to Boston and a week later she called to announce her return. "To whom shall I send the flowers?" she asked. Confused I asked her what she meant. "Well, you will probably invite me for dinner together with some of your interesting friends, and in that case, I shall send a flower arrangement." Not missing a beat, I thanked her for her gracious floral gift and thus invited her for dinner. During the next sessions, the portrait progressed rapidly, and Tina's face began to peer out of the canvas, unmistakably Tina's face. As she stood in front of the picture, she declared herself feeling shocked and confessed: "I have never known I looked so vulnerable, so sensitive, so naked and intense. I never knew or believed anyone could see this part of me."

The image was now ready to be shipped to her as soon as it was dry enough. Once it was varnished, I took photos of it, as this was how we documented our work. Tina sent a lengthy thank you letter to Alex after receiving the picture. Her husband loved the image and they wanted an unveiling, to which they invited us during the summer vacation.

Unveiling

We decided to drive East, in order to see and experience a little more of this huge country we had chosen to live in. We arrived at their house after a very long road trip in the late afternoon. Their home was a beautiful two-story structure overlooking a small lake with mountains rising behind it. Kirstin, tired from the long trip, ran out to the beach and ran barefoot through the shallow water. There were blueberry bushes on the hills and majestic ancient oaks offering their shade. We were asked inside for something to drink and were shown to our rooms. The curtains were made of heavy silk and the four-poster bed impressed Kirstin especially.

Then we went downstairs and met Donald. He was a slender, sensitive looking man. He invited us out for dinner in his favorite restaurant. Though still early, the restaurant was already filling with patrons. The menu was sumptuous and I was looking forward to a good dinner. Don suggested a first course and then ordered it for all of us. When the waiter asked what we would like as a main course, Don said this was all we needed. The look of disdain on the waiter's face told me all. After consuming the appetizer, we got up and left. Kirstin complained she was still hungry and got a glass of milk out of Tina before we all said good night.

When I pulled back the silken bedcover a rich aroma of body odors hit my nostrils. I bent down to the pillow to confirm my impression that these sheets were not clean. Then I went in search of Tina and asked her for fresh linens. "Oh, the maid must have forgotten to change them," she said, handing fresh sheets and towels from a huge linen closet. I returned to our room and changed the linen.

The next morning, when we came downstairs, Don was already making tea. There was a little round table in the spacious kitchen and old chairs, one with only three legs. Your chair is missing a leg, I said. "It is all right. We like it that way. One has to balance continuously to stay seated. I shall sit on it."

After breakfast we were guided into a large reception room where Tina's portrait hung on the wall. Tina stopped in front of the portrait. "Alex, do you realize, you painted some white hair on my head," she asked. "Where," he asked. She pointed to an area where highlights illuminated parts of her dark hair. "My dear, those are the highlights on the hair surface. Without that your hair would appear dull and lifeless. This is how your hair looks. I only painted what I saw. Hair is alive, shiny so it reflects light from its surface and it has many different tones and shades of color." Tina looked unconvinced. Alex pulled me forward into an area where light streamed through a window. "Look at her hair, there is a difference in color where the sunlight touches the hair surface. Can you see that?" I felt amazed at her inability to be able to distinguish tonal differences, while Alex continued to point out how the eye reads color and form.

Later we drove to the ocean and the huge villa Tina owned and wanted us to see and I suspect admire. It was an amazing house overlooking the ocean. Waves were gently lapping the shore and I would have loved a swim. However, Tina had to show us her property. With a small child in tow, mealtimes had to be observed and we were clearly not going to be fed lunch. We excused ourselves and found our way into the town.

That evening, Don told us a bit about himself. He had distinguished himself already as a teenager by an astute capacity to smell more than a normal person could. He was able to distinguish the fragrance of different herbs, spices, teas and coffee beans, wines and liquors. Eventually he was hired as "the nose" by a huge tea company. He bought the dried tea leaves in Asia that would become the tea varieties and combined them in creative ways to enhance their fragrance and taste.

He was widely travelled, but had never been to Africa. "I don't just want to book and go on an expensive safari. I want to experience the land and the African people, the wildlife and the jungles in the way a local can. The stocks of my wealthy grandmother have come to maturity and I wonder if you, who have lived in East Africa, would be willing to act as our guides and to join us on a three months safari. Of course, we would cover all your expenses in return. What do you think? It would give you, Ramona, a chance to visit your mother. I gather you also have an aunt and uncle living there. Perhaps we could even stay with your family, so as to live like residents in Kenya."

I could barely believe my ears. It all sounded just too good to be true. Here was a unique offer and opportunity for all of us to return to Kenya, which was a very expensive trip and one we could ill afford. It was a lot to consider and take in, so we decided to sleep on it. There would also be much to arrange in Nairobi, lodges to book, transport and safaris to arrange and we would need the help of my mother for that. In the morning I told Don that there was much to organize and I would let him know after talking all this over with my mother, as she would have to be the central person who decided our itinerary. I could arrange very little long distance. When we left, Tina asked me not to remove the bed sheets; as they would be all right for the next guests.

Heia Safari

Some weeks went by. Slowly the great safari was taking shape. We would be leaving for Kenya as soon as the summer holidays started to prepare everything for our guests. The whole offer was too good not to accept. And yet, I had some subtle doubts almost amounting to inner warnings. Tina was showing an excessive interest in Alex and Don had shown himself to be very stingy, as the example of the dinner invitation revealed. Yet, they were extremely rich people. How spoiled would they be? How much comfort would they expect? In Nairobi my mother was arranging amazing safaris and preparing rooms in her house for the guests. Tina informed us at the last minute that her 19-year-old son would also be joining us. This meant Alex, Kirstin and I would have to be accommodated in Alma and Christian's little house across the street from my mother's place, as my mother's house only had two guest rooms. How often are we given subtle signs of warning which are paid no attention to?

Tina had come for a last visit to discuss some details about the Africa safari. She was in our house when the phone rang. I handed it to her, as it was Don, but he wished to talk to me! Very puzzled I took the receiver. He said, "I need to hear your voice for assurance." "Assurance?" I asked, feeling confused. "Well, we will be together for many weeks and I hope our friendship is deep enough for growth." He rambled on about trust and intimacy, while I just listened feeling uneasy. Finally, he wanted to talk to Tina again. She returned to the living room looking bright and smiling as she said, "Well, it is all set now!" As Tina left that evening, she hugged Alex and said, "Isn't it wonderful, we will be together at last." Later we discussed these strange remarks and wrote them off as very odd. I hoped their expectations of Africa would be met with what we had to offer.

We arrived in Nairobi in June, the start of the African winter. My mother had been very busy indeed and organized wonderful events. She now suggested a very short trip to the white, tropical coast of Kenya, at the Indian Ocean, where we planned renting two houses for the visit. My mother wanted to be sure they were all right and wished to look at them first. Though I had taken anti-malaria pills, I developed a high fever on our return. We were fortunate to know the German Embassy doctor, who came promptly and examined me. The blood sample, when tested, showed no malaria.

The following days our guests from America arrived and we took off for our first safari to the Ngoro Goro Crater in Tanzania. This is a huge crater once owned by two German brothers, now a national park. It is filled with huge herds of antelopes, rhinos, and rare, black-maned lions. For two days I was too ill to do more than lie in my bed in the lodge. On our return to Nairobi the doctor came to the house to examine me again, feeling certain that I did have malaria. This time he personally examined the blood slides he had taken and spent hours searching for signs, until he finally did find malaria. "The cure feels worse than the disease," he announced the next day. "You may go blind for two weeks, but it is just temporary." He gave me my medication and further instructions. My mother and Alex took off for another safari, while I slowly healed.

I did not go blind from the medication, but something equally upsetting happened several times a day and especially at night. Suddenly the floor beneath my feet would feel as if it had dropped by several feet, while I desperately hung onto the nearest piece of furniture. Even while lying down in my bed at night, the sensation of falling would overcome me. When I had recovered sufficiently, I joined the trips into the African bush. Don insisted on sitting beside me in the rented jeep and Tina glued herself into a seat beside Alex.

Their son was a dangly 19-year-old, forever trying to get the best seat in the vehicle. He smelled unwashed, and it became clear when my mother confirmed he never had a shower. Eventually her African servant John complained, seeing lice on the bed sheets. When the young man left Africa three weeks later, his bedroom had to be fumigated because of an insect infestation. Meanwhile Tina bragged she had not washed her hair for six weeks. We drove daily with open windows through a dusty landscape of red earth and were covered by red dust by evening. One day Kirstin threw a temper tantrum in the lodge where we had stopped for lunch. She had not been able to sit beside her daddy, even in a restaurant, because Tina missed no opportunity to grab the chair beside Alex. I settled the matter fast and with authority, by giving Alex my chair and exchanging seats. Tina sulked and argued while we tried to change the subject.

Meanwhile, we had arrived in elephant country and the landscape filled with those ancient giants was magnificent. Everyone was trying to get the best view for their photographs and fighting for the best window seat. I began to find the whole situation very comical and teased Don at dinner time about it. It quickly became apparent he had no sense of the comical. That night, when we separated to go to our separate quarters, Don tried to hold my hand and put his arm around me. I slipped out of his reach. Alex told me that Tina too was making advances towards him. She confided that she and Don had had no sex in ten years, and she hoped that something might happen under the full moon in Kenya. "Why she should think I would fancy her, when I have a beautiful young wife, puzzles me," Alex said to me later.

"My Face Is Sore with Smiling"

The next day we all walked together on the snowy Diani beach. The coconut palm fronds rustled in the breeze and the Indian Ocean was purest aqua blue, merging into deepest turquoise towards the horizon. Skinny dark fishermen stood in their boats, poling themselves further out towards the reef, where the fishing was best. Don rented a native boat to go and see the reef, returning with a trophy shell, in spite of the fact that shelling was illegal. Our guests had become bolder in their demands for evening entertainment in bars, restaurants and nightclubs, which was a relief for us.

One evening after the day was complete, my mother called Alex to her hut, inviting him for a scotch with her. Since wine was the only alcohol I like, I often had the feeling that my mother considered me a bit too straight and dull. "Come join me in a scotch, Alex, my face is sore with smiling," she said as we all broke into laughter. The strain of entertaining nonstop was getting to all of us. We invented a game for Kirstin during our long safari drives, so that she did not get too bored. It was called "Who can spot the wild animal first." Usually it was the African driver, but Kirstin became outstanding. She quickly found wildlife before anyone else, especially elephants hidden among shrub palms. She established a special relationship with the pachyderms and could distinguish the rumble of their stomachs. Don politely said to her every time she pointed out an elephant," Thank you for sharing your elephant with us."

My Aunt Alma was an amazing ambassador of goodwill, and a great diplomat for all occasions. When she came to the coast to see how we were, she quickly began to entertain Tina. Quite efficient with Tarot cards, she read the cards for Tina and allowed her a glimpse into the future. Eventually a good friendship evolved over the coming years, and Alma and Christian were flown several times to the States and invited to "Permuda," as Alma called it, where they stayed in Tina's beach house. She scolded me for not using opportunities offered by these wealthy people. "They are just lonely and they will give you what you want" she insisted. In retrospect I think we had been very innocent and naïve not to have figured out that Don and Tina had expected us to be willing to switch partners with them.

Don was curiously encapsulated in his own belief systems and concepts and both were living in a make-believe world. The house we had rented for them at the coast came with an African servant-in-charge, who was responsible for cleaning, dishwashing (no dishwashers or washing machines available) and laundry. When Don discovered this man expected a gratuity for his services, he claimed he did not need help and that keeping a servant amounted to an insult to the Africans and was exploitation. In vain we explained that the owners had insisted on this arrangement to protect their property, and that Africans needed jobs to make a living. Several times Tina came to "borrow" our servant to scrub pots and pans and to wash her laundry. She never gave a tip. During our quite frequent meals in game lodges, the waiter always brought the bill for all our food to Alex. Don never offered to pay for his part of the meal, and ignored the fact he had promised this whole trip would be paid by him. At the end of the summer, we returned home with a hefty credit card debt.

There was a huge, newly built hotel on the beach, where African drumming and dancing were held nightly to amuse the tourists. Don and Tina wanted to go there and insisted we come too. Neither the music nor the food was particularly good and Alex clearly felt unwell. During the night he started vomiting and simultaneously had diarrhea. In the morning my mother looked thoughtful and worried. "I don't like this," she said. "This looks like an intestinal disorder characterized by an abnormal frequency of vomiting and loss of body fluids. The body dehydrates within 48 hours and people die of this." She offered to drive us to the hospital in Mombasa, but Alex, who had lost all bowel control, refused the indignity of wearing a towel between his legs. All fluids, all water we made him drink was instantly vomited up or excreted. His eyes became dull and he looked exhausted. He no longer reached for his habitual cigarettes, and I knew this was a bad sign. He was failing right in front of my eyes, and no amount of pleading for a drive to the hospital was accepted.

By evening he was too weak to walk. My mother got into her car. "There must be some doctor in the African villages around here," she said as she took off. I sat beside Alex feeling frustrated and worried sick. The glamour of the tropical beach faded and the cottage looked dark and gloomy. That afternoon I walked for a while along the shore, contemplating the situation. The waves rolled into shore one after another, an inevitable sequence, unstoppable motion. What if Alex died? Suddenly my whole life turned upside down. What was the purpose of living? Did life have a purpose, beyond birth moving into death? All these distractions we seek are no more than the glittering foam bubbles on the water's surface. My feet walked forward by themselves and my heart felt like an empty cavern. Oh God, don't let him die. I know what my mother suffered after my father was gone. We have such a good life together I don't want it to end, not now, not yet. The velvet breeze stroked my skin. What would my life be without him? Our child would have no father, just as I had had no father after the age of six. I don't want that fate for my child. Please Alex, live! Your life is so precious for all of us.

What If?

The servant came to bring the hurricane lamp and light. Alex looked grey and his eye sockets were hollow. He was too weak to even lift his head. My God, I thought, tomorrow I shall be a widow! Who would believe that destiny can change so quickly? I rose to look at the ocean through the open door feeling terrified, alone, desperate.

Suddenly my mother was back. Behind her walked an African of delicate build, who turned out to be a doctor trained in Czechoslovakia and who spoke German. Gently he sat down beside Alex and took his pulse. "I have a brand-new drug here from America. It is our best hope." "But he will vomit it up instantly," I said. "That is all right," he answered. "Even a moment in the stomach leaves enough of the drug to bring about a change." Alex dutifully swallowed the pill. We all waited with bated breath. Seconds later the gag reflex set in. He vomited some substance of the pill up again. The doctor was satisfied. My mother rose to take him back to the African village. Alex sank down into sleep. Our guests did not come once during this and the following days to inquire about Alex. Very slowly Alex recuperated. He still did not ask for a cigarette and I hoped he would give up smoking.

Our Africa tour was reaching its final stages and our guests would soon be leaving for the States. There was no doubt in my mind that Alex would have died without the courageous interference of my mother. Of course, it helped that she spoke fluent Kiswahili and had dared to drive into native villages at night searching for a doctor. I withdrew my attention from our American guests in a central way and rarely responded to their requests, using the excuse of Alex's illness.

Before leaving the coast, my Aunt Alma had invited all of us to dinner at the Mombasa Club, the same Old Portuguese fort where Alex and I had first talked of marriage 11 years earlier. My mother, Alex, and Kirstin stayed behind at Diani beach as we made our way to Mombasa, crossing over to the mainland by ferry. Little had changed at the club. The same old attentive African waiters guided us to the open roof terrace, where a table awaited us. A little lamp glowed in the center. A superb dinner of many courses was served and three different wines uncorked.

Alma was the perfect hostess. Tina and she talked about the Tarot cards and how the reading had affected Tina. "Oh, that was nothing," Alma said: "You should get Ramona to read your palms. She is so accurate, told me so many things about my life I had actually forgotten. Quite amazing really!" There was instant interest and Don slid his upturned palm across the table towards me. I scanned his palm for just seconds, and then placed my hand over his. As diplomatically as I could, I told him this was not an opportune time and that we should find a more suitable occasion. Never before had I seen death marked in someone's palm so clearly. He had a scant year to live! Suddenly I also understood his strange hollowness, which amounted to a lacking life force. He did indeed die, though I had hoped I would be wrong. A year later he was hit by a motorcycle as he stepped off the curb to cross a street. Death was instant.

After returning to Nairobi, the couple flew back to the USA. We stayed longer, as Alex was still very weak and recuperating from his illness. We continued to stay with my mother and to show his gratitude, he painted a beautiful half-length portrait of me to give to her. I posed beneath one of her willow trees in the garden in a powder blue dress I had sewn myself. In all the years we had been together, he had never painted me. There were two incomplete tries, and when I asked him why he did not complete the paintings, he usually claimed that he was too close to me to see me accurately. It is difficult to paint a member of one's family, and the effort is usually rewarded with failure. I had to agree, as I had tried to paint my mother.

In the picture I depicted her as sweet and gentle, missing her fiery temperament completely. In short, it did not do justice to my mother's true appearance. This portrait he painted, when I was 37 years old, now hangs in my living room and I feel very grateful to own it. At the time he worked on it, I became quite shocked to see how sensitive and vulnerable I looked. It was difficult for me to believe I looked so transparent and not at all how I saw myself. I guess, we don't want to see ourselves as we really appear, and maybe try our best to look fierce and powerful. It is hard to acknowledge that we are all far more transparent than we would like to be.

Transformation

It took Alex over a month to recuperate from his illness, and the shock of nearly losing him changed me forever. I now saw the world and life from a very different perspective. When we married, Alex had persuaded me to continue developing my artistic gift, while he "whored in the marketplace," as he put it. Over the last few years one responsibility after another was heaped onto his shoulders by the college administration. It was very clear such demands were reserved for the most able and hardworking teachers, for those most reliable. He had almost no breathing space and I suggested that he look for another position elsewhere, at another academic institution. He did look for another position, but somehow the prospect of letting go of what he had built up as a department and starting again elsewhere did not appeal to him. He was older now and weary of the illusions of success. The life he had created may have seemed more desirable than the prospect of a struggle with new challenges. At any rate, we stayed where we were. Many of our first friends had moved on.

The difference for me was that I needed to get full-time employment and we needed to own a house. We had rented the balloon construction house built in the early 20th century from Joe M. at a very reasonable price. After eight years renovations were required, which were costly and not to his liking. Among other things, the electric wiring in the house needed to be replaced. Also, the water pipes were worn and leaking, and the village of Lake Forest demanded they be replaced. Eventually a severe reprimand arrived in the mail with the threat of a fine. After weeks of doing nothing, Joe hired some cheap plumbing service. Three days into the job the police came to stop the work because the plumber was unlicensed. Then the boiler leaked and flooded the basement on the day we were leaving for our vacation. I felt grateful that we were able to leave the mess and did not have to deal with it. When we returned, Joe asked us if we would like to buy the house. Alex's private response to me was, "I would not dream of buying a wooden shack." However, as Joe obviously wished to sell the house, we needed to find another place.

Thus began an intense search in this area filled with millionaire's estates. It quickly became obvious that our income and savings were insufficient to buy a house. I needed more work and income. Alex went to the dean of Lake Forest College and asked for a full-time art teacher for the department and requested it be me. The college agreed if I would accept a part-time position, teaching one course less than a full-time lecturer. None of the benefits would be bestowed on me. That was the best they were able to offer. We accepted. As chair of the Art Department, Alex was able to arrange a teaching schedule for me that suited my needs as a mother and artist. Nonetheless, it was often a challenge.

Looking back, I don't know how I managed to accomplish the many things I did daily. I continued to paint and sell many pictures, which became part of our income. Slowly over several years we built a small base for buying a house. We curtailed our spending and for ten years did not travel outside the USA. My mother came and visited us nearly every other year from Kenya during the African winter.

Every summer we spent a full month together in Florida, mostly in Englewood on the Sarasota Key, a long stretch of island chains along the Gulf of Mexico. The water was warm and inviting there and gave us an opportunity to escape from the vicious, humid heat of the Chicago area in Illinois. By then Alex had stopped painting altogether. Our vacations during the summer were the only time he had, and I encouraged him to return to art. Over the following years he painted hundreds of watercolors and gouaches of seascapes and clouds, which are truly beautiful. My mother also began to paint during her time in Florida and gradually became a well-known artist in Nairobi, Kenya.

Buying Our First House

By 1982 we had accumulated enough funds for the down payment on a house. I asked our landlord if it was possible to buy the house Kirstin referred to as "my home." A prior search with a number of realtors had brought us to the realization that most houses in Lake Forest were beyond our means, or so badly constructed and so poorly built, they were beyond consideration. We had seen friends pour a fortune into dilapidated houses. All older buildings had very small rooms, mostly because of the difficulty of heating during the long Illinois winters. Alex was a tall man at 6 foot 2 inches and was constantly hitting his head against door frames too low for someone his height. As for me, I simply found the inner, tight spaces claustrophobic. The house at 577 East Spruce, though modest, at least stood in a very desirable location, and having rented it for so many years, we knew there would be no surprises. On February 5, 1982, my birthday, we bought it, our first house in the USA.

I don't know who was more relieved, my mother or I. Finally, we had something, a property, a home. The many years of struggle had brought a result. Our friend Michael Croydon and his wife Beverly had also acquired a home in a rural area. We helped each other out by coming together to strip walls covered with ancient wallpaper and painting rooms, windows, stairs, and kitchens. These renovations were done on weekends as a group. By Sunday evening a great deal of change had taken place. At this point we celebrated our progress with a good meal and wine and set up the following weekend for the next task. Eventually both our houses looked transformed and much more loved. The gardens too, were changed with colorful flower borders and hedges, as well as new trees. The most difficult task was changing our upstairs bathroom, a tiny space just large enough for a wash basin, bathtub and toilet. Old wallpaper had to be removed and paint stripped before anything else could be done. No wall was straight, no angle was correct. I literally had to cut large patterns of paper for the new walls. We worked on this room for five months, and Alex claimed he had not been so miserable since being in the British army. However, in the end, we had a tidy little bathroom with new fixtures and windows that could be opened and shut easily.

Our house in Lake Forest, 1960s

The Ra Festival

Michael Croydon was a very creative individual and had instigated a "Ra Festival" every June at commencement, in the last days before the summer holidays began. The festival was named after the Egyptian Sun God Ra and celebrated by the students of the large Art Department. It consisted of a parade through the little town. The students dressed in fancy costumes, created floats, arranged a band that played music, held an auction for art, and finished all with a big dance and party. After our long and cold winter, the beginning of June brought a burst of flowers, warm weather, and the start of the summer holidays. The students were ready to celebrate their freedom and so the festival was a delightful occasion. The merchants of the town joined in the activity and enough money was made to help the Fine Arts department buy new easels and art supplies for the sculpture classes. Of course, the faculty became involved also and joined the parade in fancy dress.

The auction was a highlight, and Michael Croydon imitated a colorful London auctioneer with a Cockney accent. Pottery, photographs, paintings, sculptures, and drawings had been donated for the auction and the whole affair was a fun-filled occasion. The many trees in town were flush with the first lime green leaves and some of our talented students shot amazing films of the occasion. In the evening many students gathered in our little house and projected the films they had made during the festival. I recall being awestruck by their talent and by the youthful joy and delight caught in their films. There were children singing as they danced a reel among flowers in our garden, a magnolia tree in full bloom, its pink blossoms large as saucers, students scattering flowers from atop of their float, and dancers on campus, later in the evening. The joy was catching and real, and even my garden looked so different and beautiful to me in the films.

David

As Alex's children from his prior marriage became teenagers, problems began to develop, which were not entirely unexpected. They had been living in Argentina, where Jean was an ambassador, and they paid us a visit at Christmas time after a very long interval of separation. David was now fifteen years old and Frances thirteen. Alex wisely decided we should all drive down to Captiva Island in Florida for two weeks at the ocean. The weather there was usually beautiful, which was not the case in Illinois. We were concerned with all of us becoming stir-crazy in our little house in Lake Forest. Our Citroen car drove the distance faster than ever before, and we found a wonderful contemporary house for the Christmas holiday. We had plenty of space for everyone, even on rainy days.

For Christmas, the children received tape recorders, which were a big success. Once back in Lake Forest however, they needed to record something worthwhile and this was when our friend Michael Croydon became invaluable. The college had started again and Alex and Michael would come home together after work and let loose their creativity, enhanced by a little wine. Starting their first tape recording with a farting contest, which delighted David, the recordings grew to Monty Python-like productions, which left all of us howling with mirth and were highlights of British humor and creativity. Michael was present almost daily for new sound effects and ideas. Before returning to Argentina, David learned how to bake bread and was thereafter a self-sufficient baker and very proud of it.

A year later David Mitchell fell head over heels in love with a young Argentinian girl and refused to leave the country when Jean's time as ambassador was over. David also felt that yet another change of school for him, so shortly before graduating high school, was unwise and most inconvenient. It was decided to rent a flat for David, so that he could finish his schooling where he was. This meant the sixteen-year-old was without parental supervision and living all by himself. He was even forced to cook his own meals.

Looking ahead to the future, Alex suggested David come to the USA to get his engineering degree here. As it turned out, the US consulate in Argentina mistook David F. Mitchell for an older man with a criminal record, and refused all contact with the teenager when he tried to get a visa for the USA. Alex turned to his Washington friend, Congressman Robert McClory, and asked for help. Congressman Robert McClory came through with flying colors. The mistaken identity was discovered, and David received his visa. By now he had two years of university in Buenos Aires, but he was able to finish his degree in engineering at Northwestern University. I still see David arriving at the airport in Chicago, a huge young man with a mane of long black hair, who lifted both me and Alex off the ground for a bear hug.

Frances

I recall it was very early in the morning in Lake Forest, perhaps 6 am, when a call came from Ildiko. I answered the call and then handed the receiver to Alex. She informed Alex that his daughter Frances had become impossible to control. She needed to be sent to a Swiss boarding school in Geneva, a school she had already picked out. Calmly, Alex asked for details. I sat on the steps, able to hear some of the unfolding drama. It was clear to both of us that Frances could not be sent to a top-class Swiss boarding school on a college professor's salary, which was what Ildiko was demanding. Alex refused. I pointed to the floor, saying: "She can come here." Alex understood and suggested Lake Forest, and with that the destiny of Frances abruptly changed.

By the autumn she was in the USA and being tested in a variety of high schools. It became obvious that her educational level in every subject was way above the US standard and that she was actually ready for college. To her great delight, the fifteen-year-old was accepted at Lake Forest College as a freshman. Kirstin now shared her room with Frances and the girls seemed to get along well. Even still, I established firm rules. The girls had to make their beds in the morning and all clothing had to be hung in the closet. Since Frances had so many garments the overload of her stuff had to find room in the attic. To my amazement I counted 60 pairs of jeans! And all were identical.

During her first weeks, Frances was on her best behavior, but once familiar with the routine of our lives, old habits surfaced. When she returned from classes in the late afternoon and walked through the door into the house, she dropped her coat on the floor, then her boots came off, one after the other, then her bag and her books, and then she threw herself onto the couch. In one short stride, the tiny house was reduced to looking messy. I had to be the one who asked her to pick up her stuff. Otherwise, it did not happen.

First thing in the morning, Frances felt fragile and speechless as a consequence. Her father carefully prepared her tea, making sure it was the right temperature, and he stirred in one small teaspoon of sugar. He did not insist she eat breakfast nor ask her to talk to him. Her day started quietly. Years later she still talked about how lovingly her daddy had prepared tea for her every morning, making sure the temperature was just right when she sat down to drink it. Thus, for her first year at college she lived at home and her father took care of things.

For her sixteenth birthday, Frances wanted a cowboy hat and cowboy boots. Once these items were acquired, she proudly wore them day in, day out. As a consequence, students on campus called her "Texas," and one night at a small party on campus two boys made off with her hat. An infuriated Frances stormed out to find them and her hat and when she did, she shouted in her still heavily accented English: "You fucking bastards, you stole my hat! Give it back immediately or I will tell my daddy!" The hat was instantly returned.

She remained unimpressed with much, as her travels all over the globe had given her a broader view on life. It emerged that she was experienced way beyond her years. In my opinion, Frances was a neglected child, deprived of care and unused to protection and consideration. When I showed any concern for her, she easily misinterpreted it as interference and called it bothersome.

After several months she started to suffer from nightmares. The nightmare usually started on a dark river and she was losing sight of her mother. There was a storm and a boat and then suddenly, Ildiko was swept away, perhaps drowning in the darkness, and Frances could not reach her mother or find her. She would come downstairs crying inconsolably. I recall guiding her back upstairs to her bed and stroking her back trying to sooth her, but without success. The reason for her fears became obvious. Her mother had not called her or written to her since her departure for the USA. Frances missed her mother and also missed her former lifestyle in Africa, with servants, a chauffeur, parties, lavish shopping trips, and exciting safaris in to the bush. Alex wrote a long letter to Ildiko, asking her to write to her child. He did not share the letter with me, but I am sure it was scathing in reprimand.

After staying with us for her first year of college, we decided to allow her to move onto campus and to live in the dorm there so she could be with her fellow students. She graduated with an excellent degree three years later. Her aunt and uncle, who lived in Canada, invited her for the summer after graduation to their cottage on Lake Kawagama. There she met Gordon McBride, her future husband, and moved to Canada.

Summer in Florida

The year was July 1986 and we were in Florida with my mother and Kirstin. We had just arrived at Grayton Beach in the panhandle. Friends suggested it as a wild and wonderful place. It had high white sand dunes, but the place we had rented turned out to be most inadequate. The only place for Kirstin to sleep was on a couch that was far too short for her tall frame. It was Saturday, and the realtor's office was already shut for the weekend, so we had to wait until Monday, when the office was to reopen. It was very hot and when we walked to the dunes, discarded toilets, dishwashers, laundry machines and other large trash lay about, disfiguring the landscape. The locals arrived in large four-wheel vehicles, roaring down to the beautiful open water, where they spread out sunshades and beach chairs and large ice chests filled with beer. The water was clear and fresh, but instantly I was bitten by a tiny fish whose attack I could not avoid, and Kirstin was stung by a jellyfish. Luckily, we found a pharmacy that was open on a Sunday, but this latest disaster did not bode well for us. The following morning, we arranged to return to Englewood, Florida, which we had enjoyed on previous trips.

Kirstin had grown so well. How wonderful to have her as our child...what a gift. She was still recognizable as that little face I first saw 18 years ago, with the wise look in the eyes. Now she drove our car to Englewood, just a little too fast, as impatience to get to our destination overwhelmed her. The drive seemed endless and Alex lit one cigarette after another. He never took more than two or three puffs and then put the cigarette out. A nervous habit to be sure. I tried to stop him again and again, but without success.

8 Kundalini Yoga

Three Monkeys

Many years ago on my 13th birthday, a family friend gave me a little sculpture of three ivory monkeys sitting on a black tree stump. They were called "see no evil, hear no evil, speak no evil." Their symbolism was carefully explained to me and I did understand the significance of this wise Eastern saying. Telling Alex to stop smoking had a negative impact, seeing evil or danger in his habit created fear, and listening to friends and family complaining about his smoking made me unhappy as I could not change him; he had to want to change his habits himself. I tried to follow the wisdom of the three monkeys.

At this point in time, I started to become aware of inner changes that started at about the age of forty, when my heart chakra (the emotional center) began to act up. I had been practicing hatha yoga since my 21st year and studied a lot, so it was not entirely surprising that something should shift. I pondered questions like: "What is the force behind our spiritual drive, and what does it signify?" There was dissatisfaction with where I was in my spiritual life at that time and who I seemed to be, which caused by a deep stirring within. Ambitions grew that were not there before. In my dreams I was breaking through walls, entering new and unknown spaces, seeing expansions and discovering hidden parts of my dream house that I did not know existed. I began working with my dreams, daily, consistently, and discovered two levels of reality—the one within the realm of the rational mind and one beyond the area of the mind in a realm called the subconscious. This part of life filled me with joy and illumination and creativity. How could I create a bridge between these two worlds, how could I find the connection?

I found it through a book about mantras. Neither the title nor the author of the book which I read, remain in my memory. He was a yogi, an Armenian, I think. He related that chanting the mantra Om created a memory and after chanting Om a specific number of times aloud, the mantra would chant itself. It was self-perpetuating. I took the book with me to the beach, sat down in half-lotus and carefully, as prescribed, began to repeat the sound. I had no expectations and actually did not believe that the sound once completed a number of times would sound on its own. As I sat down, I heard the waves rolling into shore and with a rushing and sucking sound being drawn back out into the ocean. With full attention I repeated Om, Om, Om, and after a while stopped. I heard the ocean again. And then, to my complete surprise, over the sound of the rolling waves I heard a clear and pristine Om. It repeated and repeated itself, eventually stopping. I recall repeating the experiment a number of times, feeling delighted and puzzled at once. How amazing!

The Bible states: "In the beginning was the Word, and the Word was with God, and the Word was God." I discovered that the concept of the Word, and its transformative power are recognized by the Dogon and Igbo people of Africa, the Karadjeri of Australia, the Mayan of Mexico, also found in Biblical sources, in the Kabbalah, as well as in Buddhist, Sufi, and Islamic traditions, quite aside from Vedic and Tantric practices.

At this point a friend gave me the gift of a pivotal book written by Swami Sivananda Radha called *Diary of a Woman's Search*. I read this story with amazement and then ordered another book by her called *Kundalini Yoga for the West*. Here was a woman and Westerner, finding her way into the complexity of yoga and succeeding in transforming her life. She had dared to open her mind and received revelation after revelation through yogic practices. It seemed intellectual knowledge is not the pinnacle of knowledge at all. Originally, we had the ability to receive higher knowing, but for some reason its energy became blocked and unavailable.

Kundalini Yoga for the West was a study book as I quickly discovered, and filled with practices. So, I threw myself into it and without hesitation began experimenting and following the prescribed exercises. To my amazement everything worked, every effort on my part was rewarded with a result. The yogis have a phrase "when the student is ready, the teacher appears." They also make a distinction between a teacher and a guru (spiritual guide) and a student and a disciple. I began to discover guidance came not only from Swami Radha's writing, but from the "teacher within."

The Divine Light Invocation

I used a practice called "The Divine Light Invocation" most frequently, and wrote down what happened and what my inner experiences were. The Divine Light Invocation is a meditative visualization, given to Swami Radha by Babaji, known as the deathless Tibetan yogi.

The practitioner is instructed to tense the whole body, much as if one is suddenly confronted by a Bengal tiger. Next one holds the breath. Now one recites the invocation and imagines and tries to see a brilliant White Light showering down over the body. A ray of this Light then enters through the crown of the head, filling every cell of the body to overflowing with brilliant light. With an exhalation one relaxes the body. A repetition of the invocation again showers Light over the body of the practitioner, but this time it brings a warm glow into the whole of one's being. This warmth is felt both within and without. Having filled every cell of the body with Light, one confirms that also every level of consciousness is now saturated with luminosity. With gratitude for this gift, the effort is now made to share the Light with other people, members of one's family, or people in need. Concerns and problems may also be placed into the Light.

In order to share the Light, one now visualizes the excess of the Light streaming out of one's spiritual heart center, seeing it becoming a clockwise spiral rising up and up. Into the spiral of Light one can then place family and friends, problems or concerns, and see them absorbed into the Light. Thus, the Light is shared with others, or can be used in healing or helping.

The coordination of tensing and relaxing and inhaling and holding the breath is somewhat complex and demands practice. However, once mastered, the Divine Light Invocation is amazing and powerful beyond belief. In the course of one year, the progress I made astonished me. From a brilliant white pinpoint of Light lasting just a brief time, I now experienced a much larger presence of Light surrounding me and also within. I often had an experience as though the sun had just come out and was pouring through the window. On opening my eyes, to my amazement, the outside world was darker than these Inner Realms. The physical sun was not shining through the window as it seemed and it was as if I were adjusting to a different reality and becoming slowly aware of an inner, unimaginably rich different State of Consciousness.

Everything in my outer world began to be affected and began to change. I saw things differently than before, my attitudes changed, my intuition became remarkably accurate. If I asked an inner question, I received answers, guidance was always available. It was as if a benevolent force had been patiently waiting to make itself known. All it gave was grace and fulfillment and joy. However, my understanding was still immature and I had to grow. I made errors; I was still in the bond of negativity. I was impatient and greedy and wanted things to go my way. I had to unlearn habits I had embraced. I had to learn not to rush and not to delay action. If I was too wrapped up in the drama of everyday affairs, I became absorbed in worldly things. I needed to slow myself down deliberately, to reflect on my desires and the actions and thoughts that followed, and redirect my attention towards my true being. It was in fact a balancing act between not being absorbed by the outer world, nor being deprived of the gifts offered by this world, but being in a state of balance and inner harmony instead.

Because I followed Swami Radha's advice and began to keep a daily spiritual diary, I now have access to many events and dreams which would have been forgotten. Being able to look up details of my life then, is a confirmation, and shows me the process of growth and development. Unfortunately, we give little credence to our subconscious workings, we deny and ridicule them and certainly don't want to talk about them. As anyone shaken by emotional turmoil knows, the sudden arising of an intense feeling colors everything and a stronger, different consciousness results. Suddenly one notices the color of the sky, the usually unobserved details of daily life jump into sharp focus, in short, everything becomes magnified. And then, slowly, almost unobtrusively, the subconscious mixes with the conscious reality; the dreams are remembered, their meaning or feeling seeps into the daylight and eventually the two separate worlds are present simultaneously. One's heart is open and one becomes receptive, so that there is awareness of layers of meaning and knowledge not usually accessible.

I had used the method of "sensing" with my body, ever since I was 15 years old. At that time, I used it to locate the whereabouts of Gamal and to find out if he was training in the club or not. I would focus on the feeling in my belly. Usually it was fuzzy, heavy, shapeless, lumpy, but quite obviously a sensation of inchoate dimension. Then I asked the feeling, "What are you, clarify yourself?" Words came and then suddenly an instant flash, a recognition of something that had bothered me.

At that time, I found a book called *Focusing*. It described the same method I played with, only the book is written by a psychologist. He used the method scientifically with a definite goal in mind. Probing into the subconscious layers may lead to beneficial change for one's personal life. I found that my intuition had much improved. I knew and felt when people thought of me, were at the other end of the phone line, or were writing to me. There are also dreams of future events. I wondered then, will they actually come true? When I practiced the Light Invocation meditation, there was now a subtle sense above and beyond my physical head. It crossed my mind that if only I had a hole in my skull (trepanation), it would be easier to get out of the body. Maybe the ancient Egyptians knew something we now no longer know, considering there are all these mummies with a carefully chiseled hole in their skulls.

A Surprise

I was asked to show in the Aery Gallery in Chicago. Alex hung the artwork in the gallery and the room became transformed. A certain elegance spread over the space and even the lighting was perfect. The paintings glowed on the walls, in spite of somewhat meager lighting. I was so fortunate to have a husband who was a museum director and was so gifted in hanging an exhibition. We arrived early to be there when the first visitors would arrive.

I had painted an abstract version of the Venus of Willendorf, a 20-thousand-year-old female sculpture, discovered in the little Austrian village of Willendorf. Our friend Ron walked in, paused in front of the painting and pulled out his checkbook. "I want this goddess because I can see the inner light in her," he said, much to my surprise.

Another couple I knew who had bought a painting from me years ago wanted the other large painting. I was thrilled to sell two large oil paintings and the evening on the whole was very positive and stimulating. There were many visitors, the conversation flowed, and after the opening we went out for a good meal with close friends in the Greek Plaka.

Visiting Lizzy in Scotland

On the 17th of May, we left for Scotland to visit my mother-in-law, Lizzie, who was now in a geriatric ward in Fife. We only saw her once a year for two weeks, as that is all we could afford, timewise. It was heartbreaking for me to see her there, bound to a wheelchair. For years I had begged her to join us in the States. "Young people should be alone and not burdened by relatives," she had said to me then and refused my offer. She was quite well for a long time and then suddenly she broke her femur, twice. Weak bones were to blame, and so she lost her ability to walk. I felt certain that had she been in the States, I would have helped her until she could walk again.

She was a wonderful spirit, and while we were there, I did my best to cheer her up. She hated her hearing aid and refused to wear it. Yet, she could hear my higher pitched voice quite well, while Alex's voice, being darker in timbre, was lost to her. We would come and pick her up at the geriatric ward and take her into the car and out for the afternoon. Fortunately, there was a charming park in Fife, with a lake, ducks and geese, a petting zoo, and a beautiful rose garden. The weather was usually perfect and so we wheeled her around the park and she enjoyed seeing the animals in the zoo, the children, and the fragrant rose garden. There was also a restaurant where we stopped for tea and cake, and sometimes we took her out to lunch.

Yet the two weeks in Europe seemed like a long time. There was little opportunity to practice hatha yoga, only meditation at dawn. Like on many trips, I gained a distance from myself and had the opportunity to evaluate my efforts in yoga and my creativity in art. Also, I now saw my husband and what he had become over the years, and I saw him with different eyes. We stayed with very good friends of his in Edinburgh. I began to notice that the smallest task was too hard for him. He was often nervous. I asked myself, why am I always so understanding and ready to bend, trying to smooth things out?

On our return flight we sat in the end section of the plane, surrounded by cigarette smoke. I began to feel really sick from it. Yet, in spite of my obvious nausea, he smoked one cigarette after another. I felt utterly poisoned by the smoke. I feared I would collapse on arrival at the O'Hare airport. Our friend Forest picked us up and I lay down on the back seat of his car. However, I remained terribly sick and felt dreadful.

The return into our little house had the usual depressing effect. It is a small, stuffed house. The garden had turned into a jungle during our absence. However, within one day I was able to revolve back to familiar reality. As I did, I asked myself if I had not, from the first moment of experiencing this house, estimated it correctly. Small and dark and confining had been my first evaluation. In the mountain of accumulated mail, we discovered that our real estate taxes had doubled. They claimed we had a fireplace, which we never ever had, and which was taxable. I exploded and felt furious. So much for mind control!

We could move and find a different house, as there is no way in which I can improve on the one we now live in. As I contemplated this situation, I became aware that moving forward was difficult for Alex. There was a fear of letting go; he was holding back and clinging to the known, to security.

Dreams and Insights

At this time, I had a very disturbing dream. Kirstin had a close friend called Jeanne. One night I told Kirstin what I had dreamt and that I felt Jeanne was in grave danger and might die. The next day, a phone call came. Jeanne almost fell out of a window on the 14th floor of a building. She was trying to clean the window, when the glass shattered and cut her legs and hands severely. She was fortunate in being able to keep her balance, as otherwise she would have plunged to her death.

The next event happened on a Monday, while I was painting the porch. The phone rang and rang. I was not answering. Then the thought rose: "Kirstin has probably had an accident;" I don't want to know! The phone continued ringing. "Perhaps she is hurt and the police wish to inform me." I pushed the thought aside. Though I knew it was Kirstin who was calling and calling, I refused to respond. I also knew she was all right. Twenty minutes later Alex came home and told me that Kirstin had just had a car crash, but was unhurt; she had tried to call me.

When I had finished reading *Kundalini Yoga for the West* and done most of the exercises in it, I turned over the last page with a sense of dread: "What do I do now? This is the end." One last sentence stood out. "Maybe now you will look for your guru." I burst into tears. The pain in my heart was a definite message. I sat down and wrote a letter to Swami Radha and sent it to her Ashram in British Columbia. I don't even recall what I said. A letter came back written by her secretary. The message struck me as so sweet. "I am interested in how you worked your way through *Kundalini Yoga for the West*. Send me all your notes typed and double spaced, so I can read them."

And so, I sat down at the typewriter and translated all my notes written in German into English, and sent her the first fat envelope. And then, the next and the next followed, and by the time I had written down everything, I was determined to go to British Columbia and to the Ashram.

Yasodhara Ashram and British Columbia

I had just sold a large painting. It allowed me to feel free to do what I wanted. I did not feel like asking Alex for permission or for money. Though he did not have a mean bone in his body and had always been more than generous to me, this decision, I felt, might not be one he would care for. I didn't want any opposition or argument. He looked at me with pity, saying, "You realize of course that you might never meet this world-famous woman; such people hold themselves aloof and separate as a rule." "I am only going for a workshop lasting four days, called An Intro to Kundalini Yoga. With the two days flying time at either end, I shall be gone for only six days." He made no further comment.

It was August, the hottest time in Illinois and we were still on summer vacation. We went to the airport at dawn.

The journey took all day. We got up at six that morning and it was nine in the evening before I arrived at Yasodhara Ashram. I reminded myself to not have expectations, preconceived ideas, hopes, or ambitions. My arrival in Vancouver was at 1:30 local time and I saw many Asians in the airport. Sikhs were tidying and sweeping the floors. The weather was overcast, 62 degrees, with light rain. When I looked into the clouds, I saw the face of Swami Radha. Here at the airport, I saw what I took to be a female Zen monk. She was a tiny creature, skin and bones, with a shaved head. It startled me to see where this soul search can lead. I hoped that my mind would be clear, and wondered what a mess it would be if I became very emotional. However, it was fun to think of all the improbable possibilities I might encounter. I felt as old as time, quite centered, but as though I had slipped into another period of history. My main fear was that I might find the guru overwhelming. Perhaps I will not meet her, as Alex predicted; however, I actually felt a wonderful surprise awaiting me.

The plane from Vancouver to the Ashram was late in departing. It rained. I sat beside a chatty engineer who had travelled all over the world. He kept my mind off my heaving stomach. But eventually, I vomited, all the same, feeling rotten. At Castelgar, I stood outside in the rain for a while and rested, thank God. The limo I was due to board was delayed, waiting for another plane to land. Then we were off down winding roads with my stomach heaving. The next stop was a town called Nelson, where we stopped at the Heritage Hotel. I had been told that someone from the Ashram might pick me up there, so I walked to the hotel desk and, just then, a man spoke my name. I had almost contemplated staying at this hotel, as it would be too late for the ferry. His name was Ian Mc...something. Then another passenger appeared and they suggested, much to my relief, to eat at the inn, as there was a late ferry in two hours' time.

A meal of red snapper and a glass of wine slowly revived my spirits. The two Canadians, both educated gentlemen, spoke in soft voices. There were silences as natural as soft rain and the conversation centered on how each one of us had discovered Swami Radha. Each man assured me of the uniqueness of the Swami and the Ashram. They told me how intensive the workshops would be and that a very good teacher called Swami Padmananda would guide the Kundalini Overview. Six persons were signed up. I told them I had worked my way through the *Kundalini Yoga for the West* volume and that it consumed a whole year. A strange look of surprise came into their faces and they laughed, saying, "Just one year! We are only at the second chakra and it has taken us five years." After five years, they said, they had not yet reached the sixth chakra.

I did not feel like a fool. I knew how her book had affected me and what I had discovered. Something inside me resembling a force was bursting to be free. I could feel that Alex was anxiously waiting for the promised phone call of my safe arrival. It would be late before I could make it. The company of the men was prompting some kind of nervous high in me. I stopped talking. We departed and eventually reached the ferry. In 45 minutes, we set off on a boat across Kootenay Bay. The night was dark and soft with wisps of clouds above the high mountains. The scenery reminded me of Austria. Once on the other side of the bay, we drove off the ferry to the Ashram through high forest and steady rain. Ian conducted me to a lodge and showed me my room, which was marked with two names, beautifully lettered in Italic hand.

Yasodhara Ashram

I called home. Kirstin answered in a sleepy voice and we talked very briefly. Then I went off to bed. I had trouble sleeping, though I felt tired to the bones. It rained steadily. I dreamt I had forgotten to feed my little lemur, the bush baby, and he had not eaten in five days. He did not leave me in peace until I gave him some nuts, which he ate in a starved fashion. I awoke, with a start. I had asked what the chances of seeing Swami Radha were and was told there were no automatic meetings between her and visitors. The dream was clear suddenly. Like a tiny starved creature, I had to beg for attention. Suddenly my mind went into a spin. A great wave of calm rolled over me, and then I felt a force that stood like an iron core and pulled me into its gravitational field. Good God, I thought, this is absolutely extraordinary. This place is a zone of energy, psychic and spiritual energy. Then my head roared, first like cymbals clashing, then like a drawn-out hooting. My senses were shaken as I sat up slipping my limbs into lotus pose and pulling my legs across each other. I started Pranayama, a yogic breathing method, to calm myself down. Finally, I must have fallen over with exhaustion and slept while a grey dawn sat in my mind. I awoke at regular intervals thinking it was dawn, but in reality, it was a pitch-black night. Eventually I rose at some ungodly hour, had a shower and found the meditation room, where I pulled myself together through meditation.

The Ashram was quite vast, with buildings scattered across the grounds, each used for a different purpose. I left the lodge and looked for the building where food was served. On the way I met a charming, sensitive-looking woman called Joann and asked for directions. The breakfast, served in the little kitchen house, was wonderful—homemade granola, yogurt, with plums and berries from the Ashram gardens. I ate a lot, but it did not seem to calm me down. Meals, as I discovered, were eaten in silence. Upon entering the dining room, one removed one's shoes. This was standard practice everywhere in the Ashram. Plates and cutlery were laid out on a long table and really excellent food was available. No talking was permitted while eating. Usually, a beautiful mantra called Hari Om was playing. I discovered that it was a healing chant and was sung by Swami Radha herself. Images of Guru Sivananda and Radha were interspaced with images of goddesses on the walls. It was good to eat in silence, feeling calm and free from obligations, the food tasted better and it enables one in addition to collect one's thoughts. The silence of nature here is a balm to the senses.

Later, having found the office, I met Swami Radha Krishnananda, recently initiated. She seemed a very level-headed, centered person. I paid my dues and asked if it was presumptuous to ask to meet Swami Sivananda Radha. She replied that Swami Radha had the visitors list, had my papers, and that she certainly would convey my request, but that it was all up to Swami Radha. I talked a little about my journey and suddenly started to cry. My reaction was not based on anything specific and took me by complete surprise. I suppose the sudden release of all the hidden, lonely inner feelings caused it. I caught myself quickly enough, apologized, and left. Her face held a startled expression. I suspected that this was likely to happen because of all my pent-up emotions and probably too much imagination. However, it was so totally unlike me to have such an emotional breakdown. It was like encountering a part of myself I did not know. I asked myself: What do you want? The answer: Nothing!! I was very happy, but some inner tension had been released. It felt like energy of a strange and unknown power. At the same time, I felt totally centered, strong and fearless.

Our Kundalini course started in the evening with an introduction into the Kundalini System. Swami Padmananda and two other teachers were present. All were sensitive, very refined women, dressed in orange silk saris and who faced us sitting on chairs. They gave us bare outlines of what to reflect upon and then assigned us a paper on the first chakra, or energy center, to be handed in at 10:00 am tomorrow.

The Seven Chakras

The first chakra is depicted as a circle containing a square, within which stands a white elephant with many trunks. It is all symbolic and we were asked to describe what in the image spoke to us. Returning to my room, I sat down at the little desk and began to write. We had been instructed to write without hesitation and without resorting to corrections. It was to be an exercise in spontaneity. Also, we were to turn in a carbon copy of our writing so the teachers had copies.

At nine o'clock in the evening we went to Satsang, translated as "the meeting of the Wise." It was at a little A-frame structure on the beach. A long path of steps descended down the hill and then one stood in front of the door. The roof was shingled and covered with moss. Upon entering, I stood in a carpeted room. A large picture window gave us a view of the beach and Kootenay Bay, with high mountains looming behind in the darkness. An altar with the bronze statue of a Tibetan deity and votive candles illuminating it stood in front of the picture window. The room was already filled with people sitting cross-legged on the carpet. Someone played a veena, and mantras were being chanted. I was already familiar with the mantras from tapes I owned, so it did not take me long to immerse myself into the chanting.

The Satsang affected me. I saw veils in my head, dark blue and a pale misty light. Its ending seemed too sudden. I wished it had gone on much longer, and once outside the prayer room, I asked the Swami who led the chanting about it. He told me he had been at the Ashram for 20 years and had come here as a young man of 21.

The following morning, I felt very emotional and teary. Writing my paper was very upsetting, demanding lots of thinking and soul-searching. The Ashram is so quiet and everything is so silent. I could hear my head droning. During the next class, aspects of the chakras were revealed. Our papers were read in class. It is a process which laid bare one's reasoning and thinking process. There is no time to revise and the results are surprisingly intense. Swami Padmanada was a woman in her sixties, very kind, firm, intelligent, and thoroughly grounded. The process was soul-searching. I had never actually examined my beliefs. By the age of eighteen I had largely rejected religion. I had not examined if there was something like a Higher Being, a Spirit, or what we call God. I had given up on religion, equating it with doctrine. That night I walked down to the dark bay and listened to the waves lapping against the shore. I felt profoundly depressed. What was the purpose of my life? How long did I have before I would be sucked into the great nothingness? Was there anything at all that gave actual meaning to life? Then, when it was evening, I went to Satsang.

It gave me a break, and then more soul-searching followed. I realized my views were extreme and upsetting. I had the Rainer Maria Rilke poetry book with me and read it after going to bed. A strange conviction grew in me, unexplainable and with a strength that was unshakable; it was a sensation of calmness and warmth, of being held in a protective embrace like a baby, of being surrounded by a power benevolent and feminine. Feminine? A fog parted in my mind; a curtain swept aside. *Who tells me thou are dark, oh my mother Divine?* The sky was dark, starless. The air was filled with a gentle warmth and softness, embracing, protecting, and enveloping me. A sense of peace and calmness filled me. I decided my paper would only seem intense to me personally; no one else would care.

The next morning Swami Padmananda asked me how I had fared. She also elected me to be the last to read my paper, after everyone else had read theirs to the class. She said not to be so extreme, and to work on developing myself through listening to mantra and practicing devotion. Her eyes were like dark pools, compassionate and wise as she looked at me. The days were intense and passed quickly. I didn't think I would meet Swami Radha and it didn't much matter at that point. I realized what the force wanted of me was to stand on my own feet. What I received here was beyond my wildest expectations and I felt completely grateful and filled with the gift of the yogic teachings. The four days sped by quickly. We concluded the Kundalini yoga course with devotional dances, which were deeply moving.

That night, during Satsang in the little prayer room overlooking the beach, they played a mantra I had not heard before. It was a Tibetan mantra called "Om Tara Tut Are So Ham." It had a strange effect on me. The light was suddenly there; a nice rounded illumination sat in my head. I held it with gratefulness. I don't remember much; the light just stayed, to my continued amazement and did not falter or fade. I decided to thank Radha for my experiences and suddenly her face was there, lit and bright, incredibly close. The chant stopped. The face slowly faded, but the light stayed. I was filled with gratitude.

Swami Radha

Later, I learned that Swami Radha had out-of-body experiences as a child. During these and also in dreams, she would visit a temple and look through the windows. Then she gradually entered the temple to discover the interior. She described all this in great detail. It was her ambition to build this temple, which she had seen and dreamt about for most of her life. I did not know any of this when the last day of my stay arrived.

When I walked through the grounds next morning, a magnificent deer stood fearlessly among the apple trees and fed on fallen fruit. He lifted his graceful head and looked calmly at me before continuing to feed. I decided this was a wonderful omen. The bay waters were blue-black and the waves left bubbles on the shore. It was so beautiful and filled with peace. Though it rained a lot that morning, I managed to sit in the sun and write one part of my paper in the fresh air. The little house that served as kitchen and dining room overlooked Kootenay Bay and had magnificent views of the shimmering lake and the high mountains beyond. A shallow stream bed carried a little river down to the lake. It was filled with huge-leafed elephant ear plants, which covered the entire area.

I learned that in the fifties a British man, retired from India, bought this place and planted elephant ear here. He called his farmstead "Yasodhara Estate." When Swami Radha saw the estate and the name, she instantly knew that this was it, this was the place she was to buy and transform into a spiritual center. Further back in time it used to be a Native holy ground. The energy in the area was so powerful; most people I met could not help but comment on it. Swami Radha worked and upheld the Ashram mostly alone for nine years, teaching people yoga and doing all the cooking for the visiting residents. Having spent my formative years in a little hotel in Cairo, run by my mother, I had a huge appreciation for Swami Radha's achievements and knew how difficult it must have been for her during her first years.

My favorite place in the Ashram was the beach prayer room. When first entering it, my instant instinct was revulsion. Here was incense, candle and idol of my Roman Catholic childhood again. I told myself to stay open-minded. These outer emblems were no more than symbols. As I learned, symbols are important in Buddhism, symbols act as reminders to keep the mind of the aspirant on the path. The mantra we chanted was like a great liberation as the mind took off and the spirit soared up. Almost always I saw light and was into another state of consciousness.

At the conclusion of our four-day course, the Swamis picked up the framed images of the chakra system. I offered my help to carry them down to a room behind the office. When we put down the last of the images, Swami Radha Krishnananda turned to me and told me that she had delivered my request to Swami Radha, but unfortunately, she was too busy and also, no longer took on pupils. I assured her that I had only wished to meet the guru, and to give her a gift I had brought with me. This news did not surprise me in the least. All I had been given here, was her work. Her blessings were attached to it like a sweet fragrance.

I went to my bedroom and commenced packing my suitcase. At seven that evening, a film was to be shown about hatha yoga and later on there was the last Satsang. A video was also shown about a temple project. As I packed, I sang a French song called: "Plaisir d'amour." So, Alex would be right after all, I would not meet the great spiritual teacher! But why should I be ungrateful, so much had been given. Somehow, beyond understanding, I felt myself to be different. Something had shifted.

I went into the bathroom and heard repeated knocking. Was someone knocking on my door? Someone called my name. A dark-haired woman called to me. "Swami Radha has time and she wants to see you." A strange sensation, a blank feeling, a vacuum inside me, surprised me. I was delighted but calm. The woman introduced herself as Julie, Swami Radha's secretary. As Swami Radha told me later on, Julie read to her the notes that I had sent.

What Is the Purpose of Your Life?

Julie led me to a large house, called "Many Mansions" and we walked up the driveway into a small room filled with discarded shoes, where I removed mine. The place had a lived-in atmosphere. I was ushered into a large living room with a view over Kootenay Bay. There was a table in the middle

Swami Sivananda Radha, 1989

and a yellow sofa along one side. I felt exceedingly hot and I removed my cardigan, which I had worn because it had been very chilly in B.C. Throughout the meeting with the guru the heat remained, almost stiflingly hot. It reminded me of Egypt. The room, probably a dining room was empty. There was a little altar. Idly I wondered what other garment I could remove, because it was so excessively hot. Then Julie reentered to let me know the guru was on her way, and would be with me in a moment.

A door opened and I saw a sight figure in a silky pink blouse glide over the step. She seemed to float. She greeted me, Indian style, hands folded in front of the face. Curly white hair cascaded on either side of her waxy-pale face. She held an aura of antiquity although she did not look old. There was an atmosphere of heat and dust, so familiar to me from Egypt. She looked like a psychic. Her hands were very slender; the palms narrow with long tapering fingers. Her eyes were the most striking, dark pools of intensity.

"I have received your papers" she said. "You have done much work." I answered that I was grateful that I was allowed to meet her and that I had brought her a gift of a poem by Rainer Maria Rilke, a very famous and much-admired poet in Germany. I had the volume in my hands, but for some reason the page and poem eluded me and I could not find it. I knew it by heart, but was unsure I could recite it. "Never mind" she said waving her hands, so I laid out the monotype picture I had brought with me.

"What is the symbolism," she inquired. "Your personal symbolism," she wanted to know. I tried to explain, never ever having thought before about symbolism in my paintings. My mind felt a bit numb, confused. Hers seemed to move rapidly. "Yes, I have Rainer Maria Rilke's work," she said as she picked up my volume, "but not this particular book. I no longer use the German language a lot. Are you an artist? Professional or amateur?" I tried to explain as best I could, and mentioned the wings of Horus around the Ra disk in my image. "Is this writing inside the orb?" she wanted to know. "I was several times in Egypt and lived there, a very interesting country. I came there via Christianity and Judaism, which led me back. I realized much came from India into those countries, in my book there is an excerpt on Katibi, *The Book of the Dead*. You might find that interesting." She spoke as if she had had many stays in Egypt, and I never questioned this impression.

I watched her and studied her face. One eye was set somewhat lower than the other and the shape of her eyes was soft, so was the color, but the look was intense. She did not look at me directly; her gaze seemed to dart from right to left, a rapid scanning...but of what? Years later I learned that this rapid method of looking back and forth was used to see the aura of a person. At the time it made me very nervous. When I was little my parents had given me a doll for Christmas. It had big eyes which rolled around inside its head whenever it was touched and moved. I reacted with terror to this doll and they had to remove it.

I noticed Swami Radha wore a broach and that her grooming was very casual, not of interest to her. I told her that I had an interest in the spiritual since my youth, but chose art instead, and maybe I should have chosen differently. She protested, telling me it was wonderful to have a creative gift. "And what is the purpose of your life?" she asked. It stopped me in my tracks; I had no idea what to say. "What is your purpose, what will you do, in the future, let's say."

"Well, I cannot retire from life in five years, which is when my husband retires. He talks of returning to Scotland; he is Scottish. It is too cold for me there, plus we have lived in the USA all these many years." As I related this, a clear impression formed itself that in five years my whole world would turn upside down, that everything would be different. "No," she responded, "you must look around. It would be too expensive to retire in the Chicago area. I have been there many times," and she mentioned the Baha'i temple. "Look in the west in a moderate climate. And your husband?"

I told her that he did not share my view. "Yes, I had two husbands, both very evolved. Do not pressure him." Her hand swept across the space in front of my eyes, as if to indicate this too would be cleared away and be of no concern. Her husbands had died. What was she telling me? Would Alex die? "Let me consider it and I shall send you a little note about places in the West, places which might be suitable for you." (Much later she did send me a note suggesting Santa Fe, New Mexico, as a good choice of a place to retire to. "It is an artistic center with many art galleries and of course artists. You might like it.")

Julie came to tell her people were waiting for her. I rose and stood before her. Although body language indicated I should stay at bay, I reached out to her hands. I recall saying that I knew she had arthritis. (How did I know this???) I focused on her one hand, which lay on the table in front of me. It twitched, as though trying to pull back. It reminded me of the movement of a snake. Then I saw my hand folding down over her hand and feeling the softness of her skin with surprise, I cupped it carefully in mine. "Yes, the body is prone to the laws of decay" she answered. "But my mind is good, like at the age of twenty, maybe better." She smiled. I thanked her again and told her the work here was extraordinary and how well Swami Padmananda had taught the Kundalini course. "Yes, she is very special to me," she said.

She rose up—she was my height—delicate and dressed in sunset pink, and folded her hands in front of her face. "Namaste" and I did the same. The eyes behind the folded hands were black, diamond-sharp, and deep. They glittered. It was a message from the soul and I responded easily—we were equals! She vanished into the other room. I did not notice her feet or her shoes. It was all seemingly totally normal, a bright old lady. But that was only the exterior. She had tried to calm me, she had talked. I had asked for nothing.

I stumbled over the threshold and noticed it was slanted. Julie stood there and I thanked her. She led me outside and asked if I could find my way. Somehow, I found my way back and realized that I had not observed etiquette. I had touched her hand; I had stood in front of her as an equal. As I walked to the lecture room for the film they planned to show, I could still feel the touch of her soft hand in mine. Then, it was as if I were back together with her. She appeared on the screen; her head framed by the softly curling white hair. There was a fierce independence, something untamable about her. I realize now how much we are caught in the body. It is our coarsest vehicle.

My right hand could still feel the touch and I curled it into a fist to hold the sensation while I sat through the hatha yoga film.

While I sat there, looking at the film, Julie suddenly came in and handed me a picture in a plastic sleeve. It was a big image of the Tibetan Goddess Tara. On the back I found a couple of messages in two different handwritings. The last two lines are a mantra signed by Swami Radha, a gift to me. This image now resides on the cover of my spiritual diary and is looked at almost daily.

Much later, I went down to the beach and stood in the misty rain. It was cold for August. The bay was calm, except for the gentle lapping of waves. It occurred to me that from Swami Radha's dining room window one had a clear view of the beach. From the heart I sent the greeting "Namaste." The Highest in me greets the Highest in you!"

The next morning, I was driven back to Nelson. In the car the conversation turned to the temple Swami Radha wished to build for the Ashram. A temple! The Rilke poem I had intended to read to her was all about a spiritual temple and its construction. How amazing! The Rilke poem had to be sent to her as quickly as possible so she would know her temple would be started soon. The poem was a message to her. Amazing to think I was the messenger. And where shall this path lead now? During the flight I chanted the mantra in my mind, until the mantra chanted itself. I had been told it was self-perpetuating.

Changed Utterly

I found myself changed. The world, after the silence I had found in the mountains at the Ashram, was unbearably noisy. There was so little silence and people were talking non-stop. I seemed to hear differently, with more attentiveness and no tolerance for empty chatter. In the past I had the radio on most of the day. Now I turned off the radio, I could not bear the invasive, constant sound. I had not expected this change and my more awakened consciousness noted many other differences.

After my return I saw Alex as a much deeper being and my daughter Kirstin as much older and more mature. I suspect my perception had become sharper. In the Ashram I had found my inner core and a confirmation of the existence of my inner world. The meeting with Swami Radha showed me the essence of an evolved, unique being, and an "old soul." What an amazing, powerful mind she had. When she returned from six months in India, the only money she had in her pocket was 25 cents. She had lived on faith only, and now owned an Ashram on 150 acres of beautiful land in British Columbia and many centers scattered all over the world. She had written a number of books and was highly regarded as one of the most important spiritual and inspirational leaders in the world. She was also the first western woman to be initiated into Sannyas.

My first dream after my return was of seeing Alex leaning against a wall. I watched, as he slowly slid to the ground. It looked so natural, that at first, I did not react, then however, I experienced panic noticing there was something terribly wrong. Then, as I continued to observe, I realized the strength and the life force comes from within, to give us the required power to live. Essentially, I cannot alter what I see happening. I cannot help or stop the energy from fading. Probably this dream is telling me of a knowledge I now have, but which I lacked before. "What is the symbolism in your paintings?" Radha had asked me. I felt confused and tongue-tied as I tried to give her some type of explanation. Now I was ready to pull up all the material of my inner world and those messages from the subconscious. It takes a conscious aim to allow those subterranean messages to speak.

I had made one fundamental mistake. I had believed that the body sustained and contained the soul. Now I know that the soul contains the body. The body is the dress of the soul. When we weaken, it is the soul that detaches itself, and then the physical energy fades.

I realized that at the Ashram there was this stillness, a silence within me. For some reason I that I could not explain, this stillness and clarity stayed with me throughout the duration of my stay. Was it the combined power of all the dedicated residents there, or was it Swami Radha that gave this gift to anyone who entered her orbit? After I left Canada, this inner state remained for about a week. All too soon, it faded, and I had to work hard to get it back. I could induce it through meditation. In my head I hear the voice of the poet Dylan Thomas saying, "Changed utterly!" And indeed, this is how I felt.

Eventually there was a problem about chanting my mantra aloud. Our house was small and there was no privacy; everyone could hear me and found it annoying. Could I chant silently? There were other changes too, for when I was alone or in the shower, I frequently just burst into tears. It was completely unpredictable and happened when I didn't expect it. I had no idea why this happened. I wrote to one of the swamis asking about this problem. I got no response. I became aware that I seemed to be stuck in the fifth chakra.

The trouble with the mind is its need for concrete evidence. It wants something tangible, and there is nothing, literally nothing to grasp at. As to connections with Swami Radha, I had been told very clearly that she no longer took students. There was nothing she could give me except her example. Why did I want to write to her? Why did I crave communication? Was this some ego gratification?

There is so much I did not know about the Ashram. Everyone I met seemed to be silent and peaceful. As a consequence, some residents exuded power, some were obviously centered, and some exuded nothing. They were almost invisible. I felt so comfortable in this environment as I felt accepted, not judged, not criticized or made self-conscious. My reaction was one of delight and feeling at home. As a matter of fact, this made me realize how uncomfortable I often felt in the world of academia.

Yoga Practice

After my visit to Yasodhara Ashram, my daily diaries were filled to overflowing with practices, their effects, dreams, and their interpretations. I studied daily in the Kundalini book and managed to cope by trial and error. Long forgotten physical problems rose. I had a swelling under one armpit. There was a healing practice which began with purification. It began with imagining myself by the ocean being washed by fresh, cool, clear salt water which penetrated and purified my whole body. From there I visualized a very green forest and met a being, symbolic for a part of me. It was a delicate and tender being, quite beautiful, which I initially did not even notice. And then, I started to pay attention to this gentle, lovely presence and it complained of my harshness, that I neglected it, never paying attention to it, even though it was my own "inner beauty." It felt neglected, overlooked, and badly treated. I immediately saw that it uttered the truth and that I had to change my attitude instantly. Miraculously my swelling under my arm was gone by the next morning.

The letter from my mother, written in Kenya, had taken 18 days to get to the States. She stumbled over a rolled carpet in the hallway, fell and fractured her hip bone. She did not complain and mentioned she was is in good spirits. I felt profoundly alarmed and it was my turn to stumble over her words in disbelief. I have had a number of dreams containing warnings about my mother's health. Intuitively, I felt she was unwell, but I had pushed the thought aside. Somewhere in the future she will die; how will I be able to cope with her death? I calculated that the flight to Nairobi takes two nights and one day in Amsterdam. What would I do for a full day in Holland? Go to a museum? Why did I instantly think the worst?

The very next day I called her. John, her African servant, answered the phone and then there was a long interval as she slowly made her way to the phone. Also, at this time, Kirstin was looking for a subject matter for a photo and took several pictures of me as I waited for my mother to pick up the phone. I heard her hesitant walk, and she sounded groggy from the painkillers. No wonder that she was in good spirits! I asked questions. Sometimes she was evasive, as when I asked who was taking care of her. "John" she said, "he even takes me to the bathroom. I said to him, John, I am an old woman and you are an old man. I have no one nearby who can assist me except you. Will you help me? I don't see any color difference; I only see human beings. I am more comfortable with his help than I would be with some British nurse."

I tried to get more information, as to how long her recovery would take, what the doctor thought. But she was more concerned that I tell no one that her African servant is nursing her. It would cause a scandal in Nairobi. I promised to be silent. She asked me when I would come to help her. It was February, and I had no idea how I could possibly cancel my classes and leave in the middle of the semester. All I could tell her was that I needed to investigate my possibilities, talk to the dean of Lake Forest College, and discuss my problem. Then I told her in detail about the Divine Light Invocation and its healing power. My mother had been very supportive of my desire to go to the Ashram and been open and interested. I asked her to be receptive to the healing vibrations I intended to send her daily, and to trust in the beneficial results of the mantra. "Let me know the effects and how you feel." With that, I let go of the connection.

My meditations and mantra sessions were improving, and there was more focus in my practice. I began to feel a sense of well-being, grace, and inner balance. I had a powerful sensation that I was being helped and was surrounded by a group of wise beings. On the second of March, I dreamt of being in a large house on a big property. It belonged to me. A part of the property was very dry, and the vegetation was severely affected by drought. I needed water. Walking about, suddenly my foot broke through the ground and into a subterranean space filled with water. The hole rapidly widened and opened up, and I realized I had found a spring. During the prior few days, I had been dreaming of moving into large, spacious rooms and leaving my narrow, tight spaces. In the dream, I found a spring and had water. This was all very positive and pointed to an improved inner situation.

At this period, at an opening exhibition in our college gallery, I met the new wife of our professor of Asian philosophy. Janet was an emergency room nurse and was filled with vitality. We immediately liked each other, and what is more, found we had a common interest in yoga. She was a disciple of Swami Muktananda, a great Yogi, someone whose books I had already read. She invited me to join her at Satsang in the city, at the Siddha Yoga center. Siddhi means to attain a special power based on an outcome of yoga.

Chanting with the Siddhas

I joined Janet for Satsang. We drove through snow and strands of light into the city and arrived just as a video, filmed in India, was starting. Then Gurumayi, the successor of Muktananda was shown. She looked slender and willowy and very lovely. The video was followed by four hours of mantra chanting. There were musicians who supported the chanters. The room was packed with people. The chant was "Om Namah Shivaya" and even though I helped myself to pillows, my pelvis began to hurt. I desperately struggled to calm my uncomfortable limbs. While I had chanted mantra before, never for four hours and there was no break in sight. I had to endure pain, stiffness, lack of concentration, and boredom, or whatever might arise. There was a large group of people sitting cross-legged in front of an empty armchair (reserved for the absent guru), and in front of the chair a votive candle on a low table has been lit.

I began to concentrate on this light. It started to become bright in my head. The luminosity fluctuated up and down, and then I suddenly came to the awareness, that I had been completely absent for a long while. Where was I, where had I been? How long had this condition lasted? And then a surge of happiness engulfed me. I was wrapped in sound; a living, moving wave of vibration, rhythm, and melody circled me like a huge hum. People got up and left the room, then returned, and I noticed it only when they brushed against me on their return. There were smells, fragrances. These came and went, making place for other smells. There was the heavy body odor, strong incense, then smells of cooking food, and perfume.

I saw myself standing beside the Cheops Pyramid and felt something, something that I also felt here. Rainbow colors manifested in front of my inner eye and a vision of Swami Muktananda stretching himself in the armchair. The chanting rhythm was intensifying and growing, faster and faster. My tongue was drumming against the roof of my mouth. I rocked back and forth to relieve the spine. The rhythm of the drumming was incredible. If I would let myself go, I would become ecstatic. Inside me it was as still and empty as the desert. Around me the mantra howled. Janet sat there, tears streaming down her face. We stretched, trying to find our way out, barely able to talk, and then, we drove back on a slow road because we were too altered to take the highway.

The next day I felt hollow and exhausted. I dreamt we had a new house and I was very happy with it. As I walked through the rooms, more and more hidden premises, new hallways, and different, surprising views emerged.

A One-Person Show

I was offered the opportunity to exhibit my work at the Gallery on campus. I had invited 43 people and expected about 30 to show up. Alex worked on campus until 10 pm in the evening, too long! The installation of the lights needed for illumination of the art was difficult. I was small and agile in climbing high ladders and adjusting the angle of the lamps so they illuminated the paintings to advantage. The lights were my job. Kirstin was a huge help in the kitchen, particularly since some of the guests arrived early. I had used the Light Invocation, the meditation I had learned from Swami Radha, and put the whole opening of the exhibition into positive vibration.

All went so well. I was astonished. It was the human factor that was particularly positive. Many acquaintances we had not seen frequently were present, and I found time to have a meaningful conversation with them all. I experienced them differently; their presence was warm and inviting. It felt as if the evening stood under a dome of blessings and protection. Even the next day the positive atmosphere continued. It was well-received by the faculty that attended.

Precognitive Dreams

My dreams continued to bring messages. In early March I had the following dream: I was pushing a wheelchair with my mother sitting inside it. She was being very difficult and she complained about everything, especially the food. We advanced towards the door, beyond which a very steep, broad set of steps led down. The stair reminded me of those found on Mexican pyramids. Suddenly I felt the weight of the wheelchair shifting and I lost control. The chair jumped forward, out of my hands and rapidly accelerating it descended the steps. I saw it catapult, and then it turned over. Far below my mother's broken body, stretched out and lifeless, lay still across a broad rock.

Shaking with horror, I could not descend over those rocks and had to take an elevator down. The elevator shook and then a corner ripped off. It was falling into a chasm and I folded my hands, waiting, waiting for the pain of the impact and certain death. We continued to fall. I silently recited a mantra. I was wondering why the crash and falling to my death takes so long. I prayed for my soul and body to disconnect quickly and easily. I then awoke, still reciting the mantra. Falling asleep once more, I was wrapping my mother's corpse into a precious silk fabric, the color of alabaster. I awoke feeling shattered in both body and mind. Clearly this was a warning dream, alerting me to my mother's death, a death that may be sudden and unexpected.

My intuition improved so that quite often I could foretell events. For instance, I knew ahead of time that some people would come for dinner. I would feel someone thinking of me, and be able to know if the thoughts were friendly or a sign of trouble. Later on, my feelings would be confirmed. I would receive a flash of a thought from a friend, and then the phone would ring and that person was on the other end of the line. When I meditated, quite often a soft glow spread inside my head, gradually turning into a bright sun and eventually into an ocean of light. The stillness inside was vast and I felt completely centered. There were some visions, too, which brought me great joy and convinced me that soul-contact is possible; for example, seeing Swami Radha appear in front of my inner eye. There were no confirmations of the authenticity of these experiences and I talked to no one about them.

April came and I felt my neck becoming intensely painful and difficult to move. I could find no reason why my neck should be so sore. During my meditation, a vision of a yogi with a dark head-covering appeared. He asked me to turn my torso to the left. I did as he asked. Then he told me to turn my torso to the right side. Again, I did as he asked. As I completed the turn, I realized that my neck was no longer stiff or sore. The vision disappeared, and indeed there was absolutely no pain left in my neck. I bowed down in gratitude.

Visiting Art Schools

Kirstin was depressed about her future. She had applied to a number of graduate schools and received acceptance from Parsons School of Design in New York City. They asked her to come for an interview and were very impressed with her talent and artistic abilities. However, the living expenses of such an environment, the difficulty of finding decent housing, and the prospect of being a poor artist discouraged her. There was another art school in Savannah, Georgia, the Savannah College of Art and Design, and an acceptance from the University of Florida, Tallahassee, to be looked at. I offered to go with her to check both places out.

On April 24, we flew to Savannah, Georgia. We rented a car and drove to Tybee Island, where we rented a room at a Days Inn hotel near the beach. I had fond memories of Savannah, where I spent a few days as a student. It was early evening as we drove into Savannah, where we investigated River Street, which as the name implies, runs along a river. There used to be a harbor there during the 18th century. The street was now home to restaurants, boutiques, and bars.

Savannah proved to be quite elegant and pretty, with lovely old houses, magnificent gardens and small squares shaded by towering, ancient old oaks dripping with Spanish moss. Kirstin managed to find her way in spite of the many one-way streets. We visited the art school, stopping first to find out what financial aid was available. There was no problem with that, and small flats were available for students to rent at moderate prices. Then we wandered through some of the art buildings. The art exhibited was not particularly high class, but the weavings and advertising were good.

We also visited an art exhibition at the artist's house. We struck up a conversation with this resident artist, who was an expert at painting fish pictures. His opinion about the school was very negative and came as quite a shock. "I would not send my daughter to be educated in this terrible school," he said without hesitation. Kirstin became quite depressed by what he told us. My response to this revelation was one of gratitude, for no one else was likely to know as much as this man did about the art school, and about what was amiss with the teaching there. We were fortunate to have had this encounter with him.

The following day we returned to Savannah College of Art and Design and searched out the Administrative Building. A young woman wearing five different earrings suggested we take a white bus and tour the campus. We were shown buildings of the art department, student halls, and another exhibition space featuring student work. What seemed to be completely missing were studios, spaces for students to use for painting, sculpture, drawing, and printmaking, something the artist had warned us of. We had actually seen some of the students standing in a stairwell or hallway with an easel, trying to work in that environment. Over lunch we discussed the situation and decided to depart for Tallahassee.

We drove through a wonderful landscape of rolling hills and forests. Tallahassee itself was a modern city with a feeling of vitality. We found the university. In the art building one of the teachers took us on a tour of the exhibition currently being shown. We saw the work of graduating students, which was very impressive. There were large terracotta sculptures, canvases with mostly abstract subject matter, and color photography. We were taken to a large warehouse, which served as studio for the students. Here, too, we saw interesting artwork. Both Kirstin and I experienced this environment as far more conducive to what we were looking for in art education than what we had experienced in Savannah. However, our efforts to get some information about financial aid were most frustrating. The office seemed to be run by students, and we were unable to get answers to our questions from them. Kirstin became very upset, and since we couldn't do anything more, we left the town and drove back.

The Okefenokee Swamp, which I had visited many years ago, was near our route and we decided to visit it. We expected the entry to be located at the lower end of the swamp and found ourselves lost in a no-man's land of denuded clear-cut forest which went on mile after mile. It took us two hours of driving time before we finally left this horror of destroyed nature. The swamp, however, was a highlight of our journey.

The water was black and like a mirror reflecting everything. There were water lilies and huge alligators, turtles, fabulous huge butterflies, even a bobcat on our boardwalk, walking ahead of us for a long time. A viewing tower gave us the opportunity to look over the treetops of dense forest of many miles. To see so much untouched beauty was truly a wonder of nature. It started to rain when we left the swamp, and again, we lost our way for a while and drove into dense traffic when we reached Savannah.

I began to have a premonition and negative feeling and begged Kirstin to allow for plenty of time to fill the car for the trip to the airport. I allowed her to drive to the gas station. The gas station she chose alarmed me, and I asked her not to go there. She ignored my warning and while I studied the map, she went to the bathroom. She returned in a huff, furious about the filthy-mouthed men in the station, who had made personal remarks about her derriere.

She slipped into her car seat and switched on the ignition, as she continued to complain about the verbal abuse, she had just experienced. The motor roared into life and out of the corner of my eye I saw the gas hose with nozzle still attached to our car ripped out of its socket, as she started off. Gas spilled out of the open hole onto the ground. The obese woman, who sat at the counter, ran out shouting abuse. We stopped our car. The owner was called: the police arrived.

All this happened so quickly. We needed to leave for the airport. The obese woman wanted my credit card number and wanted payment for the damage. She raged and ranted. I refused to give her my card. That was the moment when something amazing happened. The policeman, who so far only sat in his car, now got out and came towards me. He was short and slim and had an easy smile on his face. "They are insured," he said. "Don't under any circumstances give them your credit card. Where are you going?" "To the airport and by now we are late," I responded. "I shall guide you. I don't want you to get lost in all this traffic. Also, I think you should drive, not your daughter, as she is too upset. Have a safe journey and a good flight!"

I thanked him profusely; his open face was kind and intelligent. To me it seemed as if an angel of light had taken over and resolved the whole mess. Throughout the flight Kirstin was in a terrible state, fearful of being sued for the torn-out gas hose. I felt calm and practiced my meditation that took me so deep that I didn't even notice our plane was bobbing up and down like a cork on a rough sea.

9 Visiting Africa

A Call to Africa

The letter from my mother had taken three weeks to get to the USA. She was upbeat, sounding happy and full of energy. "You won't believe it, I myself can barely believe it, and the doctor thought it was impossible. Your Divine Light Invocation must have worked, because after two weeks my pelvis was healed. I had an x-ray and the fracture was gone. They said they had never seen a fracture heal so fast, especially on someone my age." I was so glad she was healed.

It was May, and the spring flowers were lovely; everything was in bloom. In Illinois, within only a few days, winter evolved into spring and after many months of cold, springtime was a huge gift.

I was thrilled to be returning to Kenya after quite a few years. My flight was uneventful and on my stopover in Amsterdam, I decided on a long walk. It was 7:00 in the morning and too early for any shops or museums to be open. There were hippies sleeping on the benches outside the central station. I wandered towards the Oude Kerk—the old church—in a medieval square, where the artist Rembrandt lies buried. The surprising thing about the square was that this is also the red-light district that surrounds the church. The shop windows were empty of prostitutes at this early hour. To fill my empty hours, I decided to visit the house of Anne Frank, whose diary I had read as a student. The house contained an original diary, odds and ends, photos, and some slide shows. The information was sensitively selected and powerful, and it gave me a moving impression of this terrible time and the circumstances.

After walking more and feeling footsore, I went into a pizza place for a cappuccino. It must be the badly paved surface of the cobbled sidewalks that contributes to sore leg muscles. Anyhow, I discovered that the little joint I had just entered was run by Egyptians. We started to talk and they told me that masses of people are leaving Egypt; there is no room, no work, no way of living for millions of people in the cities.

While sitting in the café, idly looking out of the window, I saw something quite incredible. An elderly woman in an orange coat stepped into the middle of the busy street, lowered white panties to below the knees, and flipped her coat and skirt with one swift gesture over her back side and proceeded to urinate. A tram car passed and the faces behind the windows registered mirth and astonishment at the full moon view she must have presented to them. It seemed as if she peed forever, before proceeding on her journey, as if she did this on a daily basis.

One of the Egyptians offered to take me to his flat so I could sleep for an hour, which is typical for this thoughtful race of people. Needless to say, I did not take his offer. Instead, I made my way back to Schiphol Airport and read my book until the flight left for Africa at midnight.

On my arrival in Nairobi, my Aunt Alma, Uncle Christian, and my mother were waiting for me. I embraced my aunt and uncle first, and finally held Leni in a long, warm hug. She felt soft, and as always exuded a beautiful fragrance. Alma and Christian were ninety years old by now, yet they looked healthy and vital and essentially unchanged. I felt grateful that they looked so well; it was a good omen. Outside the airport, the sunlight was bouncing off all surfaces, as this was the equator and the sun was straight overhead.

Nairobi looked much more African now, excitingly different from how I remembered it, and with many new buildings. We drove to Westlands and my mother's house. The grounds resembled a botanical garden with splendid plants and exotic flowers. The trees had become huge and were in bloom and the little thorn tree we had dug up 14 years ago in the Serengeti and planted here had become a huge umbrella tree shading the higher area of the garden. I laid my hands on its thick thorny trunk and, gazing up into the dense foliage above, saw a hornbill and its mate.

The altitude made me feel light-headed and brought back a familiar feeling of the wild delight and love of Africa. John, my mother's old servant, came to greet me. His hair was now white and he sported new teeth, but he was still as regal and handsome as ever. "Memsab come, I made my Kikuyu lunch for you." He had remembered my love for this special dish, called Sikumaviche. We sat under the willow tree in this tropical paradise and had lunch. Kenya coffee with its rich fragrance was served in porcelain cups. I was home again.

My mother was a wizard at transforming an environment into a haven of tranquility and luxury. Her house was filled with exotic carpets and Arab furniture from her years in Egypt. In fact, the English Colonial style house she had bought 25 years ago, when it looked like an unloved shack, had been altered completely. Old Turkish ceramic tiles with hand painted patterns now decorated the stairwell and walls of her veranda. Our dessert was a dish of spectacular mulberries from her garden. Her tree was loaded with the sweet red berries. They were heavenly. If my mother picked them and gave them to the staff to eat, they were happily consumed, she told me. However, oddly, asking the Africans to pick the fruit for themselves was below their dignity. The berries would fall and litter the ground to the delight of ants and birds.

The next morning, at my request, we went to the African market to buy papaya and mango for our breakfast. The market was spread over a wide area and was completely taken over by vendors of food, fabric, and carvings. It was colorful and so exciting that I forgot to use my camera. There were some exquisite young women with elaborate beadwork woven into their hair and wearing colorful kanga. Some of the men were Masai warriors, carrying shields and spears. We brought our fruit back to John, who was already brewing our coffee. It was amazing how exquisite the ripe fruit was and how good it tasted. It made me regret how most fruit in the States is sold in an unripe state and therefore never reaches its peak goodness.

The Goethe Institute, where I taught the German language years ago, had invited my mother to exhibit her paintings and had included me as well. The exhibition of watercolors was planned to open on May 15. My mother was unsure which paintings to choose and what to frame. I offered to take on the whole process of framing myself, as by now I have had a lot of experience with exhibitions.

She led me to a guest room, where she stored her paintings. It consisted mainly of a pile of dirty, framed pictures, which had to be taken apart, because the glass was dirty on the inside. While involved with this task, I discovered that the framer had covered up as much as one fourth of the painting surface by using a pre-cut mat of the wrong size. New mats of the correct size had to be cut for the pictures, and my mother was delighted to see her work look so much better, as she had felt that something was amiss with the work after it had been framed at the local frame store. In the end, we had fifty framed pictures in total and were ready for hanging.

Hanging the Exhibition

We rose early for the hanging of the exhibition and loaded the artwork into a big vehicle and drove into town. The German Goethe Institute was in a new building, a structure designed and built by African women. We found the big auditorium and started arranging the work along the walls. The labor went on until evening. We met the ambassador, who was to introduce the exhibition the next night. He checked out the work and walked around the show with Leni. With some help, we hung 54 images, arranged overhead lighting, and placed extra panels in the center, which featured paintings of a smaller dimension. Everyone who saw the show said it looked wonderful. My mother said she was exhausted just watching us work. She sat in a chair, her stick in her hand, and roared at anyone who disagreed with her. On one of the panels, we hung five of my own monotypes by request of the director. One of my images was of a dreaming goddess face, and it sold immediately the next day.

It was difficult not to be drawn into the whirlpool of circumstances. To remain above the fray, to recite my mantra, to meditate, I did all I could to stay collected and connected within; which was just as well, as my mother was overwhelmed at times and could become difficult. When she was nervous, she became scattered, often unable to finish a sentence. She would also hop from subject to subject. This was when she became her most trying, calling John five times within a minute, becoming impatient and irritable. He was a saint though. Mostly, he told me, he viewed it like the behavior of a child which runs this way and that way. He remains calm and was master over the situation. I for one, admired him and the wisdom of his race.

The opening of my mother's retrospective exhibition was at five o'clock. To my total surprise, 400 people came to the art opening. The big exhibition space was filled with visitors. It was very hot and humid and I was grateful that I wore thin clothing. The German ambassador gave a speech, as did the head of the Goethe Institute, Ute Graefin Baudissin. She was light and wonderfully direct, vital and a generous presence. My mother too spoke, in flawless, assured English, and was handed a big bouquet after her "thank you" speech.

Those present were very enthusiastic and full of questions about the art work. One of my mother's pictures sold, then another. There were many African artists, chatty and full of questions about techniques. I found myself surrounded by young men, some tipsy, most of them delightfully amusing. There was a sudden surprise when a group of musicians came in from the street, with their instruments in hand and now the party had truly begun. This was Africa; no tame exhibition was possible here. Before I knew it, there were people dancing, the beat became intense, and everyone was excited and enjoying themselves.

Then I remembered I had dreamt there would be an earthquake tonight. At 7:30 there was a sudden hush, then a short tremor. Someone shouted, "Earthquake," and the musicians just started playing again. Sumptuous food was offered on a large table. I did not eat anything for there was far too much going on and I was glad to be participating in such a unique event. "Is it usually like this?" I asked my mother. Then suddenly, as fast as it had started, it was all over. I was exhausted, as though the air had been let out of a balloon. The next day I felt disoriented and I lacked energy. I considered how I could direct the remainder of my time here. Leni had suggested spending some time at the coast while I was in Kenya. I brought the subject up again, indicating dates and ways of arranging a holiday by the Indian Ocean.

The Threat of Change

I think now, in retrospect, that what disturbed me was the notion of change. Change is uncomfortable and disturbs established living patterns. It jeopardizes physical security, habits, and accepted ways of life and how we act. As I observed my mother, I saw she feared losing control over her life and that would happen if she were to move into a nursing home or an assisted living situation. We discussed her options repeatedly, as there is a nursing home for British ladies in Nairobi. She told me she wanted to be pampered and taken care of, but not—as happened with my mother-in-law, Lizzie—to be moved into a nursing home. There her body would be looked after, but her spirit—her emotional and mental needs—would be subjected to a routine she found horrible. She would be surrounded by senile women and overworked nursing staff, who might pay little real attention to the aged in their care. I fully understood my mother's dilemma and wondered what she would choose; that is, if she had a choice. It was something that worried me profoundly. What I became keenly aware of was that change was in the air. My mother's situation seemed good on a superficial level, but the longer I was with her, the clearer it became that this was an illusion.

My mother was extraordinary in the way she extracted assistance everywhere, be it in shops, with acquaintances, or with her African employees. She had always been so independent and capable, so this behavior was new to me. Early in the morning her energy was high. She had her first cup of strong Kenyan tea and her first fight with John. She called him constantly for something and could not wait for anything. He was the soul of African indifference, which fueled her anger.

She shopped almost daily, so we had her driver take us into town, where we wandered from store to store. Toilet paper was bought here, lettuce there, Kleenex somewhere else. We returned glass bottles and on and on, and in no time two hours had passed and Leni was exhausted. She demanded a stool or chair in every store, and I suspected she suffered from low blood sugar. Close to noon she was in a fighting mood and needed food. However, at this stage it was already too late and she was incapable of cooking, and she collapsed on the bed. I took over the kitchen and I tried to feed her, but she asked for coffee or a gin and tonic, cheese and crackers, or pasta. I had introduced her to mixed salads, leek and potato soup, and smoothies. The question was: how long could she survive? She suffered from dizzy spells and, according to her doctor, her bones were like glass. In a sense, Leni was very fortunate to live in Kenya. In Europe or elsewhere, she would have been in a center by now, enjoying assisted living. In Kenya, servants, a chauffeur, and the way of life made existence very cushy.

Also. there were my daily visits to Alma and Christian across the road. They asked me to write letters for them or sort through odds and ends that needed attention. Alma wanted to give me a whole china set, but I didn't need that and how could I possibly take it with me? She discovered two precious carpets tucked away in her store room. The beautiful Bukhara was completely eaten up by insects. Alma had enormous energy and kept herself incredibly busy, and that meant constant visitors and invited guests. She took every opportunity to take a dig at her sister Leni. My mother then told me in painful detail how hurtful Alma was. I stayed out of these battles completely.

One Sunday, we joined a sketching group that drove to the famous Ngong Hills. Most of the members are British amateur artists and friends of my mother. When we reached our destination, we found ourselves in a beautiful open plain surrounded by low-lying hills. There were some acacia trees and cattle herds. Searching out a sun-sheltered spot under some trees, everyone put up a folding chair and easel. But we were soon discovered.

A middle-aged Kikuyu woman rushed towards us and stretched out her hand in greeting. One of the artists spoke Kikuyu and translated the message. It seems she was here with her small herd of goats. I saw the middle finger of one hand was broken and had never been set. Her face was open and flushed with excitement. Spitting into her palm she reached out to us, to shake hands with her. This is a native custom, the translator told everyone, and we should not offend her, but shake hands. Spittle is considered a substance of life force. We all steeled ourselves to the spittle handshake, and I noticed quite a few refused to shake hands. I did reach out and felt her handshake was unexpectedly limp. The Kikuyu woman was very strong physically, which reminded me of the vigor I had seen in wild animals. Later my mother felt unwell; perhaps the trip was too demanding for her. I suggested a week at the South Coast, which would be a wonderful holiday for both of us before my return to America.

Retreat to Diani Beach

Alma prepared for our trip, providing as much food as if we were to penetrate deepest, darkest Africa for there are four bags of provisions packed and waiting in the hallway. Nicholas, the young gardener, came along with us to clean fish, wash dishes, and make coffee. We took the train, which traveled overnight from the highlands down to the tropical coast. The land was still utterly beautiful, and life there was spicy and seemed much easier than elsewhere.

Of course, the phones broke down. And, there were many things that were unavailable there, but I found the griping of so many people quite unnecessary. These were usually old English settlers, who were mostly farmers. Complaining was a way of life with them and such a bore. The Kenyans were very, very ambitious in contrast and high in energy.

We took a first-class sleeper compartment. Alma handed us a bag filled with delicacies for our dinner on the train, which included a bottle of champagne. The trip was happy and uneventful. At dawn I saw the green valleys and coconut palms glittering in the sun.

I Had Dreamt of Coming to an Ocean of Light

The outskirts of Mombasa looked as if more industry had moved to the city. We took a taxi and stopped at the huge fruit and vegetable market of Mombasa, which was just as I remembered it. Unbelievable varieties of tropical fruit and vegetables were heaped into high peaks and the natives still spoke Arabic. We bought a large basket of fruit for our stay and then the old Volvo taxi took off for the snow-white coast of Diani Beach.

The house was big and it overlooked the ocean. The lawn stretched out in front of the enormous red veranda. They were not expecting us yet and the house was not ready. The sky was heavily overcast and a grey-green color scheme dominated. The air was soft and moist and sticky. The contrast of the pale green Indian Ocean under the lead-colored sky and the black-barked old trees made this landscape so very African.

There was a melancholic atmosphere to the place. At night, the ocean's roar resembled drumming and it took me a while to figure out this was a natural rhythm. After our arrival it began to rain, a steady rain which lasted all morning. We took a little stroll along the beach and met an American couple who introduced themselves as psychologists and were our neighbors. We discovered they were parapsychologists, involved in a study of the local villagers, most of whom were extremely gifted psychically and keen on witchcraft and shamanism.

During the first night of sleeping in the house I had dreams that disturbed me deeply and frightened me. My mother's helper, Nicholas, was very spiritual and talked to God every night. People respected him and seemed to know his Shamanic gifts. Here at the coast, he was sought out immediately by some villagers. My mother told me that she took him along as protection because he was so powerful. The first thing she told him at the South Coast was that he should stay with us in the house and that he was allowed to have villagers visit him, but he was not to leave us alone. He seemed to understand.

There were some extremely pretty girls here; their skin glistened like ebony, and they carried charm and grace in every movement of their lithe and slender bodies. Their voices were low and gentle. I watched them with total fascination, as they were very different from the Highland tribes, like the Kikuyu.

The place struck me as so alien and strange that I was not even tempted to swim. I was told to swim only at low tide, as the surf was quite violent. Compared to how I remembered this stretch of Diani beach, I was shocked by the changes I saw everywhere. In front of houses the jungle had been slashed back, and manicured lawns displaced the original plant life. The beautiful shells stolen from the sea were sold illegally to the tourists. Yet, there were the beautiful palms swaying gracefully and the huge baobab trees teeming with tropical birds and their many voices.

I found a good, sheltered place on the beach for practicing yoga asana and meditation. The sky was grey, but in my head, sunshine was streaming down. I was well into another level of consciousness. Every now and then, with a little jolt, I would get deeper. When I opened my eyes, instead of warm sunshine pouring down, it was grey and dark. Sometimes, I saw vividly colored orbs, sometimes a beautiful violet established itself. Then my hands tingled and I knew I was back in my body and my sense perceptions were taking over.

One afternoon my mother and I walked the white beach, toes sinking into the soft sand. She suddenly accused me of neglecting her, of not being there for her, and of being selfish. I listened in amazement and then with sadness. I suddenly saw her isolation clearly. Her desire to have her daughters with her was natural. However, the idea that I would be able to step out of my life to be with her, to protect her and to look after her, was an illusion. Beyond all that, I saw her fear of loneliness and death. Silently I walked beside her as she emptied out her feelings of anger and disappointment, of lost hopes and illusions.

That day had been particularly beautiful. Twice I had enjoyed a lengthy swim, enchanted by the coastline of softly carved sand and the gently swaying coconut palm trees with their lime green fond. I had thought of Alex; it was here, after all, in this place of beauty that our lives moved together as though joined by some amazing force of benevolence. I recall that at the time I could not believe that this grace was happening to me, that this nice man should love me, and that it should be so easy to respond. It was as if some force had always looked after me and guided me. At this point I realized I had been bitten by an insect and was covered with angry and very itchy bites.

The next day I came upon my mother in the process of scolding Nicholas. He had disobeyed her and been in the village. I listened in amazement because in no fashion could she stop a grown man from doing whatever he wanted in his free time, when not at work. He said nothing in self-defense and gave no explanation, but I could feel his hurt pride to be reprimanded like a school boy. When he was gone, I approached her and asked why she had scolded him so severely. "I am trying to educate him," was her answer.

Later I heard Nicholas chanting and groaning, sounding like a child in pain. This was his prayer and the way he dealt with his inner turmoil. It was psychic energy being rechanneled. The African has this quality of patience and further the capacity to swing to the opposite extreme of revolt and brutality. My mother said she was educating him! Educating him into what?

I felt I must warn her. He sounds possessed and he may be dangerous, especially if angry for being scolded. I can feel the force of his energy and felt most uneasy.

That night a storm rose. The houses there didn't have glass windows, only bars and shutters. The shutters had been carefully closed, but the wind squeezed through the chinks and made an eerie squealing sound. The ocean was roaring and wild and I could feel the breeze blowing through the rooms. Suddenly I heard this child's voice, chanting in repeated monotone. It sounded like some mantra. The sound repeated and repeated and with it came terror. What if Nicholas had gone mad and had come to kill my mother? With extreme self-control I left my room and managed to cross the hallway, passing his room. The wind howled and I asked how it was possible that my mother did not hear him? Without knocking I entered her room. She was lying under her mosquito net in bed and reading by the light of a hurricane lamp. I waved to her and she closed her book, saying her back hurt. Could I massage it?

There was another unoccupied bed beside her and I sat down on it. "Do you hear all this noise?" I asked her. "It's just a storm," she answered and handed me some massage cream. What was the chanting? Were they prayers? But they sound like incantations. The air seemed thick with evil. I began to repeat my mantra to calm myself and to counteract the terror I felt. Despite my mantra, despite the howling of the wind and crashing of waves and my efforts to concentrate, the child's incantation remained maddeningly present. I wondered if we would see tomorrow. Imagination fueled terror.

I began to concentrate on Swami Radha with all my might and asked for her help. Something like a radiance instantly appeared and I could see her in my mind's eye. The child's voice chanted on, but my terror slowly calmed. Then my mother began to groan. She claimed her back was in agony. I began to massage her. The pain ran to the left shoulder and down her arm. Could this be a heart attack? Did he chant a vengeful tune to punish her for this morning? Then the thought crossed my mind that these people have the patience of a rock. African witchcraft! By now he must have been chanting for three hours. I decided to ask him tomorrow, while I continued to massage her spine. At three in the morning, she took pills to counteract her pain. Shortly afterwards she fell asleep. I felt exhausted as I watched her sleep. Eventually, I extinguished the lamp.

I awoke in the bed next to my mother's, on which I had passed out, somewhere after four in the morning. It was light and birds were chirping. There was a soft lapping sound of waves against the beach. Leisurely I considered the events of the night. What was this incantation, this odd childish voice I heard for hours? Was it in my mind, or outside my mind? I meditated with all the concentration I could muster. I felt like a mere beginner in contrast to the African.

The sea was grey and a shaft of light hit it like an explosion of radiance. The ancient, rain-soaked baobab stood like a black giant before the light. Making my way into the kitchen I encountered Nicholas. "Did you hear the storm last night? It was so disturbing. Did you sleep well?" "Very well, Memsab," he answered. The whites of his eyes were yellow, as with so many Africans. Had all that psychic stuff been my imagination? I determined that I had to practice awareness while eating, reading, walking, really at any and every moment. It was important not to lose myself, not to go to sleep, not to forget myself in reverie, daydreaming, or drifting thoughts.

Second Sight

Everything was intensely felt, be it the swaying palms, the rain puddle on the red-tiled veranda floor, and my little, fierce mother. However, everything was also new and somewhat unreal. The lights I saw in meditation were mostly huge and brilliant white. In the afternoon a strong sensation of Alex suddenly established itself. There was a sense that he was irritated and did not know what to do and I instantly responded by feeling guilty. There was no rational reason why he should be irritated with me. Had he received my letters? Had something I wrote to him been a cause for disagreement? The tension mounted. Was something wrong? There wasn't a way he could contact me, no way of connecting. Essentially, I felt sad and worried.

The next few days passed uneventfully. I meditated as much as possible and went on long, solitary beach walks, as my mother seemed too fragile to walk a lot. There was an old fisherman whom I had first met years ago. He brought freshly caught fish to people who rented houses along the beach, and my mother knew him well. He came most days. Sometimes he brought lobsters, sometimes crab, sometimes ripe mangoes from the village. He arrived on an old bicycle and rang the bell several times when he stopped at the kitchen entry. We never bargained with him as his prices were unbelievably modest and his catch was always totally fresh. He had just arrived and I was the one who met him outside the kitchen entrance. We greeted each other and he showed me some lovely fish, which I purchased. My mother was just returning from a short walk and the old fisherman observed her as she staggered up the beach. "Hi, mzee Sana," he said, "mzee Sana," he repeated, looking at me. His face looked pensive and I considered the meaning of his words. He had said "She is very old, very old." Then a sudden comprehension and understanding came to me and I responded by saying; "Hi, Mama Mkubwa mezee sana." He was telling me that she was very old and dying. The Africans have almost a second sight when it comes to something like the ending of life. They can smell it and felt it. I thanked him from my heart for his prediction as he mounted his bike.

My mother was in a slightly aggressive mood and kept on picking at things. She said that this was the first time in 15 years I had come to see her, that other children did so much more for their mothers...then she said that I had positively gained a lot of weight here at the coast. She was sputtering out just about any and every irritation that entered her mind. I had talked to her about my yogic studies and she was very interested in them. Now she asked to be given my Kundalini book, but will she read and study it? It would be wonderful if she would do so. The consistent effort of daily walks had made her much stronger and she was now able to walk without feeling any pain in her back. A regular yoga practice would undoubtedly be very good for her health and general well-being.

After lunch I walked down to the beach and lay down on the soft white sand, looking at the lush tropical foliage and palm forest. The sky was azure blue. Suddenly, to my great surprise, a huge monitor lizard about four feet in length dashed out from the dense shrubbery, grabbed a sand crab, and consumed it after returning with it to higher ground. This was the first time I had ever seen one of those prehistoric monsters and I felt amazed at its size and speed of movement. It was almost as if Diani beach wanted to give me gifts to remember it before leaving. I also found a cowrie and a horse conch shell in the seaweed washed ashore by the tide. The beauty of the place sang in my soul, and my eyes felt flooded with color and my heart with gratitude.

The time came for the return to Nairobi with the evening train from Mombasa. By nightfall we reached Mombasa and the railway station. The night was blue and tropical and the sky studded with stars and a quarter moon. On the platform young Indians jested with each other, beautiful girls in saris strolled by, as well as graceful Muslims in long white gowns. There was good music playing in the station, the first time I ever encountered something like this. Then the train was off into the African night. It all felt dream-like. The mantra still sang in my head and I felt suspended by some inner joy, some inner glow and I still smelt the salt-breath of the sea.

Back in Nairobi everything changed. The mail brought two letters from Alex. This treat delighted me. But something had gone amiss. John communicated that Alex had phoned on Sunday and was urgently trying to contact me. I had felt all this and was wondering what went wrong. I had been walking the beach chanting my mantra. Now it continued in my head as it is self-perpetuating. I could not stop it. When it finally faded my hearing had cleared dramatically. I would say I could hear 20 percent better than before.

My meditation was not focused, and I was unable to relax. Perhaps the altitude was to blame. An invitation by friends of my mother brought us face to face with negativity. We were in a lovely house and in a garden filled with flowers and color. Our hosts were running down African politics and the attitude of the government. They saw everything from their superior European intellectual viewpoint. The meal was heavy, stodgy fare. I felt like an outsider. My mother had brought four beautiful mangoes and coconuts from the coast as a little gift in a basket. I don't think they saw beauty. Their negativity was upsetting. I realized how quickly one gets used to criticism and negativity and is drawn into the same mindset.

A Last Goodbye

My intuition from last weekend was correct. When I finally got in touch with Alex via phone, he told me that the realtor had cancelled our cottage in Englewood, and that we didn't have another accommodation arranged so far. Usually, the booking for a beach cottage had to be made a year ahead, so our chances of finding something suitable at such short notice were unlikely. This might jeopardize our summer vacation in Florida, which he had very much looked forward to. He and Kirstin were flying to Amsterdam the following day. I was to meet them in Holland. From there we would fly to Scotland for our annual two-week visit to see my mother-in-law. During my last night in Nairobi, nightmares invaded my sleep. I felt restless and disturbed. I awoke because I heard loud sobbing, but it was the strange bark of some creature that I initially thought was my mother.

My flight was in the evening, as most planes flew over the continent only at night. My mother and her driver took me to Nairobi airport. The formalities went quickly and then it was time to say goodbye. I stepped forward to embrace my little mother, who wore a simple little raincoat for warmth. Then the strangest thing occurred. It felt as if my chest was opening, becoming a vast space and within this vastness I felt her heart spreading out like a bird spreads its wings. There was a profound feeling of desolation and sadness and an ever-widening space and distance. "Don't grieve," I said as I kissed her. She said nothing; and in that instant, I knew I would never, ever, see her alive again. The vast space of despair was my soul reaching out to her soul for the last time.

Just Being

The next morning, I arrived at Schiphol Airport, where Alex and Kirstin were waiting for me. They had tickets for an amazing exhibition of the paintings of Franz Hals, a famous Dutch artist from the 17th century, and I enjoyed the show very much. To our delight, the weather in Holland was wonderful, and I relaxed being together with my family. Even my meditation at dawn the next day unfolded smoothly. I could feel Alex's thoughts like a tangible form in front of my face when he wanted me to stop my meditation. He confirmed that he had been very irritated when he received the news of the cancellation of our Florida cottage. My feelings, I realized, had been totally correct and he was surprised that I could feel him.

The next stage of our trip was the flight to Scotland. We drove up to see my mother-in-law. Lizzie cried with joy and was particularly pleased and happy to see her granddaughter Kirstin again. We took her out to lunch, which required me to borrow a wheelchair from the hospital. Later we drove to the park and wheeled her around the little zoo and lake, something she always enjoyed. Here again the weather was perfect, so we were very fortunate.

In Edinburgh we stayed at our usual bed and breakfast place on Pilrig Street, where Mrs. Pretty welcomed us. She had just transplanted tulips and other spring flowers in her front garden and I watched her braid the spent long tulip leaves, to tidy them up, as she said. I found the custom of the Scots' creating colorful front gardens very appealing. We went for a long walk along the road where children were sailing their boats on the shallow lake. It was getting late, close to ten o'clock, but the sun was still shining brightly, reminding us that the midnight sun would come soon. I was reminded of an air from the Isle of Eigg by Agnes Mure MacKenzie: "For days work and weeks work as

443

I go up and down, there are many gardens all about the town." Walking here was pleasant, somehow very familiar.

My meditation came easily again, and I got into a state which is like a gap in normal consciousness. There was a sense of Swami Radha, much like a guiding light. I wondered just how much she was assisting me. Is it possible that those who pursue the path are assisted, as well as pushed as hard as possible? However, it must depend on individual perseverance and determination.

During the next few days, I dreamt heavily and most of my dreams had to do with effort, with uphill struggles. Suddenly. I felt my mother. It seemed to me that the dreaming was more conscious and directed to some degree. It came as no surprise that I heard the child-like African voice with the familiar incantation returning. It is upsetting because I didn't know what caused it, or what it implied. However, I am certain that it was in some way connected with my mother and her health. I focused my mind on my mantra, and I felt relieved that the incantation stopped. My meditation was mostly deep. My body became very still, my breath shallow. The street noises were clearly heard, but my mind did not react and remained blank and unaffected. The state felt as if I were wide awake and extremely conscious. I felt my brain and the chakras in my spine. My body was without any urge to do anything, or think about anything. The state-of-awareness could be described as just "being."

My effort was to stay conscious, which was quite difficult. I realized the importance of not ever hurrying or becoming impatient with circumstances. The tendency to react in a habitual fashion, or to be mechanical, implies being asleep. I also found that I had no words for the states I was experiencing; some were instances of euphoric delight with the world where I would just soar with joy. Reciting a mantra constantly begins to build strength to stay connected "in the moment," focused on nothing more than the repetitions. It creates one-pointedness, because the mind is occupied with one aim only.

One morning towards the end of our stay, as we went for breakfast, a problem arose. The young girl who was responsible

Ramona with Alex's mother Lizzie in Scotland, 1993

for the breakfast preparation and serving the guests was ill, and Mrs. Pretty was overwhelmed with the number of guests that came. Kirstin, who had a waitressing job back in Lake Forest, recognized the situation and without saying anything, began serving coffee and tea. She also brought egg-dishes, cereals, and porridge to the tables. She was especially enchanted with the good Highland jams. It took the stress off the owners and Kirstin was applauded. Needless to say, we were very proud of our daughter.

Lizzie took our final parting with grace. We were able to take her out for a birthday lunch to a very posh restaurant, and I think she enjoyed the wonderful food. Briefly we visited the park so she could feed the ducks in the pond with the buns that she had saved.

After a couple more days, we returned to the USA. The garden was lush, overgrown, and wet. The house was dark, small, and cluttered. The usual sense of tightness began to overwhelm me. Alex noticed, of course, and became defensive. We have lived here for twenty-five years, but hard as I tried not to show it, the space depressed me. The light in summer was cut off by the tall, old trees surrounding the house. It felt a bit like living in a green, gloomy fish tank. I tried to get control over myself because I was upsetting Alex, and I went for a walk.

It was very cool for June and the temperature was similar to that in Nairobi. The gardens all looked beautifully kept. This was a prosperous town. How lucky and extraordinary to have been brought to this oasis. The absence of noise was the most obvious blessing. Just bird-sound filled the air. The mantra chanted itself even though I was so ungrateful for all that was given. We had a house to live in, how lucky we were! I tried to be grateful and gain control over the waves of emotion. And then an unexpected rush of love and light engulfed me. Gratitude swelled and a longing broke like a torrent and flooded everything. This light was like a great relief, a wave of bliss. A memory returned. At the Ashram one night, I had the vision of a Goddess. She cried and cried and tears flowed from her like rain. I witnessed her tears and I was shocked by her extraordinary grieving. "Was she always like this?" I asked. "She grieves for all humanity," was the answer.

Being back in Lake Forest meant a return to familiar tasks and functions and letting go of Africa and the impressions of Scotland. Swami Radha had recommended keeping a daily diary with the promise that an understanding would ripen and more clarity would result. It had become clear to me in dreams that my mother would die. I knew this with certainty. I just did not know when.

Surrender

One of the yogic teachings advises to submit one's will to a larger power, in essence to practice awareness. I was guided by that power not to worry about my life, my family, my art, my Florida vacation. I could flow and allow guidance, and submit my small ego. I was determined to experience what happens as a consequence and to trust this new way of not being in ultimate charge. Instead, I witnessed a choice and saw the unexpected and novel ways in which circumstances unfold. While in Scotland, I sat in semi-lotus position in the car and decided to chant mantra mentally. This kind of practice is called Japa. When I regained consciousness, we were on the outskirts of Kirkcaldy. Forty minutes had passed and I had not been aware of it.

We made the decision to drive to Florida, even if we didn't have a house of yet, and trusted we would find suitable accommodation. We also decided to investigate Kasey Key, a charming island on the West coast. It had a miniature community, one little house beside the next, picture pretty with lovely, cared for gardens. As I did so often, I wondered if we would retire to Florida, but again the sense came that we shall not choose this place. The next day a realtor showed us an old Florida cottage on the beach, quite spacious with a big veranda. After we moved in, I realized how much tension I had carried, and how readily we had found this house. Why had I ever worried? Faith without doubt brings miracles into being.

I woke early to the roar of the ocean outside the bedroom window. Rising, I walked the short stretch of sandy beach and entered the clear water for my traditional long swim. The water was delicious, transparent like glass, and soon I was swimming along the shoreline forgetting every concern or thought while feeling the freedom a fish must experience. All things and concerns became petty and negligible. I felt clear-headed, and as I swam, I could see auras around my fingers and hands.

I picked up a book by Castaneda at the library. He writes that our bodies are surrounded by a luminous egg-shape energy field. I have experienced the aura around hands, so I am curious and interested in finding out more. As I looked up from my book, my eye caught the sight of children on the beach. As I observed and started to watch them, I suddenly saw a luminous extension over one child's head. I realized I had to stop thinking and I just looked at the child as though I was looking through things and not at things. The reward was astonishing, for their bodies were now surrounded by an egg-shaped misty halo, just as Castaneda described.

While meditating, I felt a layer of something surrounding me; a mantle, a shell of some kind. It felt rounded. At night I listened to the sounds. The ocean has many threads of sounds, some high, some low. They weave into each other. Then I fancied I heard a huge sound, an enormous all-embracing Aum—the vibrations of the Supreme Spirit. It was so big; I wondered how and why I did not hear it before. Swami Radha claimed that cells have a memory. I have all sorts of memories if I listen within. For instance, I remembered hearing the mountains as a child, when we went skiing in Austria. There was also the strange humming near the Cheops pyramid. At the Red Sea, I heard the rocks. Why did I block all this? And what is wrong with my neck and throat? I do not like anyone laying a hand around my neck.

Towards the end of the month of July, I had dreams and the full conviction rose once again that something was wrong with my mother. I could sense her emotions, including her loneliness, and I realized I didn't know how to help her. At that moment I felt guilt and confusion. It was a misty, somewhat grey day and I felt my mother repeatedly. As I went deeper, a sudden vision of a rocky cove arose with waves crashing continuously into it. The sky was grey and forbidding, the sound of the rushing waves unrelenting. It was cold and damp. "A hard existence has been my lot. This brutal life-situation is the reality for most human beings. Many people value only the hardness of life." This message came across quite clearly as I looked into the ocean. The water, restlessly in motion, flowed over and into itself while absorbing new waves, swelling and ebbing.

A sudden hard push into my back brought me out of my meditation. I felt nothing else. I remembered my mother once told me that life was nothing but a constant, hard battle. "You have to be a fighter to survive." Was this message and the vision of the high, rocky cove from her? I got up to look for mail. A cable had arrived. As I held the envelope, I already knew what it would contain. I took a deep inhale. My mother was dead! She died on the first of August at 2:30 pm. The cause was a suspected heart attack.

Coming to Terms with Death

A letter from her had been lying in the mailbox since yesterday. I had had the constant feeling that there might be news for me. But why didn't I go to look in the mailbox? And now she was dead. I was grateful that it was fast and infinitely grateful that I could be with her in May. What pained me was not her going—I could accept that as part of life and she was old at 79—but the memories of all the good things she did, all the pleasures and gifts she gave. I saw the giant tree looming over her garden, a spot of beauty she created for all those who entered her orbit to enjoy. I did not cry at first. There was no rush for that and also no self-pity. I had walked the beach earlier on, feeling very, very sad. My mind was filled with death and I was trying to come to terms with loss.

Later I called my cousin Renate in Germany. "You have heard?" she asked. As gently as possible she told me about Leni. She had been found lying on the floor in her room, clutching her handbag, as if just about to go out. The dog sat beside her. The servant John had been sent to the pharmacy to get some prescription pills for her and he found her dead when he returned home. The police were called. They sealed off the house, and a guard was posted for security. What happened to the staff, John, and Nicholas, the gardener? Or to the dog? Renate continued to tell me that there was a peaceful expression and a smile on her face. She also told me that my sister in Italy, on learning of the death, had rushed to Rome, but had been unable to get a flight to Kenya. On the third day she found a flight to Paris, then Nairobi. According to my cousin Renate, my sister was devastated. She had not expected my mother to die so suddenly. She had a flight booked to arrive in Nairobi tomorrow morning.

After this, I walked to the beach. The moonlight danced on the water and I recalled the nights spent with my mother on the big porch in Diani beach. I cried. She had been a tower of strength and determination all through my life. Now she was no more. And yet, suddenly I felt her close and intensely present. Why, why do I still doubt? Energy does not disappear; it changes, transforms itself, and assumes a different form. Throughout this whole period the mantra Hari Om has been persistently chanting in my head calming me. It continued into the night. I woke several times and slept little. During my dawn meditation, the Light stayed and I felt centered, calm and unperturbed. I kept on waiting for something inside me to give or to crack. Basically, I felt and responded in a totally rational fashion. Later in the morning, I called my Aunt Alma who was sobbing and terribly upset. She kept on repeating; if only my mother had had a bell to ring for her servant to come to her!

In the evening I finally managed to connect with my sister Gabriele in Nairobi. She had just arrived and sounded depressed. Leni was in the morgue. She had seen the corpse. My mother's face looked twisted and pained. John, the servant, told her how impossible everything had been lately and my sister blamed herself for not having been there. John told her, how on the morning of the first of August, after a dinner party the prior night, my mother had felt unwell and complained her back pained her all night long. She went to the doctor, who found her EKG heart and blood pressure were normal and gave her some pills to relax her. Once back at home, she sent John to the pharmacy in Westland's to buy the prescribed pills. When John returned home, she lay dead on the floor.

There were so many decisions to be made that it was obvious I had to return to Nairobi. We decided on a flight to Kenya. The earliest I could book was for August 8. The funeral had to be by August 12. Where should she be buried? Could we have a coffin made, or could one buy one ready-made? We needed a lawyer and Gabriele discovered that only once my mother lay buried, a lawyer could start the proceedings. My mother had saved 70,000 Deutsche marks for health problems and set that sum aside in Germany. That might help my flight expenses. What a business; but first we had to pack up and drive by car back to Illinois, a trip of at least two days.

My World Turned Upside Down

As I stood on my head, I asked, how I would feel if my world were turned upside down? What feelings did yoga produce in me? Instead of emotional turmoil I experienced a measured awareness and a collected calm mind. All my responses were mature and though feeling a deep sadness inside me, I also felt gratitude for my amusing little mother and for who she had been.

We set off for our long return car journey to Lake Forest. I meditated a great deal when I was not driving. Once, I went into what I believe is a Tantric state. My left palm became extremely hot, as though a magnifying glass was projecting sunlight onto it. It was a burning sensation. I saw my mother, stretched out with eyes shut. She did not really look how I expected her to look. She was white, ghost-like, and fully stretched out on the ground. There was no grief in me. I observed her for a long time in a kind of contemplation.

Later I felt her spirit; she was inside me and looked at the landscape through my eyes. I felt quite happy. During the meditation I decided to open my eyes. There was a huge shock wave as reality hit me with great intensity. The wide panorama of the road winding through forested lands and the white clouds streaking the sky gave a curious sense of transience. It was like a film. In part it was real, in part make-believe. Then I saw my mother. She looked well and happy. I tried to hold onto the image which shifted before returning and now she looked much younger, and after a further shift, younger still. Her hair was dark again and she looked as if she was the age she had been when I was a child. How odd, but then I reasoned, if she was shaking off all of life's burdens, she was bound to become younger looking.

When we finally arrived in Lake Forest, it was humid and the garden looked very green and well kept. The house was tidy and clean. Clearly Kirstin took her duties seriously. We met Kirstin's new boyfriend, Bill. He was handsome and intelligent, seemingly a pleasant and mature person. He wore his long hair open and it cascaded down his back. In some way Kirstin and he looked alike, perhaps because both wore long open hair and had almost the same hair color. Kirstin made our dinner. After tomorrow, I would fly. The journey to Africa would take two days.

Over dinner Kirstin said that after a day, she finally cried. "I did not like my grandmother, but I loved her." When she realized that her room was filled with precious gifts from her grandmother, she broke down. She mentioned that she had written a nice letter to her towards the middle of the month and hoped my mother had received it before her death. It had arrived, for Gabriele and I found it on my mother's desk in Nairobi.

The following day there were many messages from my sister, sent from Nairobi. The messages were drawn out and confused. Gabriele came across like a stony, silent force and she was doing everything the hard way. She did not like any of the cremation places she had visited. The coffins were all inadequate; the religious services unappealing. I realized I had to accept whatever she had arranged ahead of my arrival, and that I could not unblock her mind. She would pick me up at the airport. I wanted to meet my sister with love and compassion and understanding, not some childhood rivalry, which I feared. In my altered state I could feel Gabriele quite clearly and knew there would be problems.

Before my departure, Kirstin received a letter from my mother. In it she stated that she would have lived her life differently if she could start over again. She claimed she never ever had a dream, then to her surprise dreamt that she decorated Kirstin's new flat with many African objects and treasures belonging to her. Since she had been unable to recall dreams, this was odd. In a sense she foresaw the future, as her property and her things would eventually land in Kirstin's hands and decorate her future homes.

Flight to Africa

The flight seemed easy. I sat between two Greek women, neither of whom spoke English. My limited Greek was soon exhausted. They patted my arm lovingly and covered me with a blanket when I went to sleep and were most motherly. I did not eat and slept as much as possible instead. By 11 pm the smell of fresh coffee wafted through the plane. They served strong fresh coffee, and promptly at midnight the plane landed in Amsterdam. It is somewhat unreal to land in the early morning sunshine at midnight. I have never seen a plane so filled with small children, all travelling with only their mothers. There was a young woman with three children, one baby, seated in front of me. Behind me sat a woman travelling with four very small children. The babies all cried regularly in tandem and all the mothers seemed Middle Eastern or Arab—at least the children spoke Arabic. I thought of all the care and protection Alex had lavished on me when travelling only with one child. And Kirstin never ever howled. I felt sorry for these women who never slept for even a wink during the long journey.

At Schiphol Airport, Amsterdam, I curled up on a couch in the waiting hall. It was quiet and I drifted in half sleep until 10 am local time. An Italian beauty was talking nonstop on her cell phone. She was elegant and amazing to look at and probably knew it. I found this whole situation strangely unreal. The day was sunny and the air light. It brought back memories of summers spent in Europe, and also brought a warm contentment and inner joy. I was trying to be centered within myself. The outer events passed like colored lights, neither touching nor affecting me. "Your true nature is incomprehensible to your intellect." Who said that? I watched my inner state with certain amazement. My response to my mother's death was not as expected. There is no lack of love in me, and yet I accepted her death with almost no grief, and surrendered myself to the fact. There was no pain. Behind closed lids I sensed her, an essence, a spirit, not in the least dead and gone.

I watched people walking through the airport. They moved in this "silence-cushioned hall" like figures in a silent film. Swami Radha says: "Wake up from the dream of life when it is sad and depressing. Wake up to another level of consciousness." It almost seems to me that this is exactly what has happened. I was awake in another level. The day went past quite quickly. I sat in this artificial waiting station as if I were inside an insulated time capsule.

My arrival in Nairobi was drawn out, a delay in landing, confusion in the arrival hall, and mix-ups in the luggage delivery. Gabriele was waiting for me. She looked tired and pale. Gaby had done a lot of work during the week since her arrival here and seemed well organized. Once at the house we sat down to talk. She related how she had finally made it to Nairobi from Italy, and how she was so exhausted she decided to sleep in our mother's bed. As soon as she was fast asleep something pushed her in the back and kept on pushing. Then she heard my mother's voice in her head saying: "Get out, this is my bed." She sat up in horror and left the bed.

Funeral

By late afternoon the lawyer, Murtazar Jevangee, came to discuss my mother's will. Everything went smoothly and well.

We had already gone to bed when urgent knocking came from the kitchen door. The servants John and Nicholas stood outside, each carrying a panga (sword-like weapon and digging tool). A thief had broken into the servant's cottage and stolen a bag belonging to Nicholas. The news of my mother's death must be going around, I thought, and the scavengers are beginning to gather!

In Westlands, all owners of properties paid fees to a security company, whose armed vans cruised every night through the streets until dawn. We now called "Security 4" and within minutes they arrived and searched the grounds. My mother had been robbed repeatedly over the years. On one occasion she heard thieves in her sitting room. As her dog was barking furiously, the thieves became uneasy and instead of detaching the stereo and television set from the wall socket, they raised their pangas and cut the electric power cords to the machines. As a result, electric sparks flew through the dark room and that frightened them so badly that they ran away. Most thieves are unsophisticated poor people.

The security guards found that the thieves had climbed over the garden gate, and then waited in hiding while Nicholas had his shower. Then they broke the lock to his room and entered. John heard the commotion and came to investigate, which must have frightened them. The missing bag was found tossed into the bushes. After all that excitement, no one could sleep, so we switched on the TV. In my mother's house it had become a custom for the servants to join my mother when she switched on the television. Silently advancing on bare feet, the servants came in and sat down on the floor a short distance away from the set. To my amusement, this night wasn't an exception, as both Africans silently settled down on the ground beside Gabriele and me.

The next morning, my sister and I looked through our mother's collection of Egyptian artifacts consisting of small terracotta funeral vessels, little blue faience figures, beaded necklaces, masks, dolls heads, scarabs, which were placed into the mummy bandages over the heart region, and alabaster vessels. These had been collected, bought, and even found while she lived in Cairo. We split the collection. My sister was slow and thorough in her choices. Then I cooked lunch while she created an enormous bowl of salad. With a tiny amount of help, she managed to drink a full bottle of wine. Although I was really tired after lunch, we forced ourselves to continue, nonetheless, until it was night.

The next day we paid bills all morning. Later, we had a driver come to drive us around town, paying bills in shops where they were due. In the afternoon we cleared the large veranda for the funeral service taking place tomorrow. A Roman Catholic priest called Father Specht came to see us. He was a good soul, an intelligent sensitive man. We talked about death, the *Tibetan Book of the Dead*, and the *Bardo*, and he told us about his own near-death experience. He was going to conduct the service in the cathedral tomorrow, as my mother was Catholic. At ten o'clock the coffin and body would be brought to the house so that the Africans could pay their last respects. I have no idea why this is such a strong custom here and why John insists it is the most important of all the ceremonies. The veranda was to be packed with wreaths and flowers, candles, and plants, and among all that the coffin would rest.

That evening I desperately needed to refocus myself and find my inner source of strength. I found my higher Self unperturbed and indifferent to all outer events. Sleep seemed impossible and I could hear that my sister was awake as well. She said she understood why people spent the night before a burial in mourning and stayed awake. At one point I was tempted to go to her, but in the end did not. There was nothing I could do to help her. I fell asleep at dawn.

I had realized that the events of the day would play out in a fashion that could not be shaped or controlled, least of all any emotional reaction of my own. At ten o'clock the coffin was brought to the house. The funeral director was a nice Englishman. The simple unvarnished coffin my sister had ordered would not fit through the doorway. He insisted that the ladies not be present as they turned the coffin sideways to fit it through the entrance. A stand was placed on the veranda, covered with a deep red velvet cloth, and the coffin was placed on it. The wreaths were laid on top and arranged around the stand.

The Africans started to arrive, and the room quickly filled. Most of them I did not know, though many I recognized as belonging to John's family, as they were particularly handsome people. Everyone was dressed in white. Pastor Specht, the Catholic priest, and Dr. Barbara Kiambi, the pediatrician-friend of my mother, were the only white people present besides my sister and I. John, her loyal servant of over 25 years, rose and stood beside the coffin, his hand firmly placed on top for the full duration of the ceremony. Gabriele thanked everyone for coming that day.

John's wife, Isa, a tall thin woman with a white headscarf, started a prayer for the dead in Kikuyu. It was only then I remembered that she was a healer in her tribe and knew herbal witchery. Her voice rose in a passionate intensity, a wailing such as I had never before heard. It was so sudden and unexpected; it robbed me of all time to adjust to it. The sounds, screeches, howls, hand clapping, stamping of feet and humming from the rest of the people sent me over the edge. Gabriele rolled into my arms overwhelmed with grief, and we both burst into tears, holding each other. Certainly, holding my sobbing sister did not help my self-control, and so I too, cried.

When Isa finished her lament, I felt it my duty to say something. Somehow, I found my voice and started by telling them that probably no one knew much about the life of Leni Hilpert. I briefly outlined the many events and hardships that had formed turning points in her destiny. Mostly I talked about her struggles for existence and that it was in Africa she finally found her home and support. I also mentioned that she was free of any color prejudice and loved the African people. It seems, from what Pastor Specht said in his later sermon in the church, that my summation had been very moving.

We left and drove to St. Andrews church in town. Half the church was filled with Africans, and there were a good number of European friends. The priest gave a lengthy and excellent sermon. He truly tried to do justice to this unusual woman. On her bedside table he had noticed the *Tibetan Book of the Dead* and in her bookshelf many esoteric and spiritual texts. Pastor Specht asked the African Judge Akiwumi to read a Tibetan prayer from this book, which he accomplished with great style and in a beautiful baritone voice. Then, spontaneously, the priest sang a cappella, which was a most moving tribute.

After the service, Gabriele and I thanked all the mourners and then we followed the coffin in two cars. We drove through dreadful districts to the Hindu Crematorium. The weather had been cold and the sky lead-grey since my arrival here. The shanty towns through which we drove looked dusty and hopeless. The milling crowds and busses that belched black exhaust were foul-smelling and nauseating. The trees had all been cut down, and there were just cheap buildings, shacks, dusty roads and people, people, people. Along the sidewalk, stretching for miles, so it seemed, lay colorful heaps of cloth and garments piled on the ground. Here people bought clothes, I was told. The government regularly raided and destroyed the booths that the vendors erected and confiscated their wares. It was frowned upon that the population was too poor to afford the prices in the stores in Nairobi.

We reached the Hindu Crematorium, which was set in a large tree-shaded and well-kept garden. Walkways were spread throughout the grounds. My sister said this was the most respectful and sincere crematorium she had found in town. The structure was an open-roofed enclosure with a stone-paved depression in the center. Three metal, bed-like structures provided the receptacles for the deceased. One was prepared with wood shavings and logs. Our coffin was placed on it. Gabriele laid three tropical palm blossoms onto the coffin lid. Barbara had cut three blossoms from a tree-orchid in my mother's garden, a flower she valued very much.

Somehow, I had missed out on this custom and hadn't picked any flowers. Now, suddenly aware of the need to have the gift of a blossom to place on the coffin, I found myself in an awkward situation. "I need a flower," I thought, "please spirit, give me an appropriate flower." At this point I was shuffling between people leaving the cathedral after the service. I looked down at my feet and suddenly a pink rose appeared. Bending down, I picked it up. It must have fallen from a wreath, but it was perfect. My given name was Rosemarie, because my mother loved roses. Now I had the appropriate item. I had picked up the pink rose. The color pink symbolically stands for pure love.

We stepped back as an attendant came. The fire was lit and the wood shavings quickly jumped into high flames. It became a roaring fire, white-pink and orange flames licked the black logs and sparks jumped up and trailed into air like fire flies. The heat rose and the atmosphere trembled above the coffin and spread out towards us. And, with the radiating heat, came, after a while, the familiar scent of my mother, first just faintly, but then unmistakably hers. It was not quite right; it was slightly damp and cold, like stale beer. Looking away from the bright fire, I gazed at the cool, grey-green of the surrounding bushes and suddenly, briefly, the sun came out, shedding its light like a blessing over everything. I felt a sense of triumph and relief. She was going, consumed by fire, her shell shed. A mantra sang inside my head. Outside the crematorium I had seen tablets saying: Om Shanti, Shanti, Shantihi. It was a familiar phrase meaning "Peace" and it was consoling.

Looking Back Over My Mother's Life

We returned home, once the fire went down. In the evening, Gaby and I looked at photo albums we had found tucked away, and so, once more we looked at our mother's life in pictures. Among the photos. there was a big bundle of our father's last letters, written in 1945 from the war front in Poland, before the Russian armies swept through on their way to Berlin. We read them until midnight. It was simply terrible. The letters described how my father was forced to leave for Poland a few days before Christmas in 1944. The unheated cattle barns of a big Polish farm became the barracks in which they were housed.

The recruits, consisting of teenagers and older men, had been exempt from military service due to physical reasons. They were to form a cavalry intended to fight against the advancing Russian tanks and planes. There was no ammunition left and no guns for training these men. They practiced with wooden dummy rifles. The winter of 1944-45 was extremely severe and there was no hot water for washing, no heat available. Their food was just enough to keep them alive. What a brave stand my father made, how my parents struggled! How terrible to live through such senseless destruction and death. In a way, my sister and I said goodbye to both our parents on the 14th of August 1990, and we also discovered so many things about them that we had never known before.

The following evening, we met Mehram Yaar, an Indian journalist, who wished to write an article about my mother. He knew my mother as an artist who had exhibited extensively over the past years. We gave him the information he asked for. A day later he brought an article and left. To our amazement, it was pure sentimentality. I called him to ask about changing some overstatements and inaccuracies. He claimed he had already delivered the article to the paper. Too bad! I certainly did not believe him; however, as someone once said, even poor publicity is publicity! Mehram admired Leni Hilpert and that was probably more important than anything else.

As time went by, old friends of Leni drifted in, and stories emerged about events on her death day. Indian friends who came to her house discovered her corpse about the same time as John, her servant. Since my mother was a German citizen, they called the German embassy. However, the embassy refused to take responsibility for the body. African friends were called, who immediately came to the house and made arrangements. The women washed the corpse, and then they waited until the funeral service arrived and also the police, who posted guards late at night. All of her friends said they had been very upset. Leni had not looked dead, and they found it difficult to believe she really was gone. Njoguna was so upset that he drank one scotch after another, lamenting the incompetence of so-called intelligent people who had the power to act, but refused correct action out of indifference. We thanked all who had taken care of the situation after my mother's death.

The mountain of stuff we dealt with on a daily basis took its toll. Eventually though, Gaby looked more rested, and when we were invited out to dinner, she looked very pretty. Her shorter hair made her look younger and she resembled Leni, a fact everyone commented on.

Gabriele found my mother's diary. In it were recent entries about her state of health. She mentioned heart palpitations, dizzy spells, weakness in the legs, and back pains. Clearly, there had been periods of extreme fragility and the signs of life coming to a close.

As time went by, I became more aware of the weight of this situation. I felt gratitude that Gaby and I were able to handle everything we had to attend to so smoothly and calmly and in harmony. Had the Ashram stay and the year of meditation helped me? I think so because I have an inner strength I was not aware of before.

On our last day in Kenya, we went through a comedy of errors. We required a transport permit for shipping furniture. The bank refused point blank and for no reason to give me one! Gaby somehow managed to get three forms at the bank, and so gave me one. Air France claimed Gabriele Ritter was not on their flight list. In the end, they discovered she was on their list, but that took hours to confirm and many phone calls. Our lawyer, who was Indian, expected us to come back in December with our husbands, as we women were seen as not capable of handling things. Gaby told him that our husbands asked for and expected us to come back with a Xerox of power-of-attorney authorization papers so that we had some proof in our hands. This was really clever of her, as the lawyer seemed reluctant to give us any documentation.

I was looking forward to leaving. There were gaps in my concentration and memory, indicating exhaustion. Gabriele was certainly very efficient in a dogged and persistent way. She typed all the letters for the German Banks that held accounts for Leni. I felt very bad for my mother, as she only received 700 Deutsche marks per month and must have been exceedingly careful with her money. She never complained to Gaby and me; in other words, we had no real idea she was so hard up.

We planned to return in December. In the interim, John was to stay in the house and sleep in her room. In the afternoon the gardener and another man took the wheels off the Toyota and disconnected the car battery. We found a second key for the safe, so now, both of us had a key to take away with us. The lawyer would have to pay the servants and all bills during our absence. He also had access to Leni's bank account and could take out funds once the court sessions took place.

The details of all this were endless, and I felt grateful for Gabriele's abilities. After a last dinner, we opened a bottle of champagne. At this moment, John came in and asked to have more than his salary. He had been paid most generously and my sister became very annoyed with him, as we had to leave shortly and could not focus on paying him more. Could we really trust him to take care of things when this was an example of his attitude? Eventually we rushed into the taxi and left.

The airport was disorganized and everything was handled incompetently. I hung around to make sure that my suitcase was placed on the correct conveyor belt. The official looking at my papers had an air of not knowing what to check. The plane was huge, packed with passengers, and late in departing.

I settled into my seat and looked back over the last two weeks I had just spent in Kenya. I examined the fragments of my mother's life and time and felt disturbed because it was alien and uncomfortable. Now I evaluated her differently than before, as I now knew so much more. She craved excitement and had a need for exterior stimulation in order to feel truly alive, worthwhile, and like someone of importance. Her daughters were very different.

10 Returning to America

Evaluation of My Mother's Life

Back in the States, in Lake Forest and at home, I did not feel I had reached the harbor. I felt like the Flying Dutchman, restlessly sailing the seven seas. I tried to be aware of each moment from minute to minute and tried to be grateful for the wealth in my life. Also, I felt so grateful that my dreams had warned me of my mother's impending death. I had been able to prepare my mind and heart for the huge shift that was about to happen. In contrast, I saw my sister's sadness and confusion. Once she even said to me, "Why did you not tell me of her state of health, so I could have gone to Kenya?" I knew she would not have believed me nor believed the message of my dreams, and I would have risked losing my inner voice or been ridiculed.

I sent a note to Swami Radha, telling her about my mother's death. I also included the little newspaper article written by the Indian journalist. To my great surprise, I received a letter back in a very short time. She expressed herself so touchingly, almost as if she had known Leni Hilpert when they both lived in Berlin. I felt very puzzled and came to the conclusion they might well have been moving in the same circles. Swami Radha asked me to put my mother into the Invocation of the Light as often as I could. She said that it was "my connection with the

Light I needed to put into action" and that this would affect all my actions in a very concrete way. Of course, I immediately tried it and put my mother's spirit into the Light. It was amazing, for what happened next was a sensation of intimate closeness. I felt my mother, so close to me, almost within me, and remembered Radha's words: "When we meet in the Light, that is the most intimate connection, and we are not restricted by physical boundaries." Following this experience, I made constant use of the Divine Light meditation, using it for all problems, misunderstandings, and people.

A curious letter arrived from an old friend from my student days. She was quite psychic and trustworthy, even when she made rather odd statements. She wrote that she had talked to my mother. She had a "love message" for me. My mother told her that she never talked to me of love, that she never told me in words how much she loved me. This was because in her childhood such feelings were not expressed or talked about, not by her own parents or people in general. She wanted to make sure that I knew she loved me. For this reason, she connected to my friend, so I would get a message I could trust.

"Why should she be concerned at this stage about words?" I thought to myself. I always understood she loved me, even if she did not express herself in words. The curious thing though was that my friend would send me such a message. I had never mentioned anything about my mother to my friend, and how would she therefore know, unless this contact did indeed take place. Just then I realized that it was exactly one month since my mother's funeral and cremation in Nairobi. The other oddity concerned my feelings. Reading my friend's letter and contemplating its meaning left me with a feeling of liberation and release from grief.

After my friend's letter arrived, I no longer felt burdened by my mother's death. I was able to accept it as inevitable. The many condolence letters I received embarrassed me somewhat, as I was quite proud of my mother and viewed her quick death and exit from this world as a most successful escape. She lived and died exactly as she had wished. She did not suffer some drawn-out illness, nor was she forced by circumstances to give up her lifestyle and live in a home for the aged, nor did she lose her independence, not even for even a single moment.

Though I was now back in my familiar circumstances, back teaching at Lake Forest College, being together again with my charismatic Alex and intelligent and sensitive daughter, life did not feel the same to me. I turned to the yogic teachings and to the wisdom of Swami Sivananda Radha. The firm intention began to form itself to study at Yasodhara Ashram for a longer time, maybe several months. I suddenly felt an intense desire to find my spiritual guide and to know that my probing into my soul was leading me in the right direction. I resumed my practice with renewed vigor, spending regular hours in reflection, meditation and hatha yoga. A daily spiritual diary was also part of it, as was chanting mantra. Whether it was my own mind that created visions of light or visions of Swami Radha, it was now no longer something that bothered me. I accepted that I was obviously worthy enough to have such experiences. I had to trust and to develop faith. Swami Radha repeatedly said: "Your own sincerity will protect you." The adventure had begun and I now knew that my life was altered; my conscious experiences would never be the same again. In broad daylight, with wide open eyes, I could see the Light.

Balance Between the Outer and the Inner Lives

My outer life, however, demanded staying on top of daily obligations. There was my daily painting, teaching at the college, shopping and cooking and also entertaining, as well as the chore of house cleaning. Over the years the old house had been transformed by our care and love and no longer resembled the dreary balloon construction I first entered in 1966.

In the beginning of December, Kirstin and Bill returned from Tallahassee, Florida. This had been her first half year at the university there. Looking at her face, I could see she had not had an easy time at the university; a certain amount of suffering had taken place. Bill was intelligent and talked a great deal.

Later, in the kitchen, when we were getting the food ready, Kirstin lifted her hand and said, "Look!" At first, I failed to see it. An engagement diamond ring! I don't know what she expected from me. Love and marriage were a private thing between two people, in my view. A ring is tradition. By her expression, I realized I failed to show the expected reaction. It reminded me of my own mother, when I had tried to show her the ring given to me by Joe. Furthermore, I did not think that the second-hand engagement ring of Bill's mother was a good omen. He should have bought her a new ring chosen by him or by her; at least that was my opinion.

11 Returning to Africa

The Flight to Nairobi

Alex and I had planned to fly to Nairobi over the Christmas holidays to dissolve my mother's property. We were to meet my sister and her husband there, and we were to fly on Christmas day. During the Kenya summer, the Europeans like to visit the tropical beaches of the Indian Ocean. All flights to Kenya had been booked many months before and so Christmas Day was the only day on which we still found available seats. Kirstin was not happy to see her parents go.

We flew to Paris, where we had to stay a day, and then continued flying to Africa during the night. Paris was grey, dirty and congested, and the outskirts looked ugly with bad box-like housing units spreading everywhere. There was too much traffic.

Our Air France plane had comfortable seats and really wonderful food. I managed to sleep, and at midnight we arrived in dazzling sunlight in Nairobi. Everything was brilliant with brightness, color, and warmth. My Aunt Alma and Uncle Christian came to pick us up. My mother's garden looked like an oasis with bougainvillea of all colors delighting the eye. We immediately departed for the Nairobi Club for a lunch invitation. My uncle was doing poorly and was nearly totally blind. He had trouble hearing as well. The old English Club was unchanged, except that now it was no longer for Whites only. The place was filled with African and Indian members and many children.

Quarrels, Jealousy, and Anger

By evening I felt hot and my throat was closing down and on the following day I was seriously ill. The throat was so bad I could not speak; perhaps a wise decision on my body's part, as the relationship with my sister had undergone a dramatic change. Almost the first thing she said was that our mother had only loved me. She had been abandoned and left behind in Germany in 1948. Therefore, she had certain rights regarding how we had divided our inheritance. She claimed she had functioned poorly, due to grief, when we had split inherited things following our mother's death. A whole number of items we had agreed to divide were now going to her. I could not talk and my whispered objections were not audible. I did not care about the objects, but I did care about her changing feelings towards me. I had always loved her and had helped her whenever I could or supported her. I had believed that she felt love towards me. What I saw now was a huge change and anger. I had never expected such a change in my younger sister. Now she distrusted me and accused me of taking advantage of her in her moment of profoundest grief, choosing the better deals, the more valuable objects, and cheating her wherever I could. I listened silently in shocked disbelief. I had not only lost my mother; I had also lost my sister.

I did not sleep most of the night. My head hurt, I was hot with fever, and I coughed steadily. It occurred to me that my speechlessness was a blessing. The sale of the house would be handled by my more aggressive and business-like sister. I intended to pay more attention than ever to the intuitive hints coming towards me. Sitting in the garden wrapped in a blanket, I listened to the cooing doves, the chirping of birds, and rustling leaves. I felt the goodness of this garden, created by my mother over so many years, the splendor of nature, and I briefly submerged into a feeling of gratitude and delight. I kept on wondering what my mother had felt and thought while she lived in this space. Aside from letters to people, there were no statements of her personal thoughts, no reflections on paper. There were, however, her paintings. She was almost sixty years old when she found the opportunity to return to her love for art and was able to express her feelings in images.

Moving at a Snail's Pace

It seems that we were moving at a snail's pace. Everything seemed to be turning in circles. The accountant and my sister were at loggerheads about the value of the house and property. Alex suggested going to a realtor and finding out what the value of the house actually was. My sister objected, as it would cause needless expense and there was no way to trust a realtor. My sister's evaluation was probably too high; the lawyer's evaluation was probably too low. It would not be possible for us to return in the summer, should the matter remain unresolved and the house unsold. If we were to leave the house empty, we would have to retain two servants, and that would cost money. Alex looked as if he, too, might become ill. He told me how helpless he felt, as Gabriele was directing the whole show without consulting anyone. He also found it irritating that she cut him out from conversations by speaking in German, which he could not understand.

Gabriele voiced irritation with whatever I had worked to achieve in my yoga practice and discipline. According to her, I was not critical enough. I was too easy going and avoided taking responsibilities. My simple-mindedness led me to lack aggressiveness; in short, I was a wimp. At first, my ego rose to protest, but then as she talked, I realized she was right and I agreed that I was indeed a very simple person. No need to protest! I had changed and if I was seen as a fool, so be it.

We hired packers to pack up all of Gabriele's and my inherited stuff, which would then be shipped off. However, they came before we had sorted through books and pictures and miscellaneous items. Everything was chaotic and confusing. Gabriele repeatedly informed me that I was faster and smarter in my choices, and that she had drawn the lesser deal. I tried to accommodate her, but it made little difference. Actually, I think the reverse was true.

Then she accused me of stealing some ancient Egyptian shards from a vitrine. The shards were parts of broken pots. As a consequence, she claimed it was impossible to trust me. She had to stand beside me as we each fished out our allotted number of shards. She felt certain that I would cheat and she insisted that we barely knew each other, or words to that effect. I could feel my heart contract with pain. I felt vulnerable, misunderstood, and criticized.

A headache started and I stayed. Why on earth did I deserve to be treated like an enemy? I decided to distance myself; taking this abuse was not rational or warranted. That evening after dinner, Gabriele let lose her grievances. She felt, as Leni's second daughter, she had always had the worst deal. Whenever a problem with lawyers or Leni's pension or her insurance came up, she had to deal with the legal or financial matters. I was too far away in America and been indifferent to our mother's plight. Her resentment was based on the suspicion that Leni had exploited both her and Klaus, without any signs of appreciation or gratitude. The anger and pain in Gabriele were deep-seated and festering. I listened, but made no comment. It was cathartic for her to vent her feelings fully, but it was a huge problem to resolve.

It was my sister's desire to scatter our mother's ashes into the Indian Ocean at Diani Beach. It was the place my mother had loved most and where she had spent many happy times. We had no objections to this plan and at five o'clock in the morning, on January 5th, we set off in the dark for the eight-hour trip to the coast. Klaus drove my mother's old car on a road that was, as he said, "potholes with patches of tarmac in between." We were bouncing along at a fair pace when the muffler began to sound loose. At the rest house we stopped for coffee. The place was still a peaceful haven, as it had been 26 years ago. The river was edged by papyrus reed in which yellow weaver birds had built their nests. Their lemon-yellow bodies looked like butterflies as they bounced about.

At Mtito Andei the road improved, and when we reached the outskirts of Mombasa, we found an African-Asian garage, where we stopped to have the muffler fixed. Klaus was a remarkable expert on cars. I am not sure I would have risked driving this somewhat ancient vehicle all the way for eight hours to Mombasa. The so-called garage was a compound, within which sat a large number of rotting vehicles used mostly for spare auto parts. A young slender boy slipped under our car to weld the broken muffler back together. Whenever he switched on the blow torch, he shut his eyes. He wore no protective goggles. One mistake and he would end up blind.

By late afternoon we reached Diani and its snow-white beaches. It was a great relief to plunge into the cooling aqua waters of the Indian Ocean. Alex was really ill now and he withdrew into the house. The place was the same; the glittering water, the grey sky, the baobab sentinel on the beach, but it was no longer May and my mother no longer sat on the airy veranda. I reflected with some regret that I had not fully recognized then how frail she had become. In part, her swings between energy and a total absence thereof had given me the wrong impression.

As the days went by, we all began to relax more, and since my sister's birthday had not been adequately celebrated, we decided to go out to the Baobab Hotel for dinner. This hotel is perched on higher ground overlooking the ocean. During the incoming flood time it becomes surrounded by water, much like Mont Saint Michel in France. Once a huge baobab stood at the rocky point before they built the hotel. I recalled that the vibes were very bad 25 years ago. The place held evil energy. They told me a horrible battle had taken place there, and the spirits still haunted the site. Now there was a pool, tropical plants, a jungle, delightful cottages, and an atmosphere of tropical splendor.

During the last few days there had been little opportunity to meditate, so I was aching to find a secluded spot on the white, sandy beach and to sink into my practices. The sea was slate grey and low-lying clouds touched the ocean. Later the sun burst through in metallic brightness. All was just as it had been in May with Leni. I merged into the gentle breeze as I listened to the rhythm of the ocean. Then I stood on my head, turning the world upside down. Intense joy surged through me as I absorbed the beauty all about me in gratitude. This beach and our visit here was my mother's gift to us all, at the place she loved most.

Burial at Sea

It was our intention to scatter my mother's ashes into the Indian Ocean. My sister had the vessel with the ashes with her and the idea came to send the ashes up into the sky with a balloon. Klaus had made these silken balloons before and successfully released them in Berlin at the wedding of friends. He had designed them and they looked beautiful as they drifted upwards, carried by the winds. Klaus had concluded the winds blew inland during most of the day, but at dawn the winds blew in the direction of India, away from shore.

We rented a native boat, basically a hollowed-out tree trunk with a sail. Just in case there were mishaps, we also made little paper boats, such as people used in Asia and India, into which the ashes of the deceased are sprinkled. A lit candle was placed into the paper vessel with some flowers. With the current flowing in the right direction, the little boats floated away, mostly downriver. We hoped we would not need the boats, but folded little papers anyway, just in case. To ensure their success, my sister had brought trick candles from Italy, which could only be blown out with great difficulty once they were lit. The evening before our ceremony we checked the balloon. Some of the panels, which had been glued together very carefully, had separated, probably because of the high humidity. Klaus glued them again and we all hoped for the best.

The next morning at dawn it was still dark. Alex and I staggered down the beach just as the native boat pulled into shore. We climbed into the narrow, hollowed-out boat and

LENi HiLPERT   ✳12.APR.1911 ✝1.AUG.1990

*Scattering of the ashes and flowers onto
the Indian Ocean, Kenya, 1990*

perched on the edges. We had also arranged for buckets filled
with flowers, wreaths, and garlands to be brought to the boat.
These filled all the space. The boat had a huge sail, shaped like
a scimitar. Two strong-looking fishermen now took control of
the boat and started poling us into deeper water. They were
very puzzled and I concluded they had no idea what we were
up to.

My sister unfolded the silk balloon, but the glue had not
held. Unperturbed she pulled out a needle and thread and
started to sew the panels together. Then we tried to light the
cotton inside the balloon, but there was such a strong wind that
the flame was instantly blown out. In a way, it was comical and
the Africans were beginning to find our curious performance
very amusing. At this stage we had come out far enough from
shore and were crossing over the reef, a ridge of corals and
seaweed, leading into the deeper waters of the ocean proper. A
different rhythm made the little boat rise and fall in a dramatic
way that instantly made me feel seasick.

Obviously, the idea of launching a balloon had to be abandoned and so we decided to use the little spirit boats. We unfolded them, placed a lit candle into each, and sprinkled some of my mother's ashes into each of them, then some flowers. It was difficult to drop them down to the water surface with the boat bobbing up and down so vigorously. The ocean current carried them rapidly away and we dropped flowers and wreaths alongside them. Eventually a path of colorful blossoms and spirit boats with lights formed itself, and the trailing garlands drifted away into the distance. Each one of us made a silent prayer as we released her ashes. Then the boat turned and the sail filled with wind as we headed back to shore.

The swell was making me feel nauseous. The sun had risen and the moon sliver, seen above the sail disappeared. The water was a rich emerald green and I decided to end my misery. With one swift movement I slipped over the edge of the boat into the cool water and swam the rest of the distance back to shore. The water felt magnificent and I breathed in a deep and regular rhythm, dispelling the nausea caused by the rocking boat. The boat moved no faster than I swam, so we all arrived at the same time.

That evening, we decided to go out for dinner. The Nomad was a renowned restaurant. As we got into the car, Klaus checked the tires and saw that we had a flat back tire. He had already been seated in the driver's seat and irritated with the seat belt, had thrown it back over his seat, so it now dangled behind him over the floor. Alex too, was already in the back seat of the car and as he now tried to get out, his foot got trapped in the seat belt Klaus had tossed back, and he fell heavily out of the car. It was clear to me that he was in much pain, though he made light of it. I hoped that it was only a sprain, but in my heart, I suspected that he was seriously hurt.

Mombasa Hospital Visit

That night, Alex could not sleep because of the pain and at six in the morning I went to the cottage of Simon, our servant, and asked him to phone us a taxi. By eight a rickety vehicle arrived and we took off for the Aga Khan hospital in Mombasa. We were fortunate, for the handsome Indian doctor who attended to Alex had studied in London and was excellent. Alex was x-rayed and a fracture was found in a bad place. The break was set. No pain killers were ever used. "How do you feel?" I asked, deeply concerned about the pain he must be enduring. "Surprisingly, I felt only slight discomfort," he answered. "That doctor had a healing touch." He was to have a plaster cast for six to eight weeks. We had spent most of the morning waiting, in plastic seats in a sunny little corridor of the hospital watching beautiful African and Asian women and children in vibrant clothing playing and singing and waiting for their turn to see the doctor.

Our return to Diani beach was surreal. Our vehicle was old, but we did not realize how old until we crossed an estuary on a ferry. The hold was filled with cars, including our taxi. One after another the cars were conducted to the edge of the ferry and then rolled down an incline to the road below. Our driver was terrified as he confessed to us that his brakes had given out. Once on the downward incline he could not stop the car. There were many people leaving the ferry as well, mixing themselves among the cars that were rolling slowly down to the highway. Our car could not slow down. Terrified, I recited a mantra as our vehicle left the hold and began to roll off the ferry boat. I saw a whole group of people in front of our car and expected that any moment the first bodies would be crushed beneath the wheels. To my total amazement the people in front of the car began to drift sideways, almost lifting into the air as they got out of our way, and every one of them moved aside as we thundered past them at top speed. The driver, visibly shaken, was thanking God repeatedly as we continued our journey. We sped along the coastal road towards Diani Beach.

Suddenly there were soldiers on the highway, powerfully grown men toting rifles. The driver became very nervous, and I could feel his fear. A man stepped into the road and with a raised hand signaled the driver to stop. He looked at us coldly as he opened the front door and slipped into the seat beside the driver. Looking straight ahead he gave directions as we moved back into the road. We turned away from the coast at some point and drove into fields planted with banana palms. I had no idea where we were going, and neither Alex nor I spoke a word. The road became rough and uneven and the old car seemed to find every pot hole.

Eventually, we reached a village. The uniformed man gave a signal, the driver stopped, and the soldier slid out, without uttering a single word. The driver sighed as he turned and drove back to the highway. "They are dangerous," he said to us. "They do what they want. Sometimes they make us drive for hours to some destination; they neither pay us for our time, nor for the gas. If we complain they shoot us. They have the guns; they have the power." We sighed with relief to get back to the house. My sister was angry that we had not awakened Klaus and asked him to drive us. I excused ourselves, saying the pain was too intense and we left too early. I remembered that Klaus needed his coffee first thing in the morning. So far, Alex had had no pain killers, and now he asked for a scotch. I settled him on the porch with a whisky and went into the kitchen to make us a late lunch.

Return to Nairobi and Departure to the USA

The next morning, after a leisurely start, we left the coast. Klaus did all the driving and I felt apprehensive, wondering if we would get back in one piece. There were so many lorries coming towards us and they passed us as if by a miracle. One always had the sensation that they headed straight towards our car and swerved to the side just in the last few seconds. It was a dusty, bumpy ride, and stopping for lunch at Mtito Andei was most refreshing. Twenty-five years ago, this drive had been so magical, with wild animals everywhere. Elephants often brought traffic to a full stop as they leisurely ambled across the road or stopped to feed at the edge. Back then, posters everywhere warned, "Elephants have the right of way."

Nerves were taut and tempers sharp once we arrived in Nairobi. Both Klaus and Gaby were tired and irritated. There were still mountains of work to be done and only two days left to do it all. The buyers for the house had all gone down in price with their offers and the depressing aspect that we would be unable to sell the house loomed ahead. Gaby became very aggressive due to some remark of mine, offering to throw her soup plate at my head. There came another occasion when my sister vented her anger at me, calling me names and insulting me.

Alex stepped in and said: "Your mother has died. At this time, you have no one left but each other. Is so much disagreement really called for? You only have each other, please remember that." I was grateful for his words. However, things became worse. It was a comedy of errors, delays, and frustrations. Alex and I spent nearly the whole morning labeling and cataloging Leni's paintings. The new director of the Goethe Institute was willing to mount a retrospective exhibition of her work in September, providing he could see the work. Gabriele was willing to return to Africa in September to supervise the exhibition. By noon, Dr. Eicher, the director of the Goethe Institute, and his wife arrived. We showed them the paintings and then the house and garden, as they were very interested to see an artist's home. He was a gentle man, long stationed in India and Japan. It was hard to tell if he liked my mother's paintings; however, after my Aunt Alma came over to meet him, the exhibition was firmly agreed upon. I marveled at her easy charm and how she managed to influence people.

Almost at the same time, Murtazar Jeevangee, our attorney, arrived to confirm that our best offer for the house came from an organization involved with environmental work in Kenya. It was a blessing Alex was there, as he was able to converse with the attorney in a friendly and clear-headed fashion. My sister continued to be suspicious and distrusted the Indian attorney. It seemed to occur to no one that this man had been our mother's attorney for over 25 years and had been a friend of hers over all this time.

Tempest in a Teacup

Probably the worst tempest in a teacup occurred with the moving company. My sister did not trust the African packers, who did a wonderful job, as far as I could see. She interfered with their methods and asked them to wrap her items differently, thereby slowing the process down. All my items shipped to the USA were in perfect condition, with no breakage, whereas her items met a different fate. I also think they purposely damaged some goods in retaliation for her behavior.

Our last day came. We worked relentlessly to clear the house. Alex could do little and sat with his broken arm in the sunny garden and noticed things we failed to observe. As the house was stripped of its contents it began to look old and shabby. All my mother had created disappeared, only the beauty of the garden remained. The servant John seemed confused, lost and in shock. He sat in the empty kitchen on a stool staring sadly into space. Alex talked to him, sensing his profound distress. He had worked for my mother for over 25 years. He had insisted on being given Leni's old car, in spite of the fact that he could not drive. One of his sons would drive, he assured us.

My aunt and uncle invited us to their house for yet another much-appreciated luncheon. They accepted, as yet unpacked items into their storage space, whole trunks packed with linens and towels, china and silver, and books. As the time of our departure neared, Alma began to feel one of her heart attacks, and Christian was crying, saying we would not see each other again. They had been a huge emotional support for all of us during this difficult time, and we could not have managed without them. I felt they were now at the limit of their strength and it was time to withdraw before they became even more upset.

Alex asked me to cut it short, as my elderly relatives were clearly overwhelmed. We hugged and said our goodbyes and left for the taxi, which was waiting to take us to the airport. Just then, Klaus rushed up and asked me to empty a file cabinet.

Earlier he had refused Alex's assistance with this task. At this stage, I no longer felt any hesitation and blurted out how ridiculous his whole behavior had been, how Gaby and he had created this chaos and confusion. Now this last-minute rush was the result of their disorganized minds. I refused to help and he looked shocked and not quite able to respond. Perhaps he realized this was the truth, and so we left for the airport long before they managed to go. In fact, they nearly missed the plane.

As soon as I was seated on the plane, I went to sleep. I awoke with Gaby standing in the aisle beside Alex, telling him her bag packed with silver had been forgotten and left in one of the cupboards. Probably one of the Africans would take it. A pity, for that was lovely silver. When we arrived in Paris, we said goodbye to each other, as all of us were probably glad to get out of each other's orbit. We did not even embrace. There was no feeling left in me except a profound sadness.

The plane taking us to Chicago was flying over Greenland and the North Pole. Looking out the aircraft window, the surface of the earth looked lovely with clouds drifting across it. All felt like a dream. Then the world below became white, ice covered, gleaming in the sun. What a change from the colors of Africa.

12 Aftermath

Deeply Wounded

Due to jet lag, sleep beyond three in the morning was impossible. Lying awake in my bed at home in Lake Forest, I thought about the abuse Gabriele had lavished on me and felt depressed. She had told me that I was egotistical, selfish, and domineering. Why? It did not help our relationship to feel disliked, criticized, and disapproved of. Why had she been so angry? What was I guilty of doing to her to merit such condemnation?

In the mirror I looked quite brown and had lost some weight. Outside the world was snow-covered and icy. We had returned to winter in North America. The African trip was over. But, was it over? Certainly, my heart was heavy with pain and I felt confused. My dreams were proof of that. I dreamt I was desperately looking for cover in order to hide, and I was being hunted. My crime was unclear. Alex, when I asked him if he understood what had happened, simply said my sister seemed deeply wounded to him. It was not our fault, and I was not to blame.

His arm was healing well and a first appointment with a doctor was coming up. Our classes at Lake Forest College resumed and, among other things, we had a faculty exhibition to mount at the Durand Art Institute. Since Alex could not use his right arm, I had a lot to do, which included adjusting the lights for each art work and climbing a high ladder to do so. The opening was well attended and there were many compliments.

A week later, the past events began to burden my mind once more, since I did not know how to deal with my sister. Our business was far from over; there was a substantial amount of money in the Dresdener Bank in Germany, invested sums which could not be touched until their maturity date. I had received no satisfactory statement from the bank describing the division of the sums, in spite of the fact that I was one of the heirs. In desperation I wrote to my Uncle Willy, my mother's brother in Mannheim, begging him to try to find out what arrangements my sister had made concerning the money. Fortunately, he did intercede, talked to the bank manager, and finally I received the requested statements and paper work. That experience made clear to me I had to come to a level of civilized communication with Gabriele, especially because she held a lot of the strings in her hands.

Meditation was my tool, my guidance, my teacher, and my support. I composed a letter to her in which I did not react to what had occurred, but I responded instead. I spoke of my feelings, mentioned my surprise at her unexpected accusations and asked to be forgiven for any unintended errors. Mostly I stressed that I had no intention to harm or hurt her in any way, that I did not understand what had caused her anger towards me. Having written the letter, I tore it up and started again. I began to understand that the lesson of those weeks in Kenya was to absorb all insults, all criticism my sister had directed towards me, and to let the insults go like smoke out a chimney. I had to disregard and ignore my own feelings of hurt in order to begin to understand the sources of her pain.

My birthday was in February and I wondered if Gabriele would send me birthday wishes. My mind would rise up and say: "I don't care if she does not write!" My heart, however, was sore. Eventually, I reached a stage where I grieved for the split and the seeming loss of my sister. Not only had I lost my mother, but my sister as well. Eventually I had put together a letter humble enough not to offend. I just wanted to know how she was doing and what she was feeling. Basically, I did not care about the material items left by my mother; if my sister needed them, she could have them.

I had a dream in which I bared my chest and washed it clean. Finally, I showed my heart. That day after returning from my classes at college, I found that Alex had written a letter to Gabriele. It was a good, firm letter, but it should come from me, not him. The hint was clear. I have to take a firm stand; I have to stop cringing. That evening after dinner, I sat down, and using his letter as a guide, composed of two pages to Gaby. She may hit the roof, I thought; there is no way to tell.

The dream of baring my chest and washing it clean was a clear symbol. The situation demanded to be confronted. So, I sent it. On my way to the college, the car skidded on the icy road and drove off the street and up a slope beside the church. I was not frightened for a second. Nor did the car slide into the opposite side of the street and into the truck that had just pulled up.

My Birthday

My birthday came. No card from my mother, of course. I never paid much attention to my birthday. But today, I remembered that she always sent me a card with greetings. I was her first child, and I suspect she celebrated the fact for herself as well. I hoped I helped her last May and June, I hoped something transmitted and helped her in her last hours of life.

The phone rang and I could feel the call came from far away. It was Murtaza Jeevangi, the attorney from Nairobi. He was very worried about the upcoming sale of Leni's house. He feared cheating. Even though my mother had brought the funds for the house from Europe and her living expenses were paid for from abroad, the buyers did not wish to pay in a foreign currency. Kenya money could not be transferred abroad and had no value on the international market. We needed payment for the house in foreign currency. The black-market rate for an exchange of funds meant we would lose $6,000. "That is reality." Alex said.

Later on, I called back and talked to Margaret Jeevangee, his German wife. She had just learned that my mother's handsome African servant John had died on Saturday. People joked, she said, that Leni could not stand to be in heaven without her loyal servant John. It seems that John arrived back in his village, hoping to be received in his home. During his many years of absence and service, he had faithfully sent his income to his wife, who had used the money increasing the size of their house by adding rooms and renting these out to strangers. She had cleverly added value to the property. All the many rooms of the house were rented out when John returned. His wife refused him a place to stay. To make matters worse, his youngest son crashed the car, so now John had nothing of value to his name. His wife was very clever with herbs. One morning John suffered terrible stomach cramps and they had to drive him to the nearest hospital, but he died on the way. The rumor was that his wife killed him. Poison!

I found it difficult to believe such a story, but during my time in Nairobi I heard repeatedly about poisonings. It was a favorite method used by women and poisoning as a crime was very difficult to prove. Yesterday I thought of John sitting in the dark kitchen of my mother's house, grieving for his employer. Now I grieve for John, who had been such a wise and kind soul all those many years.

Towards the middle of the month, the shipment of furniture from Nairobi arrived. However, only one container made it. We waited patiently and hoped the second container would also make it. We arranged to clear it through customs, which meant a trip to Chicago in the middle of our work week. Fortunately, the shipping company was willing to keep the first container at no cost until the second one arrived. Alex was still one-handed and I would require assistance in unpacking the containers. Thank God for friends who volunteered to help.

Where Is the Money?

The next morning an early call came from New York. A soft English voice told me that $40,000 is being transferred from Barclays Bank, NY. It should arrive any day now. We waited for our bank to call us with the confirmation. There was no further news. The bank told us they had not received the money and the days went by. Where was the money? I called almost daily. The polite answer continued to be, "Regretfully, the sum has not yet arrived."

In the middle of March, my sister called from Italy. She too, was waiting and had not received the money as of yet. In addition, the check for our expensive flights had disappeared in some bank transaction. My flight from Chicago to Nairobi and back was $4,000. I was able to stay undisturbed and free from expectations with the help of meditation.

At 7:45 am, the Sun City Trucking Firm pulled into our narrow driveway. All day long we unpacked item after item. Mountains of packing-material piled up on the porch. Friends arrived in the afternoon. When 10:00 pm came, I began to feel tired. The next day was Sunday and I began again, a little more leisurely, as I tried to control the impatience that I felt. All day long, until the arrival of midnight, the items flowed into the house. It is difficult to arrange them so that the house did not look cluttered.

I was very aware that Alex felt disturbed because his nest was being rearranged. He was also coughing too much and I felt concerned. I warned him. His smoking habit was so deeply established that he could not think of himself without a cigarette in his hand. While unpacking, he stopped every few minutes for a smoke. At night I noticed his chest making strange noises. I looked at him and saw a wonderful, valuable individual, and yet he is throwing his life away for a habit. When he sat across from me at our dining room table, I noticed a kind of dark fog over the right hemisphere of his head. It looked a bit like an upright dark plume. On the left side I saw nothing of the sort. For 26 years I have asked him to get help with his smoking habit, but he did not want to give it up. It filled me with

Gaby and Klaus on their property in Tuscany, Italy, 1991

foreboding and unease. Would he kill himself? Then I would be left behind alone. I had seen my mother and how she coped with her loneliness over so many years. It was not an easy life.

Money Problems

At this time, the house was mostly together again, but looked darker due to the Persian carpets and furniture. I felt slightly low and tired. It took a full week to put all of my mother's things somewhere. And then I received a call from my sister in Italy announcing the receipt of her money from Kenya; however, it is substantially less than she expected. She sounded extremely upset and helpless. Nothing I said would calm her. She ended up just hanging up on me!

Later, during my daily meditation, my mind again and again was drawn to my sister. I felt disturbed by distractions of this sort. When the phone rang an hour later, I made no effort to answer it. Alex did, and it was my sister. The exchange rate we had been given was not correct. We had lost money and I was to phone Murtaza. The thought of Gabriele had not been due to my wandering mind, but to actual mind-to-mind communication. I was unsure what to do now. Alex was a powerhouse of calm intelligence, and he offered to write to her.

The buyers of my mother's house had chosen a lower exchange rate than the official exchange rate. The transferred sums to my sister and me were therefore lower than expected. I felt sorry for Gabriele, as she needed the money and it was so hard to accept this intentional type of cheating. Unfortunately, there was nothing we could do. Later, when I phoned the Nairobi lawyer, he confirmed that there was nothing we could do. So now, I knew my dreams had been warning me. Part of my subconscious mind knew what was going on and what I needed to expect. I was grateful, as the dreams prepared me to expect bad news and deceit. My money was still floating somewhere in the cosmos and had not yet materialized.

Due to my yogic practices, my mind had become much more attentive to details, which I tended to overlook in the past. I was conscious of confusion in other people. I had noticed repeatedly when someone was trying to deceive me or a message was waiting to be delivered. I realized that I can now catch the negative fears, not just my own, but those of people close to me. Their thoughts slip into my awareness like a nasty smell. I also knew with absolute certainty that Gabriele would fly to Nairobi, Kenya. I could feel the agitation of the lawyer, Murtaza Jevangee, and planned to phone him to find out what was going on.

Monotypes

It rained and rained. The garden flooded. The magnolia tree, heavy with blossoms, was so loaded that branches were bending to the ground. I had to step carefully around flooded areas in the lawn, making my way towards the magnolia. As I looked down, I saw upside down trees reflected in huge puddles. It was symbolic of my state of mind and my sense of security, which was upside down. My attitude of mind was playful as I tried to stay in a positive mindset. It went to prove that I was not identifying with the mind. Actually, one part of me was watching the other part, an amusing game. Is that what the yogis called "the inner witness"? There is a lot of inner joy in me now, joy and inner gratitude beyond anything else.

I phoned Murtazar in Nairobi. He was defensive and wanted to avoid me. He gave the receiver to his wife, Margaret. So, I talked a bit to her. Either he was unable to push for a client, or he was just soft. He wanted to have nothing to do with the money. My Aunty Alma kept on phoning him about it. She insisted on knowing the truth. He insisted that Gabriele got her allotted inheritance at 45 to 46 shillings to the pound. If she only received pound 20,000, then the exchange went through the Black Market, which was known to give a poor exchange rate.

Why the hedging? Why the avoidance of contact? Was it fear of unpleasantness? Certain actions produce very unpleasant results. I had a feeling of wheels turning within wheels. Oddly, I felt untouched and protected. A shield of some quality surrounded me. One of the changes I experienced within myself was openness, a willingness to explore and to allow myself to have the personal experience. I was no longer willing to believe what I was told or to trust dogma. For example, I was reading a new book on reincarnation. How fascinating such a possibility was! In myself I found no memories of past lives. However, I did find something that itched me like an insect bite and asked for attention. It was a physical discomfort that is instantly there if someone touches my neck. Alex had found to his surprise that I would panic if he put his hand around my neck. I suppose subconsciously my body cells remember a trauma which might be from a past life. All the rules and concepts I lived by discovered a power I had feared to use and must now make use of. I chose to be an artist. The language of art speaks but is a silent tongue. My throat was sore and I asked why. Was I stifling something that needed to be expressed?

I had dreams of being strangled. Was I killed for speaking out? Why can't I speak? Is it conditioning or wrong thinking? I wondered and asked myself if I formed conflicting concepts and thoughts. And what about my beliefs and on what were they based? The trees were reflected upside down in the flooded garden-lawn. I noticed this reversal again and again, which means it spoke to me and was a symbol.

I started a whole new series of monotypes, which are unique images, single, hence the name "mono." They are printed from a plastic plate with the help of a printing press. I taught a course on monotypes at the college, and the students loved it. An artist can create a picture with printing inks on the plastic plate and then can manipulate it to her heart's content. The surprise comes with the printing, for the image is reversed in the process and no longer resembles what one was after originally.

I made images of faces, single or overlapping, and the results were entertaining to me. I preferred to work with abstractions, so these heads were novel and bore a different message. People asked if they were self-portraits, which amused me, as they looked nothing like me. In them, I expressed my imagination. I had an image of a torn-up woman, who is no longer complete, having given up her power. Some of the prints surprised me, as I didn't know where they came from. There was a dreaming face with closed eyes, surrounded with autumn leaves. Slowly a memory surfaced. I remembered that as a five-year-old, while I lived in a country inn in the Palatine, a huge rock slope beside the entry had been carved into the likeness of the German Kaiser. In the autumn, as the leaves began to fall, the face became buried under a mountain of red, yellow and brown leaves. We children gathered and had an amusing time sweeping the leaves off the stone carving. This memory surfaced and obviously inspired the monotype.

As the months went by, the relationship with my sister continued to be filled with conflict, suspicion, and confusion. Yet, all my difficulties were manageable because I could meditate and gain an inner perspective and distance. Trust and love between us had been torn apart. It caused me to question and examine how we might heal the rift caused by her belief that she had been abandoned. My mother took me with her to Egypt, leaving Gabriele behind on the farm in Frauweiler. I understood how she felt, but I did not know how to change her nor how to heal her wound.

Finding a Guru

One day I sat in the garden and chanted mantras for an hour. When Kirstin called me, I heard her voice as through a thick barrier of cotton wool, or, as from another dimension. Most strange and when I rose and walked, I felt enveloped in grace. My limbs moved as though oiled and weightless; my consciousness was altered. The grace stayed, a kind of "I" am it. "I am solid." and all else is transient and mist-like. The grace stayed for the rest of that day; nothing could shift my inner state of solidity. I felt blessed.

While in this condition, I asked to be given a sign that Radha was my guru, my guidance, and my teacher. I asked for a confirmation, a physical confirmation in the shape of a ring. In the *Autobiography of a Yogi* by Paramahansa Yogananda, I had read of a man who had asked for such a type of confirmation, and he had received it. I sent my wish into the cosmos with no expectation, and I would like to say, not much hope that such a miracle would come about.

Later that summer, I had flown to B.C. for a short stay at the Ashram. Swami Radha was celebrating her eightieth year, and a big birthday feast was planned. It turned out to be a vibrant, magical, and light-filled time. There were Indian dances and mantra chanting, and flowers were picked by everyone and turned into colorful necklaces. Every day held unexpected surprises. At the conclusion, participants were asked to write a short account of how they met Swami Radha and what had brought them to Yasodhara Ashram. I went down to the beach and found a bench and table facing the tranquil waters of Kootenay Bay and proceeded to write. I handed over 2 sheets describing my experience.

September came, Indian summer, the best part of the year in our area. I was back at the college and had just given two good lectures and then walked home. I picked up our mail and found a letter from Canada, from Julie. The letter contained a note from Swami Radha and a little box. I nearly fell over backwards when I opened the box. In it was a ring, a scarab ring, copied from an ancient Egyptian model. I was ecstatic! I had found my guru; it was Radha. In her note she said:

"Having lived in Egypt you will know that the scarab is significant of long life and eternity. Your own experiences must have shown you that changes in our human nature are very time-demanding. Old habits die slowly, so we need that longevity. I bought this ring at a museum many years ago, because I too, have spent time in Egypt. It now gives me pleasure to make this a gift to you."

OM Shanti Shanti
Swami Radha.

I sat in the living room for a while with the note and the ring, trying to get used to my "miracle" and the confirmation that Radha indeed was my guru, in spite of everything I had been told about her not accepting students any longer.

I wondered what changes this would bring to our relationship. She had sustained me, and for two years taught me through a mind-to-mind contact, or so it seems. I had the choice of telling her what her ring meant to me and thank her, or I could conceal that I asked for a sign that she is my guru. This symbolic gift had been asked for. Now it had manifested. How seriously do I take it, and she, how burdensome would it be for her to have another disciple? The ring, symbolic of my wish for a guru, had been granted. I realized that by my even raising a doubt, I showed how immature and undeserving I was.

The weather suddenly turned very hot and humid. As I meditated and relaxed, it now felt like an extraordinary release of tension. The Inner Self was clearly there and I felt on a high plateau. Everything else was insignificant, almost dreamlike. Understanding these new states came in flashes of sudden insights. I felt so open, really nothing more than an empty vessel. On September 9, I wrote to Swami Radha, accepting her ring.

This information confirmed my own experiences and therefore gave me more self-assurance. The guru, they say, can only plant the seed; the aspirant is the soil, fertile or poor in quality, in which the seed would grow. What seed did she plant? Was it Faith? Would I be able to grow spiritually? Where will all this take me? I had to get training and as yet I saw no clear path. I wrote to her again, expressing my delight with her gift of a ring, saying that I hoped I was not a burden, as I knew so little as yet and that I hoped that she was indeed my guru.

After an interval a letter came. I read the name and address feeling puzzled. It was sent by Sylvia Hellman from Burnaby. Then with a jolt I realized this was the former name of Swami Radha; her German name before her initiation into Sannyas. Her note said that if I wished for discipleship, I should ask Swami Padmananda or another person of my choice.

> "The mantra would show the way and your sincerity will guide you in your search. It is about the secret place in the mind that receives Divine knowledge."
>
> Om Shanti Shanti Shanti Hi
> Swami Radha

It felt as if a door had been slammed shut in my face. I felt a fool to have asked; it showed that I lacked faith, as I should never have doubted. And my mind questioned and questioned. My heart sang; the heart chakra was opening. A tear came. I knew nothing about the inner states as of yet or how they are reached, nothing about the necessary inner transformations. All I knew was that faith was needed and perseverance. I trusted that I had the dedication necessary. One day, for the first time, I put on the Scarab ring, the symbol of transformation. It was light metal and pleasant to wear.

Later in the day I went jogging. As I returned, running down Spruce Avenue, I became aware of a light in front of my left eye. I shut both eyes alternatively and determined the light was definitely in front of my left eye. It was an uneven circle of light with yellow edges. I wondered if the rhythmic breathing was responsible. It felt like a little sign of magic telling me I was still on the right path. Then, doubt rose, and I told myself my imagination was to blame. Instantly, I felt Swami Radha and as I did, she became visible inside the light, smiling at me. She stayed inside the light in my left eye all the way until I finally reached the house and walked up the steps to the front door. Slowly, the light faded away.

Getting My Inheritance out of Kenya

An immediate and unpleasant task was coming towards me. It was now obvious I needed to travel to Kenya in order to find some way to get the inherited money out of Africa. The lawyer claimed he could invest the sums he was holding for me, but he could not send the money out of the country. My aunt and uncle were celebrating their 50th marriage anniversary that year in Nairobi. I worried in case something happened to them before I could get to Nairobi. At the same time, I had rising fears concerning Alex. He smoked constantly, one cigarette after another. He coughed and was without force, tired and old-looking.

Meanwhile, another letter from the Nairobi lawyer arrived. Gabriele claimed the house was not yet fully paid off, and that the lawyer was charging us the cost of utilities. She suspected he and the buyers are investing the money for their own profit until a later date. I did not know what to think or believe, but found the news disturbing.

I planned to travel to Kenya during the summer for a three week stay at my aunt and uncle's place. This would give me, I hoped, enough time for a way to arrange the transfer of my inherited funds. During my meditations I got some answers, but mostly I had to confront my unease about the future. Having preconceived ideas of what should happen and how my reality should unfold created resistance to what was actually occurring. I told myself to go with an empty mind and to expect nothing. Everything comes in its own time. These inner messages made perfect sense. However, it was difficult to implement them, to stay empty of expectations, to take and accept every experience without putting a plus or minus sign in front of it. These were times when I allowed myself to be engulfed in worry, subjected to waves of fear.

The Yoga Development Course

"Put quality into your life," Swami Radha advised. What is quality? Certainly not just work, which is what we seemed to be doing. So, this was the secret, I needed to put quality into my life by living fully and with total attention. It was a daunting task.

"Emotional security has the strongest hold on most of us, and we are always looking outside ourselves for that which can only be found within. There is no security that we can really find in another person." In my communications with Swami Radha, I promised her the gift of a sculpture in clay. I had just started the piece, a female figure. I wanted her to flow organically and built the figure like a hollow pot, moving slowly from the base upwards, adding more clay parts daily, moving from level to level, up to the crown. The sculpture was hollow and of even thickness and thus easy to fire. I created her in steps, each layer having to dry to some degree before I added the next layer. I was really having a good time making this figure. I stopped painting and for that entire year as I created terra-cotta sculptures. Michael Croydon fired them for me in the big kiln of the pottery and sculpture department.

At this pivotal time in my life, I had just turned fifty; a letter arrived from Julie McKay from the Ashram. Swami Radha had some suggestions regarding the sculpture, which oddly enough, I had already begun to implement. She asked also if I had considered taking the certification course offered at the Ashram. It was called the Yoga Development Course and was necessary for anyone considering becoming a yoga teacher. I had not thought myself advanced enough, and yet here was an encouragement to forge ahead and to take the four months' program of intense yoga with the option to begin to teach later on. My heart said, "Yes."

In order to take the Ashram classes, I had to ask for a leave of absence from the college and stop teaching for the winter semester. The Ashram expenses needed to be covered by the money from my mother, which I hoped to transfer from Kenya. More complex was the question of how Alex would manage his life for the four months without me there. Fortunately, Kirstin was living at home and she agreed to take on as many responsibilities as she could. Bill was also there, which provided some distraction, as Bill and Alex got along well together. Now, every so often, I began to talk about the time being ripe for me to do some intensive yoga training. I intended to get Alex used to the idea of my absence. I certainly did not wish him to feel that I was abandoning him for some spiritual adventure. Alex had always given me the freedom to do as I chose; he did not interfere. Sometimes I was sad though, for he could be so remote; and this was becoming clearer to me now.

One evening we had a long conversation about my spiritual interests and he was vehement that he wished no contact with my "yogic interests." My inner world, my dreams and meditations, were alien to him and would never be shared interests. In fact, he made it very clear to me how offensive he found my involvement in yoga. I felt I must stop trying to share my experiences. I realized that I often bored people and that my daughter might be ashamed of her strange mother. I felt driven back into isolation. Swami Radha offered the advice that "confusion can be a very good thing. It takes away the security that we have all the answers in our pocket." I saw things from two levels, and this aroused confusion. I saw Alex as a spiritual being, but he said he was not. What level should I trust? My main effort was to bring Divine Light into my days and to share Light with other beings.

I was becoming more sensitive and vulnerable, but also stronger. I was learning to control my inner turmoil by remaining calm and centered. Responses were not based on defensive or aggressive stances. I had the choice to respond instead of reacting.

Our friend Michael Croydon had been in Normandy, France, during the summer. He wanted to retire to France. Over lunch he related how he had spontaneously joined a Catholic procession and been deeply touched, touched in the heart, as he put it. It made him realize, after much reflection, how hollow and without content his life had become. He had decided to sell his house in Illinois and to spend his coming sabbatical leave in Normandy. There he planned to look for a house and eat healthy food and live a more meaningful life. He did exactly that and bought an old manor house, which he repaired over the years and transformed into a fabulous home. Some years later he also found and married a former art student, with whom he had fallen in love, and thus completely changed his life. His faith impressed me and also his vision, which had become his reality.

The new year had come with ice and snow and our 27th wedding anniversary. I was home for the afternoon when I heard the mail drop; but did not fetch it until later. I had a feeling of expectation, a feeling that something was moving. A letter was addressed to me. The handwritten address was in Swami Radha's hand. It was a wonderful, long letter from my guru! It was warm, soothing, and kind. I sat down there and then, composing an answer and telling her I would come for the Yoga Development workshop in January 1993, the following year.

Soon, I had to start informing Alex of my decision. On a wintery morning in February, at breakfast time, I brought up the topic of Yasodhara Ashram and my wish to go to British Columbia for training. I could feel the shock wave go through Alex. He looked upset. I felt like going to him and holding him in my arms, but resisted the urge because he would have pushed me away. After all, it was I who wished to leave him for four months; he certainly would interpret it as desertion, maybe even abandonment. We discussed financial considerations. My absence from Lake Forest College would amount to losing half a year's salary. Somehow this did not touch me very much, as

I knew my decision was the perfect and right thing for me; in fact, it was my path, my dharma.

The following day, I felt a sense of strength and knew my intense yogic practices had given me a growing self-confidence. I would need it, as a storm was approaching and I needed self-reliance. Alex had been my teacher and guide throughout our years together, bringing me experiences and messages intended for my growth and development. Perhaps he was teaching me to stand up for myself and for what I understand to be my path. I had placed a small photo of Swami Radha on my bookshelf in the bedroom. One day while cleaning I removed it. The next morning, he said to me; "Where is the photo of Swami Radha? You removed it and I miss looking at her. If you had some Hindi guru on the shelf, I would throw it out. Can't stand these, but her I like. Put the picture back."

Flight to East Africa

In May I flew to Nairobi to get the inheritance left by the sale of my mother's house. I had no idea if I would be able to manage this within three weeks. I was staying with my Aunt Alma and Uncle Christian in Nairobi. They picked me up at the airport, with Ngigi, her adopted African son, driving her car. After breakfast, we talked and the shock of being back in Africa slowly sank in. The garden was lovely, full of huge fragrant roses and I walked slowly through it, bending down to inhale the rose fragrance. Things have changed here. Christian saw almost nothing now and acted the role of the helpless child, which Alma supported. Alma continued to show astonishing vigor and energy.

I phoned Murtaza Jeevangee, and his wife Margaret answered. She gave me a full-blown account of the rude behavior of Gabriele, which sounded all too probable. In the evening Murtaza came, looking well and bringing an armload of papers. He was smooth and friendly, and he eventually relaxed fully as we chatted. It seemed I could get the money out in a legal way with the loss of 22 percent. I felt very fortunate that at least for this first day all had gone smoothly. However, when

I went to my room, I discovered my bed reeked of mold. At this stage I was so exhausted I fell asleep, only to wake up a bit later with a roaring headache. I pulled the bedding onto the floor, thinking the mattress was to blame. It was 2:30 am and I felt cold. I meditated and went back to sleep at 6:30 am. The household started at 7:00 am. My head still hurt, but at least I had slept a little bit.

Alma had some ideas about how I might get my money out of Kenya, and this involved Uwe Jacob, whom I had met in Nairobi when I was 25 years old. At that time, he had been very interested in me, and I had shown him the cold shoulder as I was not interested. He had stayed in Nairobi, becoming a businessman, and now our paths crossed again. He came to collect some plants from my aunt and immediately was very keen to discuss possible ways of transferring funds and was enthusiastic and full of good ideas. Any transaction came with a fee for him, something he made very clear. However, I was very grateful to get help and suggestions, and we arranged to get together again for further negotiations.

Alma brought me a huge vase filled with roses for my room and we talked about Swami Radha and about meditation. Alma was enthusiastic and wanted to hear everything about this amazing woman and her life. The rest of the day was spent going through the remains of books, photo albums, letters and art, left by my mother. My sister had sold a lot of paintings during the autumn exhibition at the Goethe Institute. This was art created by my mother, but she shared none of the profits with me. That was to be expected; however, I felt a bit miffed to find she had box upon box of packed items belonging to our mother, which she also did not intend to share with me. It pained me to see so much grasping and it took intense meditation and mantra chanting to calm my mind. Eventually I rebalanced myself. I realized I needed to discriminate between what was essential and what was not.

Uwe came for tea and we chose to sit in the garden among the flowers. He proposed approaching some German diplomats and friends who might be willing to take Kenya shillings from me in return for Euro checks sent to my bank account in the USA. He was willing to take 60,000 shillings of my money for a start. I phoned Murtaza Jevangee the next day. Nothing had been accomplished yet, he said. The Kenya shilling is fluctuating and unsteady. It is best to wait, he advised. Then it slipped out of him that the house sale was actually completed in September of 1991. He had failed to let me know this fact, for had I known then, I could have caught a flight at Christmas time, instead of waiting until now! How could I afford to believe him or hope for help from him? I forced my mind into surrender, into calm, into trusting my inner knowing. My intuition told me to wait and wait until Uwe Jacob explained further steps tomorrow. He had been a big help explaining things to me as he did. I needed to listen with discrimination. Murtaza had stalled me for weeks by now.

Uwe Jacob came again and worked through all the papers and blockages. He also advised me on how to handle it all. After that, I called Murtaza, and asked for all the money in the form of a check in Alma's name if there was no other way to get the money out of the country. The sum would then go into her bank account. I spoke calmly, made clear demands, and hoped that my insistence would be perceived as a strength. Murtaza called the next day, asking for a postponement until later tomorrow. Then Uwe called, curious as to what had transpired.

That night my meditation was focused and intense. Was I doing the right thing in asking for a check going into my aunt's bank account? If she or my uncle died, the account would be blocked. Trusting a guiding force that would guide me correctly and would choose the right thing for me was so difficult, and the temptation to push and pull circumstances was overwhelming. To be most effective meant to be fully in control of my own emotions. Also, I must not blame myself or think myself naive or incompetent. I must not be gullible. I began to face the fact that I might fail to get the money out, and facing failure freed me. I became quite cheerful.

In the morning the phone lines were overloaded and no calls went through. I spent an hour and a half in vain trying to make calls. Then I went outside and lay on my back in the grass and looked at a soft white cloud slowly shredding in the azure blue infinity above. I observed a tree that swayed its lower branches much like the trailing seaweed at flood time. I watched birds, flowers, and soaring kites and felt the magic of being in the present moment fully. Why, oh why, could I not be in this state all the time? Then Uwe came and unpacked several deals for financial transactions. I was stunned. After I had thought that nothing would work here was the first big bite.

Murtaza was late and Alma made me phone his house. Of course, he came, he was just late. Patiently he went over the whole deal in detail, and he justified everything. His mind worked in a curious abstract way, with a great memory and tendency for detail quite alien to me. I felt bubbly and buoyant and, in the end, we parted in a light-hearted way. I was flooded by a sense of stunned disbelief and gratitude. There had been no hitch, and it all went totally smoothly. But he had forgotten the check! Just as well though, because now he will make it out in my name. Better yet, part of it will be in cash, so that I could start using the money. I will pick it all up tomorrow. He said he might even have someone who will give me dollars in cash.

As I reflected, I realized all my anxiety was based on doubt and fear, and initially started through my sister. However, it was self-created as well! What did I learn? To trust my inner knowing and the message saying, "Nothing will be denied! All will go smoothly."

That night, Christian surprised me by saying that it was time to go. "Do you wish to die?" I asked him. "Yes, if I could," he answered. I feel a deep sadness in my soul, for this was the last brief time I would share with them. They had been so generous to me in my youth, and now again, sharing the last bit of their world and values with me. The sharing had been in both directions, as I talked more than I normally would about the inner life of the soul. They were curious and open, asking to be put into a deep yogic relaxation and sleep, asking to hear mantras, asking about Swami Radha. In fact, my aunt could not hear enough about Swami Radha and I had to give her a total summary of the book *Diary of a Woman's Search*.

Alma suffered from heart problems, which were usually brought on by anxiety or tension. As a gift I gave her my mantra tape and suggested she play it and relax with the sound of the chant and that it might help her to release pressure. She was immensely impressed with the effect the chant had on her. She went to bed with the sound of Swami Radha's soothing voice sending her off into sleep. It was really touching how much Alma liked the mantra and how she sang it. She could feel the stillness and the transmission of calmness through the sound of Radha's voice. I tried to cheer her and Christian up with my chatter, songs, and stories. Christian actually thanked me for the entertainment. I teased him a lot about his reluctance to show any affection.

Alex phoned, which put me in high spirits and felt like a wonderful gift. I had once again become used to the smell of Africa, the acrid odor of fires, the scent of spices, the fragrant flowers, the crazy forms of plants, the warmth of the air, and the fertility of the soil. The old saying was true that; "One only needed to break a branch off a tree and stick it into the ground and the stick rooted itself and became a tree."

It would be strange to return to the USA, the alkaline smell of Lake Michigan and the cold coming up through the earth. As I listened to the mantra, I recognized that I was an instrument here and had a purpose, and I learned something. Perhaps I too, needed to realize how fortunate I was and to accept the beginning of a type of permanent state of joy. Alma said to me that morning, "The nice thing about you is that you are always very pleasant to people." While I cannot say I recalled previous lives; I did have some sense of an inner knowing which feels ancient. It does not have the quality of coming from the experiences of the present time. A distinct quality, with a recognizable taste or essence attached, was what I brought with me into this life. I recognized it in Radha during our brief meeting. It penetrated me, like a recognition, and felt very shocking and powerful. In fact, everything from the present time seems pale compared to the intensity of this ancient recognition. There is a little sadness within. This arbor, Alma's and Christians home, and these old people who are my relatives I shall in all likelihood, never see again. It was natural to think they might go soon, as both have reached their nineties. My inner joy remained unperturbed, however. It was an inner attitude and it colored all I saw, heard, tasted, felt, and experienced.

Friends visiting my aunt and uncle warned them of an impending oil embargo. The government was out of money and the oil ships were lying in the Mombasa harbor unable to unload their cargo. This may mean cars can't drive, cabs won't be available, and planes will stop flying. All food will be in short supply. They advised my Alma and Christian to leave for Germany and not to return to Kenya. As to what concerned me, there might not be any petrol on Tuesday, the day of my planned departure from Kenya. I did my usual yoga practice in my little room. My bags were packed and stacked in the corner. The roses Alma had placed into my room at my arrival three weeks ago look as fresh as when they had been picked. She came in and noticed how fresh the roses still were. "It must be because you practice yoga here," she said.

I woke at four in the morning from a lengthy meditation and could feel something like a fog of confusion spreading. Today would not be as expected. I needed to let go of my plans and remain open to whatever was to happen. The driver was there at 7 am and we left after lengthy goodbyes and tears. The traffic dragged along, belching black, evil smoke and fumes. At the airport I made my way to the counter. The young woman turned her head away from me and, offering no explanation, said, "The flight was cancelled." I was not surprised—only surprised that I had known. The British plane was to fly in later and leave at 11:30 at night.

Alma was genuinely happy that I was back. Friends came, we lunched, and then they went for a nap. At intervals I called for flight information. At 5 pm I finally got through to the airport. The flight was cancelled until tomorrow. Eventually I found they had rebooked me to Chicago two days later. I had lost a day. Was I internally surrendered? I was aware, conscious of my remarks, of the panic in my voice as I tried to get some clarity about the way circumstances were moving. I tried to joke and to be pleasant to the people who were trying to help. So tomorrow I would fly and sleep in some hotel in Europe and continue the journey on Thursday. I phoned Alex, who sounded like his son. Odd, I had never noticed that before.

I rose at dawn the next day, and as I was leaving, two old, frail people stood by the kitchen arbor to bid me farewell. A sense of Christian's frailty hit me more than Alma's. I had just completed living here, where I used to live 27 years ago, and with beings who were my family. My role models were these strong women. My mother now, was gone, Alma would be the next. She had been born with a certain aristocratic power, something not acquired in this life.

This time the plane left Nairobi. I sat upstairs in the first class of British Airways. It was very comfortable and luxurious. A priest sat in the aisle seat. He had been living in the humid, hot coastal plains north of Mombasa for over thirty years. He was returning to Ireland, he told me, because of the huge problems now happening in Kenya. The tribes at the coast were fighting among each other; there were raids, sickness, and starvation. Long ago I had seen the lovely, abundant land of Kenya as a paradise, but I had also seen it decline. It did not take long for everything to change, but why did corruption come so fast?

After arriving in London, I had a stop in Glasgow and a night in Scotland. Back at the airport I was heavily interrogated and my suitcase was searched; even my passport was inspected. Just when I thought all this was over, they wanted my passport again and inspected my handbag, shaking all its contents onto the counter. "Why?" I asked the young Scottish woman. "Do I look suspicious?" She never answered.

Finally, the flight descended over Illinois and I was back. Alex stood there at the arrival gate. Tall, lean, and sensitive, he exuded an air of assurance. I had missed him and was happy to be back, back to clean streets, green lawns, and huge shady trees. We sat talking, while we drank an excellent red wine. Alex looked thinner. "I am lost without you," he said. "I can survive, but my life is empty." His eyes were filled with love. "I have done a great deal of thinking during these three weeks," he told me.

Africa lay behind me like a pool of darkness, a dense shadow. To my surprise, I realized it was easier to meditate there. Though it is June, the weather in Illinois was grey and depressing and I missed the African sunshine. Then part of an empty parcel arrived from Kenya, just parts of the box and the shredded wrapping paper.

Waiting for Results

A week had gone by and the money sent from Nairobi to the Deutsche Bank in Germany did not arrive. I fought a fear that has settled in my throat and claimed that I won't get the money, and then I would not be able to go to the Ashram. We didn't have accommodations in Florida and we talked about driving to New Mexico instead. Neither one of us had ever been to the Southwest. It might be a good escape from damp, rainy, and chilly Illinois. So, should we venture forth or not? We went for a walk and I noticed how physically old and weak Alex had become. His upper thighs were without muscle and he looked drained of energy. It frightened me. I phoned bed-and-breakfast places and motels in Santa Fe, all to no avail. Accommodation there looked hopeless.

I felt ill at ease, disoriented and lost. Briefly I struggled with my mind, with the fear that the checks were lost and no money will come from Nairobi. However, I managed to overcome this concern. Eventually, the phone rang. It was a call from Germany, from the Deutsche Bank in Bonn. All but one check had arrived. Hallelujah! I felt so grateful; this indeed was like an instant answer to my anxious question and seemed almost like a miracle. I finally could relax.

Later, I was in luck and found motel accommodation in Santa Fe. We were going to the Wild West after all, and I became excited. Whenever I felt imbalanced, I took refuge in my yoga practices. When I woke up during the night, I sat in meditation for one or two hours, then returned to sleep. My dreams are often very meaningful and acted as guides. It was good that I took so many dream workshops while at Yasodhara Ashram, as they continued to provide me with answers to various problems.

At this stage we reconnected with a former student, who was an investment counselor at a bank in Lake Bluff. She helped us reorganize our mortgage payments and we managed to pay considerably less monthly. My mother's money bridged several debts and gave me some peace of mind. Alex was due to retire in three years' time and we didn't want debts then. I set aside a sum for the Ashram retreat in 1993. The last of the checks from my inheritance arrived and then the money was there, all of it! I wrote to Yasodhara Ashram. and included a deposit check. I told them I would be there for courses from January until the middle of May. Five months in all. Would it be a challenge to be cut off from family, from Alex? Would I learn and benefit? I hoped so as an inner joy bubbled up within me.

New Mexico

We set off for New Mexico the following day and made fast progress because of a very early start. By evening of the second day, the distant New Mexico Mountains loomed in pale cerulean against a huge horizon. The air was light and dry, almost like in Egypt. The landscape became more and more impressive as we neared Santa Fe. But I couldn't see a city! According to my map we were nearly there, but there weren't skyscrapers, and no high-rise towers. In fact, the city melted into the land. Most buildings were in pueblo-style, charming, organic structures, which reminded me of Egyptian villages. The motel was new, very comfortable and nice. I felt physically light-headed and slightly dizzy as I realized we were over 7500 feet above sea level here.

The next morning, we drove into the city. I was overwhelmed, disbelieving. The town was totally charming, warm and sunny. Wonderful organic structures built of adobe brick with courtyards and hollyhocks growing up beside walls greeted the eye. There were plazas and galleries with art displays in their windows, a great cathedral, and as we walked, we found shops, small bakeries, and jewelers, all within walking distance. I had forgotten how it felt to be in a town made for people, not cars.

There were people of many different ethnic backgrounds, and some were dressed in southwestern garb with big cowboy hats and boots, and some in native tribal attire. I felt as if I had stepped out of the United States into a foreign country. We found the central plaza where some musicians were playing and from there moved along a small street and found ourselves in a wonderful courtyard filled with a garden of many flowers and a splashing fountain. It was a restaurant situated inside an old mansion. I ordered a glass of white wine and Alex ordered a beer to celebrate our arrival in this magical place. We had just arrived here and yet we already felt at home.

Alex looked happy. "You know," he said: "I did not expect I would find this place so delightful. Of all the places we have visited, I like this best and I could retire here." I held my breath and almost laughed, glad that I had never told him of the letter Swami Radha had sent me in answer to my question about where we should retire. "You should try the Southwest, Santa Fe in New Mexico," she had written. She mentioned a lively art scene there, which I might find inspiring.

The next day we drove off to Abiquiu, where the artist Georgia O'Keeffe had lived and worked. The red-rock landscape was breathtaking and utterly beautiful with its mountain ranges and grand vistas. We stopped in the Ghost Ranch, impressed with the energy of calm tranquility and restfulness. The light was sensational everywhere and I could feel my longing to paint here. I managed to do some walking, which made me feel even more tempted to stay there. Alas, there were no vacancies at Ghost Ranch and we had to depart. The night skies were as clear and rich as they had been in the Egyptian desert and everything about New Mexico enchanted us.

We visited a realtor and found out how expensive houses in Santa Fe were, but he then took us to an outlying area called Eldorado, where houses were very reasonable. By now Alex had caught up with my enthusiasm and we planned to have the realtor send us information on anything suitable that came on the market. Furthermore, we intended to come back at Christmastime in 1993 to experience what winter was like. We were told that the climate was quite amazing with many more days of sunshine than elsewhere in the USA.

This was the time for the monsoons, basically afternoon showers. During the rains, we visited the museums and art galleries, of which there were many. The Indian museum had the most marvelous hand-built ceramic pots and we took further opportunities to look at adobe-style houses in Hondo Hills and Eldorado. We felt quite sure that this was the place to which we would move in three years' time. We took a last visit to homes built among hills, where silence reigns and the hot scent of pinon trees intoxicates. It felt like a dream; would it be possible that we might live here?

Alex and I went for a last drink in the enchanted courtyard of Casa Sena, the lovely place we visited on our first day. In the plaza, people gathered as some excellent musicians performed. A blind woman sang, a couple danced, children—tiny tots—hopped about, and the sun sparkled through the foliage of the old trees. A native girl leaned on her bicycle, watching. It was so moving, and I felt gratitude washing over me. We stood for a while—an appropriate goodbye to Santa Fe.

After days of intense sightseeing, we left New Mexico and drove into Colorado. Here the sky was heavy with rain clouds and the beautiful light was gone. We made the return journey home in two days. It was still summer, but the climate in Illinois was up and down, wet and hot and humid and unpredictable. When possible, I painted in the garden, as in the house there was not enough light. Friends visited, we accepted dinner invitations, and daily, I jogged along Lake Road. I spent hours chanting mantras and meditating during the nights. Basically, I lived on two levels; the outer mundane lifestyle and the inner level. I experimented and practiced and learnt to study my mind. There were experiences that guided me and brought insights. To see from the heart was all that mattered. The opportunities for practice were almost constant. I learnt to detach myself from things I could not change. Life becomes painful when one fights. So instead of opposing circumstances, I embraced them. Swami Radha had advised: "Assume you have volitional power over circumstances and over yourself. Act as though you do! Assert this power. Acting "as if" will help you over a hurdle. Circumstances will change."

And indeed, the circumstances changed. I began to understand what a difficult time Alex was experiencing. A letter from the Senior Center in Scotland informed him of his mother's rapid decline. She was up for only a few hours now, and fading slowly. However, she still enjoyed her afternoon tea. He accepted his mother's decline and the painful realization that a visit was not possible.

Not only were we considering a change of living locations but our good friend Michael Croydon had been in Normandy, France, during the summer. He wanted to retire to France. Over lunch he related how he had spontaneously joined a Catholic procession and been deeply touched, touched in the heart, as he put it. It made him realize, after much reflection, how hollow and without content his life had become. He had decided to sell his house in Illinois and to spend his coming sabbatical leave in Normandy. There he planned to look for a house and eat healthy food and live a more meaningful life. He did exactly that and bought an old manor house, which he repaired over the years and transformed into a fabulous home. Some years later he also found and married a former art student with whom he had fallen in love, and thus completely changed his life. His faith impressed me and also his vision, which had become his reality.

Gwen

Alex had asked me to look at a new candidate for the Art History department. "I would like your opinion. I am very unsure of her," he had said. I agreed, so he brought her to dinner on a hot evening in late August.

Gwen was a tall, lanky, almost beautiful woman. I felt a wave of unease as we shook hands. When I sat on the couch later, I felt self-conscious as I looked at her. Why was I so ungenerous, I thought then; my reaction to her was unbelievably nasty. God forgive me, I don't know this creature, how utterly despicable of me to not even give her a chance! Gwen was smooth, persuasive, and charming, with little-girly mannerisms. I relaxed into the role of gracious hostess and decided to ignore my intuition. By the end of the evening, I was charmed by Gwen and had no reservations about her; in fact, I completely blocked my first impression. Two years on, we realized she was not at all what she had seemed, but unscrupulous, vindictive, and corrupt, and five years later, she had managed to ruin some reputations and shorten careers. Why had I thrown all my better instincts into the wind?

Alex was personally affected by the decision to hire her and eventually, had to bravely battle horrible accusations that Gwen, now in the Art Department, was leveling against him as well as many other faculty members. Yes, she was a striking woman, a graduate of a California university, and she used this for her own agendas. Students called her "the cocktail waitress" because she came into class with a jug of water and a drinking glass and seemed to always have a dry mouth. I think they were the first to recognize what she was. She exuded a certain glamour and style and was quickly seen in the company of various wealthy male admirers. At first, we paid scant attention to the rumors that were going around, but when a parent made an appointment to see the chairman of the Art Department with severe complaints against Gwen, things changed.

As Alex was the chairman, he was responsible for the welfare of students and he had to inform the administration of any foul behavior or negligence committed by said faculty member. His position offered no protection and Gwen, once she got wind of the complaints students were making, lost no opportunity to attack Alex's reputation, accusing him of any and every wrong. She carefully maneuvered her position and, in spite of the warnings of senior faculty, the administration of the college had granted her tenure. That meant guaranteed employment for her lifetime. In my diary I had written: "Gwen got tenure. I could feel it yesterday when she received the news. It puzzles me, for the committee must be truly confused to disregard the opinion of three respected professors, all of whom gave her the worst possible evaluation, recommending she not be kept on." I felt a sense of betrayal; in fact, the entire department had been betrayed. Gwen might be persuasive and charming and attractive to look at, but why did the committee elect to keep her on? Were documents not read and evaluations ignored? Why was Alex discredited through her schemes?

Eventually, there was to be a lot of fuss about Gwen. Our friend Michael was shaking with rage. A week earlier he had become acting chair. Gwen had coldly refused his demand to alter a course with inadequate content, a course Michael felt needed updating. He went to the president of the college asking for assistance in this matter, and got absolutely no help. Alex was not surprised and, turning to Michael, said, "Well, now you can see how it is."

Meanwhile, Gwen had carefully ruined Alex's reputation, and as a consequence, he had decided to resign the chairmanship. He had built up the Fine Art Department to be one of the best in a small liberal arts college in the Midwest, and it had become the fourth largest department in the college. He was just two years from retirement when he resigned. Friends advised him to leave his job, but he decided to stay on until he was 65 years old. He neither complained nor talked much about his feelings, but to me he looked in shock and deeply wounded by this undeserved fate. It ate into him like a worm in the bud, destroying his self-esteem and love for life. Certainly, what was happening to him was beyond understanding. He had served the college loyally for nearly thirty years. Was this the right time to leave him to go to an Ashram? At that time, I was planning to leave for something that must have seemed totally irrational, and for five months at that. I wondered if he felt my coming departure as just another betrayal.

I was profoundly sad for him and was trying not to feel fear. Also, I was determined not to bother him with any criticism over his drinking and smoking. He might be killing himself, but I did not know how to stop him from these self-destructive habits. I felt adrift on a dark ocean of insecurity and danger, where I could hang onto nothing. Later, years later actually, I counted how many people, friends and members of my family, died during these few years in the 1990s. It was a time of profound change and loss so intense that I felt a deep urge to seek consolation in a spiritual retreat. I was determined to give Alex emotional support and refrain from responding to his heart's pain, for then the pain grows and feeds on imagined circumstances of loneliness and neglect.

"We dance round a ring and suppose,
But the Secret sits in the middle and knows."
                                    Robert Frost

"When we understand, we are at the center of the circle, and there we sit while Yes and No chase each other around the circumference."
                                    Chuang-Tzu

Surprise Party

Christmas came. One evening during this time, while Alex and I sat at the dining room table across from each other, he talked of his mother and father, and we were both very open-hearted and showing our feelings. Heavy with pain, I talked about my upcoming departure. I had not expected him to cry, but he did, and I was at a loss about how to respond. "You told me long ago that you would never leave me," he said. "I shall not leave you, except for a time of immersion and study of yoga.

Please do not make yourself unhappy because I am physically not beside you for a bit. I shall come back." Nonetheless, it took me a long time to calm him. It felt as if we were trying to communicate across an abyss.

We were invited to a friend's house for a farewell drink, I noticed many cars in the driveway and in a small panic, I suddenly knew it was going to be a large party. However, my mind made excuses. The cars belonged to neighbors. We were invited for just a drink. Through the window I could see into the brightly illuminated kitchen and I saw Kirstin and Bill and our friends. But, as we opened the front door, a crowd emerged and I realized this was a surprise party for me. For me? How unexpected, how surprising, and how touching!

There were hugs and more hugs, and I listened rather than talk, hearing wonderful things. Valerie, another longtime friend, hugged me and said, "I love you." Ruth said the same and so did Judy. What prompted this outpouring of affection, I wondered; This sort of thing had never happened before. What did they see and feel? I was still the same person as I have always been. However, I became aware of a tinge of some curious admiration, maybe because I was leaving for an Ashram? Particularly the women were supporting my urge to go on this spiritual journey and I thanked them for their heartfelt support. Bill was the chef in the kitchen, and Kirstin turned out one pizza after another. How wondrous all this kindness. My friend Judy brought a cheesecake from the kitchen, and everyone raised their glasses for a toast.

Over the following days, calls came from people wishing me well, presents lay at the front door, people brought gifts and books, and I felt surrounded by some form of admiration, even from strangers. Was this some Divine affirmation that my action was the right thing?

13 Yoga Training at an Ashram

Departure for British Columbia

The flight to Vancouver, BC, was long and the plane was an hour late in arriving. Everything slowed down at this point and the airport was overcrowded. I felt that I might miss my connecting flight. I noticed that this Pacific Coast airport had many Asians traveling through. The elevators were slow and crowded and I could not get up the stairs with my heavy bag. The escalators were filled with pushing and shoving travelers. I took wrong turns, broke several fingernails, and yes, my connecting flight was gone when I finally found the gate.

At the United counter, I approached a charming Asian woman and related my plight. She coldly refused to get me a hotel room. I insisted I needed to talk to the manager, who came out, heard me, and booked me into the Richmond Inn. Sometimes I am my mother's daughter! I, too, could be insistent and demand help. Night had fallen, and I was grateful as a bus took me to the hotel. I felt tired, hot, and sweaty. I sat in the hotel room with my phone card and tried for an hour to connect to the Ashram. Providing I could get a flight out in the morning, they would pick me up in Nelson. Bad weather was in the forecast.

My intuition has been correct on three counts. I knew I would miss the connecting flight. I felt I would end up in a hotel in Vancouver, and I would be picked up in Nelson by someone from the Ashram. My last phone call was to Lake Forest and to Alex. With that connection, I felt a little less lost. I finished my day with a yoga session went to sleep. Not for long though, as under my room a band started to play. I could have danced all night!

When I rose at five in the morning, the face that looked at me in the bathroom mirror looked old, tired, and wrinkled. At the airport I tried not to make mistakes and noticed how people were constantly going to the wrong counters and wrong gates. My plane to Castlebar took off in spite of poor weather conditions. It was a small plane and soon we were cruising over the Rockies. The mountains, covered with snow and fir trees, look black-grey and most dramatic. The descent to Castlebar was spectacular as the plane descended into a white bottomless hole. After a long taxi drive, I finally arrived in Nelson and enjoyed a much-needed breakfast. Not much later, a resident I had first met in 1989 came in with a big grin on her face. She was in town to do some shopping and to pick me up. I had bought a warm black quilted coat for my stay in B.C., only to find the weather was so much warmer than in Illinois. The climate was actually gentle.

Life in an Ashram

Not much later, after driving through a snowy forest, we entered the Ashram grounds. Thick snow glittered in the sun and Kootenay Bay reflected the blue sky. The door to my room had a little hand-lettered card with my name on it and the name of my roommate, who was not yet there. The accommodation was cozy. A thick carpet covered the floor and the window looked out onto trees. In the distance lay the shimmering waters of Kootenay Bay.

Before unpacking, I went outside and walked to the white temple. It had been completed only recently. Swami Radha had seen this temple in her dreams as a little girl and many times later in her life. The actual building had taken many years to be completed. I walked into the temple. Silent, white, empty space greeted me. There was a strange feeling inside me. Was it awe? This was her dream. A low, round glass table stood in the center with a single votive candle burning. This was the temple of Light, a huge domed space with unusual chandeliers cascading down from above. It overlooked Kootenay Bay on one side and there were many glass doors arranged in an attractive sequence around the entire periphery of the temple. My ears felt strange inside my head. I was not used to such deep silence.

Meals were eaten in silence, so as not to interrupt the contemplative state of mind cultivated here. When I went into the dining room, familiar faces greeted me. Swami Padmananda, wearing a green silk outfit, entered with two little dogs following alongside. As on other occasions before, I felt odd and self-conscious.

The snow had huge crystals that made it sparkle like diamonds. At eight in the morning, it was still dark, but the snow was a web of glitter. A full moon bathed this landscape. I realized that nothing here was familiar and that there was nothing I could anticipate beforehand. I met Susan, who was luminous, with kindness shining out of her eyes. She had an extra something. I told her about my meeting with Swami Radha and how much this contact had affected me. "You know, there must be a straight heart-connection between you both," she said. "Swami Radha does not write to people." This information delighted me and warmed my heart. She does not write to people; yet she wrote to me.

Later I sat in the little old prayer room and meditated. This space was cool and blue. It had been Swami Radha's room at some time in the past and had a very powerful atmosphere. Just sitting there, looking down at my hands, I saw a strange bud-like shape; an open lotus blossom formed itself beside my hand. It created itself much like a painting. I had a hard time believing my eyes, but it stayed and did not vanish as I expected it would. I went for a walk in the cold landscape and felt a bit out of breath. Thirty-five years of yoga practice had brought me here; the seeds had taken.

After dinner every night, there was a gathering of all the people for Satsang in the temple. Satsang means "the meeting of the wise." It is a time together when we chant mantra and there is usually a reading of a spiritual text or a video of Swami Radha followed by Prasad, a small sweet raisin or chocolate handed to everyone, symbolizing the sweetness of the teachings. Swami Durgananda guided us. We chanted mantras I knew and liked. It was very special. There were vibrations in my spine and, after a five-minute walk, I felt my hands tingling and vibrations going right through my whole body. Durgananda is a wondrous being, a very special swami. Her classes would start on the morrow.

While I still had the time, I wrote a letter to Alex. I felt comfortable and welcome here. Again, I assured him that I was not cold and unfeeling about leaving him; it is not a lack of love. I needed to return to my own inner source for a while because an inner shift had happened. I was still me, still warm, but I felt awake.

Don, a resident who works at the Ashram, came to suggest that we all sign up for mantra practice in the two prayer rooms or in the temple. I signed myself up for four to six o'clock in the morning in the beach prayer room. He also warned about standing up for oneself. This proved very worthwhile as the two women who moved to the adjacent room brought their computers. Suddenly there is a peace-disturbing "click-click-click" sound ringing through the walls that was going to drive me crazy. Without hesitation, I walked next door and suggested they needed to find another location for the computers, as the sound was very disturbing. Had I been compliant—for I have a tendency to comply with what others want—I would have had a real problem. The reward for being nice in oppressive circumstances is dishonesty, leading to circumstances that are disadvantageous.

The classes started and were demanding. All our notes and reflections were to be written with a carbon copy to be handed to the teachers. I found myself becoming much more watchful and even self-conscious. My new roommate, Julie, arrived. Her head had been freshly shaved and she related that she had to quit her job to come to the Ashram for the courses. She was an art historian and she worked as a curator. I was impressed with her energy and determination.

As part of our requirements for the yogic training, we wrote daily spiritual reflections. We were to practice and record them in our journals. Instantly, I felt a rising wave of subliminal discomfort. What if I fell short somehow, what if I did not measure up to the expected standards, what if I fell short in comparison to others? All these concerns amounted to a problem with self-image. Yet, at the same time, confirmation abounded that all I did with so much concern and even hesitation was accurate and correct.

We were asked to reflect and ask: "Who am I?" Working with this question, I found that I had never seriously considered "Who I am?" and my main concern was living up to the standards of other people. I have been too "nice," suppressing my own truth in favor of being acceptable.

My dreams began to give me both guidance and new material to work on. They began to speak with the symbol of "house." A "house" comments on the psychic space a person inhabits. I had a nightmare which threw me into deep shock.

In my dream, Alex and I go for a walk. It is dark and seeing is difficult. We turn a corner. I am talking, when I notice that he is not there. I turn around, turn back. Smoke curls and wafts up and says, "This is a fine way to leave me." I clearly feel his essence, though in the darkness around us I cannot see well. Suddenly he sits there, headless, a lifeless lump. I scream in agony, "Do not go my love without taking my leave!"

Then a switch occurs. I am in a bare room. He just left. I suddenly realize he has emphysema. I run out to warn him. He has already gone down the road and passed the bend. I awake crying, "Do not leave my love without taking my leave." Now fully awake, I am sobbing. I knew it, I knew it. His habits killed him.

After some time of prayer and tears, I said, "Take this life back, I surrender." It felt totally unreal to wake up in an Ashram.

I meditated for about an hour and suddenly all was stern and cold and clear. The emotion within me was gone. I was barren and cold. This, I assumed, was clarity without personal baggage or illusions left. It felt truly sobering, a shocking sensation.

That day, I battled my heart and feelings and my own mind. The dream's message was totally clear to me. It showed our future, Alex's and mine, and that I would have to face the loss of Alex. There was no doubt in my heart. This dream told me the inevitable truth. "He had already passed the bend in the road." He was beyond saving. "Take his life back," I prayed. "I surrender." What else could I do? A whole day of classes on the meaning of hatha yoga followed. The number of students in the course was small, only nine—eight women and one man from California. The turmoil of the soul had caught up with quite a few. Several women cried. I asked myself what I had expected, as I felt so out of touch with my inner self.

The buildings at the Ashram lay widely scattered throughout the landscape, and we walked from one building to the next for our various classes. The food was served in a small house overlooking Kootenay Bay. I looked down to the glacial grey waters far below. Snow gently sailed from the sky in big fluffy flakes. A supreme silence reigned. Later the sun came out. I felt tired and bored. Next morning, guided by my flashlight, I found my way down the long snowy staircase to the beach prayer room. I switched on a powerful heater and lit a candle on the low little altar. Here, sat a beautiful bronze sculpture of a Hindu Goddess, her elegant fingers in a mudra position. I started to chant the Hari Om mantra.

After one hour I was crying for my parents, for their difficult lives, their losses and cares. There was a wastepaper basket in the prayer room, nearly always filled with soggy Kleenex. Another half hour and I slid back into my coat and walked up the hill for my hatha yoga class. A young Swami taught asanas and towards the end we moved into a reflection on tadasana, the mountain, a pose demanding nothing more than just standing upright and feeling into one's body, mind and sensations. After a few moments my mind began to revolt, then complained, and the body became uncomfortable wanting release, not running somewhere, standing still, observing, feeling where am I, where do I want to go, I am standing in "the mountain."

Personal associations surfaced, such as: I am alone, feeling lost, I am by myself, and emotions arise and the mountain becomes a symbol for power and height, for overview and the ability to see the surrounding countryside. Then we were asked to write down thoughts and feelings and our conclusions. We were instructed not to edit—just to write, allowing the words to flow. Ten minutes later I had written nonstop and felt lighter, more at ease and comfortable, some inner weight was gone. I have had my first experience of using symbolism in what Swami Radha referred to as the "hidden language of hatha yoga."

After lunch we had some free time and I usually would go walking while reflecting on the events of the day and on what I had learned. Snow often fell while the sun shone. Crystals of light gently glided down from above. I felt the energy like a blessing.

That night at Satsang, a reading took place. It was from an interview with Swami Radha and it fascinated. Apparently, she was already psychic as a child and could foretell events. When she was still little, her father bought a very expensive car. He was a wealthy man and he employed a chauffeur. She warned her father that the car was dangerous and would explode. To prove her wrong, he forced her to join him in a joint drive. She felt very uneasy and then suddenly they heard ominous noises. They told the driver to stop just in the nick of time and got out of the car. Then, to everyone's horror, the vehicle burst into flames and exploded. Later, as an adult, Radha went through the war in Berlin, Germany, and had a very difficult time. She lost two husbands and two children.

After the Second World War was over, she left Germany and eventually came to Canada. There during a meditation, Swami Sivananda of Rishikesh, India, appeared to her in a vision. However, she did not know his name or how to get in touch with him until a magazine fell into her hands with an article about Swami Sivananda. She wrote to him in India. He replied that he was waiting for her and she was to come to India. Also, to remove her doubts, he informed her of many events and things in her life he could not have known. As a consequence, she gave up her job and left for India. Six months later she returned to Canada in the orange robe of a Swami and began her new life. It was amazing to discover such details of her life and it strengthened my determination. Every day brought new experiences and events beyond my expectation.

Kundalini Manifestation and Julie

We had gathered in the Beach prayer room for a class on Mantra and Meditation. It was apparent that most of us were struggling with some concern or past event. I noticed my roommate was reacting to something and felt unwell. She started to cry and sob, and then she screamed that her arms were stiffening and feeling paralyzed. This all was so sudden and it shocked us deeply. This is a primal screaming, I thought, as I watched and saw alarmed faces surrounding her. Then I saw her hands folding up into a fixed position, and only the thumb and forefinger could still move. The hands of my mother-in-law became like that during a stroke and would never regain flexibility. By now, Julie had fallen to the floor, her body writhing and moving into a curled-up posture which resembled a fetal position.

Eventually, her screams subsided. Her face had become beet-root red and almost unrecognizable. A swami covered her with a blanket and after an interval of silence asked her to talk about her experience. We all sat still, breathless and in shock. We waited and waited. Again, the swami asked her how she felt and then asked again if she would like to relate what had happened.

Hugging the blanket like a protective shell around her body, she began to talk. Some years ago, she had travelled in a mountainous country in Asia, travelling in a bus on narrow winding roads along terraced rice fields. The narrow road carved out of the hill stretched itself along steep chasms and that was where the driver lost control on a narrow curve. The vehicle went over the edge and rolled through rice paddies coming closer and closer to the rocky ledge below, where a dark chasm opened. A rock stopped the bus from rolling over the edge of this precipice. Julie said she screamed: "Buddha, if you get me out of this, I shall devote my life to you." Aside from whiplash, she was unhurt, but an orange jacket she wore that day showed a hole in the back, just at the heart center, where a metal bar would have penetrated her body had the bus not stopped just then. Five passengers died that day, and they were all transported to the nearest hospital for examination. After this experience, Julie had tried to forget the accident, until this morning, when she suddenly felt confronted by her promise to the Buddha.

The swami now told her to go "into silence" and not to talk to anyone for a specific period of time. However curious I was, I was not permitted to question her. The most perplexing change was the color of her skin. She had been beet-root red in the face during her breakdown. In the evening when I saw her change her clothes to put on a nightgown, her arms, legs, neck and back looked as if she had intense sunburn. The next day the sunburn was most obvious. She now was a deep mahogany brown. Several days later, she began to look as though she had returned from a seaside holiday and was extremely tanned. I have no explanation for this curious manifestation and the matter was never talked about.

Facing and Confronting Shortcomings

As the end of January approached, it began to snow heavily and the intensity of the spiritual practices began to tire me. I missed Alex and had the sense of having nowhere to go but inside myself. Swami Radha was not in residence at the Ashram during this winter, so it took me by surprise to see Radha in the temple at least three times. I saw her essence quite clearly before she faded from view. As I had not thought of her, it puzzled me why I should have seen her at all.

We had an interesting and intense workshop called "Life Seals." My roommate and I stayed up until way after midnight, putting together images symbolic for qualities we owned and obstacles in our life. When finally my life seals were completed, I felt relieved. The problems I faced with my sister had resolved themselves due to this process. I had shown my feelings, which I normally hide. But I had not counted on the next conflict, which was extremely perplexing. During this next workshop the swami asked me why I did not do my work! Was I really seriously involved with the inner journey and concentrated effort demanded at an Ashram? I felt stunned and confused and told her I had no idea what she was talking about.

In no sense did I feel lacking and furthermore I felt supported and carried by everything I experienced here. During Satsang that evening, a delicate, beautiful perfume filled the air. I sat in bliss as if on a cloud; feelings welled up and a sense of gratitude for everything flooded through me. It snowed six inches during the night, and the next day it was raining and the roads were slippery. I had a terrible backache on waking. During hatha yoga class the pain faded, an unexpected surprise. It was just gone. Nonetheless, I began to ask and probe into why it had manifested itself at all. The night before I had been invaded by that old feeling of worthlessness. This had not happened in such a long time. Perhaps it was caused by the swami's reaction to my Life Seal and by her questions? What was I supposed to be hiding? Why was I suspect? There were so many thoughts buzzing in my head and memories of war planes droning overhead. What was I hiding dating back to my childhood and the war? I did a lot of crying during my meditation time in the beach prayer room.

During our hatha yoga class later on, I stood on my head and reflected on what I would do if my life were turned upside-down. From the base of my skull a sensation moved up. A headache began to spread, which affected my eyesight. The voice of reason in me said: "What is this? I never have headaches? Why should this manifest?" As a consequence, my whole attention moved into the mantra Hari Om, which usually played in the classroom. Keeping my eyes tightly shut, I felt the deep urge to meditate. I craved this inner connection and did not dare to open my eyes in case the delicate thread would break.

That night was awful. I went to bed and the same incantation I had heard in 1990 in Diani Beach, Kenya, took over. Sometimes it sounded as though insects were in my pillow, buzzing and scraping against the cloth. Then I thought there were insects flying out of my pillow and again this strange droning incantation like children's voices going on and on in a discordant and irritating fashion. "What was I tapping into?" I asked myself. These sounds were extreme and unbearably intense. In Africa, I had suspected my mother's servant was aiming to punish my mother with some witchcraft, perhaps even trying to kill her. Now, more and more, it sounded like insects were flying out of my pillow. Then I saw Lizzie, my mother-in-law, clearly in my mind's eye. Instantly I knew she was dying, and that this was the message I was receiving! I sat up in bed, startled and shocked. I hoped as she died it would be easy, that she could just slip out of her shell. I wished her an easy passage into the Light and then began to chant a silent mantra for her.

The next day, mid-morning, a message was handed to me. The paper said: "Call your husband." I knew as I dialed our home number what I would hear. His voice answered, sounding tired. "My mother died last night," he said. "I could feel it," I answered. He had hoped there would be one last visit to Scotland in the spring to see her again. I felt great sadness; I loved her.

We put her into the Light during Satsang at night. I was glad she was now free of her suffering and the horrible existence she had endured in the geriatric ward in a hospital in Fife, Scotland, for nearly ten years. I could feel her spirit as I focused on her in the temple.

Susan, who was now my new friend and also a resident at the Ashram, sent me a lotus card with the promise that she would put Alex and Lizzie into the Light until February 2. This was extremely kind and generous of her and I could feel the heart-to-heart connection with her, which made me happy and gave me a warm feeling. The temple that night was wonderful. It also happened to be my wedding anniversary. Surrounded by deep snow and huge gleaming, magical crystals, I felt as if I were in a winter wonderland. The night was deep indigo and at the conclusion, the swamis and other people in the Ashram played a chant that took me right out of myself. My heart was melting, and as I walked out, I saw the faces around me glowing with an inner smile that echoed my feelings.

A new course began and I felt overwhelmed. It is Prayer Dance. Swami Radha was a professional dancer and while in India, her guru insisted that she learn Indian Prayer Dancing. Lis was teaching it to us. Lis was a heavenly candy bar—she was so sweet and her smile was uplifting and infectious. She was from Ukraine. The hand positions were very elaborate and combined with motions I found nearly impossible to grasp, let alone execute. I felt as if I were back in school trying to learn math. I felt totally overloaded, unable to remember how the movements were strung together, whether I stepped back or forwards, using the left or right foot—in short, I felt useless. I turned movements from in to out, failed to be able to visualize or feel the movements, and so what? I learned a lot in my life, maybe Indian Dancing will not be one of them. This was a learning experience about being discouraged and not acknowledging when a movement was correct. How depressing!

At night, I drank a cup of coffee and read an Ascent magazine from 1975 about how difficult it is to become a Yogi or Sanyasi. What, I asked myself, am I dreaming? What am I looking for and not finding? Why scold a rich and beautiful life, a life filled with opportunities. With three months of training, perhaps I could grow. Perhaps an answer will come to me. I tended to forget that all is given. Didn't Swami Radha write and say to me: "Great waves of Light have come your way."

During hatha yoga I had a powerful insight. There isn't one person, even a guru, who can help me to get closer to my inner self. This is all up to me, to my understanding and my perseverance in the practices. Only I can sense, feel, and establish the connection.

I decided to phone Alex. I had a feeling he was grieving and feeling low. I also thought they might have cremated Lizzie today. After Satsang I saw a note on the stairs that was for me. It said, "Phone husband." Poor Alex, he sounded so sad and heartbroken. He said he cried today. They cremated Lizzie this morning and were going to scatter her ashes in the garden of remembrance. There was no way he could have gone to Scotland for the service. The other piece of news was that Kirstin had told Bill he had to pull himself together. Alex thought the romance was fading and she might be ready to sever the relationship.

Kundalini and the Senses

In the Kundalini yoga classes, we had to deal with senses and sense perception. Apparently, due to spiritual practices, sense perceptions gradually become refined. The sense of smell, becomes keener and more discerning, taste, more selective, sight and touch, more discriminating, and hearing, much more alert. The four-day workshop focused on these ancient teachings of Kundalini yoga. A gentle, white-haired Swami; Swami Padmananda, taught the course. We were introduced to the five senses and their manifestations. The first chakra center was the sense of smell, and the second chakra was the sense of taste, and so on. Swami Padmananda gave the first exercise in smell and asked us to describe the experience but not necessarily to identify what we smelled. To my surprise, I had great problems in identifying smells. The last of the five "smell experiences" was a flower, but I had no idea what scent my nose was picking up. Swami Padmananda smiled kindly and asked me to go outside the room, walk about for a few moments and then return to the classroom with my nose in high alert. Following her instructions, I returned to the room and a wall of delicious rose scent greeted me. "Write me a little paper on what a rose means to you, whatever comes to your mind when you think of roses," she said.

My first thought was that my mother loved roses. We always had roses in our home. I was named Rosemarie. Then, in a flash, I remembered the Perfume Street in the bazaar in Cairo. My mother loved to shop for perfume and used rose essence in some deserts. The perfume venders were very liberal in offering to douse my wrist in perfume. I remember resisting because it was so expensive and I thought then, wasted on me. I wanted to smell the roses, but denied myself, frightened it would be removed like all the good things in my childhood that were taken. So that's it—seeing the impermanence of everything in life! Somehow, I had learned to deny myself what I really wanted in order to remain detached, practical, and down to earth, even to the point of denying my given name.

During these investigations, I felt dizzy and shaken up. Swami Padmananda said it was my inner self that was being shaken awake; I needed to update where I am now. She told me self-judgment takes up a great deal of energy. Seeing the impermanence of everything in life does not mean getting stuck, but being fully alive and putting life's experiences to good use. If I wanted to give things up, then I must do it in a positive, not a negative, way. What part of me was submissive? "Look inside," she said. Was it an attitude I held? My name "Rosemarie" was deemed unfitting by the students in the art school in Germany, and they changed it to Ramona. I agreed with that, not because my name was unbecoming, but because the name "Rosemarie" traditionally belonged to a blue-eyed blonde. So, the word "rose" has some connection to my self-image. Had it affected my sense of smell to the degree of blocking my nose completely?

After Satsang that evening, I walked through deep snow up the steps to the lodge and realized the woman ahead of me was Swami Padmananda. As I came closer, a beautiful fragrance filled the air. When I reached the top of the steps, I approached her and told her that I could smell the beautiful perfume she was wearing. She laughed and said, "I don't wear perfume."

The courses were not easy. Swami Padmananda was carefully edging around my touchiness, for what else could sensitivity lead to but a hyper-sensitivity. It was ego. I found myself plunging into self-defensiveness. She, in return was subtle, leaving hints all over the place for me to pick up. At first, I did not see them, and then, suddenly they stared me in the face.

Next, in our Kundalini Class, we studied each of the energy centers, called "chakras," that are associated with our physical senses and our mental and emotional bodies. When we came to the fourth of the seven chakras, called the spiritual heart center, I encountered another surprise. Because I was an artist, I had assumed my strongest sense was the ability to see: sight. However, sight did not turn out to be my strongest sense; it was touch. Again, as with every sense we investigated, we were now given tactile objects to hold and identify. Silken scarves were brought and tied around our heads to cover the eyes. We could not use our eyes to identify and describe the objects we were to examine.

My first reaction was surprise. I was given a round object with a surface that was smooth and silken. It fit into my hand; something to caress. How many of these had I painted? How many have I sunk my teeth into in my life? This object was intimate; it was one I had consumed with love and that has nourished me. I love apples. I held it between two fingers, feeling the indentation where the sharp little stalk rose. I saw apple trees in bloom, the fragrance of blossoms, and the sound of bees—an orchard painted by Van Gogh. So much about love of life was contained in the symbol of the apple. There are even "love apples"! In my mind's eye, I saw a painting of Paris offering an apple to the most beautiful of the three Graces. And now, I learned about the fourth chakra, the heart center.

The sensations of this center are fleeting, much like a beautiful dark antelope, here one second, gone the next. Feelings are like a flash, like a sudden burst of bright light, a very brief moment of sensation one is unable to capture or hold onto. The fourth chakra is associated with the largest organ of the body, the skin. The skin surrounds us, shields us against changes in temperature, holds us together as a shape, and was our body. We feel the sensation of touch, cool or warm, wet or dry, soft or hard and within the many sensations associated with touch, there is the central experience of love, which is why the fourth chakra is called the heart lotus. There is nothing as intense and delightful as touch. Air and touch are the particular expression of this chakra. Air by its very nature is lightness; it cannot be held onto. So, we learned about compassion, about healing and about pranayama, the art of breath and how to control it.

There were many courses to go through. Classes shifted to the Gita and Sutras, embracing yoga psychology and mantra chanting. Slowly, all of us lost sight of who we had been when we arrived at Yasodhara Ashram, and looked with disbelief at who we really turned out to be. We shed illusions and beliefs and eventually our concepts and habit patterns lay shattered. With our egos punctured, we became fragile like hot-house plants and vulnerable like newly hatched chicks. We had learned to be silent and to refrain from self-indulgence, especially self-defense. We could now rise at 4 am and chant for hours. We were tested by being transferred from comfortable rooms to trailers parked among trees. There were emotional outbursts and rebellious responses to contend with. In the end, everyone was licking wounds and as a group we were as close as friends could be. Opening the heart demands trust. Our ego wants life to go a certain way and in a predetermined direction. Here we have learned to trust, as there are no assurances; the heart cannot be controlled. It has an intense desire to choose what it needs.

Practicing the Invocation

We practiced an invocation called "The Divine Light Invocation" that I had first learned years ago from Swami Radha's book. Essentially, a meditation, it stresses that we are in essence, Light, created by Light, sustained by Light, protected by Light, surrounded by Light, and continuously growing into Light. I did this invocation multiple times a day and felt its power growing in me and guiding me throughout my practices.

As the days passed, the program of study and the details became more obvious. Much of our assignments consisted of written reflections on some subject leading to self-improvement and self-refinement. We were examining how our minds worked, our relationship to the outside world and to our feelings, that would provide us with pertinent details of who we were. The study of oneself was called Svadhyaya and was the most important guide to gaining insight and was an ancient Vedic practice.

We were also learning about how to develop Citta, the heart-mind connection, through reciting mantras and learning about Karma yoga, through working in the Ashram. There was a daily variety of activities displayed on a notice board. One signed up for the work of one's choice: window washing, laundry, garden work, computer work, cooking or cleaning jobs, landscaping, maintenance, or picking fruit. Most of the work was to be done in silence, a form of Tapas, or self-discipline. It was explained furthermore that we worked as a spiritual discipline, expecting neither praise, nor reward, nor pay. As a consequence, a new understanding began to form concerning how to work with total attention, avoiding all distractions.

Spirit Messenger

One afternoon I sat on the floor of the carpeted classroom among the eight other students. It rained, and then the sun came out, only to vanish again. I was tired and watched the changing light through the large glass windows. A raven flew straight through the glass and landed in the middle of our circle. "Oh, look, a raven!" No one heard me; no one seemed to see the raven. I stared at the large black bird, its feathers glistening in the afternoon sun. It hopped several times, coming closer. Then, to my horror, it picked up one of my fingers in its heavy beak, and before I had the chance to hide my hand. Its beak was sharp and the pressure extremely painful.

As I looked at my fellow students, no one seemed to be aware of the presence of the raven. The raven tugged at my finger and tried to shake it lose. I assisted its intention by shaking my hand and it let go. Again, it hopped a few paces and, turning, soared right through the windowpane that was lit by the warm afternoon sunshine. I saw it outside on the limb of a pine tree. It occurred to me to look at my finger in order to verify what I had just experienced, for after all, this was to my thinking a most unbelievable event. My finger was bruised and scraped by the sharp edges of the beak. The bird had almost broken the skin.

I was sitting in the sun, oblivious to the teacher or the class as I ruminated on my experience. I wasn't aware of a connection to ravens, except that I painted one many years ago. Clearly no one had seen the bird, so what was its message? Sense perceptions are not to be trusted, the yogis had told us. Was my experience an example of a trickster trying to shake up my belief system? Was my thinking too literal, and was there another reality where ravens could fly through glass windows? It was not altogether new to me that there were Tibetan lamas who could be seen in two locations at the same time or Tibetan yogis who dried wet sheets with the heat of their bellies during the coldest time of year. Also, I could not approach anyone in the Ashram with this puzzling event to get an explanation.

My Birthday at Yasodhara

It was my birthday and the bedside clock said 4 am. For an hour I lay in bed, reflecting on my time at the Ashram, and then I got up and dressed to go to the prayer room. Chanting was not so easy that day, and it took me a long time before I felt myself going into an altered inner state. The bay was lit by the full moon, the snow sparkled, and the stars were huge and very brilliant. I felt my heart expand in gratitude for so much beauty, so much splendor. It was the greatest gift I could have received on my birthday. I had told no one about it as I wanted no fuss over the event. I settled into my mantra chanting and felt the vibrations starting. My head hummed. The top of my head became very cold; I read about that symptom in *Chasm of Fire*, Irina Tweedy's book. The hum brought with it a feeling of profound gratitude and grace as I briefly reviewed that I had made it through 55 years of life. A wise old face reflected back to me in the glass frame standing on the altar in front of me.

Kirstin's letter came that day, and a warm feeling rushed through me. Her written gift was so heartwarming and appropriate on my birthday. I had found a special place on the wintery beach, a hidden spot, where I could sit in comfort on an ancient driftwood log, smoothed and polished by rocks and water. The sunlight was so powerful that it was blinding. Later, I returned to the Ashram grounds and noticed once again the strange heaviness like a force field pushing at me to stay away. Was it an energy repelling the unwanted visitor? I noticed this energy every time I left or reentered the Ashram grounds, but could not explain or understand what it was.

There had been so much grace that day, the grace of experiencing the pine forest, alive and fragrant, the soft rush of the waves along the shore edge of Kootenay Bay, and snow-covered mountain peaks silhouetted against a deep blue sky. That evening at Satsang I was gifted with a vision of Swami Radha. She spent the winter months in one of her other residences and we had seen nothing of her since our arrival. It now was dark and as I looked towards one of the temple windows, a figure materialized and I instantly recognized her. My heart chakra was expanding and opening wider and wider as if to fill a huge space. I felt I could breathe with this heart, which was so full of yearning and bursting with joy as well, while a deep longing shook me. I remembered thinking that feeling like this was never possible for just an ordinary human being.

My senses were definitely becoming more refined and subtle. For example, my hearing had shifted to a very subtle level. I wrote a paper because I heard the swami requesting it. She smiled broadly when I handed it in and said, "So you heard, thank you." No one else in the class handed in this paper, and I felt hot with embarrassment. That night in the temple, during Satsang, we were completing a long chant and I happened to look at Michael S., who was in our group. He was sitting on the carpeted floor and I noticed something like a pale light on his face. He looked as if he was in bliss. His face was turned inward towards his body and he seemed to be laughing into himself. Then I saw rapid flashes of light illuminating his face, as if a flashlight directed at his visage was turned on and off. It kept continuing as I walked past him. Michael had done a lot of yoga and studied with a great teacher, Iyengar, in India. His wife also was a yoga instructor in the Iyengar tradition and very advanced, I thought.

I walked back to my room through the dark, snow crunching under my feet and millions of stars blazing above. My roommate was already asleep as I slid into my bed. The air was humming. There was a sensation of power so thick, it felt as if it could be cut with a knife. My body began to move through some very strange sensations. My lower back felt a pulsation and odd agitation. My palms and the soles of my feet were being churned beyond comfort. It was as if something had taken possession of my body, even as I really did not want it, and I could not control it or stop it. If this is some Kundalini experience, I really don't want any part of it. Now my ears popped open and my hearing was enhanced and clearer. My throat seemed to gape open; there were shifts of sensation in my upper chest. My breathing seemed to concentrate itself on the heart chakra, creating a curious in-breath, a very demanding breath pattern. My mouth suddenly went dry. I did not have a drop of saliva in my mouth.

During the normal course of days, a very funny thing occurred. I noticed our shared bathrooms were becoming extremely loud as occupants farted loudly, frequently and surreptitiously. Was it the food? Was this the reason for my air-filled gut? It almost seemed as if the guys in our group suffered extreme, uncontrollable problems of indigestion. I say "guys" because the loud trumpeting seemed so unfeminine, and yet, to my surprise, I saw an elegant slim woman come out of the bathroom after one such incident.

I also decided to sign up for a Hatha Yoga Teaching Qualification. This was to happen at the end of my stay at the Ashram. A new challenge awaited me.

Hatha yoga teacher training was difficult. I had to practice a new pose, the peacock feather. My back was drenched in sweat when I lay down for a rest. My back was sore, as I had strained a muscle and my elbows were chafed. As I went into relaxation, the mantra "Hari Om" played and I drifted away on the wings of the chant. I failed to hear my teacher's request not to force the body while practicing these difficult asanas.

Later, I had a phone conversation with Alex, who sounded bored, depressed, and non-communicative. He was closing down. My experiences could not communicate to him and he felt threatened. He was uncomfortable with what I had to say, namely the spiritual things. His attitude affected me for a while. To my considerable surprise, one of the male swamis that very evening gave an impromptu speech about the isolation he experienced as a spiritual person. He also referred to the distress a husband or wife might feel, thinking their partner was leaving them to join the swamis at the Ashram. Instantly I realized I needed to be more available and show more understanding to Alex. I certainly wanted no misunderstanding to arise between us. How remarkable though, that I received such an immediate response to my concern about Alex, which allowed me to readjust my attitude and response to him.

Springtime

As time went by, winter became spring and the teachings took more solid root in me, becoming more established, and my understanding grew. The insight came that I have to take charge of my life in a different way and with a different attitude. It dawned on me how much I was already altered, yet I had no way to measure it, no full comprehension. The swamis told us it would possibly take two years before we would comprehend how much we had shifted. I still fretted about telling Alex to stop smoking; when it suddenly hit me that it was just my mind that was agitated. While it was imperative that I stood firm in my better knowing, I also practiced surrendering to a Higher Being. I did not impose my fears that he was committing slow suicide. I started writing Alex a long letter; but received one from him first, filled with pain. I was glad I had not sent my letter. When I talked to him on the phone, I heard the manipulation, saw the play for sympathy, and felt his irritation and self-justifications because his habit had been attacked. Then I understood attacking his habit was the same as attacking him.

At this juncture two people left the group; one was a psychologist who felt overwhelmed and another went to get the divorce she had hesitated with because she had lacked the courage. This gave me an example how other people had been affected and how much they were struggling. To help us with our self-inquiry and self-image, we were individually videotaped.

The next day I found the opportunity to look at my video. An Egyptian-looking face looked out to me, so Egyptian, I was stunned that I did not recognize myself. We were asked to write a paper on "How do I look to myself" and "How do I want to look." Naturally, I wanted to look relaxed and spontaneous, receptive and luminous. They asked us to remember our concern with ego, artificiality, fake smiles, and false charm and that we were carrying the Divine Light within. Can we be aware of who we truly are? Can I change what I do not want? I found it particularly strange that my youth of growing up in Egypt, should have affected me to such a degree that I managed to look Egyptian as a mature adult. I certainly had never tried to look Egyptian, so was it a past life imprint that came through? I became aware while looking at the video a second time that I stood very still, with no movement. However, my hands were most expressive and restlessly giving indication of discomfort and embarrassment. This too was a new insight. My hands were expressing more than my face.

Swami Gopalananda, a most charming human being, always carried a ready smile on his face and was very supportive of the students. It is therefore with great surprise I witnessed the female psychologist getting annoyed with him. She was really angry and she accused him of saying offensive things to her, words that I did not recall hearing. He calmly explained that every class had been taped for quality control, and that it was his desire she listen to the tape and show him, where exactly he had offended her. He handed her the tape, and she angrily left the class. Later I learned that she had not found offensive words on the tape. I felt relieved that my hearing was still reliable, but puzzled about what she thought she heard and why.

Another swami said she might have had expectations of being treated in a special way. I wondered what the "special way" implied. After all, Swami Gopalananda had been a swami for many years and had worked at the Ashram since its inception, and his whole training was about giving back, the art of selfless service leading to humility and eventually to the experience of union with the Divine. She, on the other hand, had been sort of demanding, asking constant questions. Then it clicked. He was a celibate; he did not treat her as a sex object, which she might have expected. "A woman scorned!" One other experience in his class was rather startling. I was really tired and sat across from him, about 20 feet away, feeling sleepy. For more comfort I had stretched my legs out toward this teacher and perhaps my eyes may even have closed, when suddenly something kicked the sole of my left foot, hard! Startled I looked up and he was definitely looking at me. But he was many feet away and there is no way he could have kicked me, except psychically. That was the last time I did not pay attention in his class.

Universal Prayer

There is a Universal Prayer we recited every evening. I found it to be so powerful and full of truth that I still recite it to this day:

O Adorable Lord of mercy and love
Salutations and prostrations unto Thee
Thou art Satchidananda
Thou art Omnipresent, Omnipotent and Omniscient
Thou art the Indweller of all beings.

Grant us an understanding heart
Equal vision, balanced mind,
Faith, devotion and wisdom.
Grant us inner spiritual strength
To resist temptations and to control the mind.
Free us from egoism, lust, greed, anger and hatred.
Feel our hearts with divine virtues.

Let us behold Thee in all these names and forms.
Let us serve Thee in all these names and forms.
Let us ever remember Thee.
Let us ever sing Thy glory.
Let Thy name be ever on our lips.
Let us abide in Thee for ever and ever.

Swami Sivananda

These words were no longer an abstraction for me; I could see and feel the Oneness of All.

Training to Teach Hatha Yoga

Spring was here and we were coming to the end of our Yoga Development Course. The group split into those that had completed the course and the few of us staying for the teacher training. I said goodbye to those that were leaving. We spent more talking time during our meals, which was welcome. I was now shifted into the Hatha Yoga Asana Training, which would instruct me on how to teach. Very quickly it became apparent how much I had to learn, and how much more training I would need before feeling qualified. This was not like the training I received in order to become an art teacher; rather the teaching was considered an "offering," devoid of any expectation, ego, or visible results.

My first solo class came and I was asked to demonstrate and teach the twist. I became hot and anxious and the swami asked me, "Why?" I became defensive and so we were back to square one. I was not sure I would be able to teach this, and I paid scant attention to a type of wounded pride, suggesting all this effort is nonsense and why should I subject myself to criticism! But of course, the swami was right! I was hiding my discomfort under a blanket of flip comments and a clumsy effort at humor rather than being straightforward. During this exchange, my discrediting mind had made comments which led to later events. I had received a clue that I could not teach this yoga from the head, the intellect, the mind; it had to originate elsewhere.

I became anxious about my offering at the first hatha teaching I attended, and rightly so. Two days later Elizabeth gave what I thought an entertaining, humorous, and lively demonstration. She was torn to shreds. During break, I went to the temple to chant while looking at Swami Radha's photo, crying and begging for help. Her face was changing. She looked blue-eyed and was communicating to me. Her kindness made me weep; my ineptitude made me weep. I left the temple determined that I would make my class an offering. The students were all yoga teachers. They were tired and bored and they were bad at holding the poses, which amazed me, as they all were seasoned yoga instructors. I began to respond to them by trying to help them, seeking approval by demonstrating the asana and showing how it should look, talking instead of guiding. In short, it was torture for me. And then the feedback from the seasoned experts took place.

The feedback could not have been worse. At least I had expected nothing and was not filled with self-pity. I went for a walk as I listened to the taped feedback. There wasn't a good point left. I was under some delusion if I thought I could teach this method of yoga. I had been set free. Yoga had been a joy to me...and I should therefore accept with grace and gratitude what I had learned about my abilities, and accept that this path was not for me. Those quiet-spoken Canadian women were good teachers, but not I. I considered myself to be a good teacher of art, but that did not translate into yoga and, moreover, it seemed that my pride was tied up in "teaching."

Confronting Failure

The next morning, I approached Swami R. and told her I was not evolved enough to teach and was dropping out. By evening, a head swami cornered me with the request to write a paper elaborating on the good and bad points in my experience as a yoga teacher. I sat for hours that night just writing and reflecting, and I unveiled a long-buried pain: "Rejection." It started in my childhood as rejection for being an enemy alien. Furthermore, I was a female, "not good enough and stupid." I was rejected for failing to understand a foreign language and for failure in general. Now I was ready to see Divine rejection, being not adequate or good enough. My roommate was gentle and supportive as she pointed out facts, trying to steer me off the self-abusive direction I was in.

Eventually a vision came. I was looking at a pool of brown water inside a rock, muddy water, no doubt reflective of the state of my mind. The mantra was reciting itself automatically in my mind and I was crying from frustration and exhaustion. Then I felt someone behind me, delicate, elegant, exquisitely beautiful, and filled with love. I still cry just thinking of the memory of this Being. "Who are you?" I asked again and again. It passed its arms over my shoulders and embraced me as its energy was absorbed into my back. It was penetrating me with love.

The most exquisite Being it was, and I could think of nothing else than that this must be an angel. There was an ethereal energy forming a protective cocoon around me now and it felt like wings, huge wings crossing across the front of my body disconnecting me from all prior thoughts and sensations. I was being lifted and lifted and lifted. At dawn it left me, leaving me filled with peace and bliss. The clock on my desk showed 5:00 am. I went to the beach prayer room. It was a beautiful dawn. I sat looking out over Kootenay Bay and the mountains, crying in gratitude for the revelation I had experienced during the night. The mountains reflected fully in the mirror-like surface of the bay. I had never seen it so smooth. It reflected the inner stillness in my soul.

An hour had passed and someone else came to the prayer room. I left to go outside. The first rays of the sun touched the mountain as gently as a whisper; a spreading glow expanding as the peaks lit up. When I shut my eyes and then opened them again, the world was heaven. The natural splendor was a reflection of my own inner radiance. The mountains became flushed with a soft green misty color. I had been embraced by an angel. That angel was love.

Later, two swamis with a lot of light in their eyes asked to talk to me. We chanted together, and then they told me how to avoid getting into this pit of self-negation and despair. The most interesting thing they told me was that my savasana (corpse pose), which concluded the yoga session, had been good. In fact, my voice had been soothing and there was no trace of fear. When fearful, the voice sounded harsh. This was a true insight for me. When tense, my voice became hard, and Kirstin often complained that I was shouting, even if I was not. I noticed the swamis kept their voices low, keeping out personal ambition, fear, and aggression. This was a sign to watch out for. The next day, I witnessed my roommate giving a wonderful hatha yoga class; it was taught with heart and compassion, and that gave me inspiration that someday, I too, would be able to share this gift in such a way.

Our course came to an end after three weeks and concluded very beautifully with chants in the temple. A lit candle was passed from person to person and with it a wish. I was the very last to hold the candle. My wish was for clarity of mind and the ability to carry the Light. With this in mind, I asked those with teaching experience what it was like. They told me it was very difficult to get a group of students together. People need to be drawn by something. It is fine to say the Light will draw. The Light has to be strong in an individual to attract, strong enough to convince someone to join a class and then pay money for it as well.

I reread all my reflections and letters to Alex. He was bristling with sensitivity any time we talked on the phone. My time to leave B.C. was approaching. How will I manage with his habits? Can he change? The Yoga Development Course honed my character. Perhaps now I can be more myself, less swayed by others, less fearful, more of a channel. Will I have the inner receptivity to know I need not to rush nor push, allowing an inner steadiness to guide me? I thought of roots and saw them spreading out. The "inner reality" was for me now becoming stronger than the "outer reality," especially as I saw the effect and power of the inner self. The outer shape grows from within!

> "Carried free of the old conflicts and confusions of trying to make it, and carried into the clarity of self-knowledge and service, many people find at last what they were meant to do and be."
>
> William Bridges,
> *Managing Transitions*

It was surprising how intuitive I now found myself, as I could feel my daughter and husband very clearly, almost as if there weren't a distance between us. I was becoming more secure about my inner change. As I loosened old concepts, I recognized that transitions take time. As of yet, I didn't have a handle on the new self; it is a process.

Many new faces had arrived at the Ashram. This included former Yoga Development Course students. I met them and listened to very interesting conversations about their experiences during the prior Y.D.C. I wanted to know how they coped with the return to their former lives. Bobby, who had just arrived, shared her experiences in detail. She found her many old friends were not friends any longer. They didn't have common ground with her any longer; they had nothing to share. The dependency had stopped. She began to understand that her process had started many years before she first came to the Ashram. I listened with great interest to what she said because it confirmed that I did not know how I was going to unfold. She told me to take my time, and not to rush the inner process. "Above all, you will feel detached, alone. Don't give in to the temptation to do something and act for the sake of action. Recognize why you feel uncomfortable; it is part and parcel of change. You are not yet the new you, you are still unfolding like a flower unfolding its petals. Observe yourself without expectations as what is happening is your future self. Allow, allow! All change begins with Chaos."

I recognized that, more than ever, I shall have to cultivate an empty mind, throwing out most beliefs, concepts, and views. She insisted that our culture takes endings too seriously by comparing them to finality. She was so right about that and I identified with finality, which is one of the reasons I dislike saying "goodbye" on parting. She found herself discarding and throwing out much of her former wardrobe, favoring different foods and different furniture, making an altar in her room, requiring periods of quiet for reflection and meditation. In fact, her need to call and talk to people had gone; her interests had shifted through living in the present much more and no longer making plans for the future. "There is a sort of need to stay empty, to have space, which was unknown to me before," she said. As I reflected and considered all this advice, I realized I had, at times, been unauthentic, living a limited existence. To live fully means no limits on being open and giving up limits of any sort. I have to trust the inner process and listen to the inner hint.

Nature was changing. Kootenay Bay shifted to a deep slate blue, the mountains a soft green. Buds were on the trees, leaves unfurling, dew clinging to the grass blades; it was spring. Briefly I looked and breathed in all that beauty, and then, I went to chant. I felt stronger now, more aware of who I was, less inclined to wish to be different. Perhaps the ego is less now. I looked forward to joining my family, my life partner, and my wondrous daughter Kirstin and stepping back into my transformed life.

A last lesson came: Hatha Yoga, The Hidden Language in the morning. Yes, I will teach well. I now know how it is done. I felt much more secure and strong, knowing my body will give me messages from the subconscious. I sat in lotus and felt peaceful and centered. I was ready to return, ready to test my skills and all I learned here and to learn more.

I awoke during the early hours before dawn with a start, realizing that I was to leave today. It was a grey, rainy day. Departing made easy! I said goodbye to everyone and received hugs, blessings and love. Swami R. told me to ask for help if I needed it.

By the end of four months, there was little ego left in me and a new self had surfaced—actually she had always been there, but I had denied her. She was the self that was intuitive and often psychic. She could predict future events and remembered past lives.

The return was like swimming on the surface of a wave, being carried easily and smoothly back into my former life. I searched for the difference in feeling, for the inner change in me. It was so subtle I could at first sense nothing. I was totally calm, cocooned in a centered feeling of power. Alex was all I knew him to be, a wonderful being, embracing me with an open heart, no illusion, no disappointment, his own self. Kirstin was warm and affectionate, and she had been a wonderful help during my absence.

> "If we really want to know what we should do with our lives, the first step is to reflect on the important parts of this life, and to question again and again, "Why was I born? What is the purpose of my life?"
>
> Swami Radha,
> *In the Company of the Wise*

14 Resuming Life in Lake Forest

Return to Illinois

I flowed easily into my first day back home; Kirstin had bought a sleek pair of capri pants for me and a top. She dropped them on the bed. What a thoughtful gift. After wearing the same clothes for four months, it was a welcome change to slip into something new and pleasantly cool. Oh, but this inner Light, if it is really in me, it has to manifest itself and keep on guiding me. After putting on my new clothes, I went downstairs and sat and listened to the conversation going on.

As I did, I realized all I am is borrowed: attitudes, gestures, ways of answering, and even talking. Behind and beyond all this was the inner core. Bringing that authentic part forward means tapping into a luminous, refined response and giving of that. It would also bring out the best in others; I could show how it can be done. My ego felt shattered and I was glad to notice that.

Two of my paintings were featured in a Fine Arts magazine. I registered no pride, no ambition, just a slight amusement that something like this had happened. It was, after all, the first time my work was featured. Later, Alex told me that my paintings that went into an exhibition during my absence did not go down so well. "I shall be interested to see if this experience at the Ashram enhanced your creativity and changed your imagery," he said. The positive was quickly followed by a negative, I think. It showed me how tentative everything is, and how little attention I should pay to praise or blame.

I went through a mountain of accumulated mail and by five o'clock began to feel tense. Alex noticed and sent me upstairs to meditate. Gratefully, I sank into mantra; I had no prayer room, no altar, no candlelight, and no view of Kootenay Bay. But I sank in, and the luminous orb of light sat in my head, and gratitude for my life welled up. A lot of exhaustion became apparent and for many days I went to sleep every afternoon in order to keep going. I kept dreaming of the Kootenay mountains and waking in the deep green of Lake Forest. I had to start my spiritual practice once more and dedicate time to that. In addition, I had to begin reading 36 books and write required book reports, due at the end of 12 months. Without these book reports, I would not be certified.

Though Lake Forest was a lovely place and some of the richest families of Illinois lived there, it was becoming unbearably polluted with noise. All afternoon, machines were roaring, trimming lawns and hedges and blowing leaves, and it became difficult to bear the constant sounds, especially while trying to meditate. Karma yoga was still a challenge. To work without expectations, without impatience, was hard. I found myself tense as I anticipated results or angry if the outcome was not what I wanted. I also wondered how I was going to teach hatha yoga. There was inner pressure demanding action, and ambition raised its head before I could stop it. I felt petrified and disconnected.

Someone at the Gorton Community Center needed to be asked if they were interested in a yoga teacher. My mind said I should start moving, while something within me said, "Don't bother, it will resolve itself, or there might be a better time." "Better time" meant I would worry about results again! Waiting for the combination of circumstances to feel right and thinking that everything will move as if on oiled wheels was an illusion. If I were to force circumstances, nothing would happen. It would only be a waste of energy. The community center was amply supplied with yoga teachers and so was the recreation center. I needed to offer more than just hatha yoga. This was the reality, and it felt a bit like a wake-up slap in the face. It made me feel like someone dangling with feet several inches off the ground.

Many friends old and new were very eager to connect with me and they wanted to learn about my Ashram stay and my yogic training. They were mostly intrigued by the spiritual content and not with hatha yoga aspects. They invited me to lunch, to dinner, to meet and discuss their heart- and soul-felt needs and desires, and slowly I realized that I was actually attracting people towards the Light within. I was pretty sure that I needed a spiritual attractiveness in order to direct people towards yoga. I sensed it, but I continued to struggle with self-doubt, belittling myself or assuming myself to be unimportant. I needed to purify my mind much more and get over my doubts.

There was a big contemporary art exhibition at Navy Pier in Chicago, and, as a family, we decided to visit it. Kirstin said the traffic would be awful due to road work, and we would get stuck in traffic. I told her it would not necessarily be so, as I would visualize a green open path for us. She rolled her eyes as she got into the back of the car. I started a silent mantra recitation in my head, feeling the power of the Japa-mantra, and I visualized the open, green road ahead. We encountered no delays. The traffic would just part to either side as we approached and we were allowed to magically pass through.

The exhibition was interesting but not special. It is odd to have seen so much of the best talent employed for such scant results. The soul is absent, the magic missing. We had lunch and returned, following the same open road. I felt quite excited about the visualization and the effect of the mantra, for we certainly could have become stuck several times, seriously stuck and delayed. At the Ashram, it was pointed out to us that there was always a chance to ask for help if we found we needed it. Most people don't ask. I wondered if Kirstin had noticed the ease with which we drove to Chicago and back! There was no indication that she had noticed anything.

I felt as sensitive as a hot-house plant and continued to be tired. I resumed daily hatha yoga practices and reflections, mainly reflections on the symbolism of the daily events. How they served to guide my thoughts and actions! I also used my dreams for guidance and found that many were deeply disturbing.

Alex had not asked me a single question about my time at Yasodhara Ashram. It was very obvious that he was happy I was back, but found it intolerable if I mentioned anything spiritual. Kirstin in contrast, impressed me by her vital and clear mind. I wish I could have said the same for her boyfriend Bill. He was a charming character, but beneath the surface was a suffering soul and he was drunk far too frequently.

One night, awakened by loud sounds, I found him in the kitchen noisily putting on the washing machine in order to remove some sauce spilled on his shirt while fixing a snack at two-thirty in the morning. The shirt was a gift from Kirstin and he worried lest the shirt became stained. "What about everyone upstairs being awakened?" I asked. He looked at me through a drunken haze without apology.

Sometimes, when we all gathered for breakfast in the dining room, I made the mistake of mentioning a particularly interesting dream I had. After just a few sentences, Alex would tell me that no one wanted to hear another word. In contrast to my family, I continued to be surprised at the support from other people. There was a faculty party we were invited to and I felt uneasy about accepting the invitation. It was utterly tedious, as they were faculty with which we have nothing in common. I talked very little, chanting a mantra in my head instead. Then my dear friend Emily pulled me aside, giving me a long line of praise and admiration for who and what I am, adding that she did not voice such sentiments easily. I said nothing, realizing she could feel the Light and that I was chanting a mantra inside. She connected on the level of feeling.

The next day I had agreed to go for a walk on the Lake Michigan beach with Bea. She wanted to talk to me. Normally I would refuse this opportunity; now I think perhaps I was meant to share or give back and I would see what transpired. I still found it almost impossible to believe that my words can inspire or that some inner Light was powerful enough to affect people. However, I was open to the experience. The time with Bea was light-hearted. She was a very sweet soul, and perhaps this meeting occurred for no other reason than to prove that a different "me" had been growing and I was now recognizing it.

Evaluating a House with Character

Every now and then Alex would join me for a walk. We would choose the beach or even drive to the Chicago Botanic Garden. I truly valued these occasions because in the past he consistently refused exercise in any form and had jokingly said, "The only form of exercise I take is lifting a glass." In two years, Alex would be of retirement age, and with all the recent unpleasantness in the department, he had decided that Santa Fe, NM, looked like a lovely place to move to. He also decided to give the chairmanship to our old friend Michael Croydon, the sculptor, who would take over the position of running the Art Department.

We decided to return to Santa Fe during the Christmas season to get some idea of what winter in Santa Fe was like. That brought up the next big decision, selling our house. We had improved it substantially; however, we did not add on a kitchen, which I had begged for. We needed to sell our house before we could buy something in Santa Fe. A realtor brought over four women to evaluate our house.

In their opinion, the house, an early balloon construction, dated to 1924. I believe the house was older, as there are construction details which were no longer used after the turn of the century. They suggested it might be difficult to sell because it was old. The lot size was narrow and long and did not conform to the norm. There were no other houses like it in Lake Forest. We had therefore no comparison possibilities. Despite being in a really good location and only a block from Lake Michigan, we might not get its real value. How discouraging, I thought.

However, Alex saw these points as positive; the house was unique, its location superb, it was surrounded by million-dollar homes, and it fit into the environment. Its age gave it distinction and because the lot size was narrow, the price might be affected, but that is something to discuss and evaluate later. There were huge, ancient trees surrounding the house and the garden was established. He saw the house as valuable to someone who wanted style and unique qualities and was not interested in the average home. I recalled Alex felt this house had a value I did not see when we first moved into it, and now I realized how differently he evaluated and saw the property. He saw architectural style, the inner space as rooms flowing into each other, the amount of light coming in from the windows, the rhythm of a well-placed staircase, and how easy it was to walk up or down. There also was generous space in an attic, and storage space in the basement.

The realtor came to us a day later, at night, with an estimate. The house was not worth $400,000 and we would be lucky to get $300,000. I felt shattered, my hopes dashed. She stayed late and it became clear that I had to ask all the questions. Alex did not seem capable of probing with questions and was uninterested in what the woman had to say. Kirstin came in after work and marched through, looking disturbed and angry. I could feel her fear; she did not want to lose her home.

Finally, the realtor left and we retired. I could not sleep or relax, as my mind questioned the events of the evening and the feelings it had raised. It began to rain. Why should I not look at the facts, then turn my beliefs upside down and examine the other side? This whole event could be considered a game, a test of concepts and beliefs and what direction I was willing to choose. To examine the other side was crucial. Then, I lost myself in meditation and the light stayed with me through a flowing hatha yoga session, and a bubbly joyousness invaded my mind. Where oh where had the anxiety about the high sales price for this house gone? Where was my concern that Alex was not forceful enough? All gone, I felt free in my heart. It poured rain, and then the sun came out. A new day and I phoned another realtor; and with that move, I turned everything upside down.

I had been practicing my mantra chanting, which demands uninterrupted attention and a good voice. Alex heard something I did incorrectly, so he took the time to sit and listen to me. Then he chanted the mantra himself, to show me how to do it. As an opera buff he knew an amazing amount about breath control and how to project sound. I felt touched by his concern that I would produce my voice correctly. Now hardly a day goes by without him noticing when I make an error. It actually helped me very much and made the chanting easier.

The next realtor came, and her attitude was promising, perhaps the best so far. It was an illusion; the second realtor was even worse that the first, of limited taste, and filled with verities and opinions. The house, she said, if sold by her, was worth $213,000, which would be awful. Alex and I both felt depressed. I tried to control the effect of this news and not allow it to drag me down, but clearly these matters shook me up and brought out all the old fears of homelessness and poverty in old age, not coping—all this rose up like foam on a glass of beer. Another realtor was recommended, and so Pat C. was the third expert to advise us. She felt we would be getting a fair deal if the house fetched between $325,000 and $365,000. Alex calculated that if we realized $350,000, we would be all right.

At this time, I received a letter from my Aunt Alma from Kenya, telling me my Uncle Christian had a heart attack and now slept constantly. He was 94 years old. She was deeply distressed, and she asked me to come to help her in Kenya. Then, a second very sad letter arrived from her. How could I help? I felt this was probably the end of his life. Maybe Gabriele could come to her, or my cousin Renate—they were closer to Africa than I was. Alex clearly did not wish me to go. As I looked out the window, I saw him cutting the lawn. It was humid and hot and he was looking close to physical collapse. That decided me; I had a duty here. I sensed there may not be much time left for us either. Death is inevitable, especially at 94 years. My aunt may not want to face that inevitable possibility. No one can help her with that.

Mind to Mind Connection?

I received a letter from one of the swamis telling me the Ashram would support me financially to take the training for the Hidden Language courses. That is, if I were interested and "if I am somewhere." "Where are you at?" they asked. I felt stunned. Here, I thought I was doing poorly, and yet, they thought of me highly enough to offer me a scholarship. It made me very happy and gave me a boost of confidence. However, I would have to start teaching yoga to know if I can be a channel, if the inner self knows how to transmit.

I had a dream which filled my heart and soul with love, lightness and compassion. I sat beside Swami Radha. "Can you see me as Light," she asked? I told her that I saw her in many forms, constantly changing; but not as Light; I did not see her just as Light. She was full of understanding, but I knew it meant I was not there yet. She sat down beside me; she looked at me, and it felt as though she studied me and, with each look gave to me of her power. Then, I was asked to scrub a brown rectangular stone while sitting at a long wooden table. The table looked like those found in the dining rooms of old monasteries. However, I was not alone; there was a whole group of people. When I became tired of scrubbing and polishing, the person next to me took over the job, and so the stone was passed from person to person and worked on. There was no rushing, no ambition, nothing but effort to polish this stone to one's best ability.

When I awoke from the dream, I felt this had been an actual contact with Swami Radha and that it contained a message from her. To believe this dream originated in my own mind seemed unbelievable. There was so much compassion and love in it, and I know yogis can communicate mind to mind. All day I felt uplifted by the contact with Swami Radha; all day long I felt filled with joy. It confirmed I was working on what was important, my inner transformation. Also, I was aided in my efforts. For a while I sat in the garden as night fell, chanting mantras, eyes closed. When I opened my eyes, sparkles were dancing in front of my inner vision and the light started bouncing off the grass, flowing down the green branches of trees, and vibrating everywhere I chanced to look. It was utter splendor of a kind I had never seen before. It must have been the mantra practice that had opened my ability to see this.

Holiday in Florida

June came with humidity and thunderstorms and we made the decision to drive to Florida for our seaside holidays. I hoped both of us would benefit from swimming, sunshine, and leisure. We rented a beach condo in Englewood, Florida, for our vacation, and drove two days, rising at four in the morning in order to make the trip as short as possible. Having made an excellent start, we were held up for almost an hour by a collision. Three sheet-covered bodies lay on the highway, with an arm sticking out in one case. Death, so close, so final, was sobering; it made me wonder why we were shown this event. When we arrived in Englewood, the realtor gave us an ultra-posh condo overlooking the beach. The owner had died not long ago; and so, we received a special deal. It had a plastic palm tree in the entry and plastic flowers decorated the table. A sickly-sweet smell scented the rooms. We took it; after all, it was very clean, organized, and lovingly arranged. We were meant to have it, as I have now realized.

Kirstin called at seven o'clock that evening, during a heavy thunderstorm, to tell us that Christian was dead. My uncle died on the first of July, eight days after his birthday. I felt very sad and remembered the three highway corpses. I felt heartbroken for my Aunt Alma, who had to accept this loss of her life's partner. How fortunate I had been with them for three weeks last year. Locked in my mind was an image of them sitting side by side in the little arbor in front of their kitchen. At this time the thunderstorm unleashed its power, and I had to run to close all the windows.

I awoke in the night. The thunderstorm had stopped and a nearly full-faced moon was drifting from behind clouds. The mantra Om Tara was singing in my mind and I joined with my voice in a prayer for Alma and Christian, asking the Tibetan

Goddess to protect and shield them in their hour of need. Outside, the ocean began to roar and I became aware of the night sounds joining in the melody of the mantra. This posh condo was ours for the month, and I marveled at being guided and sustained in this way. It felt like a path of miracles.

The following morning, I phoned Nairobi and talked to my older cousin Renate, who had just arrived to help my aunt. She related that Christian had died of pneumonia and old age. Alma held his hands while he died. They kept her in the hospital because she was so deeply shocked and grieving. For someone so aged, the death of a partner can extinguish their own life's light. Renate took her back to her home the next day. Alma refused to eat anything except soup, and she had no force in her voice. Since she couldn't bear to use her bedroom, Renate shifted her bed into the living room. "I seem to be psychic like all the women in our family," Renate said. "I had booked my Nairobi flight one month ago, as I felt what was going to come, and I arrived exactly on time, when my presence was needed. I felt very clearly what events were to come. Now it is important for Gabriele to fly to Africa. Also, I knew you were not meant to come to Kenya just now and your presence is not necessary."

I had never heard anyone mention before that the women of our family are psychic! She also told me that my mother's brother Willy had just suffered a heart attack. "It is the dying season," she added in a resigned voice. That evening a full moon rose, and I took myself up to the open deck on the roof, a splendid place to practice my chanting. It felt as if a broad base of bliss was rising in me, a foundation. The inner transformation was steady and taking place without my being able to see it happening. Thurston talks of "the Divine manifesting—but people not seeing it." That seems to apply to me.

The next night I again sought out the roof to meditate. The moon was throwing a broad beam of light on the Gulf of Mexico, while across the horizon, far away, a new dawn was rising. I could feel Christian, his essence, and he told me, "It is much easier, much lighter now. Give Alma my message." I tried to call her to tell her Christian had left a message for her. She was angry and refused to talk.

We began to settle into our new place and I turned off the air conditioning in favor of open windows letting in the fragrant air and the salt spray of the sea. The beach was broad and invited us for walks. The ocean, as delicious as I remembered it from past visits, drew me into long swims. Alex set up his table to paint gouaches and studied the cloud formations. As idyllic as our days were, I continued struggling with self-acceptance and with the strange inner shifts and changes. I was still searching for security and still wanted life "my way."

I forced myself to start painting. I had fun, but no results. According to Karma yoga, I am to work without reaching for the fruit of results like praise, honor, applause, financial reward, or fame. Swami Radha said, "There must be a balance between wanting to do and letting things happen."

My deepest concern was Alex, who was unwell, something I saw more clearly, and yet I said nothing. This unspoken criticism was something he felt and then we would clash. I was unable to hide my fear for him. I wondered if an instinctive sense for self-preservation was missing, for he had little or no inclination to protect his well-being through sensible choices in diet, exercise, or a balanced work schedule. Mind you, here in Florida he had stopped drinking whisky, which is hard liquor, and chose beer and wine instead. I had to disengage myself from identifying with him.

Death

My thoughts turned to Alma. She was picking up a little, I was told. However, her whole life's purpose was gone, for there wasn't a partner to look after anymore. She hung onto Renate like a drowning man clutching a piece of wood, allowing her no freedom. Renate wanted to go to a little shopping center 10 minutes' walk from the house, and Alma forbade her to leave. I was grateful I was not in Africa at this time.

The mail brought a letter from Swami Radha. It was totally unexpected. Her kindness expressed itself like a great caring and support. She wrote: "Write down your understanding in order to clarify things in your own mind. The Yoga Development Course was of great benefit to you. It is so important to keep applying in your life the insights you gained." In other words, continue to practice what you learned. Apply what you learned; use the methods of the Hidden Language when going into asana. As the days passed, I noticed inner growth and improvements and I began to trust my experiences as valid.

Alma continued to rise in my thoughts. I felt her and talked to her, urging her to accept the death of her husband. Then, on a lengthy afternoon walk, negative ideas and imaginings manifested, thoughts I pushed away. I had not come to assist my aunt in a most difficult period of need; would she seek to punish me by withdrawing an inheritance she promised me? How would I feel if this indeed would happen? Then I pushed the imagined monster away, deciding I would stay balanced in mind and refrain from plunging into hurt feelings and wounded pride. The expectations of the older generation are often unrealistic; I had already experienced this with my mother when she accused me of having neglected her by not travelling to Kenya to visit her more frequently. The fact that our budget did not permit such extravagant voyages didn't hold validity in her mind.

As I approached our condo, I saw Alex beckoning me to come quickly. I knew. "Alma is dead. She died last night," he said. The momentary shock flashed through me, and then the thought, "I am not surprised, that is why I was thinking of her." Later I talked to my cousin Renate. She told me, "Alma was in such pain—she screamed most of the day. She held my hand and hung onto it, not letting go. By six in the evening when it gets dark in Nairobi, she turned her eyes skywards and was dead. She was a very tall woman, surprisingly, because in life she did not seem so. In death she was thin and white and looking very old at the end. Yet, only yesterday she put on lipstick to meet the priest, Pater Specht, and called for her wig. Be glad you were not here. She was utterly horrible to me," said Renate. "She kept me a virtual prisoner. I was not even allowed to go out to buy toothpaste. She was so demanding and domineering. I felt homesick here. She willed herself to die, and that Christian and she shall be buried together could not be more appropriate."

My sister flew to Nairobi but arrived four hours too late, and so did not see her beloved aunt alive. I felt sad for my sister, as she had been very close to Alma. However, I had little hope of patching up the rift between my sister and me. The first concerns she voiced were, "Do you want the paintings back you gave to Alma, as gifts?" I declined. Then she offered furniture—did I want carpets? Then she mentioned that some items listed in the inventory were missing. I told her that Alma had given some things to Kirstin as gifts when Kirstin visited her at Christmas time.

Gabriele and Klaus were selected by my aunt to be executors of her will. (Christian had a separate will.) My sister was planning to come later in the year to tackle this momentous task. Renate was going to fly back to Germany during the following days, taking Christian's body and Alma's ashes with her. Christian was going to be buried in the family grave in the Rhineland. My aunt had insisted he be buried with all the pomp and ritual possible. He had on his best suit and his chest was covered with many medals and war-time insignias. To my surprise, I discovered the Water Castle, with which the German government replaced the ample properties belonging to the Muesch family, were to be gifted to the Roman Catholic Church. In other words, some considerable wealth did not go to the grandson of Christian, but to the church. Furthermore, there was a well-kept secret I only now discovered. Alma and Christian, as well of the rest of the Muesch family members, had been seriously considering making my sister their heir. Had this happened, she would now be a wealthy woman.

While struggling with loss and death, I felt particularly concerned about Kirstin. I could sense her fierce fight to succeed at the university and the drag of circumstances. I could feel the inside core or soul of people close to me. A call to Lake Forest confirmed the correctness of my intuition and that yes, she had worries on many levels. I knew her boyfriend Bill was a central problem and that only she could free herself. So I practiced my spiritual work, wrote yet another book report, and focused on being patient and grateful for the opportunities given to me. Maybe in many lifetimes I shall get somewhere.

Tests

Every morning at dawn and every evening the Turtle Patrol walked the long beaches to assist the turtles, taking care of the nests and eggs. When the new life hatched, the little turtles raced at sunset into the heaving waves to start their journey into the open sea. The turtle patrol was there to assist them and to guide stragglers and keep seabirds and crabs away from the fragile little creatures. I was full of admiration for the volunteers and their noble effort. One of my spiritual practices was "detachment." It called for choosing not to identify with confusions, emotions, upheavals of all sorts, but instead staying separate from the event. Identifying with righteousness or censure only manifests anger, and aggression is the outcome. I did not know or expect to be tested so soon. On a walk I observed a young girl taking the stake marking a turtle nest out in order to write in big letters on the beach: Dana + Don Forever! I walked past her and she smiled in greeting. I felt annoyed with her for taking the stake that marked a nest out, so that now no one would know its location. I should have discriminated; telling her with sensitivity of her mistake, while avoiding accusation or censure. It was cowardly of me to say nothing. There is so much to learn!

Two days later a maintenance man appeared on the beach and started pulling out a lovely creeper with saucer shaped leaves and lovely purple blossoms. I felt pained and thought his destruction of the plant was irrational. Why did he have to do this? Discriminate! I thought and went down to him and asked why he was pulling out this lovely plant. "They are a hazard," he said. "We like to keep them under control." Control of nature? I thought. However, he stopped. It was as if he had heard me and now changed his attitude. I understood that with just one question, just one sentence, the right amount of pressure and the right number of words, I had been able to effect change in him. I was very surprised, I must say, because I had just asked a question, which was all that was needed.

August came and with it the departure from Florida and a long hot drive back to humid Illinois. Upon our arrival home, I was greeted by the usual mountain of mail and a nasty letter from my dear Aunty Alma. Why did I not go to help her as Christian lay dying? She loved me and she wanted me. I had a dream in Florida where I had guided her to her bed, but I could not warm her.

> "I cannot thy former light relume, thy warmth restore!"
> William Shakespeare,
> paraphrase from *Othello*

In her letter she accused me of being greedy to inherit money from her and said that she was considering changing her will. Thank God, Renate was there to take care of her! I felt grateful to Renate on two counts; being with Alma for the final three weeks of her life, and telling me of this nasty last letter Alma had written to me. I battled the idea that I was cold and unfeeling for not flying to Africa, and I felt sad for letting my aunt down, but then, I never ever had the intention of going there in the first place for it was clear in my mind that I could not help her. I phoned Renate and we talked for an hour. We re-examined Alma's life and her last weeks, and I concluded she had not been ready to let go of life and was unwilling to embrace death. It had been a very hard battle for her.

Learning to Teach Yoga

Fall came and our classes at Lake Forest College resumed. Life once again became intensely busy. Alex became glum, tense, and anxious. I went with him to the doctor. The doctor had a positive attitude and the visit went smoothly, much to my relief. Five days later he went back to the doctor; something was amiss with his digestion. I suspected the sour atmosphere in the department and the corrupt behavior of a particular female faculty member, Gwen, was upsetting him.

Even my faithful practice of yoga was failing to dislodge my inner anxiety. We talked of retirement beginning the following year in May, when Alex would be 65 years of age. Alex smoked and coughed and had no interest in informing himself properly about retirement. I felt the burden was on me—the only one awake.

We went to a meeting organized for retiring faculty in the Chicago region. It was held in a very large hotel and we sat in rows in front of a platform and viewing screen. Here experts informed us about finances, social security, TIAA-CREF, health insurance, and other subjects. I took copious notes while Alex doodled and drew caricatures. Later we ran into an ex-student, who managed a bank. Alex raised the subject of needing a financial advisor for his retirement and someone to help us make the right choices. She was only too happy to assist, and she changed our financial situation from one of having large debts to one of balance. I felt enormous relief as a consequence.

I made every effort not to be critical of Alex; he had enough on his plate to cope with. He actually claimed some Shakti was transmitted to him and his intuition became sharper, much sharper; he clearly noticed the difference. I had been telling him what Radha said: "Any discovery by your Self, however small, becomes a knowing within."

The college had a yoga instructor for students on Thursday night at the chapel on campus. As a member of faculty, I could take the class for free. Not having found any opportunity to teach yoga so far, I decided to sample the classes of Jai, the instructor, just to see how he offered hatha yoga. He was young and physically very flexible and he had an alert look on his face. The students arrived and quickly filled the chapel space. Benches had been removed, so there was a large open space where the young people spread out their mats.

He must be special, I thought, as I watched students streaming in until there were about fifty bodies on the floor. He asked everyone to tell him what they hoped to get out of the yoga practice, and most people gave him an answer. He began with a pose called "Mountain," a simple standing pose, and then side stretches. He stressed the need to be aware, awake to feeling the edge of discomfort or pain, as any excess or pain was to be strictly avoided. "Release into comfort, relax, and allow the body to be at ease." He stressed the need to become aware of the contrast between comfort and forcing the body. He showed the movement flowing from one position to the other, a graceful and subtle technique. Then he asked everyone to close their eyes and to do the poses through feeling into the body, following the sensations, allowing gentle stretches. He did not concern himself with mistakes, or correct postures. His partner walked through the class, helping where needed. Eventually came the end-relaxation, called the corpse pose, and here he focused on breathing, not holding in but exhaling fully, not controlling but letting the breath flow. I felt a wave of gratitude sweep through me, as this had been a very good class, and I really looked forward to future sessions. I felt I had received a real gift.

I attended Jai's classes for at least a year and we eventually worked together. He was occasionally indisposed or unable to teach for some reason, so he would ask me to teach his class. Since enough students knew me from the Art Department, there was no awkwardness in my taking over his class. Also, his method suited me well and was much easier than the complex Hidden Language Hatha I had learned to teach at the Ashram. I was also very comfortable with a large class, something I missed later on. Jai paid no attention to time and if a class was responding and having fun, he kept the class going until 9:30 pm. It was challenging, relaxing, and very creative, especially when he tried to introduce the spiritual element by talking about awareness and the mind, ending with a read visualization. It was uplifting and joyous and very creative, and best of all I learnt a great deal.

Premonitions

Alex was very low, fragile-seeming. There was nothing I could do but not let the sense of powerlessness depress me! This was the season of autumn. I cannot put the fallen leaves on the trees. They fall because it is their time to fall. My mother died because it was time to do so. I too, am nothing but a drifting leaf in space, detached and gradually descending. I have reached a stage where little if anything tempts; not food nor love nor fame. Things have become transparent. With the death of all the family members who died so recently, I had to become more detached. Their death had taken away a part of me and I became less. I became detached. Perhaps this was what Alex felt, a sensation of being set adrift, floating through space. Lately he casually said, as if to himself: "I am dying, Egypt, dying." Am I Egypt? Is he trying to tell me something?

Kirstin started looking for a rental in Highland Park, where the apartments are more reasonable. Bill and she found something by November and we all drove there to see it. It was a cute place, perfect for young people. She rented it, but then felt sick in the pit of her stomach. Was it a step out into the cold, a step too scary? Alex had said to her that although he had carried the responsibility for supporting Bill, she would not be able to do so. Bill would have to get a steady job and pay his way. Kirstin responded: "Then I shall have to throw him out if he does not shape up!"

Since Kirstin and Bill were moving out, I considered starting a yoga course and teaching out of the upstairs bedroom. It would be enough space for seven people, a good number. There were several friends and acquaintances who might be interested. I wondered what to charge, how much, and it felt very difficult to ask people to pay. There was still considerable hesitation in me to charge for a spiritual offering. It would feel more comfortable not to put a price on my teaching. I sent a note to the Ashram, asking for advice. They replied: Under no circumstances am I to teach for nothing. They are firm and I struggled with combatting discontent and expectations that sneaked into my mind. Confronting my mind, I realized how

greedy it is. All is: "I want, I want, give me now, I need etc. etc."
I reminded myself to stay alert, to relax, to float, to feel, and
to understand that without surrender and relaxation, it was
not possible to absorb anything. Nota bene: I noticed changes
in myself that were definitely new and positive. I was no
longer annoyed with daily chores like washing dishes, glasses,
pots, and dirty drawers. Annoyance had been replaced with
acceptance. I began to understand the value of the knowledge
I was planning to offer. The teachings have a long history and
do not belong to me, but to the ancient masters and to Swami
Sivananda Radha, who spent her life making them available to
the Western mind. I was bound in a tradition and had to honor
the teachings appropriately.

My friend Ann went to a yoga retreat in Pennsylvania and
returned, excited and enthusiastic. The Ashram was very high
tech, monitoring bodies, with pranayama practices, vegetarian
food service, and body massage to release stress, and at the
conclusion of the courses she also received a mantra initiation.
I felt somehow at loose ends, as I realized that no strings
were attached to me after my time at Yasodhara Ashram; no
certifications were handed out and no initiations or Sanskrit
names given to us. Swami Radha demanded independence
from us. She insisted, "Take off your baby shoes." No mantra
initiation for me! Self-doubts still rose easily, but something
told me not to be foolish. She has been my wondrous teacher
and her work had guided me like a golden thread. She did not
allow my feelings of insecurity nor did she feed my pride. She
let me do my inner work alone, by myself. This was a path of
self-reliance; I was alone and doing it alone. I felt grateful for
her wisdom.

Eldorado

Our planned visit to Santa Fe came about during the
Christmas holidays so we could experience the winter in the
Southwest, as well as get a more intimate impression of Santa
Fe and a sense of the real estate available. On the 21st of
December we took to the sky and flew to the Southwest. We

rented a car at the Albuquerque airport and started driving north. Alex, who was driving, became very tense, blinded by the low angle of the light. The terrain looked like Egypt; orange hills, blue shadows, and vast vistas.

We had arranged to visit six adobe-style houses in Eldorado on the following day. Our realtor met us and spent the whole afternoon showing us beautiful Eldorado homes. Eldorado was a former ranch seven miles north of Santa Fe that was converted into a development. The landscape was wide and open with scattered trees, and it was home to varied wildlife. I could see us really living comfortably here in this unspoiled environment. However, thinking of this beautiful place and the possibility of living here seemed to me totally unreal. The homes we saw were truly exciting; they were uniformly designed in the adobe style, usually out of stucco, and they merged into the landscape instead of sitting on the landscape.

Ah, and the light! The sunsets were spectacular and the colors glorious. It was quite cold, but a dry cold which lacked the sting of the Illinois temperatures. We stayed warm by walking into galleries and shops and enjoying the Christmas atmosphere. The place looked lovely and Alex bought himself sunglasses and a Stetson hat. As a little boy he had played at being a cowboy. The hat suited him. For some reason, he looked impressive and, to our surprise, several times people he did not know greeted him on the street.

We spent a very pleasant day driving further north to Taos before our return flight into the Midwest. What I took away from this brief visit and what this trip taught me was to choose a lifestyle that was uplifting. The native people of the Southwest believe in a lifestyle that harmonizes with nature. The beauty and charm of the place was something I wanted to enjoy and own. Our last day was mild and sunny and our afternoon flight took us back to a grey, icy Chicago. As the plane circled the city, vast jewel chains of light stretched out beneath us and I thought back to my first arrival here in 1964. All we could find was a $60 taxi to take us back to Lake Forest. Alex was tense. We both felt disoriented, tired, and deaf from the roar of the plane. The atmosphere of New Mexico still clung on like a scent, to eventually fade. Our decision was final; we would retire to Santa Fe.

Only too quickly were we once again engaged in daily events of teaching, racing from one thing to the next, living by the clock, rushing to complete tasks, and in my case, trying to swim against the current. "No matter how the traffic flows, there is a recommended speed limit." Do I surrender in obedience or do I break the rule, ever so slightly, and speed? I decided to practice keeping to the speed limit. Then, an odd event took place. I was driving somewhere with Kirstin and she started scolding me, even shouting at me, because I did not speed. Ironically, the next day Bill was ticketed for speeding.

A Final Exhibition at the College

In March, Alex and I had a joint final exhibition in the Sonnenschein Gallery at the college, as we were both retiring at the end of the academic year, in May 1994. Alex was exhibiting a number of gouaches painted in Florida and a series of oil paintings. My work consisted mostly of abstract oils. We had to frame the pieces ourselves, as framing costs were prohibitive. Most weekends we both worked on making frames. There was a radial saw in the basement for cutting the wood for the frames. This was Alex's work, as he claimed he prefers me with all my fingers intact. The next step was gluing and nailing the frame sections together. We worked together on this task and were quite fast and efficient. Painting the frames fell into my territory, largely because I had more patience than Alex with the tedious details, and besides, he trained me well. Michael Croyden helped us with hanging the exhibition and I climbed up and down a high ladder to direct the lights towards the images.

Opening night at the gallery brought a vast number of old friends and acquaintances brimming with warmth and affection. We had known most of them since our first years in Lake Forest. I felt the exhibit was more about people than art—or maybe that was my focus. I was delighted to see whoever stood before me and the message from my heart was not missing.

Michael gave a wonderful speech, which was followed by one given by Kirstin. Experiencing my amazing daughter was always a wonderful surprise for me, and I felt so proud of her and her abilities.

I received a lot of compliments on my paintings and they were given with sincerity. Our friend Ron, God bless him, took one spin around the spacious gallery and then pulled out his checkbook and bought two paintings on the spot. My Chicago dealer materialized and expressed with great enthusiasm how much he liked the show. A messenger brought a huge bouquet of flowers from Lucy Ann, a former student. While I was searching for a vase, Julie handed me a gift of a garlic braid, a bottle of olive oil, and vinegar. Moira dropped a book into my hand and so it continued. I felt a lot of love and affection and kindness directed at us. Next, Alex gave an amazing and amusing speech, which left no doubt about what a rare creature he was. In his protective shade, I had grown these 30 years and I felt blessed for the warmth of love experienced that night. There was an abundance of light, kindness, and appreciation in the atmosphere around all of us. If only most exhibitions of art were so blessed, I thought, as I collected my coat before leaving.

The next day it really sank in what a show and what a gift of joy and appreciation the evening had been. Ron had bought two paintings, and now other people were catching up with him. There were phone calls, notes from several members of the faculty, and an amusing Stentor article by Liz, and the calls continued throughout the day. I felt I had received an abundance of gifts; such sudden wealth! It was almost unbelievable.

The book reports for my yoga certification were still not completed. I began to receive reminders from the Ashram to hurry up, that I had to complete this task. I continued to focus, often studying all day long and writing the reports at night. Increasingly, I sat back and meditated on the task and asked myself if I were actually doing this correctly. Gradually my conviction rose that I was not supposed to write an academic style paper on this spiritual material, but rather to pinpoint what my own understanding was, what I had discovered, what I had experienced. If I put my whole concentration on my intuitive understanding, the process was swift and easy. Every day, I spent time practicing the asanas and asking specific questions while in the poses. The answers came to me; some part of me gave information and advised me. How this happened I cannot tell—it was as if my mind split into a conscious part and a subconscious part. The answers or suggestions I received came from my Higher Being, my Subconscious. If I did not write it down immediately it evaporated as a dream dissolves upon waking.

One morning, I said to Alex, "My sister has probably managed to sell our Aunt Alma's house by now. I can feel it." I went to brush my teeth and she rang from Nairobi. She had sold the house and transferred the money to her sister-in-law in Washington; $25,000 was to go to me. I was amazed at my intuition! Quite a confirmation had come my way! I could actually trust my mind to know outcomes ahead of time and this meant I could know when to refrain from some action which might be unfavorable. This was an enormous gift if I took it seriously and lived by it.

I had just completed another book report when Kirstin came to talk to me. She was desperate. By now she was teaching a first grade class on the north side of Chicago, mostly African American children. Most of them were children of single teenage mothers. Quite a few were living with grandmothers; those were the lucky ones. Many came to school without proper clothes and without breakfast in their little tummies. The school lunch was perhaps the only meal they would get, but many ate it too fast, or it was too heavy for their systems and they vomited up the food as a consequence.

"I loved these kids when I first started, but now I feel they are unteachable and there isn't any discipline or interest in learning anything. I come home and head for the bathtub. There I sit drinking a beer, trying to calm down in the warm water and crying my eyes out. This is horrible and I hate it. People should have licenses before they are allowed to have babies." I tried to calm her down, without success. However, I did promise to help her out on some difficult occasions and to assist.

When Alex came home that evening, she told him she was quitting her first job as a teacher. "It is utterly horrible to have to spend time with such neglected human beings, especially if I can't help them." Alex talked about his start as a teacher in the Highlands of Scotland, obliged to teach the children of farmhands who smelled as if they had not had a bath in weeks. On rainy days it was especially bad. He had to learn to give them physical punishment, which was all they understood. And so, he learned to strike their outstretched hand with a leather belt. The first time he felt sick after hitting a child. His own parents had never ever given him physical punishment. "I know it is hard, but let me give you this advice," he said. "If somebody has to suffer, don't let it be you. My main concern is for you and at this point you have to overcome the obstacles; you cannot give up! By all means have a beer in the bathtub and cry, but do not allow defeat. You will become a superb teacher in time." He was right.

The next morning was my mother's birthday. She would have been 83 years old today. I did a little ritual with a bouquet of daffodils and placed it next to the sculpture of the Uma Goddess on my altar. I also scattered blossoms into the lap of Uma. The daffodils in the vase withered, but the blossoms in Uma's lap were still fresh two weeks later, even without water.

A Cloud of Darkness

In order to prepare the house for sale, we had several painting jobs to attend to—a bathroom, the annex to the kitchen, and a bedroom. Alex was loath to spend the little free time he had on such a chore and was constantly complaining. Once again, I was thrust face-to-face with his cigarette habit, for he smoked a whole carton in a day and a half. It was my lesson to learn not to object to the smoke and to allow him to live his life as he wanted to.

That evening, our neighbor Rick came over with a suggestion. He was a realtor and he had experience in that field, though he no longer sold houses. He offered to sell our place and suggested a value of $365,000, a price which appealed to Alex. Thus, Alex made a fast switch in giving Rick the chance to put our house on the market for the next three months. At the time it felt like a good decision with a profitable outcome, certainly better than that offered by the other realtors.

In the morning the house was on the market with a little sign beside the driveway entry. Rick and another realtor showed the house to 51 people, who walked through. At night someone from California called and wanted a chance to see the place. We got into our car and drove around for a bit, but by 7:15 pm the cars of the realtors were still in the driveway. We decided to walk in, as it was getting late. The house had a really nasty odor after all this humanity had crossed the threshold and I burnt a stick of incense, wondering if I could hold my center and stay focused and alert.

The next day I took my books and paperwork to the college, so that the house could be shown. By lunchtime, Rick informed us that people had been standing in line to get a look at the house. Later he came over to tell us there had been an offer. By evening, an agreement of $395,000 had been reached. The buyers planned to add on to the house and Thursday evening an inspection was to take place.

I felt very disturbed and weak, all without any reason. I managed to complete the latest book report and now only one book was left. When I cast a glance in the mirror at my reflection, I was startled at how tired I looked, and I decided I needed some fresh air and a walk. During the walk I contemplated the move, the sale by early June, the many shifts to come and the miracle of the high and fast sale of our house. In spite of this astonishing process, I seemed to be living under a cloud of darkness and a feeling of treachery and fear. I decided to withdraw into a lengthy meditation, which left me feeling as if I were living on two levels at the same time.

That evening, Jai and I taught a joint yoga class, which was lovely. It was a wonderful learning experience for me and as always, I felt uplifted; but in spite of this, in my soul I felt something awful was coming towards us. I waited for a dream, as so often dreams had given me a warning or an insight. It took two days before it came. An intense dream woke me. I saw myself losing Alex! Terror took hold of me. Now I knew how Alma had felt when Christian died. I told myself I had to stop fearing something that had not yet happened; after all, life was unpredictable. The next day, Alex was grading the final student papers of his art history classes. He broke his reading glasses and immediately went to the eye doctor to get replacement lenses. "You might have had a little stroke; the vision in the right eye is odd," he was told. The next step was an MRI. I stood and heard the words and my feelings were numb. I felt disconnected. I had received information about this in my dream and now angst manifested itself.

Rick phoned to let us know what had transpired with the house sale. He sounded very apologetic because the sale fell through. "These people came and behaved as though they had never seen the house before. It was quite unbelievable as they liked nothing about the place they had found so attractive on their first visit. I have never had such an experience before."

I was neither surprised nor disappointed. Their name was the sort of name that was eminently forgettable and did not stay in one's memory. I think Alex was disappointed. He had hoped for an easy and fast sale. My reaction was to put beautiful flower bouquets all over the house. One of the results of my yogic studies has been to learn to "surrender to the art of true listening." This meant "really focusing and listening to each person who talks to me so fully that I listen beyond the words." People talk to fill a vacuum, or they exaggerate to make themselves more impressive. After a while I could hear exaggerations and even lies.

I worried about Alex and his tendency not to share his fears or pains with me. We were blessed with a beautiful spring with abundant flowers everywhere. We used the opportunity to visit the Chicago Botanic Garden, as we were once again exiled from the house while it is being shown to new customers. I treasured this time spent with Alex and was grateful that he was actually willing to go for a walk.

15 A Health Challenge

Bad News

Alex had the MRI. I drove him to the hospital. It was a grey and rainy day. While he was in the MRI tube, I chanted a mantra. Then, I was told he was finished. He was completely disoriented and I helped him dress. The experience had been horrible for him, as he was very sensitive to sound. I drove us home and since both of us felt exhausted, we took a nap. The results of the MRI would be discussed with a neurosurgeon the following week.

The next day was the beginning of a weekend, and we had an invitation to drive to visit friends in Wisconsin who lived in a beautiful house overlooking a lake. It was a sunny spring day, and our young friends were impressive anthropologists who were able to have lively conversations. Ducks drifted along the shoreline followed by a chain of young ducklings. The white wine in beautiful slender glasses was superb. And then I saw Alex fall—fall backwards—and watched with instant concern wondering why—and what caused this. He was bruised and his spine was scraped. Ice bags and ointment appeared, and someone brought him a scotch to dull the pain. He got very drunk almost instantly. Fortunately, probably only I could tell how very drunk he was. His speech was unfocussed and slurred. I sat in the sun, soaking up the warmth, listening to the conversation and tried to feel beyond into the spaciousness of the lovely day. Back home that night, a call came from the hospital for Alex. The MRI showed a benign brain tumor located behind the right eye and pressing on the optical nerve. Brain surgery would be necessary or he would lose sight in his eye. Without surgery he would also lose the ability to walk.

The next day, from morning to night, people flowed in and out of the house. I had no time to stop and no time to think or to consider the news we had just received. All day I felt Alex and studied him from moment to moment. He was awake and very alert now and conscious of his vulnerable condition. He flowed with what fate dished out to him, while he smoked one cigarette after another. I felt profound compassion for him, but oddly no anxiousness.

Everything felt as if it were ordained to be just so. If I looked at anything long enough, it lost its objective reality. Nothing was fixed, nothing was permanent, and everything changed with the swish of a horse's tail, as some wise man once said. Alex was sterling—he accepted without self-pity. Probably the whisky and cigarettes were his crutch. At lunch time, for a brief moment, I felt frazzled and said, "I need a drink." But the drink had no taste, so I drank water instead. Another thing I did was to give Alex long back massages, hoping they had a healing effect. Later he confirmed that his back felt much better and the effect of the fall was lessening. In my hands I felt the need to use my energy through touch; it was almost like something giving me a little push and telling me I could help another through a force dormant in my hands.

Alex would soon celebrate his 65th birthday on May 13. This made me think about how it would be if I lost him. How would I live? His smell lingered beside me; his presence penetrated all parts of the house; his voice rang bell-like through the rooms. Our roots were totally interconnected. If he died, my life and being would be utterly destroyed. Decidedly, it was quite terrible and beyond, utterly beyond my imagination. I had no idea how I would be able to cope, and also, aside from my daughter, he was the only human being who really loved me. It was all too terrible to contemplate and I slipped into the lotus pose, seeking relief. For the first time I found the luminous inner center instantly. It was unchangeable and unaffected by circumstances and very wise-feeling. If I could only establish my mind in that core-state continuously! I still had so much to learn.

During the afternoon, we attended a luncheon at the college, followed by an invitation given by a wealthy student. Alex looked old and tired beyond his years. After he went to bed at night, I chanted and wept for over an hour. He might die, and even if he did not, 30 years of our life here in Lake Forest and, as teachers, were over.

He would have to take stock and do something with his habits and find a new way of living, with new interests and ambitions. Was he still flexible and strong enough to change? I felt unable to help him because he would not listen to me, which frustrated me. Was it his pride that stood in the way? I recalled how proud my mother had been, not sharing her pain with anyone, not letting her daughters know how she suffered with a heart condition. My mother was gone, and part of her pride had formed a barrier between us; neither of us revealed our vulnerability—she did not tell and I did not question.

Choices

Then, came the big day; a consultation with a neurosurgeon and an evaluation of the MRI. I drove us to the Evanston Hospital. A charming, super-smart doctor greeted us and rapidly explained the facts about the tumor. It was not cancerous, it was slow-growing, and surgery was the required method to remove the larger part. Not all of it was removable. It affected the optic nerve and was located behind the right eye. The surgery would last between 12 and 13 hours and be extremely sensitive. Chances of things going wrong were there; the result might be double vision or loss of movement on one side of the body. A week's stay in the hospital was required, two weeks recuperation at home, and the skull bone would require six weeks of healing time. A full physical examination was also recommended, just to know if the body would be able to take the strain of brain surgery. No part of the brain would be touched during the surgery. If Alex smoked, he would be required to give it up completely and immediately.

My head was sore as we drove back, probably from shock. Alex suggested lunch at a very elegant restaurant. I felt like saying, "I can't eat. I just want to sit in the sun!" However, I accepted the invitation as a nice idea and we enjoyed a very good lunch. My head still hurt when we got home and then I sat in the garden in the sun, chanting my mantra. Neither of us brought up the projected surgery, and neither of us felt like sifting through what promised to be a horrendous experience.

The next morning was one of those gorgeous days and I spent all morning planting flowers in the garden. What had once been an uncared-for ground had become covered with a carpet of color. It also was Alex's birthday. I awoke early and went to the kitchen to bake a birthday cake, which in spite of difficulties, turned out well—a subtle European strawberry cake. Then, surprise of surprises, a call from France, from Ildiko, wishing Alex a good start to retirement. Kirstin and Bill had extended a dinner invitation, and so we drove to their place in Highland Park. To our great surprise, Frances, her husband Gordon, and their baby Andrew suddenly emerged, and hardly had the greetings and hugs ended, when David and his wife Joyce drove up. Suddenly, Alex was surrounded by his grown children and their families.

It was a lovely evening, gentle late sunshine caressing the flowers and all these young people gathered here to celebrate Alex on his 65th Birthday. I felt sad for my mother and that Gabriele and I never made an effort to go see her on some special occasion, except for that get-together in Italy seven years ago. The following day, we were inundated with house guests, and I cooked a big lunch in my tiny kitchen. On such occasions, I often had to put pots on the floor for lack of space. The celebration was far from over, as we then returned to Kirstin's apartment for the evening.

Out of the back room a crowd of friends emerged. Bill cooked some wonderful things; the table was loaded with food and wine. Everyone seemed to have a great time. Mostly I sat still and listened, allowing the emotional waves to wash over me. Person after person came to chat. The wonderful thing is this surprise outpouring of love and affection for Alex, who stood there clearly moved by so much caring attention. I saw him and myself differently, somehow as very sensitive. Above all else, I saw what wonderful people we had raised, both children and our favorite students. Kirstin is a true heart-blossom; a giving person, kind and compassionate. Frances is full of energy, feeding and fed by all her contributions to life. David is a quiet, thoughtful force, a human being with dimension. He will achieve more, much more.

With surprise and gratitude, I noticed that, almost daily, old friends would show up or favorite former students we had not seen in years would suddenly drop by. It was most pleasant to see students from twenty years ago, and as the weather was so beautiful, we had almost daily luncheons in the garden under the blooming magnolia tree. Due to the changes in me, I was seeing so differently, noticing the human element of warmth and connection; inner tensions were recognized and frailties understood. Alex clearly cherished those contacts and I think the kindness of people supported his heart and soul.

One of these students was Wolf D., who had been buying my paintings and eventually had acquired the largest collection of my work. I talked to him for over 40 minutes one night, coming away with the conviction he was looking for the spiritual. Buying my paintings was part of this quest because he recognized something in them. The thought came to me that the energy was crossing over to him, that he was able to feel it. He told me I should start a school. My worry that I cannot transmit through teaching was perhaps unwarranted. I was also teaching several yoga classes per week at that time and my students seemed very satisfied and grateful.

Since we were both retiring from the Art Department and the college, a former student came to interview us for a newspaper. She asked Alex what his motive for life was. He answered her in the way Tosca from the Italian Opera by Verdi answers: "Vissi d'arte, vissi d'amore! I live for art, and I live for love!" When teaching, he said, he was transmitting a quality of life and a belief in being able to live with quality. Sadly, the young woman did not understand him.

In the days that followed, the strain and fear of the approaching brain surgery started to affect Alex. His mind was acting out his fears. One night he woke me, shouting: "Get away from me, leave me alone. You have deserted me because I have a hole in my head." I hugged him and told him he was safe, he was protected, as I held his shuddering body.

Samaras

Whenever time permitted, I would paint. One beautiful day followed the next and the lawn was thickly covered by the whirling samaras from our two huge maple trees. I loved the shapes of the samaras and created a composition for a large painting, which I finished rapidly. Kirstin claimed the painting later on and to this day it hangs in her living room.

Alex had received all the dates for his upcoming surgery. Frances wanted to be here to help in any way she could, which was brave of her. Alex obstinately avoided cutting back on his smoking. "I am not going to die from smoking cigarettes," he insisted. He showed how vulnerable he was and how this self-indulgent habit was taking his strength. He had to go into hospital for a chest x-ray and a heart examination. I caught myself worrying about what else they might find and if there were any hidden problems we did not even suspect. Then I caught my negative thinking and questioned where that came from. Soon, I knew I was right, for Alex knew of something else and refused the examination proposed by the doctor. The tests were beginning and I could smell his fear. He withdrew and had naps. I felt myself withdrawing as well, making the excuse that he wanted privacy. I remember sitting in an armchair and suddenly realizing he was desperate, lonely, and frightened. I went upstairs and hugged him instead, breaking his isolation while holding him so the tears he needed to release flowed freely.

The day we dreaded approached. By nine in the morning, we were at the hospital. Alex became soft-looking, almost as though wounded. Feeling his vulnerability, I held his hand. All day I sat while he lay resting after the angiogram. Half his groin was shaved, while a savage red mark showed where the tube had been pushed into the artery. The thought of the coming brain surgery made me feel sick, but I could see the right eye bulging out a bit from the pressure of the tumor behind it. So perhaps this was a grace we needed to be grateful for, that this tumor can be operated on. I faced my distress in the cafeteria and my sudden sense of futility and lost direction. I observed my feelings as they faded and became just passing clouds. The sensation of inner discomfort was based on having nothing to hold onto, nothing solid. Nothing is permanent.

I had to remain strong for him. The following afternoon, Frances arrived from Canada. I stayed quiet and centered. Alex was flowing into acceptance and indifference to most things. An inner concern was displacing the outer. Even though I did a lot of cooking and clearing dishes, I still had plenty of energy. The last day went by quickly, calls came steadily, and it rained nonstop. Alex was remote, self-controlled, and I felt his soreness. I hugged his body at night, feeling the frail remoteness. Of course, he still smoked and I could smell the foul odor of the tumor. Perhaps I could smell the fear as well. Whatever it was, it was a bad, vile odor. I prayed for him. All was projected onto Alex and his upcoming surgery and for a positive outcome.

Bill came and made a wonderful Tex-Mex dinner for everyone and even though I didn't feel like eating, I enjoyed it. Alex smoked several cigarettes and seemed withdrawn. Oddly, the insights I received now gave me a very different picture of the evolution of consciousness in life. In my vision, the outer level is taken care of so well there is no need to even think about it. No identification with the outer level is significant. The growth of anything starts with a tiny, inner seed. I needed to surrender and I needed to flow with all events, whatever may manifest.

The next day, the alarm went off at dawn and we all piled into the car. Alex smoked his last cigarette. I could feel his state of mind and the self-control he exerted. At the hospital they came with the wheelchair and he disappeared down the long hallway. We gathered together in the yellow waiting room, expecting a long day. The surgery was to last at least thirteen hours. I felt him, as if he were floating around. Could the physical boundaries which we so believe in be a delusion? He must have been sedated by then, yet he was there in the same space I was in. The volunteer lady who handled the visitors in the waiting room kept asking me: "And what is your relationship?" My relationship was to his spirit and to his inner being. At 10:10 am, she came to tell us he had just gone into surgery, which meant they had prepared him for two hours. By noon, Kirstin, with aggressive anguish, demanded lunch. Bill had been asleep in the car this whole time. We drove around and around for 30 minutes looking for a restaurant called Carmen. Kirstin was desperate, as she suffered from low blood sugar, while Bill was bad-tempered. I felt fed up with his lack of self-control and level of self-indulgence. We ended up in a Mexican place with one tire deflating. Bill took the car to have the tire pumped up so we could drive it; however, once he returned to the restaurant, he refused the food there and had lots of beer instead.

Back in the hospital, the hours crawled by and it was eight o'clock when I smelled a beautiful perfume. I had asked Swami Radha to help us, and, for a brief span of time I could feel a connection. She, too, sent gift waves, healing vibrations. Suddenly, all the tension was gone and a sensation of lightness came. Frances and Kirstin were playing cards and were in high spirits, laughing and teasing each other. It was then I knew things had gone well. My heart felt as if a big weight had been shifted away and that this meant Alex had been given back to life.

At 10:30 pm, the surgeon appeared. Alex was fine; the operation was successful. Some of the tumor around major blood vessels and nerves had been left. If it was a normal tumor it would just be watched; some other type of tumor might need radiation. He would need to sleep a lot to assist the healing. He was to be in the hospital for a week. We would be able to see him in another half hour or so. It was 11 pm, and my heart felt like a punching bag. I felt raw with a strange pain. His loneliness and the period ahead felt unreal; I was actually standing on a shifting surface without any security left, except within.

Eventually, at 12:30 am, Frances and I were admitted into intensive care and we watched Alex being wheeled into a room. He was not awake. We told the nurse who we were and she said we could come, two people at a time, to visit with him. We entered the room. His right eye looked swollen and a draining tube projected from his shaven skull, exuding pink fluid. A machine monitoring his heartbeat was attached to his chest. The chest looked thin and white. Alex opened unseeing eyes and groaned. His legs and arms moved. He looked uncomfortable, fed up physically, pained. He tried to raise his head, just as Frances said; "We love you. You are all right." He began to thrash, this time urgently and with determination. I could almost hear him say: "I want out of here. Get me up." Later, Frances said, "The fighting spirit in him was strong." I held his hand, but he could not feel mine. He was like an inchoate organism of energy struggling to gain clarity and purpose. He looked absolutely terrible—desperate, fighting, and determined to get up.

A nurse slapped a cool bandage on his head. He groaned as if in terrible pain and sank back. My poor, poor Alex! It was with great force of will that I decided he was not dying and not gone yet. He had been tortured from 8 am in the morning until 11:30 at night; how could an organism stand this? What damage would come to the soul? His mind understood what his body endured. Kirstin and Bill came, took one look at him, and ran. I only saw their backs as they disappeared. "They are too upset," said Frances. The nurses were very helpful, giving me a phone number. I had trouble driving back; I tried to go through a red light. Frances was most helpful and I was grateful for her company. When we got back, we both had a stiff drink and talked until two in the morning. It was a long day, indeed.

The sun came out and it promised to be a warm June day, but when we came to the hospital and the intensive care unit, we entered the twilight zone. When my eyes became accustomed to the dim light and I found Alex, I saw he was wired for everything: oxygen into the nose, an IV and all the monitoring devices possible, a cathedra to the bladder, even restraints on both arms. It amounted to modern torture devices. His right eye drooped and seemed too small and unfocussed. He was irritated and weak. His first request was to be rid of the restraining hand cuffs, then the oxygen, which he claimed were glasses. Then he wanted the index finger clip, which monitored his breathing, off, and finally, the catheter bothered him terribly. One by one these were removed; however, the job of peeing into a plastic gourd-bottle was not possible. Eventually he explained to the nurse, "I am a man, I can only pee standing up erect." A nurse appeared to assist in this effort. While the nurses held him upright, I played "water music" with the water tap. All this eventually did the trick and he could pee.

His next ambition was to "go home, now!" It reminded me of the plight of the geriatric patients in Scotland whose main and constant refrain had been, "I want to go home! I want to go home!" Eventually, it dawned on me that it was the irritating finger-clip he complained about, the one that measured his breathing. Damage to his lungs had reduced the expansion capacity of his lungs. The nurses gave him what they called a toy, a little tube which sent up a little ball every time he exhaled.

A monitor sounded an alarm when his breath went below the acceptable range of 90. I noted that his behavior was then most irritable and restless. He became angry whenever I encouraged him to practice his breathing and he refused to obey. Fortunately, the nurses got the results they asked for. A nurse told him straight to his face that he had damaged his lungs. "I like to smoke," he told her. "I can see you won't quit," she told him when leaving the room. I sat holding and massaging his feet, which relaxed him and even put him to sleep. He often said, "What a life," and moaned. Clearly his whole nervous system was extremely irritated and weak.

Lesson of the Day

I wondered if Alex would learn the lesson of today: humility and patience. I sat there quietly, feeling quite content, knowing this was the only place I truly wanted to be. There were no wants, no desires, only the beeps of machines, the noises of moaning patients, retching, howls of pain mingled with music from a TV, cartoons, and nurses' voices. As an environment it was very loud, filled with bustle and life. I left him after five o'clock, which was hard, but I realized I needed to refuel my own being.

It was a blessing that Kirstin and Bill had invited me to dine with them that night. I returned just in time to avoid the downpour of rain, which continued all night with lots of thunder and lightning and magnificent birdsong at five in the morning. I barely slept, and in my drifting state between sleep and wakefulness, I wondered if Alex would ever be all right again. Then my held-back tears came like a waterfall. I watched my mind with interest, aware of the swings from extreme to extreme and the inner witness observing this play of contrasts.

The next day was very hard. Alex showed personality changes to a frightening degree. He became a powerful ego—cold, determined, and without sensitivity. "Get my dressing gown. I am going downstairs for a drink." With those words he bullied his way into the hallway, restlessly in search of the elusive scotch, curious like a little boy, and difficult to control.

When Frances, Kirstin, and Bill arrived, he dressed all of us down, accusing us of neglect and letting him down. The staff explained to me that this behavior was normal after head surgery, but despite this explanation, I saw a layer manifesting in Alex that I did not know, an alien, selfish layer of domineering arrogance. He swore and called the nurses "proles." The food was rotten and where were those damned cigarettes we had hidden from him? He was like a spoiled three-year-old.

It was good I stayed late. His arm had swollen and was hot to the touch and very sore. Yet nothing was done in spite my requests. He was uncooperative and would not eat his food. Mostly he wanted his cigarettes and alcohol; probably his withdrawal symptoms were starting. This was when it became crystal clear to me that I did not wish to be an accomplice to his self-destructive behavior. If he did not change his ways, I would have to stay firm, and if necessary, leave him. I had a choice to make, just as Alex had to choose a different behavior in the immediate future; and my choice had become both clear and defined. Everything was assisting him to change his ways and take the steps towards a major transformation.

One of the doctors asked to talk to me. I left the room, and in the hallway, he asked me how much Alex drank habitually. I understated the amount. The doctor said, "This is the reason for his confusion, at least in part. He is an alcoholic and suffering from withdrawal symptoms." Would Alex have been shocked to be told he was an alcoholic? I returned to the room and Frances joined me. Alex began to pester both of us with requests for cigarettes. I told him bluntly that they had found he had emphysema and that he could never smoke again. He refused to believe this.

Frances and I talked gently to him all day long, supporting and comforting him. She stroked his arm and I stroked his leg because I sat at the end of the bed. His right eye had swollen shut. The head bandages had been taken off. A clean cut ran across his shaved head and eighteen stitches marked the operation site. There was severe bruising around his eye.

He told us that last night after we left, he got dressed to go home. They stopped him and told him to put on his nighty and go back to sleep. "I have not been ordered around like this since I was in the British army," he said. I went to the nurse to check if what he had told us was really true, and apparently it was. He had come out of his room, having detached his IV, with no notion that he looked terrible. He claimed that he needed to go out for "a drink and some fags" and that he despised this hotel because of the very poor service. The nurses thought he was very funny. He also wanted his hat. Later in the day, the doctor came and gave him a little knitted skull cap to keep his head warm. We left after 6 pm after extracting the promise that he would not try to run away again.

Back at home, a call came from David, and Frances talked to her brother, trying to explain to him how their father was doing. David seemed to be unable to understand the magnitude of the 13-hour surgery and what his father went through. He seemed to think Alex should be permitted to smoke. Frances gave him a piece of her mind before hanging up.

Party Time

That night, after the house became quiet, I went upstairs. Our bedroom looked out over the back of the garden, a long stretch of green merging into bushes and old fruit trees at the end where an old fence defines the boundary of our property. The night was filled with the sounds of creatures—frogs and squirrels—and then suddenly, from the next property, I heard laughter, cocktail glasses clinking, someone singing, an announcement over the loudspeaker, and a dance starting.

I sat on the floor in front of the open window, tired, all energy spent, listening to life, as I sat in the dark. A great weariness engulfed me and the contrast between the happy party and my exhausted mind and heart felt as vast as the universe of stars beyond the window. I crumbled into a little pile of misery and mourned the end of what had been and might never heal and never return. My life, as it had been with Alex, was over; I knew this with absolute certainty. This was the beginning of the end. A kindness was being shown to me; the process would be slow and gradual. I was being given space to accept the inevitable. Something in me was not affected, a part of me that witnessed, simply observing the manifestation of changes happening, and that part was remaining calm and serene.

I thought of a line by the great German writer Johann Wolfgang von Goethe: "Es sei wie es wolle, es war doch so schoen! Be it as it may be, it was so beautiful!" It was a mature insight by a great mind and it reverberated within me, much like a sudden understanding. The yogis refer to Purusa as a quiet, changeless part within us, which is also called the Inner Witness that watches and observes the activities passing through our mind and heart. For a year now, I had been studying so many spiritual books and writing book reports, all of which enabled me to see the effect it was having on my life and inner responses. I was actually able to connect to a deep inner part, to an inner truth, to a motionless calmness that saw clearly. There was no fear, there was no upheaval, and there was nothing but the music and laughter and sounds of night birds.

When I went to the hospital the next day, Alex seemed better, but remote. I felt cut off. He was in his own world. He felt impatient with the slowness of time as it passed. The neurosurgeon came to check on him, and I saw Alex trying to impress him. He began to sparkle with energy and stories, with humor and anecdotes. I realized that this was his way of fishing for approval and trying to get power over a situation. Alex was given assignments at the conclusion. He was asked to walk four times around the intensive care department and to eat his meals while sitting in a chair. It was explained to him that no drugs were prescribed at all at this time because his brain was so vulnerable and sensitive and anything like smoke or alcohol or drugs to control pain were counter-indicated. The doctor's other request was that Alex make sure he avoided all excitement. Anything amounting to disturbance was to be strictly avoided. This included TV. "Keep him emotionally cool," the doctor instructed me. "No excitement." Later in the day, Kirstin came with a big packet of French fries, much to her father's intense delight. He had lost four pounds, and since the hospital food was not appealing, he refused to eat it. Before leaving, Kirstin turned to me, wrapping her arms around me and sobbing: "I want my daddy back. I just want my daddy back. This is not my daddy. I want my daddy back again."

Frances went back to Canada that afternoon, and before leaving, took some photos of Alex. The images actually looked better than reality, less horrific. I felt very grateful for her wonderfully sensitive support and for coming to help, and I got rather tearful as she departed.

After a week, Alex seemed better, but nonetheless, I called the neurosurgeon's office and arranged for a consultation. I felt I needed help if I was expected to take care of Alex. In fact, I even felt he needed to be under the attention of a psychologist. In Alex I recognized a secret and truculent streak of resistance. His eyes, at least to me, looked vacant. I interpreted that dead look as being the sign of an absence within. "There is no one home!" The demand for cigarettes had not stopped. I tried very hard to watch myself and to stay aware, only speaking when necessary. However, when he again began to pester me with the command to get him cigarettes, I told him I would leave him if he smoked again. He was furious. After that we did not talk. He refused to eat the food I made and brought to the hospital, eating only the ham I had purchased. They were giving him steroid pills, as I later discovered, and the doctor said they made him truculent. Their purpose was to reduce swelling of the brain. A recent change was that Alex dozed off quite frequently. He was asleep when the doctor came in and asked me to step into the hallway.

The doctor explained how concerned he had been about the possible complications caused by the bad shape Alex's lungs were in. He held out little hope that Alex would quit smoking. He also voiced concern about Alex's drinking, insisting the alcohol intake had to be controlled until he was really healed. I asked how could I possibly cope with Alex's stubborn self-indulgence? He indicated that if I could not cope, psychiatric help would be the only alternative. However, the health insurance companies resisted such a solution and often declared it unnecessary. He promised to lay down the law, "German style," tomorrow. I was to call him instantly if Alex disobeyed. I was relieved by his assurances. He also advised a nicotine patch for Alex's addiction. As he talked to me, I noticed that he expressed himself in a direct way without trying to simplify his vocabulary.

Kirstin and Bill came, bringing a shrimp dinner for Alex. Later on, my close friend Beverly came to the hospital as well. She had flown in from California and stayed talking to me until eight o'clock, which was a great gift. That night Frances called to tell me of a teacher in her son's school who had the same surgery and also went through the delusions and traumas Alex experienced. It went on for weeks and weeks. The bones of the skull take six months to knit. She advised me to call David if I had trouble and ask him to come and help.

Release from Hospital

Upon Alex's release from the hospital, the doctor told us that he would need three full months minimum in order to return to full strength. There was not to be any booze or smoking, no mental strain of any sort like studying or reading, no excitement, no driving, and no going out. The doctor suggested the nicotine patch for control over cravings. Alex assured him he didn't need the patch and would quit without such an aid.

On the way home we had to pick up a prescription at Walgreens. When I came to the pharmacy, I parked the car, asking Alex to wait for me. Before I jumped out, he casually said, "Get me a couple of packs of cigarettes." He was furious that I refused and came back empty-handed. As we drove through familiar, deeply shaded, winding roads towards our home, I gently tried to explain that I could not and would not be able to buy him cigarettes, which, after all, had now become the tools of self-destruction for him. I loved him and wanted him healthy and alive. My conscience would not allow me to do otherwise. If he smoked again, I would leave him. I was firm and meant every word I uttered.

Once at home, his discontent continued. He barely ate any food. He searched for bottles of whisky or wine, but we had taken all temptations out of the house. Then he went for a nap and the rest of the day was calm. Many people phoned him, which really helped. Since I had a lot of work, I was genuinely tired and worn out by ten o'clock that night.

During the nights he was restless and he often had nightmares, which woke him up very early. Studying him, I realized he was in denial mode. His short-term memory was not good, and he constantly asked me for confirmation. This problem must be very upsetting for such an intelligent man, particularly as he appeared to understand his predicament. He worried me. He looked as if his light had gone out. He seemed like a hollow person. Where was his mind? He refused to talk to me, and so I determined we needed to consult with the neurosurgeon.

Alex pulled himself together for this visit; he even began to speak, but with a voice lacking the usual full power of expression. Before I could contribute anything to the conversation, Alex had managed to impress the doctor and actually convinced him of his improvement. "Yes, of course doctor, I always am ready to agree to go for a walk." However, when I suggested a walk, he always just said, "No."

It would be easy for me to go on a guilt trip, to take this burden onto myself, asking if I had failed him. Was I using the wrong approach? However, when I asked him questions, no answer was given. His eyes were dull, defeated-looking. His right eye looked much smaller than the left. He had not smoked and said it did not bother him. I suspect he resented me for not letting him smoke. He had a glass of wine, but took two sips and claimed it tasted disgusting. Sometimes I felt heartbroken for him, for all he used to enjoy was gone and no new pleasures had replaced the old. I was at a loss as to how to stimulate his mind. He often looked like his mother did just before she died, attention turned inward, all else shut out.

Meeting Amachi

My yoga students had invited me to join them for an excursion to meet an Indian female saint called Amachi, a Mahatma. She was called the "hugging saint," as she embraced people and would fill them with love. Kirstin and Bill came to entertain Alex during my absence. Ann, Alice, and I drove to the Chicago suburb of Lemont to experience this saint who was giving darshan. Amachi was a small woman with a clear complexion and was open-faced, luminous, and solidly powerful. Her whole being radiated illumination. She shared this quality by hugging a huge crowd of people, person after person without interruption, all night long. This event took place in a many-tiered Hindu temple that was hidden behind beautiful old trees. There were hundreds of people, all sorts, all sizes and types, some beautiful-looking men and women, and children with lambent eyes. All evening, I was deeply absorbed by the event—the chants, the music, the spiritual atmosphere. Present was humanity in all its colors and variety. The event was like a step back into my past, into what I knew in Egypt—mystery and magic. It was exotic and wondrous and fully absorbing.

Most of the time we were waiting for our turn to come up to the dais for the embrace of Mother, as she was called. She was seated on a stage between two giant fans with colorful silk saris hung up behind her. Dressed in gold silk with a crown on her head, she was a representation of Prakriti or Shakti. I saw her whole body constantly vibrating, which amazed me. She existed in some force field, or so I assumed. One by one, people walked up to her, to be warmly hugged and embraced. She held people and stroked their backs and blessed them. She gave off a kind of loving energy. People beamed or smiled broadly or cried or staggered and stumbled away after their embrace from Mother. It was said that they were given unconditional love. As I approached her, I felt bolder, less timid, and more assured. Once I had stepped onto the platform, I felt the vibration reaching me. Her followers sat around her.

For hours and hours radiating Shakti, she just hugged and hugged, afterwards handing out chocolate kisses and filling the air with rose scent. I folded my hands in Namaste position as I approached her and was surprised as she firmly pulled me towards her chest. I said: "Om namah Shivaya," and found my face pressed hard into her cool silk-covered arm and shoulder. I waited for fireworks, but all I felt was an empowerment and joy, assurance, and inner strength, as she murmured "Ma, Ma, Ma" repeatedly into my ear. A strong perfume of roses filled my nose, and I felt centered and peaceful as she let go of me. In my hand I clutched a foil wrapped chocolate kiss, and her scent was in my awareness and it stayed with me for days and days. In fact, anytime I thought of her, the scent of roses returned.

Like Swami Radha five years ago, she treated me as an equal. I looked into her eyes and she looked back into mine. She was all smiles and joy, and I was convinced she knew no fear. As she let go of me, I felt strength surge through me. Her gift felt familiar, like something I had experienced before. She left some essence with me, aside from the scent of roses. I recalled the stories I had heard about the Italian monk Padre Pio, who also was recognized by the scent of violets or roses.

The drive back to Lake Forest was fast as the women chatted and I was quiet. I reflected with gratitude on this strange experience and on Swami Radha, whose teachings made such an encounter with Ama possible.

Coming home, I saw the joyless expression on Alex's face. I felt emboldened, felt more like me and more detached from the difficulties in my present reality. "Let's go for a walk," I said to Alex. He did not want to, but I paid no attention to his mood. The day was beautiful, sparkling, clear and dry, and so I took him to the lake for a longer walk. He looked sullen, old, and tired. There seemed to be no joy, no emotion left in him. His energy levels must be very low, and I assumed he felt depressed, but he denied this.

When we returned home, I switched on the radio. The great pianist Alfred Brendel was talking about the Diabelli Variations, which he was about to play on the piano, plus Beethoven, Handel, and Mozart pieces. The lecture was brilliant and the humor and jokes delightful. Alex listened silently for a while; then he asked me if I could understand what Brendel said. I said, "Yes!" Then, I realized his mind could not grasp the lecture nor the musical jokes. How utterly depressing this must be for him to find his brilliant mind now incapable of understanding something that was easy for him prior to his brain surgery!

As I thought about it later, I realized his mind had been diminishing for quite a while, even before he had this surgery. I went and chanted my mantra as he slept. I hoped his mind would return to its former potential and his life force would as well. Should it remain absent, then I have lost him even as his body remains. So far, he has not demonstrated feelings, self-concern, or interest in anything. He is taciturn, sullen, and cold; this was how I saw it. All energy and joy have disappeared from him. I panicked most of the day, trying not to write to friends, trying not to give in to a cry for help. Both his older children phoned in the course of the morning, which made him happy. Still, I did not stay fully in control of my mind, and I often felt like bursting into tears. I must not react to Alex nor respond to his irritation and gloom. He is so fragile that I must not add to his irritation. Undoubtedly, this is a lesson in how to surrender my ego and my need for love and acceptance. I told myself to see reality clearly for what it is and to accept all that comes, just as it is.

Conflict

Then I felt the flu in my bones and I became ill with a nasty cough and fever, head congestion, and a sore inside, and, all this in beautiful weather. I spent parts of the day lying in the garden, thinking and re-evaluating. Where was I going? My US citizenship had come through and we would have to drive to the Chicago Federal Building to go through the ceremony with hundreds of other lucky immigrants. We started off at dawn in the rain with steady traffic congestion, which meant it took us two hours to get to the Federal Building. Somehow, I was guided to a parking lot. The courtroom was dark and filled with foreigners excited about getting their citizenships. Now I would finally be an American with all the rights. The ceremony dragged on and Alex became tired and irate. Then to my shocked surprise, Alex insisted he was going to drive us back. "Alex, you are not allowed to drive yet, please obey the rules the doctors gave you. Your brain is still fragile, your skull bone still open, and you are not supposed to have any excitement."

Yoga class in Ramona's art studio in Lake Forest, 1970's

We argued, and argued, his will against mine. I had to pull out every ounce of stubborn resistance I was capable of. Finally, I persuaded him not to sit in the driver's seat and ended up driving both of us onto the expressway and back home.

In order to save my sanity and allow him his own ways, I made the decision not to interfere with him. I decided not to force him on walks and not to correct him or to concern myself with his choices. Identification with another being and forcing that person to do something only brings pain. Thirty years with him was over—a different dawn had come. A night came, in which Alex surprised me and got drunk again! I felt so tired and dispirited I did not even chant my mantra. Some days later he complained of heartburn, but it looked more like heart pain to me. He was so exhausted that he fell asleep in the armchair. My intuition warned me not to interfere. Slowly my flu abated. As soon as I was well, I decided to strip and varnish the dining room floor. This drove Alex to the library, which was probably really good for him.

A next visit with the brain surgeon brought further warnings about the possibility of regrowth of the tumor and the negative effect of radiation treatment on the brain. I heard intuitively what the doctor did not say: "I hope this will never happen."

Since we had retired from the college, and as I was no longer teaching there, I found myself emptying out my office and clearing up my studios. I had loved teaching art and that was over now. I also had an obligation to fix the house up for the next potential buyers the realtor would bring. I remained grateful the house had not sold earlier, as it would have been terrible not to have a home during the time of the surgery and after.

I began to focus fully on the yoga classes I offered and on my many friends who took them. An upstairs bedroom was turned into a yoga studio and soon the atmosphere there felt very spiritual. I used the space for my mantra chanting and meditation, as well as my hours of daily studies. Alex liked the Chicago Botanic Garden, and to my great relief we would drive there and walk through the beautiful grounds. The love put into the growth of the plants radiated back from every flower; the colors affected and soothed the heart and soul. There were wild geese floating on the lagoon, insects humming, and birds singing, and the peace found there registered in the face of every visitor. I noticed the change and the transformation in Alex, and that he was grateful. My efforts were now focused on giving Alex the healing time he needed and giving him constructive, enjoyable tasks, such as meeting with friends and acquaintances.

With this, Kirstin and Bill were a wonderful help, as they drifted by with friends in tow, often bringing dinner or stimulation. David, too, pleased us by calling long distance for chats with his father. Many visitors came during the afternoon hours and sat in the garden with Alex, which made me realize how many friends he has and that Alex was used to being the big professor, advising students, lecturing, and guiding and helping young people. He liked and needed contact; it stimulated him and he loved to talk. Perhaps the sense of not having a purpose in life was also causing a depression.

The summer felt spent and autumn light brought a sparkling cool day. I felt cramped, inhibited, and restless. Somehow my days just flew away. Writing to friends at the Ashram helped to clear my mind. On another day, Alex became drunk by noon, even though I had his lunch in front of him within 30 minutes. However, even as I said nothing, it disturbed me how quickly he changed. Sometimes I wondered what I was doing. One night, we went to a party of mostly young people. Alex held court, knowing all the right comments and relying on his heart's language. He still had a brilliant mind, but why the self-destructive behavior? I felt that there was no lasting fulfillment. I could not control or own, plan, or direct a thing. All was just a shifting pattern. All was an end or a beginning, endlessly circling. Everything was dissolving, nothing solid was left. There was no sense of reference to where I was, standing or floating. Everything just passed through me. I had begun to understand the Buddhists. "It is our search for perfection outside ourselves that causes our suffering," said the Buddha.

Since Alex could not work, it was my job to go to the college to clear his books out. For three hours I boxed his books in the basement. We also decided to put the house back on the market. There was still some work to be done on the house to put it in the best possible shape. I worked too hard, and the strain was beginning to affect me. At this point, an old friend, Carolyn, invited me to go camping with her in the woods. What a wonderful idea, particularly since I had never camped in the USA or experienced nature in Illinois. I had been hoping for this experience for years.

At noon, people came to view the house, which meant we had to leave and spend some time away, probably at Starbucks.

Was I ready to shed this house and ready to become a gypsy? I would see how it felt to be in the woods for two days. Again, I fought some guilt at leaving Alex, but on the other hand, I would be better off not being a clinging vine.

The two days in Wisconsin with Carolyn made me feel relaxed, refreshed, and peaceful. Since she was one of my yoga students, we talked a lot about spiritual topics and practiced hatha yoga at dawn for two hours. In the evenings we chanted mantras. Those days were perfect—inspiring and wholesome. I wondered if it was a gift she gave to me or a gift from the Divine for both of us. Again, I encouraged her to visit Yasodhara Ashram, and our time together might have been a necessary encouragement.

To my great delight, Alex looked wonderful on my return. Because of the brain surgery, the college had not yet given Alex a farewell party after his many years of service. The president of the college invited us to his home for a speech and official farewell. A crowd of familiar faces greeted us, lots of faculty and lots of drinks, and then Alex received the gift of a plaid scarf and a photograph of a painting of his great-grandfather, the Reverend Alexander F. Mitchell, who had been a professor of divinity at St. Mary's College, St. Andrews, from 1848 to 1868. A number of other faculty members were celebrated and only when all was said and done, they realized that I had been overlooked. The president's wife lifted a just purchased new plant off the table and with a big smile thanked me for my 25 years as a teacher of art.

We were the last to leave, and Alex, with drink taken, continued at home. Though he said nothing, I was certain he was deeply disappointed with his gift. In Europe, such occasions provided a gold wrist watch or some other token of value and appreciation. There were other disturbing manifestations as well. He often slept very poorly and suffered nightmares. Thrashing around restlessly, he would shout: "Leave me alone, stop, get away from me," as if in great distress. When I would question him then and there, he would say, "They did such horrible things to me; they smashed and beat in my skull."

However, when I mentioned his shouts in the morning, he would deny that he recalled anything of his brain surgery. The constant repetition of being chased by a crowd of assailants in his sleep convinced me that some part of his mind did recall the surgery. He agreed eventually and stated it was better to put the whole event behind him. I replied that it seemed to me he put the event underground, which made it come up nightly from his subconscious mind. This made him irritated and impatient, and he claimed I treated him like a moron.

The house being on the market again meant frequent viewings and the need to be out of our home. I found a beautiful prairie fragrant with wildflowers for our walks. Alex insisted it smelt like an open sewer as he walked stiffly through this lovely meadow. Was this truly Alex? Perhaps I have fooled myself all my married life, believing him to be sensitive. Much of him was now indifferent to beauty. The rift between us was growing, and so far, the change in his personality had not budged an inch. The neurosurgeon had assured me he would regain his former personality in time, but when? I was increasingly becoming more restless and frustrated. What supported me were my yoga practice and the kindness of my yoga students.

I was also still teaching yoga with Jai at the chapel in the college; sometimes we had huge numbers of students. Sometimes his wife taught with him and I learnt a great deal from both of them, as the effect of their classes was truly uplifting. My mood after a yoga class would often be turned 180 degrees, and I would feel joyful and light, no matter what the prior circumstances had been. Life still could look blessed. Looking at the situation with Alex and the effect it had on our relationship, I see a greater understanding and independence in myself. Now I was able to enter deeper states of consciousness daily and know how to get there to experience the reality of this other dimension.

Though I have tried to explain some of this to Alex, he did not understand. What attracted me to him were his solid honesty, reliability, intelligence, character, and artistic sensitivity, quite aside from his joyfulness, humor, and charm. For these I admired him. From my palm reading I could conclude that even if the tumor did not regrow, a return to the former fullness of life would not be possible anymore. In fact, it would be best just to live every day to the fullest and to forgo any expectations about what the future held.

Cozumel

I determined it would be good to take Alex out of the circumstances in which he now lived and go to the seaside for a spring break. Kirstin, who was unhappy with Bill, wanted to join us and became very helpful in persuading her father that he needed a change. We chose to go to the island of Cozumel in Mexico. I found a little Mexican seaside hotel among the numerous high-rise hotels catering to tourists and felt this would be the right choice. Cozumel was once an important pilgrimage center of the ancient Mayans, who came to the island seeking to honor Ix Chel, the goddess of fertility. Now it was a favorite resort destination.

To make this decision even sweeter, one of my large paintings sold, and I did not have to ask for money to pay for the trip. I visualized a sun-drenched tropical beach and becoming one with this luminous place. Mostly I wanted the hotel to be comfortable, and I visualized the mood of the place in my mind. When we finally drove into the grounds, it was like Kenya revisited—palm-thatched roofs, tropical growth, brilliant colors, blue sparkling ocean, and sand of the softest texture. The buildings were open and spacious, and we sat in the restaurant under an open roof. A delicious meal at four in the afternoon was followed later by a refreshing swim among tropical fish. It was perfect for what I wanted Alex to experience.

I awoke in the morning to wind stirring the palm fronds, rattling the leaves, brilliant red blossoms of bougainvillea outside, and the sound of chirping. Aware of Kirstin in the bed beside us, of Alex still asleep next to me, I felt the manifestation of the love and faith between us all. It was a lovely day, and mostly we sat on the beach reading and resting. Many native people walked past, small, dark-skinned Mayans coming for a day of swimming, since it was Sunday. At night we took a cab to the town center, which brought us face-to-face to the vitality of humanity. All that energy of the little town of San Miguel surrounded us like a dream. A band of musicians, dancing children, and an anteater appeared, and vendors sold special foods. Girls looked lovely in their lace dresses, and a dog tried to get us to adopt him. We had dinner in a recommended restaurant before returning. Later on, the empty beach, I looked up at the drifting white clouds in the night sky. Clusters of luminous stars were moving behind the clouds. Both clouds and stars were in motion, but oddly it looked as if the stars were moving and the clouds were stationary. The Eternal looked transitory.

In the morning I found a new, better spot for my yoga practice under some shady trees. Later, the hotel informed me a fax had come from our realtor. I had specifically asked her not to bother us on our holiday, but she was applying pressure. I found myself totally indifferent to the urgency of the message. The house was being undervalued because of some possible problem with the narrow lot. Thinking positively meant befriending a positive attitude. Certainly $320,000 is just not enough, and that was exactly what I let the realtor know.

Kirstin and I dragged Alex to the beach for a swim, but he found the water too cold. He was resistant to even trying to get his feet wet, which was sad. We walked to an area where it was fairly quiet and one could see the most beautiful tropical fish floating just under the surface like ghosts, each fish with its own expression on its face. It was a magical world which we felt eager to investigate, and so Kirstin and I rented face masks and snorkels and spent hours in the water.

By the next day, we all began to show symptoms of illness. People had warned us to be careful not to pick up a cold or the flu on the airplane. I was grateful to be on this tropical island and allowed my fever to take its course as I lay on the beach, reading. A friend had given me a book on visualization and I was painting my dream house in Santa Fe in my mind's eye, noting all important details, such as the feeling of cool tiled floors and seeing the portals supported by carved, wooden columns, the earth-colored stucco walls, the direction the house faced, and the general landscape.

Also, to make it even more detailed, I drew a crude picture of my Santa Fe house. Years later I came across the drawing among my diary notes; the house we eventually bought even had a deck on top of the dining room, just as I had imagined. Later on, when we returned to Santa Fe to look at available houses, the house I really liked did not seem to be like the one I had imagined. My fantasy house had a south-facing back, which was curved. Only when the realtor handed us the plan for the house did I see that the back of the building was actually curved. I had not noticed this as the house was built in wedge-shaped sections; however, they did actually form a curve.

During our meals on the open portal, three native musicians would approach and play their guitars in soft harmony under the melting light. As the ocean darkened, it looked as if it were sprinkled with tiny reflections of moonlight. Boats became jewels along the horizon, and I felt the balm of the evening, a blessing of warmth, of music and love. One of the mariachi musicians with the features of an ancient Mayan was fascinating to look at. I came away with the sense that they were intuitive in a way. They were aware of Alex's pain and psychic disturbance. He always paid them handsomely when they came to our table to play and even asked for some Spanish tunes he knew.

Occasionally, Alex talked about himself. He spoke about deception, about his naivety in how he had evaluated the president and dean and so many others, and how he had been fooled by people, even friends, and been taken advantage of. Mostly I listened in silence, sad that he felt so pained by the last few years, so humiliated. It is hard to talk to him; his ego is fragile and volatile, and I seemed so often to say the wrong thing. So, I just listened. Later, I booked a trip to Tulum and Xel-Ha, just for me, as Alex did not want to join me.

Tulum

The morning of my excursion, Alex did not eat his breakfast; he was unhappy, not hungry, and he had not slept well. Sometimes, I felt guilty for feeling well, for enjoying life, for having dragged him here. Was my intention to help him futile? I tried to detach and ignore his mood. By 8:30 am I was waiting on the pier for our boat to the mainland. A white-haired man called Pinky was our guide. I sat on the deck to avoid the crowded main area, which was so air-conditioned it would keep a polar bear happy. As we left, the water turned to blue-black and the sky to pewter-coal color. Just before we arrived, I went inside, and then the tropical rain poured down. Pinky gave ten minutes of instruction, including the statement: "If you make up your mind to have a bad time, you will. It's your decision and attitude." By the time the bus came, the rain had stopped. Our arrival in Tulum was marked by brilliant sunshine. The site was spectacular. Overlooking the Caribbean, the temples rose above a breathtaking coastline. Pinky gave an excellent speech with detailed information about the site and its history.

When I got back later that afternoon, I found a feverish Alex in bed. He had slept all afternoon and had not eaten lunch. I rushed back to town to a pharmacy and bought medications and fed him the pills. We had a quiet dinner as I told him about Tulum and Xel-Ha. We are still affected by four principles: Earth, Water, Fire, Air, just as the ancients were. The doorway to the higher world of spirituality lies in the heart center, in our feelings. Mayans sacrificed human hearts, breaking the victim's neck first, so he was paralyzed but still conscious, then cutting out the heart with a stone knife. The body of the unfortunate was then rolled down the steps of the pyramid or temple. Did they try to induce feelings of compassion or awe in those who witnessed this ritual killing? Any suffering of another we feel, even fights, incite us to passion and to taking sides.

My last swim in the crystal-clear water made me grateful for such a wonderful experience. At our last meal, the three dark musicians played for us, clearly from the heart. I could feel distinctly they did not use the ego but rather some warm alive center which communicated through the music. Looking at the people of Cozumel, it became obvious that they belonged to the island and the Mexican country; there is no doubt in their minds about belonging and being whole and entitled to a full human existence. With the soft night and their voices merging, the three dark musicians played for us, and I felt moved because the sounds came from their souls. Alex said that they were like three dark angels bringing the magical joy of their own inner music to the visitors from the north. He had a sophisticated musical taste; but this was somehow moving in its simple completeness.

A last walk at dawn on the beach of Cozumel allowed me to find a sunrise-Venus shell. It lay there for me to pick up. Cozumel taught me again that heart-to-heart connections exist. After this it was time to fly back to the USA.

Back in Lake Forest, the realtor called. The couple interested in the house had made a new offer of $335,000. I turned it down, convinced in my mind that the property was worth much more. She warned me that I might not get a higher price; this was a good offer. Somehow, I seemed to lack the imagination to accept less than the full value of the property. If it was the wrong decision, then it was wrong. I wanted the house to go for the right price, for what we needed and what was in our best interests. Also, it had to be in our best interests in a higher sense. The realtor came the next day to talk to us, probably about our unrealistic expectations. However, that was not the case. I said to her, "Thought is creative! We can never have anything that we cannot imagine. My thoughts are supporting the force of my emotional desires and intention. The house price is very real to me; the value of this house is REAL to me. A lower price does not exist."

The house was shown again the very next morning. It made me realize that I had to start tidying up and getting rid of unwanted objects. Tidying up the house, I pulled out some of my paintings and looked at them. Did I really paint these? I did, and how wonderful they looked now. I felt grateful to Alex for having provided me with the opportunity to paint, for his unstinting support, and for his teaching me so many things.

I went to do some grocery shopping and ran into the realtor. The latest house offer had gone up; they are willing to pay $342,500 for the house. She urged me to accept the offer. I think I might, after a discussion with Alex. The buyers want the pipes tested for lead, but why? They were replaced three years ago, something I told them. So why do they have to test them? Odd! The house is going, and I must keep my center. Can I shift and remain detached? I went outside and, standing still, looked at the house. We have lived here for 30 years. It was a little grey house, balloon construction. Adieu.

Suddenly, everything accelerated. A house inspection was set. The man who came was intelligent and disarming in his directness. I liked him instantly. Then a call came from Fred R., the realtor in Eldorado, Santa Fe, who assured me the house prices were down nationwide; and that we certainly should find something we liked in New Mexico. Next, I talked to the moving company and emptied the stored materials in the attic and basement. I felt clear, accepting whatever manifested. I had to trust my inner guidance and my intuition.

I had been an American citizen for a full year by now, while Alex was still waiting to be accepted. Kirstin and I got in touch with Congressman McClory, our congressman-friend, about the situation. They couldn't find his papers, it seemed. Congressman McClory was very embarrassed and assured me that all would be done to accelerate the process. Alex was on some honors list for services in education and had received an award. This award made a difference, because suddenly we were called to the immigration bureau in Chicago. Alex still had difficulties with driving, so I chauffeured us into the big city. We sat for two hours in the immigration office, surrounded by tense, anxious foreigners seeking citizenship. Mostly I sat and meditated as the minutes crawled by. The drive to Chicago exhausted us both, but all was well, for they found Alex's file and the matter of citizenship could now progress. Alex finally became a legal citizen on June 8, 1995.

16 New Mexico

Choosing a House in Santa Fe

Suddenly it became urgent that we find and choose the house in Santa Fe. My friend Alicia offered to put us up in Santa Fe, so we were not obliged to stay in a hotel. She lived in an authentic, genuine adobe house with three-foot thick walls.

When we arrived in Santa Fe, the realtor picked us up and took us to see seven houses, the most expensive being the first, which was large and lovely and brand new. My heart sank when seeing the next ones, for they were all too small, though in our price range. After 30 years in a tiny box of a house in Lake Forest, I did not want another one. It seemed there was very little left in Eldorado; most of the building plots were sold by now. The next day we continued our search. It was cold and blustery and I began to wonder if we were actually meant to be here. Is it greedy to wish for the big house, for which we would have to shell out so much more?

On Saturday morning, a big open-house event in Eldorado allowed us to see everything that was available. Our realtor, Fred R., assured us that other areas in Santa Fe held nothing that we would like. Alex agreed with me, for he too liked the big house. That night I lay awake a long time, feeling tense and worried. Then, a strange dream appeared. In the dream, I feared to consider and look at a house destiny had offered and wanted me to take. I was backing away from the big house out of fear. The next morning, a call came from Fred R. The second house we had liked and considered buying, was no longer available. The pattern was shifting and very quickly. This left us with only our first choice, the big house. I phoned our financial adviser in Illinois. He advised us to take a 15-year mortgage and pay it off rapidly. I thought of my dream. Was I really meant to have the large, beautiful house? Expand your mind, I told myself. It was necessary to let go of preconceived ideas and tight attitudes. Though I could barely believe it—all signs pointed to the first house as the only choice. An old mind-set was holding me back!

Alex and I decided to look at the Eldorado house again by ourselves. We entered this beautiful, light-filled space, feeling the ambiance and imagining our possessions in it. Then we measured out the space to see where furniture would fit, looked at the view, the sunny hills, and the drifting clouds, and we made the decision to take a loan and to buy the place. That afternoon, we met with the realtor and, to our great surprise, he informed us that the owners had decided to lower the price by $18,000. This considerably improved matters for us, and we made our offer.

I felt so excited and happy. Santa Fe was luminous, fun, lively, and exotic. It was a special place and it was a grace to live there—almost unbelievable. We went out for dinner with Alicia to celebrate, and, as she had previously lived in Eldorado, she told us some of its history. Originally, it was a huge cattle ranch. In order to gain more grazing territory for cattle, the owners decided to remove the many trees, and by placing chains between trucks, they uprooted the pinyon and juniper trees. Their greedy venture did not pay off. Without the tree cover, the soil dried and grasses diminished; the cattle had insufficient pasture and the ranch had to be sold. A real estate company bought the now useless land with the intention of establishing an extension to Santa Fe. They planned to build only adobe-style homes on large plots and planned a special type of community with a swimming pool and shopping facility, as well as a wilderness area for hiking and horseback riding. This would include a community school, a senior center, a library, and a fire station. In other words, this was to be an organized community that provided cultural amenities and a beautiful environment.

The next morning, Fred R. called and confirmed that our offer had been accepted. We shall actually live here in a light-filled house and luminous environment. There was still so much to arrange and complete before we could fly back, and signs of stress showed in Alex. He had trouble with his breathing, so I was grateful that he no longer smoked. The month of May came to an end, and so did our stay in Santa Fe. At dawn we drove to Albuquerque to catch our early flight to Chicago. It was cold and grey in Illinois, and I threw myself into the task of packing up our belongings. Many times, the unexpected happened, such as when friends showed up with a ready lunch for us or Kirstin and Bill came to help with the packing. We had so much art along with big paintings in frames that were outrageously heavy. If I picked up something carelessly, my shoulder complained by evening. Having so much art brought friends and acquaintances to our house looking for sale items. I sold a lot of paintings, and that lightened the workload considerably. The money also was welcome.

June came, it was Sunday, bright and sunny, and our garden was bulging with flowers—lilac, rhododendron, wild geranium, trillium, and columbine. I went jogging and the day felt magnificent. I noticed Alex belching and belching. It was painful to hear it. I told myself to stay light, to stay detached. By late afternoon he was drunk, and even more drunk by seven o'clock, when I insisted that he eat some dinner. He looked at me lovingly and told me how much he had always loved me and how beautiful I appeared to him. I took his hand and guided him to bed and removed his clothes, and while I was briefly in the bathroom, he crashed to the floor and bruised his ribs. This was a tension I did not need, and Alex's drinking could only be stopped by him. There was no point in lecturing him. How can more value come into his life? I believed he had become very unhappy through the changes caused by the brain surgery; it had undermined his powers, his talents and abilities. Things that were once easy for him were now a challenge, like typing, balancing his checkbook, and writing. Even his driving was tentative and uncertain. I saw clearly how the mind colors everything. Our old house was filled with a soft light; it was another beautiful day with abundant birdsong, and the rhododendrons were blooming in the garden as never before. Looking back, where was I last year at this time? I was focused on the brain surgery; did I see anything at all?

While packing heavy things in the garden with a sore and increasingly painful wrist, I asked Alex to lend me a hand. He refused. I felt like crying. He had crippled himself with the intoxicating refrain of "I can't." And, in that moment, two of our best friends came by, bringing lunch. I ran to get plates, glasses, and cutlery from the house so we could eat in the garden. Alex complained of flies, insects, noise, and sun. He was drinking steadily and eating little. After a long afternoon nap, he was irritable and angry. The room full of packing cases was uncomfortable. I asked him to help with preparing some dinner. Again, he said, "I can't." Then, to my surprise, he accused me of not loving him and said that he was treated as a villain, always criticized and abused. It was no good telling him his drinking was what I criticized or that his personality changes were difficult to bear. I cried most of the evening off and on and could not stop. He went to bed at 7:30 pm and was up at 3:00 am getting scotch and milk and waking me up with the noise. I didn't know what to do. Was I meant to stay with an alcoholic? Could he change? That was when he said, "I have only a little time left. I want to die; it is not worth living like this! I want to die."

What I found so very difficult was the unpredictability of these drunken states and mood shifts. He sucked me into his states. In a fashion, all this packing was like sifting through the last 30 years of life in Lake Forest and examining who I was and what a wonderful life together my songbird Alex and I had. He was like a bird singing until our house reverberated with the sound of music. It was so difficult to watch his changes and see his despair and yet also to see his inner light still shining through his eyes.

Everything Is a Gift

I stood there helplessly observing. Was this even possible? How was this happening? Alex never returned from that brain surgery; only an incomplete Alex returned with a fractured memory and strange twists to his nature. It seemed useless to even think about it. He is obviously so unhappy. All I could do was to create an environment of love and acceptance.

I gradually came to the decision to just enjoy everything. Everything is a gift of life, whether recognized as such or not. The mind is the interpreter of all perceptions. Everything is dual and contrasting. Only I can choose on what I put value and on what I focus.

Every morning was beautiful and sunny, fragrant, filled with birdsong. And yes, life was rich and filled with blessings that were easy to overlook. There were our many friends, all concerned and trying to help, being gentle and kind. They came with gifts of food when I just needed a meal on the table and had been too busy to prepare it. Friends were sensitive enough to recognize Alex's depression and invited us to special events and parties. There was plenty of variety and boredom wasn't possible. Many times, Alex mentioned he missed his students and the lecture room. I understood teaching had been his joy and had given meaning to his life. Perhaps the most amazing two visitors were old friends, both suffering from cancer, who came one afternoon and talked to him for hours in the garden. They were at peace with where they were, and they and Alex all recognized that he did not have long to go before he, too, was looking squarely at the end.

To stay totally focused on my life and activities, I needed to make all this hard work meaningful. I thought of a Chinese slave sewing silk blouses all day long and putting love into every little stitch, for how would her life have meaning otherwise? It was Sunday again, and I went for a long meditative walk, escaping from the basement. The gardens I walked past were so lush, so

Alex's last days in Lake Forest, 1995

pristine and cared for; so much wealth lay behind that. I walked under old sheltering trees with huge canopies and marveled at how much I saw. There wasn't regret at leaving and going to the Wild West. Gratitude for the years here in Illinois and all the wonderful individuals I met was strong. I loathed saying goodbye.

My meditations during this period of deconstruction were of particular strength and power, and they furthermore gave me advice when asked for. Like dropping into a pool of liquid light, I felt wonderfully centered and blissful. My mind did not drift away but stayed fixed with what I focused on. It occurred to me that my mind only became restless because of likes and dislikes. What was I meant to learn? Was it to concentrate on the essential instead of trying to escape to some more appealing experience?

Something happened which was so surprising that I wrote it down in my daily diary. I asked the universe to help me with the task of packing, as it had become such a strain that my whole body was protesting. I asked to be given assistance and I pledged to wait until help arrived. Magically, the very next morning, Bill materialized, and within several hours all the pictures were packed. It felt like a huge burden had been lifted from my shoulders. Alex and I actually could go for a walk along the lake in the cool of early evening, and I could feel myself relaxing as I should always do, and which I don't do. The art of relaxation became possible when driving ambition was set aside and I did not ask to have my way. Without relaxation, the body and mind were tensed up and there was no space for experiencing something new or different. As we returned from our walk along the lake, the garden looked new to me. The white rhododendron blossoms had become huge and luminous in the late sparse evening light, and a lovely perfume of plants and flowers spread through the grounds.

The inevitable great garage sale followed, and again, help appeared from everywhere. I was by now more surrendered and calm. I sat in the driveway for most of the morning talking to Kirstin. That is when she told me she was thinking of breaking up her relationship with Bill. I asked questions but gave no advice. We had a beautiful champagne lunch in the garden. I opened a bottle to celebrate the completion of the garage sale. The house was now filled with packed boxes and we moved to our friend Kay's house to sleep. It was like being in a luxury hotel, and she was gracious and most generous to both of us. Kirstin phoned to let us know she had finally broken up with Bill. Bill was left crying hysterically on the floor of her apartment as she left. Alex said, "He will feel rejected by her, as he was first rejected by his father. It is an old pattern. I hope he will not harm himself in despair." Sad to say, Alex's concern was prescient.

It had become very hot and humid, and the orange day lilies were bursting into bloom, as if to celebrate. Alex complained about the humidity. It was the end of June, and a huge moving van pulled into the driveway. Three hardworking young men cheerfully emptied the house of all boxes by evening. These big guys wore shirts black with sweat as they hoisted boxes into the van. I marveled as everything flowed so smoothly, so effortlessly, and as everything assisted to make this transition easy. Even the huge amount of junk and garbage was removed from the premises. Then a thunderstorm quickly cooled and sweetened the air as we left. I looked one last time at the house, my shelter for 30 years, where I had spent so much of my life.

Departure

When we arrived at Kay's home, a group of friends and yoga students had gathered, and everyone handed me carefully chosen presents in quite amazing outpourings of love. I felt a little shocked at the unexpected intensity of love and gratitude for the yoga I had taught them. Then, bit by bit, I began to comprehend that I had managed to transmit the teachings to them and their gratitude was for the Light of the yoga teachings. The next morning, we left Lake Forest and set out on our long drive to New Mexico and our new life.

I did all the driving, but progress was slow due to some extensive road construction, so that we only covered only 300 miles on the first day. Early the next day, we crossed Texas, which struck me as huge and flat. In time we reached the border of New Mexico. The earth was no longer flat but filled with hills and mountains. It reminded me of Egypt. It was dry and the wind was warm and intense, like the desert winds of North Africa.

Eventually, we reached Santa Fe and drove to my friend's Alicia's home on Agua Fria. It was good to see Alicia and to feel the protective shell of her adobe home, which she had renovated beautifully. It was originally built in the old native pueblo style and was constructed of mud bricks. Like the Indian pueblos from which the style in part developed, these buildings derived their charm from functional materials like bricks made from earth, sand, and water, rough-hewn wood columns, and mud plaster in many warm hues. The walls are often very thick; insulating the interior with warmth in the winter, coolness in the summer, and the many sounds from outside. What I liked best was the rounded look of the houses, where inside spaces didn't have hard edges or squared-off corners. The houses seemed to expand and contract organically like the environment in which they sat. They looked like a part of the landscape. Inside the houses, the stucco-covered walls were polished to a very smooth diamond finish and had an organic silky feeling to the touch.

I had a premonition that all was not well with Kirstin and called her as soon as we arrived. She sounded shell-shocked as she related that Bill had attempted suicide. He waited until the middle of the night for this attempt, but then thankfully lost his nerve and contacted his sister, who called for help. Kirstin sounded exhausted and dispirited. She had known he would attempt something stupid and therefore waited to tell him it was over until our departure. I felt deep compassion for Kirstin and anger at Bill's thoughtless selfishness. Mostly, I felt sad for Kirstin's plight, as a psychiatrist had asked her to continue to stay with Bill for some weeks until he rebalanced spiritually and emotionally. This day, the 3rd of July, was her 27th birthday. We could neither help nor advise her but had to give her over to her fate, to her own destiny, with its upheaval and resulting lessons. During our drive to New Mexico, I had felt this intense connection to Kirstin, during which time my heart was pouring a stream of protection towards her. She confirmed she had heard my voice in her head telling her not to identify with Bill and his problems. Later during a phone conversation, she stated that she was essentially fine, but was open to the idea of having some therapy. The psychologist had suggested this might be of benefit to her.

During the night a violent thunderstorm occurred. The rain drummed against the house and the adobe walls absorbed the impact like a thick turtle shell. I felt secure and protected, a sensation I had never known in Lake Forest, where our house creaked and shivered and shook in wind and rain. In the morning, the sky was a deep blue and the sun shone as if we had never had a storm. Alicia told me that these rain storms

Santa Fe house with attached studio on right, 2014

were called monsoons because of the extreme downpour of
water. There was even a street in Santa Fe called Water Street
because during a monsoon the street actually turned into a
river.

We went back to the wonderful courtyard restaurant called
Casa Sena we'd discovered on our last visit here. In the court
center, a huge old cottonwood tree rose giant-like beside
our little table. Roses and hollyhocks filled the borders of
the garden and a fountain splashed. So many pleasures were
unfolding. After this, we drove to Eldorado. The moving van
had yet to arrive and was expected the following day. The
house looked wonderful, and it seemed unbelievable that we
should soon own it and be living there. Wherever I looked, I
was enchanted with the expanse of the high desert landscape
and the soft contours of hills. Joe, the builder, came to join us,
and Alex asked him about the possibility of adding an art studio
to the house and he agreed. To me, it looked as if the building
was not quite complete at one end, something a studio would
correct. Joe told us how he had started building the house in
1993, the same year I spent four months at Yasodhara Ashram
and when Swami Radha suggested I consider living in Santa Fe.

The closing of our house purchase went smoothly, and I told the builder how much I enjoyed the design of the house. He explained how he had broken the building into parts, aiming for more variety and that he intended to have lots of interior light within the structure and a view right through the whole house. A spaciousness resulted and I realized my visualizations while in Mexico on Cozumel Island had indeed become true. The house I had seen in my mind's eye had manifested itself.

The moving van arrived very early, and Joe came to move away some building materials left in the garage. The van had trouble getting into the long driveway, but it did manage. The men started to unload the van, but it took several days for them to complete that project. I recognized that I was becoming very anxious and needed to relax. It would be a long day and many more long days were to be expected. In the evening we sat on our portal for our first picnic meal as daylight was fading and the mountains layered themselves into stencil-like formations of the palest hue, before turning into a deep ultramarine blue. As the moon rose, I climbed up the stairs to the open-roof deck to look at the lights of near and far neighbors' houses and to hear the stillness.

Taking Possession of the House

It took two months to unpack and place all our furniture, hang curtains, put up pictures, and organize our music collection and books. The house came together bit by bit and fortunately I had my yoga mat on the deck every morning with time to reflect. Whatever I experienced on the roof was grace. It was oneness. "It comes in its own time," Swami Radha had said. It felt like waves of blessings.

Alex was the one who remembered that Eldorado had a swimming pool for its residents, and so whenever I became too tired, he took me there for a refreshing swim. My body remembered the many hours in Cairo's pools where I had trained as a swimmer. I still could move through water as easily as a fish. It was a relief and a joy to experience the coolness in the summer heat. Here I saw mountains, but the feeling was similar to what I felt so long ago. Alex sat in a lounge chair by the pool, watching me and smiling.

Living in such an attractive place as Santa Fe, we found that friends and acquaintances announced their intent to come and visit us, and suddenly we had become very popular overnight. Having houseguests made certain we did a lot of sightseeing. As a consequence, we discovered many new locations of truly amazing value, and I became more and more impressed with the beautiful state of New Mexico. Kirstin was the first person to arrive. She was now in a new relationship with a young man who had been her friend for many years. His birthday was on July 2nd and hers on July 3rd. Over the years he had been a guest at most of her birthday parties and I had no doubt that he was in love with her. Occasionally I would feel sorry for his plight, because Kirstin could be quite wild and flirty. Alex approved of Kent, saying, "He is a gentle soul and will be kind to her."

We took Kirstin to Bandelier National Monument, where the huge south-facing cliff face is perforated with natural caves once used by the ancient people as dwelling spaces. The pueblo overlooked the Frijoles Canyon and a river flowed through it. Kirstin really enjoyed the steep cliff face honeycombed with caves and perforations. A number of these caves can be entered by climbing sturdy ladders, a method used by the ancient people, which is an adventure in itself. A ceremonial cave located 140 feet up in the cliff is quite an ascent on steep ladders. A kiva is located up there and was used for the religious ceremonies of the tribes.

Trees

August arrived, and I began to plan a xeriscape garden, as we had very limited water. When the house was built, all the vegetation from the building site was removed. Now weeds were proliferating, weeds which were considered the pioneers, and if I did not want weeds, other plants had to be introduced. We lived in a high desert, and only tough plants are capable of surviving the harsh sun, wind, and limited moisture. Just at that period, Hispanic men came offering pinon trees for sale, and trees became the first thing I planted. They required watering until established, and so I bought hoses and stood outside in the evenings watering the trees. There was not a single tree on the property at the start. Looking from our portal we had a view of a bright orange house on lot over. Since the Eldorado community permits only house colors of certain hues, we were always puzzled how the owners of the orange house got away with such an outrageous color. My first trees were planted along the edge of our back boundary line so that we would eventually not have to see the orange house. In time, I planted more trees, all with the goal of covering up the view of certain houses and I succeeded magnificently. As I planted trees, I also practiced an asana called vrksasana, or the tree. I had become aware of my somewhat rootless disposition and practicing the tree pose I reflected on what it meant to be rooted.

Mantra Initiation

A most unusual thing happened. One of the swamis from Yasodhara called me to inform me that Swami Radha was going to give a mantra initiation. She felt she didn't have much time left on this earth. In a dream she found herself wearing a big pearl ring. Pearls symbolize disciples and so she chose to initiate more people onto the path. Usually only one or two disciples are chosen for a mantra initiation; rarely is a large group initiation performed.

I did some soul searching and reflected on the obligations I was committing to and what this initiation would imply. By September 9 I was on my way to Spokane. The ceremony took place in Coeur d' Alene, in the villa of close disciples of Swami Radha. The place was lush, and over 150 people were present for the event. A raised platform at one end of the room held an easy chair for the guru, who came in looking lovely. Her face was full of sweetness. From where I sat, I could catch glimpses of her. Each individual was called to come forward with their mala, a kind of rosary with 108 beads used for reciting mantras. She blessed each mala and each person and gave each one a mantra. My hands were very hot and, at times, I felt like crying. A man sitting in front of me was shaking like an aspen tree. Someone else was sobbing. Everyone was moved in a different fashion. I saw some of my friends in the gathering and a few stumbled as they made their way to Swami Radha. It was my turn and I felt intensely happy and empowered at the same time. My mala was a cheap tulsi-wood mala, and when I handed it to Radha, I was conscious of it being very tangled, so that she spent quite a while untangling it. I should have bought an expensive one at the door. Everyone had crystal or quartz-bead malas and I had such a humble one. I banned this silly thinking; after all it depends on what you do with it and not how it looks. I also presented her with the gift of a miniature rosebush. "How sweet," she said as she accepted the plant. She handed my mala back with the mantra-pronouncement. I returned to my seat. As a group, we chanted mantra for a long time. I was feeling the vibration through my whole body and down into my feet. By the end, my voice was gone and I could not speak to anyone. I stood awkwardly in silence, smiling if someone greeted me. I was unable to leave or break the spell.

Suddenly, I felt alone and separate after all the intensity of her presence. Her absence caused a sensation of abandonment, like sliding down into a deep chasm. At this stage, looking back and trying to grasp the essence of the afternoon's events, I came up with almost nothing. There were certain expressions in people's faces, inner emotions expressed in a stumble or in tears. There was a strange heat in the room, and a smell of wax from candles and perfume from flowers. I had felt tense, my palms hot and my body tired. Her forehead looked so familiar; she was my spiritual mother, or was her forehead like my actual mother's? I did not feel like leaving the grounds, I did not feel like eating, I felt lost. Then I saw the familiar face of Swami H. She talked about how the initiation had affected her some years back. "The energy is neutral," she said, quoting Swami Radha. "It is like a handful of seeds, like capital to be put to use. This is the mantra's purpose. Things will go very fast right away. The effect of the mantra will make itself known." She hugged me as I left.

I felt very depressed in my little motel room. It was as if the air has gone out of my balloon. I tried to understand what Swami H. had told me. If my inner focus was steady and unwavering, then the outer changes and events wouldn't affect me. A day later, feeling tired and spent, I was very glad to be back in Santa Fe. Alex was wonderful but fragile. A good old friend from his Kenya days had sent a letter after 18 years of silence. His wife Leda had died last March. She finished her book before cancer took her. It was odd that I felt such an urge to write to them while she was still alive and glad I did so. Now I understand why I felt an inner urge to connect. Leda pursued her talent for writing. None of us knows how much time we have left.

A few days later the news arrived that Bea V. was dying of cancer. She was our secretary in the Art Department for many years and was a friend. Alex took it poorly and was deeply upset. His upset was transferred to me, unfortunately, and he accused me of being a host of wretched qualities. He was right, he was honest, and he was very hurtful. I needed to meet myself at gut level and stop being drawn into arguments. As I watched him, I saw that he was in pain. However, if I had asked "What is wrong with you, are you in pain?" I would get nothing but annoyed denial. He refused to talk about himself and shut me out, even though I told him I felt there was something wrong. He objected passionately when I suggested he see a doctor and insisted there was nothing wrong with him.

I discovered a yoga teacher in Eldorado who had large classes and who came highly recommended. She was trained in the Iyengar style. I decided to take a class with her to find out how I would fit in as a teacher. Some of the poses were new to me, and I had to accept my limitations, realizing that the Ashram held different values, focusing much more on a spiritual approach. Thea was a veteran teacher with 16 years of experience, while I was a novice. She kindly talked to me for an hour, giving me information about pricing and the general

trends. Her students were mostly middle-aged women. Santa
Fe had 60 yoga studios, and since the summer, 20 new yoga
classes had been started. In other words, there was a glut of
yoga studios and a picky, uncommitted public. It would be
difficult to start a yoga course. I needed to wait and see how
everything shaped itself before making any decisions.

Canyon Road

On weekends, the art galleries had openings to introduce
their new artists. Alex and I began to drive into town to Canyon
Road, also called "the soul of Santa Fe." On this street there
was one gallery after another. Originally it was a street where
artists lived and worked, but over time, galleries took over the
houses. I had a wonderful time walking in the mellow autumn
light past gardens filled with golden chamisa and huge ancient
trees and visiting the various galleries. Most buildings had
attached gardens, all carefully tended and planted with lovely
flowers, particularly hollyhocks. In those days, the galleries still
offered wine to visitors. It was all very civilized and sometimes
there were bands playing music or belly dancers dancing.
We were surprised to learn that Santa Fe was the third best
market in the USA for the sale of art. Alex seemed to enjoy
going to Canyon Road as much as I did, and so we became
regular visitors to the art scene. There was one gallery I liked
in particular, and I began asking if I could interest them in my
work. I knew I would fit into this space, but I was not lucky.
Nonetheless, I knew that someday I would be accepted.

As to the countryside of Eldorado, I discovered more and
more hiking areas, uphill and downhill, arroyos and chasms,
rock formations and woods, and my walks became longer and
more interesting. It was indeed marvelous to have so many
wilderness areas to choose from and all so close to our house.
Already November approached and snow had fallen, only to
melt during the noon hour. I arranged my studio space for
painting in one of the back rooms and after eight months of not
doing any creative work, I started to paint. It felt wonderful, a
natural absorption for me. There was a certain spontaneity in

the way my hands managed the colors and how they flowed together; it was effortless.

Close to the end of the month of November I wrote a letter to Swami Radha thanking her for the mantra Initiation and telling her how it had affected me. "My present existence now has a spaciousness and ease I never knew before. And my heart is singing, singing in praise, feeling the miracle of being in this state of peace and well-being. I also feel such powerful gratitude for your teaching and to all who are such splendid examples. When I came here to Santa Fe in July, I hoped to be able to teach hatha yoga, Kundalini yoga, or dream work, anything that I was so privileged to receive through you. It has not turned out the way I thought it might. Santa Fe has over 60 yoga studios, and I have yet to find the way into teaching. We live outside town in an area called the high desert in splendid isolation, except for wonderful wildlife. Most days, the only person I talk to is Alex, and I have the privilege of time for lots of inner work." After sending the letter off, I settled down for a brief mantra practice, thinking of her. To my surprise I saw Radha very distinctly for a short period of time.

Death of the Guru

I was preparing lunch when the phone rang. It was Arnon, a resident at the Ashram in Canada. In a soft voice she told me Swami Radha had a heart attack at 6:30 am that morning. They rushed her to the hospital, but she was dead. Yesterday, she had received my letter. I thanked her for letting me know. There was an acceptance and numbness in me. They will put the body on view at the Ashram and then cremate her. Arnon was expansive and gentle, giving the message time to sink in. Would I want to come to the Ashram for the ceremonies? I said, "No." I could see my mind throughout this conversation. It was clear, a witness, watchful. The grief sat in my heart like an immense weight. I moved through my activities with awareness while reflecting on the events at the Ashram. Arnon had said they had not expected her to die. She had been listening to the Three Tenors late last night, enjoying the beautiful arias they sang.

The day passed, and I found no opportunity to grieve for this woman whom I admired and loved, and who was my spiritual mentor and guide. Now she was gone. Alex asked if I wanted to go to the Ashram and I said no, it was not necessary. I carried her in my soul, she, who had given and given. I carried her picture and her mantra. For me she had never been close physically, but certainly close at heart. "We do not meet at the personality level, we meet in the Light," she once said.

Kirstin called, saying she felt something was wrong and that she felt she needed to contact us. What was amiss? I told her Swami Radha had died. And I kept feeling her, as if she was giving from another level. I recognized a fine voice had been trying to find my ear and I had ignored it. It spoke of blessings. Is that why I cry when I think how much she gave to all who came in touch with her? I felt the in-between zone which brought insight and intuition with it. In a vision, I saw Radha lying on a bier with closed eyes. I heard her voice instructing me in Shavasana, in mantra-chanting, the voice I have listened to for six years. The organ is gone but the voice continues.

Finally, I cried for a long time while I chanted at night. I cried for the pains all those feel who are close to her, I cried for those who now must take the reins into their hands, and for the strength required, and I felt weary. For the next few days my tears were just beneath the surface, my dreams confused, my inner balance disturbed. I had a guru, a dispeller of darkness-spiritual teacher; she was now gone. I had a guru exactly from September 8th till November 30th. Such a short time! I felt left alone and abandoned, just when I expected to be taken care of spiritually. How can I ever get anywhere now?

I imagined myself standing in the temple at Kootenay Bay under the protection of the dome and saw the mellow sun reflected by the waters of the bay. If only I could go to the temple. I felt unevolved and pathetic, and I scolded myself for being ungrateful. My only choice is, "Surrender!" Be who I am meant to be, learn to follow my own drumbeat and my own needs. I cannot take my cue from anyone else and must listen to my own soul, and my inner self.

My friend Alicia invited us to a poetry reading by Rumi, the Persian mystic and poet. Alex refused, but I wanted to go and drove into town alone, something he did not approve of and perhaps had not expected I would choose to do. It was a fountain of joy; and I did the right thing in going to the Rumi poetry reading.

The Sufi spirit suffused the evening. The wisdom of a past time and a Persian poet slid into the audience like a perfume. The dancer and the musicians who acted in certain parts were just extraordinary. Zuleika undulated and stamped her feet and spun her magic until there was a standing ovation of enthusiasm flowing back from the audience. The words, dance, and music combined to produce a marvel. I felt entertained and lifted out into a starlight night into a mystic dervish dance. At the conclusion, the dancer Zuleika performed the whirl of the Sufi dervishes, spinning and spinning like a white bell, and I felt transported back in time to the whirling of Egyptian dervishes and the magic and mystery that had fed my soul. I think Alicia was delighted with my enthusiasm and gratitude, and she was glad she had invited me. Alex was furious when I got home, as I had not given him a correct time for my return. I did not know how late I would be. But I had been to the fountain of joy and the inner dance continued. It was as if I had risen above the levels that could drag me down.

We continued to have houseguests, and for Christmas Kirstin and Kent announced themselves. I was glad to have some entertainment on for Alex, and clearly, he needed people to talk to. The amount of snow that fell was amazing and the town was clad in its festive best, while the sunlight created impressionist color scenes of pink and pastel hues and deep ultramarine shadows. It was a privilege to live amidst such beauty, amidst hills of sparkling snow. Depressive thoughts of darkness still returned into my psyche every now and then, but more than not, I freed myself from that cloud of darkness and began to live in the present without fear.

I worked unrelentingly with the books and teachings of yoga, with asana and reflections, with mantra and meditation to counter the situation into which Alex was slipping. On a beautiful snowy evening, while I admired nature and the silence surrounding us, Alex started to cry about my father and his young, untimely death somewhere in Poland in 1945. He told me he was "so tired" and not grateful for his life and his achievements. I could not help him, and so I started to chant a mantra for his soul, and as I focused on the sound and vibration, peace came and transported my consciousness into compassion and love. This then became the means to slip my awareness into an inner realm, and Alex did not complain of my chanting, which he certainly had done in the past. Something intangible was transmitting to him. Yet, a few days later, he talked of suicide, saying that he should have committed it long ago.

Patsy and Nick's Visit

One morning in Santa Fe, Alex surprised me with the idea of inviting Patsy and her current husband Nick to visit New Mexico. "I would like to see her again," he said, without giving any further explanation. I knew that they were not affluent and I suspected that Alex literally invited them, plane fare included, for a month's visit. During a long walk, I came to the understanding that Alex and Patsy had unfinished business between them. Perhaps he felt he had not much time left and wanted to clear the unspoken obstacles between them.

Swami Radha, in some talk she gave, stressed the importance of symbols. The messages are there waiting for you "if you pay attention." I saw a mouse in broad daylight boldly walking across the portal tiles. The little creature had its shoulders lifted towards its ears, as though in pain. Normally a mouse will not choose to walk in an open space but scurry from one protected area to another.

As I observed Alex, I noticed his shoulders were drawn up, as though he were holding tension or pain in his sternum. He belched dramatically and painfully. Too much gas! Sometimes his speech slowed and words came only gradually. Often, he just sat in his chair, neither reading nor listening to music.

Perhaps he was listening within, as the very aged do. He ate very little; perhaps he had an obstruction in his esophagus! For breakfast he ate only half a slice of bread. At times I thought he hadn't much time left and perhaps I was seeing all the signs indicating the coming of the end. I began to understand I was indulging in an intentional blindness in refusing to see the facts. Alex was a very sick man. I have been blind, deluding myself in the hope he will get better. The brain tumor was one thing, but something else was wrong now, and facing my intentional blindness was a shocking and horrifying realization. How could I go on without him? What will my life be like as a widow? I needed to inform myself about death and dying.

Throughout it all, Alex was sweet and concerned about showing his sense of humor, and when in company, he talked and talked and managed to attract quite a few people. It happened repeatedly that when we were walking in the streets of Santa Fe, people we did not know greeted Alex. It was as if he carried some personal aura of power and this was acknowledged. Homeless people, of which there were quite a few here, also spotted him and were drawn to him like to a magnet. His pockets were never empty of some dollar notes for this special purpose.

The "banditti," as Alex called them, were a special breed of opportunists lying in wait with their trucks loaded with pinon trees. They waited for us to come home from town, a little tired and therefore more approachable, and then offered us very special deals on trees, which they planted for us. Alex would come out to the portal and bring wine glasses and a bottle to reward them for their labors. They knew everyone in the neighborhood and told him interesting snippets of information in a blend of Spanish and English. Apparently, our neighbor sells self-improvement tapes. That is why the UPS is always parked at the door. She hires a lot of workers and wears a wig when a married man, who is her lover, comes for the weekend. It must be true, as one evening we overheard a dramatic and heart-wrenching exchange. He wanted to leave her, and she was on her knees begging him not to desert her. Alex, who is a good mimic, enacted an encore for my benefit.

My gardening efforts were challenged by a severe drought, and the rainy season failed to bring the expected monsoon. We were allowed to water only between 8 pm and 6 am in the morning, and unfortunately, I had new trees to take care of. Late evenings, under an enormous blanket of huge stars, I watered all the trees several times a week. June bugs, pale fawn in color, lived in the hundreds in the pinon trees. They hummed, and the drone reminded me of a great AUM sound from a thousand voices. How extraordinary to find music chanted by bugs under this magnificent canopy of twinkling stars. "What does a tree symbolize?" I ask myself during asana practice. I have planted trees and they have to root themselves to live here. Can I do the same, accept life as it continues and root myself in this newly found reality? What I need to cultivate is the balance that a tree has so the winds of change do not blow me down.

It was a year since we moved into this house, transforming it into our home. It remained so beautiful here, so special and enchanting. Often in the morning I would find a single little white or pink flower. The area around our house was still without plant life. Only the pioneers—the weeds with huge tap roots—have invaded the area. I delighted in those little flowers called evening primrose. I ran to tell Alex to come and look at them, but they were gone by the time we returned. "That rabbit ate the flower," he said, pointing to the bunny only a few feet away.

And then the rains came, and I was surprised at how intense they could be. It leaked in the entry, in the bathroom, and in the kitchen, and water soaked into the installed carpets and tiles. I was giving a yoga class when one downpour occurred. The next day I phoned the builder, as the structure was still under warranty and now needed to be fixed. I felt vulnerable and unsure of myself, but Joe promised to be there. It was exactly a year since we bought the house, and the honeymoon was over. It was a lovely illusion, I thought, as now all its flaws were seen. I recalled the many recent dreams I had of seeping water, of ceilings dripping in a staccato rhythm, of drenched rugs. Had parts of me known this would occur? During my next meditation I came to the conviction that the outer and inner level can be clearly seen by me. I swung between the two, identifying mostly with the outer concerns. I just barely managed to hold onto the inner level, which is of so much greater importance. I desperately needed to pay attention to my intuition. No one can do a thing for me if I deny my insights, which, after all, were my guidance.

Meanwhile, the time for the visitors from Scotland came closer. Alex became more and more unwell and ate less and less. In the mornings, his pillow was damp with sweat and I smelled a sour sick smell on him. He complained about chest pain and eventually agreed that I could phone his doctor. Dr. Lopez listened carefully and suggested we go to the emergency room. We spent from four in the afternoon until nine in the evening in the hospital. He had pneumonia, which accounted for the chest pain, night sweats, and fever. I felt certain he had a high blood count. At one point, one of the doctors suggested he might have blood clots in the lungs. Alex held himself erect like a man in a strong wind, barely able to stand. Then, there was the long wait for the antibiotics. We ordered them, and I wrapped up his shivering body in my long woolen shawl and drove him home before returning to Santa Fe for the now available medication.

The moon was full, and it was late, and the landscape was so brightly lit that I switched off my headlights. The moon looked like a huge, surreal planet, quite enormous in size. The next day I tried to reach Patsy, only to discover they didn't have a phone. It meant I could not contact her to let her know Alex was so seriously ill and that their visit was inconvenient just now. I spent my day preparing the guest room for Patsy and Nick. Alex was very ill, but the antibiotics began to be effective, and I got my first full night's sleep and was no longer changing damp bed sheets.

The arrival date came and I drove with Alex to the airport. Patsy and Nick were early, and it took a bit of time to find them. It was a great reunion and clearly everyone was very happy. Alex talked a blue streak, though I could tell by the tone of his voice that he was still unwell. Everyone talked nonstop during the hour-long drive back to Eldorado, where we settled on the portal with tea and biscuits for more conversation.

Patsy looked at my big kitchen and said, "Our whole house in Scotland would fit into that space!" They were in awe, looking at the landscape in the fading light of evening, and would have stayed up even longer, had I not insisted Alex needed to go to bed. To make allowances for the high altitude here and the fact they were suffering from jet lag, we took it easy to allow them to acclimatize before doing sightseeing trips. Our first outing was to the highly recommended flea market and a lovely afternoon walk into the low sunlight. Both the grass and the clouds were illuminated with magical light, and the yellow autumn chamisa bushes were in full bloom.

Patsy was still a remarkably beautiful and amazing woman. Alex began to bloom and conversations with her were continuous, while Nick sucked his pipe. He had been a teacher of Spanish and they spent most winters in Spain to avoid the damp cold of Scotland. Neither had been to the USA, and they found New Mexico enchanting. Nick was a cancer survivor, and Patsy talked at length about the trials and tribulations of going through surgery and chemo and radiation treatments while fear gnawed on her heart that he might not make it. The most difficult were the changes Nick had to make in his daily life and the habits he had to give up. She emphasized that it took "tough love" on her part, and as the days slipped by, she began to emphasize that I, too, would be required to be more demanding with Alex: offering "tough love," in other words.

On a visit to the little El Santuario de Chimayó, a pilgrimage site that held the vibrations of all those prayers of pious souls, conflict with Alex erupted. How dare I be in agreement with Patsy concerning his choices and habits? She had no jurisdiction over him; he would do as he liked. As an aside he informed me that it was her interfering that broke up their young love affair. I let it all run down my back like water runs over a duck's feathers, for I knew the score and that there was no point in arguing with him. We had a pleasant day on the whole and Nick made a gazpacho for dinner, which was superb.

However, as the days passed, Alex found himself unable to keep up with our pace, be it in visiting Frijoles Canyon in Bandelier or in visiting Taos, and an irritation set in, caused by his continuing state of ill health, as he had never really shed his pneumonia. During the night, it became obvious to me that pneumonia was back. He ate hardly anything and was consuming alcohol in spite of taking antibiotics. I vacillated between fear for him and calmness. That night, I had a horrendous dream that foretold Alex's surgery and the flood of events that would be unstoppable. I realized I would be alone and without help, and that was sobering. I needed to surrender to events as they unfolded. That day was demanding. After having prepared a dinner, Alex finally agreed to another trip to the emergency room. He was shaking, shivery and white. How a big man can suddenly fold up like a fragile flower! It rained all day, and my drive back and forth to town was through a heavy fog, both mental and physical. Finally, at midnight I got to bed.

When I awoke, the room was filled with sunlight and bliss, and the tears and pain were simultaneous. It was all a wonderful combination of color and pattern, a blessed life. I was able to step back and see it as magical and felt infinite gratitude. After an hour of yoga, I prepared breakfast, feeling how my energy level had risen through this practice. That morning, Alex seemed better and was argumentative and accusing me of things I had not done, a good sign because it meant his feistiness was back. By evening, he did not want to eat, so Patsy took over the kitchen and made him her style of scrambled eggs, which he had not tasted since they broke up 45 years ago. Amazing grace, he ate like a trooper. Later he complained that he had to eat it, and, it was my entire fault, as we had ganged up on him.

Patsy and I had very deep conversations several times while we went walking or when I took her for a swim in the Eldorado pool. She talked about her life and I felt a deep compassion for her. It seemed to me that in comparison to what she suffered, I had been unbelievably fortunate. As Patsy and Nick's time here was slowly coming to a close, I drove them to the town for a shopping spree and helped them in finding some gifts. Downtown, the plaza was bathed in golden afternoon sunshine and the native jewelers sat in the shade of the portal of the Governor's palace, their treasures of jewelry spread out in front of them on blankets on the ground. Patsy was radiant with pleasure as she moved slowly along, admiring the crafts, and I could see her desire for some turquoise earrings she had discovered. Nick, however, was not interested in buying them. As they walked ahead to get a cup of coffee at the Casa Sena, I quickly bought the earrings for her. A food photographer was working at the big fountain, laying down flowers in the top basin. The flowers glowed in the sunlight as the fountain water sprinkled down over them. Nick sat on a stone bench sucking on his pipe, asking for nothing more to complete his happiness. Old bees in the sunshine, I thought.

I was up at 5 am the next day to take our guests back to the airport in Albuquerque. Alex stayed home and they said farewell to each other, all knowing they would never see each other again in this life. Patsy and Nick disappeared quickly at the airport and spared me any long goodbye.

During Patsy and Nick's visit, I had continued teaching yoga classes, and the number of students was increasing slowly. This meant I had a focus on something other than Alex's illness. In addition, visitors continued to be attracted to my classes and many arrived unannounced. This meant we had to be very flexible and accommodating. It was a distraction that prevented me from being completely involved with Alex, who was slipping bit by bit and hiding his pain from me. I took him to our primary care physician, a very nice young man who was so gentle and considerate and most concerned. Since Alex was in discomfort most of the night, sleep was impossible. I saw the love in the doctor and how Alex returned the love in lifting the conversations to a lighter level. He amused the doctor with stories and jokes. It could also be interpreted as a reaching out to distract others, aiming for acceptance, admittance, and coming forward due to a genuine need to give. He showed his loving disposition to anyone who came into his orbit.

The next day, it rained all day long. I saw Alex going down, his energy dropping. By evening, his fever once again had become very high. A restless night followed, with my changing sheets and shirts and awakening at dawn feeling tired. Mist was rolling in, clouds descending, strange illumination opalesque and magical. We spent the morning at the hospital. The doctor did not like the look of Alex's lungs and more x-rays and blood tests were ordered. Alex made jokes and insisted on defending his dislike of physical exercise. "My only exercise is lifting a glass," he insisted. The doctor, a woman, found that he was severely anemic and losing blood in his stool. This was a long-neglected symptom. The doctor was gentle and very competent. On Monday, further tests were ordered, and I could feel that both of us were slightly shocked by the severity of the situation. I could not help recalling my admonition to him that he was eating poorly and eating only the things he liked. Here the doctor was asking him to eat spinach, cereal, and whole wheat bread, all of which were items he avoided. So at least I had not been wrong.

Diagnosis

Monday was a fasting day, with only liquids allowed prior to his colonoscopy. I spent the morning filling out the insurance forms. Alex's mind is now incapable of grasping even the simplest forms. His friend Michael had called the prior evening, telling him that his girlfriend had just had a colonoscopy. Then Patsy called from Scotland, and she too had just undergone the very same procedure. Were these calls to be understood as a coincidence, or was he assisted by a higher power? Alex looked so thin; the skin hung off his physical frame in loose folds. Would he ever be well again?

When, after a much longer waiting time than indicated, the surgeon who had done the colonoscopy came out, his eyes told me all. They gazed at me, dark pools of compassion offering no hope. It was fourth degree colon cancer. I heard the words without surprise. All I had felt for two years was confirmed. Later I told him. At first unresponsive, Alex then rushed to the bathroom for an unexpected bowel movement predicted by the doctor. I insisted he keep the door unlocked. His white underpants were full of blood. He looked in horror. I explained that this was to be expected after the colonoscopy. He went for a nap, and I tucked the sheets in around his fragile body. I felt so frightened for him, so tearful and sore. He was shriveled-up inside in pain and fear. Even his voice was gone. I looked at his face reflected in the bathroom mirror; it looked twisted. He had cancer obstructing the bowel and under the liver. The polyps are so big and dense they would have to be removed surgically. They would have to remove a good section of the bowel, 80 to 90 percent. It has to be done quickly, within the week. The surgeon thought Wednesday was a possibility.

I phoned Vermont to talk to David. He was out and Joyce answered. Next, a call to Frances, where I left the message that it was bad news. Kirstin asked me how I was; she is the most sensitive. Waves of pain spread through me with the realization that he was going. I didn't want to believe he was dying, but I was seeing it, and oddly I couldn't reach him. He was going, his soul was going. I had to accept that his soul was departing. It was such a sweet and tender soul. I cried at dawn and could not stop. It woke Alex who was probably awake anyhow. He said, "Poor Rosie." It seemed to me that reality was an incredible manifestation of shared love and compassion. I could see love flowing out from all creatures, in manifestations, in sounds and words. I had always been aware of this ocean of love. The sweetness of love brings tears. I noticed that everyone in their own way, whether clumsy or subtle, tries to manifest loving kindness in actions or through a look or touch.

The surgery was arranged, and the next day I drove Alex in at noon. Everyone was warm and compassionate, and Alex seemed more concerned for me than for himself. I hugged him and promised to pray, and then I sat in the hospital cafeteria. There was a huge window, and I saw that the sky was swept with dark clouds. At 4 pm the surgeon came in and took a chair opposite me. "I am sorry to tell you, we had to remove most of the colon. An extensive old cancer had perforated and sat under the diaphragm. We were unable to remove this. Chemo might fix it. Innumerable polyps were present in the colon. He may have months or a couple of years to live. We are thinking of both radiation and chemo, but whatever we do, his days are numbered." I asked what his opinion was, his gut instinct, how much time did he give Alex. He paused and his eyes looked into the distance beyond the window. Perhaps he was considering his answer. Perhaps he measured my possible reaction. Then he looked into my eyes and said, "I figure, end of this month, he just might die."

I was not upset; I accepted that these would be the final weeks. It would be a battle. How does someone function without a bowel? I recalled his extended, swollen gut in January, which looked so alarming and wrong to me. Strange to think that signs come that can be seen on the outside. I had seen the esophagus cancer on my uncle and on our friend Will. I had seen the dark ray over the right hemisphere of Alex's head. After brain surgery, this dark aura was no longer there.

He was a pathetic thing when I next saw him in intensive care. I watched the nurses turn his body in bed. The nurse was very skillful. I felt her impatience with incompetence. I praised her and she began to warm up. She was most helpful to Alex and intuitive in her concern and in the way she handled situations. His condition began to improve visibly. The doctor came and told him about the results of the surgery. He reconnected the large colon to the small intestine so Alex will not need a bag. I spent the long afternoon with him and left at 7 pm to go home and make phone calls. I was grateful for my spiritual practice and the ability to regain my inner balance in times of stress.

Back home, the house looked open and bright. I sat down and cried for a while, feeling so deeply sorry for him. He was dying; part of him died already in 1994 during the brain surgery. I realized I don't need to identify with his body or his pain. It did not help him, and it only depressed me and robbed me of life force. I needed to cope with this whole situation. Also, he no longer resembled the man I married. He was changing steadily; there was only a past love relationship, a memory that I treasured, and now a soul connection. He was beginning to resemble his mother in 1993, looking like she did at the end of her life.

The days ran together. Sleeping, waking, practicing yoga, eating, making necessary calls, and spending most of the time at the hospital. Alex was terribly restless and agitated. As soon as I arrived, he would say "Get me out of here. I shall have a seizure for sure, get my shoes. I am leaving now!" It reminded me of the geriatric ward in Fife.!" Alex followed one thought only and did not hear what I said. He constantly pulled out his IV and often had to be restrained and have his ankles tied to the bed. One afternoon, I had enough and decided to take matters into my own hands. I bought him apple juice and fed him that in small sips. I bought mineral water and brought homemade avocado soup and other foods he liked. I also untied one leg and arm and then, in desperation, I chanted my mantra aloud. I did not really dare to believe this would have an effect. To my total surprise, he ate the food, drank the fluids, calmed down, and actually went to sleep.

That night there was a blizzard. Trees bent down under the weight of the snow. When I came to the hospital, Alex was better. His eyes were open, his skin was smooth, and he looked healthier in the face and less wrinkled. His mind, however, was still confused. Most of the time I sat calmly while the snow fell, listening to the beautiful taped music I had bought for him. He did not seem to pay any attention to it. I felt peaceful, surrendered, and accepting.

After two weeks, we met with doctors, and Alex was improving, so he was allowed to return home. He was to eat from a menu that included heavy fibers, and they gave him two weeks to heal. Kirstin arrived from Illinois, and it felt wonderful to have her presence and help at this difficult time. She made oatmeal cookies, which appealed to Alex. At the suggestion of my Chinese friend, we went to an Oriental doctor in Santa Fe who had some good results with herbs in treating cancer. We left with a huge bag of herbs which I cooked and strained to make tea or soup, which Alex was to drink in considerable quantity. I tasted it after spending hours making this brew, and thought it was not bad-tasting. The smell alone made Alex feel sick and he refused to touch it. He was argumentative and irritable because of the illness and his slow decline. He seemed too set in his ways to make an uncomfortable effort.

We had meeting with the doctors about the cancer treatment they wanted to prescribe. Alex needed to make a decision. The doctors planned both chemotherapy and radiation together. Their explanation was fast, leaving no time to question anything. I felt sledge-hammered. Alex was told to drink no more than one scotch per day. He was told to walk daily, and I was encouraged to use a cattle prod if he failed to obey. I very much doubted that Alex could or would obey and found the whole meeting coarse and lacking refinement. At the close they said, "Of course we intend to give you quality time for what remains of your life." "And what do you consider being 'quality time?'" Alex asked. They did not answer. I suppose words failed them.

Fortunately, both David and Frances arrived to see their father at this stage, and Frances especially—large, jolly and full of laughter—cheered him up. They brought with them an atmosphere of energy and joy. We bought her a pair of cowboy boots—an easy, quick buy, so smooth it seemed predestined. The time with them was brief. Frances was dropped off to where she took the shuttle bus to Albuquerque Airport. Alex looked frail and weak, with an expression of disgust and despair on his face. He looked like my mother did at the end, as she used all her willpower and strength to hobble along.

I realized how much energy it had cost him to be with his visitors. Staggering and unsure on his feet, he appeared weaker than I had seen him since the surgery. Did this indicate a decline or just a small dip down? We talked about dying and I told him he did not have to go through some torturous treatments for my sake. He indicated he would do what the doctors suggested. I read to him some of the cancer literature I had received, but he did not hear the warnings about the effects of chemo and radiation. It seemed as though "one day at a time" was the process.

Alex did not care to talk much. He just sat. Neither did he walk, as he was told to do. Was he defeated? I took him for a drive at sunset amidst pastel shades of mountains and a streaky sunset of molten gold with orange clouds. The shifting circumstances were shifting my values. He would die. We didn't know how soon or how difficult it would be. There was affection in him tonight and he looked more accepting.

The next day we were back in town to see the oncologist. Obviously trying not to appear impatient, he was not ready to listen to Alex's stories. He was sensitive and told us that he was ready to step away from giving the suggested treatments until later, until Alex felt better or was ready. We held eye contact, searching for more understanding. We agreed on starting the treatment in a few days; just long enough to give Alex a little more healing time or the opportunity to get used to the whole idea. Alex rose to his full height, unsteady and swaying on his feet. His voice was low again. Before leaving, I raised the problem of his fluctuating energy levels, possible depression, and his lack of appetite, and I asked that these concerns to be considered.

Later, I phoned the nice young doctor for advice. He was most generous and helpful. "No, it was not a good sign that Alex was losing vitality, not eating, barely able to walk, maybe depressed." He offered to organize a physical therapist for Alex. That night, I phoned a friend, an oncology nurse in Illinois, and told her about our problem, asking for advice and her opinion. She was wonderful, very knowledgeable and helpful, and she gave me a full account about what to expect from chemo and radiation, including all the awful side-effects, which the oncologists had not mentioned. Alex looked horrified as I related the information, and I felt sick to my heart thinking of what he was to go through. She had suggested very strongly, that he choose alternative healing methods as well, and to take something for depression and anxiety. Later on, Alex vomited. Perhaps the realization of what was to come prompted an upheaval, or he decided it would not be worth it to fight for his life.

Over the next two days, Alex deteriorated, and there was very little sleep possible for both of us. A new visit to the doctor brought me to the conviction the doctor was trying to convey a message, a message I initially failed to pick up. The doctor seemed slippery and unconvincing in what he had to say, probably because he held very little faith in the suggested treatments, but he also did not want to tell Alex the bitter truth.

Standing on my Head

Because I now needed help, a hospice service was contacted. Rachel, the nurse, came, asked questions, and took notes. Two hours later, Alex was exhausted, and I felt helpless and had questions nobody seemed willing or even able to answer. The dissolution of a human being was slow, unpredictable, and not really accessible. No one knew what to do, and no one could advise me. This then, was the moment I decided to spread out my yoga mat and stand on my head with the question: "What shall I do, now that my life is turned upside down; how do I assist Alex?" It was a method developed by Swami Radha and experienced during classes I took at Yasodhara Ashram. I was physically reversed, head on the ground, reaching up to the ceiling with my feet, motionless, but breathing and calm.

In this posture, familiar surroundings were upside down. Everything was at the opposite end from what used to be the best and only "right" way. Comfort and security were challenged. This was difficult to accept. I was standing on my head—how did my strong convictions look now? In this position, like an upside-down tree, I could not move. "Do I know where I am rooted?" "When you have your head on the ground, you cannot live in the clouds." When my feet, which are symbolically rooted in the earth, became rooted in heaven, the nourishment received was no longer intellectual or even philosophical, but spiritual. To be rooted in heaven means to receive nourishment from the inner Divine. It meant being rooted in the ideals and ethics that I had established for myself.

Swaying gently, I decided to drop back down to earth, realizing the pressure I felt on the top of my head in the asana was the weight of my own body. The burdens in life were my own; it was not my task to carry the weight or the responsibility for anyone else. Psychologically speaking, the yogic practice of standing on my head had given me an answer to my question, and I felt emotionally clearer and no longer overburdened. Then, at night, I found the stages of dissolution in *The Tibetan Book of Living and Dying*. Reading the Tibetan book, I understood more clearly how to meditate and how it was supposed to feel. I had done it many times. I also knew how the clear Light looked. Furthermore, I found information about the stages a dying person goes through, which was the information I had been seeking. Now I understood better what Alex was suffering, and chanting a mantra was the most powerful help I could give him. That night I had a dream in which Swami Radha spoke to me.

It was not long before we were back in the emergency room. David wanted to see his father again and since Alex seemed to be slipping rapidly, I did not know if he would survive for another week. David begged me to take his father to the emergency room for IV fluid, so he would not dehydrate so rapidly. At the hospital we met the surgeon, who was surprised to see Alex's condition. "Perhaps he is disintegrating faster than expected," he said. They gave him the IV fluid, but instead of perking him up, he twitched and suffered more pain, and was extremely restless all night long, which meant I didn't sleep. The physical demands on me were extreme, as I had to hold him up, guide him to the bathroom, and hold him in the shower. Since he is a big man and I am small in stature, I began to hurt myself.

At this pivotal stage, Dr. Carl Friedrichs called one evening and actually made a house call in order to give me a personal opinion about Alex. Dr. Friedrichs and Alex sat in the living room conversing. Dr. Friedrichs was a very centered and firm young man who watched and listened. Alex talked and went into his entertainment mode, surprising us with his mental agility and humor. The Dr. Friedrichs listened and observed. Patiently he waited for things to happen and unfold and did not pressure Alex in any way. Towards the end of this visit he said, "Negative experiences are often the most misleading because we usually take them as a bad sign, but in fact, the negative experiences in our practice are a blessing in disguise. Try not to react to them with aversion, as you might normally do, but recognize them instead for what they truly are, merely experiences, illusory and dreamlike. The realization of the true nature of the experience liberates you from the harm or danger of the experience itself, and as a result even a negative experience can become a source of great blessing and accomplishment." The men shook hands and Alex excused himself, saying he was tired, and he disappeared into the bedroom. Dr. Friedrichs made only one comment to me: "He is a very special being. I am so very sorry."

I was up repeatedly in the night because Alex was vomiting. He complained that he felt awful. I called our doctor, who ordered an IV. The hospice nurse came and inserted the IV. It was no sooner in position than Alex wanted it off. His back hurt, his ribs hurt, he felt sore all over. I questioned the rationale of feeding Alex intravenously when he was unable to eat or even expected to improve in the near future. The nurse agreed and explained to me what was happening to Alex, an explanation I was grateful to receive. She pointed out that in someone so severely dehydrated, nerve ends become dulled and even die and pain is numbed. "Nature is much kinder in helping along the dying process than we are. Trying to help, we interfere, making dying harder for the patient. If you want to be kind, don't interfere by reviving what is shutting down in the body. All those nerve endings become sensitive again and the general pain level increases." She instructed me in how to remove the IV, and after it was pulled out, Alex was relieved and content.

All of this was very different from what I had imagined. With one part of my being I felt at ease, and accepted what was happening, and yet in another part ambivalence and disbelief arose, and disorientation and confusion came. In so many ways this was a very important day. David and Frances were called and informed of the non-verbal commitment to let life go, and with it any efforts to help him maintain an existence deprived of quality. Alex was much more alert after the IV, which led me to believe, his attention span, memory, and awareness were slipping. During the afternoon he vomited three times.

With December approaching, David wanted to return to Santa Fe, as did Kirstin, who worried about me and what I would do later. I did some yogic breath-work with Alex, which helped very much. I noticed too that he now stood upright and straightened his back before starting to walk, as I suggested he do, to have greater balance. In the afternoon, my most kind and concerned friend Alicia, the only friend I had in Santa Fe, came by to allow me to take a walk.

The air felt wonderfully fresh on my face. When I returned, Alicia was frantic. Alex had taken a downturn, feeling he was plunging off a precipice, perhaps dying. I called the hospice; I needed more help. I was so tired by nightfall; my brain was not tracking any more. The constant sleep interruptions were taking their toll. Kirstin called with the news she had a flight in the beginning of December and that she was coming with the full understanding that he might not be alive then. She told me that she had soaked Kent's shirt the night before crying, "The daddy I knew changed as long as six years ago!" She was correct, as I had felt and noticed the same change. In 1990 I observed for the first time that he no longer had clarity of mind.

Rapid Decline

Alex was going rapidly downhill. In spite of the pain and nausea medications, he tolerated only small sips of water and that not always. The phone rang almost nonstop. Friends were calling from all over the world. I needed someone to sit with Alex, as he did not like to be left alone, and I had to go out or nap sometimes. I was relieved when the new nurse arrived. A hospice bed was also delivered, as well as a wheelchair, and we could change the bed sheets and he could be washed. Everything was now in the care of a higher force and would flow as it wanted and take its own course.

Another night followed with constantly broken sleep. I dreamed, recalling just snatches of wonderful messages. In my dream, two Tibetans arrived. They were warm, enlightened beings and carried an atmosphere of centered fearlessness and deep wisdom. They promised to guide me. Alex drifted, confused in his mind, asking if this was his house. Yesterday, he started to sweat, which meant the fire chakra was activated, according to the Tibetan interpretation of the dying process.

David, Frances, and Kirstin arrived and a quiet and peaceful day ensued. Alex somehow picked up as the energy of his children surrounded him, and he was enfolded in their care and love. We all hovered around him as he was being washed, talking and walking with him when he needed the bathroom. I asked him, "How do you feel?" He paused, as if searching for the right words. "Rotten," he answered. In my shredded emotional state, I registered a sensation of quiet acceptance. Alex was a walking skeleton by this point, and somehow it was all very real and very unreal. He asked me, "When will I get my gold watch?" He had anticipated a gift of a gold watch upon retirement.

I waited in anticipation for the return to some sense of reality, but I knew the security I had was gone forever. Soon I would be completely alone. On this day last year, Swami Sivananda Radha died, and now Alex, too, would go. The phone rang constantly as old friends connected, and even remote relatives and students somehow got the news. The days melted together, nights were shattered with broken sleep, and there was the loss of all patterns or habitual ways of living. Frances and Kirstin took over the kitchen and food preparation. Hospice nurses came and went, and the confusion mounted as too many people moved in and out of the living room. People were kind and told me how hard it is to lose a loved one. Daily, I somehow managed to practice interrupted yoga, and the soothing flow of the asana helped and returned vigor and clarity of mind to my tired brain. I found it amazing and truly marvelous.

Cynthia, the nurse, said to me, "He hangs on. He is very determined," which was true. With eyes half open, he lay there wanting to leave and go elsewhere. During the night, the strain was beginning to upset the whole family. David hugged Kirstin, sobbing bitterly. Frances had to leave the house because she felt so overwhelmed. Alex was now calling out to his Mummy, asking—no begging—to be let out. He also called for water, and his agitation was so extreme during the night that no one could sleep. At dawn came a call from Alex's former wife Ildiko in France. I held the receiver for him as Ildiko talked. He whispered, "Bye-bye," and then I took the receiver for a few closing words with Ildiko. "Imagine," she said, "if I had stayed married to him, I would now be becoming a widow."

The following morning, a glorious sunrise of fiery red and golden clouds covered the vast sky. Alex looked dead already. His eyes were turned up, and he was breathing in long gasps. No longer able to swallow, a pill given to him last night was still in his mouth, white powder dissolved, caking his tongue.

David had to go back to work, and the following day, Kirstin and Fanny also had to leave. I promised to take them out for lunch before they flew back home. Two new caretakers came, Mary and Richard. Richard was somehow special and I discovered he was a Buddhist. They would both be with Alex while I was out. Richard immediately collected all the pillows he could find and, lifting Alex's legs, back, and head, inserted support under his stiffening body, clearly making him more comfortable. Why had I not thought of that? He also told Alex that his name was Richard, that today was the 8th of December, and the time of day. While I got ready, Kirstin was holding Alex's hands, and I felt her anguish and pain. Later she told me she felt so helpless, so useless, because all she could do was to hold his hands. Little did she know that she had done the most valuable and loving deed by holding his hands in hers and supporting him by not letting go.

I intuited that Alex might go during the night that followed, so I sat and chanted my mantra aloud while holding his hand. I was alone in the house and felt teary and distraught. The crushed ice I offered to Alex for his dry mouth choked him. He could not swallow any more. His breath had become labored and while holding his hand, I notice his fingers were turning pale blue and the nails purple. His eyes had sunken in and the left eye was half open with the pupil turned upwards, as if focused on the forehead. What I assumed to be a death rattle in his throat manifested at times, and there was a curious metallic smell.

The nurse arrived. Alex had a fever and his temperature was 102 degrees, which she managed to lower within the hour with icepacks under the armpits. Then she left and Richard had not yet arrived. I thought that Alex couldn't live much longer, but that I might be wrong. At midnight, Richard came, much to my relief. He looked carefully at Alex and then proposed we meditate. Why had I not thought of this? It was an appropriate thing to do. He advised asking for help, a suggestion I found very helpful. My back had been very sore all evening, but it stopped hurting while we meditated. Richard guided the meditation briefly, and I relaxed and let go of physical fear, I transmitted this approach to Alex.

An inner assurance manifested itself and I entrusted myself to the visions that followed. I saw an elegant, long-fingered hand, almost like an ancient Egyptian hand, stroking the dome of a shaved head, suggesting release through the fontanelle. Then I invoked Swami Sivananda Radha and help from the great Guru Sivananda. He was instantly present; wearing his long dark coat. He looked into my eyes, then dipped his cupped hands into water and lifted them up allowing the water caught in his hands to run through his fingers. He repeated this process, illustrating that liquid cannot be held onto. The suggestion of release was powerful.

I saw Alex, his blue eyes. Richard later claimed he too had seen the blue eyes. We both felt his physical fear and his holding on to this concrete reality, to the known, and felt his effort to release himself into the Unknown. Eventually I came out of meditation and Richard and I compared notes. While I had not seen Swami Radha, only a spiral of smoky light, Richard claimed he had seen her. I held up a photo of her to show him as a comparison. He assured me this was precisely the same person. Then Richard told me more about himself. He had studied psychology and was fearless, using all means to gain deeper understanding.

It was late. Richard suggested I lie down and rest while he fixed himself a cup of coffee. I went to the office and lay down on the bed. Suddenly I felt restless and vulnerable. I felt a sense of Alex complaining, irritated that someone else was using his coffee grinder. Even the silence disturbed. Then I heard a knock on the door. "He left as I was making the coffee," said Richard.

Quickly, I went and looked at Alex. His one eye was half open, the lower jaw dropped down, his skin was waxen and pale, his curls were gone, and his hair hung limp and straight. His hands were still warm when I touched them, as was his forehead. All resemblance to the man I had known was gone. He looked burnt clean, burnt by the fire of fever and suffering and his skin, which had been much wrinkled, was now smooth and unmarked. He resembled his great-grandfather, with strong cheekbones and powerful features. The only part I still recognized as his were the elegant artist's hands. Those belonged to Alex. I stroked across the backs of his hands, soft skin, slightly blue, and heard the joints cracking as they had already stiffened.

"Let's meditate," said Richard's voice and so we settled down once more. "Where are you now?" I asked Alex in my mind and much to my surprise I received an instant answer. "I shall piss off to Scotland." The sensation that he had been pissed off, and so left his body; maybe even been pissed off with me, was strong. Then came a sensation he was going away, home to Scotland, to his youth, away from all this pain and struggle. Some tears came; I was alone now. Richard talked to me, which was welcome. He left at 3:20 am. Alex had died at 2:15 am. I cried.

Eventually, I passed out. I awoke to sunshine, which flooded the whole room. Across from me lay a waxen body, a stranger. I would never have recognized him as Alex. His chest, when I laid my hand on it, was still warm. His fingers and nails were blue. The second eye was partially open, too, mouth agape, slightly crooked. His hands had become stiff. I wondered if I should make a photo, but what for?

All experience was reality and of potential value. I could spare myself the corrosive effects of despair. Alex did not want to live any more. The greatest obstacles were my cycles of fear, doubt, and confusion. To live fully, I needed to let the past go and think accurately and clearly. Inside me I screamed with pain, with regret, with love for a ghost. Going, going, gone. I placed a flower on his chest.

All day long I fought the tendency to feel self-pity and an exaggerated view of my bleak future. I remembered when Alex and I first met, the early years, the joy and laughter and being young. The face that looked at me in the mirror was an old, tired stranger. By evening, his spiritual heart center was still warm, his head cold and stiff. The eyes were caving in. Many people phoned, some of them were intuitive, sensing the need to make a call. All their thoughts and words helped and supported me. I felt grateful.

Because it was Sunday, the corpse stayed here an extra day, and I felt grateful I was allowed extra time to become accustomed to the loss. The physical changes were continuous, showing me how rapidly decay set in. The next morning the funerary service arrived to collect the corpse. The men looked exactly as people who collect corpses should look. One had a long, thin, frail brown Spanish face, sensitive and serious.

He looked as if straight out of a Goya painting. They were respectful and kind. He would be cremated, and I could pick up the ashes in two weeks.

Accepting Loss

In retrospect I would say that I accepted death, and that I did not grieve excessively. Of course, I felt torn up inside and felt the loss of Alex intensely, but I also experienced his spirit as available whenever I was about to go over the edge with grief. One such occasion was during a walk into a hiking trail called "the green belt" in Eldorado. I walked to get a grip on myself and kept thinking about him. Suddenly, in front of my eyes, little pieces of something like a puzzle came together. They were alive and moving, and then, to my astonishment, I saw Alex, as clearly as the trees round about. He was smiling at me and looked happy. I saw his entire body before he vanished. This vision happened only once and I have no explanation for it.

However, when I drove the car and was focused on nothing but the road in front of me, very often I would suddenly get a sense he was sitting beside me. Several times he warned me of a dangerous traffic situation which, as a consequence, I was able to circumvent. Once, a truck was ahead of me on St. Michael's Drive. A large ladder badly tied to the truck bed was bouncing up and down. "Overtake this truck, and fast," was the urgent message I received. I obeyed instantly and then, looking back, saw that the ladder had fallen off and was lying in the path of oncoming traffic. The voice had been Alex's and I thanked him. It became easier when I allowed myself to trust my experiences, especially when they confirmed that other levels exist.

I had kept many letters Alex had written to me over the years. I began to read them again and sat there, often laughing my head off because of his wonderful sense of humor. Of course, afterwards I was sad again and people told me to "go forward." The biggest positive shift I made was when I began to thank him daily for all he had given to me, for all the joy, the laughter, the many years of love and trust and kindness. The focus was on the positive and this brought inner healing with it.

I drove to Albuquerque with the sensation of unease because I was picking up Alex's ashes and did not know my way around the city. Not having Alex to rely on means I was constantly experiencing the unknown. I fully realized that my discomfort was an illusion, but the illusion of his support had been so powerful and had made my life so easy that I now felt fragile and vulnerable. However, I found Sunrise Cremation without problem and received the ashes in a smallish cardboard box. Mister Pederson asked if he could carry the ashes, but I declined the offer. When I picked up the box it was surprisingly heavy and I almost dropped it.

The president of Lake Forest College called me to make arrangements for a memorial service the college was planning to give. He told me that, prior to his brain surgery, Alex had come to ask him to support me, should he die. It twisted my heart that in his own suffering, he had worried over me. Kirstin reminded me that Alex had really died years ago. He never really returned from that brain surgery. From then on all had been an illusion, vain hope, hanging onto the past, or trying to fix what was irreversibly draining away. Thirty years of life with him evaporated like the mist when the sun comes out. The process had been slow, which allowed me time to become used to it. What a shock a sudden loss must be, without the opportunity to say goodbye. I had been protected and shielded, something I must acknowledge.

The memorial service for Alex would be in the college chapel, followed by a dinner invitation in Glen Rowen. The dean, who was one of our friends, made the suggestion to combine these events with an exhibition of Alex's paintings in the college art gallery on campus. "You might even consider a donation of some pieces to the college," he suggested. Other work might be offered for sale during the exhibit. I approved both suggestions, as I had already thought of donating some art to the college. We also discussed an Art History Award in Alex Mitchell's name for future students graduating with

Honors in Art History. For a time, I was kept very busy with arrangements for the exhibition. I had to select the paintings, mostly gouaches, and organize their framing. My friend Kay also wished to have a large dinner party for the family and friends, including an invitation to the opera *Turandot* for us all, including Frances. The generosity of Kay was truly amazing. Returning to Illinois and a familiar environment was something I looked forward to and especially seeing Kirstin and Kent.

What to do with my life now became a big question in my mind, and I meditated on it frequently. It felt as if I had stepped from the fullness of life into a monk's cell. I longed to paint again, but art seemed such a difficult thing to return to, especially as I hadn't found a gallery on Canyon Road, the art street of Santa Fe, that was interested in my work. I began to realize I could easily become distracted by some unworthy pursuits.

One evening, I received a call from Berny V., an old friend, whose wife had died some months before Alex. He was in Bali and started by telling me what a paradise he was experiencing. "It is absolutely a place I need to share with you, I shall pay your flight and anything you need; just get your passport and come." "It is not even a month since Alex died," I told him, "I really am hardly over the shock of all that. Sorry, but I cannot accept your very generous invitation." I don't think he understood, for he kept on begging like someone deeply lost in no man's land. It made doubly clear to me that the grieving process needed to be fully experienced before any other distractions surfaced. Berny was obviously looking for a distraction.

To heal myself, I went on daily walks. My existence seemed utterly unreal and the landscape surrounding me, the mountains and drifting clouds casting ever shifting shadows, also seemed unreal. I felt numb and disconnected. I wrote a lot of thank you notes to people in response to their condolence letters and flowers, but beyond all I did was the awareness of a sense of unreality. There were also many questions in the forefront of my mind, like: Was Alex really so unaware that he did not notice the signs of his colon cancer? Was there no blood in his stool, or black excrement? No cramps or pain?

Did he choose death over the inconvenience of medical investigation and treatment? What was going on in his mind? Could it be that his mind did not function properly after his brain surgery, and did I miss out and fail to recognize something horrible?

I stood in the vacuum left by Alex. My life had been a commitment to another being who was now gone. The widow of the British poet Dylan Thomas composed a summary of her existence after his death, calling it "Leftover Life to Kill." Sometimes I was rather close to that myself. I had a nagging and almost constant suspicion that Alex kept a huge secret in his heart and soul which he did not share with me. Recently I met the doctor who diagnosed Alex's cancer and came to the house to give me an assessment of his condition in 1996. Out of the blue, he said to me, "Alex knew he had cancer, you know this, don't you?" I said, "No, I thought he was unaware of his condition!" Then I thanked him profusely, for he had freed me from the nagging doubt and suspicion that had bothered me for years. I was asking to be shown and to understand what had happened to Alex—the truth, not what I would like to see and think, but the truth!

The moment I returned to Illinois to go to the memorial service, I felt grateful not to be living there anymore. Everywhere I saw houses tightly clustered and huddled together. It is all too familiar. I spent 30 years here with Alex, who was my core, my love, and my faith, though without a physical presence, he was somehow still present. I stayed with Kirstin and Kent in Highland Park in an old, upstairs apartment, somehow charming in its old verities and comfort born of another age. Kent was a quiet man, and I noticed that as a couple they were so intuitive that they understood each other without words. We had lunch in Chicago and visited the Art Institute, where I had shown and sold my paintings for so many years.

Everything reminded me of life with Alex and of a younger, happier time. It would have been much more difficult to overcome my loss had I stayed in Illinois. The following day was spent with Kirstin in her classroom on the north side of Chicago. The children were sweet. Most of them were living with grandmothers because their mothers were young teenagers.

I helped hang the gouache images painted by Alex in the college gallery. It went very smoothly, and the show looked wonderful and contained some of his very best work. A lot of friends and faculty had connected with me in order to buy a painting before the opening, so we placed red dots on quite a few pieces.

David and Frances arrived at night. It was awful weather, driving wind and rain. David's plane was delayed for nearly four hours. The next morning, Wilson, Alex's cousin, arrived from Toronto. Alex's longtime friend Michael Croydon flew in from France. Telephone calls were almost constant. There was high energy at times and exhaustion in me with the fear I might become ill.

By early afternoon we went to the little college chapel. It felt like a vast energy field had picked me up, and all decision-making was out of my hands. Events just rolled along on oiled wheels in perfection. The first two speakers were close friends and they spoke eloquently and touchingly. Before this, Abba tenderly played the sublime "Air on a G String." Then a young woman sang "Ave Maria" with the accompaniment of Ann on piano. It was moving, and briefly it felt as if Alex's spirit was present and watching. Florrie read a brilliant tribute from her husband George.

Alex would have been proud of his two daughters. Frances, looking suave and, speaking with pointed intensity, gave account of the last days she spent with her father. She was followed by Kirstin reading a poem written two days ago on the spur of the moment. Michael then spoke, which was hard for him as he was very emotionally upset.

The tributes to Alex were deeply moving and the chapel was packed to the doors with people he had touched centrally in some way. When the Scottish piper came with familiar Gaelic tunes, Frances broke down crying. I looked at the piper's bony knees and pleated kilt and focused on breathing to keep the tears away.

At the reception that followed, I never got past the entry passage. I hugged person after person, old friends, acquaintances, and strangers. Oddly, I was not tired at all by this. Later, at a dinner party given by Kay, this trend continued. Berny was there, obviously lonely, and now he asked me to come to Florida with him. My refusal to come to Bali had not dampened his enthusiasm, and he repeatedly touched and massaged my arm and shoulder. I felt sorry for his loneliness, but I had little interest in alleviating it. Michael was visibly grieving. Everyone flowed back and forth like blossoms on a quiet bend in a stream. A former student of Alex called Angela said, "I always thought I had a very special relationship with Alex, my professor. He called me 'La Bella,' and now I discover he had this elevated kind of relationship with everyone. To me he is a very outstanding human being."

All too soon I was boarding a plane to return to an empty house in Eldorado, but with gratitude and a feeling of love for all those who had been so kind and generous in sharing my grief. They gave me an unexpected lift with their compassion and friendship.

At about this time I discovered a yoga book called *The Heart of Yoga* by T.K.V. Desikachar, the son of a legendary yogi called Krishnamacharya, who had trained almost all the most famous yogis of the 20th century. I began to study and use this book, and I wished I could meet a teacher from this lineage. Never in my wildest dreams did I think then that this wish would be granted in a very short time and be followed by many years of training by a very remarkable and amazing woman.

Throughout the difficult period of Alex's sickness and death I had been teaching yoga in Eldorado, usually three classes a week. To focus on hatha yoga and Kundalini yoga was most helpful, as it allowed me to balance my mind. The dualism in me was quite strong. Impatience with circumstances and rejection of what was difficult was splitting and dividing my mind. I really had liked the comfort and security of my marriage. Alex was my rock of Gibraltar, and now an insecure and immature part of me surfaced and wanted what was forever gone.

A false perception took over, called "avidya" in Sanskrit. Avidya is the root cause of obstacles that prevent us from recognizing things as they really are. Our vision is clouded when avidya is present, and we do not recognize the inner confusion. It also causes us to act indecisively. For most of the year I struggled with the changing circumstances in my life and focused intensely on spiritual practices. This then also became the time to venture forth to discover this amazing land of enchantment in which I had landed but had only investigated in a limited way.

I joined a hiking group, and every Sunday I ventured out to a different destination. I discovered Tent Rocks and was thrilled by the beauty of the Hoodoos. Bandelier National Monument was a next destination, and the healing mineral springs of Ojo Caliente took me by storm. I set myself the goal of venturing to a new location every weekend and hiked the back country surrounding Ghost Ranch, as well as Taos and Chaco Canyon. Most of these excursions were discoveries I made on my own. When I told some women about my hikes, I was scolded and told it was dangerous for a solitary female to take such risks. I asked what they thought of Georgia O'Keeffe driving to the badlands to paint her pictures! No comment! I did, however, leave Devil's Canyon when I found teenagers cavorting there, holding beer bottles and shooting guns at the rocks.

I met some artists and was inspired to paint again. Being an artist is a solitary occupation, and to bring myself into closer contact with the art community, I began to visit the art openings in the Santa Fe galleries. It also informed me about the different styles of painting that were successful in town—at times a depressing experience, especially when my work was not accepted. As Robert Browning said, "My business is not to remake myself, but make the absolute best of what God has made." I don't have to redo or change myself; I have to be fully what I am already.

17 Finding a New Balance

Focusing on Gratitude and Small Gifts

I continued to struggle for daily balance while painting in a small backroom with insufficient space and ventilation. I was also confronting difficulties with my yoga classes since many students proved to be quite fickle in their attendance. Hoping to gain clarity of mind, I signed up for some workshops at Yasodhara Ashram during July. Maybe I was hoping to find consolation and inner peace, maybe I thought going there would soothe my heart, but it turned out to be different. Once I arrived at Yasodhara, I was instantly adjusting to the Ashram and completely in the present moment. On the fourth day, I had a horrible dream that the house in Santa Fe was leaking from most windows, ceilings, and even inside a closet. What is my subconscious trying to tell me? The monsoon season can be intense in New Mexico. Was my house in danger of being flooded?

I had left the house in charge of a friend, an art dealer and his artist wife from Chicago, who came to spend their vacation in Santa Fe. It was not they who phoned me at breakfast time; it was Kirstin. "There is a really bad leak in the closet under the floor," she said. As it turned out, the builder had installed copper pipes made in Mexico, seemingly of poor quality. Now the floor was flooding from under the house. Since the rain was

Yoga class in the Santa Fe home

pouring in New Mexico, the windows were leaking as well and the walls were drenched. The art dealer and his wife did not know what to do aside from putting towels on the floor. Should I leave and go back to Santa Fe to deal with the mess? I could not expect my house guests to deal with this inundation!

"Learn endurance," the swamis had advised me! My usual calm was gone; there was no escape. My friends had to leave my house. It was not possible to live in it! I decided to stay at the Ashram until my departure time came and I would cope with the mess in Eldorado once I was back. My mind was clear and my decision was the right choice. The days sped past with intense lessons; I was learning to toughen up.

The flight back to New Mexico was uneventful, except that my flight was late and I missed the last shuttle bus from Albuquerque to Santa Fe. A last taxi drove up. About ten people rushed to the cab. "I shall only take the person needing the longest and most expensive trip," the driver said. I was in luck as my drive cost $100. Well after midnight we arrived at my brightly illuminated house—all the lights were on. It was very hot and airless inside, as all the windows had been shut. I had no emotional connection to the flooding damage as I pulled my suitcase over the doorstep. In the walk-in closet beside the master bedroom, I encountered a deep, freshly dug hole. Earth was piled high in a corner beside my clothes. A copper pipe with three to four pin-sized holes in it had been the culprit and the plumbers said the holes were caused by electric charges from the earth. They replaced the pipe, repaired the floor, and put the carpet back in place. The roof also had to be repaired once again.

September approached with the invitation to an exhibition of Alex's gouaches at the college, which was handled by the gallery director and dean. I accepted, the Chicago flight was fast, and before I knew it, I was looking down onto the green suburbs of Chicago. I felt happy and light, looking forward to seeing Kirstin and Kent. Kirstin picked me up and once in Highland Park, we walked through the pretty, flower-planted center of town, stopping for a coffee at Starbucks. This was wealthy America with expensive boutiques, model dresses, fancy cars, inventive and exciting stores, and old, dark, shady trees.

Kirstin and Kent's charming, second floor apartment had an aura of comfort and familiarity. It overlooked a very green oasis of a garden with old trees, a perfect place for my early morning yoga practice. Their black cat, Luna, was already in my suitcase, investigating to see if it contained anything of interest, and Kent made one of his special meals to welcome me. The love and kindness I was being showered with made me realize how much I had been missing—just a simple hug, being with family, but mostly just not being alone. In our conversations that followed, Kirstin revealed they were seriously thinking of marriage. She also would like to try for a job in Santa Fe, though she had been warned that getting a good teaching position was difficult. Kent was willing to leave the Midwest, in part because any house or flat in Illinois was prohibitively expensive and all they would be able to afford would be a fixer-upper. That meant years of trying to fix something that was way past fixing in the first place. The prospect of their coming to New Mexico was overwhelming me with joy. It would make our lives much simpler if we were closer together, especially if they had a baby.

But first, there was this whole big exhibition of Alex's work. It was being handled with attention to detail and no expense was spared. There were dinner invitations paid for by wealthy people, some I barely knew, but they knew Alex and wanted to honor him. There were luncheons with friends, speeches at the opening reception, praises for Alex and for who he was, events I never expected and which were fairly overwhelming. People I had thought little of turned out to be kind, thoughtful, generous, and warm-hearted.

Suddenly the next day, I unexpectedly found myself feeling ill and spent a whole day in bed. I lay in Kirstin and Kent's comfortable little guest room looking at the painting of the Madera Mountain that Alex painted in 1967. It was a gift to Kirstin, and it reminded me of 1967 and how a taxi drove us up to the volcano, to the peaks above the clouds, on a road lined with the most splendid hydrangea in pastel pink and sky-blue colors. The most stunning spectacle opened up as we rose above the clouds. When we got out of the car it was freezing cold at this altitude. I wore no more than a thin cotton dress, so after a few photos we snuggled back into the taxi and it took me a while to warm up again.

Alex was haunted by the peak, painting several versions of it. Kirstin was conceived that autumn, but I did not believe it until the gynecologist, a charming doctor, assured me that I was "in the family way." I looked into a lamp standing beside his desk as he told me this, seeing only the light and feeling amazement spread through me. That was 30 years ago. On the bedside table stood a photo Kirstin took in Edinburgh. It shows Alex and me and speaks so clearly of the closeness between two beings. That life was now gone forever.

My stay in Illinois was brief, and then I was home in sunny Santa Fe and glad to be back, for here was a new way of life to be built. I had the choice of facing with indifference all the unexpected events, such as the flood damage to my house, or suffering and complaining any time I had to confront difficulties.

Shouldering an uncomfortable hard task requires stamina. Rising above the negative and focusing more on gratitude and the small gifts—usually overlooked—brings one face to face with the magical. Or so I learned.

For me, my hatha yoga sessions during which I chanted the Gayatri mantra brought a certain transformation. I began to feel more, see more deeply, experience differently. I assumed the lotus pose and meditated on Light, finding tears of gratitude for the training I had received. The possibility of living in Bliss and Light is at my fingertips, available now. Hatha yoga led me into it and imperceptibly my surroundings became beautiful, even a damaged wall. I felt amazed to see such beauty, which was like a gentle, indescribable fragrance radiating out from everywhere. A luminous haze surrounded all the trees, birdsong became a symphony, and my sense perceptions were heightened to where I hear a black stink bug warning me of its presence on my yoga mat. Whole days went by in an altered awareness. New Mexico had so many interesting places for me to discover, and this I chose to take advantage of.

Discovering the Land of Enchantment

I drove to Ghost Ranch and hiked into a back area called the Box Canyon. The earth there was God's country. Ancient red rocks inspired with their unusual formations. The air, fragrant with juniper and spiced with the rich smell of earth, left me reeling with delight. The trees, so brightly yellow, felt like sunlight hitting my optic nerve. A spring ran along the path to the canyon and needed to be crossed constantly. I knew beforehand a man would be walking the same path, and so it was—a man with a dog, and fortunately the wet paw prints of the dog guided me. When I reached the Box Canyon, the ground was viridian green with lush soft grass and huge boulders that had collapsed into the canyon from above. I sat there for a bit. The spring murmured, and the leaves shivering in the breeze sounded like falling raindrops. I was glad I had made the effort to come here. I understood why mankind had built temples, stupas, domes, cathedrals, pyramids and mosques. The sheer size of a dome of rock lifts the heart in inspiration. One's own little problems dissolve when seeing greatness.

As I sat at Ghost Ranch eating my sandwich, I understood why the artist Georgia O'Keeffe had chosen to live there. It was so peaceful that even the hum of an insect gains importance and everything becomes magnified. This was spiritual country! It healed my soul. An understanding was forming in my mind. Alex was not someone I owned or was responsible for. As I continued to relinquish ownership, I began to understand his destiny better. I felt progressively freer.

Kirstin called and told me how she cried for twenty minutes about Alex's dying. To her enormous surprise, her earache and sore throat, which had been bothering her for quite a while, were gone, completely gone! Emotionally, she felt so much better. Did this experience prove that holding onto painful memories and distress created illness? It is understood that weeping in sorrow is cathartic.

Wedding Plans

For Kirstin's 31st birthday, I returned to Illinois. We went jogging together early in the morning, running past a lovely wood. It was very humid, and I was sweating for at least one hour afterwards. Kent and Kirstin were having a simple wedding party and then planned to marry in June on the island of Tortola in the British Virgin Islands. Kirstin was very tense, feeling she needed to organize every detail and make sure nothing would go wrong. Mia, a friend, offered her lovely garden for the reception. We set up the chairs and tables in the morning. The garden looked lovely with the tent and tables invitingly placed among trees and flowers. The actual event passed in a haze of activities. During this time, I met some old friends again.

Only too quickly, it was my turn to return to New Mexico, and the shift from the intensely green Midwest to the desert climate of the Southwest stood in stark contrast. I awoke under a smoky sky. The forests were burning. The land was parched, the monsoon rains had failed, and we were in a drought. The grass looked yellow. In my mind's eye, I saw the lush, green, sparkling foliage of Illinois and the view from the little bedroom onto rooftops in Highland Park. I saw the bustle of life all around, sunlight and breezes moving the heavy foliage of the trees. It suddenly hit me how much love there was in Illinois, how much caring and kindness I experienced, how warm and embracing people were, and how joyful was the event of the wedding. Alex and I had those 30 years in Lake Forest in a tight little house brimming with love. What mattered was not that at times I felt frustrated with the constriction; what mattered was the all-embracing joy of life.

New Mexico was vast open land; there was space and my house was airy and spacious. I could dance in my kitchen. Swami Radha said, "Put quality into your life." This place of mine in the high desert was very pure. I can develop here and can put high quality into my existence. Instead of aiming ambitiously for illusory goals, I can permit circumstances to unfold organically. Quality is gradually establishing itself. It started with the food. I now mostly eat vegetarian and organic. Evenings are the most difficult as my energy begins to sag. I can't afford to allow myself to get weepy and full of self-pity. For years, I did not eat dinner because of my tendency not to feel hungry at night. Now I need to eat to keep my inner balance. A small tasty meal eaten by candle light at the dining room table became standard.

I met a wonderful woman named Rebecca. She taught Reiki and healed people through touch. When Alex lay dying, I felt so useless, and my hands itched to soothe his pain. I tried passing my hands over his body, but he stopped me with a firm "Don't." He had never liked to be touched, so I was not surprised. Rebecca invited me to my first Reiki session. After climbing onto the massage table, I was covered with a sheet and told to close my eyes. The hands did not touch, but floated above my body. The energy felt boiling hot, intense, uncomfortable. Surrender to it, I told myself. Then a hand slipped under my waist. It was unexpected, and it felt good, strange, surprising. A firm palm placed itself on my head and I felt the pressure on my crown. New experiences, unexpected, different, shocking even. My guts became active, intestines gurgling. Later, Rebecca told me I needed grounding. I did not breathe fully either, which was not really surprising. However, the session had convinced me that I wanted to learn Reiki.

There were other women who formed a group and then our Reiki lessons began. Rebecca was an excellent teacher and very sensitive. She had a kind heart and she helped me in unexpected ways. For example, she recommended me to the owner in a spa called the Vista Clara Ranch. They were looking for a yoga teacher and were willing to pay well. I ended up instructing asanas to spa guests, who were curious and interested in the "experience of yoga." The drawback was that beyond a single experience there was generally no further instruction. I was always teaching beginners; no commitment or continuation was expected. Some were grateful, some said they really enjoyed yoga, some said they would try to find a teacher once they returned home, but the built-in limitation was eventually too disheartening for me. The classes were taught in a huge kiva, a round underground structure based on those built by the native populations in the past. Kivas were spiritual centers and used for prayers. Such a space was absolutely wonderful for my little classes, and I believed it impressed the spa guests.

Plans for a Trip to Egypt

One day, I heard from Kirstin, and she approached me with the request that I fulfil a promise I made to her long ago, that I would take her to Egypt and show her where I grew up. I had saved some money and the end of March during the springtime might be the best time for a visit. In May, the expected sandstorms would come and the heat would be unpleasant. I set off and picked up brochures in town. A guided group tour seemed the best way to go, if possible, with a boat voyage from Cairo to Upper Egypt. I pored over the Egypt trip information; I had not gone back in 40 years and was completely ignorant of the probable changes. I decided on adding extra days and met with a nice agent at AAA to get clearer ideas.

Many new discoveries had been made and I watched a videotape of a huge archeological find where hundreds of mummies were found near an oasis. There was a brief insert showing the Egyptian Actor Omar Sharif. He described returning to Cairo after living abroad and being shocked at his inability to recognize the city. The images of Cairo made me feel dizzy. The dusty metropolis of millions of inhabitants showed a sparkling range of skyscrapers, and I realized I was not going back to what I knew, but to a transformed country. I could not go home. At the age of 25 I had made the decision to leave and go to America. I closed my heart to this magical country that I loved like no other, and then actually found no chances for a return.

During this time, a book which I had always wanted to read, *Searching for Om Seti*, fell into my hands. Written by an English woman, it described her remarkable, strange life. It brought back memories of my own, like my obsession with Hippopotami. We are told that Egyptian women often gave birth in water, and this is why Taweret, the protector of children, is a green, female hippopotamus goddess. The only ancient piece of jewelry I wear is a pendant of a little faience hippo named Taweret. In Kenya, I picked up a huge black wood carving of a hippo and also a hippo carved of green malachite. The only item I resented losing when my sister and I split our inheritance after my mother's death was a copy of an ancient Egyptian sculpture of a faience hippo with a lotus painted on its side. I had actually bought it in Cairo, but I left it with my mother. It is not a coincidence that these figures spoke to me; rather they were part of ancient memories surfacing in this life. The first hippo I ever saw was in the Cairo Zoo, and I stood in front of it completely mesmerized by its power and stature. The color green is the color of resurrection, the color of Osiris.

Most nights I read about Egypt again. I felt terrified to go back. All had changed, and my whole past stood up before me, which was somehow overwhelming. I realized most of the people I once knew are now dead. I forged my own identity, chose what appealed to me as I grew up in Egypt. My identity thus was closely linked to this civilization. I read in the Egyptian *Book of the Dead* that "being" depends on being open. "I am the shape I made," says the consciousness that carries itself into the realest worlds. I am "becoming," always becoming, always in process.

> "That man frees himself who overcomes himself."
> J.W. von Goethe.

Funny how long it takes to pack a suitcase. Tiny decisions about what skirt is wearable with what top take up a lot of time. Finally, the suitcase is packed and a morning has passed. My mind complains, saying it should have been a lot faster. The day of the flight to Chicago came with a rush to the Albuquerque airport, then a stop in Denver and a lengthy delay. After all the rushing there was enforced leisure time. I read my book, which was stimulating. Two hours went by. We flew into heavy grey cloud formations and then we were circling over Chicago. The colors outside the window of the plane had gone to monochrome, black and white. It was snowing and raining when we finally landed. I was back to where I had lived for 30 years, an oddly familiar and at the same time unfamiliar experience. When I arrived here from Egypt 35 years ago, it was also snowing and sleeting. Kirstin picked me up.

It was good to be with my daughter and Kent, a warm, sweet couple. The apartment looked like a charming nest. Kirstin had framed many of her paintings, and they bloomed on the walls like glowing flowers. Outside it was snowing and blustery for the rest of the day.

Return to Egypt

The long flight to Cairo seemed easier than expected. Kirstin, who gets claustrophobic on planes, managed to sleep with the help of a tranquilizer. Cairo was familiar and simultaneously new and strange! We followed the line of passengers into the arrival hall when a young man offered to transport us for 30 pounds. Clearly, he was one of those sharks that offer to guide tourists. The language came flooding back to me as I bargained without hesitation to get a better price. Yes, he assured me, he had a taxi. The car was no taxi but we took it anyway. Crossing one of the bridged overpasses, the back tire blew out. He and his friend rolled out a spare and fixed the problem in minutes and then we rolled onto the island of Zamalek in the middle of the brown Nile river.

Zamalek looked tight and overbuilt; the space was gone. We had booked a few nights in the Tulip Hotel. They gave us a nice room with a corner view of the Nile. Houseboats lined it as before, but access to the water's edge was gone. All space was barred or belonged to a private club. There were plenty of cats visible everywhere. I wonder if they still remained sacred, as they had been during my childhood. Everywhere Egyptians were as sweet and courteous as I remembered them. But what happened to the women? They look like those featured in Iranian movies, drab, expressionless, a scarf wrapped tightly around the head, with no make-up, no bare skin visible on the arms or legs. Gone are the beautiful girls of 1960 with glistening black eyes enhanced with kohl, their open hair flowing down their backs.

It was hot and we decided to find some food. Night had come quickly at six o'clock, and the street lights came on, the same little street lights I remembered. They dated back to another century and gave hardly much illumination. The street was full of potholes as we skipped along, both our heads covered with shawls. I thought it wise not to stand out as tourists inviting unwanted attention, hence the shawls. We found a tiny little pizza restaurant and entered. The owner was eating his own dinner, but instantly offered to make food for us. We enjoyed a lovely meal and a lively conversation.

The next morning, we took a taxi to the pyramids. We traveled on a just-completed road flowing in serpentine fashion past huge outcroppings of apartment blocks, mostly unfinished. When the pyramids appeared, they looked majestic—grey and ancient. As we drew closer to the village lying below the monuments, I asked for the stables of Mohamed Ghunem, where my mother kept her horse and where we spent so many hours. The man whom I asked looked puzzled, and then said that the stables were long gone. A second man now walked up and explained that Mohamed was dead, and so were Said and Zakie and all others I remembered.

I felt hollow, aware that I had come too late, too late to find anyone left. How could it be they all were dead? "You want horses? I give you rides. Follow me," He said. We left the taxi and he urged us to take his horses, which were saddled and ready. Once we mounted, he said that we needed to pay him 20 pounds per horse, 30 pounds for the indispensable guide, and 60 pounds for the permit to ride on the pyramid plateau. At this point Kirstin slid off her horse, saying she felt uncomfortable. She did not want to see temples just now, nor pyramids. She only wanted to ride in the open desert and see monuments from a distance. The taxi driver had warned her about this man.

Since Kirstin refused to continue, we found another person, a man looking like a relative of Mohamed Ghunem, who was a gentle, kind man, and he helped us get over the shock of getting used to being on a horse and riding. My trot was pathetic and I seemed no longer glued to the animal's back as I had once been capable of being. Oh, but the desert, it smelled the same—it was open and expansive, and the pyramids looked magical. Beyond them rose the city of Cairo, the atmosphere hazy with pollution. Yet Cairo smelled clean. We rode for about an hour, mostly around the pyramid area, and when we had exhausted ourselves, we returned to the cab driver and I invited him to eat lunch with us, as he had been so very helpful. He suggested a restaurant which I knew from my youth, where after a morning's outing on horseback, we would stop for a wholesome breakfast. From the upper level one had a beautiful view of the pyramids. The food there was super and delicious—grilled fish, vine-ripe tomatoes, and tahini and aish baladi (local bread).

The city was like a hive of buzzing activity and energy. The driver informed us that smoking hashish is now illegal and harshly punished. People walking in the street no longer look like tired sleepwalkers as in 1965. It must become unbearably hot in all those newly erected houses resembling brick boxes. Rooftops are lined with satellite dishes; America's stamp rests on the whole world.

I noticed the air in Egypt vibrates with light and there is a sparkle of energy in the atmosphere; in fact, the air was without heaviness. In Illinois, the air was heavy, lead-like, very dense, and weighty. I loved to hear the call to prayer again, which rings out several times a day from all the minaret tops to remind people to pray to Allah. On the second day, I realized the call to prayer is now a recorded loudspeaker sound.

We decided to visit the Old Kingdom Step Pyramid of Sakkara, which lies outside Cairo and was a favorite of mine. We traveled by cab on a new ring road past what remained of the emerald green fields now squeezed by the usual unfinished high-rise apartment buildings. I wondered if they intended to plant some trees or have even a patch of garden left anywhere. This must be a hell strip during the hot summer months! Later, we passed the zoo and a fish garden.

I had tender memories of the lover's street behind the fish garden, which was unchanged. My first boyfriend and I would meet there, where the old trees had beautiful dark violet—almost black violet—blossoms, which grew into large gourds. The flowers bloomed only at night and then dropped; they also covered the sidewalk with their petals. This quiet street was a favorite place and private enough for young lovers.

When we arrived in Sakkara, the tourist buses were already lined up, and too many people crowded this ancient site, which irritated me. They were herded through the ancient monuments like sheep by a guide carrying a thin metal rod to which a bright paper flag was attached. Kirstin looked with fascination at the sand dunes. We entered the tomb of Mereruka with 31 rooms and the most beautiful ancient relief carvings on the walls.

When Kirstin saw the Step Pyramid, she remembered a recurring dream she had as a child. In her dream, she was climbing a pyramid, and the wind blew so hard she feared being blown down. She clung to the stone with her fingernails, clawing the gaps between the stone surface, desperately holding on for dear life. Interestingly, I had similar dreams of Kirstin being blown down a sheer mountain and saw her lying dead far below me.

We also saw the Tomb of Ti and then climbed up to the entrance into the Red Pyramid built by Snefru. Here, a long diagonal shaft led into the two tall chambers looking like tall gables but containing nothing. The entry into pyramids was not at the base of the monument but part way up. Kirstin refused to enter the pyramid because her claustrophobia makes her anxious in crowded tight spaces. Our next destination was the Bent Pyramid of Dahshur, which still had an intact outer stone mantle. I remembered climbing it long ago. How quickly time had passed; yet the pyramid looks unchanged. I never thought I would return to this pyramid, yet here I stood and so much time had passed, and this was the present reality. As I looked around, I blessed the desert and that I am alive to experience the present moment. I had returned to the one country that had been my home, and it was as familiar as the scent of my mother. They say, "You can't step into the same river twice," but this feels like I had arrived. I had returned with body and soul.

The next morning, with a view of the Nile River and young men rowing slender skiffs skimming over the water surface, I am looking back, remembering the past. I am impressed with who I was then, the things I did, the obstacles I overcame. Champion swimmer of Egypt at sixteen, riding horses in the desert most weekends, learning to paint and winning awards, choosing fencing and judo as sports, and becoming fluent in four languages. I now hear the clapping sound of bird wings, the familiar pigeons flying over the Nile, and the call to prayer ringing out over the vast city. From all the many minarets, the sound of "Allah ho Akbar" penetrates the day. I listen, engulfed in a sense of awe. A wave of calmness washes over me and

I feel the message to relax and to give up propelling myself forward. We have arrived.

My Old Home in Zamalek

That morning we drove to my old home in Zamalek. Ahmed, the handsome taxi driver, announced to us: "You know I am famous. The self-importance we attribute to ourselves is an obvious role and clearly seen by others. So, I am famous!" Trust Egyptians to come up with the wisdom to joke about being famous. It turns out Ahmed had lived some time in California and tried to get into movies. We drove to 6 Sharia Salah el Din, my old home. The owner, Hani, was charming, and he welcomed us like old friends. A gleaming highly polished brass plate on the entry door still reads: Leni Hilpert; Proprietor. Only in Egypt would the original owner be thus remembered and still honored after 50 years.

In the large dining room, my pharaonic wall painting was gone. It covered the whole end wall and took several days to complete. Hani made an excuse: he was Muslim and they don't make images of gods (in spite of the fact my painting was a copy from an ancient wall painting). The bathrooms looked old, and the trees between the twin structures have become huge. All were in bloom—vast white, mauve, and red flowering crowns. Hani excused himself briefly and then brought out a sculpted head my mother had made of me when I was at the age of 12. I didn't even remember it! He knew me as Rosie. "We have quite a few paintings and drawings by you, too," he said. I felt floored and confused.

He told me how my mother had come for the last time in 1974 and cried because she missed Egypt so much and had such a hard start in Kenya. "Hani, I thank you for keeping these pieces; I feel so overwhelmed seeing them again," I said. "I cannot take them with me, and don't have the time to go through a lengthy process of having them wrapped and shipped. I am sorry!" Hani led me through the place, and I looked at the rooms as we walked through the house. All looked Egyptian, a little down at the heels; none of the elegance Leni had created remained. We thanked him and he invited us to come and stay here during our future visits.

I felt torn and confused. This had been my home after all the years of being a refugee and moving from one place to the next. We had been without security, without knowing where we were going to be forced to move next. Cairo had become my shelter; this house had been my sanctuary and my home. My mother had created a wonderful, beautiful environment and shared this place with paying guests, providing a sanctuary where they were protected and comfortable. And during all her years in Cairo, she had yearned to be able to follow her creative ambition and to become an artist. Without hesitation, she had provided me with all the possible opportunities to study art and to follow my heart. At least I had not let her down. Some years later, to my amazement, I learnt that the little hotel on the Zamalek Island had been sold and had become an art gallery. My former home had become a place where artists can show and sell their work, and I know my mother would have been overjoyed.

Outside, the large trees cast their shade over us as I paused one last time to look back at what had been my home. Gone, gone, gone were the years and the time and the people I had known. I felt as if I had been in a pressure cooker. We returned to our new hotel, where we were to meet our group leader and the rest of the people who had signed up with Trafalgar Travel. We were booked into the Ramses Hilton, the tallest building in Cairo, overlooking the Medan Tahrir Square.

We stepped out of our room onto the balcony on the 26th floor. The air pollution hung like a grey curtain over the city. I was glad we were not staying there for any length of time. We left to meet our group, and a tour manager introduced himself in perfect English and guided us through an underground passage to the museum.

It was 11 am, and at this point Kirstin's blood sugar plunged. We managed to get to the Nile Hilton garden cafe just in time. Here, tranquility sat like a blessing among flowers and shrubs. Tall palm fronds rustled softly in the breeze. A sandwich brought Kirstin back into balance, after which we joined our group in the museum, where we toured the world of ancient Egypt for two hours before returning to the Hilton garden cafe once more for food. The new and powerful impressions were overwhelming for Kirstin, and I began to watch her carefully for signs of exhaustion. I promised her an exciting visit to the bazaar of Khan el Khalili, a favorite past haunt of mine, providing I could still find my way into the maze of narrow little streets.

Most women we saw wore headscarves, but not face veils. At my suggestion, Kirstin tied a headscarf over her hair and looked beautiful. In fact, she could have passed for a Syrian. We stopped at the Al Azhar Mosque, and a man appeared and offered to show us around. As it turned out, he was very educated, with a sophisticated mind, and he spoke well and from the heart. Kirstin asked all the right questions and the tour became very lively, with explanations about Muslim culture and dipping into the Islamic traditions bordering on the spiritual. The ancient mosque had been restored and cleaned, and I began to soar on the spiritual atmosphere like a bird discovering a fresh current of air. As the sky darkened, stars appeared and the white marble courtyard glowed. I watched people gliding soundlessly over the space on bare feet. I felt engulfed in the magic. We walked out into the busy street, now lit up with lights, and joined into the hustle and bustle of life. Later, we wandered through Khan El Khalili, and I discovered that I no longer remembered the network of roads and had to trust my intuition to guide us. Kirstin enjoyed it all and purchased many items at the market to take home with her. We ended the evening in a lovely restaurant with a wonderful atmosphere.

Upper Egypt

Time did not matter in Egypt and we were up at 5 am, and after a hurried breakfast, found ourselves back at the airport bound for Luxor in Upper Egypt. Our flight was very short, bringing us to a bus ride that took us to Karnak, where we visited the vast temple complex. Our group was small and consisted of Australian, Philippine, English, and American tourists. Our guide, an Egyptologist, was a very tall, stocky Egyptian called Ashraf, and he reminded me of my stepson David. Before introducing himself and starting the tour, he said, "Bism Allah, in the name of Allah," dedicating his offering. He was brilliant; he laid out the strategies of political aspirations, which could be interpreted from the Hieroglyphs left on the temple walls by pharaohs living so many centuries ago. The great pharaoh Ramses II was constantly boasting of his campaigns, his prowess, and his abilities. It was all only too human.

I enjoyed the tour of the famous temple and all the historical information and actually learned some new things. By noon we boarded our Nile boat, Miriam, and took off for Luxor to see the temple there, which was more beautiful and impressive than I remembered. We stood before huge columns and overwhelmingly large statues that were all part of a colossal layout. Was it meant to impress man or the gods? Ashraf told us that the management of the temple required the presence of 8600 priests. Considered a refuge for the pharaoh, it was a place for prayer and reflection and also a reminder of past triumphs. Pharaohs could come there to gather strength during times of difficulty and review past accomplishments while the council of the priests advised them. During the Old Kingdom, no leader was prone to boast, while during the New Kingdom, the psychology of exaggeration boosted self-esteem. Ashraf gave us a vision of the past that was both memorable and simple. At night we had a sound-and-light performance, surrounded by the colossal forest of huge columns as we sat under the open sky and the stars.

It was magical to hear poetry written by Queen Hatshepsut for the planned obelisks of Deir el Bahari. We visited her temple the next morning and were up by 5 am yet again, as Ashraf wished to avoid the crowds of tourists. The temple is located under the mountain "peak of silence," and by now mostly reconstructed by Polish stone workers under the guidance of the archeologists, a task that took many years. It was worth the whole trip to hear Kirstin gasp as she first set eyes on the long slope leading up to the terraced temple. It was moving to contemplate the ancient Queen Hatshepsut assuming leadership traditionally only granted to men and proclaiming male attributes bestowed on her by the grace of god. Yet later, on the temple wall, she was shown to be pregnant and then also depicted with her infant daughter. She did not make wars. Instead, she sent expeditions into areas along the coast of East Africa, to Punt and to many far-off islands. From these expeditions, shown on the walls, wild animals, plants, even an African queen came to Egypt, as well as exotic trees, including the date palm tree, up to then unknown in the land of the Nile. As far as I understood, the whole temple was dedicated to the cow-goddess Hathor. Everywhere we saw sculptures of the goddess Hathor carrying the moon disk between her horns.

The graves of the Nobles came next. They were brighter, lighter, and more colorful than I recall. In the Cairo Museum, I had been surprised by how large some Egyptian sculptures had become in my memory. They had grown positively huge, but in actuality, they were only small figurines. By the time we returned to our boat docked beside other Nile cruising ships, we were ready to stretch out our weary limbs. I rolled up my mat and went up to the deck. There I immersed myself into an afternoon of yoga. What a wondrous experience to go within! After not being able to do it for two days, it felt like a great gift.

The boat was sailing upriver in the direction of Aswan as we watched the villages that lined the shore speeding past, nestled in a belt of emerald green fields, with the ochre-colored desert spreading beyond. Long, long ago, when I was a teenager in Cairo, I had often looked longingly at the Nile cruise boats with their colorful tourists standing on deck enjoying the sights. I never dreamed that one day I would be one of those fortunate people, able to afford such luxury. At the time, I felt sorry for the tourists because I knew they were exposed to only a select few experiences, while I had the opportunity to actually live

Return to Egypt — Ramona with daughter Kirstin

the reality that was Egypt. I now hoped the boat would not get to Upper Egypt too quickly. I was lucky, for there was a small engine problem and the cruise was extended by several hours. The stars came out, the lamps were lit in the villages, the call for prayer rang from the little minarets, and everyone came on deck for a sundowner.

Time seemed to stand still as we sailed back into the past. Here, nothing seemed to have changed. Girls came to the shore with their ollas and filled them with water before hoisting them onto their heads, carefully balancing them as they walked back to their mudbrick homes.

In my diary notes, I asked myself the question: "What did I come back for? What am I to learn here?" The Egyptians show their humanity, and this was depicted on their temple walls, inscribed so long ago. They don't show off their wealth or power. To show off was considered coarse and vulgar. However, to have humor was considered charming.

The room service on board the ship arranged our towels differently every day. Our towels sat on the bed as kissing swans one day; then as a lotus blossom, and finally as a person wearing sunglasses. People on the street, while they are preparing to spread out their food for dinner, offered their meals to the stranger walking past. They accepted others without criticism, just as they were, and in that acceptance lies a great secret, for it makes one feel, well, it makes one feel included. They break the ice of inhibition with jokes and more jokes. "Join us, edh fadal." They show a strong tribal sense, yet are not exclusive. Their way of behaving includes the remnants of an ancient wisdom. Conquer through the charm of being, rather than through force. According to Ashraf, most of the depictions of their ancient battles seem to have elements of self-promotion rather than actual facts. They love to laugh, to love, to joke.

Among the many things to see, Edfu Temple stood out as best preserved. It was dedicated to the falcon god Horus Ptolemy III, 327 B.C. It spread out on top of the old Thutmosis III Temple, built by a previous ruler. It was a very dusty journey there, as we had to travel by horse carriage. First, we visited the Mammisi, which is Coptic for "birth house." Here was where the man chosen to become pharaoh enters, to be blessed and purified. Obviously, not all rulers were born of royal blood, but instead required a period of transformation before becoming living gods. They spent about two weeks asleep while the priests whispered sacred messages into their ears. Only then, did a man become divine. Having studied hypnotherapy, my ears picked up, as the process used in ancient Egypt sounded much like hypnotic programming for change or transformation.

I was looking forward to seeing the Temple of Philae, a Ptolemaic building. It was built on an island surrounded with black granite rocks jutting out of the Nile River. The memories of my past visit were stronger than the present reality. Many motor boats and hotels now lined the once pristine shore and the magical, languid beauty was gone. However, a trip in a felucca sailing boat compensated a bit as we drifted under the huge white sail into the deeper water. A little Arab boy in a homemade boat bobbed up and down beside us, singing a German song. He could not have been much older than nine years, and I hoped he could swim, as his boat was unsteady. He was so happy and full of joy; it was a pleasure to witness him.

Soon our voyage ended, and we flew back to Cairo for the remainder of our visit. Sakkara and the Step Pyramid of the old Kingdom were our first destination. By now we were used to awakening at five in the morning, but nevertheless it surprised me to see the pyramid shrouded in mist. Ours was the first tour bus and we entered the tomb of Mere Ruka with its wonderful depictions of animals, dancers, and images of the lifestyle of ancient Egypt. It was particularly touching to see the loving connection between a man and his wife, something not so obvious in later centuries, when the wife becomes smaller and smaller in size, indicating her loss of importance in contrast to her huge husband, as is particularly obvious in the temple complexes of Ramses.

Later we entered the pyramid of Teti, which contained walls covered with high-relief hieroglyphs called the Pyramid Texts. Kirstin still refused to go into the narrow entries of pyramids because of her claustrophobia. From Sakkara we drove to the Giza Pyramids. Although it was the end of March, it was very hot and we stood on the Giza plateau in glaring white light and heat. I noticed that I felt well in this climate and that it was so familiar. The valley temple, where I danced as a teenager, was still there, keeping company with a lot of plastic and paper garbage. A world of uncollected trash had gathered in convenient corners. Next, we visited the sacred funerary barge, the Sun Boat, first found in the early fifties and reconstructed over a period of 16 years. It was huge and amazing to look at. Only rope was used to hold it together; no nails.

After this, Ashraf led us to the huge lion-bodied, human-headed Sphinx, where he gave an impassioned speech, thereby terminating our visit to the ancient monuments. I stood once more looking at the Sphinx, at its ancient head, and time was nothing. I had stood before the Sphinx and seen it as a child, and now I was old, and nothing at all had happened and everything was just contained in the ever-continuing present moment. I moved a step closer and changed my viewpoint ever so slightly. It seems the mouth of the huge face was smiling, ever so slightly.

Cairo

Kirstin was exhausted and we decided against a planned excursion to Alexandria. Anyway, I thought it was better to stay in Cairo and rest a bit. She seemed to attract a lot of attention and many Egyptians have told her that she is beautiful. As we passed men in the street they said, "Be my queen," or "Beautiful woman." This was nothing new; they always used to comment on women, but I noticed that the once so glamorous Egyptian girls exuded no energy, no outgoing quality. Their heads were tightly wrapped and eyes downcast; they looked withdrawn—and that was in spite of Ashraf's repeated assurance of equality between men and women. A new sign that I found positive was the many young couples walking together holding hands or sitting on benches. That would not have been possible 50 years ago.

We chose to wear attractive shawls over our heads and shoulders and to be as inconspicuous as possible on our next venture, this time to visit the Citadel, the Sultan Hassan mosque, the Hanging Church of Mary in the Coptic district, and the Bazaar. The Citadel was built between 1176 and 1183 by Salah al-Din Ayyub, who became famous and known in the West as Saladin. The street on which we had lived was named after Salah al-Din, and the Citadel was the best preserved and the largest fortification in the Middle East, and it served as the home of Egypt's rulers for 700 years. One famous story that sticks to my mind is of a ruthless tyrant who came to power and wanted to fortify his position in Egypt. Therefore, he invited all the most powerful men of the land to a sumptuous dinner party in the citadel. When they had gathered, he had every one of them murdered, except one guest who jumped on his horse, forcing the animal to leap over the high wall that encloses the main structure. The horse was killed in this death leap; but the guest survived to tell the tale. The citadel with its four domes and two tall minarets was huge, and we gazed with amazement at the great marble-floored central hall.

The Mosque of Mohammed Ali is inspired by Turkish architecture and took 28 years to build. We visited the tomb of the ruler beside the entrance and briefly looked at the city of the dead, a remarkable region filled with the beautiful homes of the wealthy Arab, Mameluke, and Turkish citizens, all of whom lie buried and sealed up within their lavish homes. Some are open to visitors and some have become the living quarters of the homeless.

When I had to write a dissertation for my final degree at a university in Germany, I had chosen to write about the remarkable village of Harrania near Sakkara, where an architect, Visser Wassef, had started a weaving center. In the intervening years, this enterprise had become world-famous and the children's carpets of Harrania were sought by collectors from all over the world. Kirstin was interested in seeing this place, too, so we took a taxi and drove off into the villages along the last fields not turned into housing developments.

It proved to be a highlight of our trip, as the village was quiet and simple, just as I remembered it. A shimmering white-domed building set in a lovely garden was the perfect location to display the beautiful woven rugs, miracles of art made by children's hands. A patient, kind man who turned out to be a cousin of Visser Wassef showed us the new work, woolen rugs and smaller cotton weavings. Kirstin bought a lovely example of flying ducks made by a little girl, and I purchased two cotton ones. We visited some rooms where teenagers were working. The tranquility of the house and grounds, the gentleness of the man, and the three female weavers we met took me back to all that which had formed me and which I had loved about this country. A farmer stood beside the taxi, his dusty hand holding a bright orange tangerine. "Please for you," he said, offering his fruit. I took it, and a tear fell on its dusty skin. It was a fitting end to our visit of Egypt.

In the afternoon, Kirstin insisted on a last return to the bazar to purchase inlaid Egyptian boxes, mostly as gifts, and a beautiful chess set as Kent and she liked playing chess together. She had planned ahead and had left her suitcase more than half empty so a carpet or two could be fit in. I marveled at her good taste as she chose a lovely rug of two intertwining trees, a unique piece. She must have inherited her fondness for carpets from my mother. Later on, we found a restaurant and had a bowl of lentil soup and a glass of white wine while overlooking the traffic-laden Nile Corniche, the sailing boats sparkling like gems in the water. This concluded our last meal and event in Cairo. As I slept and dreamt, I saw ancient Egypt, figures, hieroglyphs, desert dunes, temples, and the sun rising. The city had not yet gone to sleep. Heavy traffic roared along. Most cars drove with only their parking lights on and their headlights turned off. When I lived in Cairo, the population was 3 million. Now it hovered between 15 and 18 million and the traffic flowed day and night. A grey fog now hung perpetually over the capital city. Our last day in Cairo had come. We left in the dark, at 2:30 in the morning, and I felt that this would be my last visit to this wonderful country.

Trip Home

It felt like a whirlwind of travel, and it was incomprehensible somehow to be landing in grey Frankfurt four hours later, and still later, in Chicago. I had a brief visit in Chicago with a little time to rest, then, in no time, I was back in the air and looking down on the Sandia Mountains, as the plane descended into Albuquerque, New Mexico. The first thing that fell into my hands was a bottle of Lotus perfume. I bought it for Kirstin, but she gave it back to me. The intoxicating scent was like an embrace that stayed with me, pulling my thoughts back to Egypt, back to the Nile and the sun, and it filled me with a strange longing. There was a beauty which called to my soul, penetrating the shell of indifference and dullness. There was still so much wonderful life to experience.

Kirstin and Kent Move to Santa Fe

Three weeks later I was greeted with a huge surprise. Kirstin was flying to New Mexico for an interview, as a teaching position at the Rio Grande School had opened up. It seems my Reiki teacher and friend Rebecca had introduced Kirstin to the school, having worked there herself. Finding a good teaching position in Santa Fe was not easy, and Kirstin was already teaching in a highly reputable private school in Lake Forest, so a shift would be hard. Thanks to Rebecca's help, Kirstin found her place in New Mexico, making her dreams come true, allowing for both her and Kent to relocate to Santa Fe.

She did well at the interview, I was told, and we went out for sushi to celebrate her new appointment to be the second grade teacher at this school. I had not dared to hope that she would come to New Mexico, and now, miraculously, it was happening, and I won't have to fret about her being so far away anymore. Over lunch we discussed Kent's and her future in New Mexico. He would have to leave his job in Illinois and find new employment here. I invited them to stay with me until they found a place of their own. Then, she said something to me which came as a surprise. She stated that it was amazing how I've drifted through life, which startled me. Did it appear to her that I really drifted without direction? Or was she referring to my ability to flow in a kind of trusting surrender to circumstances?

We had a quiet afternoon at home because she felt the altitude and was tired from the intense effort she put into creating a teaching portfolio, which took her many weeks—a wonderful document with images, quotes, and her teaching philosophy, all done on the computer. Kirstin and I talked about the choices of houses in Santa Fe and the job of moving all their belongings. We discussed all sorts of possibilities and became quite excited. She had the good idea of using the time before her job started here to travel to Italy with Kent. Their cats, Luna and Loco, would stay with me, and on their return, there would be no pressure to find the right house.

Invitation to Exhibit in Colorado

Close friends introduced a brilliant Israeli professor of philosophy, a former student of Lake Forest College, to my paintings. He wanted to start an art gallery in Colorado Springs. In May, he arrived in Santa Fe, accompanied by a close friend, to look at my paintings. I was nervous as I filled my large kitchen with stacks of large oil paintings, monotypes, and gouaches, preparing for his visit. He arrived carrying the largest flower bouquet I had ever seen. He had a fast and experienced eye and he made rapid selections, all the while spreading warmth with his conversation and charm. An arrangement for bringing the work to Colorado was made, and we all went out for lunch.

Later on, I felt stunned and overwhelmed. This meeting had gone beyond any expectations, and he chose 37 images to be exhibited. I was not even sure if I could fit so many pictures into my SUV. Reflecting on the events of the day and the outcome brought the conviction I must become self-reliant, and I was meant to learn this after Alex's death. I relied on Alex, on his know-how, opinion, methods and gut-instinct. He was often totally right and wise and I trusted him implicitly. Now I had to feel my way alone. I needed to release any ambition for success as it would be a barrier. I needed to embrace the moment, the opportunity to show my work, and talk to people who were interested. No expectations were allowed! I had my work cut out for myself, because now I had to start making frames and getting the paintings ready, a process I had not done all by myself before.

The Warehouse Gallery

By the 22nd of June, my pictures were framed and I set off for the Warehouse Gallery in Colorado Springs. It was a lovely drive and I listened to an audio tape that allowed me to stay relaxed. When I arrived, the place was like a market, filled with life and people coming and going. The four-story building, which contained the art gallery, had been an industrial warehouse, now renovated. The first floor contained one of the best restaurants in town, and the gallery was right next to it.

The top floor was a penthouse and apartment belonging to the professor. We unpacked my car without delay and then, equally fast, spread the paintings around the walls of the exhibition space. Not much arranging seemed necessary and with the help of a friend, the paintings were hung in fast order. Next, the lights were directed to the images and by early evening the show opened.

The public that arrived for the well-advertised exhibition were art lovers, and they were sophisticated in their taste. I had wonderful conversations, some pieces sold quickly, and the gallery was crowded. At seven o'clock we withdrew and filled a large elevator going up to the penthouse. Some special friends and collectors had been invited for dinner, which was prepared by the professor, who held an animated conversation at the same time as he prepared a fabulous dinner. I began to feel the effect of my long drive and the two glasses of wine I had consumed and was grateful to retire at the close of the evening. During the night it was hot and noisy, and I missed the silence of my house.

I had promised to guide the professor, who suffered from a cronic, painful back, through a yoga session the following morning. Probably I had never before guided someone as intelligent and focused, and the session flowed smoothly and with wonderful effectiveness. For a start, he lost his sense of time and the 90-minute yoga experience felt no longer than 10 minutes. He also felt a beneficial physical shift and a release of pain and stiffness that surprised him. A year later he told me how he had hired a yoga instructor to teach him daily at dawn. Alas, the lessons held none of the magic he had experienced with me. I could never convince him that his own mind had been responsible for the remarkable effects he had opened himself to. We became close friends after that and he would always drop by to visit me during his annual lecture in Santa Fe.

About a week after I returned from Colorado Springs, Kirstin contacted me to let me know they were all packed up and hoping to get to Santa Fe in a couple of days, probably arriving at night. They made it by 11 pm, bringing their two cats, Luna and Loco. As they opened the front door to bring in their luggage, a bird flew into the house and settled on one of the blades of the ceiling fan. So, we had to lock the cats in a spare bedroom, hoping the bird would eventually find its way through the open doorway to freedom. However, it stayed safely perched on a blade of the ceiling fan. By morning, the bird was still up there, until we disturbed it with our presence, so it began trying to fly through the clerestory window as it was unable to come down lower to locate the open door and escape into freedom. How often are we in that situation, unable to surrender our fears, unable to bow down to circumstances? Eventually, we managed to get the bird out, and the cats enjoyed roaming free around inside the house.

Invitation to Exhibit in Santa Fe

Sudden surprises came that I did not anticipate. My paintings hanging in the Warehouse Gallery in Colorado Springs were drawing attention, and an article about me had been published. One day, I received a phone call from the gallery owner. A couple had walked into his gallery and they were very impressed with the paintings, asking about the artist, and how to contact me. They had a gallery on Canyon Road in Santa Fe and wished to see more of my work. I was given their name and phone number, and because they had discovered me, this connection sounded very promising! I had learnt over the years that galleries like to discover their artists themselves, and are often uninterested in looking at unsolicited work. I phoned the gallery and talked to the director. He said he would like to come to my house during the following week to see my work. As I put down the receiver, a wave of disbelief flooded me. My expectation was negative. How do I overcome doubt and the feeling this meeting will not occur? The director might not like my work. That is the real possibility. I let go of my unease and began to feel indifferent to the outcome.

On the appointed day, the gallery director called to say he could not come and shifted the visit to the following week. So, my intuitive unease was correct; in fact, I couldn't feel a connection at all. The following week, however, both the owner and director of Horizon Gallery came to my house to look at my art. They were charming, enthusiastic, and seemingly impressed by the pictures. Eight large paintings and six monotypes were chosen. I drove them into town to the gallery. Because the images they chose were unframed, the director chose from his stash a number of large gilded frames and put some paintings into them. They really enhanced the look of the paintings, making them look more precious. Light was fading when I left and many of the paintings had already been hung. What a day! After seven years, I was finally exhibiting my work on Canyon Road.

Expectations

Over the next weeks a double opening at Horizon Gallery was planned featuring my paintings with those of another artist. This was the first exhibition for me in Santa Fe and a pleasant shift from not being shown for so long. The night of the opening, people soon began pouring into the gallery, people from the Vedic Chant Class I'd joined, from Vista Clara Ranch, where I taught yoga, and teachers from the Yoga Center, here in town, as well as from my Reiki group. Most were charming, and they praised my paintings. Those who understood the work were complimentary and stated that I was one of the better artists in Santa Fe. To my surprise, a lot of people whom I did not know arrived. It seemed to me I was riding a huge wave and talking almost nonstop. At the conclusion, I had a lovely meal at the restaurant Andiamo with a big group of friends, and it felt as if I were surrounded by a warm cocoon of enthusiastic and loving support and encouragement. I had no delusions though, for the real test of this opening was if anything would sell at the gallery.

The following day on my way back from a yoga class, I stopped at Horizon Gallery to check out how my work was doing. For a moment I felt stunned. Three-quarters of my paintings had been removed, and the dealer was in the process of hanging big, coarse paintings of masks, empty of content and brutal in impact. The artist was asking a huge price for these monsters. Just for a moment I felt disappointed and hurt, and then realized the dealer was desperate for sales. He also was very disorganized. The inventory consignment sheet made out for me could not be found. I ended up taking nine large oils back home with me. The show was over after just three days! The funny thing, though, was that I had known all along I would be disappointed by this gallery and my work once again, became unrepresented.

However, to my delight, Expressions in Fine Art, a gallery into which I had repeatedly tried to get accepted, almost immediately, picked up my work. I really liked the owner and saw she was a very successful art dealer. Eventually, and because of this exposure, my work was being shown in four different galleries in the Southwest: in Tubac and Sedona, Arizona, and in Colorado Springs and Santa Fe, New Mexico.

Two Black Cats

Once Kirstin and Kent were back from their trip to Italy, the two black cats could finally go outside. They were amazing creatures. As they knew how to climb up trees and were used to doing this in Illinois, they were not so much in danger from coyotes. They just climbed up the stucco walls of the house in seconds, and no coyote could follow them. Repeatedly the coyotes showed up in my garden, hoping to surprise the cats.

One night I had a dream. Loco was howling and his belly was dragging the ground. He was badly hurt. I almost couldn't lift him; his underside was matted, his ribs showing. Gently I tried to lay him on a table and get help. Then, I jolted awake. Not much more than a week later, I could hear Loco howling. I looked everywhere, even on the deck. I could hear the cat but couldn't see where he was.

Eventually, I went into the garage. To my horror, he was pinned to the upper end of the garage door. He must have been up on top of the open door when Kirstin left to bring things to their new house and got his leg caught in the mechanism when the garage door closed. I somehow got him out and carefully laid the poor cat on a towel on the table. Then I called Kent at work, who arrived in almost no time and took Loco to the vet. It was then I recalled my dream. The poor cat had to have surgery on the meniscus in his knee, but he lived for many years after that.

Hypnotherapy

In the meantime, I connected with the Hypnotherapy Academy of New Mexico and asked for details about their training. The head of the institute was charming and informative and told me that a past-life regression demonstration was being offered to anyone interested and would give me an impression of the power of hypnosis and what to expect. I got together with a friend who also was interested in learning about hypnotherapy, and on a cold evening, we made our way to the academy.

Several people were already waiting for the program to begin. What we experienced was a group hypnosis. I remember wondering if I would be capable of letting go as the instructor asked us to follow his suggestions that guided us into a relaxed and altered state. Then, quite suddenly, I was in a wintery place in northern Europe. The period seemed to be Romanesque, and I felt to my surprise like a big, powerful male. My face sprouted a black beard, I had hairy arms, and long black hair grew on my head. Looking down at my feet as instructed, I saw soft leather shoes on my feet. I did not wear pants but a long woolen garment. All this indicated I was wealthy. Looking about, I saw a stone hall and well-carved stone columns. As instructed, I reached into myself and examined how I felt. I was very angry and needed to make some important decisions. It was clear to me that I was a leader, and I feared betrayal.

Our instruction was to go forward to the last day of our lives and to experience the way we died. My experience was that I was asleep in a large hall when someone plunged a razor-sharp knife into my throat and cut across my neck. My hands flew up to my neck, trying to stem a soft flowing, warm liquid. I was dying, bleeding, betrayed, and voiceless. My trust had been betrayed, and I felt I was fading fast. Regretting my life, I decided never to want this type of power again. A lot of greyness surrounded me, as I slowly rose above my body, aware of being fierce and proud and knowing I had to surrender to my slow demise. I was unclear in my intentions. No doubt about it, I was a leader and a warrior, a knight. I questioned all these qualities as I died. They had not served me. There was no self-pity, no softness in me. My mind was powerful, logical, cold, clear, and analytical. I was not happy with this life, with the outcome, and I felt depressed as I slowly faded and my consciousness dissolved. My sharp mind gone, I felt disillusioned and betrayed by my beliefs, which had made my life what it became: duty-bound and limited. An intense need for freedom arose; I yearned to give back to life, to help others.

The instructor's voice guided us back into this reality and the past-life regression was over.

The group of participants looked pensive and dazed as they rose from their seats to leave. There was no small talk. Since I didn't have any doubt about my experience, I signed up for hypnotherapy courses and began a new education, one that taught me that helplessness is not one's destiny and that I could rise above the loss of my life's partner. I dipped into those inner resources that hypnosis revealed to me. The two years that followed until my certification were very demanding due to my studies, the continuation of studying and teaching yoga, and painting pictures during every spare moment I had.

18 A Life Begins

Pregnancy

Kirstin was feeling happy with her teaching position in the Rio Grande School and decided it was time for a family. With meticulous attention to detail, she started planning and arranging circumstances so that she could become pregnant and give birth with the longest maternity leave possible. By having a child in the late spring, she would add her summer vacation to the maternity leave and thus add extra weeks. She found a lovely woman from El Salvador who had experience looking after babies and who would come to the house and be with the child while she was at work. The day came when she made the joyous announcement that she was pregnant and would be expecting the birth in the spring. She and Kent were not interested in knowing the sex of the child. I was very excited, more than I expected, and looked forward to being a grandmother.

The parents of Kirstin's second grade class decided to give her a baby shower in Las Campanas, and my friend Rebecca and I were also invited. Since the place is a fair distance out of town, we drove together. The hostess was wealthy and a grandmother, raising her own grandchild alone. The guests were an amazing group of sophisticated, well-groomed, and wealthy women. It was touching how much they valued Kirstin, for their gifts were beyond generous. A baby stroller and endless garments and toys were unwrapped by Kirstin. She was charming and graceful in how she received this wave of gifts. She had inherited her father's silver tongue and also the gift of diplomacy.

As she had come straight from school to Las Campanas, she had no opportunity to eat lunch and was becoming ravenous, so we drove to town and gave her a very late lunch in Chocolate Maven. During this opportunity, I asked her if she would allow me to be at the birth and if she would like to be hypnotized during the process. I had become very excited to learn that giving birth could be made much more comfortable with hypnotic suggestions and that an increasing number of women were choosing this method. She generously gave her consent to let me help.

Some weeks before the birth, I had a dream which struck me as a warning dream. I was sitting beside Kirstin, who was holding her baby on her lap. It had an open third eye on its forehead. It would be born early and wanted his mother to know. I woke up and thought that I needed to paint this dream. She will have a son with dark hair and he knows he will be born early, earlier than expected. How remarkable! The right opportunity to tell her of this dream never came, but on February 23 I called Kirstin after waking at 7 am and asked to have breakfast with her and Kent. This gave me the opportunity to give her a hypnotherapeutic relaxation, during which she went into a deep state. I drove home feeling grateful the induction had been successful.

Time went by, and I was becoming more and more conscious of the approaching birth, as if part of me was watching every second. It had snowed and the world was a surreal, a beautiful white environment. Kirstin called to tell me she had developed high blood pressure. Her doctor ordered her to be on bed rest. Fortunately, spring break had just started. I gave her a hypnosis session to calm down her nervous system and to induce deep relaxation. Signs that indicate hypnosis are fluttering eyelids and moist, teary eyes. She had these symptoms, and on returning to full consciousness, claimed the hypnosis really had worked and that she felt deeply relaxed. Though I could not test her blood pressure, she certainly looked much calmer. I felt very grateful to have such a healing tool at my disposal and hoped I might be able to assist her during the birth.

The doctor she had chosen was the same charming doctor who had helped Alex during his last days. I felt grateful that Kirstin should be in such good hands. Two days later, Kirstin was again examined for her blood pressure. However, her blood pressure was still too elevated, which could mean the placenta was not providing enough nutrition to the child. I must confess I was beginning to become very worried, hoping she would have a safe and happy birthing experience. I realized I carried a wounded part in me, resentment about how the birth of Kirstin was decided. Sadly, I was left with a sense of disempowerment and hidden anger at being female because men had decided the whole process. Many things have changed now and fortunately for the better.

The Birth

A decision was made to induce labor, and the baby was to be born three weeks early. I remembered my dream about the early birth as I made my way to the hospital. I saw Dr. Friedrichs again, a gentle, soft-spoken man of high intelligence. He had been there to assist when Alex was dying, and now he was delivering Alex's grandchild. The doctor had an air of gentle assurance, so important at this moment. I spent the day in the hospital holding Kirstin's hand and giving her assurance. Briefly, I drove back home to cancel a yoga class and to get some food when my intuition prompted me to turn around as fast as I could to return to the hospital.

My intuition proved correct; her water had just broken and she was having strong contractions. They gave her an epidural to moderate the pain of the contractions. Medical technology had certainly made strides in alleviating pain. All through the night I gave her suggestion therapy for relaxation and for the cervix to open. Briefly, I went out in the morning to order breakfast from the Chocolate Maven. Both Kirstin and Kent were certain they would have a girl. I continued keeping my dream about the child, who would be a dark-haired boy, to myself.

One of the interesting events during the long night was my silent mantra recitation, which slowly brought about an elevated bliss level and the understanding that all was well and indeed perfect. Kirstin said she felt it too and told me she was so happy. This cocoon of protective bliss and understanding surrounded us like a blessing. The contractions became more forceful after 4 pm, and the cervix dilated. Rebecca came to give Kirstin some Reiki as I fed her ice chips, massaged her, and fussed over her. A nurse gave Kirstin instructions on how to breathe to push the baby out.

Next, the doctor arrived, and it was amazing to see a little part of the head with dark fuzz on top showing itself. With each push the little lump became bigger, increasing from coin size to fist size, until the whole head threatened to emerge. At this point, Kirstin asked for a Kleenex as she needed to blow her nose. As she blew her nose, to all our amazement, the entire body of the baby slipped out and slid into the doctors outstretched hands. She said "no" at the unexpected lunge, a "no" that held no power when the wet baby boy was placed on her chest.

This joy-filled moment was special and it stirred everyone. She looked luminous, her smooth rounded limbs glowing in the late light, the child curled up on her chest. The doctor now sucked out the child's nose and mouth, and I watched its reaction as it blinked its eyes and moved its tiny hands. It looked as soft as goose down and utterly pliable. Kirstin turned to me and said that only the yoga she had been practicing made this birth so easy. She looked lovely as she held her little boy.

Then he was examined and cleaned, and he cried a bit until Kent held its hands in his. The sound of our voices positively calmed him down and touch soothed him. It seemed to me that Kent was in a bit of a shock, so I turned to him and said,

"Congratulations, you have a son!" I felt he needed to hear this to confirm what may have seemed dreamlike. Then I took photos of him holding the baby and of Kirstin.

It was so wonderful to be a witness to this birth, and it felt like the universe opened. The magic of the experience was so obvious to me. It was in the smell of earth and blood and body. I shall never see the opening of a woman's legs as anything but a magical invitation to feast the eye and a promise of bliss. How we have undervalued the experience of birth and creation of life. Kirstin gave me the greatest joy through allowing me to witness the birth of her son. Did I enter a different state of consciousness last night? Tears were forming under closed lids. I wiped across my eyes. I felt inspired to paint the birth scene and started a picture very soon after the birth.

Perhaps the strangest coincidence was that later on I realized Benjamin's birth was on the same day on which my father, Karl Hilpert, was born. Almost a century separated the two birthdays: Ben on March 26, 2003 at 6:38 pm and Karl on March 26, 1904.

Surgery

About five weeks later, Kirstin called me at seven in the morning. Ben had been vomiting constantly, and she was in tears. I drove over, praying the baby would be all right, and he seemed to be when I looked at him. I tried to calm Kirstin down, as babies sometimes vomit very easily. The following day, after another bad night with projectile vomiting, I was back with Kirstin. She had been to the hospital, seen a doctor and a nurse, and they all told her the child was all right. Now she was using the internet for information and wondered what to do. I told her to trust her own instincts as the most accurate and reliable source of intuition.

At dawn, she called with the news that they were going to the emergency room. Ben had a fever and was still projectile vomiting. It turned out that the pyloric valve between the stomach and the small intestine had stopped working. This was called pyloric stenosis and required surgery. It is a simple procedure, but not possible in the Santa Fe hospital. Kirstin was relieved that her feelings of something being wrong were confirmed.

She and Kent drove to UNM Hospital in Albuquerque with Ben. The surgery was planned for the next day. From then on, everything happened very quickly. Ben was successfully operated on at dawn and was fine. I drew a breath of relief, grateful for this smooth surgery and the amazing surgeon. Kirstin called later and asked me to come to Albuquerque to keep her company. On the way I picked up some sushi at Wild Oats, as Kirstin did not want to eat the hospital food.

Mother and child both looked vulnerable and in shock. Ben was fed some liquid with electrolytes, which was easier to digest than breast milk, but he threw this up. Kirstin was very worried, so I recited a healing mantra for a while, of course in silence. During the course of the afternoon, Ben threw up less and less and seemed to be able to keep the liquid down, much to his mother's relief. The nurses changed his diapers frequently, and to my surprise weighed them, to know exactly how much liquid he kept down.

By evening, Ben was drinking milk without vomiting it up. He became hungry and very alert. Kirstin fed him bits of liquid at a time and he always was desperate for more, frantically sucking a pacifier to calm his hunger. When I left, he had turned the corner and would probably nurse in the night. I hugged my exhausted daughter and wished her a good night as I disappeared into the brightly lit city and returned to Santa Fe.

New Patterns

On occasion, when circumstances allowed, I would pick Ben up for some hours to give his mother a break. After being with him for a while, I would feel an inner calm within, as if his personality exuded a soothing, mesmeric effect. Often, while he slept, I would practice my yoga asanas in the same room and felt it was an honor and a gift to look after this tiny creature. To me it seemed that he radiated contentment and joy, and we giggled and laughed most of the time.

I looked forward to the special time with him, even if he slept during most of it. In the open meadow beyond the large picture window in the living room, squirrel babies appeared, and then the quail family with chicks the size of ping-pong balls rolling along behind the adults showed up. Ben was fascinated with every unusual appearance and lifted his arms to indicate he wanted to be in an upright position. Soon he learned the word "up" and in a commanding voice would shout, "Up, up, up!" especially when he heard the little train that ran not far from the house. Then we would rush up the steps to the deck, from where he could see the little train chugging along.

Meanwhile, I started having the first hypnotherapy clients and was delighted with my success. There were days when I had four clients and had to discover to my surprise that this was the limit, as I ended up being somewhat hypnotized myself, which apparently was the case with many therapists. So now, I had three jobs: artist, yoga teacher, and hypnotherapist. The Vista Clara Ranch, where I taught yoga classes, was delighted with my new ability and found many clients very eager to sample hypnosis. I was successful treating weight loss, motivation, self-esteem, past-life regression (a favorite), addictions, and pain management, just to name a few, and was also able to help people achieve relaxation and enhanced creativity. Frances, arriving for a visit, wanted to be rid of her cigarette smoking habit, and we successfully managed that with only one session. I loved being able to help people and was delighted with hypnotherapy.

I kept myself occupied, in part to distract myself from the still-present memory of Alex. The memory of a life's partner does not suddenly fade away but has a tendency to come soaring back into consciousness during the most unexpected moments. I began to practice something called "yoga nidra," a yogic method that results in an unshakable equilibrium that is present under all circumstances and situations. It is an inner peace of mind that can be activated in a relatively short span of time and leads to an inner change and allows a very different

Kirstin, Kent, and Ben

understanding of being and equanimity, states that stay active and intense even during the most difficult times.

Yoga nidra originated in the ancient Eastern teachings of yoga and tantra and brought techniques designed to extend our understanding of how to overcome the mind's penchant to separate and split into objective parts. For instance, we believe that we are solid and separate and that an external world exists beyond, independently of us. Most of us have never seriously examined our belief system or understood the nature of who we really are. Our mind usually jumps from point to point, leading to distraction and never finding any rest. Often preoccupied with innumerable opposites, we seek constant pleasure and try to avoid pain and dissatisfaction.

I became aware of my preoccupation with duality and conflict and came to the realization I was battling the ever-present opposites instead of coming to an acceptance of the truth. I had to accept that my life had changed forever, and my husband would never ever return. Most days, I was tempted to avoid reality. I had no idea how to resolve my dilemma, except that, now and then, I would encounter a deep pool of calm and soothing equanimity. It came in those moments when I was not trying to drown myself in activity and evasion. It came when I stopped and stared at a beautiful manifestation like a landscape. More and more, I allowed myself to sink into the present moment and stopped overloading my days with work.

Ben

My delightful grandchild took my hand and led me to experiences of utter simplicity and charm. One day in the garden, two lizards were mating. Ben looked at them and announced: "Grandma, look! The lizards are cuddling." His open little face held a bright smile.

One day I drove into town to pick him up and told him a story to bridge the boredom he might feel during the 20-minute drive back to my house. I had no idea if my spontaneous story was understood or welcome, as he made no comment at any time. But then, he began to insist that a certain story be repeated, and correctly, as he could not abide any omissions. That was when I realized how sharp and accurate his memory was and that he repeated details in his mind to fix them. Eventually he asked to have sleepovers, and I found that he wanted me to continue telling him stories until he finally passed out in sheer exhaustion. In that, he was not unlike his mother, who as a child had managed to get both her parents to indulge her consumption of stories for at least an hour before she finally drifted off to sleep.

It was on a weekend somewhat later that Kirstin asked me to pick Ben up for the day, and Ben requested: "Grandma, tell me another story." My little grandson was strapped into his car seat and we were preparing to drive back to my house in Eldorado. "But, not one of those fairy tales, I want a true story, like those you told me last time. I want to know all that happened and from the beginning, so don't leave anything out." And so, my stories slowly found their way not only into words, but also onto paper. They began to coalesce, to find purpose they didn't have before, because a child found them interesting. Of course, it would be many years before the stories were compiled into a book for the young man Ben has become.

Thank you, Ben.

About the Author

Ramona Mitchell is an artist and yoga teacher living in Santa Fe, New Mexico. She paints large abstract paintings and is a certified Yasodhara yoga teacher.

She was born Rosemarie Hilpert in Berlin, Germany, but spent some of her early childhood years in the Palatine area of Germany, near the French border, to escape the Allied bombs falling on Berlin. After the war, she and her mother and sister became war refugees and eventually found their way to Cairo, Egypt. In Cairo she was accepted at the Academy Des Beaux Arts and began her art studies under Jaro Hilbert for 4 years. This was followed by a scholarship at the University of Athens Georgia, USA and 4 years in the Art Academy in Kassel, Germany, earning a Master's degree in Fine Art. While in Kassel, her university friends decided she looked more like a "Ramona" than a "Rosemarie," and thus changed her name. After graduation, she briefly returned to Egypt before moving to Nairobi, Kenya, where her mother's sister lived. In Nairobi, she built an art studio and began exhibiting. It was there that she met her future husband, Alex Mitchell, a fellow artist from Scotland. When Alex received an offer to become Chairman of the Fine Arts Department at Lake Forest College in Illinois, he and Ramona relocated to Lake Forest and spent the next thirty years there. Ramona continued to paint and exhibit. She also took her studies of yoga to a new level, training at Yasodhara Ashram at Kootenay, British Columbia, Canada, and eventually receiving certification as a Yasodhara yoga teacher.

Ramona and Alex retired to Santa Fe, New Mexico, in 1994. Alex died in 1996. Today Ramona continues to paint and exhibit, as well as teach yoga in her home studio.

Made in the USA
Columbia, SC
27 April 2021